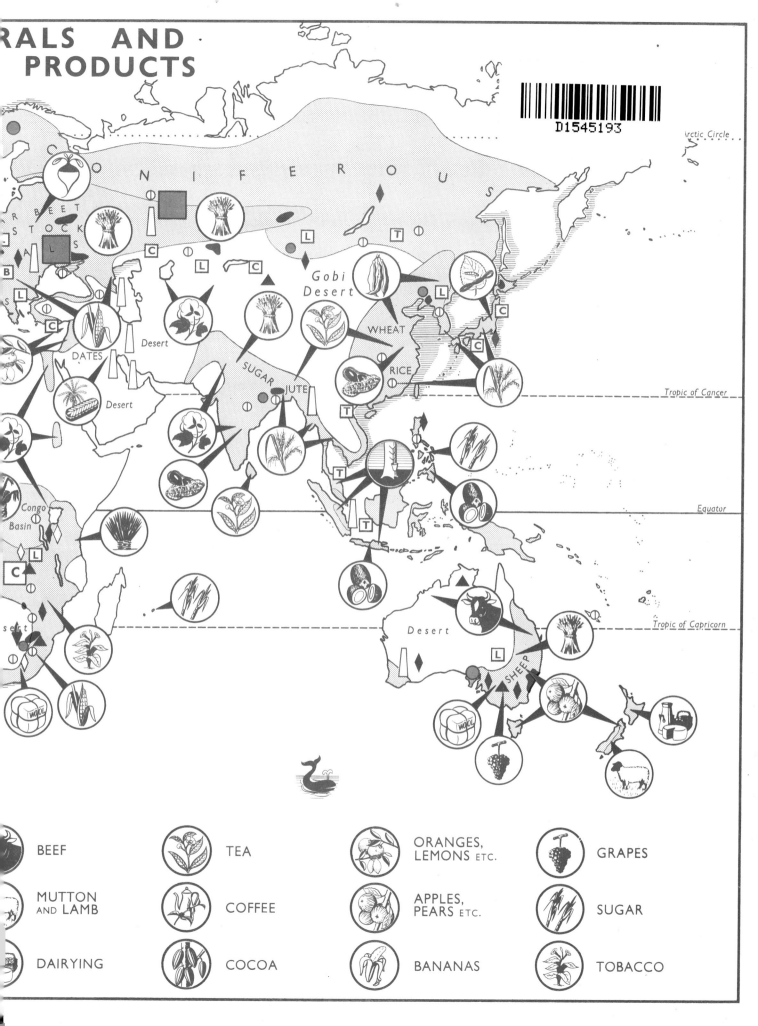

RALS AND
PRODUCTS

Arctic Circle

Gobi Desert

WHEAT

RICE

Tropic of Cancer

Desert

Desert

DATES

SUGAR JUTE

Congo Basin

Equator

Desert

Tropic of Capricorn

SHEEP

WOOL

WOOL

BEEF

TEA

ORANGES, LEMONS ETC.

GRAPES

MUTTON AND LAMB

COFFEE

APPLES, PEARS ETC.

SUGAR

DAIRYING

COCOA

BANANAS

TOBACCO

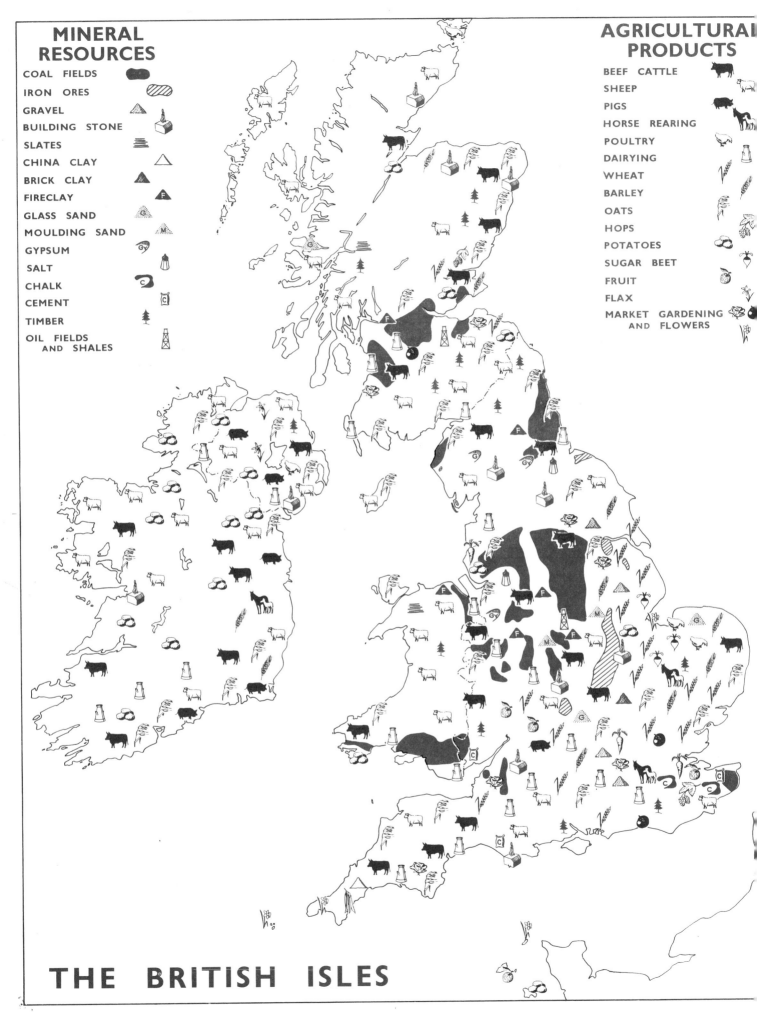

MINERAL RESOURCES

COAL FIELDS

IRON ORES

GRAVEL

BUILDING STONE

SLATES

CHINA CLAY

BRICK CLAY

FIRECLAY

GLASS SAND

MOULDING SAND

GYPSUM

SALT

CHALK

CEMENT

TIMBER

OIL FIELDS
   AND SHALES

AGRICULTURAL PRODUCTS

BEEF CATTLE

SHEEP

PIGS

HORSE REARING

POULTRY

DAIRYING

WHEAT

BARLEY

OATS

HOPS

POTATOES

SUGAR BEET

FRUIT

FLAX

MARKET GARDENING
   AND FLOWERS

THE BRITISH ISLES

Collins
GRAPHIC ATLAS

*An up-to-date World Atlas
with 64 pages of general reference maps
in full colour, an index of over
20,000 entries, two-colour endpapers and
a striking photographic supplement
'Man and Nature'*

COLLINS CLEAR-TYPE PRESS
Glasgow · London · Toronto · Sydney · Auckland · Johannesburg

FIRST PUBLISHED 1896
This Edition—the eleventh since World War II—
was published 1972

PRINTED AND BOUND IN GREAT BRITAIN
BY COLLINS CLEAR-TYPE PRESS
TX. 110

LIST OF CONTENTS

CHIEF COUNTRIES OF THE WORLD

Map	Country	Area (Sq. miles)	Population	Capital
	THE BRITISH COMMONWEALTH			
23–27	UNITED KINGDOM	94,448	54,436,000	London
66–73	CANADA	3,851,920	20,015,000	Ottawa
58–61	AUSTRALIA ...	2,968,031	11,652,000	Canberra
62, 63	NEW ZEALAND ...	103,741	2,754,000	Wellington
44, 45	INDIA	1,175,484	498,860,000	Delhi
46	PAKISTAN	365,546	102,885,000	Islamabad
45	CEYLON	25,332	10,965,000	Colombo
57	GHANA	91,846	7,945,000	Accra
57	SINGAPORE ...	224	1,940,000	Singapore
41	CYPRUS	3,600	607,000	Nicosia
57	NIGERIA	356,680	56,400,000	Lagos
57	SIERRA LEONE ...	27,925	2,450,000	Freetown
57	TANZANIA ...	362,830	10,315,000	Dar-es-Salaam
64	WESTERN SAMOA	1,097	130,000	Apia
77	JAMAICA	4,232	1,860,000	Kingston
77	TRINIDAD & TOBAGO	1,979	975,000	Port of Spain
56	UGANDA	93,983	7,740,000	Kampala
51	MALAWI	46,067	4,043,000	Zomba
47	MALAYSIA ...	128,432	9,558,000	Kuala Lumpur
56	KENYA	224,966	9,376,000	Nairobi
36	MALTA	122	330,000	Valetta
51	ZAMBIA	290,600	3,895,000	Lusaka
57	GAMBIA	4,003	316,000	Bathurst
53	LESOTHO	11,716	976,000	Maseru
42	MALDIVE ISLANDS ...	114	93,000	Malé
77	GUYANA	83,002	655,000	Georgetown
51	BOTSWANA ...	222,000	576,000	Gaberones
77	BARBADOS ...	166	246,000	Bridgetown
77	ANTIGUA ...	170	62,000	St. John's
55	SWAZILAND ...	6,703	390,000	Mbabane
19	MAURITIUS ...	809	793,000	Port Louis
77	Bahama Islands ...	4,403	138,000	Nassau
40	Bahrain	230	182,000	Manama
65	Bermuda Islands ...	21	50,000	Hamilton
47	Brunei	2,225	97,000	Brunei
78	Falkland Islands ...	4,617	2,200	Stanley
64	Fiji Islands ...	7,015	477,000	Suva
35	Gibraltar ...	2	25,000	
77	Honduras, British	8,866	114,000	Belize
48	Hong Kong ...	398	3,740,000	Victoria
64	Papua and New Guinea	178,268	2,101,000	Port Moresby
19	St. Helena ...	47	4,700	Jamestown
19	Seychelle Islands ...	156	47,000	Victoria
64	Western Pacific ...	18,000	244,000	
77	West Indies Associated States ...	947	396,000	on Barbados
	OTHER COUNTRIES OF THE WORLD			
43	Afghanistan ...	250,012	15,227,000	Kabul
37	Albania	11,100	1,814,000	Tirana
35	Algeria	952,198	12,300,000	Algiers
35	Andorra ...	174	13,000	Andorra
40	Arabia (Saudi)	870,044	6,630,000	Riyadh
79	Argentina	1,072,100	22,352,000	Buenos Aires
33	Austria	32,374	7,291,000	Vienna
30	Belgium	11,779	9,556,000	Brussels
79	Bolivia	424,175	4,330,000	La Paz
79	Brazil	3,286,572	87,000,000	Brasilia
37	Bulgaria	42,730	8,334,000	Sofia
43	Burma	261,796	25,246,000	Rangoon
47	Cambodia ...	69,900	6,300,000	Phnom Penh
57	Cameroon ...	183,000	5,550,000	Yaoundé
56	Cent. African Rep.	238,236	2,088,000	Bangui
56	Chad	495,767	2,830,000	Fort Lamy
79	Chile	286,405	8,567,000	Santiago
48	China	3,691,616	716,000,000	Peking
77	Colombia	439,525	17,787,000	Bogota
56	Congo	905,609	15,627,000	Kinshasa
56	Congo	132,049	865,000	Brazzaville
77	Costa Rica ...	19,575	1,474,000	San José
77	Cuba	44,219	7,937,000	Havana
33	Czechoslovakia ...	49,371	14,272,000	Prague
57	Dahomey ...	44,697	2,300,000	Porto Novo
29	Denmark	16,618	4,780,000	Copenhagen
28	Faeroe Islands ...	540	36,000	Torshaven
80	Greenland ...	840,025	37,000	Godthaab
77	Dominican Republic	18,816	3,619,000	Santo Domingo
78	Ecuador	109,488	5,238,000	Quito
56	Ethiopia	471,800	22,590,000	Addis Ababa
29	Finland	130,123	4,675,000	Helsinki
30–32	France	212,827	50,000,000	Paris
67	St. Pierre & Miquelon	92	5,000	St. Pierre
56	Fr. Terrs. of Afars & Issas ...	8,495	81,000	Jibuti
56	Gabon	103,319	462,000	Libreville
33	Germany (total) ...	137,400	76,812,000	
33	Eastern	41,656	17,012,000	Berlin
30	Western	95,744	59,800,000	Bonn
33	Berlin	341	3,302,000	
37	Greece	50,946	8,550,000	Athens
76	Guatemala ...	42,043	4,438,000	Guatemala City
78	Guiana, French ...	35,136	36,000	Cayenne
50	Guinea	94,968	3,420,000	Conakry
77	Haiti	10,714	4,660,000	Port-au-Prince
77	Honduras ...	43,278	2,284,000	Tegucigalpa
37	Hungary	35,919	10,164,000	Budapest
29	Iceland	39,769	197,000	Reykjavik
47	Indonesia ...	735,357	106,000,000	Jakarta
40	Iran (Persia) ...	636,312	25,781,000	Tehran
40	Iraq	173,268	8,262,000	Baghdad
27	Ireland, Rep. of ...	27,136	2,884,000	Dublin
40	Israel	7,992	2,615,000	Jerusalem
36	Italy	116,306	52,958,000	Rome
50	Ivory Coast ...	124,506	4,100,000	Abijan
49	Japan	142,730	99,720,000	Tokyo
41	Jordan	37,740	2,017,000	Amman
49	Korea (total) ...	84,602	40,450,000	
49	North	46,542	11,800,000	Pyongyang
49	South	38,060	28,650,000	Seoul
40	Kuwait	6,000	468,000	Kuwait
47	Laos	91,431	2,500,000	Vientiane
41	Lebanon	4,015	2,280,000	Beirut
57	Liberia	43,000	1,500,000	Monrovia
34	Libya	679,379	1,617,000	Beida
31	Liechtenstein ...	60	20,000	Vaduz
30	Luxembourg ...	998	332,000	Luxembourg
56	Malagasy Republic	229,233	6,548,000	Tananarive
50	Mali	476,486	4,900,000	Bamako
50	Mauritania ...	407,642	1,000,000	Nouakchott
76	Mexico	761,639	40,913,000	Mexico City
39	Mongolia	592,681	1,120,000	Ulan Bator
35	Morocco	171,842	13,323,000	Rabat
44	Nepal	54,363	9,920,000	Katmandu
30	Netherlands (Holland)	15,790	12,573,000	Amsterdam
	The Hague is the seat of Government			
77	Netherlands Antilles	371	207,000	Willemstad
78	Surinam	55,145	350,000	Paramaribo
77	Nicaragua	53,941	1,700,000	Managua
56	Niger	489,214	4,034,000	Niamey
29	Norway	125,187	3,723,000	Oslo
77	Panama	29,210	1,246,000	Panama
79	Paraguay	157,051	2,030,000	Asuncion
78	Peru	496,236	11,854,000	Lima
47	Philippine Republic	115,710	34,656,000	Manila (Quezon City)
33	Poland	124,670	31,551,000	Warsaw
35	Portugal	35,356	9,234,000	Lisbon
35	Azores & Madeira	1,236	620,000	P. Delgada & Funchal
19	Cape Verde Islands	1,557	220,000	Praia
51	Mozambique ...	302,337	6,914,000	Lourenço Marques
57	Guinea, Portugese	13,948	549,000	Bissau
56	Angola	481,365	5,119,000	Loanda
37	Romania	91,703	19,105,000	Bucharest
56	Rwanda	10,169	3,018,000	Kigali
65	Salvador	8,260	2,928,000	San Salvador
57	Senegal	76,126	3,490,000	Dakar
56	Somali Republic ...	246,208	2,500,000	Mogadishu
51–55	South Africa, Rep. of	471,466	18,298,000	Cape Town & Pretoria
50	South-West Africa	318,270	610,000	Windhoek
35	Spain	194,892	31,737,000	Madrid
50	Canary Islands ...	2,807	967,000	Las Palmas
56	Sudan	967,528	13,540,000	Khartoum
29	Sweden	173,673	7,845,000	Stockholm
31	Switzerland ...	15,942	6,080,000	Berne
41	Syria	71,482	5,634,000	Damascus
47	Thailand (Siam) ...	198,461	31,800,000	Bangkok
57	Togo	21,853	1,660,000	Lome
35	Tunisia	63,381	4,685,000	Tunis
41	Turkey	301,388	32,050,000	Ankara
40	United Arab Republic	386,112	29,600,000	Cairo
57	Upper Volta ...	105,871	4,882,000	Ouagadougou
79	Uruguay	72,174	2,715,000	Montevideo
74, 75	U.S.A.	3,615,316	200,000,000	Washington D.C.
19	Guam	211	69,000	Agana
78	Pacific Islands (Trusteeship)	830	93,000	
77	Panama Canal Zone	553	54,000	Balboa Heights
77	Puerto Rico ...	3,435	2,703,000	San Juan
18	Samoa (American)	76	23,000	Pago Pago
77	Virgin Islands ...	131	41,000	Charlotte Amalie
38, 39	U.S.S.R.	8,649,937	235,000,000	Moscow
77	Venezuela	352,153	8,880,000	Caracas
47	Viet Nam (total) ...	127,246	34,524,000	
47	North	61,296	18,400,000	Hanoi
47	South	65,950	16,124,000	Saigon
40	Yemen	75,290	5,000,000	Sana
37	Yugoslavia	98,770	19,632,000	Belgrade

ALTERNATIVE NAMES

SUPPLEMENT OF CHANGED NAMES AND NATIONAL SPELLINGS

n order to assist the reader of older books and the business-man who receives letters from abroad, the following list shows many place names which have been changed since about 1919—e.g. Constantinople, now Istanbul—and national spellings where they differ from the long-accepted English versions—e.g. Livorno, generally known as Leghorn.

Former or National Name	Present Country	New or Accepted Version
alst	Belgium	Alost
bo	Finland	Turku
drianople	Turkey	Edirne
gram	Yugoslavia	Zagreb
ix-la-Chapelle	Germany	Aachen
kmolinsk	U.S.S.R.	Tselinograd
chevsk	U.S.S.R.	Voroshilovsk
eksandropol	U.S.S.R.	Leninakan
eksandrovsk	U.S.S.R.	Zaporozhye
exandretta	Turkey	Iskenderon
lger	Algeria	Algiers
ngora	Turkey	Ankara
ntananarivo	Malagasy	Tananarive
ntioch	Turkey	Antakya
ntivari	Yugoslavia	Bar
nvers	Belgium	Antwerp
rnswalde	Poland	Choszczno
sterabad	Iran	Gurgan
ussig	Czechoslovakia	Usti
hia	Brazil	Salvador
ile Atha Cliath	Eire	Dublin
khmut	U.S.S.R.	Artemovsk
rtfa	Czechoslovakia	Bardejov
sutoland	Africa	Lesotho
tavia	Indonesia	Djakarta or Jakarta
chuanaland	Africa	Botswana
nares	India	Varanasi
ograd	Yugoslavia	Belgrade
uthen	Poland	Bytom
zawadas	India	Vijayavada
orneborg	Finland	Pori
obriki	U.S.S.R.	Novomoskovsk
ne	Algeria	Annaba
eslau	Poland	Wroclaw
it. N. Borneo	Asia	E. Malaysia (Pt.)
omberg	Poland	Bydgoszcz
zesc nad Bugiem	U.S.S.R.	Brest
ucuresti	Romania	Bucharest
alicut	India	Kozhikode
nton	China	Kwangchow
rlsbad	Czechoslovakia	Karlovy Vary
ttaro	Yugoslavia	Kotor
wnpore	India	Kanpur
ara	Brazil	Fortaleza
rnauti	U.S.S.R.	Czernowitz
emulpho	Korea	Inchon
isinau	U.S.S.R.	Kishinev
blen(ce)z	Germany	Koblenz
nstantinople	Turkey	Istanbul
rcaigh	Eire	Cork
stermansville	Congo	Bukavu
anzig	Poland	Gdansk
emerara	Guyana	Georgetown
en Haag	Netherlands	The Hague
arbekr	Turkey	Diyarbakir
rschau	Poland	Tczew
obrogea	Romania	Dobruja
orpat	U.S.S.R.	Tartu
ort	Netherlands	Dordrecht
unkerque	France	Dunkirk
vinsk	U.S.S.R.	Daugavpils
essa	Turkey	Urfa
linburghshire	Scotland	Midlothian
aterinburg	U.S.S.R.	Sverdlovsk
aterinodar	U.S.S.R.	Krasnodar
aterinoslav	U.S.S.R.	Dnepropetrovsk
ginshire	Scotland	Moray
isabethville	Congo	Lubumbashi
isavetpol	U.S.S.R.	Kirovabad
ore	India	Eluru
sinore	Denmark	Helsingör
os	Turkey	Enez
azell	Iran	Pahlevi
erjes	Czechoslovakia	Presov
zek	Yugoslavia	Osijek
tshan	China	Namhoi
rryville	Tunisia	Menzel-Bourguiba
enze	Italy	Florence
me	Yugoslavia	Rijeka
rfarshire	Scotland	Angus
rmosa	China	Taiwan
nfkirchen	Hungary	Pecs
san	Korea	Pusan
llipoli	Turkey	Gelibolu
nd	Belgium	Ghent
nova	Italy	Genoa
nsan	Korea	Wonsan
Gent	Belgium	Ghent
Gleiwitz	Poland	Gliwice
Gnesen	Poland	Gniezno
Gold Coast	Africa	Ghana
Greytown	Nicaragua	San Juan del Norte
Haddingtonshire	Scotland	East Lothian
Heijo	Korea	Pyongyang
Helsingfors	Finland	Helsinki
Heraklion	Crete	Candia
Hindenburg	Poland	Zabrze
Holland	Europe	Netherlands
Hollandia	Indonesia	Sukarnapura
Hsinking	China	Changchun
Iasi	Romania	Jassy
Iglau	Czechoslovakia	Jihlava
Insterburg	U.S.S.R.	Chernyakhovsk
Jakobstad	Finland	Pietasaari
Jakobstadt	U.S.S.R.	Jekabpils
Jesselton	Malaysia	Kota Kinabalu
Kamenskoe	U.S.S.R.	Dneprodzerzhinsk
Karafuto	U.S.S.R.	Sakhalin
Karaklis	U.S.S.R.	Kirovakan
Khibinogorsk	U.S.S.R.	Kirovsk
Khojent	U.S.S.R.	Leninabad
Kingstown	Eire	Dun Laoghaire
Kirin	China	Yungki
Kjobenhavn	Denmark	Copenhagen
Koln	Germany	Cologne
Konigsberg	U.S.S.R.	Kaliningrad
Konigshutte	Poland	Krolewska Huta
Kortrijk	Belgium	Courtrai
Kovno	U.S.S.R.	Kaunas
Kozlov	U.S.S.R.	Michurinsk
Kristiania	Norway	Oslo
Kuznetsk	U.S.S.R.	Novokuznetsk
Kyongsong	Korea	Seoul
Lagosta	Yugoslavia	Lastovo
Laibach	Yugoslavia	Ljubljana
Leitmeritz	Czechoslovakia	Litomerice
Lemberg	U.S.S.R.	Lvov
Leopoldville	Congo	Kinshasa
Leuven	Belgium	Louvain
Leva	Czechoslovakia	Levice
Libau	U.S.S.R.	Leipaja
Linlithgowshire	Scotland	West Lothian
Lisboa	Portugal	Lisbon
Livorno	Italy	Leghorn
Lucknow	India	Lakhnau
Luimneach	Eire	Limerick
Magallanes	Chile	Punta Arenas
Malaya	Asia	W. Malaysia
Mantova	Italy	Mantua
Maranhao	Brazil	São Luiz
Marburg	Yugoslavia	Maribor
Marienburg	Poland	Malbork
Marienske Lazne	Czechoslovakia	Marienbad
Mariupol	U.S.S.R.	Zhdanov
Masulipatam	India	Bandar
Mechelen / Mechlin	Belgium	Malines
Memel	U.S.S.R.	Klaipeda
Merv	U.S.S.R.	Mary
Mohammerah	Iran	Khorramshahr
Monastir	Yugoslavia	Bitolj
Montenegro	Yugoslavia	Crna Gora
Moskva	U.S.S.R.	Moscow
Moukden	China	Shenyang
Munchen	Germany	Munich
Munkacs	U.S.S.R.	Mukacevo
Napoli	Italy	Naples
Nikolsk-Ussuriisk	U.S.S.R.	Ussuriysk
Ninghsien	China	Ningpo
Nizhni Novgorod	U.S.S.R.	Gorki
Northern Rhodesia	Africa	Zambia
Novo Nikolaevsk	U.S.S.R.	Novosibirsk
Nyasaland	Africa	Malawi
Obdorsk	U.S.S.R.	Salekhard
Olmutz	Czechoslovakia	Olomouc
Oppeln	Poland	Opole
Orleansville	Algeria	El-Asnam
Padova	Italy	Padua
Para	Brazil	Belem
Parahyba	Brazil	Joao Pessoa
Pernambuco	Brazil	Recife
Pernau	U.S.S.R.	Parnu
Pernik	Bulgaria	Dimitrovo
Perovsk	U.S.S.R.	Kzyl Orda
Persia	Asia	Iran
Petro-Alexandrovsk	U.S.S.R.	Turtkul
Petrograd	U.S.S.R.	Leningrad
Petsamo	U.S.S.R.	Pechenga
Philippopolis	Bulgaria	Plovdiv
Pillau	U.S.S.R.	Baltisk
Pishpek	U.S.S.R.	Frunze
Podgorica	Yugoslavia	Titograd
Pokrovsk	U.S.S.R.	Engeis
Pola	Yugoslavia	Pula
Poltoratsk	U.S.S.R.	Ashkhabad
Port Arthur-Dairen	China	Lüta
Porto	Portugal	Oporto
Port Petrovsk	U.S.S.R.	Makhachkala
Posen	Poland	Poznan
Pressburg	Czechoslovakia	Bratislava
Puerto Mexico	Mexico	Coatzacoalcos
Queenstown	Eire	Cobh
Ragusa	Yugoslavia	Dubrovnik
Rastyapino	U.S.S.R.	Dzerzhinsk
Ratibon	Poland	Raciborz
Ratisbon	Germany	Regensburg
Reichenberg	Czechoslovakia	Liberec
Revel	U.S.S.R.	Tallinn
Rodosto	Turkey	Tekirdag
Romanovski	U.S.S.R.	Kropotkin
Ruanda-Urundi	Africa	Rwanda and Burundi
St. Petersburg	U.S.S.R.	Leningrad
Salonika	Greece	Thessaloniki
Samara	U.S.S.R.	Kuibyshev
Sarawak	Asia	E. Malaysia (Pt.)
Sergiopol	U.S.S.R.	Ayaguz
s'Gravenhage	Holland	The Hague
Shavli	U.S.S.R.	Siauliai
Shcheglovsk	U.S.S.R.	Kemerovo
Siam	Asia	Thailand
Simbirsk	U.S.S.R.	Ulyanovsk
Singora	Thailand	Songkla
Siracusa	Sicily	Syracuse
Sistova	Bulgaria	Svishtov
Smyrna	Turkey	Izmir
Sofiya	Bulgaria	Sofia
Sousse	Tunisia	Susa
Spalato	Yugoslavia	Split
Stalingrad	U.S.S.R.	Volgograd
Stanislau	U.S.S.R.	Stanislawow
Stanleyville	Congo	Kisangani
Stettin	Poland	Szczecin
Stolp	Poland	Slupsk
Stavropol	U.S.S.R.	Voroshilovsk
Swinemunde	Poland	Swinoujscie
Tadmor	Syria	Palmyra
Tammerfors	Finland	Tampere
Tanganyika	Africa	Tanzania
Tavastehus	Finland	Hameenlinna
Teschen	Poland	Cieszyn
Tetschen	Czechoslovakia	Decin
Thorn	Poland	Torun
Tiflis	U.S.S.R.	Tbilisi
Tilsit	U.S.S.R.	Sovetsk
Torino	Italy	Turin
Trebizond	Turkey	Trabzon
Trichinopoly	India	Tiruchirapalli
Troppau	Czechoslovakia	Opava
Tsaritsin	U.S.S.R.	Volgograd
Tver	U.S.S.R.	Kalinin
Uleaborg	Finland	Oulu
Ust Sysolsk	U.S.S.R.	Syktyvkar
Venezia	Italy	Venice
Verkhneudinsk	U.S.S.R.	Ulan-Ude
Viipuri	U.S.S.R.	Viborg
Vlissingen	Netherlands	Flushing
Vyatka	U.S.S.R.	Kirov
Warszawa	Poland	Warsaw
Wenchow	China	Yungkia
Wien	Austria	Vienna
Wilno	U.S.S.R.	Vilnius
Windau	U.S.S.R.	Ventspils
Xeres	Mexico	Jerez
Yunnan	China	Kunming
Yuzovka	U.S.S.R.	Donetsk
Zara	Yugoslavia	Zadar
Zaragoza	Spain	Saragossa
Zlin	Czechoslovakia	Gottwaldov
Zuider Zee	Netherlands	Ijsselmeer

NORTH EASTERN AMERICA

See inset below.

See inset above.

	Density per square mile
ARGENTINA	21
AUSTRALIA	4
AUSTRIA	225
BELGUIM	811
BOLIVIA	10
BRAZIL	27
BULGARIA	195
BURMA	96
CAMBODIA	90
CANADA	5
CHILE	30
CHINA	194
COLOMBIA	40
CUBA	180
CZECHOSLOVAKIA	289
DENMARK	287
ECUADOR	48
ETHIOPIA	48
FINLAND	36
FRANCE	235
GERMANY (E)	408
GERMANY (W)	624
GREECE	168
HUNGARY	283
INDIA	424
INDONESIA	144
IRAN (PERSIA)	41
IRELAND (REP.)	106
ITALY	455
JAPAN	698
LAOS	27
MEXICO	54
NETHERLANDS	796
NEW ZEALAND	27
NIGERIA	158
NORWAY	30
PAKISTAN	281
PERU	24
PHILIPPINES	283
POLAND	253
PORTUGAL	261
ROMANIA	208
SOUTH AFRICA	38
SPAIN	163
SWEDEN	45
SWITZERLAND	381
THAILAND	160
TURKEY	106
U.A.R. (EGYPT)	77
UNITED KINGDOM	576
UNITED STATES	55
URUGUAY	38
U.S.S.R.	27
VENEZUELA	25
YUGOSLAVIA	190

CITIES OVER 1,000,000 INHABITANTS

TOKYO, Japan
LONDON, England
NEW YORK, U.S.A.
BUENOS AIRES, Argentina
SHANGHAI, China
MOSCOW, U.S.S.R.
MEXICO CITY, Mexico
BOMBAY, India
PEKING, China
CAIRO, Egypt
JAKARTA, Indonesia
SÃO PAULO, Brazil
SEOUL, S. Korea
LENINGRAD, U.S.S.R.
CHICAGO, U.S.A.
CALCUTTA, India
BERLIN, Germany
RIO DE JANEIRO, Brazil
TIENTSIN, China
OSAKA, Japan
PARIS, France
MANILA, Philippines
SYDNEY, Australia
LOS ANGELES, U.S.A.
SHENYANG, China
DELHI, India
TEHRAN, Persia
MADRID, Spain
MONTREAL, Canada
MELBOURNE, Australia
ROME, Italy
WUHAN, China
CHUNGKING, China
SANTIAGO, Chile
PHILADELPHIA, U.S.A.
SAIGON, S. Vietnam
NAGOYA, Japan
KARACHI, Pakistan
YOKOHAMA, Japan
BUDAPEST, Hungary
HAMBURG, Germany
ATHENS, Greece
KWANGCHOW
  (CANTON), China
TORONTO, Canada
ISTANBUL, Turkey
SINGAPORE
MADRAS, India

LIMA, Peru
DETROIT, U.S.A.
VIENNA, Austria
MILAN, Italy
BANGKOK, Thailand
BARCELONA, Spain
HARBIN, China
ALEXANDRIA, U.A.R.
BUCHAREST, Romania
LUTA, China
CARACAS, Venezuela
PUSAN, S. Korea
KIEV, U.S.S.R.
NANKING, China
BOGOTA, Colombia
KYOTO, Japan
STOCKHOLM, Sweden
SIAN, China
LAHORE, Pakistan
COPENHAGEN, Denmark
HYDERABAD, India
TASHKENT, U.S.S.R.
KOBE, Japan
BAKU, U.S.S.R.
MUNICH, Germany
WARSAW, Poland
NAPLES, Italy
CASABLANCA, Morocco
MONTEVIDEO, Uruguay
TAIPEH, Formosa
KHARKOV, U.S.S.R.
TSINGTAO, China
GORKI, U.S.S.R.
JOHANNESBURG, S. Africa
CHENGTU, China
BIRMINGHAM, England
KINSHASA, Congo
BRUSSELS, Belgium
NOVOSIBIRSK, U.S.S.R.
PRAGUE, Czechoslovakia
TAIYUAN, China
TURIN, Italy
BAGHDAD, Iraq
KUIBYSHEV, U.S.S.R.
GLASGOW, Scotland
KITAKYUSHU, Japan
KANPUR, India
SURABAYA, Indonesia

The densities shown on this map have been carefully selected. They correspond broadly with the major human occupations as shown below.

Persons per sq. mile

Under 2	Virtually uninhabited. Nomadic hunters & herds. Isolated mining settlement & oases.
2- 20	Grazing; forestry; shifting cultivation. Extensive grain farming (N.America & Australia).
20 - 100	Mixed farming. Extensive farming (U.S.S.R. etc.).
100 - 400	Arable cultivation. Small scale industries.
Over 400	Intensive cultivation (Asia, Egypt etc.) Major industrial & urban

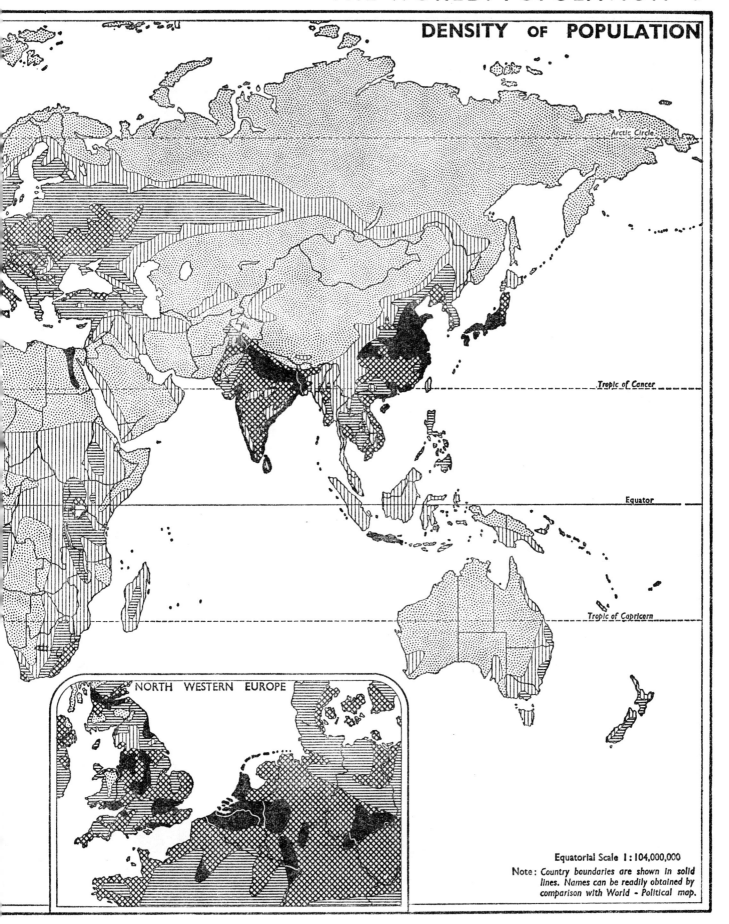

DENSITY OF POPULATION

NORTH WESTERN EUROPE

Equatorial Scale 1:104,000,000

Note: *Country boundaries are shown in solid lines. Names can be readily obtained by comparison with World - Political map.*

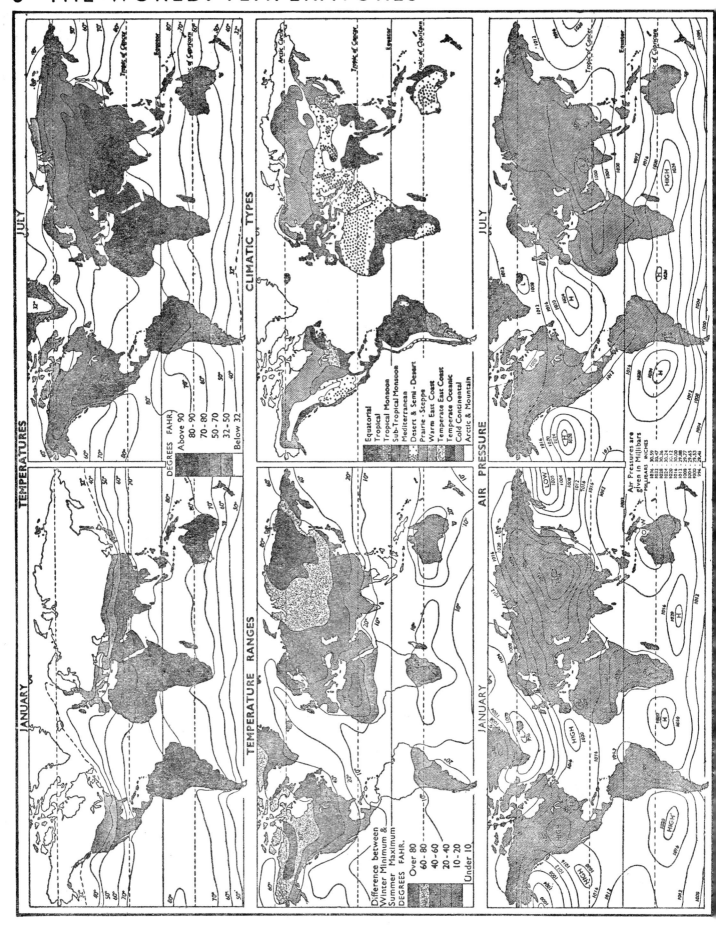

TEMPERATURES

JULY

JANUARY

DEGREES FAHR.
Above 90
80 - 90
70 - 80
50 - 70
32 - 50
Below 32

CLIMATIC TYPES

Equatorial
Tropical
Tropical Monsoon
Sub-Tropical Monsoon
Mediterranean
Desert & Semi - Desert
Prairie - Steppe
Warm East Coast
Temperate East Coast
Temperate Oceanic
Cold Continental
Arctic & Mountain

TEMPERATURE RANGES

Difference between
Winter Minimum &
Summer Maximum
DEGREES FAHR.
Over 80
60 - 80
40 - 60
20 - 40
10 - 20
Under 10

AIR PRESSURE

JULY

JANUARY

Air Pressures are
given in Millibars
MILLIBARS   INCHES
1036   30.59
1032   30.47
1028   30.36
1024   30.24
1020   30.12
1016   30.00
1012   29.88
1008   29.77
1004   29.65
1000   29.53
996   29.41
992   29.29
988   29.18

ANNUAL RAINFALL

ARCTIC OCEAN

PACIFIC OCEAN

Arctic Circle

Tropic of Cancer

Equator

Tropic of Capricorn

Kuro Siwo

West Wind Drift

ATLANTIC OCEAN

INDIAN OCEAN

North Atlantic Drift

Labrador Current

Gulf Stream

Canaries Current

North Equatorial Current

South Equatorial Current

Benguela Current

Brazil Current

West Australia Current

Equatorial Current

Australia Current

OCEAN

North Pacific Current

California Current

North Equatorial Current

Equatorial Counter Current

South Equatorial Current

Peruvian Current

West Wind Drift

PACIFIC OCEAN

Note:— Currents in the Northern Indian Ocean flow in reverse direction during the summer (monsoon) season.

Inches per annum
Over 80
40-80
20-40
10-20
Under 10

Ocean currents
Relatively Warm
Relatively Cool

SEASONAL RAINFALL AND WINDS

SUMMER (Northern Hemisphere)

July Winds

Arctic Circle

SOUTH EAST MONSOON

SOUTH WEST MONSOON

Tropic of Cancer

Doldrums

Equator

SOUTH EAST MONSOON

SOUTH EAST TRADES

Tropic of Capricorn

Roaring Forties

Westerlies

Horse Latitudes

NORTH EAST TRADES

Doldrums

SOUTH EAST TRADES

Horse Latitudes

Westerlies

NORTH EAST TRADES

Doldrums

SOUTH EAST TRADES

Inches per annum
Over 40
20-40
10-20
5-10
Under 5

WINTER (Northern Hemisphere)

January Winds

Westerlies

NORTH EAST TRADES

NORTH EAST TRADES

NORTH MONSOON

Calms

SOUTH EAST TRADES

Roaring Forties

Westerlies

Horse Latitudes

NORTH EAST TRADES

Doldrums

SOUTH EAST TRADES

Horse Latitudes

Westerlies

Westerlies

NORTH EAST TRADES

Doldrums

SOUTH EAST TRADES

Westerlies

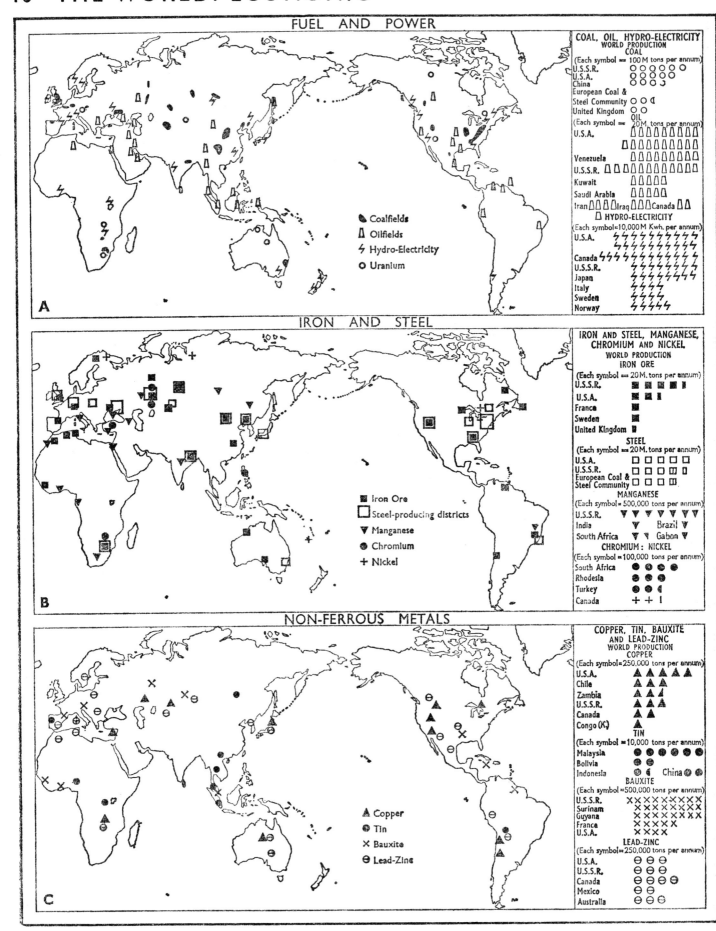

FUEL AND POWER

COAL, OIL, HYDRO-ELECTRICITY
WORLD PRODUCTION
COAL
(Each symbol = 100 M tons per annum)
U.S.S.R.
U.S.A.
China
European Coal &
Steel Community
United Kingdom
OIL
(Each symbol = 20 M. tons per annum)
U.S.A.
Venezuela
U.S.S.R.
Kuwait
Saudi Arabia
Iran   Iraq   Canada
HYDRO-ELECTRICITY
(Each symbol = 10,000 M Kwh. per annum)
U.S.A.
Canada
U.S.S.R.
Japan
Italy
Sweden
Norway

- Coalfields
- Oilfields
- Hydro-Electricity
- Uranium

A

IRON AND STEEL

IRON AND STEEL, MANGANESE, CHROMIUM AND NICKEL
WORLD PRODUCTION
IRON ORE
(Each symbol = 20 M. tons per annum)
U.S.S.R.
U.S.A.
France
Sweden
United Kingdom
STEEL
(Each symbol = 20 M. tons per annum)
U.S.A.
U.S.S.R.
European Coal &
Steel Community
MANGANESE
(Each symbol = 500,000 tons per annum)
U.S.S.R.
India   Brazil
South Africa   Gabon
CHROMIUM : NICKEL
(Each symbol = 100,000 tons per annum)
South Africa
Rhodesia
Turkey
Canada

- Iron Ore
- Steel-producing districts
- Manganese
- Chromium
- Nickel

B

NON-FERROUS METALS

COPPER, TIN, BAUXITE AND LEAD-ZINC
WORLD PRODUCTION
COPPER
(Each symbol = 250,000 tons per annum)
U.S.A.
Chile
Zambia
U.S.S.R.
Canada
Congo (K.)
TIN
(Each symbol = 10,000 tons per annum)
Malaysia
Bolivia
Indonesia   China
BAUXITE
(Each symbol = 500,000 tons per annum)
U.S.S.R.
Surinam
Guyana
France
U.S.A.
LEAD-ZINC
(Each symbol = 250,000 tons per annum)
U.S.A.
U.S.S.R.
Canada
Mexico
Australia

- Copper
- Tin
- Bauxite
- Lead-Zinc

C

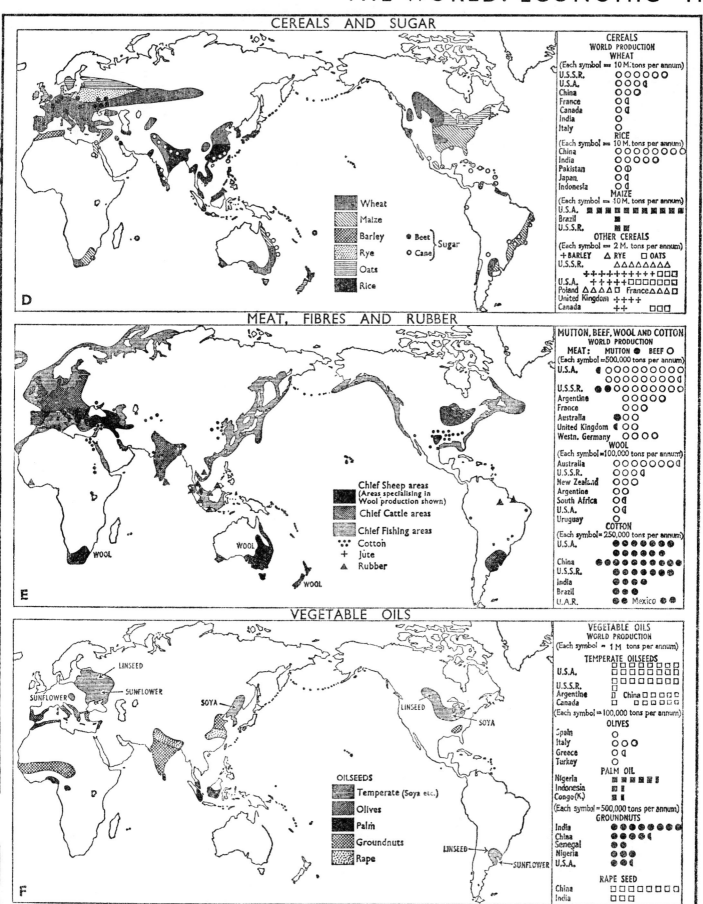

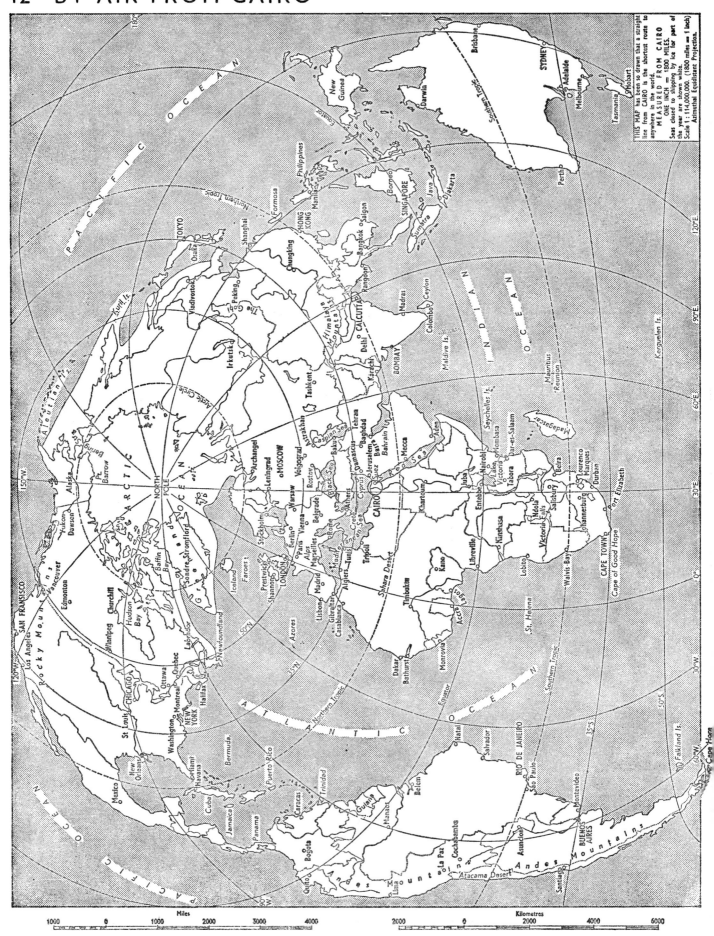

THIS MAP has been so drawn that a straight
line from CAIRO is the shortest route to
anywhere in the world.
MEASURED FROM CAIRO
ONE INCH = 1800 MILES.
Seas closed to shipping by ice for part of
the year are shown white.
Scale 1 : 114,000,000. (1800 miles = 1 inch).
Azimuthal Equidistant Projection.

Miles
1000   0   1000   2000   3000   4000

Kilometres
2000   0   2000   4000   6000

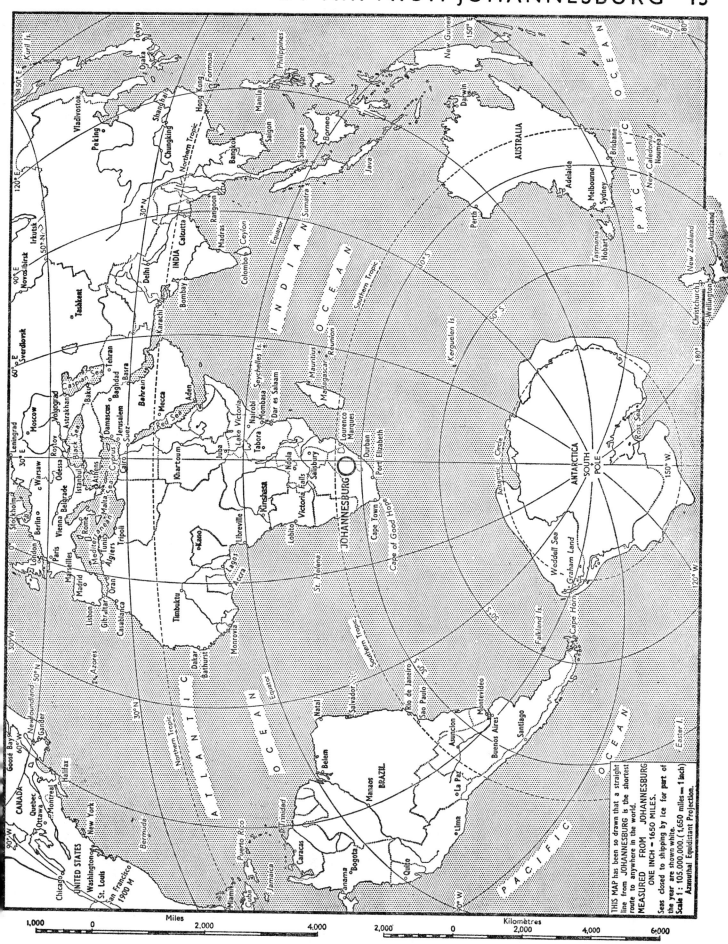

THIS MAP has been so drawn that a straight line from JOHANNESBURG is the shortest route to anywhere in the world.
MEASURED FROM JOHANNESBURG
ONE INCH = 1650 MILES.
Seas closed to shipping by ice for part of the year are shown white.
Scale 1: 105,000,000. (1,650 miles = 1 inch)
Azimuthal Equidistant Projection.

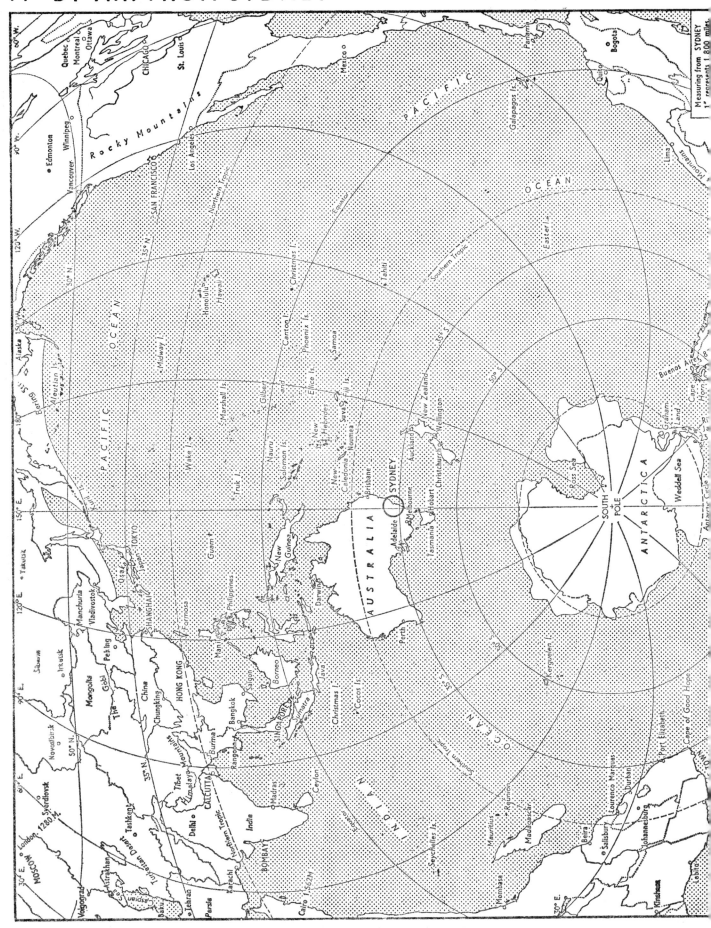

Measuring from SYDNEY
1" represents 1,800 miles.

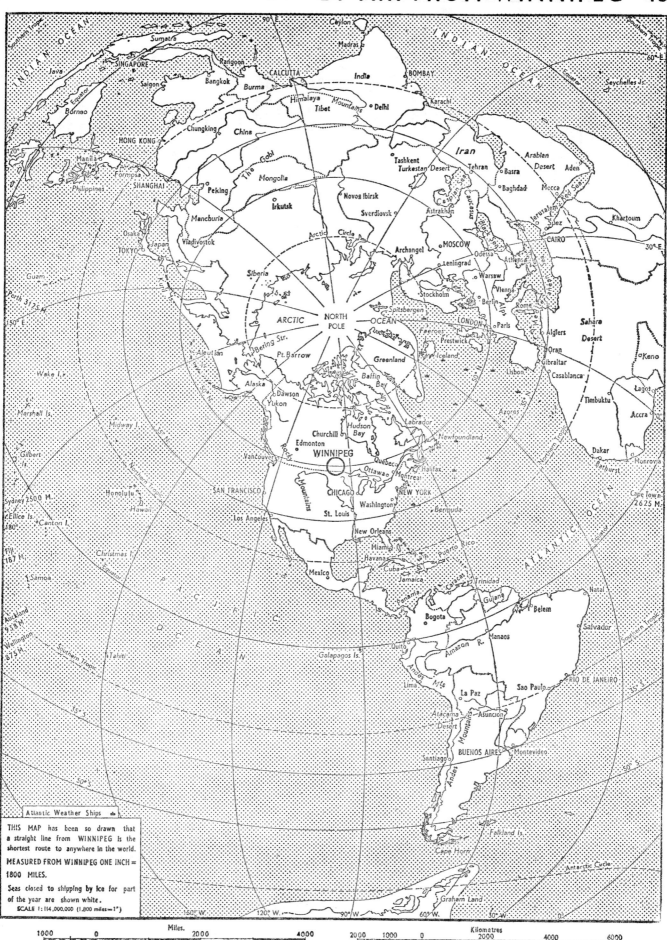

Atlantic Weather Ships ⚓

THIS MAP has been so drawn that a straight line from WINNIPEG is the shortest route to anywhere in the world.

MEASURED FROM WINNIPEG ONE INCH = 1800 MILES.

Seas closed to shipping by ice for part of the year are shown white.

SCALE 1: 114,000,000 (1,800 miles = 1")

Miles.
1000   0   2000   4000

Kilometres
2000   1000   0   2000   4000   6000

TABLE OF AIRLINE DISTANCES BETWEEN THE PRINCIPAL CITIES OF THE WORLD

City	Amsterdam	Auckland	Berlin	Bombay	Buenos Aires	Cairo	Calcutta	Chicago	Copenhagen	Dakar	Hamburg	Hong Kong	Honolulu	Johannesburg	Karachi	Lisbon	LONDON	Mexico City	Montreal	Moscow	Nairobi	New York	Panama City	Paris	Rio de Janeiro	Rome	San Francisco	Singapore	Sydney	Tokyo
Winnipeg	4043	8375	4356	9584	7253	6981	10375	700	4267	5101	4279	7653	3872	9611	8717	4503	3920	1756	1248	6056	9481	1299	3255	4682	6152	4805	1967	10745	9015	5866
Tokyo	8974	7085	9324	4887	11748	7416	3852	6305	8961	11923	9160	1787	3848	9949	5205	10000	8642	7149	7161	8297	7908	2116	9621	8224	13285	8576	6244	3748	6379	
Sydney	11112	1333	11501	6913	14439	9281	6045	12023	11491	13041	11621	4592	5142	8503	7456	10994	11503	9255	10310	10323	8684	10110	10893	11042	14238	10536	7538	4149		
Singapore	7433	5542	6542	2455	13984	5366	1836	11358	7576	9259	7472	1961	6673	7285	2998	7530	7463	12650	12040	6911	10739	10029	12624	6860	12558	6621	10367			
San Francisco	5706	6205	6529	11043	7083	7635	9132	2091	5954	6382	6388	8031	2394	10859	10277	7180	5354	1899	2532	5865	8159	2680	3377	6686	7041	6362				
Rome	805	12108	748	3854	7091	1320	4730	4839	955	2708	851	6789	9425	4889	3297	1142	885	6864	4113	1531	3355	4271	6115	681	5958					
Rio de Janeiro	6239	13757	6238	9876	1312	7192	10686	5875	6774	3124	6161	13260	9435	5886	5916	4795	5834	5481	5163	7221	11283	4830	3664	5669						
Paris	231	12789	539	5183	7030	1990	4163	4140	637	2613	465	7707	8601	5489	4011	894	208	5716	3806	1532	4036	3625	5912							
Panama City	5848	9410	5848	5183	2186	7383	13630	724	6426	6642	6053	11408	5771	10213	9428	4875	5700	1499	3806	10393	11145	2791								
New York	3639	8800	3969	7999	5954	5607	8228	713	3649	3802	3806	8031	4976	8289	7697	3254	3442	2092	333	4999	8159									
Nairobi	4160	11267	4103	3021	8756	2203	4056	8883	4175	4357	4126	6121	12661	1809	2790	4744	4240	9654	8492	4889										
Moscow	1329	13642	966	5123	8549	1968	3518	5723	956	4379	1153	6592	7037	6930	3367	2413	1557	7284	4808											
Montreal	3421	9425	3119	6804	4399	5732	7527	745	3649	4135	3806	7707	4926	8581	7434	3254	3251	2307												
Mexico City	5727	8607	6331	8486	4693	8865	11620	1056	6651	8141	6204	8936	4293	10349	10847	6138	5821													
LONDON	229	13006	690	5410	7157	2184	5626	3944	610	2703	462	7591	7750	5698	4172	966														
Lisbon	1148	13250	1443	5081	6136	2478	5872	3978	1538	1737	1366	7685	9575	5138	4599															
Karachi	4115	8732	5673	543	10596	2206	1354	8502	4285	6305	4148	3225	8816	4599																
Johannesburg	5694	7170	5673	4830	4068	4022	6865	9003	5771	4477	5722	8162	8228																	
Honolulu	7613	4499	9006	8531	9297	9458	7507	4483	8348	8776	9065	5636																		
Hong Kong	7694	5925	7537	3332	13536	5688	2297	8087	7744	9959	7373																			
Hamburg	235	12959	163	4705	7502	2187	5581	4587	173	3515																				
Dakar	2874	14801	3119	6804	4068	2029	5765	4373	3515																					
Copenhagen	393	13017	226	4729	8120	2029	6765	4373																						
Chicago	4395	8644	4693	8486	6435	6138	10632																							
Calcutta	5535	7378	5478	1035	11961	3565																								
Cairo	2042	10783	2478	2699	7157																									
Buenos Aires	7513	13926	7457	11203																										
Bombay	4659	7997	4602																											
Berlin	363	12599																												
Auckland	12016																													

EXPLANATORY NOTES

The table of airline distances between the principal cities of the world has been most carefully compiled from the latest available list of airlines. The distances are as given in current commercial timetables and not calculated on the map. Distances quoted are in statute miles.

Where there is a choice of routes the shortest is given, but even so, many distances exceed that of half-way round the world (12,500 miles). In some cases political factors prevent the establishment of airlines, e.g., from Peking to Tokyo, which would shorten long over-land journeys, whilst in other cases economic factors discourage traffic, e.g., directly between S. Africa and S. America. New routes are however continually being developed, e.g., from Amsterdam to Vancouver via the North Pole.

Note that the names in the top row are alphabetical from left to right, while the same names in the side column are arranged alphabetically from the foot upwards. To find the distance between any two names, take one of the names in the top row and read down the figure column till opposite the appropriate name. Should this not give the answer, repeat the process with the other name. For example, the Lisbon-Cairo distance is obtained by finding Cairo in the top row and reading down the figure column till opposite Lisbon; if the Lisbon entry in the top row is used no distance will be found opposite Cairo.

LONDON to

British Isles

Aberdeen ..	429
Belfast ..	322
Dublin ..	279
Glasgow ..	327
Jersey ..	180
Kirkwall ..	557
Lerwick ..	652
Liverpool ..	165
Manchester ..	152
Prestwick ..	350
Stornoway ..	566

Europe

Athens ..	1,535
Brussels ..	219
Geneva ..	469
Madrid ..	778
Oslo ..	727
Prague ..	672
Stockholm ..	908
Vienna ..	864

For Amsterdam, Berlin, Lisbon, Paris, see above.

NEW YORK to

U.S.A.

Baltimore ..	178
Boston ..	184
Cleveland ..	404
Los Angeles ..	2,930
Miami ..	1,091
New Orleans	1,185
Philadelphia ..	101
Salt Lake C. ..	2,087
Seattle ..	2,434
Washington ..	202

Americas

Barranquilla ..	2,160
Bermudas ..	762
Curacao ..	1,990
Jamaica ..	1,635
Lima ..	4,092
Santiago ..	5,311
Toronto ..	365

For San Francisco, Buenos Aires, Rio de Janeiro, Montreal, Chicago, see above.

TORONTO to

Canada

Calgary ..	1,672
Churchill ..	1,799
Edmonton ..	1,674
Gander ..	1,254
Goose Bay ..	1,131
Halifax ..	1,053
Montreal ..	324
Ottawa ..	243
Quebec ..	486
Regina ..	1,274
St. John's ..	1,612
Vancouver ..	2,188
Winnipeg ..	934

U.S.A.

Chicago ..	421
Cleveland ..	214
Miami ..	1,357
New Orleans	1,251
New York ..	365
San Francisco	2,177

SYDNEY (Australia) to

Adelaide ..	717
Alice Springs	1,565
Brisbane ..	428
Cairns ..	1,333
Canberra ..	148
Darwin ..	1,961
Hobart ..	647
Melbourne ..	455
Norfolk Is. ..	1,048
Perth ..	2,037
Port Moresby	1,766
Rockhampton	803
Tennant Cr. ..	1,400

AUCKLAND (N.Z.) to

Christchurch ..	475
Dunedin ..	673
Gisborne ..	225
Invercargill	1,251
New Plymouth	158
Palmerston N.	250
Wellington ..	287

KARACHI to

Ahmedabad ..	369
Colombo ..	1,514
Delhi ..	665
Jhodpur ..	382
Madras ..	1,186

For Bombay and Calcutta, see main table.

DELHI to

Bombay ..	708
Calcutta ..	816
Colombo ..	1,530
Lahore ..	260
Madras ..	1,110
Nagpur ..	530
Peshawar ..	522
Srinagar ..	430

BOMBAY to

Colombo ..	970
Madras ..	642
Nagpur ..	287

JOHANNESBURG to

Bloemfontein ..	232
Bulawayo ..	224
Capetown ..	798
Durban ..	305
Kimberley ..	230
Livingstone ..	594
N'dola ..	910
Port Elizabeth	566
Salisbury ..	600
Windhoek ..	740

ANKARA to

Adana ..	249
Athens ..	521
Baghdad ..	1,008
Basra ..	1,249
Beirut ..	492
Belgrade ..	722
Cairo ..	970
Istanbul ..	642
Nicosia ..	426

Important Airports

Airport	City
Schiphol	Amsterdam
Whenuapai	Auckland
Templehof	Berlin
Santa Cruz	Bombay
Ezeiza	Buenos Aires
Dum Dum	Calcutta
Kastrup	Copenhagen
Kai Tak	Hong Kong
Yesilköy	Istanbul
Portela	Lisbon
Heathrow	London
Dorval	Montreal
Domodedovo	Moscow
Embakasi	Nairobi
John F. Kennedy	New York
Orly	Paris
Galeao	Rio de Janeiro
Leo. da Vinci	Rome
Kallang	Singapore
Arlanda	Stockholm
Mascot	Sydney
Haneda	Tokyo

TRAVEL BY AIR can be much more direct than by land or sea. Great circles drawn around the curve of the globe are always the shortest distances between places. But on small-scale maps drawn to show true shapes or equal areas the shortest route is usually NOT a straight line.

THIS MAP has been so drawn that a straight line from LONDON is the shortest route to anywhere in the world.

MEASURED FROM LONDON ONE INCH = 1600 MILES. The land is coloured in concentric circles round London. To the inside edges of the green is 2500 miles; the red : 5000 miles; yellow : 6250 miles (Quarter way round the earth)

AS the map projection would distort to un-recognisable shapes the land areas of New Zea-land and Australia some important places are named outside the map to show true direction from London and the distance in miles from the edge of the map.

THIS MAP also serves to show the world's land hemisphere with Western Europe at its centre. North Polar seas closed to ships by ice for part of the year are shown white.

THIS MAP DOES NOT SHOW the shortest routes or correct dis-tances between places unless both are in a straight line with London.

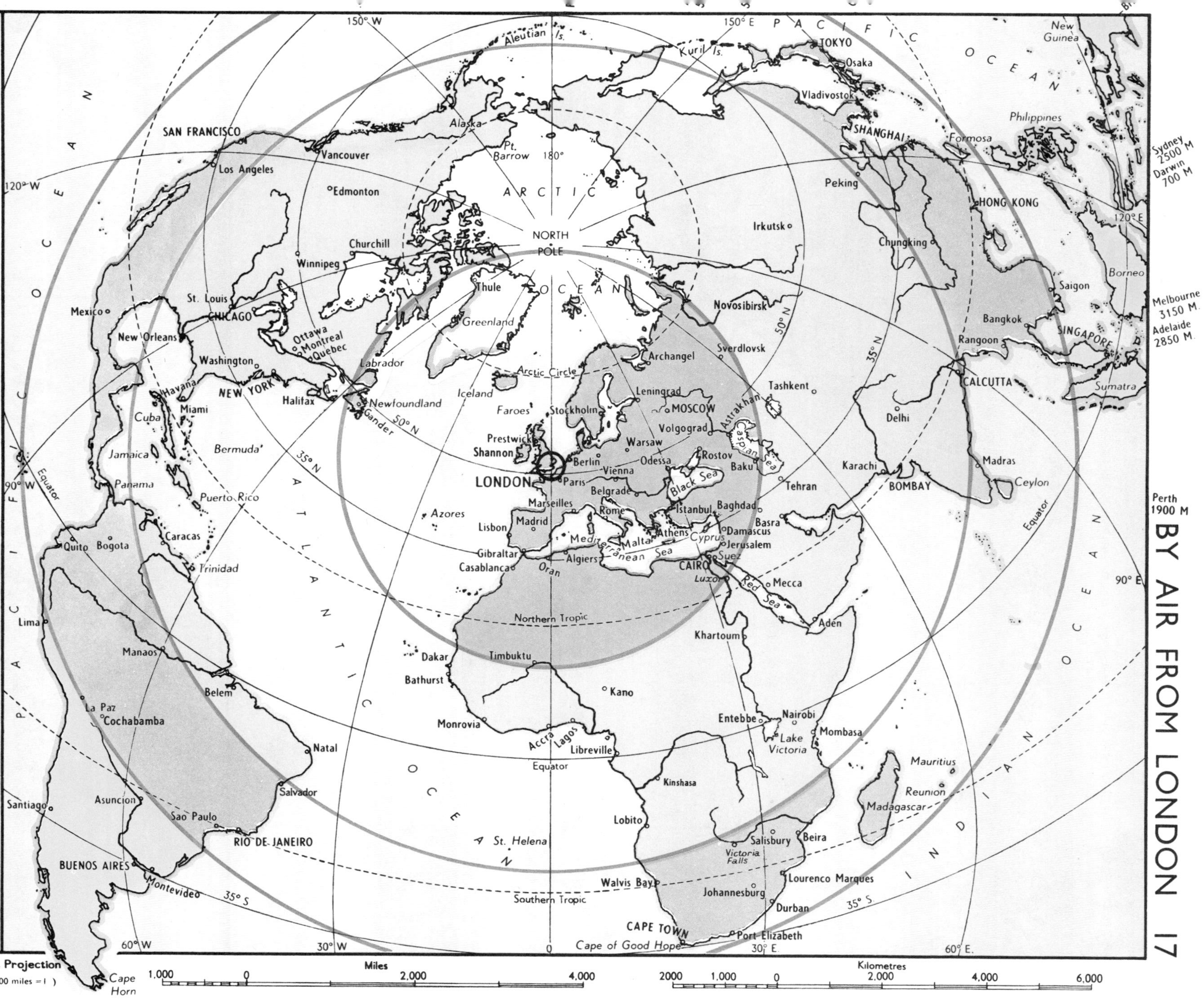

Azimuthal Equidistant Projection

SCALE 1 : 100,000,000 (1,600 miles = 1")

MH/68

Sydney 2500 M   Darwin 700 M   Melbourne 3150 M   Adelaide 2850 M   Perth 1900 M

Kilometres
6,000
4,000
2,000
0
2000
4,000

Miles
2,000
1,000
0
1,000
2,000

NORTH POLE

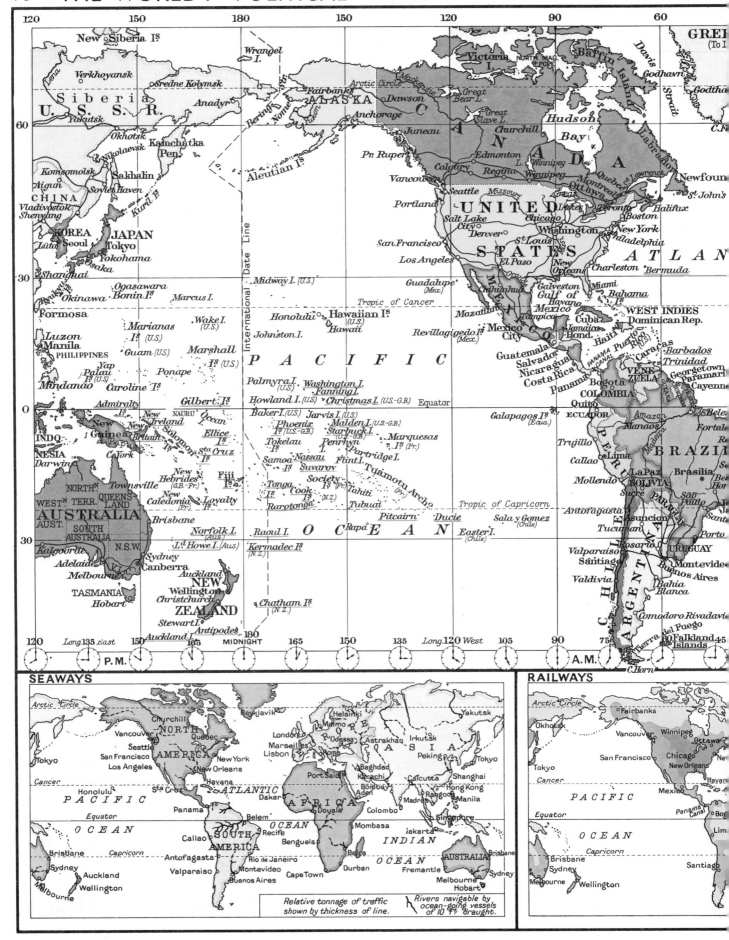

Relative tonnage of traffic shown by thickness of line.

Rivers navigable by ocean-going vessels of 10 ft draught.

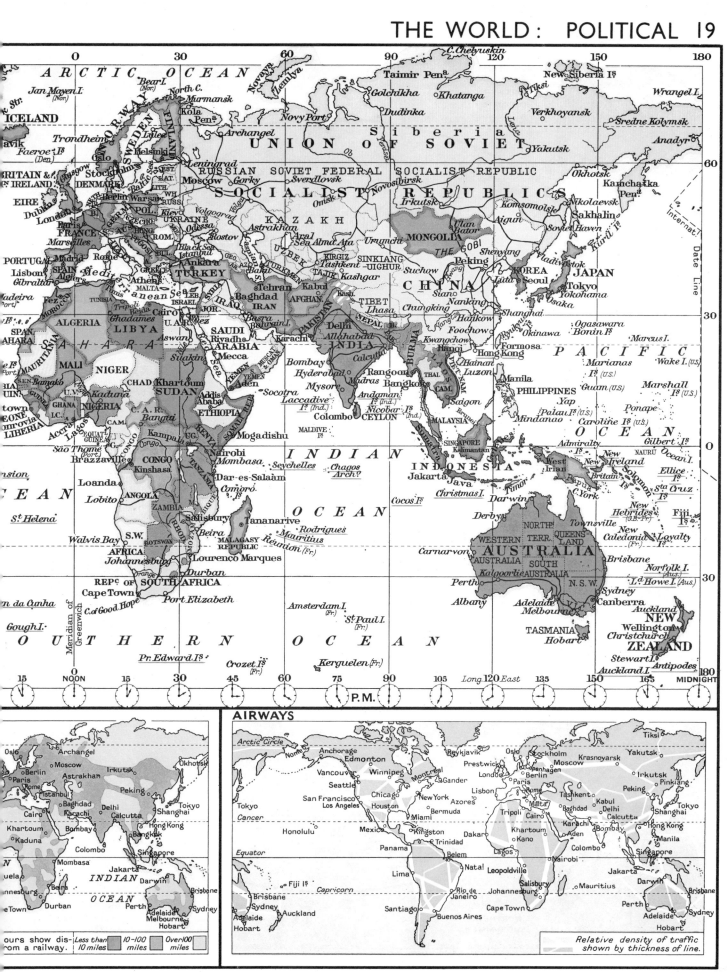

Relative density of traffic shown by thickness of line.

hours show dis- Less than 10-100 Over 100
from a railway. 10 miles miles miles

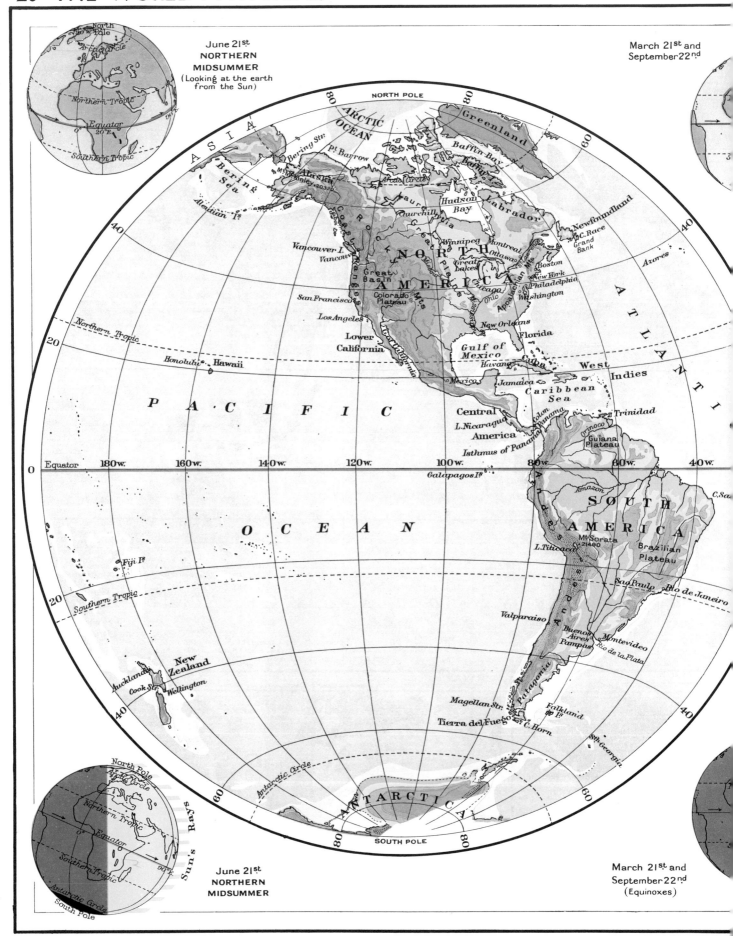

June 21st
NORTHERN
MIDSUMMER
(Looking at the earth
from the Sun)

March 21st and
September 22nd

NORTH POLE

ARCTIC OCEAN

ASIA

Bering Str.
Pt. Barrow
Bering Sea
Mt. McKinley .20320
Alaska
Aleutian Is.

Greenland

Baffin Bay
Baffin
Arctic Circle

Hudson Bay
Labrador
Churchill

Newfoundland
C. Race
Grand Bank

NORTH AMERICA

Vancouver I.
Vancouver
Great Basin
Colorado Plateau
San Francisco
Los Angeles

Winnipeg
Montreal
Ottawa
Great Lakes
Chicago
Ohio
Missouri
Appalachian Mts.
Boston
New York
Philadelphia
Washington

Azores

ATLANTIC

40

Northern Tropic
Lower California

New Orleans
Florida

Gulf of Mexico
Havana
Mexico
Cuba
Jamaica
Caribbean Sea
West Indies

Honolulu
Hawaii

20

PACIFIC

Central America
L. Nicaragua
Colon
Panama
Isthmus of Panama

Trinidad
Orinoco
Guiana Plateau

Equator
180 w.
160 w.
140 w.
120 w.
100 w.
80 w.
60 w.
40 w.
0

Galapagos Is.

Amazon
SOUTH AMERICA
C. Sa

OCEAN

Mt. Sorata
Ct. 21490
L. Titicaca
Brazilian Plateau

Fiji Is.

Sao Paulo
Rio de Janeiro

20
Southern Tropic

Valparaiso

Andes
Buenos Aires
Pampas
Montevideo
Rio de la Plata

New Zealand
Auckland
Cook Str.
Wellington

Patagonia

Magellan Str.
Tierra del Fuego
C. Horn
Falkland Is.
Sth. Georgia

40

Antarctic Circle

60
ANTARCTICA

80
SOUTH POLE
80

June 21st
NORTHERN
MIDSUMMER

Sun's Rays

North Pole
Arctic Circle
Northern Tropic
Equator
Southern Tropic
Antarctic Circle
South Pole

March 21st and
September 22nd
(Equinoxes)

Over 12,000'   12,000'–6,000'   6,000'–3,000'   3,000'–1,500'   1,500'–600'

Zenithal
Scale

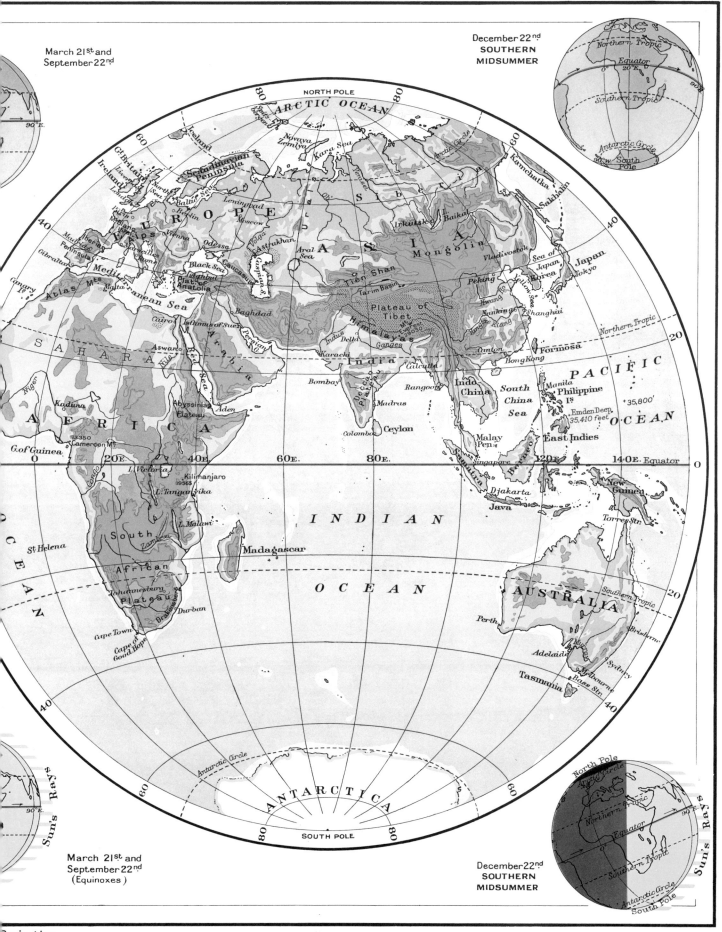

March 21st and
September 22nd

December 22nd
SOUTHERN
MIDSUMMER

NORTH POLE
ARCTIC OCEAN
Spits bergen
Iceland
Novaya
Zemlya
Kara Sea
S I B E R I A
Kamchatka
Sakhalin
Gt Britain
Scandinavian
Peninsula
North Sea
Ireland
Irish Sea
Baltic Sea
Berlin
Leningrad
E U R O P E
Vienna
Moscow
Madrid
Iberian
Peninsula
Marseilles
Rhine
Odessa
Volga
Astrakhan
A S I A
Irkutsk
L. Baikal
Mongolia
Vladivostok
Sea of
Japan
Japan
Tokyo
Gibraltar
Pyrenees
Corsica
Black Sea
Caucasus
Aral
Sea
Caspian S.
Tien Shan
Peking
Korea
Yellow Sea
Canary
Is.
Atlas Mts
Mediterranean Sea
Malta
Sicily
Plateau of
Anatolia
Baghdad
Tarim Basin
Plateau of
Tibet
Nanking
Shanghai
Cairo
Isthmus of Suez
Himalayas
Mt Everest
29030
Yangtze Kiang
Hwang Ho
Northern Tropic
20
S A H A R A
Arabia
Persian
G.
Indus
Delhi
Ganges
Canton
Formosa
Aswan
Nile
Karachi
India
Calcutta
Hong Kong
PACIFIC
Niger
Red
Sea
Bombay
Deccan
Plateau
Madras
Rangoon
Indo
China
South
China
Sea
Manila
Philippine
Is
+35,800'
OCEAN
Kaduna
A F R I C A
Aden
Abyssinian
Plateau
13350
Cameroon Mt
Colombo
Ceylon
Malay
Pen
Emden Deep
35,410 feet
East Indies
G.of Guinea
0
20E
40E
60E.
80E.
Singapore
Borneo
120E
140E. Equator
0
Congo
L.Victoria
Kilimanjaro
19565
L.Tanganyika
Sumatra
Djakarta
Java
New
Guinea
Torres Str.
L. Malawi
I N D I A N
St Helena
South
Zambesi
Madagascar
O C E A N
A F R I C A N
Johannesburg
Plateau
Drakensberg
Durban
A U S T R A L I A
Southern Tropic
20
O C E A N
Perth
Brisbane
Cape Town
Cape of
Good Hope
Adelaide
Murray
Sydney
40
Tasmania
Melbourne
Bass Str.
40
Antarctic Circle
A N T A R C T I C A
80
SOUTH POLE
80
60

March 21st and
September 22nd
(Equinoxes)

December 22nd
SOUTHERN
MIDSUMMER

Sun's Rays
90°E.

Sun's Rays

Projection
OOO

600-0   Land below sea level   0-100 Fathoms   100-1,000 Fathoms   below 1,000 Fathoms

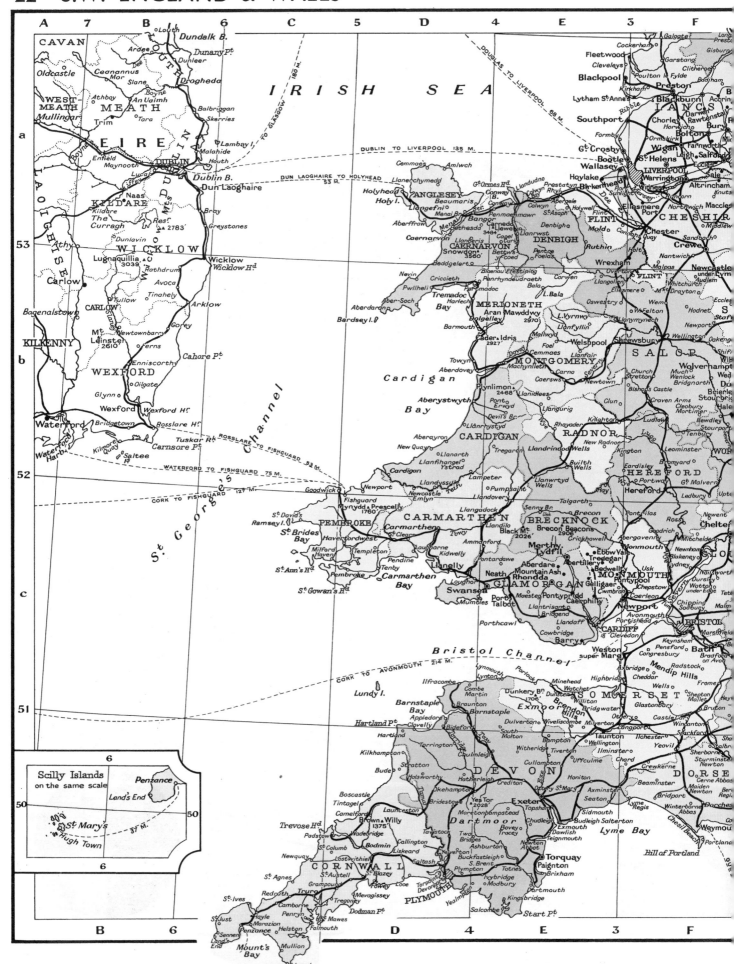

Scale, 1:1,750,000 = 28 miles to 1 inch

Miles
10 0 20 40 60 80

Kilomètres
20 0 40 80 120

Principal Railways ⌒ Steamer Routes NAUT. MLS.

Long. 2 East

NORTH SEA

ENGLISH CHANNEL

Strait of Dover

FRANCE

BELGIUM

HULL TO BERGEN 470 M.

HULL TO TRÖNDHEIM 744 M.

HULL TO CUXHAVEN 350 M.

HULL TO AMSTERDAM 192 M.

HARWICH TO ESBJERG 355 M.

HARWICH TO LEITH 391 M.

HARWICH TO HOOK OF HOLLAND 106 M.

61 M.

38 M.

22 M.

CHERBOURG 83 M.

TO LE HAVRE 114 M.

TO DIEPPE 64 M.

Counties and regions: West Riding, East Riding, Lindsey, Kesteven, Holland, Derby, Nottingham, Leicester, Rutland, Soke of Peterborough, Isle of Ely, Norfolk, Suffolk West, Suffolk East, Huntingdon, Northampton, Warwick, Bedford, Cambridge, Oxford, Bucks, Hertford, Essex, Berks, Surrey, Kent, Sussex West, Sussex East, Hants, Isle of Wight, Greater London, The Wash, The Broads, The Fens, South Downs

Place names (selection): Harrogate, Otley, Ilkley, Wetherby, York, Tadcaster, Leeds, Selby, Morley, Batley, Wakefield, Castleford, Pontefract, Barnsley, Huddersfield, Holmfirth, Penistone, Rotherham, Sheffield, Chesterfield, Dronfield, Doncaster, Mexborough, Bawtry, Epworth, Crowle, Scunthorpe, Brigg, Grimsby, Cleethorpes, Immingham, Barton, Hull, Hedon, Withernsea, Patrington, Spurn Hd, Saltfleet, Louth, Mablethorpe, Sutton on Sea, Market Rasen, Wragby, Lincoln, Horncastle, Alford, Spilsby, Skegness, Wainfleet, Burgh le Marsh, Boston, Spalding, Holbeach, Sutterton, Donington, Kings Lynn, Hunstanton, Heacham, Dersingham, Castle Rising, Downham Market, Swaffham, Fakenham, Walsingham, Blakeney, Cley, Holt, Sheringham, Cromer, Mundesley, N. Walsham, Stalham, Aylsham, Reepham, E. Dereham, Wymondham, Norwich, Acle, Gt. Yarmouth, Loddon, Stratton, Long Stratton, Beccles, Lowestoft, Bungay, Wrentham, Southwold, Halesworth, Saxmundham, Aldeburgh, Framlingham, Wickham Mkt., Woodbridge, Orford, Ipswich, Felixstowe, Harwich, Walton on the Naze, Frinton on Sea, Clacton on Sea, Colchester, Brightlingsea, Manningtree, Weeley, Maldon, Witham, Chelmsford, Braintree, Halstead, Sudbury, Hadleigh, Bury St. Edmunds, Newmarket, Mildenhall, Thetford, Brandon, Diss, Eye, Debenham, Laxfield, Haverhill, Clare, Newport, Saffron Walden, Royston, Baldock, Cambridge, St. Neots, Huntingdon, St. Ives, Ely, Chatteris, March, Wisbech, Whittlesey, Peterborough, Oundle, Corby, Stamford, Oakham, Melton Mowbray, Loughborough, Coalville, Leicester, Market Harborough, Kettering, Wellingborough, Rushden, Northampton, Rugby, Lutterworth, Hinckley, Nuneaton, Birmingham, Coventry, Solihull, Kenilworth, Warwick, Leamington, Stratford on Avon, Banbury, Brackley, Buckingham, Bicester, Woodstock, Oxford, Abingdon, Witney, Faringdon, Wantage, Newbury, Reading, Maidenhead, Windsor, Slough, Uxbridge, Watford, St. Albans, Hemel Hempstead, Berkhamsted, Tring, Aylesbury, Leighton Buzzard, Luton, Dunstable, Hitchin, Stevenage, Hertford, Ware, Bishops Stortford, Harlow, Epping, Enfield, Barnet, Harrow, Ealing, London, Ilford, Romford, Brentwood, Billericay, Rayleigh, Southend, Shoeburyness, Canvey I., Gravesend, Rochester, Chatham, Gillingham, Sittingbourne, Faversham, Whitstable, Herne Bay, Margate, Ramsgate, Broadstairs, Sandwich, Deal, Walmer, Dover, Folkestone, Sandgate, Hythe, New Romney, Dungeness, Rye, Winchelsea, Hastings, Bexhill, Eastbourne, Beachy Hd., Pevensey, Battle, Northiam, Tenterden, Ashford, Canterbury, Maidstone, Tunbridge Wells, Crowborough, Uckfield, Lewes, Newhaven, Seaford, Brighton, Hove, Worthing, Littlehampton, Bognor Regis, Chichester, Arundel, Goodwood, Midhurst, Petersfield, Petworth, Horsham, Crawley, Haywards Heath, Burgess Hill, Ringmer, East Grinstead, Edenbridge, Sevenoaks, Reigate, Redhill, Dorking, Leatherhead, Croydon, Bromley, Purley, Caterham, Godstone, Guildford, Godalming, Haslemere, Hindhead, Liphook, Alton, Basingstoke, Farnham, Aldershot, Farnborough, Woking, Chertsey, Kingston, Richmond, Wimbledon, Winchester, Eastleigh, Southampton, Fareham, Gosport, Portsmouth, Havant, Hayling I., Selsey Bill, Isle of Wight, Newport, Ryde, Sandown, Shanklin, Ventnor, St. Catherines Pt., Cowes, Lymington, Christchurch, Bournemouth, New Forest, Ringwood, Lyndhurst

Calais, Boulogne, Dunkirk, Ostend, St. Omer, Armentières, Béthune, Lens, Le Touquet, C. Gris Nez

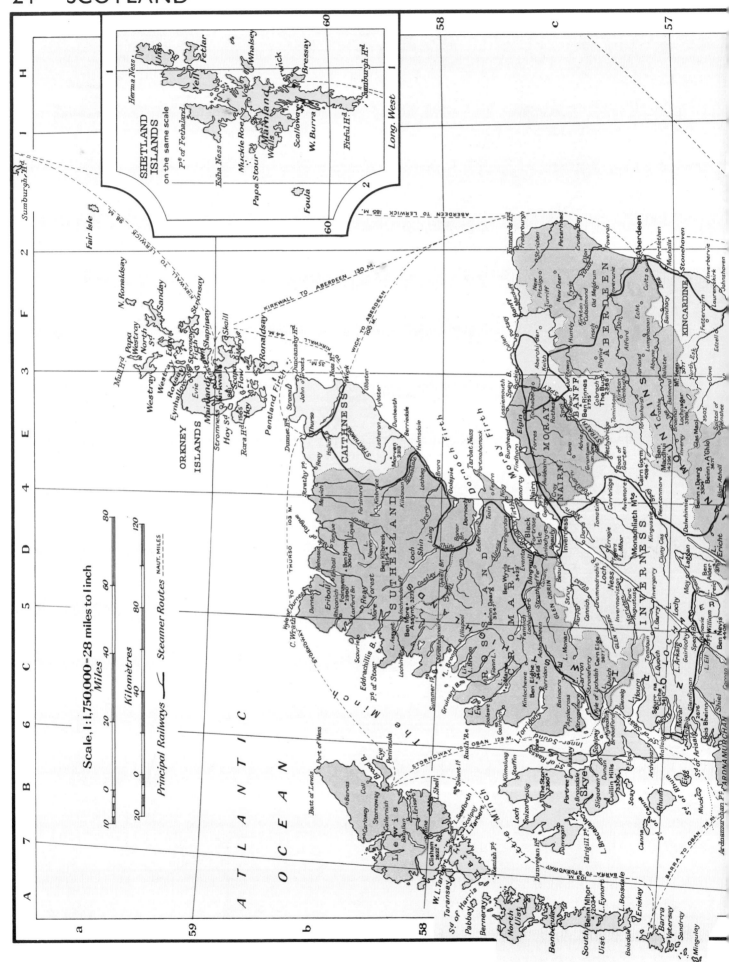

SHETLAND ISLANDS
on the same scale

Herma Ness I.
Unst
Fetlar
Yell
Whalsey
Pt. of Fethaland
Esha Ness
Muckle Roe
Papa Stour
Walls
Mainland
Scalloway
W. Burra
Fitful Hd.
Foula
Sumburgh Hd.
Long. West

ABERDEEN TO LERWICK 185 M.

Scale, 1:1,750,000=28 miles to 1inch

Miles
Kilometres
NAUT. MILES

Principal Railways
Steamer Routes

ATLANTIC OCEAN

ORKNEY ISLANDS

N. Ronaldsay
Sanday
Papa Westray
North Ronaldsay
Westray
Eday
Stronsay
Shapinsay
Rousay
Eynhallow
Evie
Mainland
Kirkwall
Stromness
Scapa Flow
Hoy Sd.
Hoy
S. Ronaldsay
Rora Hd.
Skaill
Pentland Firth
Stroma
Duncansby Hd.
John o' Groats

Fair Isle

Sumburgh Hd.

KIRKWALL TO ABERDEEN 130 M.
WICK TO ABERDEEN 100 M.

CAITHNESS
Thurso
Reay
Dunnet Hd.
Wick
Ulbster
Lybster
Latheron
Dunbeath
Berriedale
Helmsdale

SUTHERLAND
C. Wrath
Kyle of Durness
Durness
Rhiconich
Eriboll
L. Eriboll
Ben Hope
Loyal
Tongue
Melness
Loch Naver
Kinbrace
Forsinard
Strathy Pt.
Melvich

Butt of Lewis
Port of Ness
Eye Peninsula

Lewis
Stornoway
Carloway
Callernish

ROSS AND CROMARTY

MORAY
Elgin
Forres
Nairn

BANFF
Banff
Macduff

ABERDEEN
Peterhead
Fraserburgh
KINCARDINE
Stonehaven

INVERNESS

Ben Nevis

Skye
Portree

NAIRN

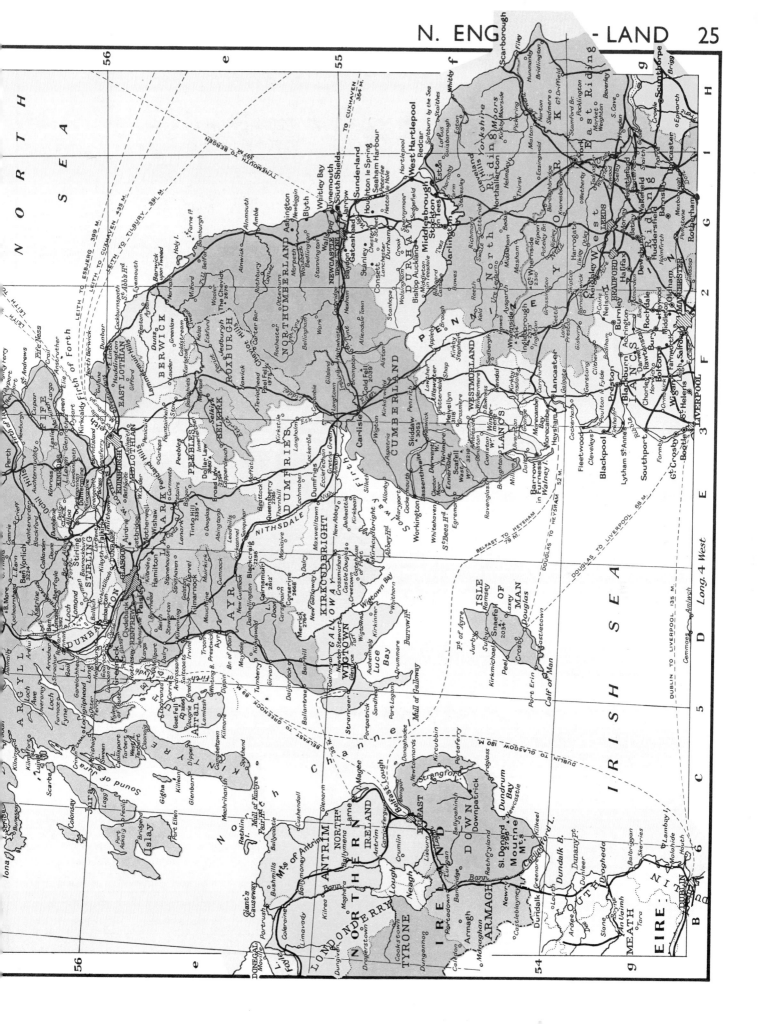

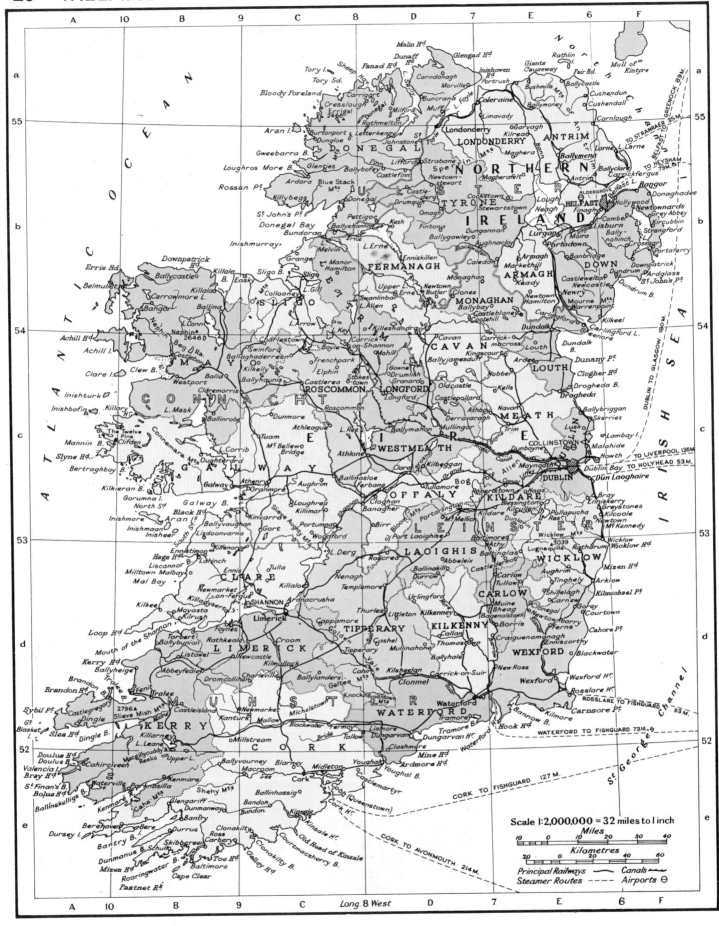

Scale 1:2,000,000 = 32 miles to 1 inch

Miles

Kilometres

Principal Railways —— Canals ——
Steamer Routes ---- Airports ⊖

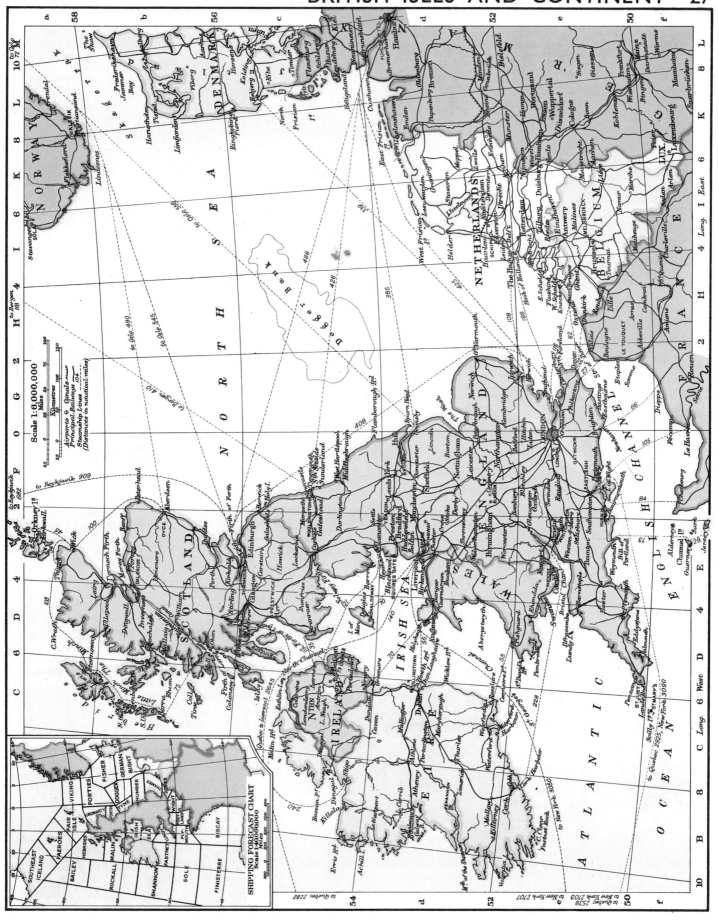

Scale 1:6,000,000

Airports ⊕ Canals
Principal Railways
Steamship Lines 104
(Distances in nautical miles)

SHIPPING FORECAST CHART
Scale 1:40000000

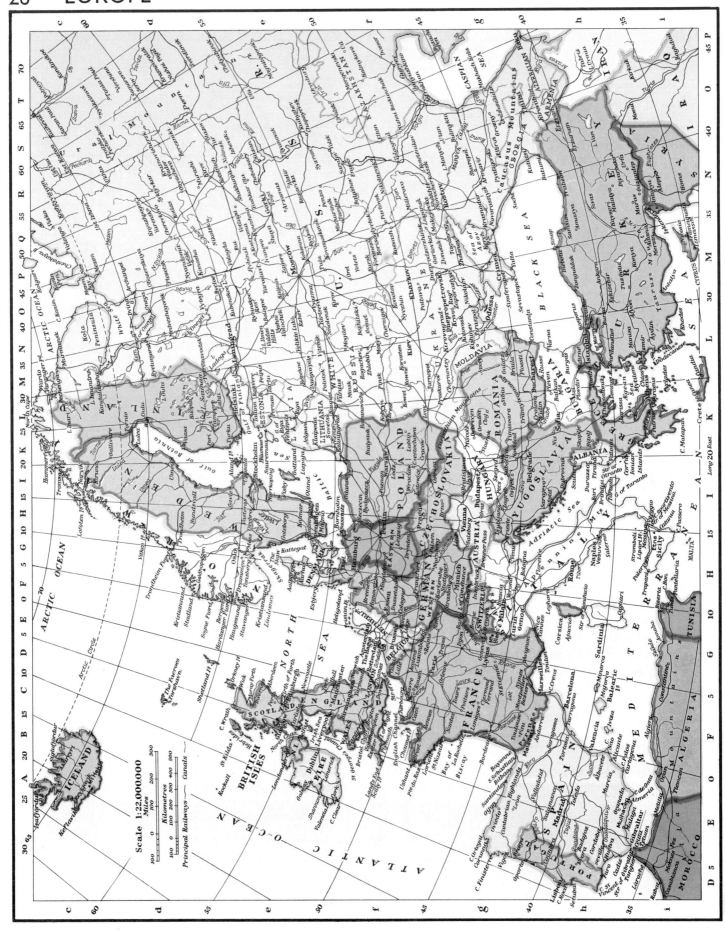

Scale 1:22,000,000

Miles
100   200   300

Kilometres
100 200 300 400 500

Principal Railways —— Canals

ARCTIC OCEAN

ICELAND *on same scale*

THE FAEROES *on same scale*

ATLANTIC OCEAN

NORTH SEA

SKAGERRAK

KATTEGAT

GULF OF BOTHNIA

GULF OF FINLAND

ESTONIA

LATVIA

LITHUANIA

WHITE RUSSIA

DENMARK

NORWAY

SWEDEN

FINLAND

U. S. S. R.

GERMANY

POLAND

NETHERLANDS

Scale 1:9,250,000

Long East

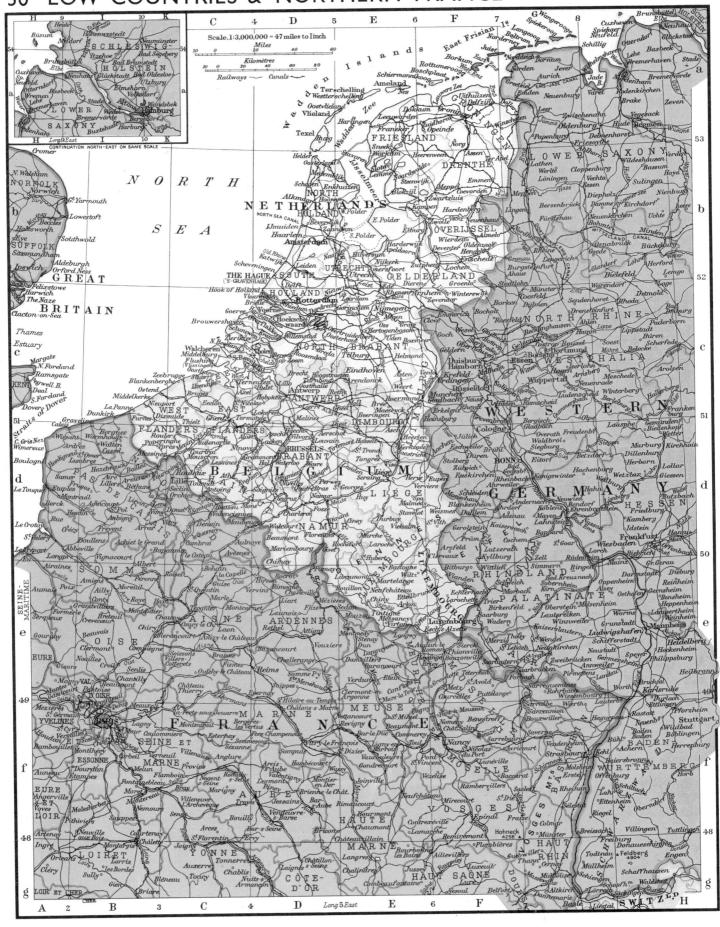

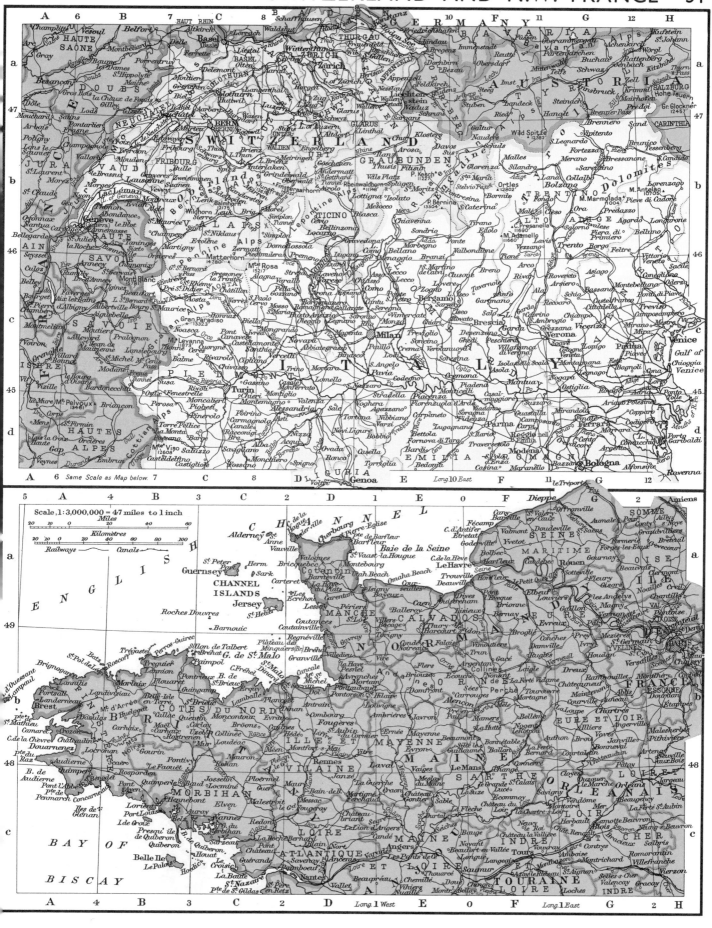

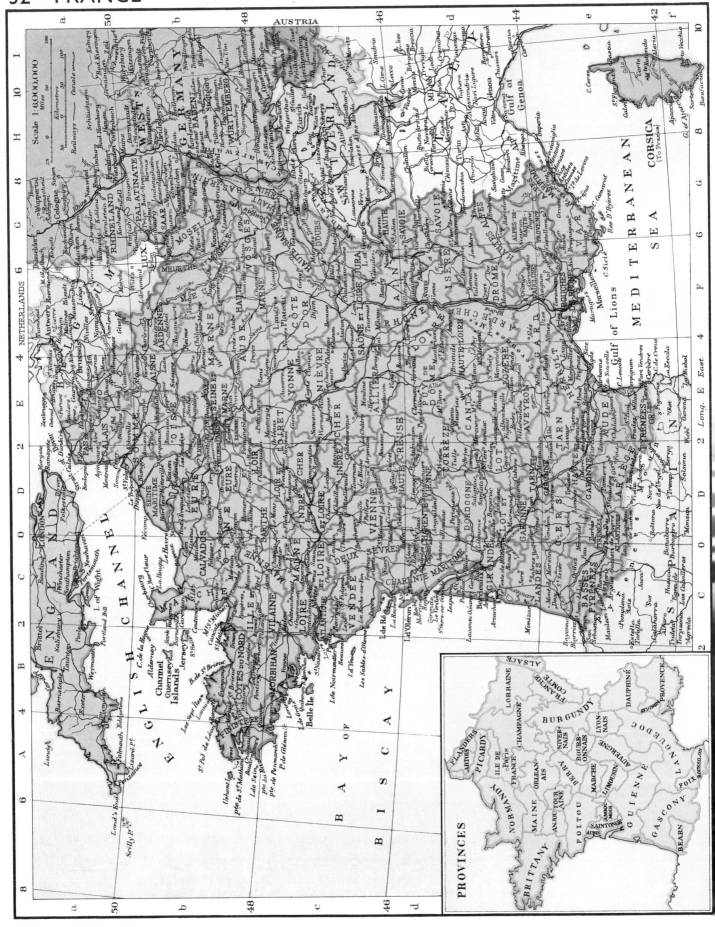

PROVINCES

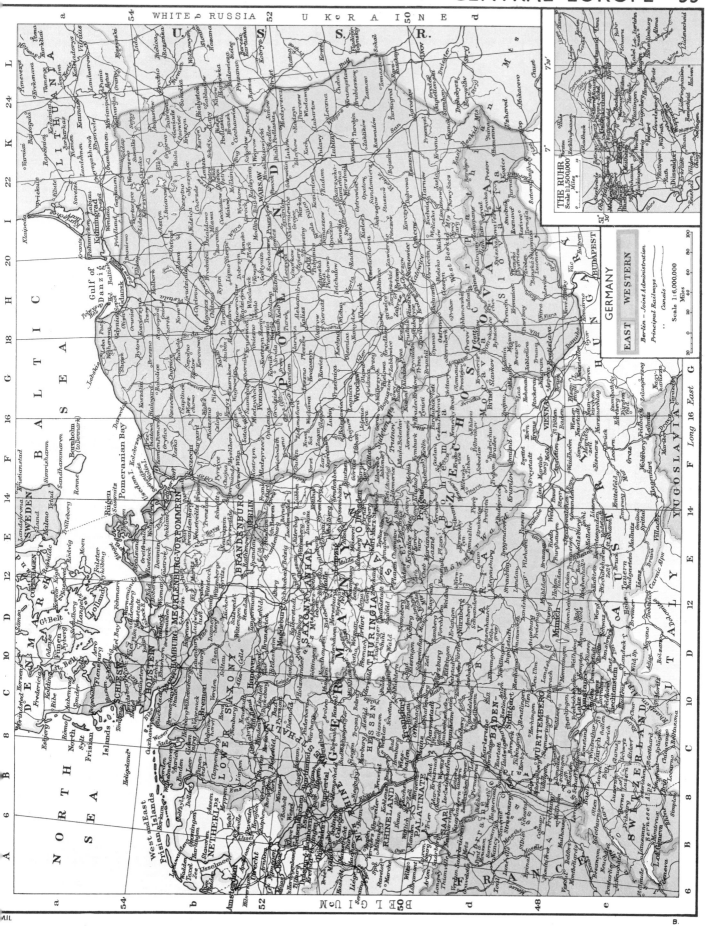

THE RUHR
Scale 1:1,500,000

GERMANY
EAST WESTERN
Berlin - Joint Administration.
Principal Railways
Canals
Scale 1:6,000,000

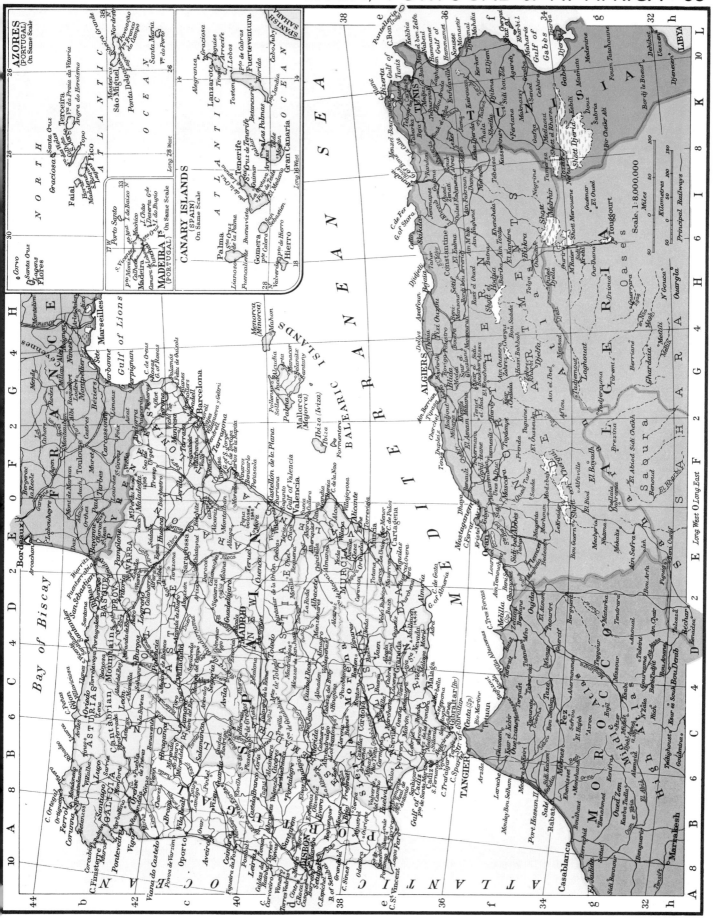

Scale, 1 : 5,250,000

Miles
20   0   20   40   80   100

Kilomètres
50   0   50   100   150

Principal Railways

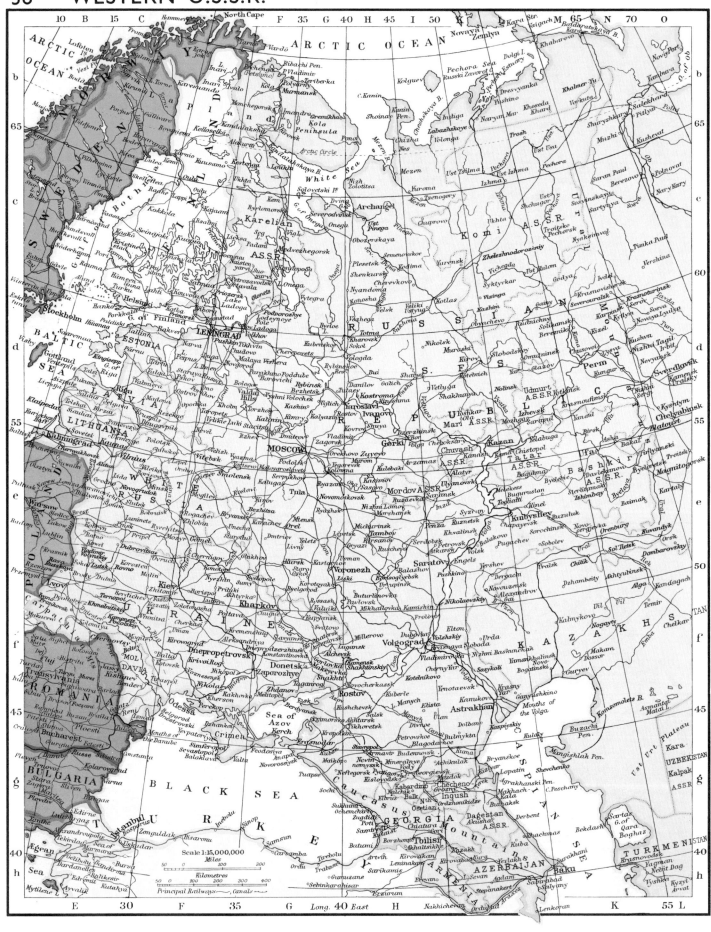

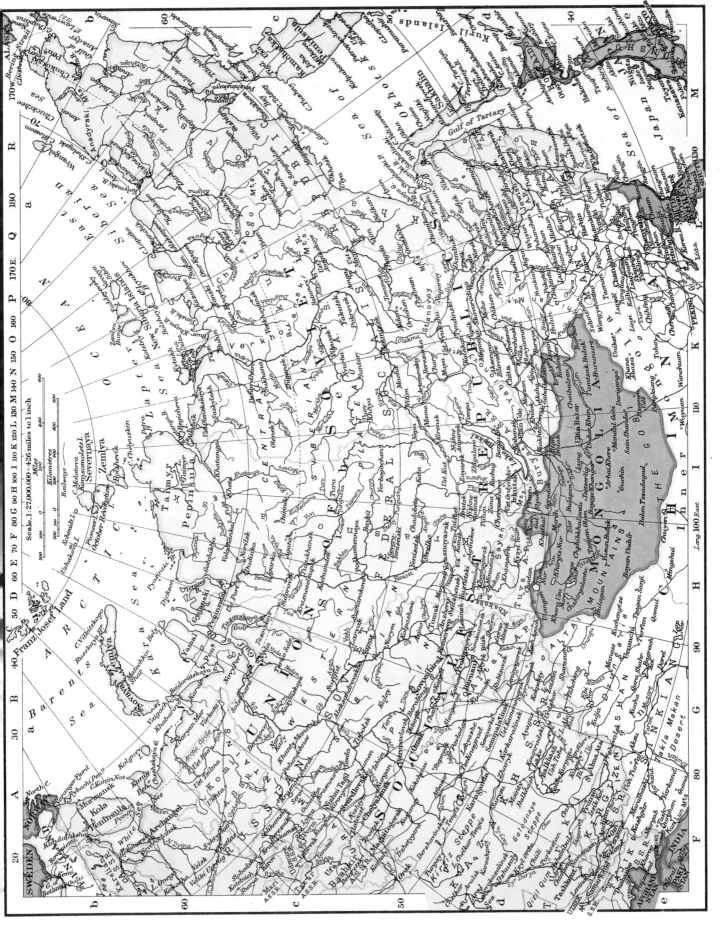

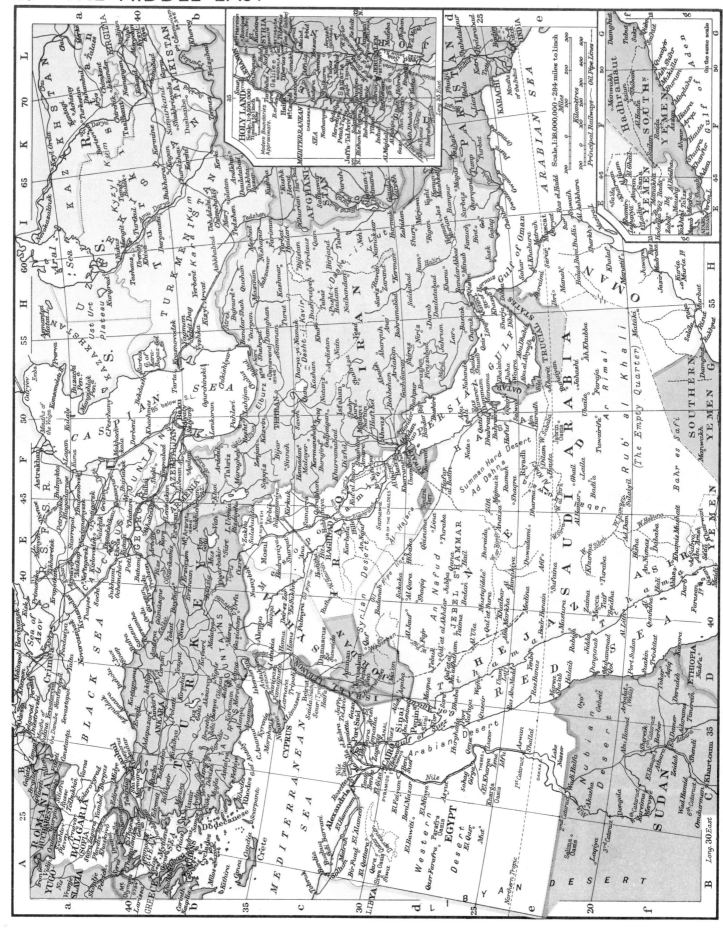

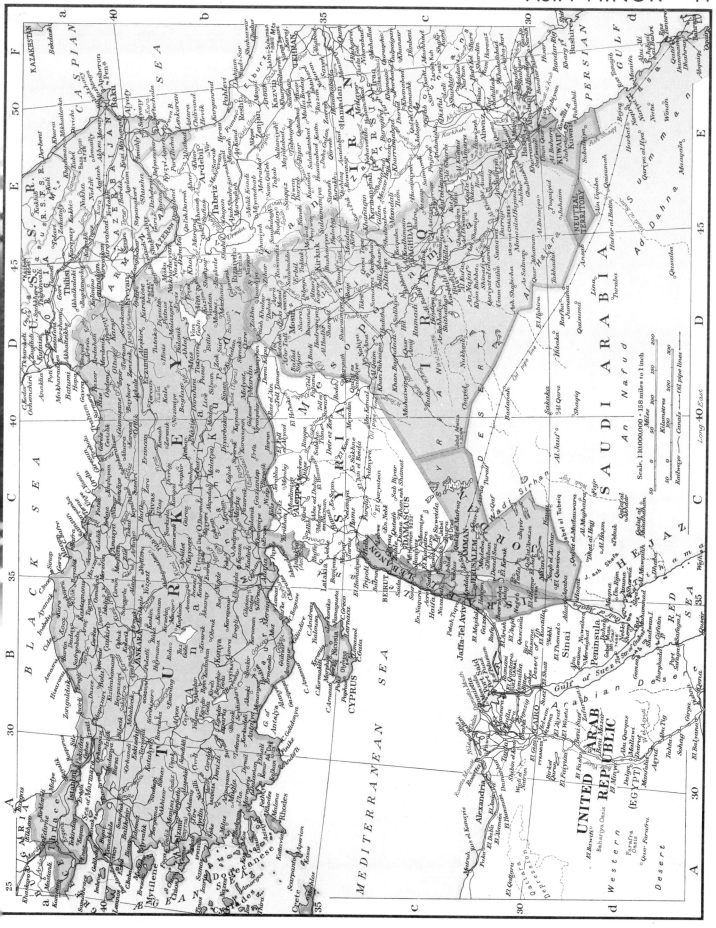

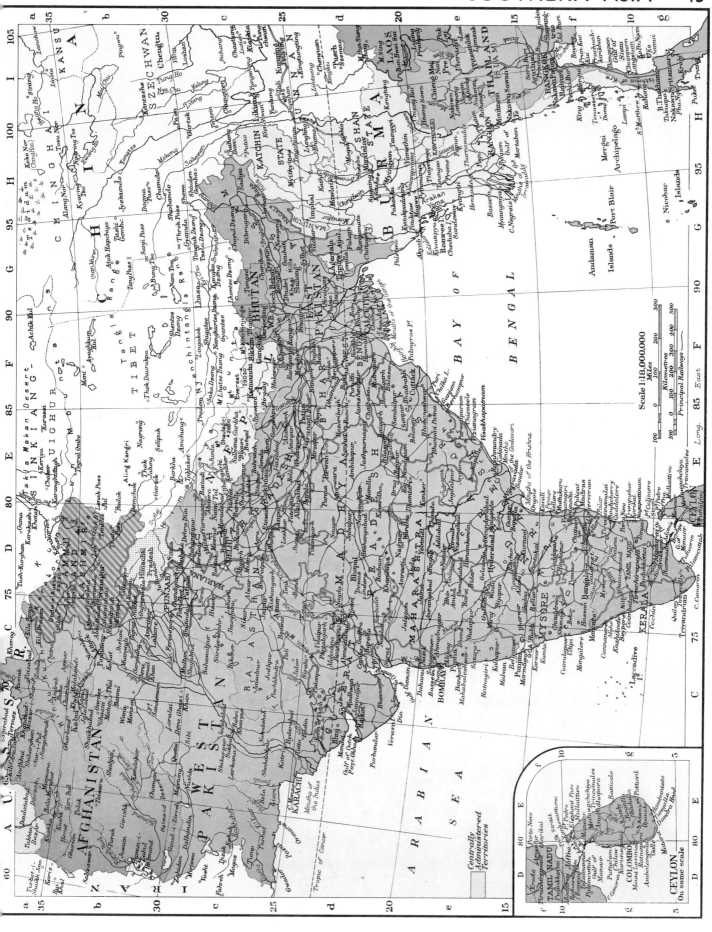

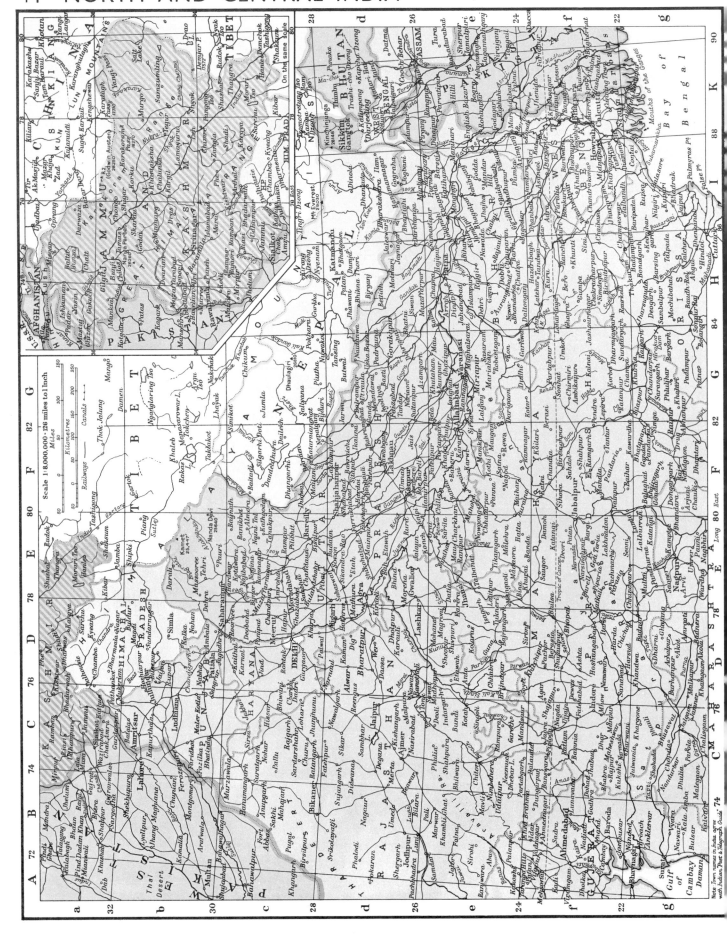

CEYLON
Scale, 1:4,000,000 - 63 miles to 1 inch

India

Town spellings are in agreement
with the Indian Post Office Guide.

☐ Centrally administered
Territories

Scale, 1:8,000,000 - 126 miles to 1 inch

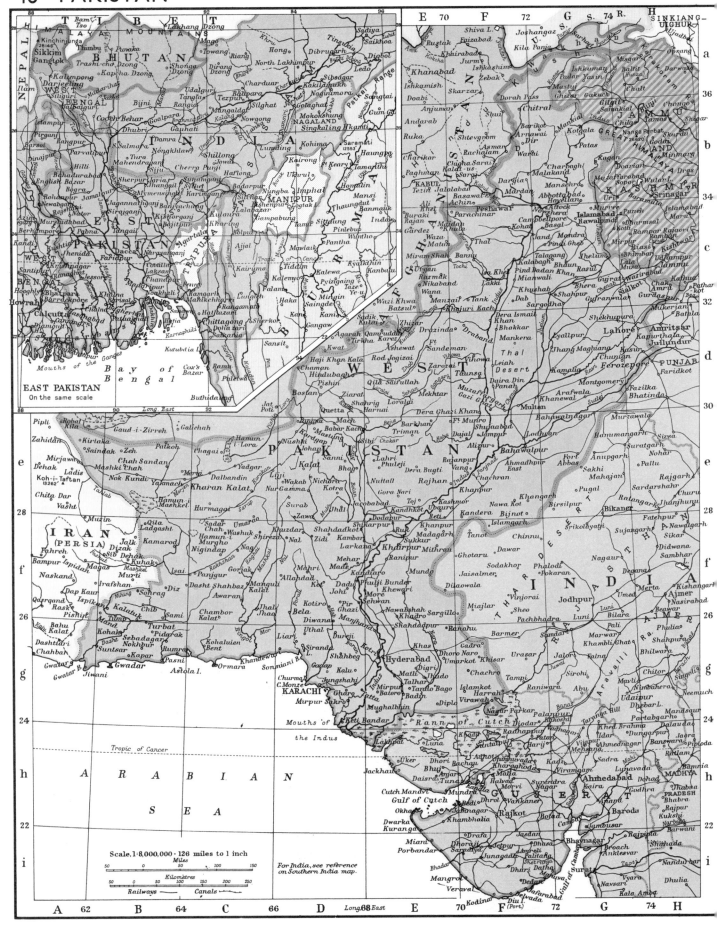

EAST PAKISTAN
On the same scale

Scale, 1:8,000,000 · 126 miles to 1 inch

Miles

Kilometres

Railways   Canals

For India, see reference
on Southern India map.

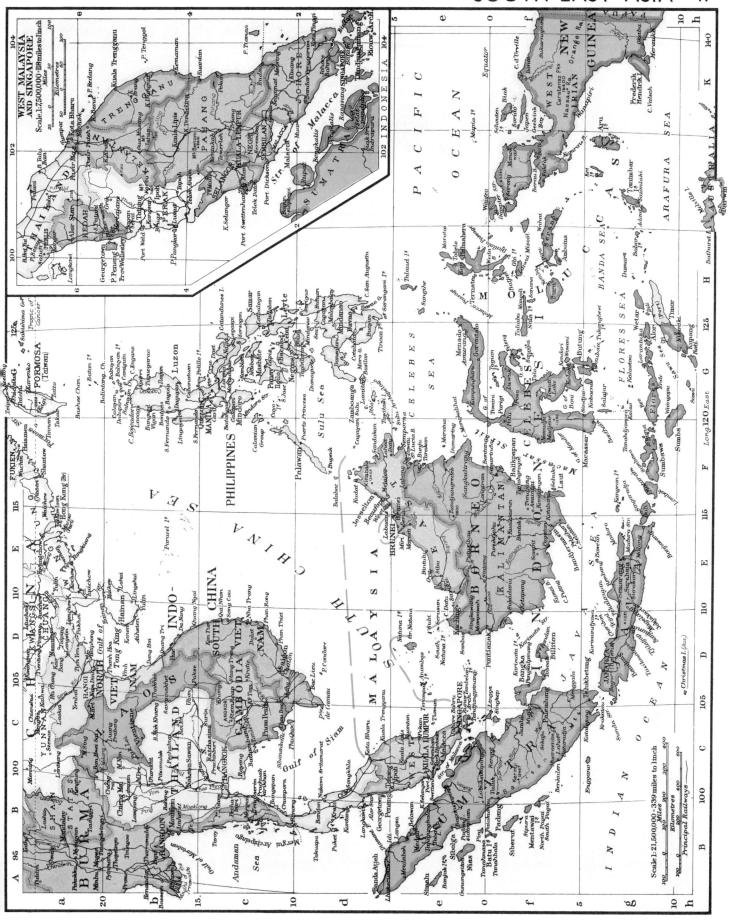

WEST MALAYSIA AND SINGAPORE

Scale 1:7,500,000=118 miles to 1 inch

Miles
Kilometres

Scale 1:21,500,000=339 miles to 1 inch

Miles

Kilometres

Principal Railways

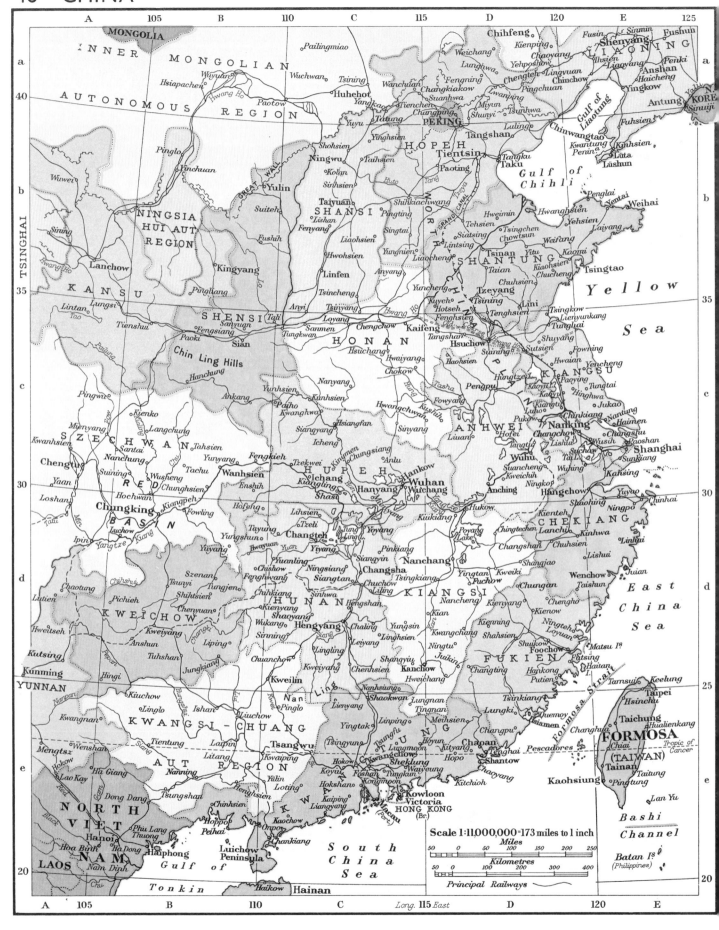

Scale 1:11,000,000=173 miles to 1 inch

Miles
50 0 50 100 150 200 250

Kilometres
50 0 100 200 300 400

Principal Railways

Long. 115 East

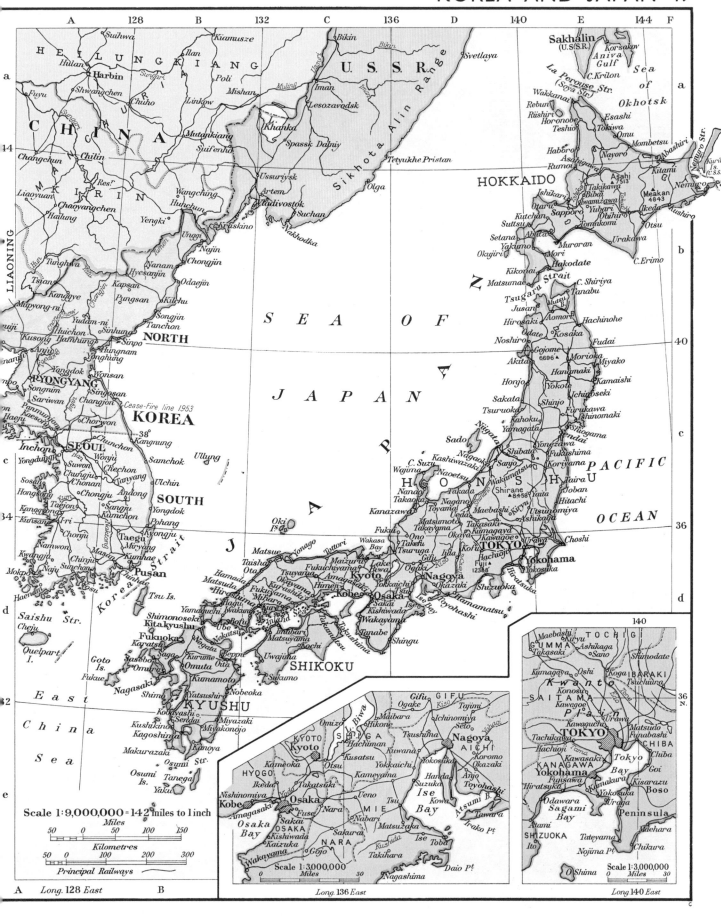

Scale 1:9,000,000 = 142 miles to 1 inch

Miles
50 0 50 100 150

Kilometres
50 0 100 200 300

Principal Railways

Scale 1:3,000,000
Miles
0 50

Scale 1:3,000,000
Miles
0 30

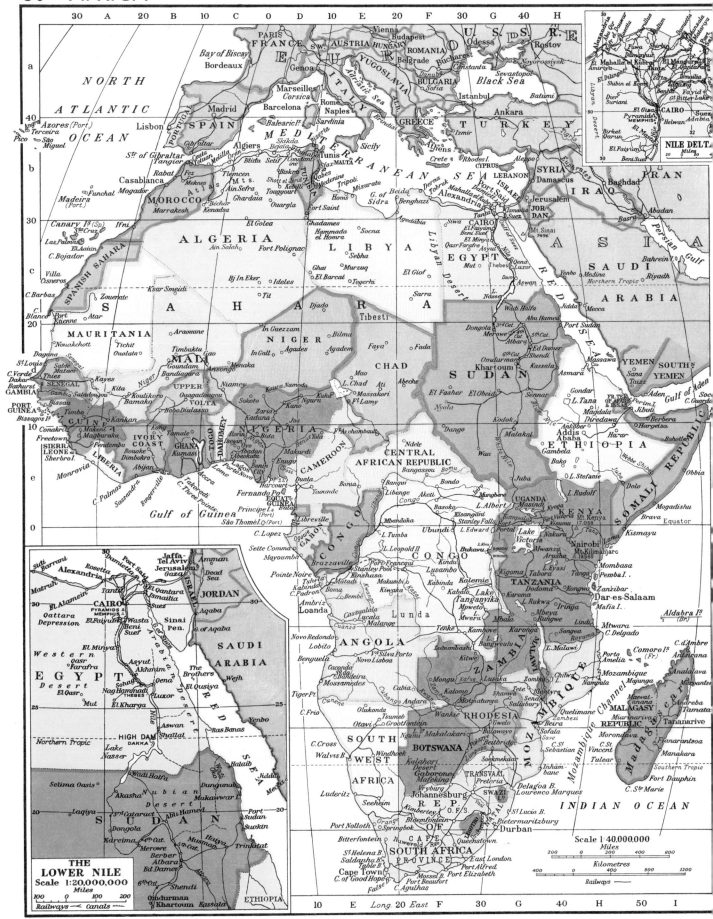

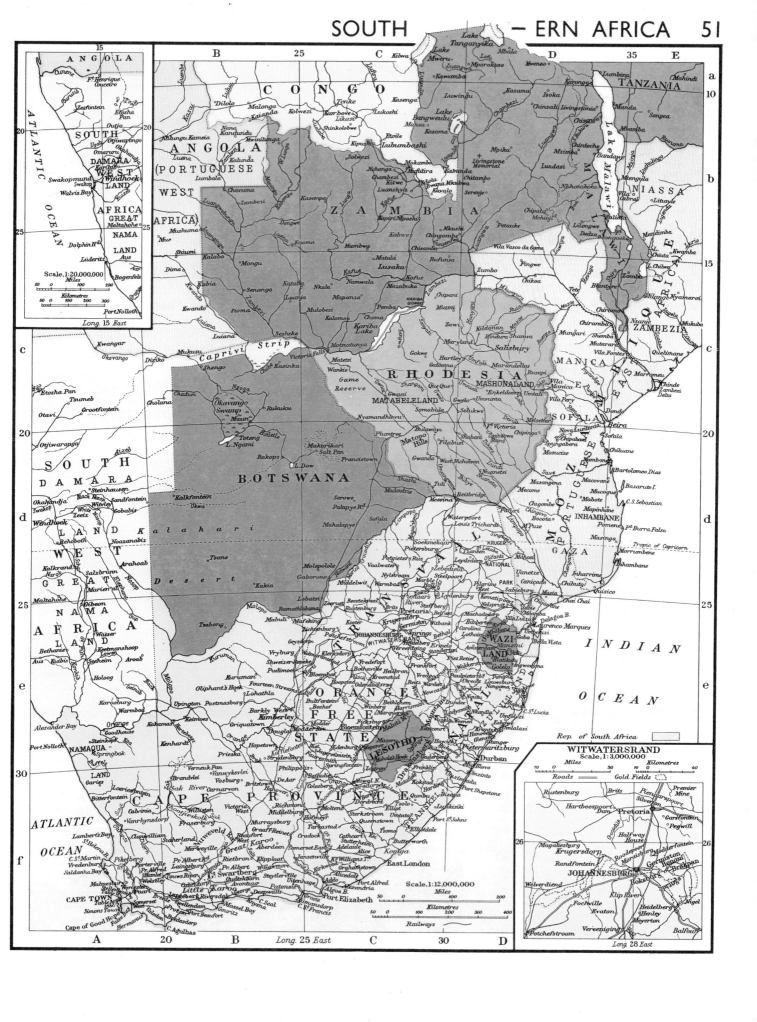

ORANGE FREE STATE

Kimberley
Beaconsfield

BLOEMFONTEIN

Thaba Nchu

NATAL

Ladysmith
Harrismith
Colenso

LESOTHO

Mt. Aux Sources 10761

Giants Castle 10868

Thabana Ntlenyana 11425

Ben MacDhui 10095

QUTHING

DRAKENSBERG

Griqualand East

CURRIE
MOUNT
ALFRED

Kokstad

ALBERT

Burgersdorp

WODEHOUSE

Stormberg

Queenstown

GLEN GREY

Fingoland

Umtata

Graaff-Reinet

Sneeuberg

Compass Berg 8209

MARAISBURG

TARKA

Cradock

Somerset East

Transkei

Butterworth

Kentani

ALBANY

King William's Town

East London

Grahamstown

Port Alfred

Uitenhage

Algoa Bay

Port Elizabeth

Jeffreys Bay
C. St. Francis

INDIAN OCEAN

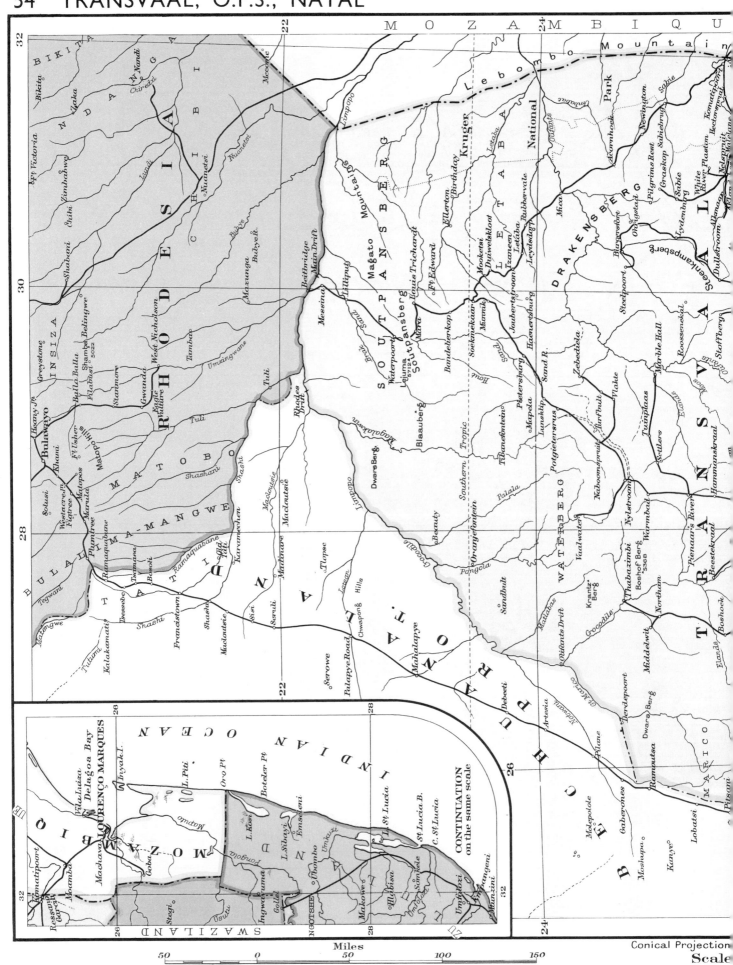

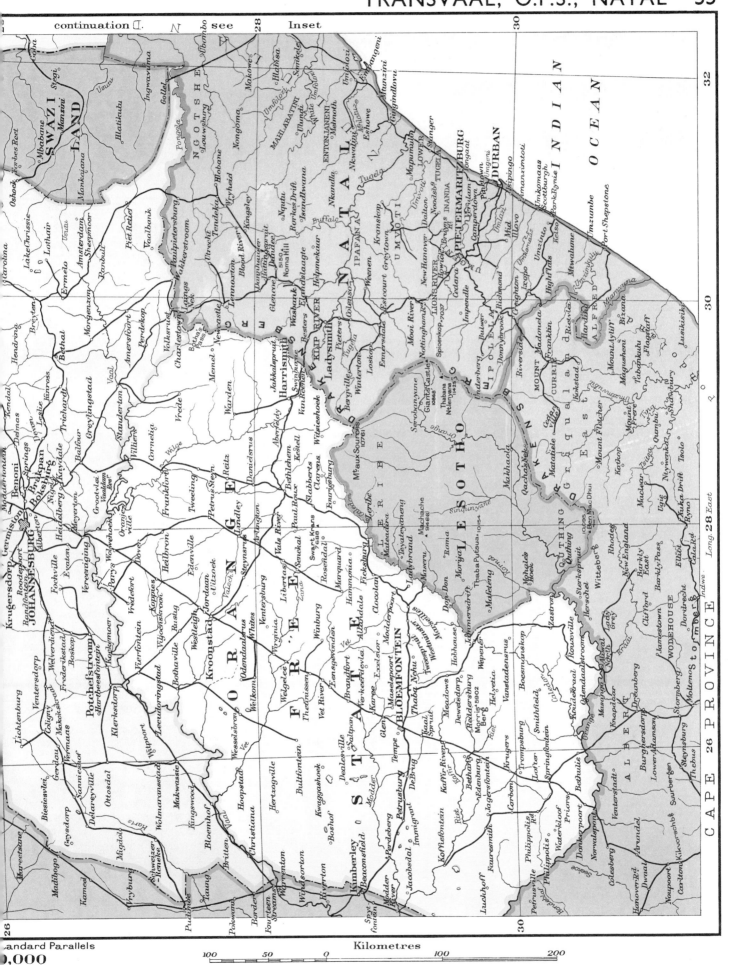

continuation II.   see Inset

SWAZI LAND

NGOTSHE

N A T A L

I P A F A N A

U M V O T I

I N D I A N   O C E A N

DURBAN

PIETERMARITZBURG

O R A N G E   F R E E   S T A T E

BLOEMFONTEIN

Kimberley

LESOTHO

C A P E   26   P R O V I N C E

Long. 28 East

Kilometres
100   50   0   100   200

andard Parallels
0,000

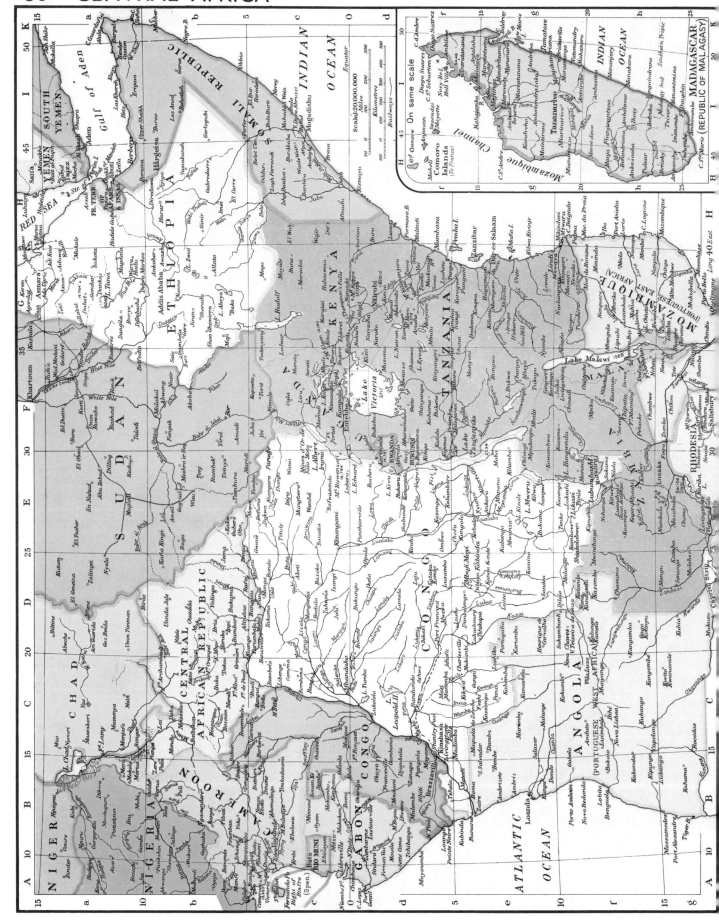

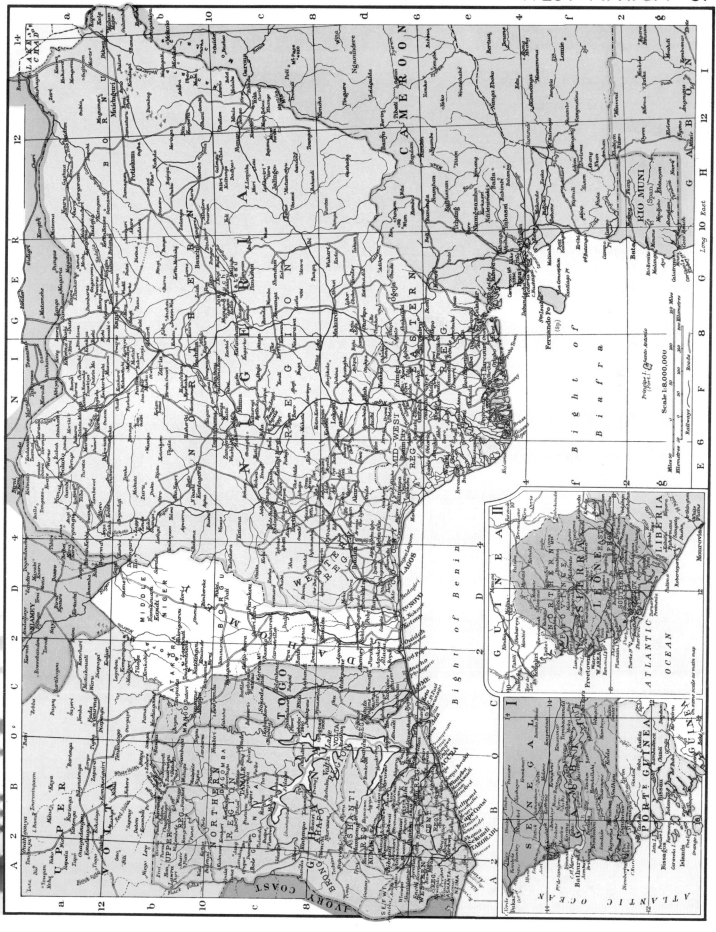

TASMANIA
on the same scale

Scale, 1:10,000,000

Scale 1:10,000,000

Scale 1:20,000,000
Miles
Kilometres
Principal Railways

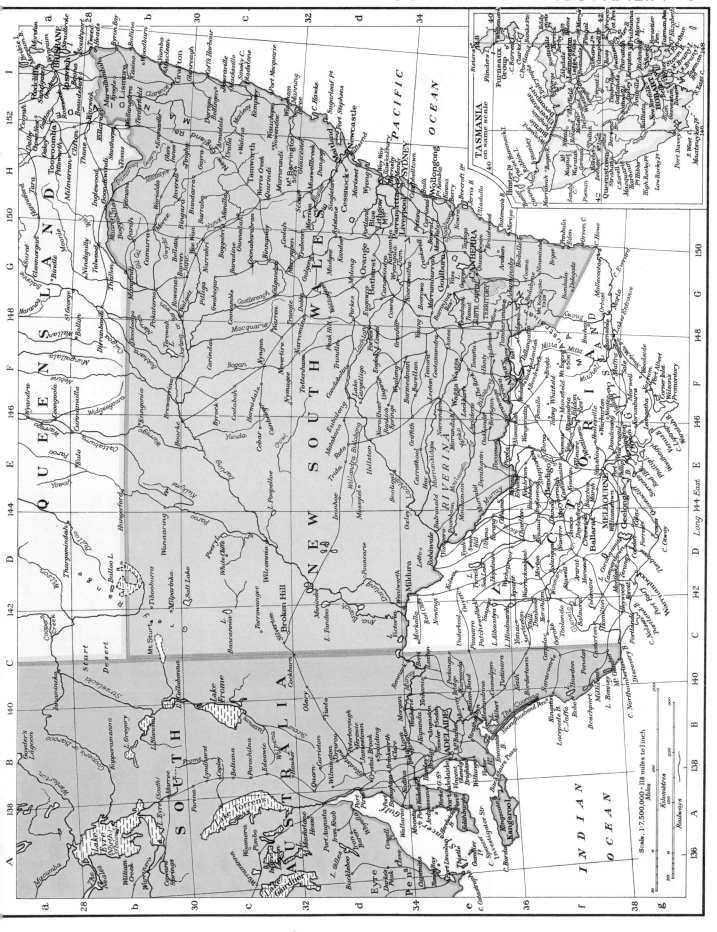

TASMANIA
on same scale

Scale, 1:7,500,000 = 118 miles to 1 inch

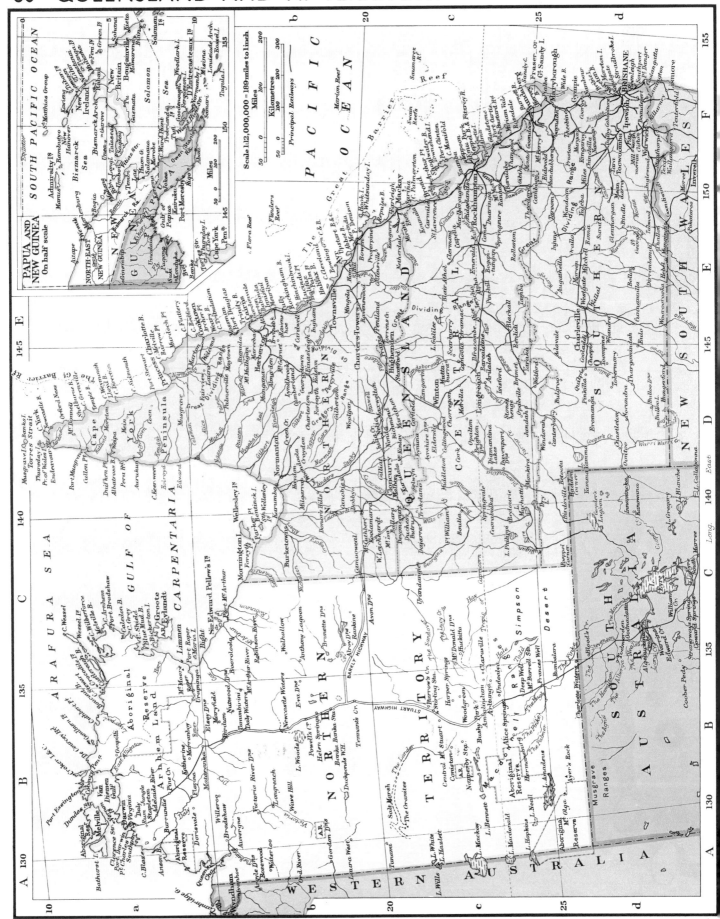

INDIAN OCEAN

THE KIMBERLEYS
on half scale

INDIAN
OCEAN

SCALE. 1: 7,500,000 = 118 miles to 1 inch

Gibson Desert

Great Victoria

Desert

INDIAN

OCEAN

Great Australian

Bight

PERTH
Fremantle

Northam

Kalgoorlie

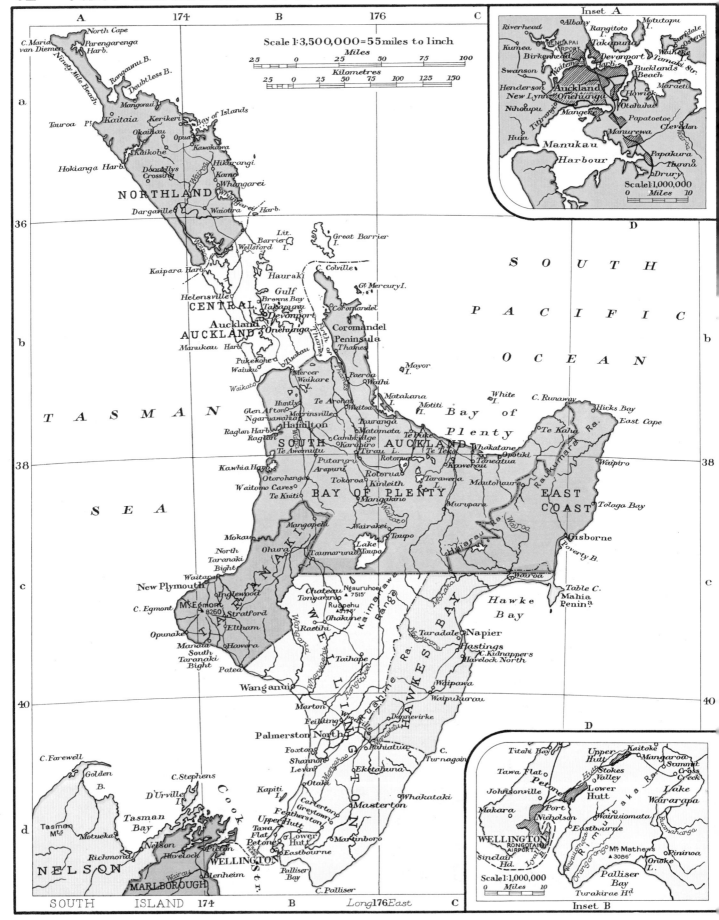

Scale 1:3,500,000 = 55 miles to 1 inch

Miles

25 0 25 50 75 100

Kilometres

25 0 25 50 75 100 125 150

Inset A

Riverhead · Albany · Rangitoto I. · Motutapu I.
WHENUAPAI AIRPORT · Takapuna · Surfdale · Ostend
Kumeu · Birkenhead · Devonport · Waiheke I. · Tamaki Str.
Swanson · Waitemata Harb. · Bucklands Beach
Henderson · Auckland · Howick · Meraeti
New Lynn · Onehunga · Otahuhu
Nihotupu · Tiropanga · Mangere · Papatoetoe · Clevedon
Huia · Manurewa · Papakura · Tuina
Manukau Harbour · Drury

Scale 1:1,000,000
0 Miles 10

Inset A map labels:

NORTHLAND
North Cape
C. Maria van Diemen
Parengarenga Harb.
Rangaunu B.
Ninety Mile Beach
Doubtless B.
Tauroa Pt.
Mangonui
Kaitaia
Kerikeri
Okaihau
Opua
Bay of Islands
Kawakawa
Kaikohe
Hikurangi
Kamo
Hokianga Harb.
Donnellys Crossing
Whangarei
Dargaville
Waiotira
Whangarei Harb.

SOUTH PACIFIC OCEAN

Lit. Barrier I.
Wellsford
Great Barrier I.
Kaipara Harb.
Hauraki
C. Colville
Helensville
Gulf
Gt Mercury I.
Browns Bay
CENTRAL
Coromandel
Takapuna
AUCKLAND
Devonport
Auckland
Onehunga
Coromandel Peninsula
Manukau Harb.
Thames
Firth of Thames
Pukekohe
Mayor I.
Waiuku
Mercer
Paeroa
Waikato
Waikare L.
Waihi
TASMAN
Huntly
Te Aroha
Matakana
White I.
C. Runaway
Hicks Bay
SEA
Glen Afton
Whitoa
Motiti I.
East Cape
Ngaruawahia
Morrinsville
Bay of
Te Kaha
Raglan Harb.
Hamilton
Tauranga
Plenty
Raglan
Cambridge
Matamata
Te Puke
Whakatane
SOUTH
Karapiro
AUCKLAND
Opotiki
Te Awamutu
Tirau
Rotorua
Te Teko
Waipiro
Kawhia Harb.
Putaruru
Taneatua
Arapuni
Rotorua
Otorohanga
Tokoroa
Kinleith
Tarawera L.
EAST
Waitomo Caves
Mautohaura
COAST
Te Kuiti
Mangakino
Tolaga Bay
Mokau
Mangapehi
Wairakei
Murupara
North Taranaki Bight
Ohura
Taupo
Waikato
Gisborne
Waitara
Lake Taupo
Poverty B.
New Plymouth
Taumarunui
Wairoa
Inglewood
Chateau
Ngauruhoe 7515'
Table C.
C. Egmont
Mt Egmont 8260
Tongariro
Ruapehu 9175'
Mahia Penin.
Stratford
Ohakune
Hawke Bay
Eltham
Raetihi
Opunake
Wanganui
Taradale
Napier
Manaia
Hawera
Taihape
Hastings
South Taranaki Bight
C. Kidnappers
Patea
Havelock North
Wanganui
Waipawa
Marton
Waipukurau
Feilding
Dannevirke
Palmerston North
HAWKES BAY
Foxton
Pahiatua
Shannon
Turnagain
Levin
Eketahuna
Otaki
Kapiti I.
Carterton
Whakataki
Greytown
Masterton
Featherston
Upper Hutt
Tawa Flat
Petone
Lower Hutt
Martinboro
Eastbourne
Palliser Bay
C. Palliser

TASMAN SEA

C. Farewell
Golden B.
C. Stephens
D'Urville I.
Cook
Tasman Mts
Tasman Bay
Motueka
Nelson
Str.
Richmond
Havelock
Picton
d
NELSON
Blenheim
WELLINGTON
MARLBOROUGH
Wairau

SOUTH ISLAND 174

Long 176 East

Inset B

Titahi Bay
Upper Hutt
Kaitoke
Tawa Flat
Petone
Stokes Valley
Mangaroa
Johnsonville
Lower Hutt
Summit
Cross Creek
Makara
Port Nicholson
Wainuiomata
Lake Wairarapa
WELLINGTON
RONGOTAI AIRPORT
Eastbourne
Ruamahanga
Sinclair Hd.
Lyall
Mt Mathews 3086'
Pirinoa
Orongorongo
Onoke L.
Palliser Bay
Scale 1:1,000,000
0 Miles 10
Turakirae Hd.

A 174 B 176 C
a
36
b
38
c
40
D
D

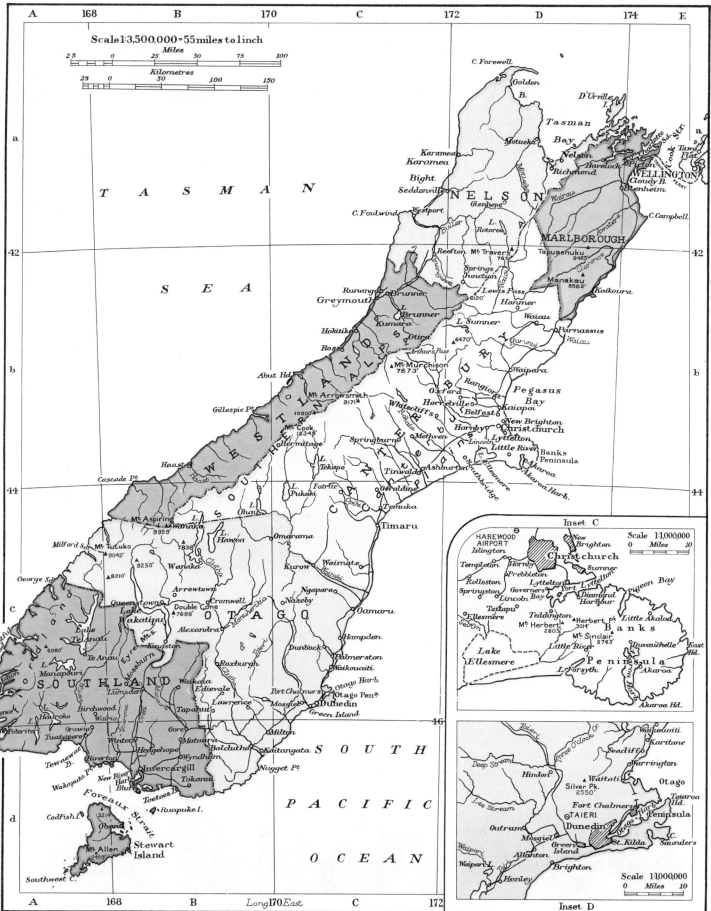

Scale 1:3,500,000 = 55 miles to 1 inch

Miles
25 0 25 50 75 100

Kilometres
25 0 50 100 150

T A S M A N

S E A

C. Farewell

Golden
B.

D'Urville
I.

Karamea
Karamea
Bight

Motueka

Seddonville

Richmond

Havelock

Picton

WELLINGTON

Cloudy B.

Blenheim

C. Foulwind

Westport

Glenhope

Wairau

MARLBOROUGH

C. Campbell

Reefton

Mt Travers
7671'

Tapuaenuku
9465'

Springs
Junction

Lewis Pass
6120'

Hanmer

Manakau
8562'

Kaikoura

Runanga
Brunner

Greymouth

L.
Brunner

Hokitika

Kumara

Otira

L. Sumner

Waiau

Parnassus

Waiau

Ross

Arthur's Pass

6470'

Hurunui

Waipara

Abut Hd.

Mt Murchison
7873'

Oxford

Rangiora

Pegasus

Bay

Mt Arrowsmith
9171'

Horrelville

Belfast

Kaiapoi

Gillespie Pt.

10200'

Mt Cook
12349'

Whitecliffs

Methven

Hornby

New Brighton
Christchurch

Lyttelton

Little River

Akaroa

Springburn

Lincoln

Banks
Peninsula

Hermitage

L. Tekapo

Tinwald

Ashburton

L. Ellesmere

Akaroa Harb.

Haast

Southbridge

Cascade Pt.

L.
Pukaki

Fairlie

Geraldine

L.
Ohau

Temuka

Mt Aspiring
9959'

L.
Wanaka

Opihi

Timaru

Milford Sd.

Mt Tutuko
9042'

7838'

L.
Hawea

Omarama

8210'

Wanaka

9250'

Arrowtown

Cromwell

Kurow

Waimate

Waitaki

Ngapara

George Sd.

Double Cone
7688'

Naseby

Oamaru

6080'

Queenstown
Lake
Wakatipu

Alexandra

O T A G O

Hampden

Lake
Te Anau

Kingston

Roxburgh

Dunback

Palmerston

Te Anau

Manapouri

Lumsden

Lawrence

Waikouaiti

Otago Harb.

S O U T H L A N D

Waikaia
Edievale

Port Chalmers

Otago Pena.

Mosgiel
Dunedin

Hauroko

Birdwood
Wairio

Tapanui

Green Island

Poteriteri

Orawia
Tuatapere

Wintor
Hedgehope
Wyndham

Gore
Mataura
Balclutha

Milton

Kaitangata

S O U T H

Tewaewae
B.

Riverton

Invercargill

Tokanui

Nugget Pt.

Wakaputa Pt.
New River
Harb.
Bluff

P A C I F I C

Foveaux Strait

Toetoes B.

Codfish I.

3214'

Oban

Ruapuke I.

Mt Allen
2459'

Stewart
Island

O C E A N

Southwest C.

Inset C

Scale 1:1,000,000
0   Miles   10

HAREWOOD
AIRPORT
Islington

New
Brighton

Christchurch

Templeton

Hornby

Sumner

Prebbleton

Lyttelton

Rolleston

Governers
Bay

Port
Lyttelton

Pigeon Bay

Springston

Lincoln

Diamond
Harbour

Taitapu

Teddington

Herbert Pk.
3014'

Little Akaloa

Ellesmere

Mt Herbert
2805'

B a n k s

Sedwyn

Mt Sinclair
2763'

Duvauchelle

East
Hd.

Lake
Ellesmere

Little River

P e n i n s u l a

Akaroa

L. Forsyth

Akaroa Hd.

Taieri

Waikouaiti

Three O'Clock

Karitane

Seacliff

Warrington

Deep Stream

Hindon

Waitati

Silver Pk.
2550'

Otago

Lee Stream

Port Chalmers

Taiaroa
Hd.

Outram

TAIERI

Dunedin

Peninsula

Waipori

Mosgiel

Otago Harb.

C.
Saunders

Allanton

Green
Island

St. Kilda

Waipori L.

Brighton

Henley

Scale 1:1,000,000
0   Miles   10

Inset D

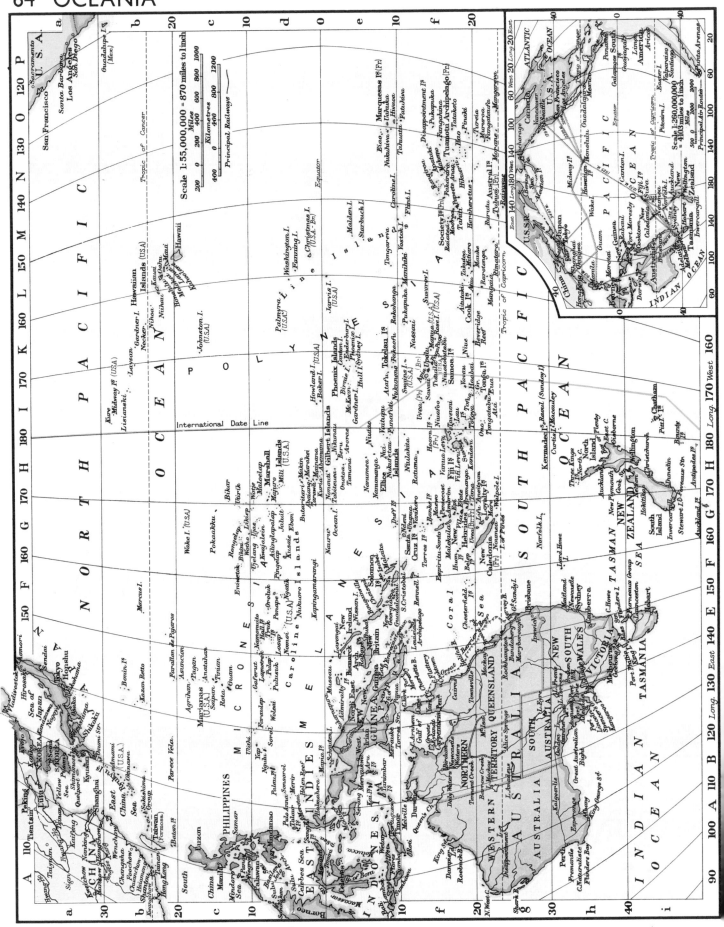

Scale 1:35,000,000

Miles 100 | 0 100 200 300 400 500 600 700 Miles
Kilometres 100 | 0 100 | 500 | 1000 Kilometres

Main Railways —— Roads (where shown) ≈≈ Main Canals ....

Bonne Projection

CONTINUATION on same scale

Long. West 100 of Greenwich

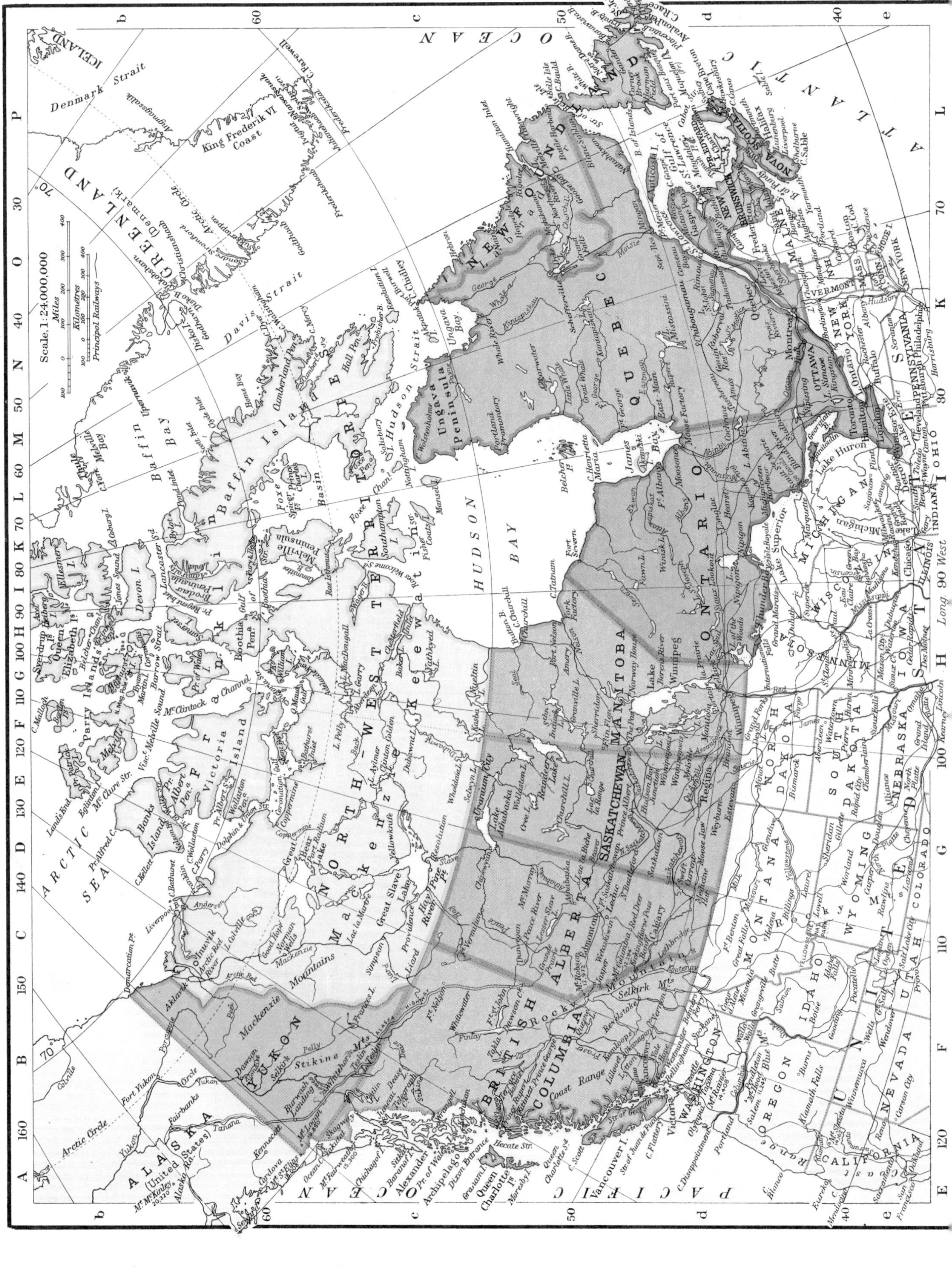

ICELAND

GREENLAND (Arctic. Great. Denmark)

King Frederik VI Coast

Denmark Strait

Davis Strait

Scale 1:24,000,000

Miles
Kilometres
Principal Railways

Baffin Bay

Baffin Island

Cumberland Peninsula

Foxe Basin

Melville Peninsula

Hudson Strait

Ungava Peninsula

Ungava Bay

NEWFOUNDLAND

QUEBEC

HUDSON BAY

James Bay

Southampton I.

ARCTIC OCEAN

Ellesmere I.

Queen Elizabeth Is.

Devon I.

Boothia Gulf of Pen. Boothia

Prince of Wales I.

ARCTIC SEA

Banks Island

Victoria Island

Prince Albert Pen.

NORTH-WEST TERRITORIES

Keewatin

Mackenzie

Mackenzie Mountains

Great Bear Lake

Great Slave Lake

Lake Athabaska

YUKON

Stikine Mts.

Rocky Mts.

BRITISH COLUMBIA

ALBERTA

SASKATCHEWAN

MANITOBA

ONTARIO

Lake Winnipeg

Selkirk Mts.

Coast Range

Vancouver I.

Queen Charlotte Is.

Alexander Archipelago

ALASKA (United States)
Mt. McKinley 20,320

Arctic Circle

PACIFIC OCEAN

Hecate Str.

Lake Superior

Lake Huron

Lake Michigan

Lake Erie

Lake Ontario

OTTAWA

Montreal

Toronto

Quebec

NEW BRUNSWICK

NOVA SCOTIA

MAINE

VERMONT

NEW HAMPSHIRE

MASS.

CONN.

NEW YORK

PENNSYLVANIA

Philadelphia

New York

Boston

OHIO

INDIANA

ILLINOIS

WISCONSIN

MICHIGAN

IOWA

MINNESOTA

NORTH DAKOTA

SOUTH DAKOTA

NEBRASKA

WYOMING

MONTANA

IDAHO

WASHINGTON

OREGON

NEVADA

UTAH

COLORADO

CALIFORNIA

UNITED STATES

Long. 90 West

Atlantic OCEAN

Gulf of St. Lawrence

St. Lawrence

Cape Race

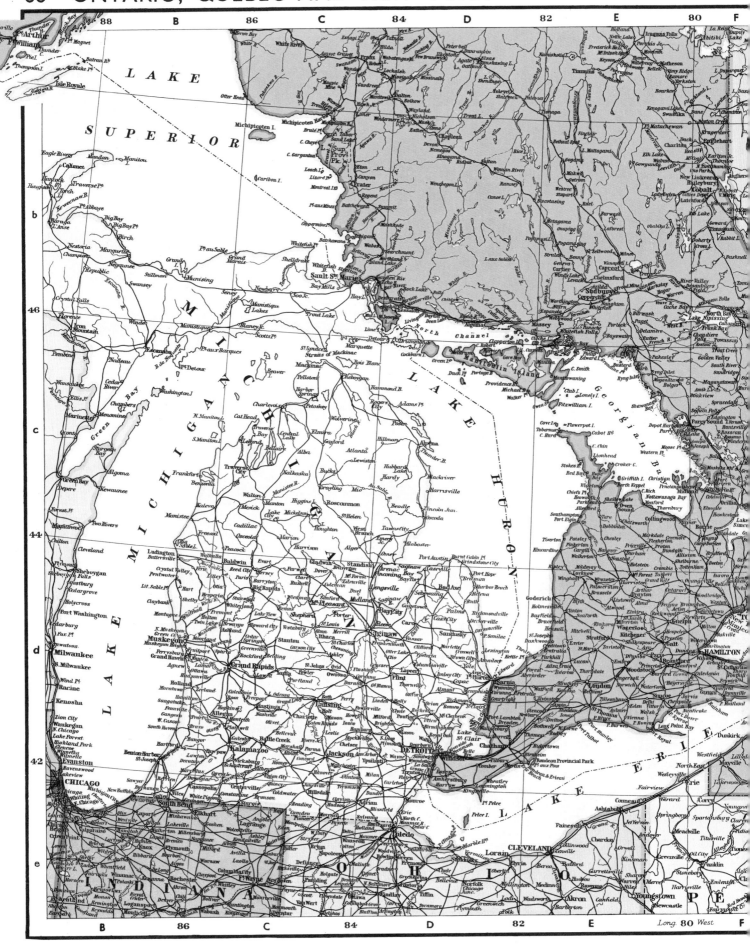

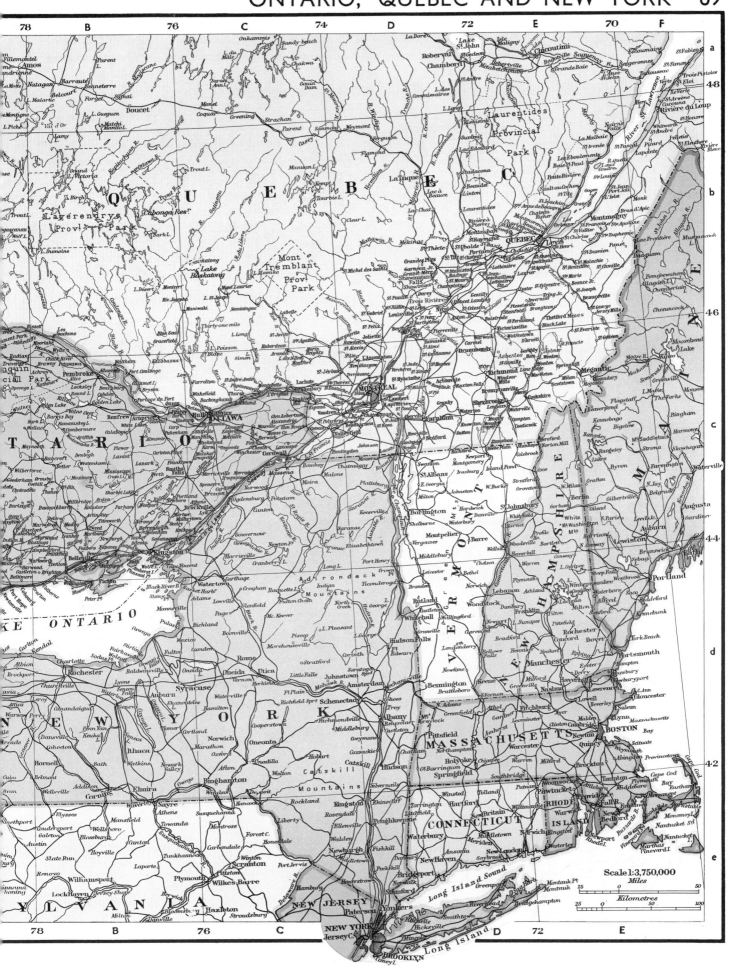

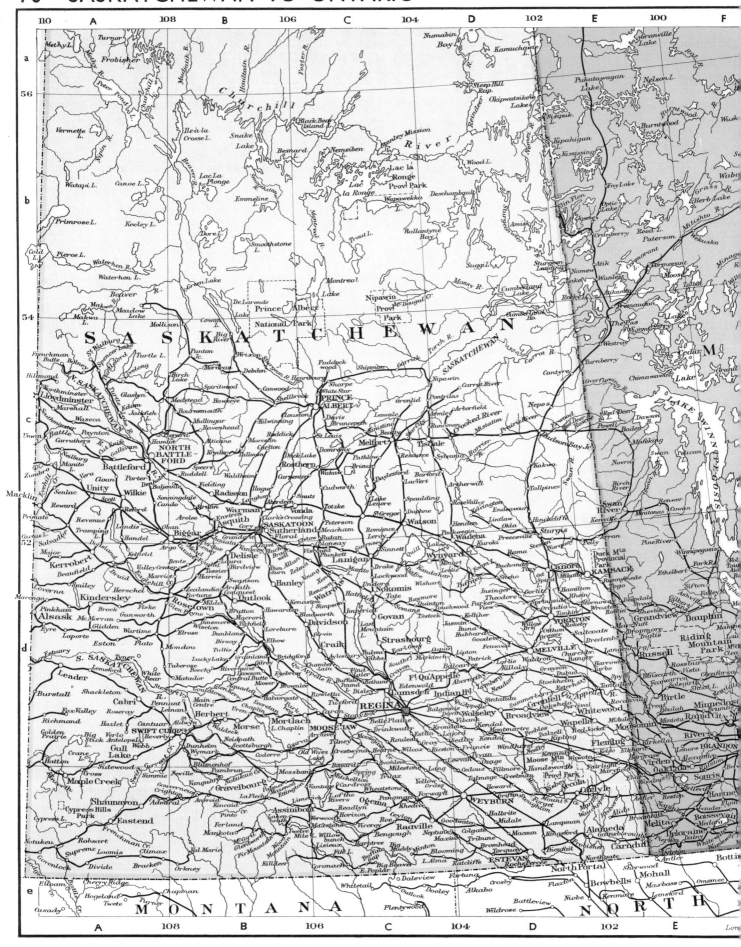

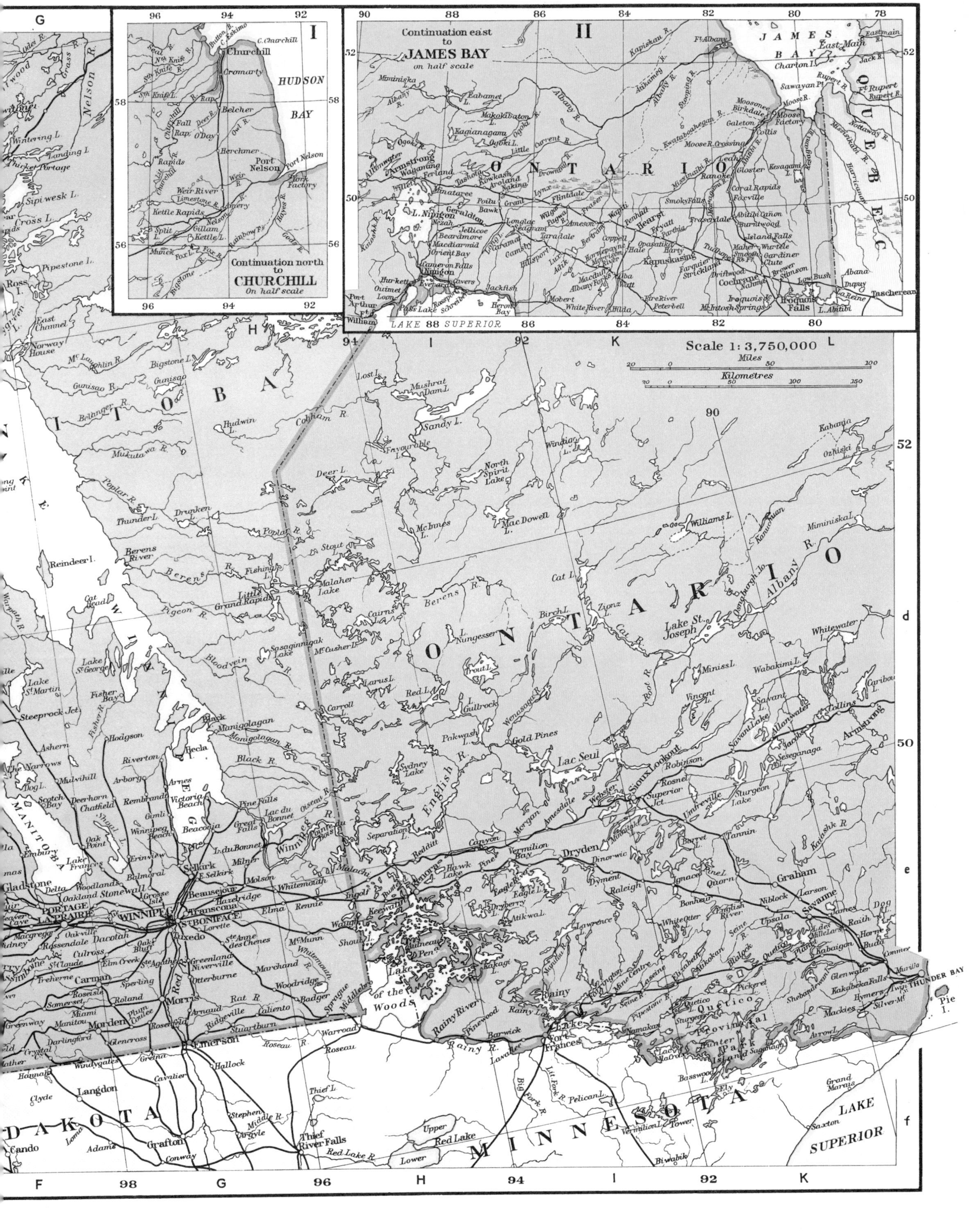

Scale 1:3,750,000

Miles

Kilométres

I Continuation north to CHURCHILL On half scale

II Continuation east to JAMES BAY on half scale

HUDSON BAY

JAMES BAY

QUEBEC

ONTARIO

MANITOBA

DAKOTA

MINNESOTA

LAKE SUPERIOR

LAKE OF THE WOODS

WINNIPEG

PORTAGE LA PRAIRIE

THUNDER BAY

Churchill · Port Nelson · York Factory

Nelson R. · Hudwin L. · Deer L. · Favourable L. · Sandy I. · North Spirit Lake · Mac Dowell L. · Williams L. · Kabania

Berens R. · English R. · Lac Seul · Lake St. Joseph · Albany R. · Armstrong · Whitewater L. · Caribou L.

Lake of the Woods · Rainy River · Rainy Lake · Fort Frances · Quetico Provincial Park · Kakabeka Falls

Fort William · Port Arthur · Lake Nipigon · Geraldton · Hearst · Kapuskasing · Cochrane · L. Abitibi

St. Boniface · Selkirk · Stonewall · Emerson · Morris · Morden · Carman

Scale 1: 3,750,000
Miles
Kilometres

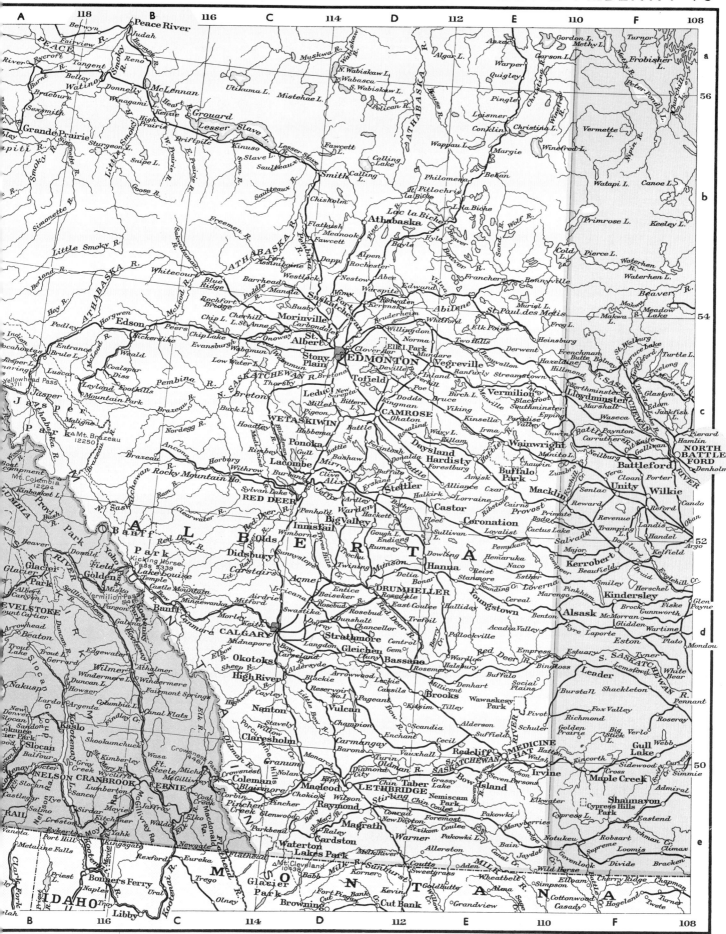

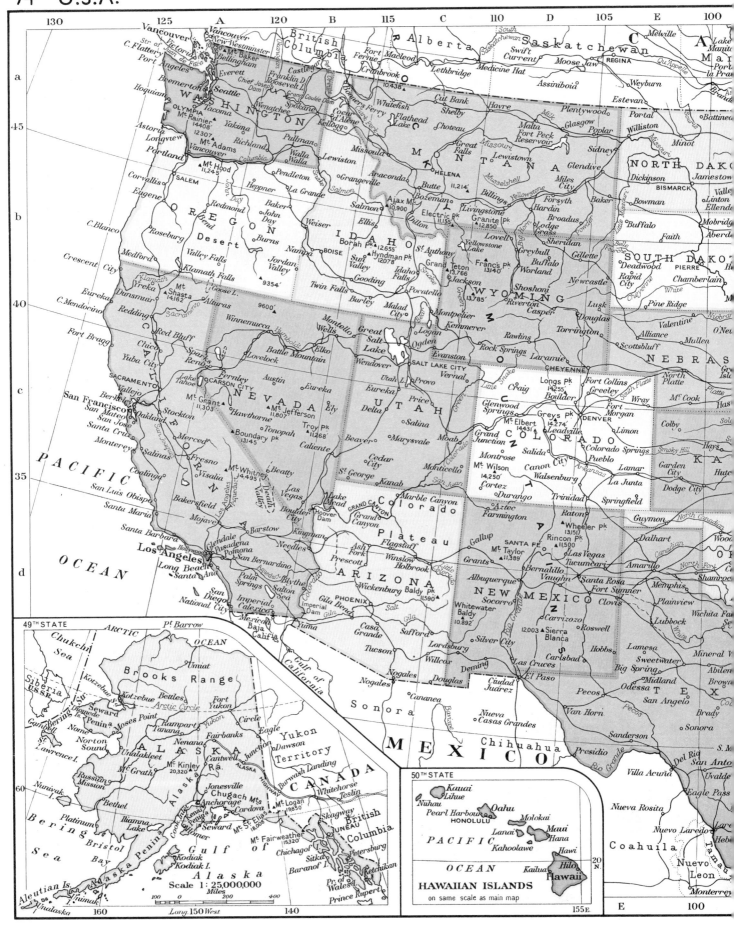

Scale 1:12,500,000 = 197 miles to 1 inch

Miles
100   0   100   200   300   400

Kilometres
100   0   200   400   600

Principal Railways   Canals   Dams
State Capitals shown thus - DES MOINES

NEW YORK
Scale 1:2,500,000
Miles
0   25

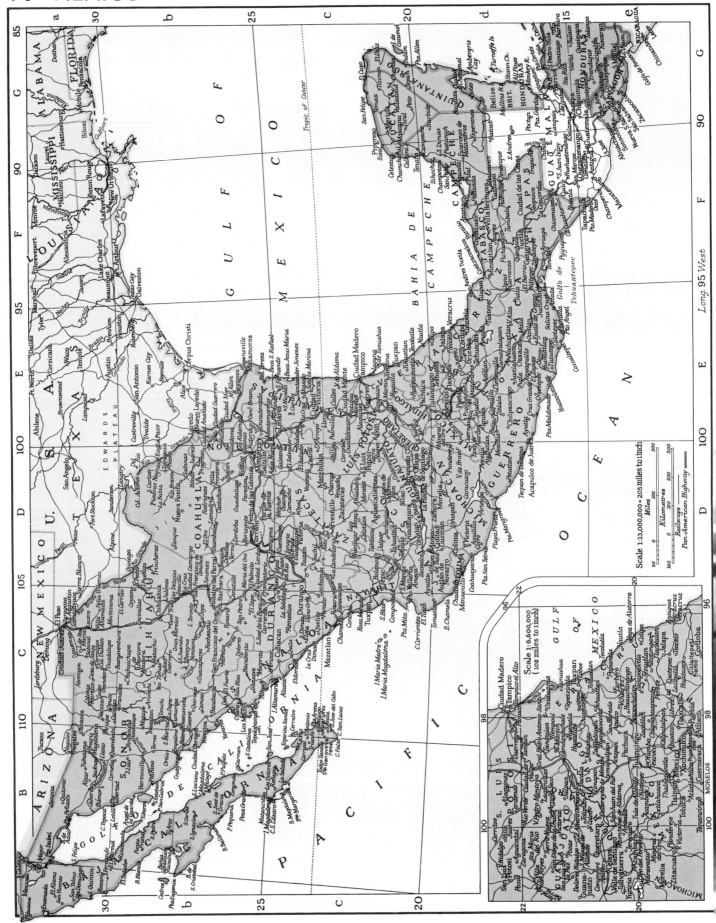

Scale 1:13,000,000 = 205 miles to 1 inch

Railways
Pan-American Highway

Scale 1:6,500,000 (102 miles to 1 inch)

Long. 95 West

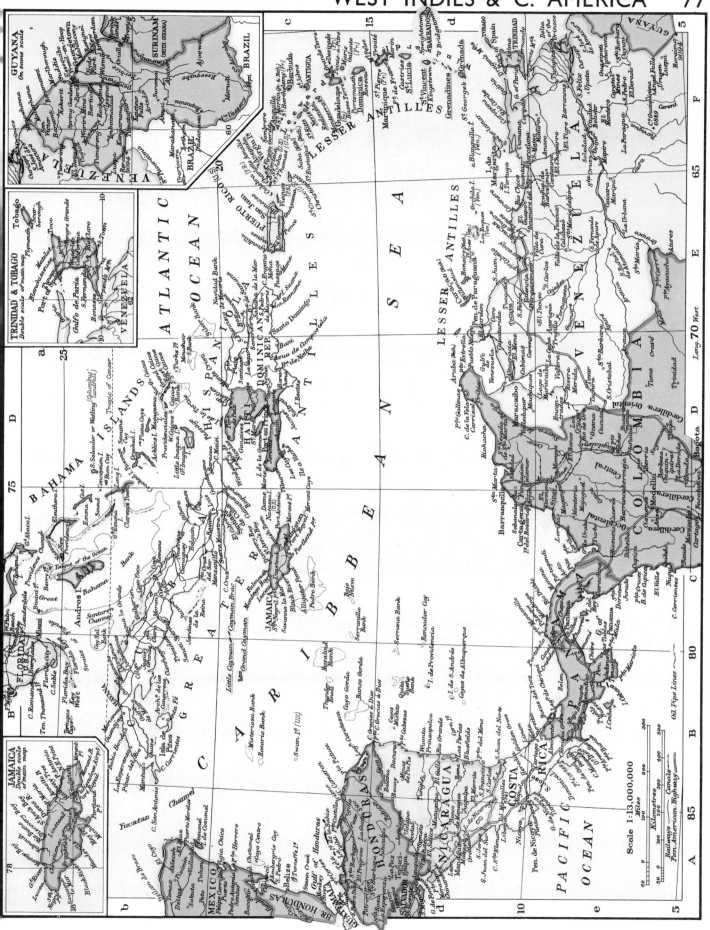

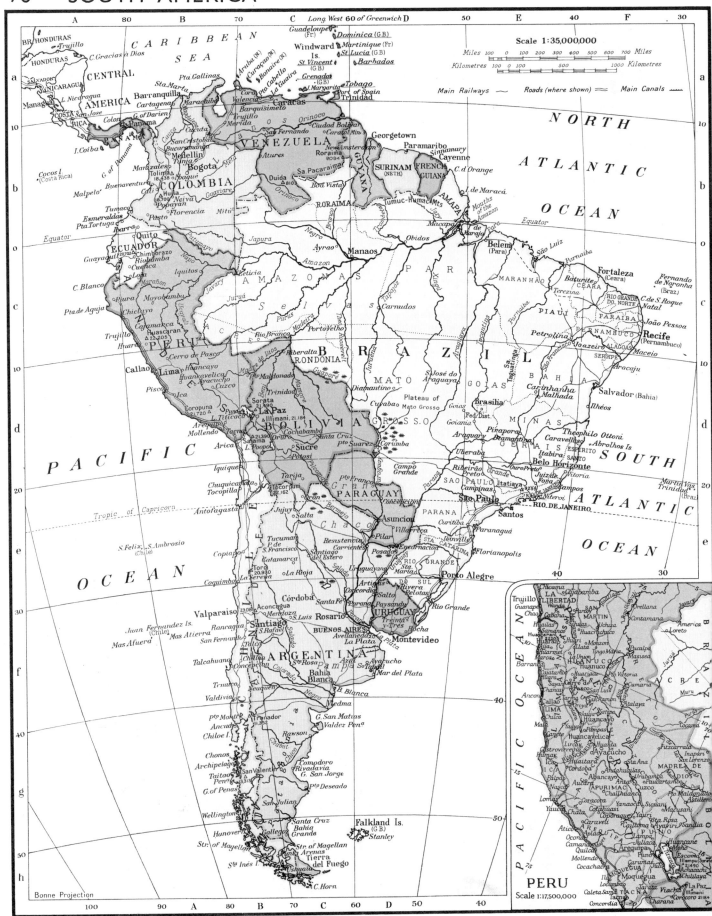

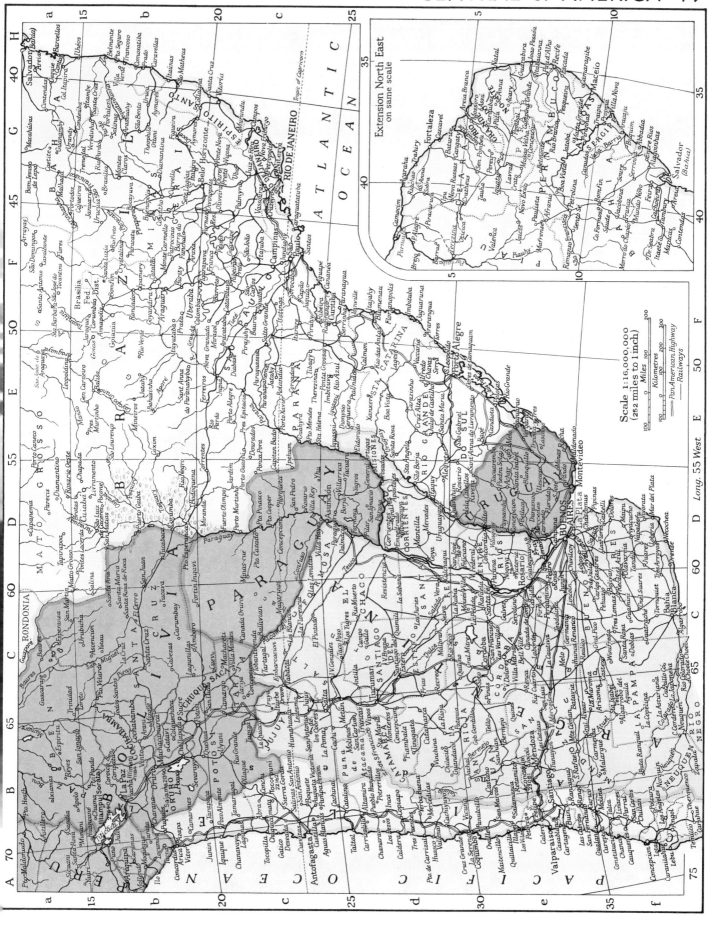

Extension North East
on same scale

Scale 1:16,000,000
(252 miles to 1 inch)
Miles
Kilometres
= Pan-American Highway
— Railways

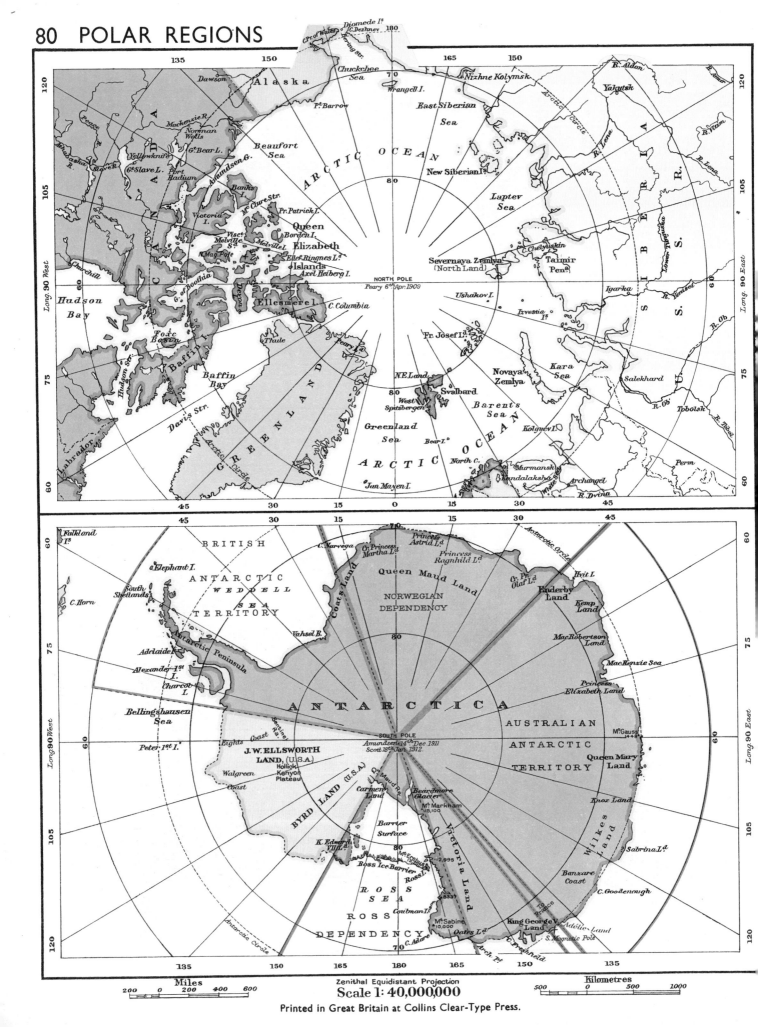

Top map (Arctic) labels:

Diomede Is.
C. Dezhnev
C. Pr. of Wales
Bering Str.
180
135
150
165
150
Dawson
Alaska
Chuckchee Sea
70
Wrangell I.
Nizhne Kolymsk
R. Aldan
Yakutsk
R. Amur
120
120
Peace
Mackenzie R.
Norman Wells
Pt. Barrow
East Siberian Sea
R. Lena
R. Vitim
Athabaska R.
Gt. Bear L.
Fort Radium
Beaufort Sea
Arctic Circle
R. Lena
Lower Tunguska
Yellowknife
Gt. Slave L.
Banks I.
Amundsen G.
ARCTIC OCEAN
80
New Siberian Is.
Laptev Sea
R. Vilui
105
105
Victoria I.
McClure Str.
Pr. Patrick I.
Melville I.
Borden I.
Queen
Severnaya Zemlya (North Land)
C. Chelyuskin
Taimir Pen.
Igarka
R. Yenisei
R. Ob
Vsct. Melville Sd.
Mag. Pole
Ellef Ringnes L.
Axel Heiberg I.
Elizabeth
Islands
NORTH POLE
Peary 6th Apr. 1909
Ushakov I.
Irvestia Is.
SIBERIA
U.S.S.R.
60
60
Churchill
G. of Boothia
Devon
Ellesmere I.
C. Columbia
Fr. Josef Ld.
Salekhard
R. Ob
Hudson Bay
Foxe Basin
Baffin I.
Thule
Peary Ld.
80
NE Land
Kara Sea
Tobolsk
R. Tobol
75
75
Davis Str.
Hudson Str.
Baffin Bay
West Spitsbergen
Svalbard
Novaya Zemlya
Barents Sea
Perm
Labrador
GREENLAND
Greenland Sea
Bear I.
North C.
Kolguev I.
Murmansk
Archangel
60
60
Arctic Circle
Jan Mayen I.
ARCTIC OCEAN
Kandalaksha
White Sea
R. Dvina
45
30
15
0
15
30
45

Bottom map (Antarctic) labels:

60
60
Falkland Is.
45
30
15
70
15
30
45
BRITISH
C. Narvega
Cr. Princess Martha Ld.
Princess Astrid Ld.
Princess Ragnhild Ld.
Antarctic Circle
Elephant I.
ANTARCTIC
Queen Maud Land
Cr. Pr. Olaf Ld.
Hvit I.
Enderby Land
C. Horn
South Shetlands
WEDDELL SEA TERRITORY
Coats Land
NORWEGIAN DEPENDENCY
Kemp Land
75
75
Adelaide I.
Antarctic Peninsula
Vahsel B.
80
MacRobertson Land
MacKenzie Sea
Alexander 1st I.
Charcot I.
Princess Elizabeth Land
Bellingshausen Sea
Sentinel Ra.
ANTARCTICA
SOUTH POLE
Amundsen 14th Dec. 1911
Scott 18th Jan. 1912
AUSTRALIAN
Mt. Gauss
(1448)
Peter 1st I.
Eights Coast
J. W. ELLSWORTH LAND (U.S.A.)
Hollick Kenyon Plateau
Qn. Maud Ra.
ANTARCTIC
Queen Mary Land
90
90
Walgreen Coast
BYRD LAND (U.S.A.)
Carmen Land
Beardmore Glacier
Mt. Markham 15,100
TERRITORY
Knox Land
Wilkes Land
Sabrina Ld.
105
105
K. Edward VII Ld.
Barrier Surface
80
Victoria Land
Banzare Coast
C. Goodenough
Ross Ice Barrier
Ross I.
ROSS SEA
Coulman I.
Mt. Sabine 10,000
King George V Land
Adélie Land
S. Magnetic Pole
120
120
ROSS DEPENDENCY
C. Adare
Oates Ld.
70
135
150
165
180
165
150
135

Miles
200   0   200   400   600
Kilometres
500   0   500   1000
Zenithal Equidistant Projection
Scale 1 : 40,000,000
Printed in Great Britain at Collins Clear-Type Press.

KARIBA: Power for Central Africa

The Zambezi is a truly great river—1750 miles long, and its central section forms the boundary between Zambia and Rhodesia. There, amidst remote bush country, and at the lower end of the long, narrow Kariba Gorge, the dam has been built. The associated power-house will supply urgently needed extra power to enable the Rhodesian Copperbelt and other industrial areas to sustain their remarkable development.

Work was started in 1956 before either of the access roads had been built across the rugged, forested country to the distant railheads and existing main roads. 1960 was set as the deadline for the completion of the dam and first power-house, thus the enormous physical difficulties were heightened by a race against time.

Above Looking across the Kariba Gorge before building actually started in 1956.

Below The " pure arch " dam, containing over three million tons of concrete, rises 420 feet above the river bed. The crest of the dam is 2025 feet long and carries a forty-foot road. (*Both Federal Information Dept.*)

The access roads were completed in a matter of months and were in continuous use for four years carrying immense loads of steel, cement (500,000 tons) and other materials, transformers, generators, turbines, flood gates, all construction equipment and plant, as well as all food and necessities for the 10,000 men engaged. Airstrips and later an aerodrome were built, and two towns with all modern amenities.

As the dam wall rose, the impounded waters of the Zambezi started to form " Lake Kariba " which has now become the largest reservoir in the world, 175 miles long and 20 wide. Some 50,000 Africans had to be moved and re-settled, bush had to be cleared to prevent underwater obstructions, and game rescued or driven out. Meanwhile the first of two underground power-houses was being excavated in the solid rock. (The machine hall is 460 feet long, 75 feet wide and 132 feet high, and contains six 140,000. b.h.p. turbines each driving a 100-megawatt alternator.)

Despite the unprecedented floods of 1957 and 1958, the work was completed on time due largely to two factors: the use of construction machinery and plant on a scale rarely known before, certainly not in Africa, and the fanatical determination of all employed—African and European alike.

THE ST. LAWRENCE SEAWAY

A new ocean link

The five great Lakes of North America which are joined to the Atlantic Ocean by the St. Lawrence River are, unfortunately, at different levels. Thus considerable obstacles to navigation exist between the lakes and in the St. Lawrence itself. The surmounting of these obstacles to provide a deep water route into the heart of the American continent was for centuries the dream of explorers and commercial interests—a dream which became a reality in 1959 with the opening of the St. Lawrence Seaway; this provides a 27-foot channel from the Atlantic to Duluth, some 2,300 miles. Since, with the dredging of certain sections, this channel already existed above Prescott and below Montreal, the St. Lawrence Seaway Development Corporation, established by Canada and the U.S. in 1954, concentrated its attention on the river between these towns where the canals by-passing rapids, etc., were only 14 feet deep. Works carried out in this section are estimated to have cost Canada $200 million and the U.S. $100 million. At the same time a great international power development project was undertaken near Cornwall (*see inset map*).

Some idea of the work undertaken can be obtained by taking an imaginary voyage upstream from Montreal to Lake Ontario. Three miles upstream from the pool of Montreal harbour is the first of the seven new locks—the St. Lambert Lock, which lifts the ship 15 feet to the level of the La Prairie Basin—a turning-round basin through which the ship-channel passes to the second lock, Côte Ste Catherine Lock. The function of this lock is to by-pass the Lachine Rapids, and it raises the ship 30 feet to the level of Lake St. Louis. It is of the same dimensions as the other new locks on the St. Lawrence and the eight locks of the Welland Ship Canal i.e. 730 feet long, 80 feet wide, and with 30 feet of water over the lock sills. The 24 million gallons of water required to fill it can be let in or out in 10 minutes. Beyond this lock the ship proceeds by overland canal for 7½ miles to Lake St. Louis and thence by dredged channels to the Power Canal which by-passes the Beauharnois Power House; the two locks on this canal raise the ship a further 82 feet to the level of Lake St. Francis. The ship traverses this lake to cross the international boundary near Cornwall thus passing out of a section of wholly Canadian constructions into the International Rapids

The Iroquois Lock (the highest of the new locks) enables shipping to by-pass the Iroquois Control Dam which can be seen on the right and which controls the outflow of Lake Ontario into the newly-formed lake St. Lawrence.

(*High Commissioner for Canada*)

MASSENA INTAKE
INGLESIDE
CANADA
LONG SAULT ISLANDS
LONG SAULT DAM
EISENHOWER LOCK
TOWN OF LONG SAULT
SHEEK ISLAND
BARNHART BRIDGE
LEY DONDERO CANAL
ST. LAWRENCE POWER DAM
CLOSURE STRUCTURE
CORNWALL DYKE
TAILRACE EXCAVATION
LOCK 19
POLLEY'S GUT
CORNWALL CANAL

A panoramic view of the International Rapids section looking towards Lake Ontario (see inset map). The " Wiley-Dondero Canal " is now the American Canal. Some idea of the vast scale of the undertaking may be gained by bearing in mind that the St. Lawrence Power Dam (centre), is 1,100 yards long, and the Long Sault Dam (upper centre), though smaller, is still only 130 yards under half a mile in length. *(High Commissioner for Canada)*

section where all navigational projects are on U.S. soil and were undertaken by that country.

This section, which contains the most extensive new works of the Seaway, also contains the great international hydro-power project—the Barnhart-Cornwall Power House with its two associated control dams, one at the Power House site, and the other the spillway dam upstream at Long Sault. This Power House, which is one of the greatest in the world, makes use of the energy formerly dissipated in the Long Sault Rapids. Its foundations are sunk 90 feet in the riverbed, and 4 million tons of concrete were used in its construction. The Power House Dam is 162 feet above foundation and 3,300 feet long; the Long Sault Dam, which is 2,250 feet long and 145 feet above foundation, holds up Lake St. Lawrence—a 40 mile long reservoir created to suppy the enormous quantities of water used in the turbines. When the dam was closed, about 20,000 acres on the north shore were flooded, but 6,500 people had previously been resettled farther inland in new villages (over 500 buildings were also physically removed) and both roads and railways were re-routed. The whole power project is estimated to have cost $600 million, split equally between Canada and the U.S. and will supply each country with 850,000 kWs. of electricity.

The ship by-passes this one mile to the south, by means of the 10 miles long American Canal with its two locks—the Snell with a lift of 45 feet and the Eisenhower which lifts the ship another 38 feet into Lake St. Lawrence. At the head of the lake is another control dam—the Iroquois—to regulate the flow from Lake Ontario, and the ship must by-pass this by means of the Iroquois Lock, the highest of the new locks. Thence we proceed through the Thousand Islands to Lake Ontario, 246 feet above sea-level.

Between Lakes Ontario and Erie there is a difference of level of 326 feet, partly due to the Niagara Falls. This is overcome by the eight locks of the 27 miles long Welland Ship Canal, which has now been deepened to 27 feet.

The new Seaway will facilitate the movement of bulky products, particularly grain, iron-ore and coal, and it is estimated that the traffic will increase to approximately four times the pre-1959 volume. It is probable that a large fleet of specially constructed ships will operate between the Atlantic and Duluth with cargoes transhipped at Montreal or the coast, rather than that ocean-ships will make the voyage into the heart of the continent to any great extent. Whatever develops, it is certain that the industrial areas fringing the Great Lakes will be greatly benefited as will more distant parts by this great international achievement.

Electricity from the VOLGA RIVER

INDUS WATERS

Neighbours in Agreement

The Nangal Dam (on the left) is an already completed barrage on the Sutlej River which controls irrigation in India in the upper Punjab. Water is diverted first into the 40-miles long Hydel Canal the headgates of which form the foreground of the photograph on the right. (*Press Information Bureau, India*)

As part of the industrial and agricultural programmes of the U.S.S.R., gigantic "hydropower" stations are being built on the main rivers which are being transformed as very long sections broaden out to form a series of enormous reservoirs. The map shows principal dams and reservoirs in Western U.S.S.R.

The station on the Volga, near Kuibyshev, seen in the photograph (*Soviet Weekly*) below, is said to be the largest in the world. It took seven years to build and generates 2,300,000 kWs., and was named the "Volga-Lenin Hydro-power Station".

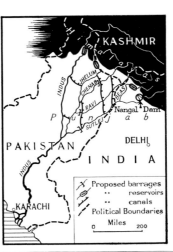

The signing of the Indus Waters Treaty marks the beginning of a momentous irrigation and power project for India and Pakistan. The Indus with five main tributaries comprises one of the great river systems of the world with an annual flow twice that of the Nile. The rivers rise outside Pakistan in the Himalayan rainbelt before coming down to the dry plains of the Punjab where they are greatly used for irrigation and support forty million people in Pakistan and ten million in India.

The sharing of the Indus waters has been a matter of dispute for many years and since 1947 the chief cause of strained relations between the two countries. Under the new plan the waters of the three eastern rivers, Ravi, Beas, and Sutlej, will

ocated to India, and that of the three western,
enab, Jhelum, and Indus, to Pakistan. Since India
l intercept waters previously used lower down by
<istan, a series of great feeder canals will conduct
ter from the western rivers into the Pakistan
tions of the eastern rivers. These canals, although
Pakistan, will be paid for by India. Besides greatly
anding the area under irrigation in both countries
1 improving existing systems, the project will
ovide much needed power—300,000 kWs., for
<istan and 200,000 for India.

A notable feature is that the plan is being
anced internationally by loans and grants from six
untries and the World Bank, which has sponsored
e project.

United Nations plans for the
RIVER MEKONG

Four great rivers flow out from Tibet. One of these, the Mekong, flows through China in its upper reaches, then forms part of the boundaries of Burma before entering Indo-China where it flows through and sometimes between four countries often in the news: Laos, Cambodia, Viet Nam, and Siam. Within this area twenty million people are estimated to be dependent on the river or liable to be effected by its development.

The United Nations, through its various agencies, has undertaken a comprehensive programme for the overall development of the Mekong Basin with the object of raising standards of life throughout the area.

The present plan is to construct, as a first phase, four dams on the main river—one for the benefit of each country. Later three more dams are proposed. The purpose of the dams will be fourfold. They will prevent the periodic and disastrous floods which at present occur, and they will, by submerging rapids, facilitate transport in an area where this essential is gravely lacking (for example all exports from Laos at present have to cross into Siam to proceed by rail to Bangkok). They will also fulfil the vital function of storing water for irrigation and industry. Agriculture, particularly the growing of sugar, maize, and fruits, could be greatly expanded in many areas of potentially fertile but unwatered soils. Local minerals may be used to develop a canning industry. Finally, tremendous amounts of hydro-electric power will be generated and supplied to farms and factories, and will also supply power for railways in an area deficient in fuels.

The idea of developing as a unit, within the framework of a comprehensive plan, a complete river basin is not new (e.g. the Tennessee Valley in the U.S.A.) but such an ambitious international project under the direction of a world authority is revolutionary.

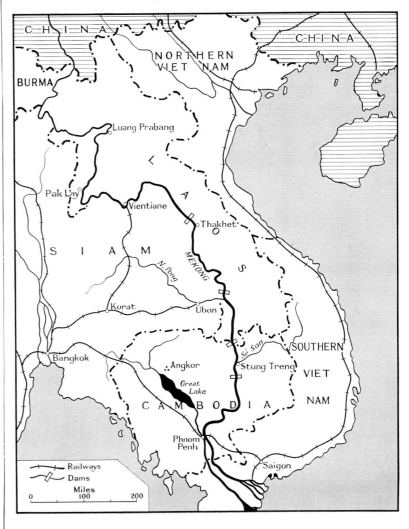

BRASILIA: A beautiful new capital.

In the past, capitals of countries—especially young federal countries such as Australia, South Africa, India, U.S.A.—have been moved to existing or newly created towns usually in order to forestall dangerous rivalry between established cities. This reason has not been paramount in the creation of Brasilia, the new capital of Brazil; furthermore, unlike previous examples, the new city has been totally planned and set in a hitherto undeveloped region, and largely built as a single major operation within the space of three years. It is also indisputably unique in the style of its buildings and the attempt—in its overall design—to make a city both functionally perfect and beautiful.

Its location may be said to be geographically logical—near the physical centre of the country and close to the trans-continental highway which has just been built from Belem in the north to the extreme south. Brasilia in fact should be instrumental in opening up two million square miles of virgin territory by drawing in people from the over-crowded coastal zone. Also, by focusing routes on itself, it will effectively link up and unify for the first time the several remote industrial and commercial regions of Brazil. Add to this the advantages of abundant space, congenial climate, and the opportunity to create anew and you have the material reasons at least which justify the building of Brasilia.

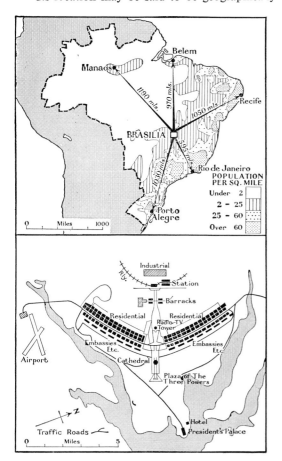

There are however deeper reasons: Brasilia is intended by the country's leaders to be both dedication and symbol of the " coming-of-age " of a great nation. The people of Brazil are a truly harmonious blend of races, colours and creeds, and they have developed—as no other similar country has succeeded in doing—a community of ideals and national traditions which has been paralleled since the war by a remarkable economic expansion. Brasilia has become an ideal in itself and has thereby transcended argument which has raged about the cost of the project, its timing, or indeed the physical necessity of such a move.

The actual site chosen was bounded on two sides by rivers. From the outset the general plan was that the resultant triangular, slightly domed piece of land should be limited on its third side by the service or industrial sector of the town and the two rivers dammed to form an artificial lake set in parkland. The final design was the subject of a national competition which was won by Lucio Costa, an eminent Brazilian architect. The basic shape he has imparted is that of an open cross (also described as a " bow-and-arrow " or " aeroplane ") with a distinctive silhouette from nearly every point of view. The E-W axis comprises Government buildings, with the highest structure—a radio-TV tower—at its centre, and is raised on an embanked platform. The curved N-S axis comprises the eight-mile residential zone. This will embrace numerous individual residential areas or " super-blocks "—groups of very large apartment buildings facing outwards to main streets and inwards to private and public gardens, schools, and shopping centres free of traffic. Each " block " will have its own " greenbelt " of trees and these will unify and formalise the whole zone whilst allowing each block to develop internally on its own lines. One of the great benefits of the " total " method of town planning is that the traffic problem, so acute elsewhere, can be planned out of existence. In Brasilia this has been achieved by segregating classes of traffic on three levels.

The historic photograph on the left shows the building of the " Plaza of the Three Powers " against the background of the surrounding bush country. The " saucer " is the Chamber of Deputies, whilst the " dome " is the Senate. At the back are the twin blocks of administrative offices and the chief executive building. The drawing above is of the Cathedral, a most revolutionary building with ribs of concrete and walls of glass. On the right is the President's " Palace of the Dawn " with adjoining private chapel, which was one of the first buildings to be completed, and is typical of the many brilliant conceptions of Oscar Niemeyer, who also designed the Cathedral.   (*Brazilian Government*)

THE YANGTZE SPANNED

This huge bridge at Wuhan is some 1,300 yards long and although hundreds of miles from the sea, is the lowest point at which the river is spanned. The Peking to Canton Railway uses the lower deck and the upper deck is a roadway.　　(*Camera Press Ltd.*)

UIDER ZEE RECLAIMED

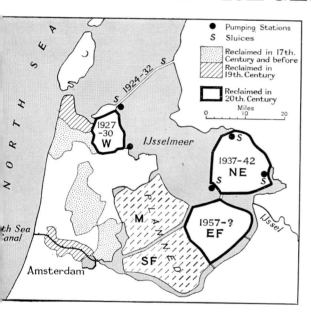

thereby forms the foundation of the whole project. Along its crest runs a wide road and it has let into it two giant sluices which control the level of the Ijsselmeer (as the lake is now called) as well as locks for the passage of ships.

Wieringermeer was brought under full cultivation in 1941 after the soil had been slowly purged of its salt content. In 1945, a few days before the end of the war, it was flooded by the Germans; it took twelve months to pump dry again and all buildings had to be rebuilt. Now it is a prosperous land of crops and pasture. The North East Polder benefited from the transformation of the Ijsselmeer to fresh water. It was soon brought under the plough and now supports a population of 30,000.

Wieringerwerf, one of three new villages built in Wieringermeer Polder. Complete in 1935 it had to be completely rebuilt after the flooding of 1945.　　(*Aerofilm Ltd.*)

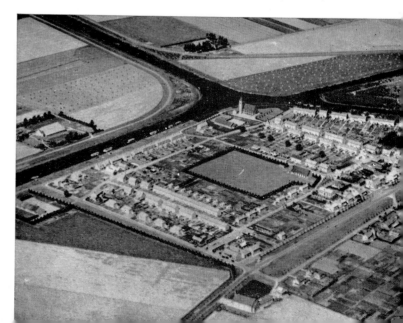

Holland is one of the smallest countries in the world but even more than half its area has been won by man from marsh and sea. Draining, dyking and reclamation have been going on for a thousand years despite many setbacks.

Since 1923 vast areas of the former Zuider Zee have been closed and drained in the most ambitious scheme of its kind yet attempted. Three of the five planned " polders " or enclosures have been pumped dry, amounting in all to 300,000 acres, equivalent to twice the area of Middlesex. These are the Wieringermeer, North East, and East Flevoland Polders and of these the first two are now in full production. Markerwaard and South Flevoland are still in prospect and will add another 244,000 acres.

The great enclosing dam, twenty miles long, which was completed in 1932 shuts off the North Sea from the former Zuider Zee (the latter gradually becoming a fresh water lake) and

NATURE WINS

In these days Man can split the atom and can destroy vast areas of the world at the touch of a switch. As we have shown in the preceeding seven pages, he can harness rivers to control floods, to create electric energy and can bring ocean-going vessels to the heart of a continent. Man may therefore feel all-conquering, but lest he be too smug we are concluding with this page.

Although many of the difficulties which condemned early Man to a primitive life have been overcome— every now and then Nature unleashes again these elemental powers and wipes out Man's puny achievements.

Above EARTHQUAKE. This picture shows the roof of what used to be a block of shops and flats leaning over at a crazy angle and threatening to fall at any moment as a result of the earthquake which destroyed the Moroccan port of Agadir early in March 1960. *(Central Press Photos Ltd.)*

Left LOCUSTS have been a scourge to mankind since the age of Moses and before. In spite of the efforts made internationally for locust control, a migration such as this on the Kenya-Uganda border can cause damage amounting to millions of pounds. The usual breeding grounds are in the Somali peninsula though they menace vast areas of Africa and Asia. *(Paul Popper Ltd.)*

Below TYPHOON in the Philippines in June 1960. The car had been swept some $2\frac{1}{2}$ miles and the waters had reached a depth of some ten feet at this spot near Manilla. Typhoons in this area and Tornadoes in the Caribbean and America can cause terrifying destruction in a very short time in spite of the elaborate warning systems now in existence. *(Central Press Photos Ltd.)*

WORLD INDEX

This index has been completely revised and brought up-to-date and contains over 20,000 entries. Each place name is immediately followed by a brief location guide such as *France*, *N.S.W.* New South Wales, *W.I.* West Indies. Thereafter the Latitude and Longitude are given and in bold figures the page number of the largest scale map. Throughout the index, to save lines and get the maximum number of entries into the space available, the normal geographical contractions such as R. for river and I. for island are used. Countries and their major divisions such as states or counties appear in small capitals but the easiest way to find the best map or maps of any country is to refer to the Countries of the World list at the beginning of this atlas.

Place	Lat.	Long.	No.
AABENRAA, Denmark.	55N	9½E	**33**
Aachen, Germany.	50¾N	6E	**33**
Aalborg, Denmark.	57¼N	10E	**29**
Aalen, Germany.	48¾N	10E	**33**
Aalesund, Norway.	62½N	6¼E	**29**
Aarau, Switzerland.	47½N	8E	**31**
Aarberg, Switzerland.	47N	7¼E	**31**
Aargau, Switzerland.	47½N	8¼E	**31**
Aarhus, Denmark.	56¼N	10¼E	**29**
Aasnes, Norway.	60½N	12E	**29**
Aba, Nigeria.	5N	7¼E	**57**
Abaco Is., Gr., Bahamas.	26½N	77¼W	**75**
Abadan, Iran.	30¼N	48¼E	**40**
Abaiang I., Pacific.	2N	172E	**64**
Abakan, U.S.S.R.	53¾N	91½E	**39**
Abadeh, Iran.	31N	52E	**40**
Abancay, Peru.	13¾S	73W	**78**
Abarquh, Iran.	31N	53E	**40**
Abashiri, Japan.	44N	144E	**49**
Abau, Papua (inset).	10S	148E	**60**
Abemama I., Pacific.	0	173E	**64**
Abbeville, France.	50¼N	1¾E	**32**
Abbeyfeale, Ireland.	52¼N	9¼W	**26**
Abbey Hd., Scotland.	54¾N	4W	**25**
Abbeyleix, Eire.	53N	7½W	**26**
Abbiategrasso, Italy.	45½N	8½E	**31**
Abbot B., Queens., Aust.	20S	148E	**60**
Abbotsford, Br. Col.	49N	122¼W	**72**
Abbottabad, Pakistan.	34¼N	73¼E	**46**
Abbotts, W. Aust.	26½S	118E	**61**
Abeche, Chad.	13¾N	20¾E	**56**
Abeokuta, Nigeria.	7N	3½E	**57**
Aberavon, Wales.	51½N	3¾W	**22**
Aberayron, Wales.	52¼N	4¼W	**22**
Abercarn, Wales.	51¾N	3¼W	**22**
Aberchirder, Scotland.	57½N	2½W	**24**
Abercorn, see MBALA.	9S	31E	**51**
Aberdeen, C. Pr., S.Afr.	32½S	24E	**53**
Aberdeen, N.S.W.	32¼S	150¾E	**59**
Aberdeen, Sask., Can.	52¼N	106¼W	**70**
Aberdeen & Tn., Scot.	57¼N	2W	**24**
Aberdeen, S. Dak., U.S.	45½N	98½W	**74**
Aberdeen, L., N.W. Can.	64N	100W	**66**
Aberdovey, Wales.	52½N	4W	**22**
Aberfeldy, O.F.S.	28¼S	29E	**55**
Aberfeldy, Scotland.	56½N	3¾W	**24**
Aberfoyle, Scotland.	56¼N	4½W	**25**
Aberffraw, England.	53¼N	4½W	**22**
Abergavenny, Eng.	51¾N	3W	**22**
Abergele, Wales.	53¼N	3¾W	**22**
Aberlour, Scotland.	57½N	3¼W	**24**
Abersoch, Wales.	52½N	4¾W	**22**
Abersychan, England.	51¾N	3W	**22**
Abertillery, England.	51¾N	3¼W	**22**
Aberystwyth, Wales.	52½N	4W	**22**
Abeya, L., Ethiopia.	6N	37½E	**56**
Abidjan, Ivory Coast.	5½N	4W	**50**
Abha, Arabia.	18N	42½E	**40**
Abilene, Alb., Can.	54N	111½W	**73**
Abilene, Texas, U.S.A.	32½N	100W	**74**
Abingdon, England.	51¾N	1¼W	**23**
Abington, Scotland.	55½N	3¾W	**25**
Abinsi, Nigeria.	7¾N	9E	**57**
Abitibi, L., Ont. Can.	48¾N	79¾W	**71**
Abitibi, R., Ont., Can.	51N	81W	**71**
Ablis, France.	48½N	1¾E	**31**
Abnazan, Spain.	41½N	2½W	**35**
Abo, see TURKU.			
Aboh, Nigeria.	5½N	6½E	**57**
Abolo, Congo (B.)	0	14E	**56**
Abomey, Dahomey.	7¼N	2E	**57**
Abondance, France.	46¼N	6¾E	**31**
Aboso, Ghana.	5N	2W	**57**
Aboyne, Scotland.	57N	2¾W	**24**
Abraka, Nigeria.	5¾N	6E	**57**
Abrantes, Portugal.	39½N	8¼W	**35**
Abrolhos Is., Brazil.	17S	39W	**78**
ABRUZZI, Italy.	42N	14E	**36**
Abu Al Abyadh, Arab.	24½N	54E	**40**
Abu Ali, Arabia.	27N	49E	**41**
Abu Arish, Saudi Arab.	16¾N	42¾E	**40**
Abu Dhabi, Arabia.	24½N	54½E	**40**
Abu Hamed, Sudan.	19½N	33¼E	**50**
Abuja, Nigeria.	9¼N	7¼E	**57**
Abu Markha, Arabia.	25N	38E	**40**
Abu Qir, U.A.R. (inset).	31½N	30E	**50**
Abuta, Japan.	42½N	141E	**49**
Abut Hd., S.I., N.Z.	43¼N	170¼E	**63**
Abu Zabad, Sudan.	12N	29E	**56**
Abu Zenima, U.A.R.	28¾N	33E	**41**

Place	Lat.	Long.	No.
Abwong, Sudan.	9¼N	32E	**56**
Acambaro, Mexico.	20N	100¾W	**76**
Acapulco, Mexico.	16¾N	100W	**76**
Acarahu, Brazil.	2¾S	40W	**79**
Acarigua, Venezuela.	10N	69W	**77**
Accra, Ghana.	5¾N	¼W	**57**
Accrington, England.	53¾N	2¼W	**22**
Acerra, Italy.	41N	14¼E	**36**
Achalpur, India.	21¼N	77½E	**44**
Achenkirch, Austria.	47½N	11¾E	**31**
Achern, Germany.	48½N	8E	**30**
Achik Kul, L., China.	37N	89E	**43**
Achiet, Le Grand, Fr.	50¼N	2¾E	**30**
Achikulak, U.S.S.R.	44½N	45E	**38**
Achill, Eire.	54N	10¼W	**26**
Achill, I. & Hd., Eire.	54N	10W	**26**
Achnasheen, Scotland.	57½N	5W	**24**
Acireale, Sicily.	37½N	15¼E	**36**
Acklin I., Bahama Is.	22¼N	74W	**77**
Acle, England.	52¾N	1½E	**23**
Acme, Alberta, Can.	51½N	113½W	**73**
Aconcagua, Mt., Arg.	32½S	70W	**79**
Acornhoek, Transvaal.	24½S	31E	**54**
Acquapendente, Italy.	42¾N	11E	**36**
Acqui, Italy.	44¾N	8½E	**36**
Acre, Brazil.	10S	70W	**78**
Acre, B. of, Israel (ins.).	32¾N	35E	**40**
Acre, Israel.	33N	35E	**40**
Acri, Italy.	39½N	16½E	**36**
Acta, Panama.	8½N	78W	**77**
Acton, Ontario, Can.	43¾N	80W	**68**
Actonvale, Que., Can.	45½N	72¼W	**69**
Ada, Ghana.	5¾N	¾E	**57**
Adabia, U.A.R. (inset).	30N	32½E	**50**
Adaja R., Spain.	41¼N	5W	**35**
Adamello, Mt., Italy.	46¼N	10½E	**31**
Adaminaby, N.S.W.	36S	148¾E	**59**
Adams Bridge, Ceylon.	9¼N	79½E	**45**
Adams, Mt., U.S.A.	46½N	122½W	**74**
Adams Peak, Ceylon.	6¾N	80½E	**45**
Adana, Turkey.	37N	35¼E	**41**
Adapazari, Turkey.	40¾N	30½E	**41**
Adarama, Sudan.	17N	35E	**40**
Adare C., Antarctica.	71S	173E	**80**
Adavale, Queens., Aust.	26S	144½E	**60**
Adda R., Italy.	46¼N	9¼E	**36**
Ad Dahna, D. Saudi Arabia.	27N	47E	**40**
Addis Ababa, Ethiopia.	9N	38¾E	**56**
Addo, C. Pr., S. Africa.	33½S	25¾E	**53**
Adelaide, C. Pr., S.Afr.	32¾S	26¼E	**53**
Adelaide, S. Australia.	35S	138¾E	**59**
Adelaide I., Antarctica.	67S	68½W	**80**
Adelaide Penin., Can.	68N	98W	**66**
Adelaide R., Australia.	13¼S	131E	**60**
Adelboden, Switz.	46½N	7½E	**31**
Adel Edjele, Algeria.	28N	9¾E	**34**
Adele I., W. Aust. (ins.).	16S	123E	**61**
Adelie Land, Antarctica.	67S	140E	**80**
Aden, S. Yemen.	12½N	45E	**40**
Adena, Germany.	50½N	7E	**30**
Adendorp, C. Province.	32¼S	24½E	**53**
Adh Dhahiriya, Israel.	31½N	34¾E	**40**
Adi Ugri, Ethiopia.	15N	38½E	**56**
Adigasawa, Japan.	40¾N	140¼E	**49**
Adige R., Italy.	45¼N	12¼E	**36**
Adilabad, India.	19½N	78½E	**45**
Adirondack Mts., U.S.A.	44N	74W	**69**
Adiyaman, Turkey.	37½N	38E	**41**
Adjud, Romania.	46N	27E	**37**
Admiral, Sask., Can.	49¾N	108W	**70**
Admiralty, G., W. Aust.	14S	126E	**61**
Admiralty Inlet, Can.	72N	86W	**66**
Admiralty Inlet, U.S.A.	48N	122½W	**72**
Admiralty I., Pacific.	2S	147E	**64**
Adoni, India.	15¾N	77¼E	**45**
Adorf, Germany.	50¼N	12¼E	**33**
Adour, R., France.	43¾N	1¼W	**32**
Adra, Spain.	36¾N	3W	**35**
Adrano, Sicily.	37¾N	14¾E	**36**
Adria, Italy.	45N	12E	**31**
Adrian, Mich., U.S.A.	41¾N	84W	**68**
Adrianople, see EDIRNE.			
Adriatic Sea, Italy.	43N	16E	**36**
Aduwa, Ethiopia.	14N	38¾E	**56**
Advance, C. Pr., S. Afr.	31¼S	21½E	**52**
Advie, Scotland.	57½N	3½W	**24**
Adycha Riv., U.S.S.R.	69N	135E	**39**
Aegades Is., Sicily.	38N	12E	**36**
Aegean Sea, Greece.	39N	25E	**37**
Aegina, I. of, Greece.	37½N	23½E	**37**

Place	Lat.	Long.	No.
Aero, I. of, Denmark.	55N	10½E	**33**
Aerschot, Belgium.	51N	5E	**30**
Afago, Nigeria.	10½N	8E	**57**
Afars & Issas, Fr. Terr. of Africa.	12N	42¾E	**56**
Affula, Israel (inset).	32½N	35¼E	**40**
AFGHANISTAN, Asia.	33N	65E	**43**
Afgoi, Somali Republic.	2¼N	45E	**56**
Afif, Arabia.	23½N	42½E	**40**
Afikpo, Nigeria.	6N	8E	**57**
Aflou, Algeria.	34N	2E	**35**
Afmadu, Somali Republic.	½N	42E	**56**
Aframso. Ghana.	7¼N	1½W	**57**
Afyon, Turkey.	38¾N	30½E	**41**
Agadem, Niger.	17N	13¼E	**50**
Agades, Niger.	17N	8E	**50**
Agan, Riv., U.S.S.R.	62N	75E	**39**
Agana Guam. I., Pac.	13½N	144¾E	**64**
Agata, U.S.S.R.	67N	92E	**39**
Agazzano, Italy.	45N	9½E	**31**
Agdam, U.S.S.R.	40N	47E	**38**
Agde, France.	43¼N	3½E	**32**
Agedabia, Libya.	31N	20E	**34**
Agen, France.	44¼N	¾E	**32**
Agenebode, Nigeria.	7N	6½E	**57**
Agincourt, France.	50½N	2E	**32**
Aginskoe, U.S.S.R.	51N	114E	**39**
Aginskoe, U.S.S.R.	55N	95E	**39**
Agnes Riv., S. Aust.	27S	132¾E	**60**
Agordat, Ethiopia.	15¾N	37½E	**56**
Agordo, Italy.	46¼N	12E	**31**
Agra, India.	27¼N	78E	**44**
Agrakhanski, P., U.S.S.R.	43½N	48E	**38**
Agreda, Spain.	42N	2W	**32**
Agrihan I., Pacific.	19N	143E	**64**
Agri R., Italy.	40¼N	16¾E	**36**
Agrigento, Sicily.	37¼N	13½E	**36**
Agrinion, Greece.	38½N	21¼E	**37**
Agropoli, Italy.	40¼N	15E	**37**
Aguadilla, Puerto Rico.	18N	67½W	**77**
Aguascalientes, Mex.	21¾N	102½W	**76**
Aguilas, Spain.	37½N	1½W	**35**
Aguja, Pta. de, Peru	5S	81W	**78**
Agulhas, C., C. Pr.	34¾S	20E	**52**
Agwarra, Nigeria.	10½N	4½E	**57**
Ahaus, Germany.	52N	7E	**30**
Ahirli, Turkey.	38½N	26½E	**37**
Ah Khubba, Arabia.	22N	52½E	**40**
Ahlen, Germany.	51¾N	8E	**30**
Ahlhorn, Germany.	52¾N	8¼E	**30**
Ahmedabad, India.	23N	72¾E	**44**
Ahmednagar, India.	19¼N	74¾E	**45**
Ahoada, Nigeria.	5N	6¾E	**57**
Ahrdorf, Germany.	50½N	6¾E	**30**
Ahr Riv., Germany.	50½N	7¼E	**30**
Ahrweiler, Germany.	50½N	7E	**30**
Ahuachapan, Salvador.	13½N	90W	**76**
Ahualulco, Mexico.	22¼N	101¼W	**76**
Ahumada, Mexico.	30½N	106¾W	**76**
Ahwar, S. Yemen.	14½N	46½E	**40**
Ahwaz, Iran.	31¼N	48¾E	**40**
Aigle, Switzerland.	46¼N	7E	**31**
Aiguebelle, France.	45½N	6½E	**31**
Aigun, China.	50N	127½E	**39**
Aijal, India.	23½N	92½E	**43**
Ailat, Israel.	29N	35E	**41**
Ailinglapalap I., Pac.	8N	168E	**64**
Aillevillers, France.	48N	6¼E	**30**
Ailly, France.	49¾N	2¼E	**30**
Aim, U.S.S.R.	59N	134E	**39**
Ain, France.	46N	5¼E	**32**
Ain Haradh, Arabia.	24N	49E	**40**
Ain Sefra, Algeria.	32¾N	½W	**35**
Ain Touta, Algeria.	30N	1½E	**34**
Airaines, France.	50N	1¾E	**30**
Aidrie, Scotland.	55¾N	4W	**25**
Aire, France.	50¾N	2¼E	**30**
Aire, R., England.	53¾N	1W	**23**
Airolo, Switzerland.	46½N	8½E	**31**
Aisne, P. & R., France.	49½N	3½E	**32**
Aitape, New Guinea (ins.).	3S	142E	**60**
Aitutaki I., Pacific.	19S	161W	**64**
Aiud, Romania.	46¼N	23½E	**37**
Aix (en Provence), Fr.	43½N	5½E	**32**
Aix-la-Chapelle, see AACHEN.			
Aix-les-Bains, France.	45½N	6E	**32**
Aiyion, Greece.	38¼N	22E	**37**
Aizeb, Riv., S.W. Africa.	21S	19E	**51**
Aizpute, U.S.S.R.	56¾N	21½E	**38**
Ajaccio, Corsica.	42N	8¾E	**36**

Place	Lat.	Long.	No.
Ajana, W. Australia.	28S	114½E	**61**
Ajax, Mt., Mon., U.S.A.	45¼N	114W	**74**
Ajmer, India.	26½N	74¾E	**44**
Ajoewa, Surinam.	2½N	56W	**77**
Akaroa, S.I., N.Z.	43¾S	173E	**63**
Akasha, Sudan.	21N	31E	**40**
Akassa, Nigeria.	4¼N	6E	**57**
Aketi, Congo.	2¾N	23¾E	**56**
Akhaltsikhe, U.S.S.R.	42N	43E	**38**
Akheloos, Greece.	38¼N	21E	**37**
Akhisar, Turkey.	39N	27¾E	**41**
Akhtyrka, U.S.S.R.	50½N	35E	**38**
Akhtyubinsk, U.S.S.R.	50½N	57E	**38**
Akimiski I., N.W. Can.	53N	81½W	**66**
Akita, Japan.	39¾N	140E	**49**
Akkerman, U.S.S.R.	46½N	30E	**38**
Akkoy, Turkey.	37½N	27½E	**37**
Aklavik, N.W. Can.	68N	135W	**66**
Akobo, Sudan.	7¾N	33E	**56**
Akola, India.	20½N	77E	**45**
Akomolingo, Cameroon.	4N	12E	**56**
Akpatok I., N.W. Can.	60¼N	68W	**66**
Akron, Ohio, U.S.A.	41N	82½W	**75**
Aksaray, Turkey.	38N	34E	**41**
Aksenovo-Zilovskoe, U.S.S.R.	53N	111E	**39**
Aksha, U.S.S.R.	50N	112E	**39**
Aksu, China.	41N	80E	**39**
Akureyri, Iceland (ins.).	65¾N	18W	**29**
Akure, Nigeria.	7¼N	5¼E	**57**
Akuse, Ghana.	6N	¼E	**57**
Akusha, U.S.S.R.	42N	47½E	**38**
Akwanga, Nigeria.	9N	8½E	**57**
Akyab, Burma.	20¼N	92¾E	**43**
Ala, Italy.	45¾N	11E	**31**
Ala Pt., Italy.	42¾N	10¾E	**36**
Ala Kul, L., U.S.S.R.	46N	81E	**39**
ALABAMA, U.S.A.	33N	87W	**75**
Alabama R., Ala., U.S.A.	31N	87W	**75**
Alaca, Turkey.	40¼N	34¾E	**41**
Alacati, Turkey.	38¼N	26½E	**37**
Alagna, Italy.	46N	8E	**31**
Alagoas, Brazil.	9½S	36½W	**78**
Alagon, Riv., Spain.	39¾N	7W	**35**
Alajuela, Costa Rica.	10N	84W	**77**
Alameda, Sask., Can.	49¼N	102¼W	**70**
Aland I., Finland.	60¼N	20E	**29**
Alang Nor, L., China.	35N	97E	**43**
Alanya, Turkey.	36½N	32E	**41**
Alapa, Nigeria.	8¾N	4½E	**57**
Alaquines, Mexico.	22¼N	99½W	**76**
Alar Del Rey, Spain.	43N	4½W	**35**
Alasehir, Turkey.	38¼N	28½E	**37**
Al Ashkhara, Arabia.	22N	59E	**40**
ALASKA, U.S.A.	65N	150W	**74**
Alatyr, U.S.S.R.	55N	46½E	**38**
Albacete, Spain.	39N	1¾W	**35**
Albacutya L., Victoria.	35¾S	142E	**59**
Alba Iulia, Romania.	46N	23½E	**37**
ALBANIA, Europe.	41N	20E	**37**
Albany, Ga., U.S.A.	31¾N	84¼W	**75**
Albany, N.I., N.Z. (inset A).			**62**
Albany, N.Y., U.S.A.	42¾N	73¾W	**69**
Albany, W. Australia.	35S	118E	**61**
Albany R., Ont., Can.	52¼N	82W	**66**
Albany R., Ont., Can.	51¼N	90W	**71**
Albatross B., Queens.	12S	141¾E	**60**
Albatross Pt., N.I., N.Z.	38S	174½E	**62**
Al Beidha, Yemen (ins.).	14N	45¾E	**40**
Albenga, Italy.	44N	8¼E	**36**
Alberche, Riv., Spain.	40N	5W	**35**
Alberga Riv., S. Aust.	27½S	136E	**60**
Alberique, Spain.	39N	½W	**35**
Alberni, Br. Col., Can.	49¼N	124¾W	**72**
Albert, France.	50N	2¾E	**30**
Albert Canal, Belgium.	51N	5E	**30**
Albert, L., S. Aust.	35¾S	139E	**59**
Albert, L., Uganda.	2N	31E	**56**
Albert Nile, Uganda.	2N	31½E	**56**
Albert Riv., Queensland.	17S	139¾E	**60**
ALBERTA, Canada.	54N	115W	**66**
Albertinia, C. Prov.	34¼S	21½E	**52**
Alberton, Canada.	46¾N	64W	**67**
Albertville, Congo (K.)	6S	29¼E	**56**
Albertville, France.	45½N	6¼E	**32**
Albi, France	44N	2¼E	**32**
Albion, N.Y., U.S.A.	43¼N	78¼W	**69**
Albo, Mt., Sardinia.	40½N	9½E	**36**
Albreda, Br. Col., Can.	52¾N	119¼W	**72**
Albuera, La, Spain.	38¾N	7W	**35**
Albuquerque, U.S.A.	35N	106¾W	**74**

[90] Albury—Apsley

Place	Lat.	Long.	No.
Albury, *N.S.W., Aust.*	36S	147E	59
Alcala, *Spain.*	40½N	3½W	35
Alcala La Real, *Spain.*	37½N	4W	35
Alcamo, *Sicily.*	38N	13E	36
Alcaniz, *Spain.*	41¼N	¼W	35
Alcantara, *Spain.*	39¾N	7W	35
Alcaraz, *Spain.*	38¾N	2½W	35
Alcester *England.*	52¼N	1¾W	23
Alchevsk, *U.S.S.R.*	48½N	39E	38
Alcira, *Spain.*	39¼N	½W	35
Alcoy, *Spain.*	38¾N	½W	35
Alcudia, *Majorca I.*	39¾N	3¼E	35
Aldabra Is., *Indian Oc.*	9½S	46½E	50
Aldan, *U.S.S.R.*	58½N	125½E	39
Aldan Riv., *U.S.S.R.*	64N	130E	39
Aldborough, *England.*	53¾N	0	23
Aldeburgh, *England.*	52¼N	1½E	23
Alderney, *Channel Is.*	49¾N	2¼W	31
Aldershot, *England.*	51¼N	¾W	23
Alderson, *Alb., Can.*	50¼N	111¼W	73
Aldridge, *England.*	52½N	2W	23
Alegranza I., *Canary Is.*	29½N	13½W	35
Alegrete, *Brazil.*	30S	56W	79
Aleksandriya, *U.S.S.R.*	48N	33E	38
Aleksandrovsk, *U.S.S.R.*	51N	142E	39
Aleksandrovskoe, *U.S.S.R.*	60N	78E	39
Aleksandrow, *Poland.*	51¾N	19¼E	33
Aleksandrow, *Poland.*	52¾N	18¾E	33
Alekseyevo, *U.S.S.R.*	70N	149E	39
Aleksinac, *Yugoslavia.*	43½N	22E	37
Alemsid, *Morocco.*	32½N	6W	34
Alencon, *France.*	48½N	0	32
Aleppo, *Syria.*	36¼N	37E	41
Aleria, *Corsica.*	42N	9½E	36
Alert B., *Br. Col., Can.*	50½N	127W	72
Ales, *France.*	44N	4E	32
Ales, *Sardinia.*	39¾N	8¾E	36
Alessandria, *Italy.*	45N	8¾E	36
Autelian Is., *Alaska.*	57N	168W	74
Alevina, C., *U.S.S.R.*	59N	150½E	39
Alexander Arch., *U.S.A.*	55N	135W	66
Alexander Bay, *C. Pr.*	28¾S	16½E	52
Alexander Ist L., *Antarc.*	69S	70W	80
Alexandra, *S.I., N.Z.*	45¼S	169¼E	63
Alexandra, *Vict., Aust.*	37¼S	145¾E	59
Alexandretta, see ISKENDERON.			
Alexandria, *C. Pr.*	33¾S	26½E	53
Alexandria, *U.A.R.*	31¼N	30E	50
Alexandria, *La., U.S.A.*	31¼N	92½W	75
Alexandria, *Ont., Can.*	45¼N	74¾W	69
Alexandria, *Va., U.S.A.*	38¾N	77W	75
Alexandrina L., *S. Aust.*	35½S	139E	59
Alexandroupolis, *Gr.*	40¾N	26E	37
Alexandrov Gai, *U.S.S.R.*	50½N	49E	38
Alexis Creek, *Br. Col.*	52¼N	123¼W	72
Aleysk, *U.S.S.R.*	52N	82E	39
Al Faluja, *Israel* (ins.).	31½N	34¾E	40
Alfaro, *Spain.*	42¼N	2W	35
Alfatar, *Bulgaria.*	44N	27E	37
Alflos, Riv., *Greece.*	37½N	21¼E	37
Alfonsine, *Italy.*	44½N	12E	31
Alford, *England.*	53¼N	¼E	23
Alford, *Scotland.*	57½N	2¾W	24
Alfreton, *England.*	53N	1½W	23
Alga, *U.S.S.R.*	49¾N	57½E	38
Algebuckina, *S. Aust.*	27½S	136¼E	60
Algeciras, *Spain.*	36¼N	5½W	35
ALGERIA, *N. Africa.*	33N	3E	50
Al Ghail, *Yemen* (ins.).	15¼N	45E	40
Alghero, *Sardinia.*	40½N	8¼E	36
Algiers, *Algeria.*	36¾N	3E	35
Algoa B., *C. Pr., S. Afr.*	33¾S	25¾E	53
Algoma, *Ont., Can.*	46¼N	82¾W	68
Algonquin Park, *Can.*	45½N	78¾W	69
Al Hamar, *Arabia.*	22½N	46E	40
Al Hanakiya, *Arabia.*	25N	46E	40
Al Hauta, *S. Yem.* (ins.)	15¾N	48E	40
Aliaga, *Spain.*	40¾N	¾W	35
Aliaga, *Turkey.*	38¾N	27E	37
Aliakmon Riv., *Greece.*	40½N	21½E	37
Alibag, *India.*	18½N	73E	45
Alicante, *Spain.*	38¼N	½W	35
Alice, *C. Pr., S. Africa.*	32¾S	27E	53
Alice, *Queens., Aust.*	23½S	146E	60
Alice, *Texas, U.S.A.*	27½N	98W	74
Alice Downs, *W. Aust.*	18S	128E	61
Alice Springs, *N. Terr.*	23¾S	134E	60
Alicedale, *C. Pr., S. Afr.*	33¼S	26E	53
Alicudi I., *Italy.*	38½N	14½E	36
Alida, *Sask., Canada.*	49¼N	102W	70
Aliero, *Nigeria.*	12¼N	4½E	57
Aligarh, *India.*	28N	78E	44
Alima Riv., *Congo (B.)*	2S	17E	56
Alindao, *Cent. Afr. Rep.*	5N	21E	56
Aline, *Scotland.*	58N	6½W	24
Aling Kangri Mt., *China.*	33N	81E	43
Aliverion, *Greece.*	38½N	24E	37
Aliwal North, *C. Pr.*	30¾N	26¾E	53
Alix, *Alberta, Canada.*	52½N	113¼W	73
Al Jauf, *Saudi Arabia.*	29¾N	39½E	40
Aljustrel, *Portugal.*	38N	8E	35
Al Khabura, *Mus. & Om.*	24N	57E	40
Alkmaar, *Netherlands.*	52¾N	4¾E	30
Alkmaar, *Transvaal.*	25½S	30¾E	54
Allada, *Dahomey.*	6¾N	2E	57
Allahabad, *India.*	25½N	82E	44
Allahdad, *Pakistan.*	27N	66E	46
Allakh Yun, *U.S.S.R.*	60N	135E	39
Allan, *Sask., Canada.*	52N	106W	70
Allandale, *O.F.S.*	28¾S	27E	55
Allanwater, *Ont., Can.*	50½N	90¼W	71
Allata, *Ethiopia.*	6¾N	38¼E	56
Allanton, *S.I., N.Z.*	(inset D).		63
Allegheny Mts., *U.S.A.*	38N	80W	75
Allen, Bog of, *Ireland.*	53½N	7W	26
Allen, L., *Ireland*	54N	8W	26
Allen Mt., *N.Z*	47½S	168E	63
Allendale, *England.*	54¾N	2¼W	25
Allentown, *Pa., U.S.A.*	40½N	75½W	75
Alleppey, *India.*	9½N	76½E	45
Aller, Riv., *Germany.*	53N	8¼E	33
Allevard, *France.*	45½N	6E	31
Alliance, *Neb., U.S.A.*	42½N	102½W	74
Allier, Riv., *France.*	46N	3¼E	32
ALLIER, *France.*	46¼N	3¼E	32
Alligator Pond, *Jamaica.*	18N	77½W	77
Allison Harb., *Canada.*	51N	127½W	72
Alliston, *Ontario, Can.*	44¼N	80W	68
Al Lith, *Saudi Arabia.*	20N	40E	40
Alloa, *Scotland.*	56¼N	3¾W	24
Allonby, *England.*	54¾N	3½W	25
All Pines, *Br. Hond.*	16¾N	88½W	76
Alma, *New Bruns., Can.*	45¾N	65W	67
Alma Ata, *U.S.S.R.*	43½N	77E	39
Almaden, *Spain.*	38¾N	4¾W	35
Almaden, *Queensland.*	17S	144½E	60
Almagro, *Spain.*	39N	3¾W	35
Al Majdal, *Israel*, (ins.).	31¾N	34½E	40
Almansa, *Spain.*	38¾N	1W	35
Al Marj, *Libya.*	32½N	21E	34
Almelo, *Netherlands.*	52¼N	6½E	30
Almendralejo, *Spain.*	38¾N	6½W	35
Almeria, *Spain.*	36¾N	2½W	35
Almeria, G. of, *Spain.*	36¾N	2½W	35
Almirante, *Panama.*	9¼N	82½W	77
Almiros, *Greece.*	39¼N	23E	37
Almond R., *Scot.*	56½N	3½W	25
Almonte, *Ontario, Can.*	45½N	76½W	69
Almora, *India.*	29¾N	79¾E	44
Alness, R., *Scot.*	57¾N	4¼W	24
Alnmouth, *England.*	55½N	1½W	25
Alnwick, *England.*	55½N	1¾W	25
Alonsa, *Manitoba, Can.*	50¾N	99W	71
Alor I., *Indonesia.*	8¼S	124½E	47
Alor Star, *Malaysia.*	6¼N	100¼E	47
Alost, *Belgium.*	51N	4E	30
Alpes Maritimes, *Fr.*	43¾N	7E	34
Alps, The, *Europe.*	46N	7E	32
Alpha, *Queens., Aus.*	23¾S	146¾E	60
Al Qara, *Saudi Arabia.*	30N	40E	41
Al Qunfidha, *Saudi Arabia.*	19N	41E	40
Al Qurna, *Iraq.*	31N	47½E	40
ALSACE, *France.*	48N	7½E	32
Alsask, *Sask., Canada.*	51½N	110W	70
Alsfeld, *Germany.*	50¾N	9E	33
Al Shaab, *S. Yemen.*	13N	44¾E	56
Alstahaug, *Norway.*	65½N	12E	29
Alston, *England.*	54¾N	2½W	25
Alta, *Norway.*	70N	23½E	29
Alta Lake, *Br. Col., Can.*	50¼N	123W	72
Altagracia, *Venezuela.*	11N	71½W	77
ALTAI, *U.S.S.R.*	52N	85E	39
Altai Mts., *Mongolia.*	48N	92E	39
Altan Bulak, *Mongolia.*	50N	106E	39
Altamura, *Italy.*	40¾N	16½E	36
Altar, *Mexico.*	30¾N	112W	76
Altata, *Mexico.*	24½N	108W	76
Altdorf, *Switzerland.*	46¾N	8¾E	31
Altena, *Germany.*	51¼N	7¾E	33
Altenburg, *Germany.*	51N	12½E	33
Alt Fiord, *Norway.*	70N	23E	29
Altkirch, *France.*	47¾N	7E	30
Alto Molokwe, *Moz.*	16S	37½E	56
Alton, *England.*	51¼N	1W	23
Altona, *Germany.*	53½N	10E	33
Altoona, *Pa., U.S.A.*	40½N	78¼W	75
Altrincham, *England.*	53½N	2¼W	22
Alturas, *Cal., U.S.A.*	42N	120½W	74
Al Ula, *Saudi Arabia.*	27N	38E	40
Alula, *Somali Rep.*	12N	50½E	56
Alvdalen, *Sweden.*	61N	14E	29
Alvesta, *Sweden.*	56½N	15E	29
Alvinston, *Ont., Can.*	42¾N	81¾W	68
Alwar, *India.*	27¾N	76¾E	44
Al Yahudiyah, *Israel.*	32N	35E	40
Alyth, *Scotland.*	56¾N	3¼W	24
Alytus, *Lith, U.S.S.R.*	54½N	24E	33
Alzey, *Germany.*	49¾N	8E	30
Amabele, *C. Province.*	32¾S	27½E	53
Amadeus, L., *Aust.*	24¾S	131E	60
Amadi, *Sudan.*	5½N	30¼E	56
Amagasaki, *Japan.*	34¾N	135½E	49
Amager I., *Denmark.*	55¾N	12¾E	29
Amalias, *Greece.*	37¾N	21½E	37
Amami Group, *Japan.*	28¼N	130E	64
Amanzimtoti, *Natal.*	30S	31E	55
Amapala, *Honduras.*	13¼N	87¾W	77
Amara, *Iraq.*	32N	47E	41
Amarillo, *Tex., U.S.A.*	35¼N	101¾W	74
Amasya, *Turkey.*	40¾N	36E	41
Amazon, Riv., *Brazil.*	0	50W	78
AMAZONAS, *Brazil.*	4S	64W	78
Amba, *India.*	18¾N	76¼E	45
Ambala, *India.*	30½N	76¾E	44
Ambalangoda, *Ceylon.*	6¼N	80E	45
Ambalavao, *Malagasy.*	21¼S	47E	56
Ambarchik, *U.S.S.R.*	79¾N	162½E	39
Ambato-Boueni, *Malagasy.*	16½S	46¾E	56
Ambatondrazaka, *Malagasy.*	18S	48E	56
Amberg, *Germany.*	49¼N	11½E	33
Ambergris Cay I., *W.I.*	18N	88W	77
Amberley, *S.I., N.Z.*	43¼S	172¾E	63
Ambikapur, *India.*	23N	83E	44
Ambilobe, *Malagasy.*	13¼S	49E	56
Amble, *England.*	55¼N	1½W	25
Ambleside, *England.*	54½N	3W	25
Amboina, *Indonesia.*	3¾S	128¼E	47
Amboise, *France.*	47½N	1E	31
Ambositra, *Malagasy.*	20½S	47¼E	56
Ambovombe, *Malagasy.*	25S	45½E	56
Ambre, C. d', *Malagasy.*	12S	49¼E	56
Ambrieres, *France.*	48½N	¾W	31
Ambrim I., *Pacific.*	18S	169E	64
Ambrizete, *Angola.*	7S	13E	56
Ambriz, *Angola.*	7¾S	13E	56
Amchung, *Tibet.*	31N	83¾E	43
Ameca, *Mexico.*	20½N	104W	76
Ameland, Is. *Neth.*	53½N	5¾E	30
Amen, *U.S.S.R.*	68N	180	39
Amersfoort, *Neth.*	52¼N	5¾E	30
Amersfoort, *Trans.*	27S	29¾E	55
Amery, *Man., Canada.*	56½N	94¼W	71
Amesbury, *England.*	51¼N	1¾W	23
Amfiklia, *Greece.*	38½N	22½E	37
Amfilokhia, *Greece.*	39N	21E	37
Amfipolis, *Greece.*	40¾N	24E	37
Amfissa, *Greece.*	38½N	22½E	37
Amga, Riv., *U.S.S.R.*	63N	135E	39
Amga, *U.S.S.R.*	61N	132E	39
Am Guerida, *Chad.*	13N	21E	56
Amguid Bordj, *Algeria.*	26½N	5½E	34
Amgu, *U.S.S.R.*	46N	138E	39
Amgun Riv., *U.S.S.R.*	53N	141E	39
Amguyema R., *U.S.S.R.*	68N	179W	39
Amherst, *N.S., Can.*	45¾N	64¼W	67
Amherstburg, *Ont.*	42¼N	83W	68
Amiens, *France.*	49¾N	2¼E	32
Amlwch, *Wales.*	53½N	4½W	22
Amman, *Jordan.*	32N	36E	40
Ammanford, *Wales.*	51¾N	4W	22
Amorgos, I., *Aegean S.*	36¾N	26E	37
Amos, *Que., Canada.*	48½N	78W	69
Amoy, see HSIAMEN.			
Ampanihy, *Malagasy.*	25S	45E	56
Ampthill, *England.*	52N	½W	23
Amran, *Yemen* (inset).	15¼N	44½E	40
Amraoti, *India.*	21N	77¾E	44
Amristar, *India.*	31¾N	75E	44
Amsterdam, *Holland.*	52½N	4¾E	30
Amsterdam, *N.Y., U.S.*	43N	74¼W	69
Amsterdam, *Trans.*	26¾S	30¾E	55
Amstetten, *Austria.*	48¼N	14¾E	33
Amu-Darya, *Afghan.*	37½N	66E	43
Amu Darya, R., *U.S.S.R.*	44N	59E	42
Amundsen B., *Antarc.*	67½S	50E	80
Amundsen S., *Antarctic.*	70S	110W	80
Amur, R., *U.S.S.R.*	53N	141E	39
Amurang, *Celebes, Indon.*	1N	124E	47
Anaa I., *Pacific.*	18S	145W	64
Anabar, Riv., *U.S.S.R.*	73N	113E	39
Ana Branch R., *N.S.W.*	34S	141½E	59
Anaconda, *Mon., U.S.A.*	46N	113½W	74
Anaco, *Venezuela.*	9N	64W	77
Anadyr Gulf, *U.S.S.R.*	64N	180E	39
Anadyr & R., *U.S.S.R.*	65N	179E	39
Anadyrski Mts., *U.S.S.R.*	67N	175E	39
Anafi, I. of, *Greece.*	36½N	26E	37
Ana, *Iraq.*	34½N	42E	40
Anaiza, *Saudi Arabia.*	26N	45E	40
Anakapalle, *India.*	17½N	83E	45
Analalava, *Malagasy.*	14¾S	47¾E	56
Anambas Is., *S. China S.*	3N	106E	47
Anamur & C., *Turkey.*	36N	32¾E	41
Anantapur, *India.*	14¾N	77¾E	45
Anapa, *U.S.S.R.*	45N	37½E	38
Anar, *Iran.*	31N	55E	40
Anatahan I., *Pacific.*	15N	145E	64
Ancenis, *France.*	47¼N	1¼W	31
Anchau, *Nigeria.*	11N	8¼E	57
Anching, *China.*	30½N	117E	48
Anchorage, *Alaska, U.S.*	61N	150W	74
Ancona, *Italy.*	43¾N	13½E	36
Ancud, *Chile.*	42S	74W	78
Andalsnes, *Norway.*	62½N	7½E	29
ANDALUSIA, *Spain.*	37½N	5W	35
Andaman Is., *B. of Beng.*	12N	92½E	43
Andermatt, *Switzer.*	46¾N	8½E	31
Andernach, *Germany.*	50½N	7½E	30
Anderson, R., *N.W. Can.*	70N	129W	66
Anderson, *S.C., U.S.A.*	34½N	82½W	75
Andes Mts., *S. America.*	27S	68W	78
Andhra, *India.*	17N	80E	45
Andijan, *U.S.S.R.*	41N	72E	39
Andkhui, *Afghanistan.*	36½N	65E	43
Ando I., *Norway.*	69N	16½E	29
Andong, *Korea.*	37N	129E	49
Andorra, *Spain.*	42½N	1½E	35
Andover, *England.*	51¼N	1½W	23
Andrab, *Afghanistan.*	35½N	70E	43
Andreas, C., *Cyprus.*	36N	34E	41
Andreba, *Malagasy.*	17½S	48E	56
Andria, *Italy.*	41¼N	16¼E	36
Andros I., *Bahamas.*	24½N	78W	77
Andros, I. of, *Greece.*	38N	25E	37
Anduto, *Angola.*	12S	17E	56
Anecho, *Togo.*	6¼N	1½E	57
Anegada I., *W.I.*	18½N	64W	77
Aneityum, *Pacific.*	20S	170E	64
Anenous, *C. Pr.*	29¼S	17½E	52
Aneroid, *Sask.*	49¾N	107¼W	70
Anfo, *Italy.*	45¾N	10½E	31
Angara, Riv., *U.S.S.R.*	57N	103E	39
Angaston, *S. Aust.*	34½S	139E	59
Angel Falls, *Venezuela.*	6½N	63W	77
Angelholm, *Sweden.*	56¼N	12¾E	29
Angelo, Riv., *W. Aust.*	23½S	117½E	61
Angerman R., *Sweden.*	63N	17E	38
Angermunde, *Germany.*	53N	14E	33
Angers, *France.*	47½N	¾W	3
Angerville, *France.*	48¼N	2E	3
Angkor, *Cambodia.*	14N	104E	4
Anglesey I., *Wales.*	53¼N	4½W	2
Anglure, *France.*	48½N	3¾E	3
Angmagssalik, *Green.*	65½N	37½W	6
Angol, *Chile.*	37¾S	73W	7
Angouleme, *France.*	45¾N	¼E	3
ANGOUMOIS Prov., *Fr.*	45¾N	¼E	3
Anguilla Is., *W.I.*	18N	63W	77
Angus, *Scotland.*	56¾N	3W	2
Anholt, *Denmark.*	56½N	11½E	2
ANHWEI, *China.*	32¼N	117E	4
Aniene, Riv., *Italy.*	41¾N	12¼E	3
Anina, *Romania.*	45N	21¾E	3
Aniva, C., *U.S.S.R.*	46N	144E	3
Anizy le Chateau, *Fr.*	49½N	3½E	3
Anjar, *India.*	23¼N	70E	4
Anjouan I., *Malagasy.*	12½S	45E	5
ANJOU, *France.*	47¼N	½W	3
Anju, *Korea.*	39½N	125½E	4
Ankang, *China.*	32½N	109¾E	4
Anka, *Nigeria.*	12N	6E	5
Ankaratra Mts., *Malag.*	19S	47E	5
Ankara, *Turkey.*	40N	33E	4
Ankazoaba, *Malagasy.*	22½S	44¾E	5
Anketell, *W. Aust.*	28S	119E	6
Anklam, *Germany.*	53¾N	13¾E	3
Ankober, *Ethiopia.*	9½N	40E	5
Ankola, *India.*	14¾N	74¼E	4
Anlu, *China.*	31N	113E	4
Annaba, *Algeria.*	36¾N	7¾N	3
Annaberg, *Germany.*	50½N	13E	3
An Nafud. D., *Arabia.*	28N	40E	4
Annai, *Guyana.* (inset).	4N	59W	7
An Najaf, *Iraq.*	32N	44E	4
Annalee, R., *Ireland.*	54N	8¼W	2
Annan, *Scotland.*	55N	3¼W	2
Annapolis, *Md., U.S.A.*	38N	76½W	7
Annapolis, *Nova Scotia.*	44¾N	65½W	6
Ann Arbor, *Mich. U.S.*	42¼N	83¾W	6
An Nasiriya, *Iraq.*	31½N	46½E	4
Annecy, *France.*	46N	6¼E	3
Annecy, L de, *France.*	45¾N	6¼E	3
Annecy, *France.*	45¾N	6¼E	3
Annemasse, *France.*	46¼N	6¼E	3
Anniston, *Ala., U.S.A.*	33¾N	86W	7
Annonay, *France.*	45¼N	4¾E	3
An Numas, *Arabia.*	19N	42E	4
Annweiler, *Germany.*	49¼N	8E	3
Ansbach, *Germany.*	49¼N	10½E	3
Anshan, *China.*	41¼N	123E	4
Anshun, *China.*	26¼N	106E	4
Anson B., *N. Terr.*	13S	130E	6
Ansongo, *Mali.*	16N	0	5
Anstruther, *Scotland.*	56¼N	2¾W	2
Antakya, *Turkey.*	36¼N	36E	4
Antalaha, *Malagasy.*	15S	50¼E	5
Antalya & G., *Turkey.*	37N	30¾E	4
Antarctic Peninsula, *Antarctica.*	67S	65W	8
Antelao, Mt., *Italy.*	46½N	12¼E	3
Antequera, *Spain.*	37N	4½W	3
Anthony Lag., *Austr.*	18S	135½E	6
Antibes, *France.*	43½N	5¼E	3
Anticosti I., *Quebec.*	49½N	63W	6
Antigonish, *Nova Scot.*	45¾N	62W	6
Antigua I., *W. Indies.*	17N	61¾W	7
Antifer, C. de, *France.*	49¾N	¼E	3
Antigua, *Guatemala.*	14½N	91W	7
Antilla, *Argentina.*	26½S	64½W	7
Antilles, Lesser, *W. Ind.*	15N	63W	7
Antioch, see ANTAKYA.			
Antivari, see BAR.			
Antipodes I., *S. Pacific.*	49¾S	178½E	6
Antofagasta, *Chile.*	23¾S	70½W	7
Antoing, *Belgium.*	50½N	3½E	3
Antongil B., *Malagasy.*	15½S	50E	5
Antrain, *France.*	48½N	1¼W	3
Antrim Mts., *Ireland.*	55¼N	6¼W	2
ANTRIM, *N. Ireland.*	54¾N	6¼W	2
Antsirabe, *Malagasy.*	20S	47E	5
Antsirane, *Malagasy.*	12¼S	49¼E	5
Antung, *China.*	40N	124½E	4
Antwerp, *Belgium.*	51¼N	4½E	3
An Uaimh, *Eire.*	53¾N	6¾W	2
Anuradhapura, *Ceylon.*	8¼N	80½E	4
Anyang, *China.*	36¼N	114¼E	4
Any, *China.*	35N	110½E	4
Anza, *Colombia.*	6¾N	76W	7
Anzhero Sudzhensk, *U.S.S.R.*	56¼N	86E	3
Anzio, *Italy.*	41½N	12½E	3
Aoiz, *Spain.*	42¾N	1¼W	3
Aomori, *Japan.*	40¾N	140¾E	4
Aosta, *Italy.*	45¾N	7¼E	3
Aosta, *Italy.*	45¾N	7¼E	3
Aparima R., *S.I., N.Z.*	46¼S	168¼E	6
Aparri, *Luzon, P.I.*	18¼N	121¾E	4
Apataki I., *Pacific.*	15S	145W	6
Apatin, *Yugo.*	45½N	19E	3
Apeldoorn, *Nether.*	52¼N	6E	3
Apennine Mts., *Italy.*	43N	12E	3
Aperion, *Greece.*	35½N	27E	4
Apia, *Samoa, Pacific.*	13¾S	172W	6
Apoteri, *Guyana.* (ins.).	3½N	58W	7
Appalachian Mts., *U.S.*	36N	82W	6
Appenzell, *Switzer.*	47¼N	9½E	3
Appiano, *Italy.*	45¾N	9E	3
Appin, *Scotland.*	56½N	5½W	2
Appleby, *England.*	54½N	2½W	2
Applecross, *Scotland.*	57½N	5¾W	2
Appledore, *England.*	51N	4¼W	2
Appleton, *Wis., U.S.A.*	44¼N	88½W	7
Apsley, *Tasmania.*	42½S	147¼E	5

Place	Lat.	Long.	No.
Apt, France.	43¾N	5½E	32
PULIA, Italy.	41N	17E	36
Apure, Riv., Venezuela.	8N	66W	77
Aqaba & G., Jordan.	29N	35E	41
Aqiq, Sudan.	18N	38E	40
Aquila, Italy.	42¼N	13½E	36
Aquililla, Mexico.	18½N	102¾W	76
Aquin, Haiti.	18¼N	73½W	77
ARABIA, SAUDI. Asia.	24N	45E	40
Arabian Desert, U.A.R	28N	33E	41
Arabian Sea, Asia.	15N	65E	43
Aracaju, Brazil.	11S	37W	79
Aracena, Spain.	38N	6¾W	35
Arad, Romania.	46¼N	21¼E	37
Arafura S., Indonesia.	8S	134E	47
Aragano, Sicily.	37¼N	13¾E	36
ARAGON & Riv., Spain.	41½N	1W	35
Araguari, Brazil.	18¾S	48¼W	79
Araguaya, Riv., Brazil.	4S	49W	78
Arahoab, S.W. Africa.	24S	19E	51
Arakan Yoma, Burma.	19N	94½E	47
Aral Sea, U.S.S.R.	45N	60E	40
Aralsk, U.S.S.R.	46¾N	62½E	39
Araluen, N.S.W.	35½S	149¾E	59
Aramac, Queensland.	23S	145¼E	60
Aran Is., Eire.	53½N	9¾W	26
Aran I., Eire.	55N	8¾W	26
Aran Mawddwy, Wales.	52¾N	4W	22
Aranda de Duero, Sp.	41¾N	4W	35
Aranjuez, Spain.	40N	3¾W	35
Araouane, Mali.	18½N	4W	50
Arapuni, N.I., N.Z.	38S	175¾E	62
Ararat, Victoria.	37¼S	143E	59
Ararat, Mt., Turkey.	39¾N	44¼E	41
Arauca, Riv., Venezuela.	7½N	67W	77
Aravalli Ra., India.	25N	73½E	44
Araxes, Riv., Iran. U.S.S.R.	39N	49E	41
Arbai Khere, Mongolia.	47N	103E	39
Arbalat, Sudan.	20N	36½E	40
Arborg, Manitoba.	51N	97¼W	70
Arbois, France.	47N	5¾E	31
Arbroath, Scotland.	56½N	2½W	25
Arces, France.	48¼N	3½E	30
Arc, France.	47½N	5½E	31
Archer Pt., Queensland.	16S	145½E	60
Arch Pt., Antarctica.	69S	160E	80
Archangel, U.S.S.R.	64½N	40¾E	38
Archer, Riv., Queens.	13S	141¾E	60
Arcis-s-Aube, France.	48½N	4¼E	30
Arco, Italy.	46N	11E	31
Arcola, Sask.	49¾N	102½W	70
Arcos, Spain.	36¾N	5¾W	35
Arcot, India.	12¾N	79¼E	45
Arctic Red, R., Can.	68N	136W	66
Ardakan, Iran.	30N	53E	40
Ardara, Ireland.	54¾N	8½W	26
Ardebil, Iran.	38¼N	48½E	40
ARDECHE, France.	44¾N	4½E	32
Ardee, Eire.	53¾N	6½W	26
Ardennes Mts., France-Belgium.	50N	5½E	30
ARDENNES, France.	49¾N	4¾E	32
Ardglass, N. Ireland.	54¼N	5½W	26
Ardila, Riv., Portugal.	37N	7½W	35
Ardistan, Iran.	33½N	52E	40
Ardlui, Scotland.	56¼N	4¾W	24
Ardmore Hd., Ireland.	52N	7¾W	26
Ardnacrusha, Eire.	52¾N	8¾W	26
ArdnamurchanPt., Sco.	56¾N	6W	24
Ardnaree, Ireland.	54N	9W	26
Ardres, France.	51N	2E	30
Ardrishaig, Scotland.	56N	5½W	25
Ardrossan, S. Australia.	34½S	138E	59
Ardrossan, Scotland.	55¾N	4¾W	25
Ardvasar, Scotland.	57N	6W	24
Are, R., France.	45½N	6½E	31
Arendal, Norway.	58½N	8¾E	29
Arendonck, Belgium.	51¼N	5¼E	30
Areopolis, Greece.	36½N	22½E	37
Arequipa, Peru.	16½S	71½W	78
Ares, France.	45N	1¼W	32
Arevalo, Spain.	41¼N	5W	35
Arezzo, Italy.	43½N	12E	36
Argenta, Italy.	44½N	11¾E	31
Argentan, France.	48¾N	0	32
Argenteuil, France.	49N	2¼E	32
ARGENTINA, S. America.	40S	66W	78
Argentia, Newfound.	47¼N	54W	67
Argentino, L., Argen.	50¼S	72½W	78
Argenton, France.	46½N	1½E	32
Argesul, Riv., Romania.	44N	26½E	37
Arghandab, Afghan.	32N	65E	43
Argolis, G. of, Greece.	37N	23E	37
Argos, Greece.	37¾N	22¾E	37
Argungu, Nigeria.	12¾N	4¼E	57
Argun, Riv., China.	52½N	121E	39
Argyle Dns., W. Aust.	16½S	128¾E	60
ARGYLL, Scotland.	56½N	5½W	25
Argyrokastron, Alb.	40¼N	20¼E	37
Ariano Polesine, Italy.	45N	12E	31
Arica, Chile.	18½S	70½W	79
Arid, C., W. Australia.	34S	123¼E	61
ARIEGE, France.	43N	1½E	32
Arigna, Ireland.	54N	8½W	26
Arilalah, Queensland.	23½S	143½E	60
Arima, Trinidad.	11½N	60½W	77
Arinda, Guyana. (ins.).	5N	59W	77
Arinno, W. Australia.	29½S	115½E	61
Arisaig, Scotland.	56¾N	5¾W	24
Arisaig, Sd. of, Scotland.	57N	6W	24
Arisio, Riv., Italy.	46¼N	11¼E	31
Arispe, Mexico.	30½N	110½W	76
Aristazabal I., Br. Col.	52¾N	129¾W	72
Aritzo, Sardinia.	40N	9¼E	36
Arivechi, Mexico.	29N	109W	76
Ariza, Spain.	41½N	2W	35
ARIZONA (State), U.S.A.	35N	112W	74
Arjona, Colombia.	10N	75W	77
Arkadelphia, Ark., U.S.	34N	93W	75
ARKANSAS & R., U.S.A.	35N	92½W	75
Arklow, Eire.	52¾N	6¼W	26
Arkonam, India.	13N	79½E	45
Arlanzon, Riv., Spain.	42N	4¾W	35
Arlberg Tunl., Austria.	47½N	10¼E	31
Arles, France.	43¾N	4¾E	25
Arlington, O.F.S.	28S	27¾E	53
Arlon, Belgium.	49¾N	5¾E	30
Arltunga, N. Terr.	23½S	134½E	60
Armadale, W. Aust.	32¼S	116E	61
ARMAGH, N. Ireland.	54¼N	6¾W	26
Armancon, R., France.	47¾N	3½E	30
Armavir, U.S.S.R.	45N	41E	38
ARMENIA, U.S.S.R.	40N	45E	38
Armentieres, France.	50¾N	2½E	23
Armidale, N.S.W.	30½S	151¾E	59
Armoed, C. Pr.	33¾S	22E	52
Armstrong, Br. Col.	50½N	119¼W	72
Armstrong, Ont., Can.	50½N	89W	71
Arnauti, C. of, Cyprus.	35N	32E	41
Arnhem. C., N. Terr.	12S	137E	60
Arnhem, Netherlands.	52N	6E	30
Arnhem Land, N. Terr.	13½S	133½E	60
Arniston, C. Pr.	34¾S	20¼E	52
Arno R., Italy.	43¾N	10¼E	36
Arnprior, Ont., Can.	45½N	76½W	69
Arnsberg, Germany.	51½N	8E	30
Aroab, S.W. Africa.	26¾S	19¾E	51
Arolsen, Germany.	51½N	9E	30
Arorae, Pacific.	3S	176E	64
Arosa, Switzerland.	46¾N	9¾E	31
Arock, Oreg., U.S.A.	42¾N	117½W	74
Arona, Italy.	45¾N	8½E	31
Arpino, Italy.	41¾N	13½E	36
Arqa, S. Yemen. (ins.).	14¾N	47E	40
Arran, I. of, Scotland.	55¾N	5¼W	25
Arras, France.	50¼N	2¾E	32
Arrecife, Canary Is. (ins.)	29N	13½W	35
Arree, Mt. de, France.	48½N	4W	31
Arriaga, Mexico.	16¼N	93½W	76
Arrochar, Scotland.	56¼N	4¾W	25
Arrow Lough, Eire.	54¼N	8¼W	26
Arrowhead, Br. Col.	50¾N	118W	73
Arrowsmith, Mt., S.I., N.Z.	43½S	171E	63
Arrowtown, S.I., N.Z.	45S	168¾E	63
Arrowwood, Alberta.	50¾N	113¼W	73
Arsiero, Italy.	45¾N	11¼E	31
Arta, Majorca.	39¾N	3½E	35
Arta, Greece.	39¼N	21E	37
Artem, U.S.S.R.	43½N	132E	49
Artemovsk, U.S.S.R.	48½N	38E	38
Artemovsk, U.S.S.R.	54N	92E	39
Artemovskiy, U.S.S.R.	58N	115E	39
Artenay, France.	48N	1¾E	30
Artesia, Botswana.	24S	26½E	54
Arthal, Kashmir (ins.).	33N	76¼E	44
Arth, Switzerland.	47N	8½E	31
Arthur Pass, S.I., N.Z.	42¾S	172E	63
Arthur Pt., Queensland.	22S	150E	60
Artigas, Uruguay.	30S	58W	78
ARTOIS, France.	50½N	2½E	32
Artvin, Turkey.	41½N	42E	41
Aruba I., W. Indies.	12½N	70W	77
Arucas, Canary Is. (ins.).	28¼N	15¼W	35
Aru Is., Indonesia.	6S	134½E	47
Arun, R., England.	50¾N	½W	23
Arundel, England.	50¾N	½W	23
Arusha, Tanzania.	3¼S	36¾E	56
Aruvi-Aru, Riv., Ceylon.	8¾N	79¾E	45
Arve, R., France.	46¼N	6E	31
Arvida, Quebec.	48½N	71¼W	69
Arvika, Sweden.	59¾N	13E	29
Arys, U.S.S.R.	43N	69E	39
Arzamas, U.S.S.R.	55½N	43¾E	38
Arzew, Algeria.	35¾N	¼W	35
Arzfeld, Germany.	50¼N	6¼E	30
Asaba, Nigeria.	6¼N	6½E	57
Asahigawa, Japan.	43¾N	142¼E	49
Asahi, Mt., Japan.	43N	143E	49
Asbestos, Quebec.	45¾N	72W	69
Ascension, Mexico.	31½N	108W	76
Ascension I., Atlantic.	8S	15W	19
Asch, Belgium.	51N	5½E	30
Asch, Czechoslovakia.	50¼N	12¼E	33
Aschaffenburg, Ger.	50N	9¼E	33
Aschersleben, Germany.	51¾N	11½E	33
Ascoli Piceno, Italy.	42¾N	13½E	36
Ascot, England.	51½N	¾W	23
Asele, Sweden.	64N	17E	29
ASHANTI, Ghana.	7N	2W	57
Asha, U.S.S.R.	55N	57E	38
Ashbourne, England.	53N	1¾W	23
Ashburton, England.	50½N	3¾W	22
Ashburton, S.I., N.Z.	43¾S	171¾E	63
Ashburton, R., W. Aust.	22¾S	115E	61
Ashby-de-la-Zouch, England.	52¾N	1½W	23
Ashcroft, Br. Col.	50½N	121¼W	72
Ashern, Manitoba.	51¼N	98¼W	71
Asheville, N.C., U.S.A.	35½N	82½W	75
Ashford, England.	51¼N	¾E	23
Ashfork, Ariz., U.S.A.	35¼N	112½W	25
Ashington, England.	55¼N	1½W	74
Ashikaga, Japan.	36½N	139½E	49
Ashkhabad, U.S.S.R.	38N	58E	40
Ashland, Maine, U.S.A.	46½N	68¼W	67
Ash Shihr, S. Yemen.	15N	49¾E	40
Ashton, C. Pr.	33¾S	20¼E	52
Asiago, Italy.	45¾N	11½E	31
Asinara I. & G., Italy.	41N	8¼E	36
Asino, U.S.S.R.	57N	87E	39
ASIR, Saudi Arabia.	18½N	42½E	40
Ask I., Norway.	60¾N	4¾E	29
Asmara, Ethiopia.	15¼N	39E	56
Asmar, Afghanistan.	35N	70½E	43
Asnen, L., Sweden.	56½N	14¾E	29
Asola, Italy.	45¼N	10½E	31
Aspatria, England.	54¾N	3½W	25
Aspern, Austria.	48¼N	16½E	33
Aspiring, Mt., N.I. N.Z.	44½S	168¾E	63
Asquith, Sask.	52¼N	107¼W	70
Assab, Ethiopia.	13N	42½E	56
As Sabya, Saudi Arabia.	17N	42½E	40
ASSAM, India.	27N	94E	43
Assche, Belgium.	51N	4¼E	30
Assen, Netherlands.	53N	6½E	30
Assiniboia, Sask.	49¾N	106W	70
Assiniboine R., Ont.	50N	98W	66
Asso, Italy.	45¾N	9¼E	31
Astakos, Greece.	38½N	21E	37
Astara. Iran.	38½N	48¾E	40
Asten Netherlands.	51¼N	5½E	30
Asti, Italy.	45N	8¼E	36
Astipalaia, I. of, Greece.	36½N	26½E	37
Astorga, Spain.	42¾N	6W	35
Astoria, Oreg., U.S.A.	46¼N	123¾W	74
Astor, Kashmir.	35¼N	75E	43
Astrakhan, U.S.S.R.	46½N	48E	38
Astrida, Burundi.	2½S	29¾E	56
Astros, Greece.	37½N	22¾E	37
ASTURIAS, Spain.	43½N	6W	35
Asuncion I., Pacific.	19¾N	145E	64
Asuncion, Paraguay.	25¼S	57¾W	79
Aswan, U.A.R.	24N	33E	50
Asyut, U.A.R.	27¼N	31E	50
Atacama Desert, Chile.	26S	67½W	79
Ata I., Pacific.	22S	178W	64
Atafu I., Pacific.	9S	172W	64
Atak Hapchiga, China.	33N	92½E	43
Atakpame, Togo.	7½N	1E	57
Atar, Mauritania.	20¾N	13¼W	50
Atbara, Sudan.	17¾N	34E	50
Atbara, Riv., Sudan.	18N	34E	40
Atbasar, U.S.S.R.	51¾N	68½E	39
Atebubu, Ghana.	7¾N	1W	57
Ath, Belgium.	50½N	3¾E	30
Athabaska, Alberta.	54¾N	113¼W	73
Athabaska, L., Sask.	59½N	109W	66
Athabaska, R., Alberta.	56N	112W	66
Athboy, Eire.	53½N	6¾W	22
Athboy, Eire.	53¾N	6¾W	26
Athenry, Eire.	53¼N	8¾W	26
Athens, Ga., U.S.A.	34N	83½W	75
Athens, Greece.	38N	23¾E	37
Athens, Ontario.	44¾N	76W	69
Atherly, Ontario.	44½N	79¼W	68
Atherton, Queensland.	17¼S	145½E	60
Athi, Riv., Kenya.	2S	37½E	56
Athleague, Ireland.	53½N	8¼W	26
Athlone, Eire.	53½N	8W	26
Athos, Mt., Greece.	40½N	24E	37
Athy, Eire.	53N	7W	26
Atikokan, Ontario.	48¾N	91¾W	71
Atiu I., Pacific.	20S	160W	64
Atkarsk, U.S.S.R.	52N	45E	38
Atlanta, Ga., U.S.A.	33¾N	84½W	75
Atlantic, Iowa, U.S.A.	42N	95W	75
Atlantic City, N.J., U.S.A.	39½N	74½W	75
Atlas Mts., N. Africa.	33N	0	50
Atlin & L., Br. Col.	59½N	133½W	66
Atrek, Riv., Iran.	37N	54E	40
Attack, Pakistan.	34N	72¼E	43
Attawapiskat R., Can.	53N	81W	66
Attigny, France.	49½N	4½E	30
Attleboro, Mass., U.S.A.	42N	71¼W	69
Attleborough, Eng.	52½N	1E	23
Attock, Pakistan.	33¾N	72¼E	46
Atuntze, China.	28N	99E	43
Atures, Venezuela.	6N	69W	77
Aubagne, France.	43¼N	5½E	32
AUBE & R., France.	48½N	4¼E	32
Aubigny, France.	50¼N	2½E	30
Auburn, Maine, U.S.A.	44N	70¼W	69
Auburn, N.Y., U.S.A.	43N	76½W	69
Aubusson, France.	46N	2¼E	32
Auch, France.	43¾N	½E	32
Auchi, Nigeria.	7N	6¼E	57
Auchenmalg, Scotland.	54¾N	4¾W	25
Auchterarder, Scotland.	56¼N	3¾W	25
Auchtermuchty, Scot.	56¼N	3¼W	25
Auckland, N.I., N.Z.	37S	174¾E	62
AUCKLAND, CENTRAL, N.I., N.Z.	38S	176E	62
Auckland Is., S. Pacific.	51S	166E	64
AUDE, France.	43N	2¼E	32
Audegle, Somali. Rep.	2¼N	45E	56
Audenarde, Belgium.	51N	3½E	30
Auderville, France.	49¾N	2W	31
Audierne, France.	48N	4½W	31
Audlem, England.	53N	2½W	22
Audierne, B. de, France.	48N	4¾W	31
Audun-le-Roman, Fr.	49½N	6E	30
Auga, Israel (inset).	32N	34¾E	40
Augathella, Queens.	26S	147E	60
Aughmacloy, Ireland.	54½N	7W	26
Aughrim, Ireland.	52¾N	6½W	26
Aughrim, Ireland.	53½N	8½W	26
Aughty, Ireland.	53N	8½W	26
Augi, Nigeria.	13N	4½E	57
Augsburg, Germany.	48½N	10¾E	33
Augusta, Maine, U.S.A.	44N	70W	75
Augusta, Sicily.	37¼N	15¼E	36
Augusta, Ga., U.S.A.	33½N	82W	75
Augusta, Me., U.S.A.	44¼N	69¾W	69
Augusta, W. Aust.	34½S	115E	61
Augustow, Poland.	53¾N	23E	33
Augustus I., W. Aust.	16S	125E	61
Augustus, Mt., W.Aust.	24½S	116E	61
Aujila, Libya.	29N	21½E	34
Auldearn, Scotland.	57½N	3¾W	24
Aulla, Italy.	44¼N	10E	36
Aulne, R., France.	48¼N	4¼W	31
Aulnoye, France.	50¼N	4E	30
Aumale, France.	49¾N	1¾E	30
Auneau, France.	48½N	1¾E	30
AUNIS, France (inset).	46¼N	1½E	32
Aunis, France.	46¼N	1W	32
Aurangabad, India.	19¾N	76½E	45
Aurich, Germany.	53½N	7½E	33
Aurillac, France.	45N	2½E	32
Aurora, Ill., U.S.A.	41¾N	88¼W	75
Aurora, C. Pr.	32¾S	18½E	52
Aurora, Ontario.	44N	79½W	68
Aurukun, Queensland.	12½S	142E	60
Aus. S.W. Africa.	26¾S	16¼E	51
Austerlitz. see SLAVKOV.			
Austin, Minn., U.S.A.	43½N	93W	75
Austin, Nev., U.S.A.	39½N	117W	74
Austin, Texas, U.S.A.	30¼N	97¾W	75
Austin, Pa., U.S.A.	41¾N	78W	69
Austin L., W. Aust.	27¾S	117¾E	61
Austin, W. Australia.	27½S	118E	61
Austral Is., Pacific.	21S	140W	64
AUSTRALIA	25S	135E	58
Australian Alps, Vict.	37S	148E	59
AUSTRIA. Europe.	47N	14E	33
Authon, France.	48¼N	1E	31
Autlan de Novarro, Mexico.	19¾N	104½W	76
Autun, France.	47N	4¼E	32
AUVERGNE, France.	45½N	3E	32
Auvergne, N. Terr.	16S	130E	60
Aux Sources, Mt., Lesotho.	28¾S	28¾E	55
Auxerre, France.	47¾N	3½E	32
Avallaneda, Arg.	35S	58W	79
Avallon, France.	47½N	3¾E	32
Avalon Pen., Newf.	47N	53½W	67
Avebury, England.	51½N	1¾W	23
Aveiro, Portugal.	40¾N	9W	35
Avellino, Italy.	41N	14¾E	36
Avero I., Norway.	63N	7¾E	29
Aversa, Italy.	41N	14¼	36
Aves Is., Venezuela.	12½N	67½W	77
Avesnes, France.	50N	4E	30
AVEYRON, France.	44¼N	2¾E	32
Avezzano, Italy.	42N	13½E	36
Avia, Greece.	39¾N	22¾E	37
Aviemore, Scotland.	57¼N	3¾W	24
Avigliano, Italy.	40¾N	15¾E	36
Avignon, France.	44N	4¾E	32
AVIGNON, France (ins.).	44¼N	6E	32
Avila, Spain.	40¾N	4¾W	35
Aviles, Spain.	43½N	6W	35
Avoca, Eire.	53N	6¼W	22
Avoca, Victoria.	37S	143½E	49
Avoca, Riv., Victoria.	36½S	143¾E	59
Avola, Br. Col.	51¾N	119½W	72
Avon Downs, N. Terr.	20S	137½E	60
Avon, R., England.	52½N	1W	23
Avonlea, Sask.	50N	105W	70
Avonmouth, England.	51½N	2¾W	22
Avontuur, C. Pr.	33¾S	23E	52
Avranches, France.	48¾N	1¼W	32
Avre, R., France.	49¾N	2½E	30
Avricourt, France.	48½N	6¾E	30
Awash & Riv., Eth	9N	40E	56
Awaso, Ghana.	6¼N	2¼W	57
Awatere, R., S.I., N.Z.	41¾S	174¼E	63
Aweil, Sudan.	9¾N	27½E	56
Awe, L., Scotland.	56¼N	5¼W	25
Awka, Nigeria.	6N	7E	57
Awunaga, Ghana.	6N	1E	57
Axar Fiord, Iceland.	66½N	17W	29
Axbridge, England.	51¼N	2¾W	22
Axel, Netherlands.	51½N	3¾E	30
Axel Heiberg, I., Can.	78N	90W	66
Axim, Ghana.	5N	2¼W	57
Axminster, England.	50¾N	3W	22
Axum, Eth.	13½N	38E	56
Ayacucho, Arg.	37S	58W	79
Ayacucho, Peru.	13S	74W	78
Ayaghkum Kul, Tibet.	34N	88E	43
Ayaguz, U.S.S.R.	48N	80½E	39
Ayamonte, Spain.	37N	7¼W	35
Ayangba, Nigeria.	7½N	7¼E	57
Ayan, U.S.S.R.	56½N	138E	39
Ayas, Turkey.	40N	32½E	41
Aydin, Turkey.	37¾N	28E	41
Ayenfuri, Ghana.	6N	2W	57
Ayers Rock Mt., Aust.	26S	131¾E	60
Ayios Evstratios I., Gr.	39½N	25E	37
Aylesbury, England.	51¾N	¾W	23
Aylmer, Ontario.	42¾N	81W	68
Aylmer, L., N.W. Can.	64N	109W	66
Aylsham, England.	52¾N	1E	23
Aynho, England.	52N	1¼W	23
Ayodhya, India.	26¾N	82¼E	44
Ayon I., U.S.S.R.	70N	169E	39
Ayrao, Brazil.	3S	61W	78
Ayr, Queensland.	19½S	147½E	60
AYR & Town, Scotland.	55½N	4¾W	25
Ayre, Pt. of, Isle of Man	54½N	4½W	25
Ayrshire Dns., Queens.	22S	142½E	60
Aysgarth, England.	54¼N	2¼W	25
Ayton, Scotland.	55¾N	2W	25
Ayuthia, Thailand.	14½N	100½E	47

Place	Lat.	Long.	No.
Ayvalik, *Turkey*.	39¼N	26¾E	41
Azamgarh, *India*.	26N	83E	44
Azare, *Nigeria*.	11½N	10¼E	57
Azay le Rideau, *France*.	47¼N	½E	31
AZERBAIJAN, *U.S.S.R.*	40N	47E	38
Aziziye, *Turkey*.	36½N	27½E	41
Azores Is., *Atlantic*.	38N	29W	35
Azov, Sea of, *U.S.S.R.*	46N	37E	38
Azov, *U.S.S.R.*	47N	39½E	38
Azuero, Pen. of, *Pan.*	7½N	81W	77
Azul, *Argentina*.	37S	60W	79
Azzan, *S. Yemen*. (ins.).	14¾N	48E	40
BABA, C., *Turkey*.	39½N	26E	37
Babadag, *Romania*.	45N	28¾E	37
Babakin, *W. Australia*.	32¼S	118E	61
Babar Is., *Indonesia*.	7¾S	130E	47
Bab el Mandeb Str., *Red Sea*.	12½N	42½E	56
Babinda, *Queensland*.	17¼S	146E	60
Babine, L., *Br. Col. Can.*	55N	126W	72
Babo, *New Guinea*.	2½S	133½E	47
Babul, *Iran*.	36¾N	52¾E	40
Babuyan Is., *P.I.*	19N	122E	47
Babylon, *Iraq*.	32½N	44E	40
Bacalar, *Mexico*.	18½N	88W	76
Bacau, *Romania*.	46½N	27E	37
Baccarat, *France*.	48½N	6¾E	30
Bacchus Marsh, *Vict.*	37¾S	144½E	59
Bachok, *Malaysia*.	6N	102¼E	47
Back, Riv., *S.W. Africa*.	28S	20E	51
Back, Riv., *N.W. Can.*	67N	101½W	66
Backstairs Pass., *S.Aust.*	35½S	138¼E	59
Bac Lieu, *Indo-China*.	9N	106E	47
Bacolod, *Negros, P.I.*	10¾N	123E	47
Bacubiritu, *Mexico*.	25¾N	107½W	76
Bacup, *England*.	53¾N	2¼W	22
Badagara, *India*.	11½N	75½E	45
Badagri, *Nigeria*.	6½N	3E	57
Badajoz, *Spain*.	38¾N	7W	35
Badanah, *Saudi Arabia*.	31½N	41½E	41
Bad Bramstadt, *Ger.*	54N	10E	30
Bad Briburg, *Germany*.	51¾N	9E	30
Baddeck, *C. Breton I.*	46¼N	60¾W	67
Bad Doberan, *Germany*.	54N	12E	33
Bad Ems, *Germany*.	50½N	7½E	30
Baden, *Austria*.	48N	16¼E	33
Baden Baden, *Germany*.	48¾N	8¼E	30
BADEN-WURTTEMBERG, *Germany*.	43½N	8½E	30
Badgastein, *Austria*.	47N	13E	33
Bad Godesburg, *Ger.*	50¾N	7E	30
Bad Homburg, *Ger.*	50¼N	8¼E	33
Badia, *Saudi Arabia*.	22N	46½E	40
Badin, *Pakistan*.	24¾N	68¾E	43
Bad Kissingen, *Ger.*	50¼N	10½E	33
Bad Kreuznach, *Ger.*	49¾N	8E	33
Badnur, *India*.	22N	78E	44
Bad Pyrmont, *Germany*.	52N	9¼E	33
Bad Reichenhall, *Ger.*	47¾N	12¾E	33
Badr Hunain, *Sau. Arab.*	23½N	39E	40
Bad Segeberg, *Germany*.	54N	10¼E	30
Bad Tolz, *Germany*.	47¾N	11½E	33
Badulla, *Ceylon*.	7N	81½E	45
Bad Wildungen, *Ger.*	51N	9E	33
Baebriggan, *Eire*.	53½N	6¼W	22
Baena, *Spain*.	37¾N	4¼W	35
Baeze, *Spain*.	38N	3½W	35
Bafata, *Port Guin.*(ins.).	12N	14¾W	57
Baffin Bay, *Arctic*.	70N	60W	80
Baffin I., *N.W.T.*	66N	70W	80
Bafoussam, *Cameroon*.	5½N	10½E	57
Bafra & C., *Turkey*.	41¾N	36E	41
Bagamoyo, *Tanzania*.	6½S	39E	56
Bagan Serai, *Malaysia*.	5¼N	100¼E	47
Bagansiapion, *Sum. E.I.*	2N	101E	47
Bage, *Brazil*.	31½S	54¼W	79
Bagenalstown, see MUINE BHEAG.			
Baghdad, *Iraq*.	33½N	44½E	40
Bagheria, *Sicily*.	38N	13½E	36
Bagneres-de-Bigorre, *France*.	43N	¼E	32
Bagneres-de-Luchon, *France*.	42¾N	½E	32
Bagnoli, *Italy*.	45¼N	11¾E	31
Bagrach Kol, L., *China*.	42N	87E	39
Baguio, *Luzon, P.I.*	16N	120E	47
Bahama Is., *W. Indies*.	25N	75W	77
Bahawalnagar, *Pak.*	30N	73E	46
Bahawalpur, *Pakistan*.	29½N	71¾E	44
BAHIA *Brazil*.	13S	42W	78
Bahia, see SALVADOR.			
Bahia, Is. de la, *Hond.*	16N	87W	77
Bahia Blanca, *Arg.*	38¾S	62W	78
Bahia de Neiba, *Dom.*	18N	72W	77
Bahia de Samana, *Dom.*	19N	69W	77
Bahia Escocesa, *Dom.*	19N	69¾W	77
Bahia Honda, *Cuba*.	22½N	84W	77
Bahr Auk, R., *C.Afr.Rep.*	8½N	19E	56
Bahr el Arab, R., *Sudan*.	10N	26E	56
Bahr el Ghazal, *Sudan*.	9¾N	30E	56
Bahr el Jebel, *Sudan*.	9¾N	30½E	56
Bahraich, *India*.	27½N	81½E	44
Bahrain I., *Persian Gulf*.	26N	50½E	40
Bahramabad, *Iran*.	30N	56E	40
Baia-Mare, *Romania*.	47¾N	23½E	37
Baibokun, *C. Afr. Rep.*	7¾N	15¾E	56
Baiersbronn, *Germany*.	48½N	8½E	30
Baikal, L., *U.S.S.R.*	53N	109E	39
Baile Atha Cliath, see DUBLIN.			
Bailen, *Spain*.	38½N	3¾W	35
Bailesti, *Romania*.	44N	23½E	37
Bailey, *C. Pr.*	31¾S	26¾E	53
Bailleu, *France*	50¾N	2¾E	30
Baimak, *U.S.S.R.*	52½N	58E	38
Bain-de-B., *France*.	47¾N	1¾W	31
Baines Riv., The, *Aust.*	16S	130E	60
Bainham, *S.I., N.Z.*	40¾S	172½E	63
Bairnsdale, *Victoria*.	37¾S	147½E	59
Baisogala, *U.S.S.R.*	55¾N	23¾E	33
Baitadi, *Nepal*.	29½N	80½E	44
Baixo, I. do, *Madeira Is.*	33N	16W	35
Baja, *Hungary*.	46¼N	19E	37
Bajil, *Yemen* (inset).	15N	44E	40
Bajo Boquete, *Panama*.	8½N	82½W	77
Bakal, *U.S.S.R.*	55N	59E	38
Baker, *Mont., U.S.A.*	46¾N	104¼W	74
Baker, *Oregon, U.S.A.*	45N	117½W	74
Baker I., *Pacific*.	0	177W	64
Baker Lake, *N.W.T.*	64¼N	95W	66
Baker, Mt., *Wash., U.S.*	48¾N	122¼W	74
Bakersfield, *Calif., U.S.*	35½N	119W	74
Bakewell, *England*.	53¼N	1¾W	23
Bakhta, Riv., *U.S.S.R.*	63N	89E	39
Bako, *Ethiopia*.	5¾N	36½E	56
Baku, *U.S.S.R.*	40½N	50E	38
Bakuma, *Cent. Afr. Rep.*	6N	23E	56
Bakundi, *Nigeria*.	8N	10¾E	57
Bakura, *Nigeria*.	12¾N	6E	57
Bala, *Ontario*.	45N	79½W	68
Bala, *Wales*.	52¾N	3¾W	22
Bala, L., *Wales*.	52¾N	3¾W	22
Balabac I., *P.I.*	8N	117E	47
Balad, *Somali Republic*.	2¾E	45¾N	56
Balad Bani Bu Ali, *Muscat & Oman*.	22N	59E	40
Balaklava, *S. Aust.*	34¼S	138½E	59
Balaklava, *U.S.S.R.*	44½N	33½E	38
Balakovo, *U.S.S.R.*	52N	48E	38
Balallan, *Scotland*.	58¼N	6½W	24
Bala Murghat, *Afghan.*	35N	63½E	43
Balana, *Nicaragua*.	14¾N	84¾W	77
Balancan, *Mexico*.	17¾N	92W	76
Balashov, *U.S.S.R.*	51½N	43½E	38
Balasore, *India*.	21½N	87E	44
Balassagyarmat, *Hung.*	48N	19¼E	37
Balaton, L., *Hungary*.	47N	17¾E	37
Balboa, *Panama*.	9N	79¼W	77
Balbriggan, *Eire*.	53½N	6¼W	26
Balcarres, *Sask.*	50¾N	103½W	70
Balcic, *Bulgaria*.	43½N	28E	37
Balclutha, *S.I., N.Z.*	46¼S	169¾E	63
Bald Hd., *W. Australia*.	35S	118E	61
Baldaratskaya B., *U.S.S.R.*	69N	67E	38
Baldock, *England*.	52N	¼W	23
Baldrisy C., *Malagasy*.	16S	50E	56
Baldwin, *N.Y., U.S.A.*	40¾N	74¼W	75
Baldy Pk., *Ariz., U.S.A.*	34N	110W	74
Balearic Is., *Mediter.*	39½N	3E	35
Balfate, *Honduras*.	16N	86W	77
Balfour, *C. Pr.*	32½S	26¾E	53
Balfour, *Transvaal*.	26¾S	28½E	55
Balfour Dns., *W. Aust.*	22½S	121E	61
Balgonnie, *Sask.*	50½N	104¼W	70
Bali I., *Indonesia*.	8½S	115E	47
Balikesir, *Turkey*.	39½N	27¾E	41
Balikpapan, *Borneo*.	1¼S	117E	47
Balintang Ch., *Philip.*	20N	122E	47
Balkhash, L., *U.S.S.R.*	46½N	75E	39
Balkhash, *U.S.S.R.*	47N	75E	39
Balkan Mts., *Bulgaria*.	43N	25E	37
Balla Balla, *W. Aust.*	21S	117½E	61
Ballachulish, *Scotland*.	56¾N	5W	24
Ballaghaderreen, *Ire.*	54N	9W	26
Ballantrae, *Scotland*.	55¼N	5W	25
Ballara, *Queensland*.	20½S	140E	60
Ballarat, *Victoria*.	37½S	143¾E	59
Ballard, L., *W. Aust.*	29S	121E	61
Ballater, *Scotland*.	57N	3W	24
Balleroy, *France*.	49¼N	¾W	31
Ballina, *Ireland*.	54¼N	9¼W	26
Ballina, *N.S.W.*	28¾S	153½E	59
Ballinakill, *Ireland*.	52¾N	7¼W	26
Ballinasloe, *Ireland*.	53¼N	8¼W	26
Ballingeary, *Ireland*.	51¾N	9¼W	26
Ballinhassie, *Ireland*.	51¾N	8½W	26
Ballinrobe, *Ireland*.	53½N	9¼W	26
Ballinskelligs B., *Ire.*	51¾N	10¼W	26
Balloch, *Scotland*.	56N	4¾W	25
Ballon, *France*.	48¼N	¼E	31
Ballybunion, *Ireland*.	52½N	9½W	26
Ballybay, *Ireland*.	54N	7W	26
Ballybofey, *Ireland*.	54¾N	7¾W	26
Ballycastle, *Ireland*.	54¼N	9½W	26
Ballycastle, *N. Ireland*.	55¼N	6¼W	26
Ballyclare, *Ireland*.	54¾N	6W	26
Ballygawley, *Ireland*.	54½N	7¼W	26
Ballyhale, *Ireland*.	52½N	7¼W	26
Ballyhaunis, *Ireland*.	53¾N	8¾W	26
Ballyheige, *Ireland*.	52½N	9¾W	26
Ballyjamesduff, *Ire.*	53¾N	7¼W	26
Ballylanders, *Ireland*.	52¼N	8½W	26
Ballymahon, *Ireland*.	53½N	7½W	26
Ballymena, *N. Ireland*.	54¾N	6¼W	26
Ballymoney, *Ireland*.	55N	6½W	26
Ballyragget, *Ireland*.	52¾N	7¼W	26
Ballynahinch, *Ireland*.	54½N	6W	25
Ballyshannon, *Ireland*.	54½N	8¼W	26
Ballyvagh, *Ireland*.	53¼N	9¼W	26
Ballyvourney, *Ireland*.	52N	9W	26
Balme, *Italy*.	45¼N	7¼E	31
Balmhorn, Mt., *Switz.*	46½N	7½E	31
Balmoral, *Scotland*.	57N	3¼W	24
Balmoral, *Victoria*.	37¼S	141¾E	59
Balnacra, *Scotland*.	57½N	5½W	24
Balonne, *Queensland*.	27½S	148E	60
Balovale, *Zambia*.	13S	23E	51
Balrampur, *India*.	27½N	82¼E	44
Balranald, *N.S.W.*	34½S	143½E	59
Balsas, Riv., *Mexico*.	18N	102W	76
Balta, *U.S.S.R.*	48N	29½E	38
BALTIC SEA, *N. Europe*.			29
Baltim, *U.A.R.*	31½N	31½E	50
Baltimore, *Eire*.	53N	7W	26
Baltimore, *Md., U.S.A.*	39¼N	76½W	75
Baltimore, *Eire*.	51½N	9¼W	26
Baltinglass, *Eire*.	52¾N	7W	26
Baltisk, *U.S.S.R.*	54¾N	20E	33
Baltiski, *U.S.S.R.*	59½N	24¼E	38
Baltit, *Kashmir* (inset).	36½N	74½E	44
Baltrum, I. of, *Ger.*	53¾N	7½E	30
Balya, *Turkey*.	39¾N	27½E	37
Bam, *Iran*.	29N	58E	40
Bamako, *Mali*.	13N	8W	50
Bambari, *Cent. Afr. Rep.*	5¾N	20½E	56
Bamberg, *Germany*.	49¾N	10¾E	33
Bamboo, *W. Aust.*	21S	120½E	61
Bamburgh, *England*.	55¾N	1¾W	25
Bamenda, *Cameroon*.	6N	10½E	57
Bamfield, *Br. Col.*	48¾N	125W	72
Bamingi, R., *C. Afr. Rep.*	8N	19E	56
Bamori, *Mexico*.	31N	111½W	76
Bampton, *England*.	51N	3½W	22
Bampur, *Iran*.	27½N	60E	40
Banagher, *Ireland*.	53¼N	8W	26
Banas, Riv., *India*.	26N	77E	44
BANAT, *Romania*.	45½N	21E	37
Banavie, *Scotland*.	56¾N	5W	24
Banbridge, *N. Ireland*.	54¼N	6¼W	26
Banbury, *England*.	52N	1¼W	23
Bancannia, L., *N.S.W.*	31S	142E	59
Banchory, *Scotland*.	57N	2½W	24
Bancroft, *Ontario*.	45¼N	77¾W	69
Banco Gorda, *Carib. S.*	15N	82W	77
Banda, *India*.	25½N	80½E	43
Banda Atjeh, *Sumatra*.	5½N	95½E	47
Banda Is., *Indonesia*.	4½S	129¾E	47
Banda Sea, *Indonesia*.	6S	130E	47
Bandar, *India*.	16¼N	81¼E	45
Bandar Abbas, *Iran*.	27¼N	56½E	40
Bandar Penggaram, *Mal.*	1¾N	103E	47
Bandar Rig, *Iran*.	29¾N	51E	41
Bandar Shah, *Iran*.	37N	54¼E	40
Bandar Shahpur, *Iran*.	30½N	49½E	40
Bandarawela, *Ceylon*.	6¾N	81E	45
Bandiagara, *Mali*.	14N	3W	50
Bandirma, *Turkey*.	40½N	28E	37
Bandjermasin, *Borneo*.	3½S	114½E	47
Bandolierkop, *T'vaal.*	23½S	29¾E	54
Bandon, *Thailand*.	8N	99E	47
Bandon, *Eire*.	51¾N	8¾W	26
Bandra, *India*.	19N	72¾E	45
Bandung, *Java*.	7S	107½E	47
Bandundu, *Congo. (K.)*	3½S	17¾E	56
Banes, *Cuba, W. Indies*.	21N	76W	77
Baneza, La, *Spain*.	42¼N	6W	35
Banff, *Alberta*.	51¼N	115¾W	73
Banff Park, *Alb., Can.*	51¾N	116W	73
Banff, *Scotland*.	57¾N	2½W	24
BANFF, *Scotland*.	57½N	3W	24
Bangalore, *India*.	13N	77½E	45
Bangasu, *C. Afr. Rep.*	4¾N	22¾E	56
Bangemall, *W. Aust.*	24½S	116½E	61
Banggai Is., *Indonesia*.	1¾S	123½E	47
Bangka I., *Sumatra*.	2½S	106E	47
Bangkok, *Thailand*.	13½N	100½E	47
Bangor, *Ireland*.	54¼N	9¾W	26
Bangor, *Maine, U.S.A.*	45N	69W	75
Bangor, *N. Ireland*.	54¾N	5¾W	26
Bangor, *Wales*.	53¼N	4¼W	22
Bangspan, *Thailand*.	12N	100E	43
Bangued, *Luzon, P.I.*	17½N	120E	47
Banguey I., *Borneo*.	7½N	117¼E	47
Bangui, *C. Afr. Rep.*	4½N	18½E	56
Bangweulu L., *Zambia*	11½S	30E	51
Ban Hwei Sai, *Laos*.	20N	101E	47
Banj, *Dom. Rep.*	18N	70½W	77
Baniyas, *Syria*.	35N	36E	41
Baniyas, *Syria* (inset).	33¼N	35½E	40
Banjak Is., *Sumatra*.	2¼N	97¼E	47
Banjaluka, *Yugoslavia*.	44¾N	17¼E	36
Banjumas, *Java*.	7½S	109¼E	47
Banjuwangi, *Java*.	8¼S	114½E	47
Banka Banka Sta., *Aust.*	19S	134E	60
Bankot, *India*.	18N	73E	45
Banks I., *Br. Col.*	53¼N	130W	72
Banks I., *N.W.T.*	73½N	120W	66
Banks Is., *Pacific*.	13¾S	167½E	64
Banks I., *Queensland*.	10S	142E	60
Banks, Pen., *S.I., N.Z.*	43¾S	173E	63
Banks Strait, *Tasmania*.	40½S	148E	59
Bankura, *India*.	23¼N	87E	44
Ban Mak Khaeng, *Thai.*	17½N	103E	47
Bann, R., *N. Ireland*.	54¾N	6½W	26
Bannockburn, *Scotland*.	56N	4W	25
Bannu, *Pakistan*.	33¼N	70¼E	43
Banska Bystrica, *Czech.*	48¾N	19¼E	33
Banska Stiavnica, *Czechoslovakia*.	48½N	19E	33
Banswara, *India*.	23½N	74½E	44
Bantry, *Eire*.	51¾N	9½W	26
Bantry B., *Ireland*.	51¾N	9¾W	26
Banyo, *Cameroon*.	7N	12E	56
Banzare Coast, *Antarc.*	66¾S	125E	80
Bapatla, *India*.	16N	80½E	45
Bapaume, *France*.	50N	3E	30
Bar, *Yugoslavia*.	42N	19E	37
Bar-le-Duc, *France*.	48¾N	5¼E	32
Bara, *Sudan*.	13¾N	30¼E	56
Barabinsk, *U.S.S.R.*	55¼N	78¼E	39
Baracoa, *Cuba*.	20¼N	74½W	77
Baradine, *N.S.W.*	31S	149E	59
Barahona, *Dom. Rep.*	17½N	71¼W	77
Baralaba, *Queensland*.	24¼S	149¾E	60
Barama, Riv. *Guyana*.	9N	60W	77
Baramanni, *Guyana*.	8N	59W	77
Baramula, *Kashmir*.	34N	75E	43
Baranof I., *Alas., U.S.A.*	57N	137W	74
Baranovichi, *U.S.S.R.*	53¼N	26E	38
Barbas, C., *Sp. Sahara*.	22N	18W	50
Barbados I., *W. Indies*.	13¼N	59½W	77
Barbastro, *Spain*.	42N	0	35
Barberton, *Transvaal*.	25¾S	31E	55
Barbosa, *Colombia*.	6N	74¾W	77
Barbuda I., *W. Indies*.	17½N	61¾W	77
Barcaldine, *Queens.*	23½S	145¼E	60
Barcellona, *Sicily*.	38¼N	15¼E	36
Barcelona, *Spain*.	41½N	2¼E	35
Barcelona, *Venezuela*.	10¼N	64½W	77
Barcelonette, *France*.	44½N	6¾E	32
Barcoo, R., *Queensland*.	24S	144E	60
Barcs, *Hungary*.	46N	17½E	37
Bardejov, *Czecho.*	49¼N	21¼E	33
Bardera, *Somali. Rep.*	2½N	42¼E	56
Bardi, *Italy*.	44¾N	9¾E	31
Bardia, *Libya*.	32N	25E	40
Bardoc, *W. Australia*.	30¼S	121¼E	61
Bardonecchia, *Italy*.	45N	6½E	31
Bardsey I., *Wales*.	52¾N	4¾W	22
Bardswell Group, Is., *Br. Col., Canada*.	52¼N	128¼W	72
Bareilly, *India*.	28¼N	79½E	44
Barellan, *N.S.W.*	34¼S	146½E	59
Barents Sea, *Arctic*.	75N	45E	80
Barfleur, *France*.	49¾N	1¼W	31
Barfleur, C., *France*.	49¾N	1¼W	32
Bargal, *Somali. Rep.*	11½N	51E	56
Barge, *Italy*.	44¾N	7¼E	31
Barguzin, *U.S.S.R.*	53N	110E	39
Barisal, *Pakistan*.	22½N	91E	43
Barrancas, *Venezuela*.	8½N	62W	77
Barrhill, *Scotland*.	55¼N	4¾W	25
Bari, *Italy*.	41¼N	17E	36
Barisan Mts., *Sumatra*.	4½S	102½E	47
Barito, R., *Borneo*.	3½S	114½E	47
Barkerville, *Br. Col.*	53N	121½W	72
Barkha, *Tibet*.	31¼N	82E	43
Barkly Br., *C. Pr.*	33½S	25¾E	53
Barkly East, *C. Pr.*	31S	27½E	53
Barkly Pass, *C. Pr.*	31¼S	27¾E	53
Barkly West, *C. Pr.*	28½S	24½E	56
Barkly Highway, *Aust.*	20S	135E	61
Barlad, *Romania*.	46¼N	27½E	33
Barlee, L., *W. Aust.*	28S	119E	63
Barletta, *Italy*.	41¼N	16½E	30
Barlow, *W. Australia*.	27S	121½E	67
Barmedman, *N.S.W.*	34¼S	147½E	51
Barmer, *India*.	25¾N	71½E	46
Barmouth, *Wales*.	52¾N	4W	21
Barnard Castle, *Eng.*	54½N	2W	29
Barnaul, *U.S.S.R.*	53¼N	83½E	36
Barnet, *England*.	51¾N	¼W	22
Barneville, *France*.	49½N	1¾W	35
Barnsley, *England*.	53½N	1½W	29
Barnoldswick, *Eng.*	54N	2W	23
Barnouic, *France*.	49N	2¾W	32
Barnstaple, *England*.	51N	4W	23
Barnstaple Bay, *Eng.*	51N	4½W	22
Baro, Riv., *Ethiopia*.	8N	34E	52
Barstow, *Cal., U.S.A.*	35N	117½W	72
Baro, *Nigeria*.	8½N	6½E	54
Baroda, *C. Pr.*	32S	25½E	57
Baroda, *India*.	22¼N	73¼E	44
Baroncourt, *France*.	49½N	5½E	30
Barons, *Alberta*.	50N	113W	73
Barquisimeto, *Venez.*	10N	69W	77
Barra, I. of, *Scotland*.	57N	7½W	24
Barraba, *N.S.W.*	30¼S	150½E	59
Barrackpore, *India*.	22½N	88¼E	44
Barrancabermeja, *Col.*	7N	74W	77
Barranquilla, *Col.*	11¼N	75W	77
Barre, *Vt., U.S.A.*	44¼N	72½W	69
Barreiro, *Portugal*.	38½N	9¼W	35
Barretos, *Brazil*.	20¾S	48½W	79
Barrhead, *Scotland*.	55¾N	4½W	25
Barrhead, *Alberta*.	54¼N	114½W	73
Barrie, *Ontario*.	44½N	79¾W	68
Barriere, *Br. Col.*	51¼N	120W	72
Barrington, Mt., *N.S.W.*	32S	151½E	59
Barrow B., *Ireland*.	52½N	6¾W	26
Barrow's Creek, *Aust.*	21½S	134E	60
Barrow I., *W. Aust.*	20¾S	115¼E	61
Barrow Pt., *Queensland*.	14½S	145E	60
Barrow Pt., *Alaska, U.S.*	70N	158W	74
Barrow, R., *Eire*.	52½N	7W	26
Barrow Str., *N.W.T.*	74¼N	97W	66
Barrow-in-Furness, *England*.	54¼N	3¼W	25
Barry, *Wales*.	51½N	3¼W	22
Barrydale, *C. Pr.*	34S	20¾E	52
Bar-s-Aube, *France*.	48¼N	4¾E	30
Bar-s-Seine, *France*.	48N	4½E	30
Barsi, *India*.	18N	76E	48
Barth, *Germany*.	54¼N	12¾E	33
Bartica, *Guyana*. (ins.).	6½N	58W	77
Bartin, *Turkey*.	42N	32¼E	41
Bartlesville, *Okla., U.S.A.*	37N	96W	57
Bartolomeo Dias, *Moz.*	21½S	35½E	51
Barton, *England*.	53¾N	½W	23
Barton, *S. Australia*.	30½S	132¾E	58
Bartoszyce, *Poland*.	54¼N	20¾E	33
Baruth, *Germany*.	52¼N	13½E	33
Baruva, *India*.	18¾N	84¾E	45
Barvas, *Scotland*.	58¼N	6½W	24
Barwani, *India*.	22N	75E	44
Barwon, R., *N.S.W.*	30S	148E	59
BAS RHIN, *France*.	48½N	7½E	32
Basankusu, *Congo. (K.)*	1¼N	19¾E	56
Basbeck, *Germany*.	53¾N	9E	30

Basento—Bhadarwah [93]

Place	Lat.	Long.	No.
Basento, Italy.	40½N	16¾E	36
Bashaw, Alberta.	52½N	113W	73
Bashi Chan, China Sea.	21N	121E	48
BASHKIR, U.S.S.R.	54N	56E	38
Basilan I., P.I.	6¾N	122E	47
Basildon, England.	51½N	½E	23
BASILICATA, Italy.	40½N	16E	36
Basingstoke, England.	51¼N	1¼W	23
Basle, Switzerland.	47½N	7½E	31
BASQUE, Spain.	43N	3W	35
Basra, Iraq.	30½N	47¾E	40
Bass Strait, Tasmania.	40S	146E	58
Bassano, Alberta.	50¾N	112¼W	73
Bassano, Italy.	45¾N	11½E	31
Basse Terre, Guadeloupe.	16N	61¾W	77
Bassein, Burma.	17N	94¾E	43
Bassein, India.	19¼N	72¾E	45
Bassenthwaite, Eng.	54½N	3¼W	25
BASSES ALPES, France.	44N	6¼E	32
BASSES PYRENEES, Fr.	43N	1W	32
Bassum, Germany.	52¾N	8¾E	30
Bastak, Iran.	27½N	54¾E	40
Basti, India.	26¾N	82½E	44
Bastia, Corsica.	42¾N	9½E	36
Bastogne, Belgium.	50N	5¾E	30
BASUTOLAND, see LESOTHO.			
Bata, Rio Muni.	2N	9¾E	57
Batamay, U.S.S.R.	63¾N	129¾E	39
Batan Is., P.I.	20¾N	122E	47
Batang, see PA'AN.			
Batangas, P.I.	13½N	121¼E	47
Batavia, Riv., Queens.	11S	142F	60
Batcab, Guatemala.	17½N	90W	76
Batchawana, Ontario.	47N	84½W	68
Bateman's Bay, N.S.W.	35¾S	150¼E	59
Bath, England.	51½N	2½W	22
Bathgate, Scotland.	55¾N	3¾W	25
Bathurst, C. Pr.	33½S	26¾E	53
Bathurst, Gambia.	13½N	16¾W	57
Bathurst, New Bruns.	47¾N	65¾W	67
Bathurst, N.S.W.	33½S	149½E	59
Bathurst, C., N.W. Can.	71N	129W	66
Bathurst Inlet, Canada.	66N	108W	66
Bathurst I., Australia.	11½S	130E	60
Bathurst I., N.W. Can.	76N	100W	66
Batia, Cameroon.	4½N	11E	56
Batjan Is., Indonesia.	½S	127½E	47
Batley, England.	53¾N	1¾W	23
Batlow, N.S.W.	35½S	148E	59
Batna, Algeria.	35½N	6E	35
Baton Rouge, La., U.S.	30½N	91¼W	75
Batouri, Cameroon.	4½N	14¾E	56
Battambang, Cambodia	13½N	103¼E	47
Batthenmurnana, Mt., W. Australia.	25S	119E	61
Batticaloa, Ceylon.	7¾N	81¾E	45
Battineau, N.D., U.S.A.	48N	100W	74
Battle, England.	50¾N	½E	23
Battle Creek, U.S.A.	42¼N	85¼W	68
Battle Harbour, Newf.	52N	56W	67
Battle Mountain, U.S.A.	41N	117½W	74
Battle, R., Alberta.	52¾N	111W	73
Battleford, Sask.	52¾N	108¼W	70
Batu Is., Sumatra.	½S	98½E	74
Batumi, U.S.S.R.	41¾N	41½E	38
Baturadja, Sumatra.	4S	104E	47
Baturite, Brazil.	4S	38¾W	79
Batz, France.	48¾N	4W	31
Bauchi, Nigeria.	10½N	9¾E	57
Baud, France.	48N	3W	31
Baudo, Colombia.	5½N	77W	77
Bauge, France.	47½N	0	31
Bauld, C., Newf., Can.	51½N	55½W	67
Baume les Dames, Fr.	47¼N	6¼E	31
Bavarian Alps, Ger.	47½N	11½E	31
BAVARIA, Germany.	49N	11E	33
Bauru, Brazil.	22¼S	49W	79
Bautzen, Germany.	51¼N	14½E	33
Bawean I., Indonesia.	6S	112½E	47
Bawku, Ghana.	11N	½E	57
Bawtry, England.	53½N	1W	23
Bayan Khongor Mong.	47N	100E	39
Bayan Undur, Mongolia.	46N	99E	39
Bayardi, U.S.S.R.	46½N	53E	38
Bayburt, Turkey.	40½N	40½E	41
Bay City, Mich., U.S.A.	43½N	83¾W	68
Bayamo, Cuba.	20¼N	76¾W	77
Bayeux, France.	49¼N	¾W	32
Baykit, U.S.S.R.	62N	97E	39
Bayonne, France.	43½N	1½W	32
Bayreuth, Germany.	50N	11½E	33
Baza, Spain.	37½N	2¾W	35
Bazancourt, France.	49¼N	4¼E	30
Bazar Dara, Kashmir.	36½N	77E	44
Bazaruto I., Moz.	22S	36E	51
Bazas, France.	44¾N	¼W	32
Bazoko, Congo (K.).	1½N	23E	56
Bazzano, Italy.	44¼N	11E	31
Beachport, S. Aust.	37½S	140E	59
Beachy Head, England.	50¾N	¼E	23
Beacon, W. Aust.	30¼S	117½E	61
Beaconsfield, C. Pr.	28¾S	24¾E	53
Beaconsfield, England.	51½N	¾W	23
Beaminster, England.	50¾N	2¾W	22
Bear, Riv., Utah, U.S.A.	41N	113W	74
Bear I., Antarctica.	74½S	109W	80
Bear I., Arctic.	75N	16E	80
Beardmore Glacier, Antarctica.	84½S	170E	80
BEARN, France.	43N	1W	32
Beas, R., India.	32N	76E	44
Beata, I. Dom. Rep.	17½N	72W	77
Beatrice, Neb., U.S.A.	40N	96½W	75
Beattock, Scotland.	55¼N	3½W	25
Beatty, Nevada, U.S.A.	37N	117W	74
Beauceville, Quebec.	46¼N	70¾W	69
Beaudesert, Queensland.	28S	153E	60
Beaufort, Malasyia.	5¼N	115¾E	47
Beaufort-en-Vallee, Fr.	47½N	¼W	31
Beaufort S., Arctic Oc.	72N	135W	80
Beaufort West, C. Pr.	32¼S	22½E	52
Beaufort, France.	45¾N	6½E	31
Beaugency, France.	47¾N	1¾E	31
Beaugency, France.	47¾N	1½E	32
Beauharnois, Quebec.	45¼N	74W	69
Beauly & Firth, Scot.	57½N	4½W	24
Beaumaris, Wales.	53¼N	4¼W	22
Beaumont, Belgium	50¼N	4¼E	30
Beaumont, France.	48¼N	0	31
Beaumont, France.	49N	2¼E	30
Beaumont, France.	49N	5¾E	30
Beaumont, Tex., U.S.A.	30N	94¼W	75
Beaune, France.	47N	4¾E	32
Beaurreau, France.	47½N	1W	31
Beausejour, Manitoba.	50N	96½W	71
Beauty, Transvaal.	23¼S	28E	54
Beauvais, France.	49½N	2¼E	32
Beauvoir, France.	47N	2W	32
Beaver, Utah, U.S.A.	38¼N	112¾W	74
Beaverton, Ontario.	44½N	79¼W	68
Beawar, India.	26¼N	74½E	44
Bebra, Germany.	51N	9½E	33
Beccles, England.	52½N	1½E	23
Béchar, Algeria.	31¾N	2¼W	35
BECHUANALAND. see BOTSWANA.			
Beclean, Romania.	47¼N	24¼E	37
Bedale. England.	54¼N	1½W	25
Bedan, Saudi Arabia.	27½N	41E	40
Beddgelert, Wales.	53N	4¼W	22
Bedford, C. Pr.	32¾S	26½E	53
BEDFORD, England.	52¼N	½W	23
Bedford, N.Y., U.S.A.	41N	74W	75
Bedford, Quebec, Can.	45N	73W	69
Bedford, C., Queensland.	15S	145½E	60
Bedlington, England.	55¼N	1½W	25
Bedonia, Italy.	44½N	9½E	31
Bedourie, Queensland.	24¼S	139½E	60
Bedwellty, Wales.	51½N	3W	22
Beechworth, Victoria.	36½S	146½E	59
Beecroft Hd., N.S.W.	35S	150¾E	59
Beenleigh, Queensland.	27½S	153E	60
Beeringen, Belgium.	51N	5½E	30
Beersheba, Israel	31¼N	34¾E	41
Beestekraal, T'vaal.	25½S	27½E	54
Beeston, England.	52¾N	1¼W	23
Befandriana, Malagasy.	22S	44¾E	56
Bega, New S. Wales.	36¾S	149¾E	59
Begicheva I., U.S.S.R.	74N	11E	39
Behbehan, Iran.	31N	50½E	40
Beida, Libya	32½N	21¼E	34
Beidha, Saudi Arabia.	21N	40E	40
Beilngries, Germany.	49N	11½E	33
Beinn a Ghlo, Scot.	56¾N	3½W	24
Beinn Dearg, Scotland.	56¾N	3¾W	24
Beinn Dearg, Scotland.	57¾N	5W	24
Beinn Mhor, Scotland.	56½N	7¼W	24
Beira, Mozambique.	19¾S	35E	51
Beirut. Lebanon.	34N	35½E	41
Beisan, Israel (inset).	32½N	35½E	40
Beiseker, Alberta.	51½N	113½W	73
Beitbridge, Rhodesia.	22¼S	30E	51
Beith, Scotland.	55¾N	4½W	25
Beit Jibrin, Israel (ins.).	31½N	35E	40
Beius, Romania.	46¾N	22½E	37
Beja, Portugal.	38N	8W	35
Bejaïa, Algeria.	36½N	5E	35
Bejar, Spain.	40½N	6W	35
Bekdash, U.S.S.R.	42N	52½E	38
Bekes, Hungary.	46¾N	21¼E	37
Bekescsaba, Hungary.	46¾N	21E	37
Bekwai, Ghana.	6½N	1½W	57
Bela, Bulgaria.	43½N	25¾E	37
Bela, Pakistan.	26N	66E	43
Bela, India.	26N	82E	44
Bela Crkva, Yugoslavia.	45N	21¼E	37
Belawan, Sumatra.	3¾N	98½E	47
Belchatow, Poland.	51¼N	19¼E	33
Belcher Ch., N.W. Can.	77N	98W	66
Belcher Is., Canada.	56½N	79½W	66
Belcher, Man., Canada.	58N	94W	71
Belchite, Spain.	41¼N	¾W	35
Belecke, Germany.	51½N	8½E	30
Belem, Brazil.	1½S	48½W	78
Belen, Panama.	8½N	81½W	77
Belep Is., Pacific.	20S	161E	64
Belet Ven, Somali Rep.	5N	45E	56
Belfast, Maine, U.S.A.	44N	69W	75
Belfast & L., N. Ire.	54½N	6W	26
Belfast, S.I., N.Z.	43½S	172½E	63
Belfast, Transvaal.	25¾S	30E	54
Belfodio, Ethiopia.	10½N	35E	56
Belford, England.	55½N	1¾W	25
Belfort, France.	47¾N	7E	32
Belgaum, India.	15¾N	74½E	45
BELGUIM. Europe.	50½N	4½E	30
Belgrade, Yugoslavia.	44¾N	20½E	37
Belitong I., see BILLITON.			
Belize, Br. Honduras.	17½N	88W	77
Belka, W. Australia.	32S	118E	61
Bell, C. Pr.	33¼S	27¼E	53
Bellac, France.	46¼N	1¼E	32
Bellanagh, Ireland.	53¾N	7¼W	26
Bellano, Italy.	46N	9¼E	31
Bella Vista, Moz.	26½S	32½E	51
Belle-Isle-en-Terre, Fr.	48½N	3½W	31
Bell Ville, Argentina.	33S	63W	79
Bella Bella, Br. Col.	52¼N	128W	72
Bella Coola, Br. Col.	52¼N	127W	72
Bellary, India.	15¼N	77E	45
Bellata, New S. Wales.	30S	149¾E	59
Bellegarde, France.	46¼N	5¾E	31
Belle Ile, France.	47¼N	3W	32
Belle I., Newfoundland.	52N	55W	66
Belle Isle, Str. of, Newf.	51½N	56½W	67
Belleme, France.	48½N	½E	31
Bellerive, Tasmania.	42¾S	147½E	59
Belleville, Ill., U.S.A.	38½N	90W	75
Belleville, Ontario.	44¼N	77½W	69
Belley, France.	45¾N	5¾E	32
Bellingen, N.S.W.	30½S	153E	59
Bellingham, Wash., U.S.	48¾N	122½W	74
Bellingham, England.	55¼N	2¼W	25
Bellingshausen S., Ant.	70S	85W	80
Bellinzona, Switz.	46¼N	9E	31
Belluno, Italy.	46¼N	12¼E	31
Belluno, Italy.	46¼N	12¼E	36
Bellville, C. Pr.	34S	18½E	52
Belmez, Spain.	38¼N	5¼W	35
Belmont, C. Pr.	29½S	24¼E	53
Belmullet, Ireland.	54¼N	10W	26
Belo Horizonte, Brazil.	20S	44W	79
Beloit, Wis., U.S.A.	42½N	89W	75
Belomorsk, U.S.S.R.	64½N	35E	29
Belper, England.	53N	1½W	23
Beltana, S. Australia.	30¾S	138½E	59
Beltsy, U.S.S.R.	47¾N	28E	37
Belturbet, Ireland.	54¼N	7½W	26
Belur, India.	13N	76E	43
Belvedere Marittimo, Italy.	39½N	15¾E	36
Bely I., U.S.S.R.	73N	70E	39
Belzig, Germany.	52¼N	12½E	33
Bembe, Angola.	7S	15E	56
Bemidji, Minn., U.S.A.	47½N	95W	75
Benabarre, Spain.	42N	½E	32
Ben Alder, Scotland.	56¾N	4½W	24
Benalla, Victoria.	36½S	146E	59
Benares, see VARANASI.			
Benavente, Spain.	42N	6W	35
Benbecula I., Scotland.	57½N	7½W	24
Ben Chonzie, Scotland.	56½N	4W	25
Ben Cruachan, Scot.	56½N	5¼W	25
Bencubbin, W. Aust.	30¾S	117¾E	61
Bend, Oregon, U.S.A.	43¾N	122W	74
Bende, Nigeria.	5¾N	7½E	57
Bender Kassim, Somali Republic.	11½N	49½E	56
Benderi, U.S.S.R.	46¾N	29½E	38
Bendering, W. Aust.	33S	118½E	61
Bendigo, Victoria.	36¾S	144½E	59
Bendorf, Germany.	50½N	7¾E	30
Ben Eighe, Scotland.	57½N	5½W	24
Benesov, Czecho.	49¾N	14½E	33
Benestroff, France.	48¾N	6¾E	30
Benevento, Italy.	41¼N	14¾E	36
Bengal, B. of, India.	18N	90E	42
BENGAL, E., Pakistan.	24N	90E	43
BENGAL, W., India.	23N	86E	43
Ben Gardane, Tunisia.	33N	11½E	34
Benghazi, Libya.	32¼N	20E	34
Bengough, Sask.	49½N	105½W	70
Benguela, Angola.	12½S	13½E	56
Benha, U.A.R. (inset.)	30½N	31½E	50
Ben Hope, Scotland.	58½N	4½W	24
Beni, Riv., Brazil.	10S	65W	78
Beni Abbes, Algeria.	30N	2W	34
Benicarlo. Spain.	40½N	½E	35
Beni Mazar, U.A.R.	28N	31E	40
Beni Saf, Algeria.	35¼N	1½W	35
Benin City, Nigeria.	6½N	5¾E	57
Benina, Libya.	32¼N	20¼E	34
Beni Suef, U.A.R.	29N	31E	50
Beni Ulid, Libya.	32N	14E	34
Benkulen, Sumatra.	3¾S	102½E	47
Ben Lawers, Scotland.	56½N	4¼W	25
Benlidi, Queensland.	24½S	145E	60
Ben Lomond, Scotland.	56¼N	4¾W	25
Ben Macdhui, Lesotho.	30¾S	28E	55
Ben Macdhui, Scotland.	57N	3¾W	24
Ben McDhui, C. Pr.	30½S	28E	53
Ben More Assynt, Scot.	58¼N	5W	24
Ben More Scotland.	56½N	4¼W	25
Ben More, Scotland.	56½N	6W	25
Bennett, L., N. Terr.	23S	131E	60
Ben Nevis, Scotland.	56¾N	5W	24
Bennington, Ut., U.S.A.	42¾N	73¼W	69
Benodet, France.	48N	4W	31
Benom, Mt., Malaysia.	3¾N	102E	47
Benoni, Transvaal.	26¼S	28½E	55
Ben Rinnes, Scotland.	57½N	3¼W	24
Bensheim, Germany.	49¾N	8¾E	30
Bentinck I., Queens.	16½S	140E	60
Bentota, Ceylon.	6½N	80E	45
Benue, R., Nigeria.	7¾N	6¾E	57
Ben Vorlich, Scotland.	56¼N	4¼W	25
Benwee Hd., Ireland.	54¼N	10W	26
Ben Wyvis, Scotland.	57¾N	4½W	24
Beograd, see BELGRADE.			
Beppu, Japan.	33N	131E	49
Berat, Albania.	40¾N	20E	37
Berau B., New Guinea.	2½S	133E	47
Berber. Sudan.	18N	34E	40
Berbera, Somali Rep.	10½N	45E	56
Berberati, C. Afr. Rep.	4¼N	15¾E	56
Berbice, R., Guyana.	6½N	56W	77
Berchtesgaden, Ger.	47¾N	13E	33
Berck, France.	50½N	1¾E	30
Berdichev. U.S.S.R.	50N	28½E	38
Berdyansk, U.S.S.R	46½N	36¾E	38
Bere I., Ireland.	51¾N	9¾W	26
Berehaven, Eire.	51¾N	10W	26
Berehovo, U.S.S.R.	48¼N	22½E	37
Berens River, Man.	52¼N	97W	71
Bere Regis, England.	50¾N	2¼W	22
Beresti, Romania.	46N	28E	37
Bereza Kartuska, U.S.S.R.	52½N	25E	33
Berezina, R., U.S.S.R.	52½N	30E	38
Berezovka, U.S.S.R.	57N	115E	39
Berezniki, U.S.S.R.	59½N	56¼E	38
Berezovo, U.S.S.R.	64N	65E	38
Bergama, Turkey.	39N	27E	41
Berga, Spain.	42¼N	1½E	32
Bergamo, Italy.	45¾N	9¾E	36
Bergedorf, Ger. (ins.).	53½N	10E	30
Bergen, Germany.	54½N	13½E	33
BERGEN & Tn., Nor.	60½N	5¼E	29
Bergen-op-Zoom, Neth.	51½N	4¼E	30
Bergerac, France.	44¾N	½E	30
Bergeres les Vertus, France	48¾N	4E	30
Bergisch-Gladbach, Ger.	51N	7¼E	30
Bergues, France.	51N	2½E	30
Bergville, Natal.	28¾S	29¼E	55
Berhampore, India.	24N	88¼E	44
Berhampur, India.	19¼N	85E	45
Bering Sea, N. Pacific.	56N	180E	20
Bering Strait, U.S.A.-U.S.S.R.	66N	170W	20
Berkel, Riv., Germany.	52¼N	6½E	30
Berkeley, Calif., U.S.A.	37¾N	122½W	74
Berkhamsted, England.	51¾N	½W	23
Berkovitza, Bulgaria	43¼N	23E	37
BERKSHIRE CO., Eng.	51½N	1½W	23
Berleburg, Germany.	51N	8¼E	30
Berlin, C. Pr.	33S	27½E	53
Berlin, Germany.	52½N	13½E	33
Berlin, N.H., U.S.A.	44½N	71¼W	69
Bermejo, Riv., Arg.	27S	59W	78
Bermuda, Atlantic.	32N	65W	18
Bernadillo, N.Mex., U.S.	35N	106W	74
Bernay, France.	49¼N	½E	31
Bernburg, Germany.	51¾N	11¾E	33
Berne, Switzerland.	47N	7½E	31
Berneck, Germany.	48¼N	8½E	33
Berneray I., Scotland.	57¾N	7¼W	24
Bernese Alps, Switz.	46½N	7½E	31
Bernier I., W. Aust.	25S	114¼E	61
Bernina, Mt., Switz.	46½N	10E	31
Bernin Kebbi, Nigeria.	12½N	4¼E	57
Beroun, Czechoslovakia.	50N	14E	33
Berounka, Riv., Czecho.	50N	14½E	33
Berri, S. Australia.	34¼S	140½E	59
Berriedale, Scotland.	58¼N	3½W	24
Berrigan, N.S.W.	35¾S	145¾E	59
BERRY, France.	47N	2E	32
Berry, N.S.W.	34¾S	150¾E	59
Berry Is., Bahamas.	26N	77½W	77
Bersenbruck, Germany.	52½N	8E	30
Berthier, Quebec.	46½N	73¼W	69
Bertholet, C., W. Aust.	17S	122E	61
Bertoua, Cameroon.	4½N	13¾E	57
Bertraghboy B., Ire.	53½N	10W	26
Beru I., Pacific.	2S	176E	64
BERWICK, Scotland.	55¾N	2½W	25
Berwick-upon-Tweed, England.	55¾N	2W	25
Besancon, France.	47¼N	6E	32
BESSARABIA, U.S.S.R.	48¼N	27½E	37
Bessemer, Ala., U.S.A.	33½N	87W	75
Besters, Natal.	28½S	29½E	55
Betancuria, Canary Is.	28½N	14W	35
Betanzos, Spain.	43½N	9W	35
Betare, Cameroon.	6N	14E	56
Bethal, Transvaal.	26½S	29½E	55
Bethals Dorp, C. Pr.	33¾S	25½E	53
Bethanie, S.W. Africa.	26½S	17½E	51
Bethany, Jordan (ins.).	31¾N	35¼E	40
Bethany, O.F.S.	29½S	26E	55
Bethel, Alaska, U.S.A.	60N	160½W	74
Bethesda, Wales.	53¼N	4W	22
Bethesda Rd., C. Pr.	32S	24¾E	53
Bethlehem, Pa., U.S.A.	40½N	75½W	75
Bethlehem, O.F.S.	28½S	28¼E	55
Bethlehem, Jordan.	31¾N	35¼E	40
Bethsaida, Israel (inset)	32¾N	35½E	40
Bethulie, O.F.S.	30½S	26E	55
Bethune, France.	50½N	2½E	23
Bethune, Sask.	50¾N	105¼W	70
Bethune, R., France	50N	1E	31
Betioky, Malagasy.	24S	44¾E	56
Betoota, Queensland.	25¾S	140¾E	60
Betroka, Malagasy.	23¼S	46¼E	56
Bettiah, India.	26¾N	84¾E	44
Bettie, W. Australia.	27½S	114¾E	61
Bettles, Alaska, U.S.A.	66½N	151W	74
Bettola, Italy.	44¾N	9½E	31
Bettws-y-Coed, Wales.	53N	3¾W	22
Betzdorf, Germany.	50¾N	8E	30
Beuthen, see BYTOM.			
Beuvron, R., France.	47½N	1½E	31
Beveland Is., Neth.	51½N	4E	30
Beveridge Reef, Pacific.	20S	168W	64
Beverley, England.	53¾N	½W	23
Beverley, Mass., U.S.A.	42¾N	70¾W	69
Beverley, W. Australia.	32½S	117E	61
Beverwijk, Neth.	52½N	4½E	30
Bewdley, England.	52¼N	2¼W	22
Bexhill, England.	50¾N	½E	23
Beynosa, Mexico.	26½N	98W	76
Beyoglu, Turkey.	41¼N	29E	37
Beypazari, Turkey.	40½N	31¾E	41
Beypore, India	11¼N	75¾E	45
Beysehir, Turkey.	37¾N	31¾E	41
Bezau, Austria.	47½N	9¾E	31
Bezhetsk, U.S.S.R.	57¾N	36½E	38
Bezhitsa, U.S.S.R.	53N	34E	38
Beziers, France.	43¼N	3¼E	32
Bezwada, see VIJAYAVADA.			
Bhadarwah, Kashmir.	32¾N	76E	44

Place	Lat.	Long	No.
Bhadrak, *India.*	21N	86½E	44
Bhagalpur, *India.*	25¼N	87E	44
Bhamo, *Burma.*	24¼N	97¼E	43
Bhandara, *India.*	21¼N	79¾E	44
Bharatpur, *India.*	27¼N	77½E	44
Bhatinda, *India.*	30¼N	75E	44
Bhatpara, *India.*	23N	88½E	44
Bhavnagar, *India.*	21¾N	72¼E	44
Bhawani Patna, *India.*	20N	83¼E	44
Bhilsa, *India.*	23½N	77¾E	44
Bhima, Riv., *India.*	16¼N	77E	45
Bhir, *India.*	19N	75¾E	45
Bhiwani, *India.*	28¾N	76¼E	44
Bhopal, *India.*	23¼N	77½E	44
Bhubaneshwar, *India.*	20N	86E	43
Bhuj, *India.*	23¼N	69¾	46
BHUTAN, *Asia.*	27½N	90E	43
Biafra, Bight of, *Africa.*	3N	6½E	57
Biasca, *Switzerland.*	46¼N	9E	31
Biala, *Poland.*	53½N	22E	33
Biala Podlaska, *Poland.*	52N	23¼E	33
Bialogard, *Poland.*	54N	16E	33
Bialowieza, *Poland.*	52¾N	23¾E	33
Bialystok, *Poland.*	53¼N	23¼E	33
Biarritz, *France.*	43½N	1½W	32
Bibai, *Japan.*	43N	142E	49
Biberach, *Germany.*	48N	9¾E	33
Bibbiena, *Italy.*	43¾N	12E	36
Bibiani, *Ghana.*	6½N	2½W	57
Bibile, *Ceylon.*	7¼N	81¼E	45
Bic, *Quebec.*	48¼N	68¾W	67
Bicester, *England.*	51¾N	1¼W	23
Bickerton I., *N. Terr.*	13¼S	136E	60
Bida, *Nigeria.*	9N	6E	57
Bidar, *India.*	18N	77½E	45
Biddeford, *Me., U.S.A.*	43½N	70½W	69
Bideford, *England.*	51N	4¼W	22
Biebrich, *Germany.*	50N	8¼E	30
Biedenkopf, *Germany.*	51N	8½E	30
Biel, *Switzerland.*	47¼N	7¼E	31
Biel, L. of, *Switz.*	47¼N	7¼E	31
Biella, *Italy.*	45½N	8E	31
Bielefeld, *Germany.*	52N	8½E	33
Bielica, *U.S.S.R.*	53¾N	24½E	33
Bielowa, *Poland.*	50¾N	16¾E	33
Bielsk Podlaski, *Pol.*	52¾N	23¼E	33
Bielsko, *Poland.*	49¾N	19E	33
Bienfait, *Sask.*	49¼N	102¾W	70
Biesjespoort, *C. Pr.*	31¾S	23¼E	52
Biesjesvlei, *Transvaal.*	26¼S	26E	55
Biferno, Riv., *Italy.*	42N	15E	36
Big Bell, *W. Australia.*	27½S	118E	61
Big River, *Sask.*	53¾N	107W	70
Big Horn R., *U.S.A.*	46N	108W	74
Big Sable Pt., *U.S.A.*	44N	86½W	68
Big Sioux R., *U.S.A.*	43N	97W	74
Big Spring, *Tex., U.S.A.*	32¼N	102W	74
Big Umgazi, *C. Pr.*	31¾S	29¼E	53
Big Valley, *Alberta.*	52N	112¾W	73
Biggar, *Sask.*	52N	108W	70
Biggar, *Scotland.*	55½N	3½W	25
Biggleswade, *England.*	52¼N	¼W	23
Bignona, *Senegal.*	12¾N	16¼W	57
Bihac, *Yugoslavia.*	44¾N	16E	36
Bihar, *India.*	25¼N	85½E	44
BIHAR, *India.*	24N	85E	43
Biharamulo, *Tanzania.*	2½S	31¼E	56
Bihe, *Angola.*	12½S	17E	56
Biisk, *U.S.S.R.*	52¾N	85E	39
Bijapur, *India.*	16¾N	75¾E	45
Bijar, *Iran.*	36N	47½E	41
Bijauri, *Nepal.*	28N	82E	44
Bijelo Polje, *Yugo.*	43N	19¾E	37
Bijistan, *Iran.*	34¾N	58E	40
Bikaner, *India.*	28N	73¼E	44
Bikar I., *Pacific.*	13N	170E	64
Bikan & Riv., *U.S.S.R.*	47½N	134E	39
Bikini Atoll, *Pacific.*	12N	162E	64
Bilaspur, *India.*	22N	82E	44
Bilbao, *Spain.*	43½N	3W	35
Bilecik, *Turkey.*	40¼N	30E	41
Bilin, *Czechoslovakia.*	50¼N	13¾E	33
Billabong Riv., see Moulamein Riv.			
Billericay, *England.*	51½N	½E	23
Billings, *Mont., U.S.A.*	45¾N	108½W	74
Billingshurst, *England.*	51N	½W	23
Billiton, I. *Sumatra.*	3S	107½E	47
Billy Billong, *W. Aust.*	27½S	116E	61
Bilma, *Niger.*	18¾N	13½E	50
Biloxi, *Miss., U.S.A.*	30½N	88¾W	75
Biltine, *Chad.*	15N	21E	56
Bima, *Indonesia.*	8½S	118¾E	47
Bimbila, *Ghana.*	8¾N	0	57
Bimini Is., *Bahamas.*	26N	78W	77
Binasco, *Italy.*	45¼N	9E	31
Bindle, *Queensland.*	27½S	148¾E	59
Bindura, *Rhodesia.*	17¼S	31¼E	51
Bingara, *N.S.W.*	29¾S	150½E	59
Bingen, *Germany.*	50N	8E	33
Bingerville, *Ivory C.*	5½N	3¾W	50
Bingham, *England.*	53N	1W	23
Binghamton, *N.Y., U.S.*	42¼N	76W	69
Binnaway, *N.S.W.*	31½S	149½E	59
Binscarth, *Manitoba.*	50¾N	101¼W	70
Bint, *Iran.*	26N	59¾E	40
Bintan I., *Indonesia.*	1N	104½E	47
Bintulu, *Malaysia.*	3¼N	113E	47
Bin Yauri, *Nigeria.*	10¾N	4¾E	57
Birao, *Cent. Afr. Rep.*	10N	23E	56
Birchwood, *S.I., N.Z.*	46S	167¾E	63
Birdsville, *Queensland.*	26S	139¾E	60
Birdum, *N. Terr.*	16S	133¼E	60
Bir Fuad, *U.A.R.*	31N	26½E	40
Birganj, *Nepal.*	27N	85E	44
Birjand, *Iran.*	33N	59E	40

Place	Lat.	Long	No.
Birkenfeld, *Germany.*	49½N	7E	30
Birkenhead, *England.*	53½N	3W	22
Birkenhead, *N.I., N.Z* (inset A).			62
Birket Qarun L., *U.A.R.*	29½N	30½E	50
Birmingham, *Ala., U.S.*	33½N	86¾W	75
Birmingham, *Eng.*	52½N	1¾W	23
Birnie I., *Pacific.*	4S	171W	64
Birobijan, *U.S.S.R.*	48¾N	133E	39
Birr, *Eire.*	53N	8W	26
Birringarra, *W. Aust.*	26½S	117E	61
Birsk, *U.S.S.R.*	55½N	55½E	38
Birthday, *Transvaal.*	23¼S	30¾E	54
Birtle, *Manitoba.*	50½N	101W	70
Birzai, *U.S.S.R.*	56¼N	24¾E	38
Birzula, *U.S.S.R.*	47¾N	29½E	37
Biscay, Bay of, *France.*	46N	4W	34
Bisceglie, *Italy.*	41¼N	16¾E	36
Bischofshofen, *Austria.*	47½N	13¼E	33
Bisha, *Saudi Arabia.*	20N	43E	40
Bishop Auckland, *Eng.*	54¾N	1¾W	25
Bishop's Castle, *Eng.*	52½N	3W	22
Bishop's Stortford, *Eng.*	51¾N	¼E	23
Bishop's Waltham, *Eng.*	51N	1¼W	23
Biskra, *Algeria.*	34¾N	5¾E	35
Bismarck Arch., *Pac.*	3S	148E	64
Bismarck, *N.D., U.S.A.*	47½N	101W	74
Bismarck Ra., *N. Guinea.*	6S	145E	60
Bissagos Is. *P. Guin.*	11½N	16¼W	50
Bissau, *Port. Guinea.*	12N	15½W	50
Bistrita, *Romania.*	47N	24½E	37
Bistrita, Riv., *Rom.*	46½N	27E	37
Bitburg, *Germany.*	50N	6½E	30
Bitlis, *Turkey.*	38¼N	42E	41
Bitolj, *Yugoslavia.*	41N	21¼E	37
Bitonto, *Italy.*	41¼N	16¾E	36
Bitterfeld, *Germany.*	51½N	12¼E	33
Bitterfontein, *C. Pr.*	31S	18¼E	52
Bitterworth, *Malaysia.*	5½N	100¼E	47
Bityi, *C. Pr.*	31¾S	28½E	53
Biv, *Nigeria.*	10½N	12¼E	57
Biwa, L., *Japan.*	35½N	136E	49
Biya, R., *U.S.S.R.*	52½N	87E	39
Bizana, *C. Pr.*	30½S	30E	53
Bizerta, *Tunisia.*	37¼N	10E	35
Bjelovar, *Yugoslavia.*	46N	16¾E	36
Bj In Eker, *Algeria.*	24N	5E	50
Bjorneborg, see PORI.			
Bjuro, C., *Sweden.*	64½N	21E	29
Blaafield, *Norway.*	64N	12½E	29
Black Riv., *Ark., U.S.A.*	34N	91W	75
Black Riv., *China.*	21N	105E	48
Black River, *Jamaica.*	18N	78W	77
Blackall, *Queensland.*	24½S	145½E	60
Blackburn, *England.*	53¾N	2½W	22
Blackcraig, Mt., *Scot.*	55½N	4¼W	25
Blackford, *Scotland.*	56¼N	3¾W	25
Black Forest, see Schwarzwald.			
Black Head, *Ireland.*	53¼N	9¼W	26
Blackie, *Alberta.*	50½N	113½W	73
Black Isle, *Scotland.*	57½N	4¼W	24
Black Lake, *Quebec.*	46N	71¼W	69
Black Mts., *Wales.*	51¾N	3¼W	22
Blackpool, *England.*	53¾N	3W	22
Black Sea, *Europe-Asia.*	43N	35E	38
Blacksod Bay, *Eire.*	54¼N	10W	26
Blackwater, *Br. Col.*	53¼N	123W	73
Blackwater, *Eire.*	52¼N	6¼W	26
Blackwater, R., *Eng.*	51¾N	1E	23
Blackwater, R., *Ire.*	54¼N	7W	26
Blackwater, R., *Ire.*	52¼N	8½W	26
Blaenau-Ffestiniog, *Wales.*	53N	3¾W	22
Blagodarnoe, *U.S.S.R.*	45N	43E	38
Blagoveshchensk, *U.S.S.R.*	50¼N	127½E	39
Blain *France.*	47½N	1¾W	31
Blair Athol, *Queens.*	22¾S	147½E	60
Blair Atholl, *Scotland.*	56¾N	3¾W	24
Blairgowrie, *Scotland.*	56½N	3½W	24
Blairmore, *Alberta.*	49½N	114¼W	73
Blaj, *Romania.*	46¼N	24E	37
Blakeney, *England.*	51¾N	2¾W	22
Blakeney, *England.*	53N	1E	23
Blanc, C., *Tunis.*	37¼N	10E	35
Blanc, Mt., *France.*	45¾N	6¾E	31
Blanca B., *Argentina.*	40S	61W	78
Blanche, L., *S. Aust.*	29¼S	139¾E	59
Blanchisseuse, *Trin.*	11½N	61W	77
Blanco, *C. Pr.*	34S	22½E	52
Blanco, C., *Sp. Sahara.*	21N	17W	50
Blanco, C., *Peru.*	4S	81W	78
Blanco, C., *Ore., U.S.A.*	42¾N	124½W	74
Blanc Sablon, *Quebec.*	51½N	57¼W	67
Blandford, *England.*	50¾N	2¼W	22
Blanes, *Spain.*	41½N	3E	35
Blaney Jn., *C. Pr.*	33S	27½E	53
Blangy, *France.*	50N	1¾E	32
Blankenberghe, *Belg.*	51¼N	3¼E	30
Blankenheim, *Ger.*	50½N	6½E	30
Blanquilla I., *Venez.*	12N	64½W	77
Blantyre, *Malawi.*	15¾S	35E	51
Blanzac, *France.*	45¼N	0	32
Blarney, *Eire.*	52N	8¾W	26
Blavet, R., *France.*	47¾N	3¼W	31
Blaydon, *England.*	55N	1¾W	25
Blaye, *France.*	45N	¾W	32
Blayney, *N.S.W.* (ins.).	33½S	149E	60
Blaze, C., *N. Terr.*	13S	130¼E	60
Bleneau, *France.*	47¾N	3E	30
Blenheim, *Germany.*	48¾N	11E	33
Blenheim, *Ontario.*	42¼N	82W	68
Blenheim, *S.I., N.Z.*	41½S	174E	63
Blerancourt, *France.*	49½N	3¼E	30
Blessington, *Ireland.*	53¼N	6½W	26

Place	Lat.	Lang.	No.
Blida, *Algeria.*	36½N	2¾E	35
Blind River, *Ontario.*	46¼N	83W	68
Blinkwater *C. Pr.*	32¾S	26½E	53
Blisworth, *England.*	52¼N	1W	23
Bloemfontein, *O.F.S.*	29S	26¼E	53
Bloemhof, *Transvaal.*	27¾S	25½E	55
Blois, *France.*	47½N	1¼E	32
Blokzijl, *Neth.*	52½N	6E	30
Blood River, *Natal.*	27¾S	30½E	55
Blood's Creek, *S. Aust.*	23½S	135½E	60
Bloody Foreland, *Eire.*	55¼N	8½W	26
Bloomington, *Ill., U.S.*	40½N	89W	75
Bludenz, *Austria.*	47¼N	9¾E	33
Bluecleiff, *C. Pr.*	33½S	25½E	53
Bluefield, *Va., U.S.A.*	37¼N	81¼W	75
Bluefields, *Nicaragua.*	12N	84W	77
Blue Mts., *N.S.W.*	33S	150E	59
Blue Mud Bay, *N. Terr.*	13S	135¾E	60
Blue Nile, R., *Africa.*	10¼N	36E	50
Blue River, *Br. Col.*	52¼N	119¼W	72
Blue, Riv., *Kan., U.S.A.*	39N	96W	75
Blue Stack Mts., *Eire.*	54¾N	8¼W	26
Bluff, *S.I., N.Z.*	46½S	168¼E	63
Bluff Pt., *W. Australia.*	27½S	114E	61
Bluff Knoll, *W. Aust.*	34¾S	118E	61
Blumenau, *Brazil.*	27S	49W	79
Blythe, *Cal., U.S.A.*	33N	115W	74
Blyth, *England.*	55¼N	1½W	25
Blyth, *Ontario.*	43¾N	81½W	68
Blytheville, *Ark., U.S.A.*	36N	90W	75
Bo, *Sierra Leone.*	8N	11¾W	57
Boacu, *Nicaragua.*	12N	85½W	77
Boat of Garten, *Scot.*	57¼N	3¾W	24
Boa Vista, *Brazil.*	2¾N	60¾W	78
Bobbio, *Italy.*	44¾N	9¼E	31
Bobcaygeon, *Ontario.*	44½N	78½W	69
Boblingen, *Germany.*	48¾N	9E	30
Bobodiulasso, *Up. Volta.*	11N	4½W	50
Bobolice, *Poland.*	54N	16½E	33
Bobruisk, *U.S.S.R.*	53¼N	29¼E	38
Bocas Del Toro, *Panama.*	9N	82W	77
Bocay, *Nicaragua.*	14¾N	85W	77
Bochnia, *Poland.*	50N	20½E	33
Bocholt, *Germany.*	51¾N	6¾E	33
Bochum, *Germany.*	51½N	7¼E	33
Boda, *Congo* (*B.*).	4N	18E	56
Bodalla, *N.S.W.*	36S	150E	59
Boden, *Sweden.*	66N	22E	38
Boderg, L., *Ireland.*	53¾N	8W	26
Bode Sadu, *Nigeria.*	9N	4¾E	57
Bodiam, *C. Pr.*	33¼S	27½E	53
Bodinayakanur, *India.*	10N	77½E	45
Bodmin, *England.*	50½N	4¾W	22
Bodo, *Norway.*	67¼N	14¼E	29
Bodrum, *Turkey.*	37N	27½E	37
Boeni, *Gabon.*	0	13E	56
Boeo, C. of, *Sicily.*	37¾N	12½E	36
Boesmanskop, *O.F.S.*	30S	27E	55
Bofu, *Japan.*	34N	132E	49
Bogan Riv., *N.S.W.*	30S	146¼E	59
Bogantungan, *Queens.*	23¾S	147¼E	60
Bogenfels, *S.W. Africa.*	27S	15E	51
Boggabilla, *N.S.W.*	28½S	150½E	59
Boggabri, *N.S.W.*	30¾S	150E	59
Boggola, *W. Australia.*	24S	117½E	61
Bogia, *N. Guinea* (ins.).	4S	145E	60
Bognor Regis, *Eng.*	50¾N	¾W	23
Bogong, Mt., *Victoria.*	37S	147¼E	59
Bogota, *Colombia.*	4¾N	74W	78
Boguszow, *Poland.*	50¾N	16¼E	33
Bohain, *France.*	50N	3½E	30
BOHEMIA, *Czecho.*	49¾N	15E	33
Bohmer Wald, *Germany-Czecho.*	49¼N	13E	33
Bohmte, *Germany.*	52½N	8¼E	30
Bohol I., *Philippines.*	10N	124E	47
Boiestown, *N. Bruns.*	46½N	66½W	67
Boileau, C., *W. Aust.*	18S	122E	61
Boisdale & L. *Scotland.*	57N	7¼W	24
Boise, *Idaho, U.S.A.*	43¾N	116¼W	74
Boissevain, *Manitoba.*	49¼N	100W	70
Bojador, C., *Sp. Sahara.*	26N	14½W	50
Bojanow, *Poland.*	50¼N	22E	33
Bokani, *Nigeria.*	9½N	5E	57
Bokerboom, *S.W. Afr.*	28S	19½E	52
Bokhara Riv., *N.S.W.*	29¾S	147E	59
Bokn Fd., *Norway.*	59¼N	5¾E	29
Bokoio, *Angola.*	12½S	14E	56
Boksburg, *Transvaal.*	26¼S	28¼E	55
Bolama, *Port. Guinea.*	11½N	15½W	57
Bolangir, *India.*	21½N	83½E	44
Bolangum, *Victoria.*	37S	143E	59
Bolanos, *Mexico.*	22N	104¼W	76
Bolbec, *France.*	49¾N	¼E	31
Bolbo, Riv., *Italy.*	44¾N	8½E	31
Bole, *Ghana.*	9N	2¼W	57
Boleslawiec, *Poland.*	51¼N	15½E	33
Bolgrad, *U.S.S.R.*	45½N	28½E	37
Bolivar, *Argentina.*	36½S	61W	79
BOLIVIA, *S. America.*	18S	69W	78
Bollnas, *Sweden.*	61N	16E	29
Bollon, *Queensland.*	28S	147½E	60
Bolmen, L., *Sweden.*	57N	13¾E	29
Bologna, *Italy.*	44½N	11¼E	36
Bologoe, *U.S.S.R.*	58N	34E	38
Bolotwa, *C. Pr.*	32S	27¼E	53
Bolsena L., *Italy.*	42½N	12E	36
Bolshaya Riv., *U.S.S.R.*	64N	178E	39
Bolshevik I., *U.S.S.R.*	78½N	102½E	39
Bolshoy I., *U.S.S.R.*	74N	141E	39
Bolsover, *England.*	53¼N	1¼W	23
Boltana, *Spain.*	42½N	0	32
Bolton, *England.*	53½N	2½W	22
Bolu, *Turkey.*	40¾N	31½E	41
Bolus Hd., *Ireland.*	51¾N	10¼W	26

Place	Lat.	Long.	No.
Bolzano, *Italy.*	46½N	11¼E	3
Bomarsund, *Finland.*	60N	20E	2
Bombala, *N.S.W.*	37S	149¼E	5
Bombay, *India.*	19N	72¾E	4
BOMBAY, *India.*	22N	72½E	4
Bomfin, *Brazil.*	10½S	40W	7
Bomlo I., *Norway.*	59¾N	5E	2
Bompas Hill, *W. Aust.*	27½S	115½E	6
Bon, C., *Tunisia.*	37N	11E	3
Bonaigarh, *India.*	22N	85E	4
Bonaire I., *W. Indies.*	12¼N	68W	7
Bonar Bridge, *Scot.*	57¾N	4¼W	2
Bonasse, *Trinidad.*	10N	62W	7
Bonavista & B., *Can.*	48½N	53½W	6
Bondo, *Congo.* (*K.*).	4N	24E	5
Bone, see ANNABA			
Bone, Gulf of, *Alg.*	36¾N	7¾E	3
Bo'ness, *Scotland.*	56N	3½W	2
Bongor, *Chad.*	10¼N	15½E	5
Boni, Gulf of, *Celebes.*	4S	121E	4
Bonifacio, *Corsica.*	41¼N	9E	3
Bonilly, *France.*	48¼N	4E	3
Bonin Is., *Pacific.*	27N	142½E	6
Bonn, *Germany.*	50¾N	7E	3
Bonne, *France.*	45½N	7E	3
Bonne Bay, *Newf.*	49½N	58W	6
Bonners Ferry, *U.S.A.*	48¼N	116W	7
Bonnetable, *France.*	48¼N	½E	3
Bonneville, *France.*	46N	6¼E	3
Bonneval, *France.*	48¼N	1¼E	3
Bonney, L., *S. Aust.*	37¾S	140¼E	5
Bonnie Rock, *W. Aust.*	30½S	118¼E	6
Bonnievale, *C. Pr.*	34S	20E	5
Bonny, *Nigeria.*	4½N	7¼E	5
Bonnyville, *Alberta.*	54¼N	110¾W	7
Bontassieve, *Italy.*	43¾N	11¼E	3
Bontoc, *Luzon P.I.*	16½N	120¼E	4
Boolathanna, *W. Aust.*	24¾S	114E	6
Booligal, *N.S.W.*	34S	144½E	5
Boomi, *N.S.W.*	28¾S	149½E	5
Boona, *Queensland.*	28S	152¾E	5
Boons, *Transvaal.*	26S	27¼E	5
Boonville, *N.Y., U.S.A.*	43½N	75¼W	6
Boorabbin, *W. Aust.*	31¼S	120¼E	6
Booroloola, *N. Terr.*	16S	136¼E	6
Boorowa, *N.S.W.*	34½S	148¾E	5
Boothia, G. of, *N.W.T.*	70N	88W	6
Boothia Pen., *N.W.T.*	71N	94W	6
Bootle, *England.*	53½N	3W	2
Boppard, *Germany.*	50¼N	7½E	3
Boqueron, *Cuba, W.I.*	20N	75W	7
Bor, *U.S.S.R.*	56½N	44E	3
Borah Pk., *Id., U.S.A.*	44N	114W	7
Borama, *Somali Rep.*	10N	43½E	5
Boras, *Sweden.*	57¾N	13E	2
Borazjan, *Iran.*	29¾N	51E	4
Borda, C., *S. Aust.*	35¾S	136¼E	5
Bordeaux, *France.*	44¾N	¾W	3
Borden Is., *N.W. Can.*	77N	110W	6
Border, *C. Pr.*	28S	24¾E	5
Bordertown, *S. Aust.*	36¼S	140¾E	5
Bordj Berresof, *Alg.*	32¼N	8E	3
Bordj Le Boeuf, *Tunis.*	32¼N	10E	3
Borg, *Iceland* (inset).	64N	22W	2
Borga, *Finland.*	60½N	25E	2
Borgholm, *Sweden.*	57N	16¾E	2
Borgo, *Italy.*	46N	11½E	3
Borgomanero, *Italy.*	45¾N	8½E	3
Borgotaro, *Italy.*	44½N	9½E	3
Borisoglebsk, *U.S.S.R.*	51½N	42E	3
Borisov, *U.S.S.R.*	54¼N	28½E	3
Borispol, *U.S.S.R.*	50½N	31E	3
Borken, *Germany.*	52N	6¾E	3
Borkum, *Germany.*	53½N	6¾E	3
Borlu, *Turkey.*	38¾N	28½E	3
Bormida Riv., *Italy.*	45N	8½E	3
Bormio, *Italy.*	46½N	10½E	3
BORNEO ISLAND. *E. Indies.*	0	115E	4
Bornholm I., *Denmark.*	55¼N	15E	2
Bor Nor, *Mongolia.*	47½N	118E	3
BORNU, *Nigeria.*	12N	12E	5
Boroughbridge, *Eng.*	54¼N	1½W	2
Borovichi, *U.S.S.R.*	58½N	34E	3
Boros, *Norway.*	62½N	11E	2
Borris, *Ireland.*	52½N	7W	2
Boryslav, *U.S.S.R.*	49¼N	23½E	3
Borzhomi, *U.S.S.R.*	42N	43E	3
Borzo S. Lorenzo, *Italy.*	44N	11¼E	3
Borzya, *U.S.S.R.*	50½N	116½E	3
Bosa, *Sardinia.*	40¼N	8½E	3
Bosanski Novi, *Yugo.*	45N	16½E	3
Boscastle, *England.*	50¾N	4¾W	2
Boschplaat, *Neth.*	53½N	6¼E	3
Bosembele, *C. Afr. Rep.*	5N	17½E	5
Boskoek, *Transvaal.*	25½S	27E	5
Boshof, *O.F.S.*	28½S	25¼E	5
Boshof Berg, *T'vaal.*	24¾S	27½E	5
Boskop, *Transvaal.*	26½S	27E	5
Bosna Riv., *Yugoslavia.*	45N	18¼E	3
BOSNIA & HERCEGOVINA, *Yugoslavia.*	44¼N	17¼E	3
Bosoli, *Botswana.*	21S	27¾E	5
Bosporus, The, *Turkey.*	41¼N	29¼E	4
Bossangoa, *C. Afr. Rep.*	6½N	17¼E	5
Bossut, C., *W. Aust.*	18½S	122E	6
Boston, *England.*	53N	0	2
Boston, *Mass., U.S.A.*	42¼N	71W	7
Boteler Pt., *Natal.*	27¼S	32¾E	5
Botersleegte, *C. Pr.*	30½S	21¼E	5
Botesdale, *England.*	52¼N	1E	2
Bothaville, *O.F.S.*	27½S	26½E	5
Bothnia, G. of, *Baltic S.*	62N	20E	2
Bothwell, *Tasmania.*	42½S	147E	5
Botletle, R., *Botswana.*	20¼S	24E	5

Place	Lat.	Long.	No.
Botosani, Romania.	47¾N	26¾E	37
Bot River, C. Pr.	34¼S	19¼E	52
BOTSWANA, Africa.	22S	24E	51
Bottrop, Germany.	51½N	7E	30
Botwood, Newfound.	49¼N	55½W	67
Bou Arfa, Morocco.	32½N	2W	34
Bouake, Ivory Coast.	7N	5W	50
Boucaut B., N. Terr.	12S	134½E	60
Bouches Du Rhone, Fr.	43¾N	5E	32
Bocota, Mozambique.	22½S	33E	51
Bou Denib, Morocco.	32N	3½W	34
Bougainville I., Pacific.	6S	155E	64
Bougainville, C., W.A.	13½S	126½E	61
Bougie, see BEJAIA.			
Bouillon, Belgium.	49¾N	5E	30
Boulder, Col., U.S.A.	40N	105W	74
Boulder, W. Australia.	31S	122E	61
Boulder City, U.S.A.	36¼N	114¾W	74
Boulder Dam, see HOOVER DAM.			
Boulia, Queensland.	23S	140E	60
Boullens, France.	50¼N	2½E	30
Boulogne, France.	50¾N	1½E	32
Boumba, Niger.	12½N	2¾E	57
Boundary Pk., U.S.A.	37½N	118W	74
Bounty I., S. Pacific.	48S	179E	64
BOURBONNAIS, France.	46N	3E	32
Bourbonne les Bains, Fr.	48N	5¾E	30
Bourg, France.	46¼N	5¼E	32
Bourg St. Maurice, Fr.	45½N	6¾E	31
Bourges, France.	47N	2½E	32
Bourget, L. du, France.	45¾N	5¾E	31
Bourgneuf, France.	47N	2W	32
Bourke, N.S.W.	30S	146E	59
Bourmont, France.	48¼N	5½E	30
Bourne, England.	52¾N	¼W	23
Bournemouth, Eng.	50¾N	1¾W	23
Bou Saada, Algeria.	35¼N	4E	35
Boussac, France.	46¼N	2¼E	32
Boussu, Belgium.	50½N	3¾E	30
Bouxwiller, France.	49N	7½E	30
Bou Zengane, Morocco.	31N	6W	34
Bouzonville, France.	49¼N	6½E	30
Bovey Tracey, Eng.	50½N	3¾W	22
Bovre Field, Norway.	62½N	9E	29
Bow Island, Alberta.	49¾N	111¼W	73
Bow R., Alberta.	50½N	112¼W	73
Bowden, C. Pr.	33S	26½E	53
Bowelling, W. Aust.	33½S	116½E	61
Bowen, Riv., Queens.	21S	147½E	60
Bowen, Queensland.	20S	148¼E	60
Bowes, England.	54½N	2W	25
Bowesdorp, C. Pr.	30½S	18E	52
Bowling Green, U.S.A.	37N	86W	75
Bowman, N.Dak., U.S.	47N	104W	74
Bowmanville, Ontario.	44N	78¾W	69
Bowness, England.	54½N	3W	25
Bowral, N.S.W.	34½S	150½E	59
Bowraville, N.S.W.	30½S	152¾E	59
Box, England.	51½N	2¼W	22
Boxmeer, Netherlands.	51½N	6E	30
Boyalik, Turkey.	42N	28½E	41
Boyanup, W. Australia.	33½S	115¾E	61
Boyle, Eire.	54N	8¼W	26
Boyne, R., Eire.	53½N	6¾W	26
Boyup Brook, W. Aust.	33¾S	116E	61
Bozeman, Mon., U.S.A.	45½N	111W	74
Bozoum, Cent. Afr. Rep.	6½N	16½E	56
Bra, Italy.	44¾N	8E	36
BRABANT, Belgium.	50¾N	4½E	30
BRABANT, N., Neth.	51½N	5½E	30
Brac I., Yugoslavia.	43¼N	16¾E	37
Bracadale & L., Scot.	57½N	6¼W	24
Bracciano, L., Italy.	42¼N	12¼E	36
Bracebridge, Ontario.	45N	79¼W	68
Brach, Libya.	27½N	15E	34
Bracieux, France.	47½N	1½E	31
Bracke, Sweden.	62½N	15E	29
Brackley, England.	52N	1W	23
Bracknell, England.	51½N	¾W	23
Brad, Romania.	46¼N	22¾E	37
Bradano, Riv., Italy.	40½N	17E	37
Bradford, England.	53¾N	1¾W	25
Bradford, Ontario.	44¼N	79½W	68
Bradford-on-Avon, England.	51¼N	2¼W	22
Bradshaw, N. Terr.	15½S	130½E	60
Brady, Texas, U.S.A.	31½N	99¾W	74
Braemar, Scotland.	57N	3½W	24
Braga, Portugal.	41½N	8¼W	35
Braganca, Portugal.	41¾N	7W	35
Brahmani R., India.	21N	85E	44
Brahmaputra R., Ind.	26¼N	91E	44
Braidwood, N.S.W.	35½S	149¾E	59
Braila, Romania.	45¼N	28E	37
Brainerd, Minn., U.S.A.	46½N	94W	75
Braintree, England.	51¾N	½E	23
Braisne, France.	49¼N	3½E	30
Brake, Germany.	53¼N	8½E	30
Brakpan, Transvaal.	26¼S	28¼E	55
Brakpoort, C. Pr.	31¼S	23¼E	52
Brampton, England.	55N	2¾W	25
Brampton, Ontario.	43¾N	79¾W	68
Branco, Riv., Brazil.	2S	62W	78
Brandenburg, Ger.	52½N	12½E	33
Brandfort, O.F.S.	28¾S	26½E	55
Brandon, England.	52½N	¾E	23
Brandon Hd. & B., Ire.	52¼N	10¼W	26
Brandon, Manitoba.	49¾N	100W	70
Brandon, Vt., U.S.A.	43¾N	73¼W	69
Brandvlei, C. Pr.	30½S	20½E	52
Braniewo, Poland.	54½N	19¾E	33
Bransk, Poland.	52¾N	22¾E	33
Brantford, Ontario.	43¼N	80¼W	68
Branzi, Italy.	46N	9¾E	31
Brasilia, Brazil.	15¾S	47¾W	78

Place	Lat.	Long.	No.
Brasov, Romania.	45¾N	25½E	37
Brass, Nigeria.	4½N	6¼E	57
Brassus, le, Switz.	46½N	6¼E	31
Bratislava, Czecho.	48¼N	17E	33
Bratsk, U.S.S.R.	56N	101¾E	39
Braunau, Austria.	48¼N	13E	33
Braunschweig, C. Pr.	32¾S	27½E	53
Braunton, England.	51N	4¼W	22
Brava, Somali Rep.	1¼N	44E	56
Braviken Fiord, Swe.	59N	17E	29
Bray, France.	48¼N	3½E	30
Bray, Ireland.	53¼N	6W	26
Bray Head, Ireland.	52N	10¼W	26
Brazeau, Alberta.	52½N	116W	73
Brazeau, Mt., Alberta.	52½N	117¼W	73
BRAZIL, S. America.	12S	54W	78
Brazos, Texas, U.S.A.	29N	95W	75
Brazos R., Tex., U.S.A.	32N	95½W	75
Brazzaville, Congo (B.)	4¼S	15E	56
Brcko, Yugoslavia.	45N	19E	36
Brda Riv., Poland	53N	18E	33
Breaden, L., W. Aust.	26S	126E	61
Breaker Inlet, W. Aust.	20S	119E	61
Brechin, Scotland.	56¾N	2¾W	24
Brecht, Netherlands.	51¼N	4½E	30
BRECKNOCK, Wales.	52N	3½W	22
Brecon, Wales.	52N	3½W	22
Brecon Beacons, Wales.	51¾N	3½W	22
Breda, Netherlands.	51½N	4¾E	30
Bredasdorp, C. Pr.	34½S	20E	52
Bredenbury, Sask.	51N	102W	70
Bree, Belgium.	51¼N	5½E	30
Breede, Riv., C. Pr.	34¼S	20¾E	52
Bregenz, Austria.	47½N	9¾E	33
Brehal, France.	48¾N	1½W	31
Brehat, France.	48¾N	3W	31
Breidha Fiord, Iceland.	65¾N	24W	29
Breissach, Germany.	48N	7½E	30
Bremangerland I., Nor.	62N	4½E	29
Bremen, Germany.	53N	8¾E	33
Bremer, W. Australia.	34¾S	119E	61
Bremerhaven, Ger.	53½N	8½E	33
Bremerton, U.S.A.	47½N	122¾W	74
Bremervorde, Germany.	53½N	9½E	30
Brendon Hills, Eng.	51N	3¼W	22
Brenner Pass, Austr.-It.	47N	11½E	33
Brennero, Italy.	47N	11½E	31
Breno, Italy.	46N	10½E	31
Brenta Riv., Italy.	45½N	12¼E	31
Brentwood, England.	51½N	¼E	23
Brescia, Italy.	45½N	10¼E	35
Breslau, see WROCLAW.			
Bresle R., France.	50N	1¾E	30
Bressanone, Italy.	46¾N	11¾E	31
Bressay, Scotland.	60¼N	1W	24
Bressuire, France.	47N	¼W	32
Brest, France.	48½N	4½W	32
Brest (Litovsk), U.S.S.R.	52N	23¾E	33
Breteuil, France.	49¾N	2¼E	30
Brewarrina, N.S.W.	30S	146¾E	59
Breyten, Transvaal.	26¼S	30E	55
Brezina, Algeria.	33¼N	1½E	35
Brezova, Czecho.	48¾N	17½E	33
Bria, Cent. Afr. Rep.	6½N	22E	56
Briancon, France.	45N	6¾E	32
Briare, France.	47¾N	2¾E	30
Bribie I., Queensland.	26½S	153¼E	59
Brickaville, Malagasy.	18¾S	49E	56
Bricon, France.	48N	5E	30
Bridestowe, England.	50½N	4¼W	22
Bridgeburg, Ontario.	43N	79W	69
Bridgend, Scotland.	55¾N	6¼W	25
Bridgend, Wales.	51½N	3½W	22
Bridge of Allan, Scot.	56¼N	4W	25
Bridge of Doon, Scot.	55½N	4½W	25
Bridge of Orchy, Scot.	56½N	4¾W	25
Bridgeport, Conn., U.S.	41¼N	73¼W	75
Bridgetown, W. Aust.	34S	116½E	61
Bridgetown, Barbados.	13N	59½W	77
Bridgetown, Eire.	52¼N	6½W	22
Bridgewater, N.S., Can.	44¼N	64½W	67
Bridgnorth, England.	52½N	2½W	22
Bridgwater, England.	51¼N	3W	22
Bridlington, England.	54¼N	¼W	25
Bridport, England.	50¾N	2¾W	22
Brielle, Netherlands.	51¾N	4¼E	30
Brienne-le-Chat, Fr.	48¼N	4½E	30
Brienz, L. of, Switz.	46½N	8E	31
Brienz, Switzerland.	46¾N	8E	31
Brierley Hill, England.	52½N	2W	22
Briey, France.	49¼N	6E	30
Brig, Switzerland.	46¼N	8E	31
Brigg, England.	53½N	½W	23
Brigge I., W. Aust.	14S	125E	61
Bright, Victoria.	36¾S	147E	59
Brightlingsea, Eng.	51¾N	1E	23
Brighton, England.	50¾N	¼W	23
Brighton, Ontario.	44N	77¾W	69
Brighton, S. Australia.	35S	138½E	59
Brighton Dns., Queens.	23½S	142E	60
Brighton, S.I., N.Z.	(inset D).		63
Brignogan, France.	48¾N	4¼W	31
Brindisi, Italy.	40¾N	18E	36
Brinkworth, S. Aust.	33¾S	138½E	59
Brionne, France.	49¼N	½E	31
Brioude, France.	45¼N	3½E	32
Briouze, France.	48¾N	½W	31
Briquebec, France.	49½N	1½W	31
Brisbane, Queensland.	27½S	153E	60
Brisbane R., Queens.	27½S	153E	60
Bristol, Tenn., U.S.A.	36½N	82¼W	75
Bristol, England.	51½N	2½W	22
Bristol Bay, Alaska, U.S.	59N	160W	74
BRITISH COLUMBIA, Can.	54N	124W	66

Place	Lat.	Long.	No.
BRITISH HONDURAS, Cent. America.	17N	88¾W	76
Brits, Transvaal.	25½S	27¾E	54
Britstown, C. Pr.	30½S	23½E	52
BRITTANY, France.	48N	3W	32
Britten, Transvaal.	27¾S	25½E	55
Brive, France.	45¼N	1½E	32
Brixham, England.	50½N	3½W	22
Brno, Czechoslovakia.	49¼N	16½E	33
Broach, India.	21¾N	73E	44
Broad Arrow, W. Aust.	30½S	121½E	61
Broad B., Scotland.	58¼N	6¼W	24
Broad Sd., Queensland.	22S	149E	60
Broadford, Scotland.	57¼N	5¾W	24
Broad Law Mt., Scot.	55½N	3½W	25
Broadstairs, England.	51½N	1½E	23
Broadus, Mont., U.S.A.	46N	106W	74
Broadview, Sask.	50½N	103½W	70
Broadway, England.	52N	1¾W	23
Brockman, Mt., W. Aust.	22S	116E	61
Brockton, Mass., U.S.A.	42¼N	70¾W	69
Brockville, Ontario.	44½N	75¾W	69
Brod, Yugoslavia.	45¼N	18E	37
Brodeur Pen., N.W.T.	73N	88W	66
Brodick, Scotland.	55½N	5¼W	24
Brodnica, Poland.	53¼N	19½E	33
Brody, U.S.S.R.	50N	25E	38
Broglie, France.	49N	½E	31
Broken Hill, N.S.W.	32S	141½E	59
Broken Hill, see KABWE	14½S	28½E	56
Bromberg, see BYDGOSZCZ.			
Bromley, England.	51½N	0E	23
Bromptonville, Que.	45½N	72W	69
Bromsgrove, England.	52¼N	2W	23
Bromyard, Wales.	52¼N	3W	22
Bronkhorstspruit, S.Af.	25¾S	28¾E	55
Bronnoysund, Norway.	65N	12E	29
Bronx, N.Y., U.S.A.	41N	74W	75
Brooklyn, N.Y., U.S.A.	40¾N	73¾W	69
Brooks, Alberta.	50¾N	111¾W	73
Brookes Inlet, W. Aust.	35S	116E	61
Brooks Range, U.S.A.	68N	150W	74
Brookton, W. Aust.	32¼S	117E	61
Brookville, Pa., U.S.A.	41¼N	79W	68
Broome, W. Australia.	18S	122¼E	61
Broons, France.	48¼N	2¼W	31
Brora & Riv., Scotland.	58N	3¾W	24
Brosna, R., Ireland.	53½N	7½W	26
Brou, France.	48¼N	1¼E	31
Brough, England.	54½N	2¼W	25
Broughton, England.	54¼N	3¼W	25
Broughty Ferry, Scot.	56½N	2¾W	25
Brouwershaven, Neth.	51¾N	3¾E	30
Browns B., N.I., N.Z.	36¾S	174¾E	62
Brownsville, Tex., U.S.	26N	97½W	74
Brown Willy, Mt., Eng.	50½N	4¾W	22
Brownwood, Tex., U.S.	32N	99¾W	74
Bruas, Malaysia (inset).	4½N	100½E	47
Bruce, Ontario.	46¼N	83¾W	68
Bruce, Mt., W. Aust.	22½S	117½E	61
Bruce Rock, W. Aust.	31¾S	118E	61
Bruchsal, Germany.	49N	8½E	30
Bruck, Austria.	48N	16¾E	33
Bruck, Austria.	47½N	15¼E	33
Bruel, Germany.	53¾N	11¾E	33
Bruges, Belgium.	51¼N	3¼E	30
Brugg, Switzerland.	47½N	8¼E	31
Bruhl, Germany.	50¾N	7E	30
BRUNEI, East Indies.	4½N	114½E	47
Brunette Dns., N. Terr.	18¾S	136E	60
Brunico, Italy.	46¾N	12E	31
Brunner, S.I., N.Z.	42½S	171½E	63
Brunsbuttel, Germany.	54N	9¼E	30
Brunswick, Germany.	52¼N	10½E	33
Brunswick B., W. Aust.	15S	125E	61
Brunswick Junction, W. Australia.	33¼S	115½E	61
Bruntal, Czecho.	50N	17½E	33
Bruny Is., Tasmania.	43¼S	147½E	59
Brus, Yugoslavia.	43¼N	21¼E	37
Brussels, Belgium.	50¾N	4½E	30
Brussels, Ontario.	43¾N	81¼W	68
Brussow, Germany.	53½N	14E	33
Bruton, England.	51¼N	2½W	22
Brux, Czechoslovakia.	50½N	13¾E	33
Bruyns Hill, Natal.	29½S	30¾E	55
Bryansk, U.S.S.R.	53¼N	34½E	38
Bryanskoe, U.S.S.R.	44N	47½E	38
Brzeg, Poland.	50¾N	17½E	33
Brzezno, Poland.	54N	17¼E	33
B. Thakham, Thailand.	9N	99E	43
Buali, Cent. Afr. Rep.	5N	18E	56
Buayan, Mindanao, P.I.	6N	125E	47
Buba, Port. Guinea.	11¾N	15W	57
Bubye Riv., Rhodesia.	22S	31½E	51
Bucaramanga, Col.	7N	73¾W	77
Buccaneer Arch., W.Aus.	16S	123E	61
Buchan, Victoria.	37½S	148¼E	59
Buchan Ness, Scotland.	57½N	1¾W	24
Buchanan, Sask.	51¾N	102¾W	70
Bucharest, Romania.	44½N	26E	37
Buchau, Austria.	47½N	11¾E	31
Buckeburg, Germany.	52¼N	9E	33
Buckfastleigh, Eng.	50½N	4W	22
Buckie, Scotland.	57¾N	3W	24
BUCKINGHAMSHIRE, Eng	51¾N	¾W	23
Buckingham, Eng.	51¾N	¾W	23
Bucklands Beach, N.I., N.Z. (ins. A).			62
Buckleboo, S. Australia.	33S	136¼E	59
Bucksport, Me., U.S.A.	44¾N	68¾W	67
Buctouche, N. Bruns.	46½N	64¾W	67
Budapest, Hungary.	47½N	19E	37
Budawn, India.	28N	79¼E	44
Budd Coast, Antarctica.	66S	52E	80

Place	Lat.	Long.	No.
Bude, England.	50¾N	4½W	22
Budejovice, Czecho.	49N	14½E	33
Budennovsk, U.S.S.R.	45N	44E	38
Budleigh Salterton, England.	50½N	3½W	22
Buea, Nigeria.	4¼N	9½E	57
Buenaventura, Col.	4N	77W	78
Buenadventura, Mex.	30N	107½W	76
Buenavista, Canary Is.	28½N	16¾W	35
Buenavista, Mexico.	28N	110W	74
Buenos Aires, Arg.	34¾S	58½W	79
Buffalo, N.Y., U.S.A.	43N	78¾W	73
Buffalo, S.Dak., U.S.A.	46N	103½W	74
Buffalo, Wyo., U.S.A.	44¼N	106¾W	74
Buffalo Park, Alberta.	52½N	111W	73
Buffalo R., Natal.	28½S	30½E	55
Bug, R., Pol.-U.S.S.R.	52½N	20¾E	33
Buga, Nigeria.	8½N	7½E	57
Bugio, I. do, Madeira.	32½N	16½W	35
Bugi, Papua (inset).	9S	143E	60
Bugojna, Yugoslavia.	44N	17½E	36
Bugsuk I., Philippines.	8N	117E	47
Bugulma, U.S.S.R.	54N	53E	38
Buguruslan, U.S.S.R.	53¾N	52½E	38
Buhl, Germany.	48¾N	8½E	30
Bui, U.S.S.R.	58½N	41½E	38
Builth Wells, Wales.	52¼N	3½W	22
Buin, Solomon Is. (ins.).	7S	15E	60
Buinaksk, U.S.S.R.	43N	47E	38
Bujnurd, Iran.	37½N	57E	48
Buka I., Solomons, Pac.	5½S	154½E	64
Buka, Cent. Afr. Rep.	7N	18E	56
Bukavu, Congo (K.).	2½S	28¾E	56
Bukene, Tanzania.	4S	33E	56
Bukhara, U.S.S.R.	40N	65E	48
Bukoba, Tanzania.	11S	31¾E	56
BUKOVINA, U.S.S.R.	47½N	25E	37
Bukwium, Nigeria.	12N	5½E	57
Bulagan, Mongolia.	47N	91E	39
Bulagan, Mongolia.	48N	103E	39
Bulawayo, Rhodesia.	20¼S	28½E	54
BULGARIA, Europe.			37
Bulgroo, Queensland.	25¾S	144E	60
Bullara, W. Australia.	22½S	114E	61
Bulle, Switzerland.	46¾N	7E	31
Bullen Hill, W. Aust.	24½S	121E	61
Buller, R., S.I., N.Z.	41¾S	171½E	63
Bullfinch, W. Australia.	31S	119E	61
Bulli, N.S.W.	34¼S	151E	59
Bullo, L., Queensland.	29S	142¼E	59
Bulloo Riv., Queensland.	28S	144E	59
Bulmen, Germany.	51¾N	7½E	30
Bulmykta, U.S.S.R.	45½N	46E	38
Bulo Burti, Somali Rep.	4N	45½E	56
Bultfontein, O.F.S.	28¼S	26¼E	55
Bulun, U.S.S.R.	70¾N	127¼E	39
Bulwer, Natal.	29¾S	29¾E	55
Bulyea, Sask.	51N	104¾W	70
Bun, Riv., Mozambique.	20S	34E	51
Buna, Kenya.	2¾N	39½E	56
Bunaiyan, Saudi Arabia.	22!N	51E	40
Bunbury, W. Aust.	33½S	115½E	29
Buncrana, Ireland.	55N	7½W	68
Bundaberg, Queens.	24¾S	152¼E	58
Bundarra, N.S.W.	30½S	151E	24
Bunessen, Scotland.	56¼N	6¼W	46
Bundi, India.	25½N	75¾E	23
Bundoran, Eire.	54½N	8¼W	21
Bungay, England.	52½N	1½E	64
Bu Ngem, Libya.	31N	15½E	33
Bung Tso, L., China.	43N	91E	46
Bunji, Kashmir (inset).	35¾N	74½E	44
Bunnarroo, W. Aust.	28½S	117½E	61
Buntine, W. Australia.	30S	116½E	61
Buntingford, England.	52N	0	23
Buntok, Borneo.	2S	114¾E	47
Buqbuq, U.A.R.	32N	25½E	34
Bura, Kenya.	2S	40E	56
Bur Akaba, Somali Rep.	3N	44E	56
Burao, Somali Rep.	9½N	45½E	56
Buraida, Saudi Arabia.	27½N	44E	40
Buraimi, Trucial S.	24N	55½E	40
Burakin, W. Australia.	30½S	117¼E	61
Burbage, England.	51½N	1½W	23
Burdekin, Riv., Queens.	20S	147½E	69
Burdwan, India.	23¼N	87¾E	44
Bure, R., England.	52½N	1½E	23
Buren, Germany.	51½N	8½E	30
Bureya R., U.S.S.R.	51N	132½E	39
Burford, England.	51¾N	1½W	23
Burg, Germany.	52¼N	11¾E	33
Burg, Netherlands.	53N	5E	30
Burgas, Bulgaria.	42½N	27½E	37
Burgdorf, Germany.	52½N	10E	33
Burgdorf, Switzerland.	47N	7½E	31
Burgersfort, T'vaal.	24¾S	30½E	54
Burgerville, C. Pr.	30½S	24½E	53
Burgess Hill, England.	50¾N	¼W	23
Burghausen, Germany.	48¼N	12¾E	33
Burghead, Scotland.	57¾N	3½W	24
Burghersdorp, C. Pr.	31S	26½E	53
Burgh le Marsh, Eng.	53¼N	½E	23
Burgos, Spain.	42½N	3¾W	35
Burgsteinfurt, Ger.	52½N	7½E	33
BURGUNDY, France.	47N	4½E	32
Burhanpur, India.	21½N	76½E	44
Burica, Pta., Panama.	8N	83W	77
Burin, Pen., Newf., Can.	47N	55½W	67
Burke Creek, Queens.	23½S	139¾E	60
Burketown, Queens.	17¾S	139½E	60
Burks Falls, Ontario.	45¾N	79½W	68
Burley, Idaho, U.S.A.	42½N	114W	74
Burlington, Ia., U.S.A.	40¾N	91¼W	75
Burlington, Vt., U.S.A.	44½N	73¼W	69
BURMA, Asia.			43

Place	Lat.	Long.	No.
Burnabimbie, W. Aust.	28S	117½E	61
Burnett Riv., Queens.	25S	153¾E	60
Burnham Market, Eng.	52¾N	¾E	23
Burnham-on-Crouch, England.	51¾N	¾E	23
Burnie, Tasmania.	41S	146E	59
Burnley, England.	53¾N	2¼W	25
Burns, Oregon, U.S.A.	44N	119W	74
Burns Lake, Br. Col.	54¼N	125¾W	72
Burntisland, Scotland.	56N	3¼W	24
Burracoppin, W. Aust.	31½S	118½E	61
Burra Falsa Pt., Moz.	22½S	36E	51
Burren Junc., N.S.W.	30S	149E	59
Burriana Spain.	40N	0	35
Burrinjuck, N.S.W.	35S	148½E	59
Burrow Hd., Scotland.	54½N	4½W	25
Burrundie, N. Terr.	13½S	131¾E	60
Bursa, Turkey.	40¼N	29E	41
Burstall, Sask. Canada.	50¾N	109¾W	70
Burtonport, Ireland.	55N	8½W	26
Burton-upon-Trent, England.	52¾N	1¾W	23
Buru I., Indonesia.	3½S	127E	47
Burujird, Iran.	33½N	48¾E	41
Burullus, L., U.A.R.	31½N	31E	50
Burum, S. Yemen.	14¾N	49¾E	40
BURUNDI, C. Africa.	3½S	30E	56
Burunurt, Mongolia.	47N	111E	39
Burwash Landing, Can.	61N	138¾W	66
Bury, England.	53¾N	2¼W	25
BURYAT A.S.S.R., U.S.S.R.	53N	110E	39
Bury St. Edmunds, England.	52¼N	¾E	23
Burye, Ethiopia.	10¾N	37¼E	56
Bushire, Iran.	29N	51E	40
Bushmills, Ireland.	55¼N	6½W	26
Bushruiyeh, Iran.	34N	57½E	40
Bushy Park, N. Terr.	23S	133½E	60
Busie, Ghana.	10½N	2½W	57
Bussa, Nigeria.	10N	4½E	57
Busselton, W. Aust.	33¾S	115½E	61
Bustard Hd., Queens.	24S	152E	60
Busto Arsizio, Italy.	45¾N	8¾E	31
Busum, I. of, Germany.	54¼N	9E	30
Buta, Congo (K.).	2¾N	24¾E	56
Butaritari, Pacific.	4N	173E	64
Bute, Scotland.	55¾N	5¼W	24
Bute Inlet, Br. Col.	50¾N	125W	72
Butedale, Br. Col.	53¼N	128¾W	72
Butere, Kenya.	0	34E	56
Butru, Queensland.	21½S	139¾E	60
Butt of Lewis, Scot.	58½N	6½W	24
Butterfly, W. Aust.	29½S	121½E	61
Butte, Mont., U.S.A.	46N	112½W	74
Butterworth, C. Pr.	32¼S	28¼E	53
Button B., Manitoba.	58¾N	94W	71
Butuan, Mindanao. P.I.	9N	125½E	47
Butung I., Celebes, Indon.	5S	123E	47
Buturlinovka, U.S.S.R.	50¾N	40½E	38
Butwal, Nepal.	27½N	83½E	44
Butzbach, Germany.	50½N	8¾E	30
Buxtehude, Ger. (ins.).	53½N	9¾E	30
Buxton, England.	53¼N	1¾W	23
Buyaga, U.S.S.R.	60N	126E	39
Buzachi Pen., U.S.S.R.	45N	52E	38
Buzau, Romania.	45¼N	26¾E	37
B. Uzen Riv., U.S.S.R.	48½N	50E	38
Buzuluk, U.S.S.R.	53N	52½E	38
Buor-Khaya B., U.S.S.R.	72N	131E	39
Bwana Mkubwa, Zam.	13S	28¾E	51
Byam Martin, I., Can.	73N	105W	66
Byantay Riv., U.S.S.R.	69N	135E	39
Bydgoszcz, Poland.	53N	18E	33
Byelaya Riv., U.S.S.R.	56N	54E	38
Byelebie, U.S.S.R.	54N	54E	38
Byelgorod, U.S.S.R.	50½N	36½E	38
Byeloe, L., U.S.S.R.	60¼N	37½E	38
Byelopole, U.S.S.R.	51½N	34E	38
Byeloretsk, U.S.S.R.	54N	58E	38
Bylnice, Czecho.	49N	18E	33
Bylot I., N.W. Canada.	73N	79W	66
Byrd Land, Antarctica.	80S	135W	80
Byrock, N.S.W.	30¾S	146½E	59
Byron Bay, N.S.W.	28¾S	153½E	59
Bytom, Poland.	50¼N	19E	33
Bytow, Poland.	54¼N	17½E	33
CABANTUAN, P.I.	15½N	121E	47
Cabanintha, W. Aust.	27S	118E	61
Cabeza De Buey, Spain.	38¾N	5¼W	35
Cabimas, Venezuela.	10½N	71½W	77
Cabo Juby, Sp. Sahara.	28N	13W	35
Caboolture, Queensland.	27S	153E	60
Cabot Str., Canada.	47½N	60W	66
Cabra, Spain.	37¾N	4½W	35
Cabrach, Scotland.	57½N	3W	24
Cabri, Sask., Canada.	50¾N	108½W	70
Cacak, Yugoslavia.	44N	20½E	37
Caccia, C., Sardinia.	40½N	8E	36
Caceres, Colombia.	7½N	75W	77
Caceres, Spain.	39¾N	6¼W	35
Cachalot, Br. Col., Can.	50N	127¼W	72
Cacheu, Port. Guinea.	12¼N	16¼W	57
Cachinal, Chile.	25S	69¼W	79
Cachoeira, Brazil.	12½S	39W	79
Cadca, Czechoslovakia.	49½N	18¾E	33
Cader Idris, Mt., Wales.	52¾N	3¾W	22
Cadillac, Mich., U.S.A.	44¼N	85½W	69
Cadiz & G., Spain.	36¾N	6¼W	35
Cadnam, England.	51N	1½W	23
Caen, France.	49¼N	¼W	32
Caerleon, England.	51½N	3W	22
CAERNARVON, Wales.	53¼N	4¼W	22
Caerphilly, Wales.	51½N	3¼W	22
Caersws, Wales.	52½N	3½W	22
Caesarea, Israel (inset).	32½N	35E	40
Cagayan, Mindanao, P.I.	8½N	124¾E	47
Cagayan R., Luzon, P.I.	18¼N	121½E	47
Cagayan Sulu, I., P.I.	7N	118E	47
Cagli, Italy.	43¾N	12½E	36
Cagliari, Italy.	39¼N	9E	36
Caha Mts., Eire.	51¾N	9¾W	26
Cahir, Eire.	52¼N	7¾W	26
Cahirciveen, Eire.	52N	10¼W	26
Cahore Pt., Eire.	52½N	6¼W	22
Cahors, France.	44½N	1½E	32
Caibarien, Cuba.	22½N	79½W	77
Caicara, Venezuela.	8N	66W	77
Caicos Is., W. Indies.	22N	71½W	77
Caimanera, Cuba.	20N	75¼W	77
Cairn Gorm Mt., Scot.	57½N	3½W	24
Cairn Ryan, Scotland.	55N	5W	24
Cairns, Queens.. Aust.	17S	145¾E	60
Cairnsmuir Mt., Scot.	55¼N	4¼W	25
Cairo, U.A.R.	30N	31¼E	80
Caister-on-Sea, Eng.	52¾N	1¾E	23
Caistor, England.	53½N	¼W	23
CAITHNESS, Scotland.	58½N	3¼W	24
Cajamarca, Peru.	7S	79W	78
Cajarc, France.	44½N	1¾E	32
Cala, C. Pr., S. Africa.	31½S	27¾E	53
Calabar, Nigeria.	5N	8¼E	57
Calabozo, Venezuela.	9N	67½W	77
CALABRIA, Italy.	39N	16½E	36
Calafat, Romania.	44N	23E	37
Calahorra, Spain.	42¼N	2W	35
Calais, France.	51N	1¾E	32
Calais, Maine, U.S.A.	45N	67W	75
Calamar, Colombia.	10¼N	75W	77
Calamian Is., P.I.	12N	120E	47
Calamocha, Spain.	41N	1¼W	35
Calapan, Mindoro, P.I.	13½N	121¼E	47
Calarasi, Romania.	44¼N	27¼E	37
Calarasi, U.S.S.R.	47¼N	28¼E	37
Calatafini, Sicily.	37¾N	13E	36
Calatayud, Spain.	41½N	1½W	35
Calayan I., Philip. Is.	19N	121E	47
Calcutta, India.	22¾N	88¼E	44
Caldas Da Rainha, Portugal.	39½N	9¼W	35
Caldera, Chile.	27S	71W	79
Caldy I., Wales.	51¾N	4¾W	22
Caledon, C. Pr., S. Afr.	34¼S	19½E	52
Caledon, Ireland.	54¼N	6¾W	25
Calera Pte., Canary Is.	28N	17W	35
Calf of Man, England.	54N	4¾W	25
Calgary, Alberta, Can.	51N	114¼W	73
Calgary, Scotland.	56½N	6¼W	24
Calexico, Calif., U.S.A.	32¾N	115½W	74
Calheta, Azores (inset).	38¾N	28W	35
Calheta, Madeira Is.	33N	17¼W	35
Caliacra, C., Bulgaria.	43½N	28½E	37
Cali, Colombia.	3½N	76½W	78
Caliente, Nev., U.S.A.	37¾N	114½W	74
California, G. de, Mex.	27½N	112½W	76
California, Trin. (ins.).	11N	61W	77
CALIFORNIA, U.S.A.	36N	118W	74
Calimere Pt., India.	10¼N	79¾E	45
Calingiri, W. Aust.	31S	116½E	61
Calitri, Italy.	41N	15E	37
Calitzdorp, C. Pr.	33½S	21¾E	52
Callabonna, L., S. Aust.	30S	140E	59
Callac, France.	48½N	3½W	31
Callan, Eire.	52½N	7¼W	26
Callander, Ont., Can.	46¼N	79¼W	68
Callander, Scotland.	56¼N	4¼W	24
Callao, Peru.	12S	77W	78
Callernish, Scotland.	58¼N	6¾W	24
Calles, Mexico.	23N	98W	76
Callington, England.	50½N	4¼W	22
Calne, England.	51½N	2W	22
Caltagirone, Sicily.	37¼N	14½E	36
Caltanissetta, Sicily.	37½N	14¼E	36
Calumet, Mich., U.S.A.	47¼N	88½W	68
Calvados, France.	49N	0	32
Calvert I., Br. Col., Can.	51½N	128W	72
Calvi, Corsica.	42½N	8¾E	36
Calvinia, C. Pr., S. Afr.	31½S	19¾E	52
Camaguey, Cuba.	21½N	77½W	77
Camalore, Italy.	44N	10¼E	36
Camara, Madeira Is.	32¾N	17W	35
Camarat, C., France.	43¼N	6¾E	32
Camarel, France.	48¼N	4½W	31
Camargo, Bolivia.	21S	65¼W	79
Camargo, Mexico.	27¾N	105¼W	76
Camaron, C., Honduras.	16N	85W	77
Cambay, India.	22¼N	72¾E	44
CAMBODIA, Indo-China.	12½N	105E	47
Camboon, Queensland.	25S	150½E	60
Camborne, England.	50¼N	5¼W	22
Cambrai, France.	50¼N	3E	32
Cambria, C. Pr., S. Afr.	33¾S	24½E	53
Cambridge, Cape Pr.	33S	28E	53
CAMBRIDGE & Tn., Eng.	52¼N	½E	23
Cambridge, G., W. Aust.	15S	128E	60
Cambridge, Mass., U.S.	42½N	71W	75
Cambridge, N.I., N.Z.	38S	175½E	62
Camden, Ark., U.S.A.	33½N	92¾W	75
Camden, N.J., U.S.A.	39¾N	75W	75
Camden, N.S.W., Aust.	34S	150¾E	58
Camelford, England.	50¾N	4¾W	22
CAMEROON, Africa.	5N	12E	57
Cameroon, Mt., Nigeria.	4½N	9E	57
Camiguin I., Luzon, P.I.	18N	122E	47
Camocim, Brazil.	3S	41W	79
Camoola, Queens., Aust.	23S	144E	60
Camooweal, Queens.	20S	138½E	60
Campana, Argentina.	34¼S	59W	79
CAMPANIA, Italy.	41N	15E	36
Campbell, Alaska, U.S.	64N	170W	74
Campbell, Cape Pr.	28¾S	23¾E	53
Campbell, C., S.I., N.Z.	41¾S	174E	63
Campbell Riv., Br. Col.	50N	125¼W	72
Campbellford, Ont.	44¼N	77¾W	69
Campbellpore, Pakis.	33¾N	72¼E	44
Campbellton, Canada.	48N	66¾W	67
Campbelltown, N.S.W.	34S	150¾E	59
Campbell Town, Aust.	42S	147½E	59
Campbeltown, Scot.	55½N	5½W	24
Campeche, Mexico.	20N	90¾W	76
CAMPECHE, Mexico.	18N	91W	76
Campeche, G. of, Mex.	20N	93W	76
Camperdown, Natal.	29¾S	30½E	55
Camperdown, Victoria.	38¼S	143¼E	59
Campina Romania.	45N	25¾E	37
Campinas, Brazil.	23S	47W	79
Campobasso, Italy.	41½N	14¾E	36
Campo Grande, Brazil.	20S	54W	78
Campos, Brazil.	23S	42W	79
Camposampiero, Italy.	45½N	11¾E	31
Camposanto, Italy.	44¾N	11¼E	31
Campsie Fells, Scotland.	56N	4W	24
Campulung, Romania.	45¼N	25E	37
Campulung, Romania.	47½N	25½E	37
Camrose, Alberta, Can.	53N	112¾W	73
Camurra, N.S.W., Aust.	29½S	149¾E	59
Can, Turkey.	40N	27E	37
Canadian Riv., U.S.A.	35½N	95½W	75
Canakkale, Turkey.	40¼N	26½E	37
Canale, Italy.	44¾N	8E	31
Cananea, Mexico.	31N	110¼W	76
Canary Islands, Africa.	28N	16W	50
CANARY IS., Atlantic.	28N	16W	35
Canbelego, N.S.W.	31½S	146½E	59
CANBERRA, Australia.	35½S	149E	59
Cancale, France.	48¾N	2W	31
Canche, R., France.	50¼N	1¾E	30
Cande, France.	47½N	1W	31
Candia, see IRAKLION.			
Cane Riv., W. Aust.	21½S	116E	61
Canea, I. of, Crete.	35½N	24E	37
Canete, Peru.	13¼S	76½W	78
Canicado, Mozambique.	24½S	33E	51
Canicatti, Sicily.	37½N	13¾E	36
Canim, L., Br. Col.	51¾N	121W	72
Cankiri, Turkey.	40½N	33½E	41
Canna, I. & Sd. of, Scot.	57N	6½W	24
Cannanore, India.	11¾N	75¼E	45
Canna, W. Australia.	28½S	116E	61
Cannes, France.	43¾N	7E	32
Cannich, Scotland.	57½N	4¾W	24
Cannock, England.	52¾N	2W	22
Canobie, Queens., Aust.	19S	141E	60
Canon City, Col., U.S.A.	37¾N	105W	74
Canonbie, Scotland.	55N	2¾W	25
Canora, Sask., Can.	51¾N	102¼W	70
Canowindra, N.S.W.	33¾S	148½E	59
Canso & C., Canada.	45¼N	61W	67
Cantabrian Mts., Spain.	43N	5W	35
Cantal, Mt., France.	45N	2¾E	32
CANTAL, France.	45N	2¾E	32
Cantaura, Venezuela.	9N	64W	77
Canterbury, England.	51¼N	1¼E	23
Canterbury Plains, S.I., N.Z.	43¾S	172E	63
Canterbury, Queens.	25½S	142E	60
CANTERBURY, S.I., N.Z.	43½S	172E	63
Canterbury Bight, N.Z.	44½S	172E	63
Canton, see Kwangchow.			
Canton I., Pacific.	1S	171W	64
Canton, Ohio, U.S.A.	40¾N	81¼W	75
Cantu, Italy.	45¾N	9¼E	31
Cantwell, Alaska.	63N	150W	74
Canutillo, Mexico.	26N	105W	76
Canvey I., England.	51½N	¾E	23
Canwood, Sask., Can.	53½N	106¾W	70
Cany-Barville, France.	49¾N	½E	30
Capatarida, Venezuela.	11N	70½W	77
Cape Barren I., Aust.	40¼S	148¼E	59
Cape Breton I., Canada.	46N	61W	67
Cape Coast, Ghana.	5N	1¼W	57
Cape Girardeau, U.S.A.	36½N	89½W	75
Cape Horn, Chile.	56S	67¼W	78
Cape of Good Hope, South Africa.	34¼S	18½E	52
Cape Town, Cape Pr.	34S	18½E	52
Cape Verde I., Atlantic.	16½N	25¼W	19
Cape York Pen., Aust.	12S	142E	60
Capel, England.	51¼N	¼W	23
Capel Curig, Wales.	53¼N	4W	22
Capella, Queens., Aust.	23S	148E	60
Capelongo, Angola.	15S	15E	56
Capernaum, Isr. (ins.).	33N	35¼E	40
Cap Haitien, Haiti.	19¾N	72½W	77
Capitignano, Italy.	42½N	13¼E	36
Capiz, Panay, P.I.	11½N	122¾E	47
Cappercleuch, Scot.	55½N	3½W	25
Capraia I., Corsica.	43N	9¾E	36
Capreot, Ont., Can.	46¾N	81W	68
Caprera, I. of, Sardinia.	41¼N	9¼E	36
Capri I., Italy.	40½N	14¼E	36
Capricorn Ra., W. Aust.	23½S	117½E	61
Caprino, Italy.	45½N	10¾E	31
Caprivi Strip, S.W. Afr.	17½S	22E	56
Capua, Italy.	41N	14¼E	36
Caracal, Romania.	44¼N	24¼E	37
Caracas, Venezuela.	10½N	67W	77
Caransebes, Romania.	45½N	22¼E	37
Caraquet, New Bruns.	47¾N	65W	67
Caratal Mines, Venez.	7¼N	62½W	77
Caravaca, Spain.	38N	1¾W	35
Caravellas, Brazil.	17¾S	39¼W	79
Carballino, Spain.	42½N	8W	35
Carberry, Man., Can.	49¾N	99¼W	71
Carbery, Ireland.	51¾N	9W	26
Carbon, O.F.S., S. Afr.	30S	25½E	55
Carbon Blanc, France.	44¾N	1W	32
Carbonara, C., Sardinia.	39N	9½E	36
Carbonia, Sardinia.	39¼N	8½E	36
Carbonear, Newf., Can.	47¾N	53¼W	67
Carcassone, France.	43¼N	2¼E	32
Cardenas, Cuba	23N	81¼W	77
Cardiff, Wales.	51½N	3¼W	22
CARDIGAN, Wales.	52¼N	4W	22
Cardigan Bay, Wales.	52½N	4½W	22
Cardross, Sask., Can.	49¾N	105½W	70
Cardston, Alb., Can.	49¼N	113¼W	73
Cardwell, Queens., Aust.	18¼S	146E	60
Carei, Romania.	47¾N	22½E	37
Carenero, Venezuela.	10½N	66W	77
Carentan, France.	49½N	1¼W	31
Carey, L., W. Aust.	28½S	122½E	61
Cargese, Corsica.	42N	8½E	36
Carhaix, France.	48¼N	3¾W	31
Cariati, Italy.	39½N	17E	37
Caribana Pta., Colombia.	9N	76¾W	77
Caribbean S., W. Indies.	15N	75W	77
Cariboo Mts., Br. Col.	53N	120½W	72
Carinda, N.S.W., Aust.	30½S	147¾E	59
Carinhanha, Brazil.	13S	44W	78
Carini, Sicily.	38N	13¼E	36
CARINTHIA, Austria.	47N	12½E	31
Caripe, Venezuela.	10N	63½W	77
Carleton, Que., Can.	48¼N	66W	67
Carlingford, N. Ireland.	54N	6W	26
Carlisle, England.	54¾N	3W	25
Carloforte, Sardinia.	39¼N	8¼E	36
Carlops, Scotland.	55¾N	3½W	25
Carlos De La Rapita, Spain.	40¾N	¾E	35
Carlow, Eire.	52¾N	6¾W	26
Carloway, Scotland.	58¼N	6¾W	24
Carlow, Eire.	52½N	6¾W	22
Carlsbad, see KARLOVY VARY.			
Carlsbad, N.Mex., U.S.	32¼N	104¼W	74
Carlton, England.	53N	1W	23
Carlton, C. Pr., S. Afr.	31¼S	25E	53
Carlton, Sask., Can.	52¾N	106½W	70
Carlyle, Sask., Can.	49¾N	102¼W	70
Carmagnola, Italy.	44¾N	7¾E	31
Carman, Man., Can.	49½N	98W	71
Carmangay, Alb., Can.	50¼N	113W	73
CARMARTHEN & Town & Bay, Wales.	51¾N	4¼W	22
Carmel, Mt., Isr. (ins.).	32¾N	35E	40
Carmen Land, Antarc.	85S	157½W	80
Carmila, Queens., Aust.	22S	149½E	60
Carmona, Spain.	37½N	5¾W	35
Carn Eige, Scotland.	57¼N	5W	24
Carnamah, W. Aust.	29¾S	115¾E	61
Carnarvon, Cape Pr.	31S	22E	52
Carnarvon, W. Aust.	25S	113¾E	61
Carnatic, India.	12½N	79E	43
Carndonagh, Eire.	55¼N	7¼W	26
Carnduff, Sask., Can.	49¼N	101¾W	70
Carnedd Llewellyn, Mt., Wales.	53¼N	4W	22
Carnegie, L., W. Aust.	26½S	122½E	61
Carnew, Ireland.	52¾N	6½W	26
Carnforth, England.	54¼N	2¾W	25
Carnic Alps, Italy.	46½N	13E	36
Carnlough & B., Ire.	55N	6W	26
Carno, Wales.	52½N	3½W	22
Carnot, Cent. Afr. Rep.	5N	15¾E	56
Carnot B., W. Aust.	17S	122E	61
Carnoustie, Scotland.	56½N	2¾W	24
Carnsore Pt., Eire.	52¼N	6¼W	22
Carnudos, Brazil.	7¼S	57¼W	78
Carnwath, Scotland.	55¾N	3½W	25
Carolina, T'vaal, S. Afr.	26S	30¼E	55
Caroline Is., Pacific.	5N	150E	64
Caroline I., Pacific.	10S	150W	64
Carora, Venezuela.	10N	70W	77
Caroni, Riv., Venezuela.	8N	63W	77
Caron, Sask., Canada.	50½N	105¾W	70
Carouge, Switzerland.	46¼N	6E	31
Carpaneto, Italy.	45N	9¾E	31
Carpathian Mts., Europe	49N	20E	33
Carpentaria, G. of, Aust.	14S	139E	58
Carpentras, France.	44¼N	5E	32
Carpi, Italy.	44½N	10¾E	31
Carpolac, Vict., Aust.	36¾S	141¼E	59
Carra, L., Ireland.	53¾N	9¼W	26
Carrantuohill, Ireland.	52N	9¾W	26
Carrara, Italy.	44N	10E	36
Carrathool, N.S.W.	34¼S	145¼E	59
Carrbridge, Scotland.	57¼N	3¾W	24
Carrickfergus, N. Ire.	54¾N	5¾W	26
Carrickmacross, Ire.	54N	6¾W	26
Carrick-on-Shannon, Ireland.	54N	8W	26
Carrick-on-Suir, Ire.	52¼N	7½W	26
Carrieton, S. Aust.	32½S	138¼E	59
Carrigart, Ireland.	55N	7¾W	26
Carrington, U.S.A.	47½N	99¼W	74
Carrizal, Colombia.	12½N	72¼W	77
Carrizo, El, Mexico.	30N	105W	76
Carrizozo, N.Mex., U.S.	33N	105½W	74
Carroll, Iowa, U.S.A.	42¼N	95W	75
Carron, R., Scotland.	57¾N	4½W	24
Carrouges, France.	48½N	¼W	31
Carrowmore, L., Ire.	54¼N	9¾W	26
Carsamba, Turkey.	41½N	36¾E	41
Carson City, Nev., U.S.	39¼N	119¾W	74
Carsphairn, Scotland.	55¼N	4½W	25
Carstairs, Alberta, Can.	51½N	114¼W	73
Carstairs, Scotland.	55¾N	3¾W	24
Cartagena, Colombia.	10½N	75½W	77
Cartagena, Spain.	37¾N	1W	35

Cartago—China Sea. [97]

Place	Lat.	Long.	No.
Cartago, Colombia.	4¾N	76W	77
Cartago, Costa Rica.	9¾N	84W	77
Carter Bar, England.	55N	2½W	25
Carteret, France.	49¼N	1¾W	31
Carterton, N.I., N.Z.	41S	175½E	62
Carthage, Miss., U.S.A.	37½N	95W	75
Carthage, N.Y., U.S.A.	44N	75½W	69
Cartier, Ontario, Can.	46½N	81¼W	68
Cartwright, Labrador.	53¾N	57W	66
Carupano, Venezuela.	10¾N	63W	77
Carvoeiro, C., Port.	39¼N	9½W	35
Casa Grande, Ariz., U.S.	33N	112W	74
Casablanca, Morocco.	33¾N	7½W	35
Casale Monferrato, It.	45¼N	8½E	31
Casalmaggiore, Italy.	45N	10½E	31
Casamozza, Corsica.	42½N	9½E	36
Cascade Pt., S.I., N.Z.	44S	168½E	63
Cascade Ra., U.S.A.-Can.	47N	121W	72
Cascaes, Portugal.	38¾N	9½W	35
Casella, Italy.	44½N	9E	31
Caserta, Italy.	41N	14¼E	36
Cas Fiorentino, Italy.	43½N	12E	36
Cashel, Eire.	52½N	7¾W	26
Casina, Italy.	44½N	10½E	31
Casino, N.S.W., Aust.	28¾S	153E	59
Caslav, Czechoslovakia.	50N	15½E	33
Caspe, Spain.	41¼N	0	35
Casper, Wyo., U.S.A.	42¾N	106¼W	74
Caspian Sea, S.W. Asia.	43N	51E	40
Cassel, France.	50¾N	2½E	30
Cassino, Italy.	41½N	13¾E	36
Casteldelfino, Italy.	44½N	7½E	31
Castel del Rio, Italy.	44¼N	11½E	36
Castelfranco, Italy.	45¾N	12E	31
Castellammare, Italy.	40¾N	14½E	36
Castellammare G., It.	38N	13E	36
Castellamonte, Italy.	45¼N	7¾E	31
Castellana, Italy.	40¾N	17E	36
Castellane, France.	43¾N	6½E	32
Castellon de la Plana, Spain.	40N	0	35
Castelmoron, France.	44¼N	½E	32
Castelnaudary, France.	43¼N	1¾E	32
Castelo Branco, Port.	39¾N	7½W	35
Castelvetrano, Sicily.	37½N	12¾E	36
Casterton, Vict., Aust.	37½S	141½E	59
Castigliole, Italy.	44¾N	7½E	31
CASTILE, Spain	39¾N	3¾W	35
Castlebar, Ireland.	53¾N	9¼W	26
Castleblayney, Ireland.	54¼N	6¾W	25
Castle Cary, England.	51N	2½W	22
Castlederg, Ireland.	54¾N	7¾W	26
Castledermot, Ireland.	52¾N	7W	26
Castle Douglas, Scot.	55N	4W	24
Castlefinn, Ireland.	54¾N	7¾W	26
Castleford, England.	53¾N	1¼W	25
Castlegar, Br. Col., Can.	49¼N	117¾W	73
Castlegregory, Ireland.	52¼N	10W	26
Castleisland, Ireland.	52¼N	9½W	26
Castlemaine, Victoria.	37S	144¼E	59
Castlemartyr, Ireland.	52N	8W	26
Castle, Mt., Alb., Can.	51¼N	115¾W	73
Castle Pollard, Ireland.	53¾N	7¼W	26
Castlerea, Ireland.	53¾N	8½W	26
Castlereagh B., Aust.	12¼S	135E	60
Castlereagh R., N.S.W.	30½S	147½E	59
Castle Rising, England.	52¾N	½E	23
Castletown, I. of Man.	54¼N	4¾W	25
Castlewellan, Ireland.	54¼N	6W	26
Castor, Alberta, Can.	52¼N	111¾W	73
Castres, France.	43½N	2¼E	32
Castries, St. Lucia, W.I.	14N	61W	77
Castrop-Rauxel, Ger.	51½N	7¼E	30
Castrovillari, Italy.	39¾N	16¼E	36
Castuera, Spain.	38¾N	5½W	35
Catalca, Turkey.	41N	28½E	37
Cat I., Bahamas.	24¼N	76W	75
Catalao, Brazil.	18S	48W	79
CATALONIA, Spain.	41¼N	1E	35
Catamarca, Argentina.	28½S	65¾W	79
Catanduanes I., P.I.	13¾N	124½E	47
Catania, Sicily.	37½N	15E	36
Catanzaro, Italy.	39N	16½E	36
Catastrophe, C., S. Aust.	35S	136E	59
Catbalogan, Samar, P.I.	11¾N	125E	47
Caterham, England.	51¼N	0	25
Cathcart, C. Pr., S. Afr.	32½S	27½E	53
Catskill Mts., U.S.A.	42N	74¼W	69
Catterick, England.	54¼N	1¾W	25
Cauca Riv., Colombia.	9N	74W	77
Caucasus Mts., U.S.S.R.	42½N	44E	38
Caudebec, France.	49½N	¾E	31
Caulnes, France.	48¼N	2¼W	31
Caura, Riv., Venezuela.	7N	65W	77
Cauvery, Riv., India.	13N	76½E	45
Cavalese, Italy.	46¼N	11½E	31
CAVAN, Ireland.	54N	7¼W	26
Cavite, Luzon, P.I.	14½N	121E	47
Cawnpore, see KANPUR.			
Cawood, England.	53¾N	1¼W	25
Cax, Riv., N. Terr., Aust.	15S	136E	60
Cayenne, Fr. Guiana.	5N	52¼W	78
Cayman Is., W. Indies.	19¼N	80W	77
Cayo, Br. Honduras.	17N	90W	77
Cayo Coco, Cuba, W.I.	22N	78W	77
Cayo Gorda, Carib. S.	16N	82W	77
Cayo Romano, Cuba.	22N	77W	77
Cazalla, Spain.	38N	5¾W	35
Ceanannus Mor, Eire.	53¾N	6¾W	26
CEARA, Brazil.	5S	40W	79
Ceara, see FORTALEZA.			
Cebaco I., Panama.	8N	81W	77
Cebu, Philippines.	10¼N	123E	47
Ceccano, Italy.	41½N	13½E	36
Cecil Rhodes Mt., W. Aust.	26S	122E	61
Cecina, Italy.	43¼N	10½E	36
Cedar City, Ut., U.S.A.	37¾N	113W	74
Cedar, L., Man. Can.	53¼N	100W	70
Cedar Rapids, U.S.A.	42N	91½W	75
Cedar R., Iowa, U.S.A.	41¼N	91W	75
Cedara, Natal.	29½S	30¼E	55
Cedarville, Cape Pr.	30½S	29E	53
Cedros I., Mexico.	28N	115¼W	76
Cefalu, Sicily.	38N	14E	36
Cega Riv., Spain.	41¼N	5W	35
Cegled, Hungary.	47¼N	19¾E	37
Ceiba, La, Venezuela.	9¼N	71W	77
Celaya, Mexico.	20½N	101W	76
CELEBES I., Indonesia.	2S	120E	47
Celebes Sea, Indonesia.	4N	122E	47
Celje, Yugoslavia.	46¼N	15¼E	36
Celle, Germany.	52¾N	10½E	33
Cemmaes, England.	53¼N	4¼W	22
Cemmaes, Wales.	52¾N	3¾W	22
Cenis Pass, Mt., France.	45¼N	7E	31
Ceno, Riv., Italy.	44½N	10E	31
Cento, Italy.	44¾N	11¼E	31
CENT. AFRICAN REP.	7N	20E	56
Central Butte, Sask.	51N	106¼W	70
Centralia, Ill., U.S.A.	38N	89W	75
Cephalonia, Greece.	38¼N	20½E	37
Cerbere, France.	42½N	3¼E	32
Cereal, Alberta, Can.	51¼N	110¾W	73
Ceres, C. Pr., S. Africa.	33½S	19¼E	52
Ceres, Italy.	45¼N	7¼E	31
Ceret, France.	42½N	2¾E	32
Cerignola, Italy.	41¼N	16E	36
Cernavoda, Romania.	44¼N	28E	37
Cernay, France.	47¾N	7¼E	30
Cerne Abbas, England.	50¾N	2½W	22
Cerro de Pasco, Peru.	10½S	76W	78
Cervaro, Riv., Italy.	41¼N	16E	36
Cesar, Riv., Colombia.	9N	74W	77
Cesena, Italy.	44¼N	12¼E	36
Ceska Trebova, Czecho.	49¾N	16¼E	33
Cesme, Turkey.	38N	26E	41
Cessnock, N.S.W., Aust.	33S	151¼E	59
Cetinje, Yugoslavia.	42½N	19E	37
Ceuta, Morocco.	35¾N	5¼W	35
Cevennes Mts., France.	44¼N	4E	32
Cevio, Switzerland.	46¼N	8½E	31
Ceylon, Indian Ocean.	7N	81E	45
Ceylon, Sask., Canada.	49½N	104½W	70
Chablis, France.	47¾N	3¾E	30
Chaco, Gran. Par.-Arg.	25S	62W	78
CHAD, Africa.	13N	17E	56
Chad L., Africa.	14N	14E	50
Chadan, U.S.S.R.	51N	91E	39
Chadobets, U.S.S.R.	59N	99E	39
Chadum Riv., Bots.	19S	22E	51
Chafe, Nigeria.	12N	6½E	57
Chagda, U.S.S.R.	59N	130E	39
Chagos, Arch., Ind. Oc.	5S	72E	42
Chahbar, Iran.	25¼N	60½E	40
Chahong Dam, Burma.	28N	97½E	43
Chai Chai, Moz.	25¼S	34E	51
Chaibasa, India.	22½N	86E	44
Chaivo, U.S.S.R.	52N	144E	39
Chakar, China.	36N	81E	43
Chalabre, France.	43N	2E	32
Chalantun, China.	48N	122E	39
Chalette, France.	48N	3E	30
Chaleur, B. de, Canada.	48N	65½W	67
Chalindrey, France.	47¾N	5½E	30
Chaling, China.	27N	113E	48
Challerange, France.	49¼N	4½E	30
Chalna, Pakistan.	22½N	89½E	43
Chalonnes (s-Loire), Fr.	47½N	¾W	32
Chalons-s-Marne, Fr.	49N	4½E	32
Chalon-s-Saone, Fr.	46¾N	4¾E	32
Chalt, Kashmir (inset).	36¼N	74¼E	44
Chalunka, Kash. (ins.).	35N	77E	44
Chalus, Iran.	36N	51½E	41
Cham, Germany.	49¼N	12¾E	33
Chaman, Afghanistan.	30¾N	66½E	43
Chamba, India.	32½N	76¼E	44
Chambal R., India.	26½N	77E	44
Chamben, Zambia.	13S	28E	51
Chamberlain, S. Dak., U.S.A.	43¾N	99¼W	74
Chamberlain R., W. Aust.	16S	128E	61
Chambery, France.	45½N	5¾E	31
Chambord, Que., Can.	48¼N	72W	69
Chambwe, Moz.	15S	32E	56
Chamdo, China.	31¼N	97E	43
Chamonix, France.	46N	6¾E	31
CHAMPAGNE, France.	49N	4E	32
Champagnole, France.	46¾N	6E	31
Champeric, Guatemala.	14¼N	92W	76
Champery, Switz.	46¼N	6¾E	31
Champion, Alb., Can.	50¼N	113W	73
Champlain, L., U.S.A.	45N	73W	75
Champlitte, France.	47½N	5½E	31
Champoton, Mexico.	19¼N	90¾W	76
Chanaral, Chile.	27S	71W	79
Chanda, India.	20N	79½E	45
Chandarpur, India.	21¼N	83¼E	44
Chandigarh, India.	30¾N	77E	44
Chandler, Que., Can.	48¼N	64¾W	67
Chandpur, E. Pakistan.	23¼N	89½E	46
Chandra, R., Kashmir.	33N	76E	44
Chang Chenmo, Riv., Kashmir (inset).	34¼N	78E	44
Changchow, China.	31¾N	120E	48
Changchun, China.	44N	125E	49
Change, France.	48N	¼E	31
Changhua, Formosa.	24N	120½E	48
Changjin, Riv., Korea.	41¼N	128E	48
Changjon, Korea.	39N	128E	49
Changki, Riv., China.	27N	109½E	49
Changkiakow, China.	41¼N	115E	48
Changping, China.	40¼N	116E	48
Changpu, China.	24¼N	118E	48
Changsha, China.	28¼N	112½E	48
Changshan, China.	28¼N	118E	48
Changshu, China.	32N	121E	48
Changte, see ANYANG.			
Changteh, China.	29N	111½E	48
Changting, China.	26N	116E	48
Changyon, Korea.	38N	125E	49
Chankiang, China.	21N	110½E	48
CHANNEL IS. (Br.).	49¼N	2½W	31
Chantilly, France.	49¼N	2½E	32
Chany, L., U.S.S.R.	54¾N	77½E	39
Chaoan, China.	23¼N	116E	48
Chao I., Madeira Is.	32¼N	16¼W	35
Chaoyang, China.	22¼N	117E	48
Chaoyang, China.	42¼N	120E	48
Chaoyangchen, China.	42¾N	126½E	49
Chapayevsk, U.S.S.R.	53N	50E	38
Chapel-en-le-Frith, England.	53¼N	1¾W	23
Chapleau, Ont., Can.	47¾N	83¼W	68
Chapra, India.	25¾N	84¾E	44
Chara, U.S.S.R.	56N	118½E	39
Charak, Iran.	27N	54E	40
Charana, Bolivia.	17½S	69¼W	79
Charcas, Mexico.	23¼N	101¼W	76
Charcot I., Antarctica.	70S	75W	80
Chard, England.	50¾N	3W	22
Charduar, India.	27N	93E	43
Chardzhou, U.S.S.R.	39N	62E	40
CHARENTE, France.	45¾N	0	32
CHARENTE MARITIME, France.	45¾N	1W	32
Charente, R., France.	45¾N	1W	32
Charikar, Afghanistan.	35N	70E	43
Charing, England.	51¼N	¾E	23
Charleroi, Belgium.	50½N	4½E	30
Charles, Mt., W. Aust.	28S	117½E	61
Charles Pk., Mt., W. Aust.	33S	121E	61
Charleston, U.S.A.	38¼N	81¼W	75
Charleston, Queensland.	18½S	143½E	60
Charlestown, Ireland.	54N	8¾W	26
Charlestown, Natal.	27½S	29½E	55
Charlesville, Congo (K.)	5½S	21E	56
Charleville, Eire.	52¼N	8¾W	26
Charleville, France.	49¾N	4¾E	30
Charleville, Queensland.	26½S	146½E	60
Charlotte, N. Car., U.S.	35¼N	80¾W	75
Charlotte Amalie, W.I.	18N	65W	77
Charlotte Waters, Aust.	26S	135E	60
Charlottesville, U.S.A.	38N	78½W	75
Charlottetown, Can.	46¼N	63¼W	67
Charlton, Ont., Can.	47¾N	80W	68
Charlton, Vict., Aust.	36½S	143¼E	59
Charters Towers, Aust.	20S	146¼E	60
Chartres, France.	48½N	1½E	32
Chascomus, Argentina.	35½S	58W	79
Chastleton, Queensland.	27½S	142E	60
Chateaubriant, France.	47¾N	1¼W	31
Chateau Chinon, Fr.	47N	4E	32
Chateau du Loir, Fr.	47¾N	½E	31
Chateaudun, France.	48¼N	1¼E	32
Chateau Gontier, Fr.	47¾N	¾W	31
Chateau la Valliere, Fr.	47½N	½E	31
Chateaulin, France.	48¼N	4W	31
Chateauneuf, France.	48¼N	1¼E	31
Chateauroux, France.	46¾N	1¾E	32
Chateau Salins, France.	48¾N	6½E	30
Chateau Thierry, Fr.	49N	3½E	30
Chateau Tongariro, Mt., N.I., N.Z.	39S	175½E	62
Chateauvillain, France.	48N	5E	30
Chatellerault, France.	46¾N	½E	32
Chatham, England.	51½N	½E	23
Chatham, New Bruns.	47¼N	65½W	67
Chatham, Ont., Can.	42¼N	82¼W	68
Chatham Is., Pacific.	43½S	178W	64
Chatillon, France.	47N	1½E	32
Chatillon, Italy.	45¾N	7¾E	31
Chatillon-s-Seine, Fr.	48N	4½E	30
Chat Renault, France.	47¼N	1E	31
Chattahoochee R., U.S.	30N	85W	75
Chattanooga, U.S.A.	35N	85¼W	75
Chatteris, England.	52½N	0	23
Chau Doc, Vietnam.	11N	105E	47
Chaumont, France.	48¼N	5½E	32
Chauny, France.	49¾N	3¼E	30
Chauvin, Alberta, Can.	52¾N	110¼W	73
Chaux de Fonds, La, Switzerland.	47¼N	6¾E	31
Chaves, Portugal.	41¾N	7¼W	35
Chavuma, Zambia.	13S	22½E	51
Chayul Dzong, Tibet.	28N	93E	43
Chazni, Afghanistan.	33N	68¼E	43
Cheadle, England.	53N	2W	23
Cheboksary, U.S.S.R.	56¼N	47¼E	38
Chechon, Korea.	37N	128E	49
Cheddar, England.	51¼N	2¾W	22
Cheduba I., Burma.	18¾N	93½E	43
Cheepie, Queens., Aust.	26½S	145E	60
Chefoo, see YENTAI.			
Cheim, L. of, Germany.	48N	12½E	33
Cheju, Korea.	33½N	127E	49
CHEKIANG, China.	29N	120E	48
Chekunda, U.S.S.R.	51N	131E	39
Chelesai, U.S.S.R.	48N	55E	38
Chelkar, U.S.S.R.	47¾N	59½E	38
Chelkar-Tengiz, L., U.S.S.R.	48N	63E	39
Chellala, Algeria.	35N	2E	34
Chelm, Poland.	51¼N	23½E	33
Chelmno, Poland.	53¼N	18½E	33
Chelmsford, England.	51¾N	½E	23
Chelmsford, Ont., Can.	46½N	81¼W	68
Chelmza, Poland.	53¼N	18½E	33
Cheltenham, England.	51¾N	2¼W	22
Chelva, Spain.	39¾N	1W	35
Chelyabinsk, U.S.S.R.	55¼N	61½E	38
Chelyuskin, C., U.S.S.R.	77¾N	104½E	39
Chemille, France.	47¼N	¾W	31
Chemnitz, Germany.	50¾N	13E	33
Chemulpo, see INCHON.			
Chenab, R., Pakistan.	32¼N	73½E	46
Chengane, Riv., Moz.	25S	33½E	51
Chengchow, China.	34¾N	114E	48
Chengho, China.	27N	118½E	48
Chengteh, China.	41¾N	118E	48
Chengtu, China.	30¾N	104E	48
Chenhsien, China.	26N	112½E	48
Chenpien, China.	22¾N	100E	43
Chenyuan, China.	27¼N	108E	48
Chenyuanting, China.	23¼N	101E	43
Chepo, Panama.	9N	79W	77
Chepstow, England.	51¾N	2¾W	22
CHER, & R., France.	47N	2½E	32
Cheranchi, Nigeria.	12¾N	7½E	57
Cherbourg, France.	49¾N	1¾W	32
Cheremkhovo, U.S.S.R.	53N	103E	39
Cherepovets, U.S.S.R.	59N	38E	38
Cherevkovo, U.S.S.R.	62N	45E	38
Cheribon, Java.	6¾S	108½E	47
Cherkasi, U.S.S.R.	49½N	32E	38
Chernigov, U.S.S.R.	52N	31½E	38
Chernogorsk, U.S.S.R.	53¾N	91½E	39
Chernovtsy, U.S.S.R.	48¼N	26E	38
Cherny Yar, U.S.S.R.	48N	46E	38
Chernyakhovsk, Lith., U.S.S.R.	54½N	22E	33
Cherskogo Mts., U.S.S.R.	68N	142E	39
Chertsey, England.	51¼N	½W	23
Chesapeake Bay, U.S.A.	38N	76W	75
Chesham, England.	51¾N	¾W	23
CHESHIRE, England.	53¼N	2¾W	22
Cheshskaya B., U.S.S.R.	68N	48E	38
Chesil Bank, England.	50¾N	2½W	22
Chesley, Ont., Can.	44¼N	81¼W	68
Chester, England.	53¼N	2¾W	22
Chesterfield, England.	53¼N	1½W	23
Chesterfield Inlet, Can.	63¾N	92W	66
Chesterfield Is., Pacific.	19½S	158½E	64
Chester-le-Street, Eng.	54¾N	1½W	25
Cheticamp, C., Canada.	46¾N	61W	67
Cheviot Hills, England-Scotland.	55¼N	2¼W	25
Cheviot, The, Mt., Eng.	55½N	2W	25
Chewelah, Wash., U.S.	48N	117¾W	73
Cheyenne, Wyo., U.S.A.	41¼N	104¾W	74
Cheyenne Riv., U.S.A.	45N	101W	74
Cheyne B., W. Aust.	34½S	118½E	61
Chezacut, Br. Col., Can.	52¼N	124W	72
Chhabra, India.	24¾N	76¾E	44
Chhindwara, India.	22N	79E	44
Chiai, Formosa.	24N	120½E	48
Chiampo, Italy.	45½N	11¼E	31
CHIAPAS, Mexico.	17N	92¼W	76
Chiari, Italy.	45½N	10E	31
Chiasso, Switzerland.	45¾N	9E	31
Chiatura, U.S.S.R.	41¾N	43½E	38
Chiavari, Italy.	44¼N	9½E	36
Chiavenna, Italy.	46¼N	9½E	31
Chiba, Japan.	35½N	140¼E	49
Chibuto, Mozambique.	24½S	34E	51
Chicago, Ill., U.S.A.	41¾N	87¾W	75
Chichagof I., Alaska.	58N	138W	74
Chichester, England.	50¾N	¾W	23
Chiclayo, Peru.	7S	80W	78
Chico, Calif., U.S.A.	39¾N	122W	74
Chico Riv., Arg.	43S	63W	78
Chicomuselo, Mexico.	15¾N	92¼W	76
Chicopee, Mass., U.S.A.	42¼N	72¼W	75
Chicoutimi, Que., Can.	48½N	71¼W	69
Chidley, C., Canada.	60½N	64W	67
Chief Joseph Dam, Washington, U.S.A.	48N	119W	74
Chieng Mai, Thailand.	19N	99E	47
Chieng Rai, Thailand.	20N	100E	43
Chieri, Italy.	45N	7¾E	31
Chieti, Italy.	42¼N	14¼E	36
Chihfeng, China.	42¼N	119E	48
Chihkiang, China.	27¼N	110E	48
Chihli, G. of, China.	39N	119E	48
Chihsui, Riv., China.	29N	106E	48
Chihuahua, Mexico.	28N	106W	76
Chiili, U.S.S.R.	44N	67E	39
Chikien, China.	53N	120E	39
Chikmagalur, India.	13¼N	75¾E	45
Chikoa, Mozambique.	15½S	32E	51
Chilas, India.	35¼N	74E	44
Chilaw, Ceylon.	7¾N	79¾E	45
CHILE, S. America.	33S	71W	78
Chilik, U.S.S.R.	51¼N	54½E	36
Chilin, China.	44N	126½E	49
Chilivani, Sardinia.	40¾N	8½E	36
Chilka, L., India.	19¾N	85½E	45
Chillan, Chile.	36½S	72W	79
Chilliwack, Br. Col.	49¼N	122W	72
Chiloe I., Chile.	42½S	74W	78
Chilpancingo, Mex.	17½N	99¼W	76
Chiltern Hills, Eng.	51¾N	¾W	23
Chiluane, Moz.	21S	35E	51
Chilwa, L., Malawi.	15½S	35½E	51
Chimay, Belgium.	50N	4½E	30
Chimborazo, Mt., Ecua.	1½S	79W	78
Chimkent, U.S.S.R.	42¼N	69½E	39
Chimre, Kashmir (ins.).	34N	78E	44
Chin Ling Hills, China.	34N	107½E	48
CHINA, Asia.	30N	110E	48
China Sea, East	27½N	125E	48

[98] China Sea—Conon R.

Place	Lat.	Long.	No.
China Sea, South.	21N	115E	48
Chinaja, Guatemala.	16½N	90W	76
Chinandega, Nicarag.	12½N	87W	77
Chinavane, Moz.	25S	32½E	51
Chinchilla, Queensland.	26¾S	150½E	60
Chinchilla, Spain.	39N	1¾W	35
Chinchoua, Gabon.	0	10E	56
Chinchow, China.	41N	121E	48
Chinde, Mozambique.	18½S	36½E	51
Chindio, Mozambique.	17S	35E	56
Chindwin R., Burma.	23N	95¼E	43
Chinga, Mozambique.	15¼S	38¾E	56
Chinginarra, W. Aust.	21½S	116E	61
Chingombe, Zambia.	14S	30E	51
Chingovo, Riv., Moz.	22½S	33E	51
Ching-Hai, China.	37N	100E	43
CHINGHAI, China.	35N	97E	43
Chingleput, India.	12¾N	80E	45
Chingtechen, China.	29½N	117¼E	48
Chinhae, Korea.	35N	129E	49
Chinhai, China.	30N	121¾E	48
Chinhsien, China.	22N	108½E	48
Chinju, Korea.	35¼N	128E	49
Chinnur, India.	18¾N	79¾E	45
Chinon, France.	47¼N	¼E	31
Chinsali, Zambia.	11S	32½E	51
Chinteche, Malawi.	11¾S	34¼E	51
Chinwangtao, China.	40N	119½E	48
Chiny, Belgium.	49¾N	5¼E	30
Chioggia, Italy.	45¼N	12¼E	36
Chios I. Greece.	38¼N	26E	37
Chipabava Moz.	20½S	33½E	51
Chipani, Rhodesia.	17S	29E	51
Chipata, Zambia.	13½S	32¾E	51
Chipewyan, Alb., Can.	58¾N	111¼W	66
Chipinga, Rhodesia.	20¼S	32½E	51
Chipman, New Bruns.	46¼N	65¾W	67
Chippenham, England.	51½N	2¼W	22
Chipping Norton, Eng.	51¾N	1½W	23
Chipping Sodbury, England.	51½N	2½W	22
Chiquimula, Guatemala.	15N	90W	76
Chiquinquira, Colombia.	5¼N	74W	77
Chiramba, Mozambique.	17S	35E	51
Chirinda, U.S.S.R.	67N	100E	39
Chiriqui, L. de, Panama.	9N	82W	77
Chiriqui Grande, Pan.	8½N	82W	77
Chiromo, Malawi.	16½S	35¼E	51
Chirpan, Bulgaria.	42¼N	25½E	37
Chiry, France.	49½N	3E	30
Chisamba, Zambia.	15S	28¼E	51
Chishow, China.	28¼N	109¾E	48
Chistopol, U.S.S.R.	55½N	50½E	38
Chita, U.S.S.R.	52N	113E	39
Chitambo, Zambia.	13S	31E	51
Chitradurga, India.	14¼N	76¼E	45
Chitral, Pakistan.	36N	72E	43
Chitre, Panama.	8N	80W	77
Chittagong, Pakistan.	22N	92E	43
Chittoor, India.	13¼N	79¼E	45
Chiuta, L., Malawi.	14¾S	35¾E	51
Chiva, Spain.	39½N	½W	35
Chivasso, Italy.	45¼N	8E	31
Chivilcoy, Argentina.	35S	60W	79
Chizha, U.S.S.R.	67N	45E	38
Chobe, Riv., Botswana.	18S	25E	51
Choele Choel, Arg.	39¼S	65½W	79
Choibalsan, Mongolia.	48N	115E	39
Choiseul I., Pacific.	7S	157E	64
Choisy, France.	48¾N	2½E	30
Chojna, Poland.	53N	14½E	33
Chojnice, Poland.	53¾N	17½E	33
Chojnow, Poland.	51¼N	16E	33
Cholana, S.W. Africa.	19S	21E	51
Cholet, France.	47N	¾W	32
Cholon, Vietnam.	10¾N	106½E	47
Choluteca, Honduras.	13N	87W	77
Choma, Zambia.	16¾S	27E	51
Chomutov, Czecho.	50½N	13½E	33
Chona, Riv., U.S.S.R.	63N	111E	39
Chonan, Korea.	37N	127E	49
Chongchow R., Korea.	39½N	125E	49
Chongjin, Korea.	41¾N	129¾E	49
Chongo, Kashmir (ins.)	35¾N	75¾E	44
Chonju, Korea.	36N	127E	49
Chonos Arch., Chile.	45S	76W	78
Chorley, England.	53¾N	2¾W	25
Chorregon, Australia.	23S	143½E	60
Chorwon, Korea.	38N	127½E	49
Chorzele, Poland.	53¼N	21E	33
Chorzow, Poland.	50¼N	19E	33
Choshi, Japan.	35¾N	140¾E	49
Choszczno, Poland.	53¼N	15½E	33
Choteau, Mon., U.S.A.	47N	111½W	74
Chowie Riv., China.	46N	124E	39
Chowkiow, China.	34¼N	115E	48
Chowtsun, China.	37N	118E	48
Christchurch, England.	50¾N	1¾W	23
Christchurch, S.I., N.Z.	43½S	172¾E	63
Christiana, Jamaica.	18¼N	77½W	77
Christiana, Transvaal.	28S	25¼E	55
Christianshaab, Green.	68¾N	51W	66
Christiansted, W.I.	17½N	65W	77
Christmas Crk., W.Aust.	19S	126E	61
Christmas I., Ind. Oc.	10½S	105¾E	47
Christmas I., Pacific.	2¼N	157¾W	64
Chu Riv., China.	30N	106E	48
Chu, Riv., U.S.S.R.	42N	76E	39
Chuanchow, China.	26N	110½E	48
Chubut Riv., Arg.	43S	64W	78
Chucheng, China.	36N	119¼E	48
Chuchiliga, Ghana.	11N	1¼W	57
Chuchow, China.	28N	113E	48
Chuckchee S., U.S.S.R.	69N	175W	39
Chudleigh, England.	50½N	3½W	22
Chudovo, U.S.S.R.	59N	31¾E	38
Chugach Mts., Alaska.	61N	145W	74
Chuguev, U.S.S.R.	50N	37E	38
Chuho, China.	45½N	128E	49
Chuhuichupa, Mexico.	29¾N	109W	76
Chuhsien, China.	28¾N	119E	48
Chuhsien, China.	35½N	119E	48
Chukotski Pen, U.S.S.R.	66½N	175W	39
Chulman, U.S.S.R.	56N	124E	39
Chulmleigh, England.	50¾N	3¾W	22
Chulym R., U.S.S.R.	57¾N	87E	39
Chumikan, U.S.S.R.	54N	135E	39
Chumporn, Thailand.	10½N	99¼E	47
Chuna, Riv., U.S.S.R.	58N	93E	39
Chunchon, Korea.	38N	128E	49
Chungan, China.	27½N	117½E	48
Chungsiang, China.	31¼N	112½E	48
Chunghsien, China.	30N	107½E	48
Chungju, Korea.	37N	128E	49
Chungking, China.	29¾N	106¾E	48
Chungtienting, China.	27½N	100E	43
Chunya, Tanzania.	8½S	33½E	56
Chunya, Riv., U.S.S.R.	62N	96E	39
Chuprovo, U.S.S.R.	64N	46E	38
Chuquicamata, Chile.	22¼S	69W	79
Chur, Switzerland.	46¾N	9½E	31
Churchill, Man., Can.	58¾N	94W	71
Churchill, L., Sask.	56N	108¼W	70
Churchill, R. Newf. Can.	53N	60W	67
Church Stretton, Wales.	52½N	3W	22
Churu, India.	28¼N	74¾E	44
Chusovoi, U.S.S.R.	58N	58E	38
Chust, U.S.S.R.	48¼N	23¼E	33
CHUVASH, U.S.S.R.	56N	47E	38
Chuyen, China.	43N	101E	39
Chzhibkhalantu, Mong.	47¾N	96¾E	39
Chzhirgalantu, Mong.	48N	91E	39
Ciechanow, Poland.	53N	20½E	33
Ciechanowiec, Poland.	52¾N	22½E	33
Ciego de Avila, Cuba.	22N	78W	77
Cienfuegos, Cuba.	22¼N	80½W	77
Cieszyn, Poland.	49¾N	18¾E	33
Cieza, Spain.	38¼N	1¼W	35
Cigliano, Italy.	45¼N	8E	31
Cilician Gates, Turkey.	37N	35E	41
Cinca, Mt., Yugo.	43¾N	17E	36
Cincinnati, Ohio, U.S.	39¼N	84½W	75
Cine, Turkey.	37½N	28E	37
Ciney, Belgium.	50¼N	5¼E	30
Cinto, Mt., Corsica.	42¼N	9E	36
Cintra, Portugal.	38¾N	9½W	35
Ciralia, W. Australia.	22½S	114E	61
Cirars, India.	17½N	82½E	43
Circle, Alaska, U.S.A.	66N	145W	74
Cirencester, England.	51¾N	2W	23
Ciro, Italy.	39½N	17E	37
Cisneros, Colombia.	7N	75W	77
Citrusdal, South Africa.	32½S	19E	52
Cittadella, Italy.	45½N	11¾E	31
Ciudad Anahuac, Mex.	27N	100W	76
Ciudad Bolivar, Venez.	8N	63W	77
Ciudad Juarez, Mexico.	32N	106¾W	76
Ciudad Madero, Mexico.	22N	97½W	76
Ciudad Mante, Mexico.	23N	98½W	76
Ciudad Obregon, Mex.	27½N	110W	76
Ciudad Real, Spain.	39N	4W	35
Ciudad Rodrigo, Spain.	40¾N	6¾W	35
Cividale, Italy.	46N	13¼E	36
Civita Castellana, It.	42¼N	12½E	36
Civitavecchia, Italy.	42N	11¾E	36
Civray, France.	46¼N	½E	32
Cizre, Turkey.	37½N	42¼E	41
Cizycko, Poland.	54N	21¾E	33
Clackline, W. Aust.	31¾S	116¼E	61
CLACKMANNAN, Scot.	56¼N	3¾W	25
Clacton-on-Sea, Eng.	51¾N	1¼E	23
Clairault, C., W. Aust.	33½S	115E	61
Clamecy, France.	47½N	3½E	32
Clanwilliam, C. Pr.	32¼S	19E	52
Claonaig, Scotland.	55¾N	5½W	25
Clara, Ireland.	53¼N	7½W	26
Clara, Riv., Queensland.	19S	143E	60
Claraville, N. Terr.	23S	135E	60
Clarecastle, Eire.	19S	143E	60
CLARE, Eire.	52¾N	9W	26
Clare, England.	52¼N	½E	23
Clare, S. Australia.	33¾S	138½E	59
Clare I., Eire.	53¾N	10W	26
Clare, R., Eire.	53½N	9W	26
Claremorris, Eire.	53¾N	9W	26
Clarence Riv., N.S.W.	29¼S	153½E	59
Clarence R., S.I., N.Z.	42¼S	173¾E	63
Clarence Str., Aust.	12S	131E	60
Clarence Tn., Bahamas.	24N	75W	77
Clarens, O.F.S., S. Afr.	28½S	28½E	55
Claresholm, Alb., Can.	50N	113½W	73
Clark Fork R., U.S.A.	47½N	115W	74
Clarke City, Que., Can.	50¼N	66½W	67
Clarke I., Tas., Aust.	40½S	148¼E	59
Clarksburg, U.S.A.	39¼N	80¼W	75
Clarksdale, Miss., U.S.A.	34N	91W	75
Clarkson, C. Pr., S. Afr.	34S	24¼E	53
Clarkson, Mt., W.Aust.	17½S	123E	61
Clarksville, Tenn., U.S.	36½N	87W	75
Clashmore, Ireland.	52N	7¾W	26
Clayoquot, Br. Col.	49¼N	126W	72
Clear, C., Ireland.	51½N	9½W	26
Clearwater, Br. Col.	51¾N	120W	72
Clearwater, L., Quebec.	55N	75W	66
Cleator Moor, Eng.	54½N	3½W	25
Cleethorpes, England.	53½N	0	23
Cleobury Mortimer, England.	52½N	2½W	22
Clerf, R., Luxembourg.	50N	6E	30
Clermont, France.	49½N	2¼E	32
Clermont-en-Argonne, France.	49N	5E	30
Clermont, Queensland.	22¾S	147¾E	60
Clermont Ferrand, Fr.	45¾N	3¼E	32
Clervaux, Luxembourg.	50N	6E	30
Clery, France.	47¾N	1¾E	30
Cleso, Italy.	46½N	11E	31
Cleve, Germany.	51¾N	6E	30
Cleve, S. Australia.	33¾S	136½E	59
Clevedon, England.	51½N	2¾W	22
Clevedon, N.I., N.Z.	(inset A).		62
Cleveland, Ohio, U.S.A.	41½N	81½W	75
Cleveland, C., Aust.	19S	147E	60
Cleveland Hills, Eng.	54¼N	1¼W	25
Cleveleys, England.	53¾N	3W	22
Clew B., Eire.	53¾N	9¾W	26
Clifden, Eire.	53½N	10W	26
Clifford, C. Pr., S. Afr.	31S	27½E	53
Cliffy Hd., W. Aust.	35S	116¼E	61
Clifton, Queens., Aust.	28S	152E	60
Climax, Sask., Canada.	49¼N	108¼W	70
Clinton, Br. Col., Can	51½N	121½W	72
Clinton, Iowa, U.S.A.	41¾N	90¼W	75
Clinton, Okl., U.S.A.	35½N	99½W	74
Clinton, Ont., Can.	43¾N	81½W	68
Clinton Colden, L., Can.	63N	108W	66
Clisham, Mt., Scotland.	58N	6¾W	24
Clitheroe, England.	53¾N	2¼W	25
Clive, Alberta, Canada.	52½N	113½W	73
Clocolan, O.F.S., S. Afr.	29S	27½E	55
Cloghan, Eire.	53¼N	7¾W	26
Clogher Pt., Eire.	53¾N	6¼W	26
Clonakilty, Eire.	51½N	8¾W	26
Cloncurry, Queensland.	20¾S	140½E	60
Cloncurry Riv., Aust.	20S	141¼E	60
Clonegall, Eire.	52¾N	6½W	26
Clones, Eire.	54¼N	7¼W	26
Clonmel, Eire.	52¼N	7¾W	26
Cloppenburg, Ger.	52¾N	8E	30
Close, C., Antarctica.	66S	52½E	80
Cloudy Bay, S.I., N.Z.	41¼S	174E	63
Clova, Scotland.	56¾N	3W	24
Clovelly, England.	51N	4½W	22
Clovis, N. Mex., U.S.A.	34¾N	104W	74
Cloyes, France.	48N	1¼E	31
Cluj, Romania.	46¾N	23½E	37
Clun, Wales.	52¼N	3W	22
Clunes, Vict., Aust. (ins.)	37¼S	143¾E	58
Cluny Cas, Scotland.	57N	4¼W	24
Clusone, Italy.	45¾N	10E	31
Clutha Riv., S.I., N.Z.	46½S	169¾E	63
Clyde Inlet, N.W. Can.	71N	69W	66
Clyde, Firth of, Scot.	55½N	5W	25
Clydebank, Scotland.	56N	4½W	25
COAHUILA, Mexico.	27N	102½W	76
Coalinga, Calif., U.S.A.	36N	121W	74
Coalville, England.	52¾N	1¼W	23
COAST, N.I., N.Z.	38½S	177¾E	62
Coast Mts., Br. Col.	54N	128W	72
Coatbridge, Scotland.	55¾N	4W	25
Coaticook, Que., Can.	45N	71¾W	69
Coats I., N.W.T., Can.	62½N	83W	66
Coats Land, Antarctica.	76S	28W	80
Coatzacoalcos, Mex.	18¼N	94½W	76
Cobalt, Ontario, Can.	47¼N	79¾W	68
Cobar, N.S.W., Aust.	31½S	145¾E	59
Cobden, Ontario, Can.	45¾N	77W	69
Cobden, Victoria, Aust.	38¼S	143E	59
Cobh, Eire.	51¾N	8¼W	26
Coblenz, see KOBLENZ.			
Cobourg, Ont., Can.	44N	78W	69
Cobourg Pen., Aust.	11½S	132E	60
Cobra, El, Cuba, W.I.	20N	76W	77
Coburg I., N.W. Can.	78N	80W	66
Cochabamba, Bolivia.	17½S	66½W	79
Cochem, Germany.	50¼N	7¼E	30
Cochin, India.	10N	76¼E	45
Cochrane, Ont., Can.	49N	81W	71
Cockburn, S. Australia.	32S	141E	59
Cockburnspath, Scot.	56N	2¼W	25
Cockerham, England.	54N	3W	22
Cockermouth, Eng.	54¾N	3¼W	25
Cocos Is., Indian Ocean.	12S	96¾E	19
Cocos Is., Pacific.	5¼N	87¼W	78
Cod, C., Mass., U.S.A.	42N	70W	69
Codegno, Italy.	45¼N	9½E	31
Codfish I., S.I., N.Z.	47S	167¾E	63
Codigoro, Italy.	44¾N	12¼E	31
Codroipo, Italy.	46N	13E	36
Coen, Queens., Aust.	14S	143¼E	60
Coen Riv., Queens., Aust.	13S	142E	60
Coesfeld, Germany.	52N	7¼E	30
Coeur d'Alene, U.S.A.	48N	116½W	74
Coevorden, Nether.	52¾N	6¾E	62
Coff's Harbour, N.S.W.	30¼S	153E	59
Cofimvaba, Cape Pr.	32S	27½E	53
Cognac, France.	45¾N	¼W	32
Cohoes, N.Y., U.S.A.	42¾N	73¾W	69
Cohuna, Vict., Aust.	35¾S	144¼E	59
Coiba I., Panama.	7½N	82W	77
Coimbatore, India.	11N	77E	45
Coimbra, Portugal.	40½N	8½W	35
Cojedes, Riv., Venez.	8N	68W	77
Cojutepeque, Salvador.	13½N	89W	76
Colac, Victoria, Aust.	38¼S	143½E	59
Colborne, Ontario, Can.	44N	77¾W	69
Colby, Kansas, U.S.A.	39¼N	101W	74
Colchester, Cape Pr.	33¾S	25¾E	53
Colchester, England.	51¾N	¾E	23
Cold Fell, Mt., Eng.	54¾N	2½W	25
Cold Lake, Alb.-Sask.	54½N	110¼W	73
Coldstream, Cape Pr.	34S	23¾E	53
Coldstream, Scotland.	55¾N	2¼W	25
Colebrook, U.S.A.	44¾N	71½W	69
Coleman, Alberta, Can.	49¾N	114¼W	73
Coleman Riv., Queens.	15S	141½E	60
Colenso, Natal.	28¾S	29¾E	55
Coleraine, N. Ireland.	55¼N	6¾W	26
Coleraine, Vict., Aust.	37½S	141¾E	59
Coleroon R., India.	11¼N	79¾E	45
Colesberg, Cape Pr.	30¾S	25E	53
Coligny, T'vaal, S. Afr.	26¼S	26¼E	55
COLIMA, Mexico.	19N	104W	76
Colima, Mexico.	19¼N	103¾W	76
Coll, Scotland.	58¼N	6½W	24
Coll I., Scotland.	56¾N	6½W	24
Collalbo, Italy.	46½N	11½E	31
Collie, W. Australia.	33¼S	116¼E	61
Collier B., W. Aust.	17S	124E	61
Collinee, France.	48¼N	2½W	31
Collines de Perche, Fr.	48¾N	¼E	31
Collingwood, Ont.	44½N	80¼W	68
Collingwood, Queens.	22½S	141E	60
Collins, Ontario, Can.	50¼N	89½W	71
Collinstown, Eire.	53½N	6¼W	26
Collinsville, Queens.	20½S	147¾E	60
Collooney, Ireland.	54¼N	8½W	26
Colmar, France.	48N	7¼E	30
Colmenar Viejo, Spain.	41N	4W	35
Colne, England.	53¾N	2¼W	22
Colne, R., England.	51¾N	1E	23
Cologna Veneta, Italy.	45¼N	11½E	31
Cologne, Germany.	51N	7E	30
COLOMBIA, S. America.	3½N	72W	78
Colombo, Ceylon.	7N	79¾E	45
Colon, Cuba, W. Indies.	22½N	81W	77
Colon, Panama.	9½N	79¾W	77
Colonia Marina, Italy.	41½N	12½E	36
Colonne, C., Italy.	39N	17¼E	36
Colonsay, I. of, Scot.	56N	6¼W	25
COLORADO, U.S.A.	39N	105W	74
Colorado R., Arg.	37¾S	68W	79
Colorado R., Tex., U.S.	31N	98W	74
Colorado R., Utah, U.S.	37N	111W	74
Colorado Springs, Colorado, U.S.A.	38¾N	104¾W	74
Colotlan, Mexico.	22N	103W	76
Colsterworth, Eng.	52¾N	¾W	23
Columbia, Mo., U.S.A.	39N	92¼W	75
Columbia, S.C., U.S.A.	34N	81W	75
Columbia, Mt., Can.	52¼N	117¼W	73
Columbia R., U.S.A. Canada.	46¼N	123½W	66
Columbus, Geo., U.S.A.	32½N	85W	75
Columbus, Miss., U.S.A.	33N	88½W	75
Columbus, Ohio, U.S.A.	40N	83W	75
Colville, C., N.I., N.Z.	36½S	175¼E	62
Colville, L., N.W. Can.	67N	125W	66
Colville R., Alaska, U.S.	70N	150W	66
Colwyn & B., Wales.	53¼N	3¾W	22
Comacchio, & L., Italy.	44¾N	12E	31
Comalapa. Guatemala.	15N	91W	76
Coman, Mt., Antarc.	74½S	65W	80
Combe Martin, Eng.	51¼N	4W	22
Combeaufontaine, Fr.	47¾N	6E	30
Comber, Ireland.	54½N	5¾W	26
Combourg, France.	48½N	1¾W	31
Comeau B., Que., Can.	49¼N	68W	67
Comet, Queens., Aust.	23½S	148½E	60
Comet Vale, W. Aust.	30S	121E	61
Comilla, Pakistan.	23½N	91¼E	46
Comino, C., Sardinia.	40½N	9¾E	36
Commercy, France.	48¾N	5½E	32
Committee B., Canada.	68N	86W	66
Como, & Lake, Italy.	46N	9¼E	36
Comodoro Rivadavia, Argentina.	46S	67½W	78
Comorin, C., India.	8¼N	77½E	45
Comoro Is., Moz. Chan.	12S	44E	56
Compiegne, France	49¼N	2¾E	32
Compostela, Mexico.	21¼N	105W	76
Comrie, Scotland.	56½N	4W	25
Cona, Italy.	45¼N	12E	31
Conara Jn., Tasmania.	41¾S	147½E	59
Concarneau, France.	48N	4W	31
Concepcion, Arg.	27¼S	65¼W	79
Concepcion, Chile.	37½S	73½W	79
Concepcion, Paraguay.	23½S	57½W	79
Conception B., Newf.	47¾N	53W	67
Conception I., Bahamas.	24N	75W	77
Conches, France.	49N	1E	31
Concord, N.H., U.S.A.	43¼N	71½W	69
Concordia, Argentina.	31¼S	58¼W	79
Condamine, R., Aust.	27S	150E	60
Conde-s-Noireau, Fr.	49N	½W	31
Condobolin, N.S.W.	33S	147¼E	59
Condom, France.	44N	½E	32
Conecuh R., Fla., U.S.A.	31N	87W	75
Conegliano, Italy.	45¾N	12¼E	31
Conflans, France.	49¼N	5¾E	30
Confolens, France.	46N	¾E	32
Congleton, England.	53N	2¼W	22
CONGO, (Kinshasa) Afr.	2½S	22½E	56
CONGO, (Brazzaville) Afr.	2½S	15E	56
Congo R., Africa.	3S	16E	56
Congresbury, Eng.	51¼N	2¾W	22
Coniston, England.	54¼N	3¼W	25
Coniston, N. Terr.	22½S	132½E	60
Conjeeveram, India.	13N	79½E	45
Conklin, Alb., Canada.	55¾N	111W	73
Conn, L., Ireland.	54N	9¼W	26
Connah's Quay, Wales.	53¼N	3W	22
CONNACHT, Eire.	53½N	9W	26
CONNECTICUT, U.S.A.	41½N	72½W	69
Connel, Scotland.	56½N	5½W	25
Connemara Mts., Eire.	53¼N	9½W	26
Connerre, France.	48N	½E	31
Connor, Mt., W. Aust.	15S	126E	61
Conon, R., Scotland.	57½N	4½W	24

Place	Lat.	Long.	No.
Conquest, Sask., Can.	51¼N	107¼W	70
Consett, England.	54¾N	1¾W	25
Constance, L. of, Germany-Switz.	47½N	9¼E	31
Constanta, Romania.	44¼N	28¼E	37
Constantine, Algeria.	36¼N	6¼E	35
Constantinople, see ISTANBUL.			
Constitucion, Chile.	35¼S	72¼W	79
Contres, France.	47¼N	1¼E	31
Conty, France.	49¼N	2¼E	30
Conversano, Italy.	41N	17E	36
Conway Ark., U.S.A.	35N	92¼W	75
Conway B., Wales.	53¼N	4W	22
Conway, C. Pr., S. Afr.	31¾S	25¼E	53
Conway, N.H., U.S.A.	44N	71W	69
Coober Pedy, S. Aust.	29S	134E	60
Cooch Behar, India.	26¼N	89¼E	44
Cook Inlet, Alaska.	60N	151W	74
Cook Is., S. Pacific.	20S	158W	64
Cook Strait, N.Z.	41¼S	174¼E	62
Cookhouse, Cape Pr.	32¼S	25¼E	53
Cookshire, Que., Can.	45¼N	71¼W	69
Cookstown, Ireland.	54¼N	6¼W	25
Cooktown, Queensland.	15¼S	145¼E	60
Coolabah, N.S.W., Aust.	31S	146¼E	59
Cooladdi, Queens.,Aust.	26¼S	145¼E	60
Coolah, N.S.W., Aust.	31¼S	149¼E	59
Coolangatta, Queens.	28¼S	153¼E	60
Coolgardie, W. Aust.	31S	121¼E	61
Coolup, W. Australia.	32¼S	115¼E	61
Cooma, N.S.W., Aust.	36¼S	149¼E	59
Coonabarabran, Aust.	31¼S	149¼E	59
Coonalpyn, S. Aust.	35¼S	139¼E	59
Coonamble, N.S.W.	31S	148¼E	59
Coondapoor, India.	13¼N	74¼E	45
Coongan, R., W. Aust.	20¼S	119E	61
Coongoola, Queens.	27¼S	146E	59
Cooper's Creek, S. Aust.	28S	139F	59
Coorabulka, Queens.	24S	140¼E	60
Coorow, W. Australia.	30S	116¼E	61
Cooroy, Queens., Aust.	26¼S	153E	60
Coosa, Riv., U.S.A.	32¼N	86W	75
Cootamundra, Aust.	34¼S	148E	59
Cootehill, Ireland.	54N	7W	26
Cooyah, Queens., Aust.	27S	151¼E	60
Cop, Czechoslovakia.	48¼N	22¼E	33
Copenhagen, Denmark.	55¼N	12¼E	29
Copertino, Italy.	40¼N	18E	36
Copiapo, Chile.	27¼S	70W	79
Copley, S. Australia.	30¼S	138¼E	59
Copparo, Italy.	44¼N	11¼E	31
Copper Harbour, U.S.A.	47N	88W	75
Coppercliff, Ont., Can.	46¼N	81¼W	68
Coppermine & R., N.W.T., Canada.	67¼N	115¼W	66
Coquet, R., England.	55¼N	2W	25
Coquilhatville, see MBANDAKA.			
Coquimbo, Chile.	30S	71¼W	79
Corabia, Romania.	43¼N	24¼E	37
Coral Rapids, Ontario.	50¼N	81¼W	71
Coral Sea, S. Pacific.	17S	155E	64
Corangamite, L., Aust.	38S	143¼E	59
Corato, Italy.	41¼N	16¼E	36
Corbeil, France.	48¼N	2¼E	30
Corbin, Ky., U.S.A.	37N	84W	75
Corbridge, England.	55N	2W	25
Corby, England.	52¼N	1¼W	23
Corcubion, Spain.	43N	9¼W	35
Cordele, Ga., U.S.A.	32N	83¼W	75
Cordoba, Argentina.	31¼S	64W	79
Cordoba, Mexico.	18¼N	97W	76
Cordoba, Mexico.	26¼N	103W	76
Cordoba, Spain.	38N	4¼W	35
Cordova, Alaska,U.S.A.	61N	146¼E	66
Corfe Cas., England.	50¼N	2W	22
Corfield, Queens., Aust.	21¼S	143¼E	60
Corfu I., Greece.	39¼N	19¼E	37
Coria, Spain.	40N	6¼W	35
Corinna, Tasmania.	41¼S	145¼E	59
Corinth, Miss., U.S.A.	35N	88¼W	75
Corinth, Greece.	38N	22¼E	37
Corinth, N.Y., U.S.A.	43¼N	73¼W	69
Corinth, G. of, Greece.	38¼N	22¼E	37
Corinthia, W. Aust.	31S	119¼E	61
Cork, Queens., Aust.	22¼S	141¼E	60
CORK & Town, Eire.	51¼N	8¼W	26
Corlay, France.	48¼N	3W	31
Corleone, Sicily.	37¼N	13¼E	36
Corlu, Turkey.	41¼N	27¼E	37
Cormorant, Man., Can.	54¼N	100¼W	70
Corn Is., W. Indies.	12N	83W	77
Cornelia, O.F.S., S. Afr.	27¼S	28¼E	55
Cornelio, Mexico.	30N	111W	76
Corner Brook, Newf.	49N	58W	67
Corner Inlet, Australia.	38¼S	146¼E	59
Cornie, C., W. Aust.	21¼S	115¼E	61
Corno, Mt., Italy.	42¼N	13¼F	36
CORNWALL, England.	50¼N	5W	22
Cornwall, Ont., Can.	45¼N	74¼W	69
Cornwallis I., Canada.	75N	95W	66
Coro, Venezuela.	11¼N	69¼W	78
Corocoro, Bolivia.	17¼S	68¼W	78
Coromandel, N.I., N.Z.	36¼S	175¼E	62
Coromandel Coast, Ind.	12N	81E	45
Coronation, Alb., Can.	52N	111¼W	73
Coronation, G., Canada.	68N	110W	66
Coronel, Chile.	37S	73W	79
Coropuna, Mt., Peru.	16S	73W	78
Corowa, N.S.W., Aust.	36S	146¼E	59
Corps, France.	44¼N	6E	31
Corpus Christi, U.S.A.	27¼N	97¼W	75
Corran, Scotland.	56¼N	5¼W	24
CORREZE, France.	45¼N	2E	32
Corrie, Scotland.	55¼N	5¼W	25
Corrib Lough. Eire.	53¼N	9¼W	26
Corrientes, Argentina.	27¼S	58¼W	79
Corrientes, C., Col.	5¼N	77¼W	77
Corrientes, C., Cuba.	22N	84¼W	77
Corrientes, C., Mexico.	20¼N	105¼W	76
Corrigin, W. Australia.	32¼S	117¼E	61
Corrimal, N.S.W., Aust.	34¼S	150¼E	59
Corrofin, Ireland.	53N	9W	26
Corry, Penn., U.S.A.	42N	79¼W	68
Corse, C., Corsica.	43N	9¼E	36
Corserine, Mt., Scot.	55¼N	4¼W	25
Corsham, England.	51¼N	2¼W	22
CORSICA, Mediterranean.	42¼N	9E	34
Corte, Corsica.	42¼N	9¼E	36
Cortez, C., U.S.A.	38N	108W	74
Corum, Turkey.	40¼N	35E	41
Corumba, Brazil.	19S	57¼W	79
Corunna, Spain.	43¼N	8¼W	35
Corvallis, Ore., U.S.A.	44¼N	123¼W	74
Corvo I., Azores (inset).	40N	31W	35
Corwen, Wales.	53N	3¼W	22
Cosenza, Italy.	39¼N	16¼E	36
Cosne, France.	47¼N	2¼E	32
COSTA RICA, C. America.	9N	84W	77
Costermansville, see BUKAVU.			
Cotabato, Mind., P.I.	7¼N	124¼E	47
COTE D'OR, France.	47¼N	4¼E	32
Cotentin, France.	49¼N	1¼W	31
COTES DU NORD, Fr.	48¼N	3W	31
Cotopaxi, Mt., Ecuador.	1S	78¼W	78
Cotswold Hills, Eng.	52N	1¼W	22
Cottian Alps, France-Switzerland.	44¼N	7E	31
Coucy-le-Chateau, Fr.	49¼N	3¼E	30
Coulee Dam, U.S.A.	48¼N	118¼W	74
Coulman I., Antarc.	73¼S	170E	80
Coulommiers, France.	48¼N	3E	30
Council Bluffs, U.S.A.	41¼N	95¼W	75
Coupar Angus, Scot.	56¼N	3¼W	25
Courantyne Riv., Surinam. (inset.)	6N	56W	77
Courcelles, France.	49N	6¼E	30
Courseulles, France.	49¼N	¼W	31
Courtalain, France.	48¼N	1¼E	31
Courtenay, Br. Col.	49¼N	125W	72
Courtenay, France.	48N	3E	30
Courtmacsherry B., Ireland.	51¼N	8¼W	26
Courtown Harb., Ire.	52¼N	6¼W	26
Courtrai, Belgium.	50¼N	3¼E	30
Courville, France.	48¼N	1¼E	31
Coutainville, France.	49N	1¼W	31
Coutances, France.	49N	1¼W	31
Covilha, Portugal.	40¼N	7¼W	35
Covington, Ky., U.S.A.	39N	84¼W	75
Cowal, L., Australia.	33¼S	147¼E	59
Cowan, L., W. Aust.	32S	122E	61
Cowaramup, W. Aust.	33¼S	115E	61
Coward Springs, South Australia.	29¼S	137¼E	59
Cowbridge, Wales.	51¼N	3¼W	22
Cowdenbeath, Scotland.	56N	3¼W	25
Cowell, S. Australia.	33¼S	137E	59
Cowes, I. of W., Eng.	50¼N	1¼W	22
Cowra, N.S.W., Aust.	33¼S	148¼E	59
Cox's Bazar, Pakistan.	21¼N	92E	46
Cozumel, I. de, Mexico.	20N	87W	76
Craboon, N.S.W., Aust.	32S	149¼E	59
Cracow, Poland.	50N	20E	33
Cradle, Mt., Tas. Aust.	41¼S	146E	59
Cradock, C. Pr., S. Afr.	32¼S	25¼E	53
Craig, Colorado, U.S.A.	40¼N	107W	74
Craigieburn, S.I., N.Z.	43S	171¼E	63
Craiguenamanagh, Ireland.	52¼N	7¼W	26
Craig Rennie, C. Pr.,	32¼S	26E	53
Craik, Sask., Canada.	51¼N	105¼W	70
Crail, Scotland.	56¼N	2¼W	25
Craiova, Romania.	44¼N	23¼E	37
Cranbrook, Br. Col.	49¼N	115¼W	73
Cranbrook, England.	51¼N	¼E	23
Cranbrook, W. Aust.	34¼S	117¼E	61
Craon, France.	47¼N	1W	31
Cratheus, Brazil.	5S	40¼W	79
Crathie, Scotland.	57¼N	3¼W	24
Crato, Brazil.	7¼S	39¼W	79
Craven Arms, Wales.	52¼N	3W	22
Cravo, Colombia.	6N	70W	77
Crawley, England.	51N	3¼W	22
Crecy, France.	50¼N	1¼E	32
Crediton, England.	50¼N	3¼W	22
Cree, L., Sask., Canada.	57N	107W	66
Creen Creek, Queens.	17¼S	142E	60
Creetown, Scotland.	55N	4¼W	25
Creighton, Natal.	30S	29¼E	55
Creil, France.	49¼N	2¼E	30
Crema, Italy.	45¼N	9¼E	31
Cremona, Italy.	45N	10E	36
Crescent City, U.S.A.	41¼N	124W	74
Cres Is., Yugoslavia.	44¼N	14¼E	36
Cressy, Australia (ins.).	38¼S	144¼E	58
Crest, France.	44¼N	5E	32
Creston, Br. Col., Can.	49¼N	116¼W	73
Creston, Iowa, U.S.A.	41N	94W	75
Creswick, Vict., Aust.	37¼S	143¼E	59
Crete, I., Greece.	35N	25E	37
Creus, C. de, Spain.	42¼N	2¼E	35
CREUSE, France.	46N	2E	32
Creuse, Riv., France.	47¼N	0	30
Crevalcore, Italy.	44¼N	11¼E	31
Crevecoeur, France.	49¼N	2E	30
Crewe, England.	53¼N	2¼W	22
Crewkerne, England.	50¼N	2¼W	22
Crianlarich, Scotland.	56¼N	4¼W	25
Criccieth, Wales.	53N	4¼W	22
Crickhowell, Wales.	51¼N	3W	22
Cricklade, England.	51¼N	1¼W	23
Crieff, Scotland.	56¼N	3¼W	25
Crimea, U.S.S.R.	45N	34E	38
Crinan & Canal, Scot.	56N	5¼W	25
Cristobal, Panama.	9N	80W	77
Croagh Patrick, Mt., Ireland.	53¼N	9¼W	26
CROATIA, Yugoslavia.	45¼N	15¼E	37
Crocodile Is., Australia.	12S	135E	60
Crocodile R., S. Africa.	24¼S	27¼E	54
Croker, I. &C., N. Terr.	12S	132¼E	60
Cromarty, Scotland.	57¼N	4W	24
Cromarty Firth, Scot.	57¼N	4¼W	24
Cromarty, S.I., N.Z.	46¼S	167¼E	63
Cromer, England.	53N	1¼E	23
Cromwell, S.I., N.Z.	45S	169¼E	63
Crook, England.	54¼N	1¼W	25
Crooked I., Bahamas.	23N	74W	77
Crookston, Minn.,U.S.A.	48N	97W	75
Crookwell, N.S.W.	34¼S	149¼E	59
Crosby, England.	53¼N	4¼W	25
Cross Creek, N.I., N.Z. (inset B)			62
Cross Riv., Nigeria.	5N	8E	57
Crosset, Ark., U.S.A.	33N	92W	75
Crossgar, Ireland.	54¼N	6W	26
Crossmichael, Scotland.	55N	4W	25
Crotone, Italy.	39N	17E	36
Crotoy, le, France.	50¼N	1¼E	30
Crouch, R., England.	51¼N	¼E	23
Crowborough, Eng.	51N	¼E	23
Crowes, Vict., Aust.	38¼S	143¼E	59
Crowle, England.	53¼N	¾W	23
Crowsnest Pass, Can.	49¼N	114¼W	73
Croy, Scotland.	57¼N	4W	24
Croydon, England.	51¼N	0	23
Croydon, Queens., Aust.	18S	142E	60
Croydon, W. Aust.	32¼S	117¼E	61
Crozon, France.	48¼N	4¼W	31
Cruces Pta., Colombia.	6N	77¼W	77
Cruden Bay, Scotland.	57¼N	1¼W	24
Crumlin, Ireland.	54¼N	6¼W	25
Cruz, C., Cuba, W. In.	20N	78¼W	77
Crystal Brook, S. Aust.	33¼S	138¼E	59
Cuamba, see KWAMBA.			
Cuango, Riv., Congo (K.)	3S	17E	56
Cuanza R., Angola.	2S	16¼E	56
CUBA, West Indies.	22N	79W	77
Cuckney, England.	53¼N	1W	23
Cucuta, Colombia.	8N	72¼W	77
Cuddalore, India.	11¼N	79¼E	45
Cuddapah, India.	14¼N	78¼E	45
Cuddingwarra,W.Aust.	27¼S	117¼E	61
Cudgewa, Vict., Aust.	36¼S	147¼E	59
Cudworth, Sask., Can.	52¼N	105W	70
Cue, W. Australia.	27¼S	118E	61
Cuenca, Ecuador.	3S	79W	78
Cuencame, Mexico.	24¼N	103¼W	76
Cuernavaca, Mexico.	18¼N	99W	76
Cuilco, Guatemala.	15¼N	92W	76
Cuillin Hills, Scotland.	57¼N	6¼W	24
Culaba, Brazil.	15¼S	56W	78
Culebra, I., Puerto Rico.	18N	65W	77
Culgoa R., N.S.W.	28¼S	147¼E	59
Culiacan, Mexico.	24¼N	107¼W	76
Cullen, Scotland.	57¼N	2¼W	24
Cullen Pt., Queensland.	12S	142E	60
Cullinan, T'vaal, S. Afr.	25¼S	28¼E	54
Cullompton, England.	50¼N	3¼W	22
Culoz, France.	45¼N	5¼E	31
Cults, Scotland.	57N	2¼W	24
Culver Pt., W. Aust.	33S	125E	61
Culverden, S.I., N.Z.	42¼S	172¼E	63
Cumana, Venezuela.	10¼N	64¼W	77
Cumberland, Br. Col.	49¼N	124¼W	72
CUMBERLAND, England.	54¼N	3W	25
Cumberland, U.S.A.	39¼N	78¼W	75
Cumberland, Australia.	18S	143E	60
Cumberland Pen., Can.	67N	65W	66
Cumberland R., U.S.A.	37¼N	85W	75
Cumberland Sd., Can.	66N	68W	66
Cummins, S. Aust.	34¼S	135¼E	59
Cumnock, Scotland.	55¼N	4¼W	25
Cumuripa, Mexico.	28N	110W	76
Cuneo, Italy.	44¼N	7¼E	36
Cunnamulla, Queens.	28S	145¼E	60
Cuorgne, Italy.	45¼N	7¼E	31
Cupar, Sask., Can.	51N	104¼W	70
Cupar, Scotland.	56¼N	3¼W	25
Cupica, Colombia.	7N	77¼W	77
Cupica, B. de, Colombia.	6N	77¼W	77
Curacao I., Carib. Sea.	12N	69W	77
Curiapo, Venezuela.	8¼N	61W	77
Curico, Chile.	35S	71¼W	79
Curitiba, Brazil.	25S	49W	79
Curragh Res., Eire.	53N	6¼W	22
Curtis I., Queens., Aust.	23¼S	151E	60
Cushendall, Ireland.	55¼N	6W	26
Cushendun, Ireland.	55N	6W	26
Cut Bank, Mon., U.S.A.	48N	111W	74
Cut Knife, Sask., Can.	52¼N	109W	70
Cutch, G. of, India.	22¼N	69¼E	46
Cuthbert Pt., Australia.	11S	134E	60
Cuttack, India.	20¼N	86E	45
Cuvier, C., W. Aust.	24¼S	114E	61
Cuxhaven, Germany.	53¼N	8¼E	33
Cuyo Is., P.I.	10¼N	121E	47
Cuyuni Riv., Guyana.	7N	58W	77
Cuzco, Peru.	13¼S	72W	78
Cwmbran, Wales.	51¼N	3W	22
Cyclades Is., Greece.	37N	25E	37
Cygnet, Tas., Aust.	43¼S	147E	59
Cypress Hills Pk., Can.	49¼N	109¼W	70
CYPRUS, Mediterranean.	35N	33E	41
Cyrene, Libya.	33N	22E	34
Czaplinek, Poland.	53¼N	16E	33
Czarnkow, Poland.	53N	16¼E	33
CZECHOSLOVAKIA. Eur.	49N	18E	33
Czersk, Poland.	53¼N	18E	33
Czestochowa, Poland.	50¼N	19E	33
Czlopa, Poland.	53N	16E	33
DABABA, Saudi Arabia.	19N	43E	40
Dabat, Ethiopia.	12¼N	37¼E	56
Dabeiba, Colombia.	8N	76W	77
Dabrowa, Poland.	50¼N	21E	33
Dabrowa, Poland.	53¼N	23¼E	33
Dacca, Pakistan.	23¼N	90¼E	46
Dacura, Nicaragua.	14¼N	83W	77
Dadessa Riv., Ethiopia.	10N	36E	56
Daet, Luzon, P.I.	14N	123E	47
Dagana, Senegal.	16N	15W	50
Dagebull, Germany.	54¼N	9E	33
Dagenham, England.	51¼N	¼E	23
DAGESTAN, U.S.S.R.	42¼N	47E	38
Dagupan, Luzon, P.I.	16N	121E	47
Dahanu, India.	20N	73E	45
Dahlem, Germany.	50¼N	6¼E	30
DAHOMEY, W. Africa.	9N	2E	57
Dairen, see LUTA.			
Dajarra, Queens., Aust.	21¼S	139¼E	60
Dakar, Senegal.	14¼N	17¼W	50
Dakka, U.A.R.	23N	32¼E	40
Dal Riv., Sweden.	60N	17E	29
Dalan Tszadagad, Mongolia.	44N	105E	39
Dalat, Viet Nam.	12N	108¼E	47
Dalbandin, Pakistan.	29N	64E	43
Dalbeattie, Scotland.	55N	3¼W	25
Dalby, Queens., Aust.	27¼S	151¼E	60
Dalen, Norway.	59¼N	8E	29
Dalhart, Texas, U.S.A.	36N	102¼W	74
Dalhousie, Canada.	48N	66¼W	67
Daljarrock, Scotland.	55¼N	4¼W	25
Dalkeith, Scotland.	55¼N	3W	25
Dallas, Texas, U.S.A.	32¼N	96¼W	75
Dalmally, Scotland.	56¼N	5W	24
DALMATIA, Yugoslavia.	43N	16E	37
Dalmellington, Scot.	55¼N	4¼W	25
Dalry, Scotland.	55¼N	4¼W	25
Dalrymple P., Australia.	41S	146¼E	59
Dals Ed, Sweden.	59N	12E	29
Dalton, England.	54¼N	3¼W	25
Dalton, Ga., U.S.A.	34¼N	85W	75
Dalton, Natal.	29¼S	30¼E	55
Dalupiri I., Luzon, P.I.	19N	121E	47
Dalwallinu, W. Aust.	30¼S	116¼E	61
Dalwhinnie, Scotland.	57N	4¼W	24
Daly & R., N. Terr.	12¼S	132E	60
Daly Waters, Australia.	16¼S	133¼E	60
Dam, Ad, Saudi Arabia.	20¼N	44¼E	40
Daman, India.	20¼N	72¼E	45
Damanhur, U.A.R.	31¼N	30¼E	41
Damar I., Indonesia.	7S	128E	47
Damara Ld., S.W. Afr.	22¼S	15E	51
Damascus, Syria.	33¼N	36¼E	41
Damba, Angola.	7S	15¼E	56
Dambacha, Ethiopia.	10¼N	37E	56
D'Ambre, C., Malagasy.	12S	49¼E	56
Dambuki, U.S.S.R.	54N	127E	39
Dame Marie, Haiti,W.I.	18N	74¼W	77
Damghan, Iran.	36N	55E	40
Damghut, S. Yemen.	16¼N	51E	40
Damietta, U.A.R.	31¼N	31¼E	50
Dammam, Saudi Arabia.	26N	50E	41
Damme, Germany.	52¼N	8¼E	30
Damodar R., India.	23¼N	86E	44
Damoh, India.	23¼N	79¼E	44
Dampier Arch., Aust.	20¼S	116E	61
Dampier Ld., W. Aust.	17¼S	122¼E	60
Dampier Str., N. Guinea.	2S	130¼E	47
Damslaagte, Cape Pr.	32¼S	20¼E	52
Damville, France.	49N	1E	31
Damvillers, France.	49¼N	5¼E	30
Da Nang, Vietnam.	16N	108¼E	47
Danbury, U.S.A. (ins.).	41¼N	74¼W	68
Dandaragan, W. Aust.	30¼S	115¼E	61
Dandenong, Victoria.	38S	145¼E	59
Dange, France.	47N	¼E	32
Dangila, Ethiopia.	11¼N	36¼E	56
Dango, Sudan.	10N	24¼E	56
Danielskuil, Cape Pr.	28¼S	23¼E	53
Danielsrus, O.F.S.	28S	28¼E	55
Danilov, U.S.S.R.	58N	40E	38
Dankaz, Ethiopia.	12N	37¼E	56
Dannemarie, France.	47¼N	7E	30
Dannemora, Sweden.	61N	17E	29
Dannenberg, Germany.	53N	11E	33
Dannevirke, N.I., N.Z.	40¼S	176¼E	62
Dannhauser, Natal.	28S	30E	55
Dansalan, Mind., P.I.	7¼N	124E	47
Danube, R., Europe.	45N	29¼E	38
Danville, Ill., U.S.A.	40N	87¼W	75
Danzig, see GDANSK.			
Daoud, Algeria.	35¼N	7¼E	35
Daoulas, France.	48¼N	4¼W	31
Darab, Iran.	29N	54¼E	40
Darb, Saudi Arabia.	17N	42E	40
Darbhanga, India.	26¼N	86E	44
Dardanelles, Turkey.	40¼N	26¼E	37
Dar-es-Salaam, Tanz.	6¼S	39¼E	56
Darganata, U.S.S.R.	41N	62E	40
Dargaville, N.I., N.Z.	36S	173¼E	62
Dariganga, Mongolia.	45N	112E	39
Darien, G. of, Colombia.	10N	77W	77
Darjeeling, India.	27¼N	88¼E	44
Darke's Peak, S. Aust.	33¼S	136E	59

Place	Lat.	Long.	No.
Darling, C. Pr., S. Afr.	33¼s	18½E	52
Darling Ra., W. Aust.	32½s	116E	61
Darling R., N.S.W.	33¾s	142¼E	59
Darlington, England.	54½N	1½W	25
Darlot, L., W. Aust.	27½s	122E	61
Darmstadt, Germany.	49¾N	8¾E	33
Daroca, Spain.	41¼N	1¼W	35
Dartford, England.	51½N	¼E	23
Dartmoor, England.	50½N	4W	22
Dartmouth, England.	50¼N	3½W	22
Darvel, Scotland.	55½N	4¼W	25
Darventa, Yugoslavia.	45N	18E	36
Darwaza, Kash. (ins.).	36½N	76E	44
Darwen, England	53¾N	2½W	25
Darwin, N. Terr., Aust.	12½s	131E	58
Darwin, Mt., Rhod.	16¾s	31½E	51
Darwolo, Poland.	54½N	16¼E	33
Darya-yi-namak, Iran.	35N	54E	40
Darzab, Afghanistan.	35½N	65E	43
Dasht R., Pakistan.	25N	61½E	43
Dasht-i-Kavir, Iran.	34¾N	55E	40
Dassen I., C. Pr., S. Afr.	33½s	18E	52
Dassiedeur, Cape Pr.	32½s	25¾E	53
Datia, India.	25½N	78½E	44
Datu, C., Malaysia.	2N	109¾E	47
Daugavpils, U.S.S.R.	55¾N	26½E	38
Daulatabad, Iran.	28½N	56E	40
Daun, Germany.	50¼N	7E	33
Dauphin & L., Canada.	51¼N	100W	70
DAUPHINE, France.	44¾N	6¼E	32
Dava, Scotland.	57½N	3½W	24
Davao, Mindanao, P.I.	7N	125½E	47
Davenport, Ia., U.S.A.	41½N	90½W	75
Davenport Downs, Queensland, Aust.	24¼s	141¼E	60
Daventry, England.	52¼N	1¼W	23
David, Panama.	8½N	82½W	77
Davidson, Sask., Can.	51¼N	106W	70
Davis Sea, Antarctica.	66s	93E	80
Davis Str., N. Atlantic.	65N	60W	66
Davlekanovo, U.S.S.R.	54N	55E	38
Davos Platz, Switz.	46¾N	9¾E	31
Davyhurst, W. Aust.	30s	121E	61
Dawa, Ghana.	6N	½E	57
Dawa, R., Ethiopia.	4¾N	42E	56
Dawlish, England.	50½N	3½W	22
Dawson, Yukon.	64N	139¼W	66
Dawson Creek, Can.	56¼N	120¼W	66
Dax, France.	43¾N	1W	32
Day Dawn, W. Aust.	27½s	117½E	61
Daylesford, Vict., Aust.	37¼s	144¼E	59
Daysland, Alb., Can.	52¾N	112¼W	73
Dayton, Ohio, U.S.A.	39½N	84¼W	75
Daytona Beach, U.S.A.	29¼N	81W	75
De Aar, C. Pr., S. Afr.	30¾s	24E	53
Dead Sea, Isr.-Jordan.	31½N	35½E	41
Deadwood, U.S.A.	44½N	103¾W	74
Deakin, W. Aust.	30¾s	128½E	58
Deal, England.	51¼N	1½E	23
Dealesville, O.F.S.	28½s	25¾E	55
Dearborn, Mich., U.S.A.	42¼N	83½W	75
Dease, L., Br. Col., Can.	58¾N	130¼W	66
Dease R., Br. Col., Can.	60N	129W	66
Death Valley, U.S.A.	36¼N	116¾W	74
Deauville, France.	49½N	0	31
Debar, Yugoslavia.	41½N	20½E	37
Debden, Sask., Canada.	53¾N	106¾W	70
Debenham, England.	52¼N	1E	23
Deborah, L., W. Aust.	31s	118½E	61
Debra Markos, Ethio.	10¼N	37¾E	56
Debrecen, Hungary.	47½N	21½E	37
De Brug, O.F.S., S. Afr.	29¼s	25¾E	55
Decatur, Ill., U.S.A.	39½N	88¾W	75
Decazeville, France.	44½N	2¼E	32
Deccan Plateau, India.	18N	78E	43
Decimomannu, Sard.	39¼N	9E	36
Decize, France.	46¾N	3½E	32
Decoral, Iowa, U.S.A.	43N	92W	75
De Courcey Hd, Aust.	11s	132½E	60
Deddington, England.	52N	1¼W	23
De Doorns, Cape Pr.	33½s	19½E	52
Dedza, Malawi.	14¼s	34½E	55
Dee, R., Scotland.	57¼N	2¼W	24
Dee, R., Scotland.	55N	4W	25
Dee, R., England.	53¼N	3W	22
Dee, R., Eire.	53¾N	6½W	26
Deelfontein, Cape Pr.	31s	23¾E	53
Deep Stream R., S.I., N.Z. (inset D)			63
Deep Well, Australia.	24¼s	134E	60
Degema, Nigeria.	4½N	6¾E	57
Deggendorf, Germany.	48¾N	13E	33
De Grey Riv., W. Aust.	20½s	119E	61
Dehibat, Tunisia.	32N	10¾E	35
Dehra, India.	30¼N	78E	44
Deir ez Zor, Syria.	35¼N	40E	41
Dej, Romania.	47¼N	23¾E	37
Dekina, Nigeria.	7½N	7E	57
Dekoa, Cent. Afr. Rep.	6½N	19E	56
Delagoa B., Moz.	26s	33E	51
Delange, C. Pr., S. Afr.	33¼s	25¼E	53
Delareyville, T'vaal.	26¾s	25¼E	53
Delatyn, U.S.S.R.	48½N	24½E	37
DELAWARE, U.S.A.	39N	75¾W	75
Delaware R., U.S.A.	42N	75W	75
Delegate, N.S.W., Aust.	37¼s	149E	59
Delemont, Switz.	47¼N	7¼E	31
Delft. Netherlands.	52N	4¼E	30
Delfzijl, Netherlands.	53½N	6¾E	30
Delgado, C., Moz.	10½s	40½E	56
Delhi, India.	28¾N	77¼E	43
Delia, Alberta, Canada.	51¾N	112¼W	73
Delisle, Sask., Canada.	51¾N	107¼W	70
Delle, France.	47½N	7E	31
Dellys, Algeria.	37N	4E	35
Delmas, T'vaal, S. Afr.	26¼s	28¾E	55
Delmenhorst, Germany.	53N	8¼E	30
Deloraine, Man., Can.	49¼N	100½W	70
Deloraine, Tas., Aust.	41½s	146¾E	59
Delportshoop, S.Africa.	28½s	24¼E	53
Delta, Utah, U.S.A.	39N	112½W	74
Delvine, Albania.	40N	20E	37
Demarcation Pt., Can.	70N	140W	66
Demavend, Mt., Iran.	36N	53E	40
Demchok, China.	32½N	79¾E	43
Demerara R., Guy. (ins.)	6½N	57W	77
Deming, U.S.A.	33N	108½E	74
Demirci, Turkey.	39N	28½E	37
Demmin, Germany.	53¾N	13E	33
Denain, France.	50¼N	3½E	30
Denbigh & Tn., Wales.	53¼N	3½W	22
Dendre, R., Belgium.	51¼N	4¼E	30
Dengdeng, Cameroon.	5N	13½E	56
Denge, Nigeria.	13N	5½E	57
Denham & Sd., W. Aust.	25½s	114E	61
Denholm, Sask., Can.	52¾N	108W	70
Denia, Spain.	39N	0	35
Deniliquin, N.S.W.	35½s	145E	59
Denison Pt., Queens.	20s	148E	60
Denison, W. Australia.	29¼s	115E	61
Denison Downs, W.Aust.	19s	128E	61
Denizli, Turkey.	37½N	29E	41
DENMARK, Europe.	56N	10E	29
Denmark Str., Atlantic.	66N	20W	19
Denmark, W. Aust.	35s	117¼E	61
Denniston, S.I., N.Z.	41¾s	171¼E	63
Denton, Texas, U.S.A.	33N	97W	75
Dent du Midi, Switz.	46N	6¾E	31
D'Entrecasteaux Is., Pac.	10s	151E	60
Denver, Col., U.S.A.	39¾N	105W	74
Deo, R., Cameroon.	9N	13E	56
De Put, C. Pr., S. Afr.	30¾s	24E	53
Dera Ghazi Khan, Pak.	30N	70¾E	46
Dera Ismail Khan, Pak.	31¾N	70¾E	46
Derbent, U.S.S.R.	42N	48¼E	38
DERBY & Town, Eng.	52¾N	1½W	23
Derby, Tas., Aust. (ins.).	41s	148E	59
Derby, W. Australia.	17¼s	123½E	58
Derdepoort, T'vaal.	24½s	26½E	54
Derg, Libya.	30N	10E	34
Derg, L., Eire.	53N	8¼W	26
Derg, R., Eire.	54¾N	7½W	26
Dergachi, U.S.S.R.	51N	48E	38
Derna, Libya.	32¾N	22½E	34
De Ridder, La., U.S.A.	31N	93W	75
Derravaragh, L., Ire.	53¾N	7½W	26
Dersingham, England.	52¾N	½E	23
Derudeb, Sudan.	17½N	36E	40
De Rust, C. Pr., S. Afr.	33½s	22½E	52
Derwent Bridge, Tas.	42¼s	146E	59
Derwent, R., England.	54½N	3¼W	25
Derwent, R., Tasmania.	43s	147¾E	59
Derwentwater, Eng.	54½N	3¼W	25
Derzhavinskoe, U.S.S.R.	51N	66E	39
Deschaillons, Quebec.	46½N	72W	69
Desenzano, Italy.	45½N	10½E	31
Deseronto, Ont., Can.	44¼N	77W	69
Desirade, Guadeloupe.	16½N	61W	77
Des Moines & R., U.S.	41¾N	93¾W	75
Desna, R., U.S.S.R.	51¾N	32½E	38
Dessau, Germany.	51¾N	12¼E	33
Deta, Romania.	45½N	21¼E	37
Detmold, Germany.	52N	8¾E	33
Detour, Mich., U.S.A.	46N	84W	68
Detroit, Mich., U.S.A.	42¼N	83W	75
Detroit, Minn., U.S.A.	47N	95W	75
Deux Rivieres, Canada.	46¼N	78½W	69
DEUX SEVRES, France.	46½N	¼W	32
Deva, Romania.	45¾N	22¾E	37
Devarkonda, India.	16¾N	79E	45
Devdelija, Yugoslavia.	41¼N	22½E	37
Deventer, Nether.	52¼N	6¼E	30
Devgarh, India.	16¼N	73¼E	45
Devil's Bridge, Wales.	52½N	3¾W	22
Devil's Lake, U.S.A.	48N	99W	74
Devizes, England.	51¼N	2W	23
De Vlakte, C. Pr., S. Afr.	33½s	23½E	53
DEVON, England.	50¾N	3¾W	22
Devon, T'vaal, S. Afr.	26¼s	28¾E	55
Devon I., N.W.T., Can.	75N	86W	66
Devoncourt, Queens.	21¼s	140¼E	60
Devonport, England.	50¼N	4¼W	22
Devonport, Tas., Aust.	41N	146¼E	59
Devuli R., Rhodesia.	20s	33E	51
Dewas, India.	23N	76E	44
Dewetsdorp, O.F.S.	29½s	26½E	55
De Wildt, Transvaal.	25½s	28E	54
Dewsbury, England.	53¾N	1½W	23
Deynze, Belgium.	51N	3½E	30
Dezhneva, C., U.S.S.R.	66N	170W	39
Dha'ain, Saudi Arabia.	26N	51E	40
Dhaba, Saudi Arabia.	27N	36E	41
Dhahran, Saudi Arabia.	26N	50E	40
Dhamtari, India.	20¾N	81½E	45
Dhanbad, India.	24N	86½E	44
Dhangarhi, Nepal.	28¾N	80½E	44
Dhar, India.	22½N	75½E	44
Dharma, Saudi Arabia.	24½N	46E	40
Dharwar, India.	15½N	75E	45
Dhaulagiri, Mt., India.	28¾N	83½E	44
Dhiban, Jordan (ins.).	31½N	36E	40
Dholka, India.	22¾N	72½E	44
Dholpur, India.	26¾N	77¾E	44
Dhomokos, Greece.	39N	22¼E	37
Dhoraji, India.	21¾N	70½E	46
Dhubri, India.	26N	90E	43
Dhulia, India.	21¼N	74¾E	44
Dia, I. of, Crete.	34¼N	25½E	37
Diamant Pt., Indonesia.	5N	97½E	47
Diamantina, Brazil.	18s	43½W	79
Diamantina R., Aust.	26½s	139E	60
Diamantino, Brazil.	14½s	57W	79
Diamond Harb., S.I., N.Z. (inset C)			63
Dibai, Trucial States.	25N	55E	40
Dibaya, Congo (K.).	6½s	23E	56
Dibba, Trucial States.	25½N	56E	40
Dibrugarh, India.	27½N	94¾E	46
Dickinson, U.S.A.	47N	103W	74
Dickson, U.S.S.R.	73½N	80¼E	39
Didsbury, Alb., Can.	51¾N	114¼W	73
Die, France.	44¾N	5½E	32
Dieburg, Germany.	49¾N	8¾E	30
Diego Suarez, Malag.	12½s	49E	56
Diemel, R., Germany.	51½N	9E	30
Diepholz, Germany.	52¾N	8¼E	30
Dieppe, France.	50N	1E	32
Dieren, Netherlands.	52N	6E	30
Dier Suriani, U.A.R.	30½N	30½E	50
Diest, Belgium.	51N	5E	30
Dieuze, France.	48¾N	6¾E	30
Dif, Kenya.	2N	41E	56
Differdange, Luxem.	49½N	6E	30
Digby, N.S., Canada.	44¾N	65¾W	76
Digne, France.	44N	6¼E	32
Digul, R., N. Guinea.	7¼s	140E	47
Dijon, France.	47¼N	5E	32
Dikwa, Nigeria.	12N	14E	57
Dilam, Saudi Arabia.	24N	47E	40
Dili, Timor, E. Indies.	8½s	125½E	47
Dillenburg, Germany.	50¾N	8¼E	30
Dilling, Sudan.	12N	29¾E	56
Dillon, Mon., U.S.A.	45¼N	112¾W	74
Dilolo, Congo (K.).	10½s	22½E	56
Dimbelenge, Congo (K.)	5½s	23E	56
Dimbokro, Ivory Coast.	7N	5W	50
Dimboola, Vict., Aust.	36½s	142E	59
Dimitrovgrad, Bulg.	42N	25¾E	37
Din, India.	21N	71½E	43
Dinajpur, Pakistan.	25½N	88½E	44
Dinan, France.	48½N	2W	32
Dinant, Belgium.	50¼N	5E	30
Dinard, France.	48½N	2W	31
Dinaric Alps, Yugo.	43¾N	16¾E	37
Dinder & Riv., Sudan.	13N	33E	56
Dindigul, India.	10½N	78E	45
Dingle & Bay, Eire.	52½N	10¼W	26
Dingwall, Scotland.	57½N	4¼W	24
Dinorwic, Ont., Can	49¾N	92½W	71
Dinsmore, Sask., Can.	51¼N	107½W	70
Diomede Is., Alaska.	65N	169W	74
Diplo, Pakistan.	24¼N	69¾E	46
Dippin, Scotland.	55½N	5¼W	25
Dipton, S.I., N.Z.	46s	168¼E	63
Direction, C., Queens.	12½s	143½E	60
Diredawa, Ethiopia.	10N	42E	56
Dirk Hartog I., W. Aust.	25¾s	114E	61
Dirranbandi, Queens.	28½s	148¼E	60
Disappointment Is., Pac.	12s	140W	64
Discovery B., Jamaica.	18¼N	77½W	77
Discovery B., Victoria.	38s	141E	59
Disko B., Greenland.	69¼N	52W	66
Disko I., Greenland.	69½N	53½W	66
Diss, England.	52½N	1¼E	23
Diu I., India.	20¾N	71E	46
Divenie, Gabon.	2½s	12E	56
Dives & R., France.	49¼N	0	31
Divnoe, U.S.S.R.	46N	43¼E	38
Dixcove, Ghana.	5N	2W	57
Dixmude, Belgium.	51N	3E	30
Dixon Entrance, Can.	54½N	132W	66
Diyarbakir, Turkey.	38N	40¼E	41
Dizful, Iran.	32¼N	48¼E	41
Dja, R., Cameroon.	2N	16E	56
Djado, Niger.	21½N	12½E	50
Djambala, Congo (B.).	2½s	14¾E	56
Djelfa, Algeria.	34¾N	3¼E	35
Djeneien, Tunisia.	31¾N	10E	35
Djerba I., Tunisia.	33¾N	10½E	35
Djidjelli, Algeria.	36¾N	6E	35
Djupivogur, Iceland.	65N	15W	29
Dmitriev, U.S.S.R.	52¼N	35E	38
Dmitrov, U.S.S.R.	56¼N	37½E	38
Dneprodzerzhinsk, U.S.S.R.	48½N	34½E	38
Dnepropetrovsk, U.S.S.R.	48½N	35E	38
Dnieper, R., U.S.S.R.	46½N	32½E	38
Dniester, R., U.S.S.R.	46½N	30E	38
Dno, U.S.S.R.	57½N	30E	38
Doarian, Kash. (ins.).	34¾N	74E	44
Doba, Chad.	8¾N	17E	56
Dobbiaco, Italy.	47N	12¼E	33
Dobbyn, Queens., Aust.	19¾s	140E	60
Doboj, Yugoslavia.	44¾N	18E	36
DOBRUJA, Romania.	44½N	28½E	37
Dobrzyn, Poland.	52¾N	19¼E	33
Dodecanese Is., Greece.	36½N	27E	37
Dodge City, U.S.A.	37¾N	100W	74
Dodman Pt., England.	51¼N	4¾W	22
Dodoma, Tanzania.	6s	36E	56
Dodsland, Sask., Can.	51¾N	108¾W	70
Dog Creek, Canada.	51½N	122¼W	72
Dogger Bank, N. Sea.	55N	3E	27
Dogma Pass, China.	32N	96E	43
Doha, Qatar.	25¼N	51½E	40
Dokkum, Netherlands.	53¼N	6E	30
Dol, France.	48½N	1¾W	31
Dolban, U.S.S.R.	46N	47E	38
Dole, France.	47N	5¾E	32
Dolgelley, Wales.	52¾N	4W	22
Dolgi I., U.S.S.R.	69N	58E	38
Dolinsk, U.S.S.R.	47N	143E	39
Dollar, Scotland.	56¼N	3½W	25
Dollar Law, Scotland.	55½N	3¼W	25
Dolo, Ethiopia.	5N	42E	56
Dolomite Mts., Italy.	46¼N	12E	36
Dolores, Argentina.	37s	57W	79
Dolores, Mexico.	26½N	107W	76
Dolphin Head, S.W.Afr.	26s	15E	51
Domazlice, Czecho.	49½N	13E	33
Dombarovkiy, U.S.S.R.	51N	59E	38
Dombas, Norway.	62N	9E	29
Dombovar, Hungary.	46½N	18E	36
Dome I., Burma.	12N	98E	43
Domfront, France.	48½N	¾W	31
Dominica I., W. Indies.	15½N	61½W	77
Dominical, Costa Rica.	9¾N	84W	77
DOMINICAN REPUBLIC. Caribbean.	18N	70W	77
Domira B., Malawi.	13½s	34½E	56
Domitz, Germany.	53¼N	11¼E	33
Dommel, R., Nether.	51¾N	4¾E	30
Domodossola, Italy.	46¼N	8¼E	31
Don, R., England.	53½N	1W	25
Don, R., France.	47½N	2W	31
Don, R., Scotland.	57¼N	2½W	24
Don, R., U.S.S.R.	47N	43E	38
Donaghadee, N. Ire.	54¾N	5½W	26
Donald, Br. Col., Can.	51½N	117W	73
Donalda, Alberta, Can.	52½N	112½W	73
Donaueschingen, Ger.	48N	8½E	33
Donauworth, Germany.	48¾N	10¾E	33
Don Benito, Spain.	39N	5¾W	35
Doncaster, England.	53½N	1¼W	23
Dondo, Angola.	9¾s	14½E	56
Dondo, Mozambique.	19½s	35E	51
Don-Don, O.F.S., S. Afr.	29½s	27¼E	55
Dondra Head, Ceylon.	6N	80½E	45
DONEGAL & Tn., Eire.	54¾N	8W	26
Donets, R., U.S.S.R.	47¾N	37E	38
Donetsk, U.S.S.R.	48N	37¾E	38
Dongara, W. Aust.	29¼s	115E	61
Dong Dang, China.	22N	106E	48
Dong Hoi, Vietnam.	17½N	107E	47
Dongola, Sudan.	19¼N	30E	50
Dongwe, R., Zambia.	14s	23E	51
Donington, England.	52¾N	¼W	23
Donkerpoort, O.F.S.	30½s	25½E	55
Donkins B., Cape Pr.	31¾s	18¼E	52
Donna I., Norway.	66N	12E	29
Donnaz, Italy.	45¾N	7¾E	31
Donnelly's Crossing, N.I., N.Z.	35¾s	173¾E	62
Donnybrook, Natal.	30s	29¾E	55
Donnybrook, W. Aust.	33½s	116E	61
Donor's Hills, Aust.	18s	141E	60
Doon L., Scotland.	55¼N	4½W	25
Doon, R., Scotland.	55½N	4¾W	25
Doore I., W. Australia.	25¼s	114E	61
Dora Baltea Riv., Italy.	45¼N	8E	31
D'Orange, C., Brazil.	5N	51W	78
Doringdraai, C. Pr.	32¾s	23¾E	53
Dora Riparia R., Italy.	45¼N	7¾E	31
Dorchester, England.	50¾N	2½W	22
DORDOGNE & R., Fr.	44¾N	1E	32
Dordrecht, C. Pr., S.Af.	31½s	27E	53
Dordrecht, Nether.	51¾N	4½E	30
Dorel, China.	41N	87E	39
Dore, Mt., France.	45¾N	2¾E	32
Dores, Scotland.	57½N	4¼W	24
Dori, Pakistan.	31N	66¼E	43
Doring R., C. Pr., S. Afr.	31¾s	18½E	52
Dorisvale, N.Terr., Aust.	14s	131½E	60
Dorking, England.	51¼N	¼W	23
Dormans, France.	49N	3½E	30
Dornbirn, Austria.	47½N	9¾E	33
Dornoch, Scotland.	57¾N	4W	24
Dornoch Firth, Scot.	58N	3¾W	24
Dornum, Germany.	53½N	7½E	30
Dorohoi, Romania.	48N	26½E	37
Dorothea, L., W. Aust.	26½s	123E	61
Dorrigo, N.S.W., Aust.	30½s	152¾E	59
DORSET, England.	50¾N	2½W	22
Dorsten, Ger. (inset).	51¾N	7E	33
Dortmund, Germany.	51½N	7½E	33
Dortmund-Ems Canal, Germany.	52¼N	7¼E	30
Dossor, U.S.S.R.	47½N	53E	38
Dothan, Alaska, U.S.A.	31¼N	85½W	75
Douai, France.	50¼N	3E	30
Double Cone Mt., N.Z.	45s	168¾E	63
DOUBS, France.	47N	6½E	32
Doubs, R., France.	47¼N	6½E	32
Doubtful Bay, W. Aust.	33¾s	119E	61
Doubtful Sd., S.I., N.Z.	45¼s	166¾E	63
Doubtless B., N.I., N.Z.	35s	173½E	62
Doucet, Quebec, Can.	48¼N	76½W	69
Doudeville, France.	49¾N	¾E	31
Doue, France.	47¼N	¼W	31
Douglas, C. Pr., S. Afr.	29s	23¾E	53
Douglas, Ariz., U.S.A.	31½N	109½W	74
Douglas, I. of Man.	54¼N	4½W	25
Dougrie, Scotland.	55½N	5½W	25
Doulus B. & Hd., Ire.	52N	10½W	26
Doume, Cameroon.	4½N	13½E	56
Doune, Scotland.	56¼N	4W	25
Douro, R., Portugal.	41¼N	7¾W	35
Dove, R., England.	52¾N	1¾W	23
Dover Pt., W. Aust.	32½s	126E	61
Dover & Straits, Eng.	51¼N	1¼E	23
Dover, Del., U.S.A.	39¼N	75½W	75
Dover, O.F.S., S. Africa.	27s	27¾E	55
Dover, Tas., Aust.	43¼s	147E	59
Dovey, R., Wales.	52½N	3¾W	22
Dowa, Malawi.	13½s	34E	56
Dow, L., Botswana.	22s	25E	51
DOWN, N. Ireland.	54¼N	6W	26
Downham Market, England.	52½N	½E	23
Downpatrick, N. Ire.	54¼N	5¾W	26
Downpatrick Hd., Ire.	54¼N	9½W	26

Place	Lat.	Long.	No.
Downs, North, *Eng.*	51¼N	¼E	23
Downs, South, *Eng.*	50¼N	¼W	23
Drac R., *France.*	45N	6E	31
Dragasani, *Romania.*	44¼N	24¼E	37
Draghoender, *C. Pr.*	29¼s	22E	52
Dragon's Mths., *Venez.*	11N	62W	77
Draguignan, *France.*	43¼N	6¼E	32
Drakensberg Mts.,*S.Af.*	24¼s	30E	54
Drama, *Greece.*	41¼N	24¼E	37
Drammen, *Norway.*	59¼N	10¼E	29
Draperstown, *Ireland.*	54¼N	6¼W	25
Dras, *Kashmir* (inset).	34¼N	75¼E	44
Drava, R.,*Yugoslavia.*	46¼N	14E	37
Drawa, R., *Poland.*	54¼N	15¼E	33
Drenovo, *Bulgaria.*	43N	25¼E	37
Drensteinfurt, *Ger.*	51¼N	7¼E	33
Drenthe, *Holland.*	52¼N	6¼E	30
Dresden, *Germany.*	51N	13¼E	30
Dresden, *Ontario, Can.*	42¼N	82¼W	68
Dresvyanka, *U.S.S.R.*	68N	55E	38
Dreunberg, *Cape Pr.*	31s	26¼E	52
Dreux, *France.*	48¼N	1¼E	32
Drew, *C. Pr., S. Africa.*	34s	20¼E	52
Drin, R., *Albania.*	41¼N	19¼E	37
Drina, R., *Yugoslavia.*	45N	19¼E	37
Drnis, *Yugoslavia.*	43¼N	16¼E	37
Drogheda & B., *Eire.*	53¼N	6¼W	26
Drohobycz, *U.S.S.R.*	49¼N	23¼E	38
Droitwich, *England.*	52¼N	2¼W	22
Dromcolliher, *Ireland.*	52¼N	8¼W	26
DROME, *France.*	44¼N	5E	33
Dronfield, *England.*	53¼N	1¼W	23
Droogegrond, *C. Pr.*	29¼s	20¼E	52
Drozdovka, *U.S.S.R.*	68N	38E	29
Drug, *India.*	21N	81¼E	44
Drumheller, *Alb., Can.*	51¼N	112¼W	73
Drumlish, *Ireland.*	53¾N	7¾W	26
Drummondy,*Que.,Can.*	45¼N	72¼W	69
Drummore, *Scotland.*	54¾N	4¾W	25
Drumnadrochit, *Scot.*	57¼N	4¼W	24
Drumquin, *Ireland.*	54¼N	7¼W	26
Drury, *N.I., N.Z.*	(inset A).		62
Drweca R., *Poland.*	53N	19E	33
Dryden, *Ontario, Can.*	49¼N	92¼W	71
Dry, L., *Queens., Aust.*	25s	140E	60
Dry, R., *N. Terr., Aust.*	14s	131¼E	60
Drygalski I., *Antarc.*	65¼s	92¼E	80
Drymen, *Scotland.*	56N	4¼W	25
Drysdale &R., *W. Aust.*	14s	126¼E	61
Duala, *Cameroon.*	4N	9¼E	56
Duaringa, *Queens.,Aust.*	23¼s	149¼E	60
Dubawnt, L. & R., *Can.*	64N	102W	66
Dublin & Bay, *Eire.*	53¼N	6¼W	26
Dubno, *U.S.S.R.*	51N	26E	38
Dubois, *Penn., U.S.A.*	41¼N	78¼W	69
Dubovka, *U.S.S.R.*	48¼N	45E	38
Dubrovitsa, *U.S.S.R.*	51¼N	26¼E	38
Dubrovnik, *Yugo.*	42¼N	18E	37
Dubuc, *Sask., Canada.*	50¼N	102¼W	70
Dubuque, *Iowa, U.S.A.*	42¼N	90¼W	75
Duchess, *Queens., Aust.*	21¼s	140E	60
Ducie I., *S. Pacific.*	24¼s	125W	18
Duck Lake, *Sask., Can.*	52¼N	106¼W	70
Duckponds, *W.H., Aust.*	19s	131¼E	60
Duddington, *England.*	52¼N	¼W	23
Dudinka, *U.S.S.R.*	69¼N	86¼E	39
Dudley, *England.*	52¼N	2W	22
Dudypta, R., *U.S.S.R.*	70N	85E	39
Duff Is., *Pacific.*	10s	166E	64
Dufftown, *Scotland.*	57¼N	3¼W	24
Dufile, *Uganda.*	3¼N	32E	56
Dugi Otok Is., *Yugo.*	44N	15E	36
Duida, Mt., *Venezuela.*	4N	66W	78
Duifken Pt., *Queens.*	11¼s	142E	60
Duisburg-Hamborn, *Germany.*	51¼N	6¼E	33
Duiwelskloof, *T'vaal.*	23¼s	30¼E	54
Dukati, *Albania.*	40¼N	19¼E	37
Dulce, G. of, *Costa Rica.*	9N	83¼W	77
Dulgalakh R.,*U.S.S.R.*	69N	135¼E	39
Dullstroom, *Transvaal.*	25¼s	30E	54
Duluth, *Minn., U.S.A.*	46¼N	92¼W	75
Dulverton, *England.*	51N	3¼W	22
Dumaguete, *Phil. Is.*	9¼N	123¼E	47
Dumaresq R., *Queens.*	28¼s	150¼E	59
Dumbarton, *Scotland.*	56N	4¼W	25
Dumbleyung, *W. Aust.*	33¼s	117¼E	61
Dumfries, *Scotland.*	55¼N	3¼W	25
DUMFRIES, *Scotland.*	55¼N	3¼W	25
Dumka, *India.*	24¼N	87¼E	44
Dummer See, *Ger.*	52¼N	8¼E	30
Dun, *France.*	49¼N	5¼E	30
Dunaff Head, *Ireland.*	55¼N	7¼W	26
Dunafoldvar, *Hung.*	46¼N	19E	37
Dunajec, R., *Poland.*	50¼N	21E	33
Dunan, *Scotland.*	57¼N	6W	24
Dunany Pt., *Eire.*	53¼N	6¼W	26
Dunback, *S.I., N.Z.*	45¼s	170¼E	63
Dunbar, *Scotland.*	56N	2¼W	25
DUNBARTON, *Scotland.*	56N	4¼W	25
Dunbeath, *Scotland.*	58¼N	3¼W	24
Dunblane, *Sask., Can.*	51¼N	107W	70
Dunblane, *Scotland.*	56N	3¼W	25
Dunboyne, *Eire.*	53¼N	6¼W	26
Duncan, *Okla., U.S.A.*	34¼N	98W	74
Duncansby Hd., *Scot.*	58¼N	3W	24
Dundalk & Bay, *Eire.*	54N	6¼W	26
Dundas & L., *W. Aust.*	32¼s	121¼E	61
Dundas Str., *N. Terr.*	11¼s	131¼E	60
Dundee, *Natal, S. Afr.*	28¼s	30¼E	55
Dundee, *Scotland.*	56¼N	3W	25
Dundrum & B., *N. Ire.*	54¼N	5¼W	26
Dundurn, *Sask., Can.*	51¼N	106¼W	70
Duneannon, *Eire.*	52¼N	7W	26
Dunedin, *C. Pr., S. Afr.*	32s	22¼E	52
Dunedin, *S.I., N.Z.*	46s	170¼E	63
Dunfermline, *Scotland.*	56N	3¼W	25
Dungannon, *N. Ire.*	54¼N	6¼W	26
Dungarvan, *Eire.*	52N	7¼W	26
Dungarvan Harb., *Ire.*	52N	7¼W	26
Dungeness, *England.*	51N	1E	23
Dungiven, *Ireland.*	54¼N	7W	25
Dungloe, *Ireland.*	55N	8¼W	26
Dungog, *N.S.W., Aust.*	32¼s	151¼E	59
Dungunab, *Sudan.*	22N	37E	40
Dunkeld, *Scotland.*	56¼N	3¼W	25
Dunkery Beacon, *Eng.*	51¼N	3¼W	22
Dunkirk, *France.*	51N	2¼E	32
Dunkwa, *Ghana.*	6N	1¼W	57
Dun Laoghaire, *Ire.*	53¼N	6¼W	26
Dunlavin, *Ireland.*	53N	6¼W	26
Dunleer, *Ireland.*	53¼N	6¼W	25
Dun Manus B., *Ireland.*	51¼N	9¼W	26
Dunmanway, *Ireland.*	51¼N	9W	26
Dunmore, *Ireland.*	53¼N	8¼W	26
Dunnet Hd., *Scotland.*	58¼N	3¼W	24
Dunns Riv., *Jamaica.*	18¼N	77¼W	77
Dunnville, *Ont., Can.*	43N	79¼W	68
Dunolly, *Vict., Aust.*	36¼s	143¼E	59
Dunoon, *Scotland.*	56N	5W	25
Duns, *Scotland.*	55¼N	2¼W	25
Dunstable, *England.*	51¼N	¼W	23
Dunster, *England.*	51¼N	3¼W	22
Dunvegan, *Alb., Can.*	56N	118¼W	66
Dunvegan, *Scotland.*	57¼N	6¼W	24
Dunvegan Hd., *Scot.*	57¼N	6¼W	24
Durack Ra., Mts., *W. Aust.* (inset).	17s	128E	61
Durack, Riv., *W. Aust.*	16s	129E	61
Durance, R., *France.*	44¼N	6E	31
Durango, *Col., U.S.A.*	37¼N	107¼W	74
DURANGO, *Mexico.*	24N	104¼W	76
Durango, *Spain.*	43¼N	2¼W	35
Duras, *France.*	44¼N	¼E	32
Durazno, *Uruguay.*	33¼s	56¼W	79
Durazzo, *Albania.*	41¼N	19¼E	37
Durban, *Natal.*	29¼s	31E	55
Durbanville, *C. Pr.*	33¼s	18¼E	52
Durbuy, *Belgium.*	50¼N	5¼E	30
Duren, *Germany.*	50¼N	6¼E	33
Durgapur, *India.*	23¼N	87¼E	44
Durge Nur, L., *Mong.*	48N	93E	39
Durham & Tn., *Eng.*	54¼N	1¼W	25
DURHAM, *N.C., U.S.A.*	36N	78¼W	75
Durlach, *Germany.*	49N	8¼E	30
Durness, *Scotland.*	58¼N	4¼W	24
Durrow, *Ireland.*	52¼N	7¼W	26
Durrus Ross, *Ireland.*	51¼N	9¼W	26
Dursey I., *Ireland.*	51¼N	10¼W	26
Dursley, *England.*	51¼N	2¼W	22
Dursunbey, *Turkey.*	39¼N	28¼E	37
Durtal, *France.*	47¼N	1W	31
D'Urville, C., *New Guin.*	2s	137¼E	47
D'Urville I., *S.I., N.Z.*	40¼s	174E	63
Dushambe, *U.S.S.R.*	38N	69E	39
Dusseldorf, *Germany.*	51¼N	6¼E	33
Duwadami, *Saudi Arabia.*	24¼N	44E	40
Dvina R. &G.,*U.S.S.R.*	64¼N	42E	38
Dwaal, *C. Pr., S. Afr.*	31s	24¼E	53
Dwarka, *India.*	22¼N	69E	46
Dwars Berg, *T'vaal.*	22¼s	28¼E	54
Dwyka, *C. Pr., S. Afr.*	33s	21¼E	52
Dyer, C., *N.W. Canada.*	67N	60W	66
Dyersburg, *Tenn., U.S.A.*	36N	89¼W	75
Dyke, L., *Newfound-land, Can.* (inset).	54¼N	66W	67
Dysart, *Scotland.*	56¼N	3¼W	24
Dzamyn Ude, *Mong.*	43N	111E	39
Dzaoudzi, *Comoro Is.* (inset).	12¼s	45¼E	56
Dzepa, *Yugoslavia.*	42¼N	22E	37
Dzerzhinsk, *U.S.S.R.*	56¼N	43¼E	38
Dzhambeity, *U.S.S.R.*	50N	52¼E	38
Dzhambul, *U.S.S.R.*	43N	71¼E	39
Dzhankoi, *U.S.S.R.*	46N	34E	38
Dzhardhan, *U.S.S.R.*	68¼N	124E	39
Dzhetygara, *U.S.S.R.*	52N	61E	39
Dzhusaly, *U.S.S.R.*	46N	63E	39
Dzialdowo, *Poland.*	53¼N	20¼E	33
Dzungaria, *China.*	45N	83E	39
EAGLE, *Alaska, U.S.A.*	65N	142W	74
Eagle Pass, *Tex., U.S.A.*	29N	100W	74
Eagle Vulture, *Rhod.*	21s	29E	54
Ealing, *England.*	51¼N	¼W	23
Eardisley, *Wales.*	52¼N	3W	22
Earl Grey, *Sask., Can.*	51N	104¼W	70
Earlston, *Scotland.*	55¼N	2¼W	25
Earn, L., *Scotland.*	56¼N	4¼W	25
Easingwold, *England.*	54¼N	1¼W	25
Easky, *Ireland.*	54¼N	9W	26
East Alligator R., *Aust.*	12s	132¼E	60
East Beskid Mts., *Poland-Czecho.*	49¼N	22E	33
East Head, *S.I., N.Z.* (inset C).			63
Eastbourne, *England.*	50¼N	¼E	23
Eastbourne, *N.I., N.Z.*	41¼s	174¼E	62
East Cape, *N.I., N.Z.*	37¼s	178¼E	62
East China Sea, *Asia.*	30N	125E	48
East Dereham, *Eng.*	52¼N	1E	23
East End, *Sask., Can.*	49¼N	108¼W	70
EAST FLANDERS, *Belg.*	51N	3¼E	30
Easter I., *Pacific.*	27s	110W	18
East Grinstead, *Eng.*	51¼N	0	23
East Harling, *Eng.*	52¼N	1E	23
East Ilsley, *England.*	51¼N	1¼W	23
East Kilbride, *Scot.*	55¼N	4W	25
Eastleigh, *England.*	51N	1¼W	23
East Linton, *Scotland.*	56N	2¼W	25
East London, *C. Pr.*	33s	28E	53
East Looe, *England.*	50¼N	4¼W	23
EAST LOTHIAN, *Scot.*	56N	2¼W	24
Eastmain & R., *Quebec.*	52¼N	78¼W	66
EAST MALAYSIA, *S.E. Asia.*	4N	114E	47
Eastpoort, *C. Pr., S.Afr.*	32¼s	26E	53
East Retford, *England.*	53¼N	2W	23
East Riding, *England.*	54N	2W	23
East Siberian S., *U.S.S.R.*	73N	160E	39
East St. Louis, *Ill., U.S.*	38N	90W	75
Eau Claire, *Wis., U.S.A.*	44¼N	91¼W	75
Ebbw Vale, *Wales.*	51¼N	3¼W	22
Ebenrode, *U.S.S.R.*	54¼N	22¼E	33
Eberswalde, *Germany.*	52¼N	13¼E	33
Ebi Nor, L., *China.*	46N	83E	39
Ebinoyon, *Rio Muni.*	1N	10¼E	57
Eboli, *Italy.*	40¼N	15E	36
Ebolowa, *Cameroon.*	3N	12E	56
El Banco, *Colombia.*	9N	74¼W	77
El Barcat, *Libya.*	24N	11E	50
Ebon I., *Pacific.*	5N	168E	64
Ecclefechan, *Scotland.*	55N	3¼W	25
Eccles, *England.*	53¼N	2¼W	22
Eccleshall, *England.*	52¼N	2¼W	22
Echt, *Scotland.*	57¼N	2¼W	24
Echternach, *Luxem.*	49¼N	6¼E	30
Echuca, *Vict., Aust.*	36s	144¼E	59
Eckford, *Scotland.*	55¼N	2¼W	25
Ecommoy, *France.*	47¼N	0	31
Ecouche, *France.*	48¼N	0	31
ECUADOR, *S. America.*	2s	77W	78
Edah, *W. Australia.*	28s	117¼E	61
Edam, *Sask., Canada.*	53¼N	108¼W	70
Eday, I., *Scotland.*	59¼N	2¼W	24
Ed Damer, *Sudan.*	17¼N	34E	50
Edderton, *Scotland.*	57¼N	4¼W	24
Eddrachillis B., *Scot.*	58¼N	5¼W	24
Ed Dueim, *Sudan.*	14¼N	32E	56
Eddystone L'house, *England.*	50¼N	4¼W	27
Eddystone Pt., *Aust.*	41s	148¼E	59
Ede, *Netherlands.*	52N	5¼E	30
Ede, *Nigeria.*	7¼N	4¼E	57
Edea, *Cameroon.*	4N	10E	56
Edeback, *Sweden.*	60N	14E	29
Edel Land, *W. Aust.*	26s	114E	61
Eden, *N.S.W., Aust.*	37s	150E	59
Eden, R., *England.*	54¼N	2¼W	25
Edenbridge, *England.*	51¼N	¼E	23
Edenburg, *O.F.S.*	29¼s	26E	55
Edenderry, *Eire.*	53¼N	7W	26
Edenville, *O.F.S.,S.Afr.*	27¼s	27¼E	55
Edeowie, *S. Aust.*	31¼s	138¼E	59
Eder, Riv., *Germany.*	51N	9¼E	33
Eder, Riv., *Mongolia.*	49N	102E	39
Edgewood, *Canada.*	49¼N	118¼W	73
Edhessa, *Greece.*	40¼N	22E	37
Edievale, *S.I., N.Z.*	45¼s	169¼E	63
Edinburgh, *Scotland.*	56N	3¼W	24
Edirne, *Turkey.*	41¼N	26¼E	37
Edith Ronne Land, *Ant.*	81s	45W	80
Edithburgh, *S. Aust.*	35s	137¼E	59
Edjudina, *W. Aust.*	29¼s	123E	61
Edmonton, *Alb., Can.*	53¼N	113¼W	73
Edmundston, *Canada.*	47¼N	68¼W	67
Edolo, *Italy.*	46¼N	10¼E	31
Edremit & G., *Turkey.*	39¼N	27E	37
Edri, *Libya.*	27N	13¼E	34
Edsel Ford Ranges, *Antarctica.*	78s	145W	80
Edson, *Alberta, Can.*	53¼N	116¼W	73
Edward Creek, *S. Aust.*	28¼s	135¼E	60
Edward, L., *Uganda.*	¼s	29¼E	56
Edward, Riv., *Aust.*	14¼s	141¼E	60
Edzell, *Scotland.*	56¼N	2¼W	24
Eecloo, *Belgium.*	51¼N	3¼E	30
Eendekuil, *C. Pr.,S.Afr.*	32¼s	19E	52
Eensgevonden, *O.F.S.*	28¼s	26¼E	53
Efate I., *N.Heb., Pacif.*	17¼s	168¼E	64
Egbe, *Nigeria.*	8¼N	5¼E	57
Egea, *Spain.*	42N	1¼W	35
Eger, *Czechoslovakia.*	50N	12¼E	33
Eger, Riv., *Czecho.*	50¼N	14E	33
Eger, *Hungary.*	48N	20¼E	37
Egersund, *Norway.*	58¼N	6E	29
Egerton, Mt., *W. Aust.*	25s	117¼E	61
Eggan, *Nigeria.*	8¼N	6¼E	57
Eggiwil, *Switzerland.*	47N	7¼E	31
Egham, *England.*	51¼N	¼W	23
Eglinton I., *N.W. Can.*	74N	120W	66
Egmont, C., *N.I., N.Z.*	39¼s	173¼E	62
Egmont, Mt., *N.I., N.Z.*	39¼s	174E	62
Egremont, *England.*	54¼N	3¼W	25
Egridir, *Turkey.*	37¼N	30¼E	41
Egton, *England.*	54¼N	¼W	25
Egyn, Riv., *Mongolia.*	49N	103E	39
EGYPT, see UNITED ARAB REPUBLIC			
Ehrenbreitstein, *Ger.*	50¼N	7¼E	30
Eiao I., *Pacific.*	9s	141W	64
Eidsvold, *Queens., Aust.*	25¼s	151¼E	60
EIFEL, *Germany.*	50N	7E	30
Eigg I., *Scotland.*	56¼N	6¼W	24
Eights Coast, *Antarc.*	73s	93W	80
Eighty Mile Beach, *W. Aust.* (inset).	20s	120E	61
Eil, Loch, *Scotland.*	56¼N	5¼W	24
Eilenburg, *Germany.*	51¼N	12¼E	33
Einasleigh, *Australia.*	18¼s	144E	60
Eindhoven, *Netherlands.*	51¼N	5¼E	30
Einsiedeln, *Switz.*	47¼N	8¼E	31
Eisenach, *Germany.*	51N	10¼E	33
Eisenerz, *Austria.*	47¼N	15E	33
Eisenstadt, *Austria.*	47¼N	16¼E	33
Eisk, *U.S.S.R.*	46¼N	38¼E	38
Eisleben, *Germany.*	51¼N	11¼E	33
Eitorf *Germany.*	50¼N	7¼E	30
Ejszyszki, *U.S.S.R.*	54¼N	25E	33
Ejutla De Crespo, *Mex.*	16¼N	97W	76
Eket, *Nigeria.*	4¼N	8E	57
Eketahuna, *N.I., N.Z.*	40¼s	175¼E	62
Ekimchan, *U.S.S.R.*	54N	133E	39
Ekwan Riv., *Ont., Can.*	51¼N	82W	66
Elafos, I. of, *Greece.*	36¼N	23E	37
El Ageila, *Libya.*	30N	19¼E	34
El-Asham, *Algeria.*	36N	1¼E	35
El Alamein, *U.A.R.*	30¼N	29E	41
El Alamo, *Mexico.*	31N	116¼W	76
El Amiriya, *U.A.R.* (ins.)	31N	30E	50
Elandshoek, *T'vaal.*	25¼s	30¼E	54
Elandslaagte, *Natal.*	28¼s	30E	55
Elandsvlei, *Cape Pr.*	32¼s	19¼E	52
El Arish, *U.A.R.*	31¼N	34E	41
El Asnam, *Algeria.*	36¼N	1¼E	35
Elayu, *Somali Rep.*	11N	48¼E	41
Elazig, *Turkey.*	38¼N	39¼E	41
Elba, I., *Italy.*	42¼N	10¼E	36
Elbasan, *Albania.*	41N	20E	37
El Bauga, *Sudan.*	18N	33¼E	40
El Bawiti, *U.A.R.*	27¼N	28¼E	41
El Bayadh, *Algeria.*	33¼N	1E	35
Elbe, R., *Germany.*	53¼N	9¼E	33
Elberfeld, see WUPPERTAL			
Elbert, Mt., *Col., U.S.A.*	39N	108W	74
Elbeuf, *France.*	49¼N	¼E	31
Elblag, *Poland.*	54¼N	19¼E	33
Elbow, *Sask., Canada.*	51¼N	106¼W	70
El Brega, *Libya.*	30¼N	20E	34
Elbrus, Mt., *U.S.S.R.*	43¼N	42¼E	38
El Bur, *Somali Rep.*	5N	46E	56
Elburg, *Netherlands.*	52¼N	5¼E	30
Elburz Mts., *Iran.*	36N	52E	41
El Cardon, *Venezuela.*	12N	70W	77
El Carmen, *Colombia.*	10N	75W	77
El Carre, *Ethiopia.*	5¼N	42E	56
El Chaparro, *Venez.*	9N	65W	77
Elche, *Spain.*	38¼N	¼w	35
El Daba, *U.A.R.*	31N	28¼E	41
Elde, Riv., *Germany.*	53¼N	11¼E	33
Elderslie, *Queens., Aust.*	22¼s	142¼E	60
El Dlingat, *U.A.R.*	31N	30¼E	50
El Dorado, *Ark., U.S.A.*	33N	93W	75
Eldorado, *Mexico.*	24N	107¼W	76
Eldorado, *Venezuela.*	7N	62W	77
Eldoret, *Kenya.*	¼N	35¼E	56
Electric Pk., *Mont., U.S.*	45N	111W	74
Elena, *Italy.*	41¼N	13¼E	36
Elephant I., *Antarc.*	61¼s	55W	80
Elephant Pass, *Ceylon.*	9¼N	80¼E	43
Elephant, Riv., *S.W.Afr.*	26s	19E	51
Eleuthera I., *Bahamas.*	25¼N	76¼W	77
El Erg, *Libya.*	29N	21¼E	34
Elevsis, *Greece.*	38N	23¼E	37
El Faiyum, *U.A.R.*	29N	31E	41
El Fasher, *Sudan.*	13¼N	25¼E	50
El Fuerte, *Mexico.*	26¼N	108¼W	76
El Fugha, *Libya.*	28N	17E	34
El Gallo, *Nicaragua.*	12¼N	84¼W	77
El Geddahia, *Libya.*	32N	15E	34
El Geneina, *Sudan.*	13¼N	22¼E	56
El Geria Esh Shergia, *Libya.*	30¼N	13¼E	34
Elgin, *Illinois, U.S.A.*	42N	88W	75
ELGIN, *Scotland.*	57¼N	3¼W	24
El Giof, *Libya.*	24N	23E	50
El Giza, *U.A.R.*	30N	31¼E	41
El Golea, *Algeria.*	30¼N	3E	34
Elgol, *Scotland.*	57¼N	6W	24
Elgon, Mt., *Uganda.*	1¼N	34¼E	56
El Guapo, *Venezuela.*	10N	66W	77
El Hammam, *U.A.R.*	30¼N	29¼E	41
Elhovo, *Bulgaria.*	42¼N	26¼E	37
Elie, *Scotland.*	56¼N	2¼W	24
Elim, *C. Pr., S. Africa.*	34¼s	19¼E	52
Elisabethville, see LUBUMBASHI.			
Elista, *U.S.S.R.*	46N	44E	38
Elizabeth, *U.S.* (ins.).	40¼N	74¼W	75
Elk, *Poland.*	53¼N	22¼E	33
El Kharga, *U.A.R.*	25¼N	30¼E	40
Elkhart, *Ind., U.S.A.*	41¼N	86W	68
Elkhorn, *Man., Can.*	50N	101¼W	70
Elk Lake, *Ont., Can.*	47¼N	80¼W	68
Elko, *Br. Col., Can.*	49¼N	115¼W	73
Elko, *Nevada, U.S.A.*	40¼N	115¼W	74
El Kuneitra, *Syria* (ins.).	33¼N	35¼E	40
Ella Valla, *W. Aust.*	25s	114¼E	61
Elleker, *W. Aust.*	35s	117¼E	61
Ellendale, *N.Dak.,U.S.A.*	46N	99W	74
Ellerton, *T'vaal, S.Afr.*	23¼s	30¼E	54
Ellesmere, *England.*	52¼N	2¼W	22
Ellesmere, *S.I., N.Z.*	(inset C).		63
Ellesmere I., *N.W. Can.*	78N	81W	66
Ellesmere, *S.I., N.Z.*	44¼s	172¼E	63
Ellesmere Port, *Eng.*	53¼N	3W	22
Ellice Is., *Pacific.*	8s	178¼E	18
Elliot, *C. Pr., S. Africa.*	31¼s	27¼E	53
Elliot Dale, *Cape Pr.*	32¼s	28¼E	53
Ellis, *Idaho, U.S.A.*	44¼N	114¼W	74
Ellon, *Scotland.*	57¼N	2W	24
Ellsworth Highland, *Antarctica.*	75s	105W	80
Ellwangen, *Germany.*	49N	10¼E	33
Elma, *Manitoba, Can.*	49¼N	95¼W	71
El Manteco, *Venezuela.*	7¼N	63W	77
El Mansura, *U.A.R.*	31N	31¼E	41
El Masta, *U.A.R.* (ins.)	29N	31¼E	50
El Medano, *Canary Is.*	28N	16¼W	35
El Mekili, *Libya.*	32N	22E	34
El Mene, *Venezuela.*	11N	71W	77
Elmina, *Ghana.*	5N	1¼W	57
El Minya, *U.A.R.*	28N	30¼E	41

[102] Elmira—Fiera

Place	Lat.	Long.	No.
Elmira, Ontario, Can.	43¾N	80½W	68
Elmira, N.Y., U.S.A.	42N	76¾W	69
Elmira, Pr. Ed. I., Can.	46½N	62W	67
El Morrito, Nicaragua.	11½N	85W	77
Elmshorn, Germany.	53¾N	9¾E	33
El Obeid, Sudan.	13¼N	30¼E	56
El Oued, Algeria.	33½N	7E	35
El Paso, Mexico.	32N	106½W	76
Elphin, Ireland.	53¾N	8¼W	26
El Qantra, U.A.R. (ins.).	31N	32½E	50
El Qasr, U.A.R.	26N	28E	40
El Qattara, U.A.R.	30¾N	27E	41
Elrose, Sask., Canada.	51¼N	108W	70
El Sauce, Nicaragua.	13N	86½W	77
Elsey Dns., N. Terr.	15S	134E	60
Eltham, N.I., N.Z.	39½S	174¼E	62
El Tigre, Venezuela.	8½N	64W	77
Elton, U.S.S.R.	48½N	46½E	38
El Tocuyo, Venezuela.	10N	70W	77
Eluru, India.	16¾N	81¼E	45
El Valle, Colombia.	5¾N	77W	77
Elvas, Portugal.	39N	7W	35
Elven, France.	47¾N	2¼W	31
Elverum, Norway.	60¼N	11½E	29
Elvire, Mt., W. Aust.	22S	117E	61
Elvo, Riv., Italy.	45¼N	8¾E	31
El Wak, Kenya.	3N	41E	56
El Wejh, Saudi Arabia.	26½N	36½E	40
Ely, England.	52¼N	¼E	23
Ely, Nevada, U.S.A.	39¼N	114¾W	74
Elyria, Ohio, U.S.A.	41¼N	82W	68
El Zapote, Mexico.	17N	98W	76
Emba & R., U.S.S.R.	47N	56E	38
Embrun, France.	44½N	6½E	31
Emden, Germany.	53½N	7¼E	33
Emerald, Queens., Aust.	23½S	148E	60
Emerson, Man., Can.	49N	97W	71
EMILIA-ROMAGNA, Italy.	44½N	10½E	31
Emine, C., Bulgaria.	42¾N	28E	37
Emman, Riv., Sweden.	57N	17E	29
Emmaville, N.S.W.	29½S	151½E	59
Emmen, Netherlands.	52¾N	7E	29
Emmerich, Germany.	51¾N	6¼E	30
Emmet, Queens., Aust.	24½S	144E	60
Empoli, Italy.	43¾N	11E	36
Emporia, Kan., U.S.A.	38N	96½W	75
Empress, Alberta, Can.	51N	110W	73
Ems, R., Germany.	53N	7¼E	30
Ems Dollart, R., Neth.	53¼N	7E	30
Emseleni, Natal (ins.).	27½S	32½E	54
Ems-Jade Canal, Ger.	53¼N	7½E	30
Emu Park, Queensland.	23¼S	150¾E	60
Enard Bay, Scotland.	58¼N	5¼W	24
Enchi, Ghana.	6N	3W	57
Encinillas, Mexico.	29¼N	106¼W	76
Encontrados, Venez.	9N	72½W	77
Encounter B., S. Aust.	35¾S	138¾E	59
Endau, Malaysia (inset).	2½N	103½E	47
Endako, Br. Col., Can.	54N	125W	72
Ende, Indonesia.	9S	122E	47
Endeavour Str., Queens.	10½S	142E	60
Enderbury I., Pacific.	2S	171W	64
Enderby, Br. Col., Can.	50½N	119W	72
Enderby Ld., Antarc.	66½S	51½E	80
Enez, Turkey.	40¾N	26E	41
Enfidaville, Tunisia.	36¼N	10¼E	35
Enfield, Eire.	53½N	6¾W	22
Enfield, England.	51¾N	0	25
Engadine, Switz.	46¾N	10E	31
Engano, C., Dom. Rep.	18N	68W	77
Engano, C., Luzon, P.I.	18½N	122¼E	47
Engcobo, C. Pr., S.Afr.	31¾S	28E	53
Engedi, Jordan (inset).	31½N	35¼E	40
Engelberg, Switz.	46¾N	8½E	31
Engels, U.S.S.R.	51¾N	46¼E	38
Engen, Germany.	47¾N	8¾E	30
Enggano I., Sumatra.	5½S	102¼E	47
Enghien, Belgium.	50¾N	4E	30
Englehart, Ont., Can.	47¾N	79¾W	68
English Bazar, India.	25N	88E	44
English Channel.	50N	0W	23
English, Riv., Ont. Can.	50½N	94W	71
Enid, Oklahoma, U.S.A.	36½N	97¾W	74
Eniwetok I., Pacific.	11N	161E	64
Enkeldoorn, Rhodesia.	19S	31E	51
Enkhuizen, Nether.	52¾N	5E	30
Enna, Sicily.	37½N	14¼E	36
En Nagura, Leb. (ins.).	33¼N	35¼E	40
En Nahad, Sudan.	12½N	26½E	56
Ennepe R., Ger. (ins.).	50½N	7½E	33
En Nofuia, Libya.	31N	18E	34
Ennerdale, England.	54½N	3¼W	25
Ennersdale, Natal.	29S	29¾E	55
Enngonia, N.S.W.	29¼S	145¾E	59
Ennis, Ireland.	52¾N	9W	26
Enniscorthy, Ireland.	52½N	6½W	26
Enniskerry, Ireland.	53¼N	6¼W	26
Enniskillen, N. Ire.	54¼N	7¾W	26
Enns & Riv., Austria.	48¼N	14½E	33
Enos, see ENEZ.			
Enontekis, Finland.	68N	23E	29
Enschede, Nether.	52¼N	6¾E	30
Ensenada, Mexico.	32N	117W	76
Enshih, China.	30¼N	109½E	48
Entebbe, Uganda.	0	32½E	56
Entre Rios, Argentina.	31S	60W	79
Entreves, Italy.	45¾N	7E	31
Enugu, Nigeria.	6½N	7½E	57
Enza, Riv., Italy.	45N	10¼E	36
Epanomi, Greece.	40½N	23E	37
Epernay, France.	49¼N	4E	32
Epi I., Pacific.	18S	169E	64
Epinal, France.	48¼N	6¾E	32
Epping, England.	51¾N	¼E	23
Epsom, England.	51¼N	¼W	23
Epworth, England.	53¾N	¾W	23
Erandique, Honduras.	14½N	88½W	76
Erasmia, T'vaal, S.Afr.	25¾S	28¾E	55
Erbil, Iraq.	36¼N	44E	41
Erciyas Dagi, Mt., Turkey.	38½N	35½E	41
Erdek & G. of, Turkey.	40½N	27½E	37
Erdre, R., France.	47¼N	1½W	31
Erebus, Mt., Antarc.	77½S	167E	80
Eregli, Turkey.	41N	28E	41
Eregli, Turkey.	41¼N	31½E	41
Erenkoy, Turkey.	40N	26½E	37
Erentsab, Mongolia.	50N	116E	39
Eresmia, Riv., Spain.	41½N	5W	35
Eresos, Mytilene I., Gr.	39N	26E	41
Erevan, U.S.S.R.	40¼N	44½E	38
Erft, Riv., Germany.	51¼N	6¾E	30
Erfurt, Germany.	51N	11E	33
Ergene, Riv., Turkey.	41N	26E	41
Erquy, France.	48½N	2½W	31
Eriboll & L., Scotland.	58½N	4½W	24
Ericht, Loch, Scotland.	56¾N	4¼W	24
Erie, Penn., U.S.A.	42¼N	80W	75
Erie, L., U.S.A.-Can.	42¼N	82W	69
Erigavo, Somali Rep.	10½N	47½E	56
Erimo, C., Japan.	42N	143E	49
Eriskay I., Scotland.	57N	7¼W	24
Erisort, Loch, Scot.	58¼N	6½W	24
Erith, England.	51½N	¼E	23
Erkelenz, Germany.	51N	6¼E	30
Erkrath, Germany. (inset).	50¾N	6¾E	33
Erlangen, Germany.	49½N	11E	33
Erlistoun, W. Aust.	28S	122½E	61
Ermelo, T'vaal, S. Afr.	26½S	30E	55
Erne, L., N. Ireland.	54½N	7¾W	26
Erne, R., N. Ireland.	54½N	8W	26
Ernee, France.	48¼N	1W	31
Ernest Giles Ra., Aust.	27S	124E	61
Eromanga, Queens.	26¾S	143¼E	60
Eromanga I., Pacific.	18¾S	169¼E	64
Errigal, Mt., Ireland.	55N	8¼W	26
Erris Head, Ireland.	54¼N	10W	26
Errogie, Scotland.	57¼N	4½W	24
Erstein, France.	48½N	7½E	30
Ervy, France.	48N	4E	30
Erz Mts., Ger.-Czecho.	50½N	13E	33
Erzincan, Turkey.	39¾N	39½E	41
Erzurum, Turkey.	39¾N	41¼E	41
Esashi, Japan.	45N	143E	49
Esbjerg, Denmark.	55½N	8½E	33
Escalon, Mexico.	26¾N	104¼W	76
Escalona, Spain.	40N	4½W	35
Escanaba, Mich., U.S.A.	45¾N	87W	68
Escaut R., France.	50¼N	3¼E	30
Esch-s-Alzette, Lux.	49½N	6¼E	30
Eschweiler, Germany.	50¾N	6¼E	30
Escorial, Spain.	40½N	4W	35
Escuinapa, Mexico.	22¾N	105¾W	76
Esha Ness, Scotland.	60½N	1½W	24
Eshowe, Natal.	28¾S	31½E	55
Esk, R., Scotland.	55N	3W	25
Eskilstuna, Sweden.	59½N	16¾E	29
Eskimo, C., Can. (ins.).	59N	94W	71
Eskisehir, Turkey.	39¾N	30½E	41
Esla, Riv., Spain.	41½N	6W	35
Esmeraldas, Ecuador.	1N	79¾W	78
Espalion, France.	44½N	2¾E	32
Espanola, Ont., Can.	46¼N	81¾W	68
Esperance B., W. Aust.	33¾S	122E	61
Esperanza, La, Cuba.	22½N	84W	77
Esperanza, La, Hond.	14N	88W	77
Espichel, C., Portugal.	38¼N	9W	35
ESPIRITO SANTO, Brazil.	20S	40½W	79
Espiritu Santo I., Pac.	15½S	167E	64
Es Salt, Jordan (inset).	32N	35½E	40
Essen, Germany.	52¾N	8E	30
Essendon, Mt., W. Aust.	25S	121E	61
Essequibo, Riv., Guy.	7N	58W	78
ESSEX, England.	51¾N	½E	23
Essex, Ontario, Can.	42¼N	82¾W	68
Esslingen, Germany.	48¾N	9¼E	33
Es Sukhne, Syria.	35N	39E	41
Es Suweida, Syria.	32½N	36½E	41
Estavayer, Switz.	46¾N	7E	31
Estcourt, Natal.	29S	30E	55
Este, Italy.	45¼N	11¾E	31
Estella, Spain.	42½N	2W	35
Estepona, Spain.	36½N	5W	35
Esterhazy, Sask., Can.	50¾N	102W	70
Esternay, France.	48¾N	3½E	30
Estevan Is., Br. Col.	53N	129½W	72
Estevan, Sask., Can.	49¼N	103W	70
Eston, Sask., Canada.	51¼N	108¾W	70
Eston, England.	54½N	1¼W	25
ESTONIA, U.S.S.R.	58N	25E	38
ESTREMADURA, Spain.	38¾N	7W	35
Estremoz, Portugal.	39N	7¾W	35
Etain, France.	49¼N	5½E	30
Etampes, France.	48½N	2¼E	30
Etaples, France.	50½N	1¾E	30
Etawah, India.	26¾N	79E	44
Ethel Riv., W. Aust.	24S	118E	61
ETHIOPIA, N.E. Africa.	10N	40E	56
Etive, Loch, Scotland.	56½N	5¼W	25
Etna, Mt., Sicily.	37¾N	15E	36
Eton, England.	51½N	¾W	23
Eton, Queens., Aust.	21½S	149E	60
Etosha Pan, S.W. Afr.	19S	16½E	51
Etretat, France.	49¾N	0	31
Ettellbruck, Lux.	49¾N	6E	30
Ettenheim, Germany.	48¼N	7¾E	30
Ettrick, R., Scotland.	55½N	3W	25
Ettrick, W. Australia.	20¾S	120E	61
Eu, France.	50N	1½E	30
Euabalong, N.S.W.	33S	146½E	59
Eua I., Pacific.	21S	177W	64
Euboea I., Greece.	38½N	23¾E	37
Eucla, W. Australia.	31¾S	129E	58
Eugene, Oregon, U.S.A.	44N	124W	74
Euglo, N.S.W., Aust.	33½S	147¼E	59
Eugowra, N.S.W., Aust.	33½S	148½E	59
Eulo, Queens., Aust.	28¼S	145E	60
Eupen, Belgium.	50¾N	6E	30
Euphrates R., Iraq-Syr.	35¼N	40E	41
EURE, France.	49N	1E	32
EURE ET LOIRE, France.	48½N	1½E	32
Eureka, Calif., U.S.A.	40¾N	124W	74
Eureka, Nevada, U.S.A.	39½N	116W	74
Euroa, Victoria, Aust.	36¾S	145½E	59
Euskirchen, Germany.	50½N	6¾E	30
Euston, N.S.W., Aust.	34½S	142¾E	59
Eutin, Germany.	54N	10¾E	33
Eva Dns. N. Terr., Aust.	18S	134¾E	60
Evandale, Tas., Aust.	41½S	147¼E	59
Evanston, Wyo., U.S.A.	41¾N	111W	74
Evansville, Ind., U.S.A.	37N	87½W	75
Evanton, Scotland.	57½N	4½W	24
Evaton, T'vaal, S. Afr.	26½S	28E	55
Everard, C., Vict., Aust.	37¾S	149½E	59
Everest, Mt., Nepal Tibet.	28N	87E	43
Everett, Wash., U.S.A.	48N	122¼W	74
Everglades, The, U.S.A.	26½N	80¾W	75
Evesham, England.	52¼N	2W	23
Evian, France.	46¼N	6½E	31
Evie, Scotland.	59N	3¼W	24
Evolene, Switzerland.	46¼N	7½E	31
Evora, Portugal.	38¾N	8W	35
Evran, France.	48½N	2W	31
Evreux, France.	49N	1¼E	31
Evron, France.	48¼N	½W	31
Evrotus Riv., Greece.	36¾N	23E	37
Evvoia, G. of, Greece.	38¾N	23E	37
Ewe, Loch, Scotland.	57¾N	5¾W	24
Ewell, England.	51½N	1¼E	23
Excelsior, O.F.S., S. Afr.	29S	27E	55
Exe, R., England.	50¾N	3½W	22
Exeter, England.	50¾N	3½W	22
Exeter, Ontario, Can.	43½N	81½W	68
Exmoor, England.	51¼N	3¾W	22
Exmouth, England.	50½N	3½W	22
Exmouth G., W. Aust.	22½S	114E	61
Exuma Sd., Bahamas.	24N	76W	77
Eyasi, L., Tanzania.	3½S	35E	56
Eye, England.	52½N	1¼E	23
Eyebrow, Sask., Can.	51N	106¼W	70
Eyemouth, Scotland.	55¾N	2¼W	25
Eye Penin., Scotland.	58¼N	6¼W	24
Eynhallow Sd., Scot.	59N	3W	24
Eynort, Loch, Scot.	57¼N	7¼W	24
Eyre, W. Australia.	32¼S	126¼E	58
Eyre Creek, Queens.	25S	138E	60
Eyre, L., S. Australia.	28½S	137¼E	58
Eyre Mts., S.I., N.Z.	45¼S	168½E	63
Eyre Penin., S. Aust.	33S	136E	59
Ezine, Turkey.	39½N	26½E	37
FABRIANO, Italy.	43½N	13E	36
Facatativ, Colombia.	5N	74¾W	77
Faddeyevsky I., U.S.S.R.	74N	143E	39
Faemunden, L., Nor.	62N	12E	29
Faenza, Italy.	44¼N	11¾E	36
Faeroes, The, Europe.	62N	7W	28
Fafan Riv., Ethiopia.	5½N	45E	56
Fagaras, Romania.	45½N	25E	37
Fahsien, China.	23½N	113E	48
Faial I., Azores (inset).	38¾N	28½W	35
Fairbanks, Alaska, U.S.	64¾N	148½W	74
Fairford, England.	51¾N	1¾W	23
Fair Head, N. Ireland.	55¼N	6¼W	22
Fair Isle, Scotland.	59½N	1½W	24
Fairlie, S.I., N.Z.	44S	170¾E	63
Fairview, Alb., Can.	56¼N	118¼W	73
Fairview, Queens., Aust.	15½S	144¼E	60
Fairweather, Mt., U.S.	59N	139W	74
Faith, S. Dak., U.S.A.	45N	102W	74
Faizabad, Afghanistan.	37N	70E	43
Faizabad, India.	26¾N	82E	44
Fajr, Saudi Arabia.	28½N	37½E	41
Fakaofu I., Pacific.	10S	171W	64
Fakarara I., Pacific.	17S	145W	64
Fakenham, England.	52¾N	¾E	23
Fakfak, N. Guinea, E.I.	3S	133E	47
Fal, R., England.	50¼N	5W	22
Falaba, S. Leone (ins.).	9¾N	11¼W	57
Falaise, France.	48¾N	¼W	31
Falam, Burma.	23N	93¾E	43
Falciu, Romania.	46½N	28E	37
Falkenberg, Sweden.	57N	12½E	29
Falkirk, Scotland.	56N	3¾W	25
Falkland Is., S. Amer.	51S	59¾W	78
Fall R., Mass., U.S.A.	41¾N	71W	69
Falmouth, England.	50¼N	5W	22
Falmouth, Jamaica.	18½N	77¾W	77
False Bay, C.Pr., S.Afr.	34¼S	18¾E	51
Falster, Denmark.	55N	12E	33
Falsterbo, Sweden.	55½N	13E	29
Falun, Sweden.	61N	16E	29
Famagusta, Cyprus.	35¼N	34E	41
Fanad Head, Ireland.	55¼N	7¾W	26
Fangahina I., Pacific.	15S	140W	64
Fangak, Sudan.	9¾N	31E	56
Fangataufa I., Pacific.	21S	139W	64
Fannich, Loch, Scot.	57¾N	4¾W	24
Fanning I., Pacific.	4¼N	159¾W	18
Fano, Italy.	43¾N	13E	36
Fanuch, Iran.	26½N	60E	40
Fao, Iraq.	30N	48½E	41
Faradje, Congo (K.).	3¾N	29¾E	56
Farafra Oasis, U.A.R.	26½N	28E	41
Farah & R., Afghan.	32½N	62¼E	43
Faraja, Saudi Arabia.	22N	51E	40
Farallon de Pajaros, I., Pacific.	20N	145E	64
Farasan Is., Saudi Arabia.	17N	42E	40
Faraulep I., Pacific.	9N	140E	64
Fareham, England.	50¾N	1¼W	23
Farewell, C., Green.	59¾N	43¾W	66
Farewell, C., S.I., N.Z.	40½S	172¾E	63
Fargo, N. Dak., U.S.A.	47N	96¾W	75
Faridkot, India.	30½N	74½E	44
Faridput, E. Pak. (ins.).	23¾N	89¾E	46
Farim, Port. Guinea.	12½N	15W	57
Farimun, Iran.	35½N	60E	40
Farina, S. Australia.	30S	138¼E	59
Faringdon, England.	51¾N	1½W	23
Farleigh, Queens., Aust.	21½S	149½E	60
Farmington, U.S.A.	37N	108¼W	74
Farnborough, Eng.	51¼N	¾W	23
Farne Is., England.	55¾N	1½W	25
Farnham, England.	51¼N	¾W	23
Farnham, Quebec, Can.	45¼N	73W	69
Farnworth, England.	53½N	2½W	22
Faro, Portugal.	37N	8W	35
Faro I., Sweden.	58N	20E	29
Faro, Riv., Cameroon.	9N	13E	56
Farquhar, C., W. Aust.	24S	114E	61
Farrar Creek, Queens.	25S	141E	60
Farrar, R., Scotland.	57½N	5W	24
Farrukhabad, India.	27½N	79½E	44
Farsala, Greece.	39¼N	22½E	37
Farsund, Norway.	58N	6¾E	29
Fasano, Italy.	40¾N	17½E	37
Fastnet Rock, Eire.	51½N	9½W	26
Fastov, U.S.S.R.	50N	30E	38
Fatehpur, India.	26N	80¾E	44
Fatsing, China.	26N	120E	48
Fatuhiva I., Pacific.	10S	139W	64
Faure I., W. Australia.	25½S	114E	61
Fauresmith, O.F.S.	29¾S	25¼E	55
Faverges, France.	45½N	6¼E	31
Faverney R., France.	48N	6E	30
Faversham, England.	51¼N	¾E	23
Favignana I., Sicily.	38N	12½E	36
Fawcett, Alb., Can.	54½N	114¼W	73
Fawn, I., Ont., Can.	53N	90W	66
Faya, Chad.	18N	19E	50
Fayetteville, N.C., U.S.	35N	78¾W	75
Fayetteville, Ark., U.S.A.	36N	94W	75
Fayid, U.A.R. (inset).	30½N	32½E	50
Fearn, Scotland.	57¾N	3¾W	24
Featherston, N.I., N.Z.	41S	175¼E	62
Fecamp, France.	49¾N	½E	31
Fehmarn, I. of, Ger.	54½N	11E	33
Feilding, N.I., N.Z.	40¼S	175½E	62
Felanitx, Majorca.	39½N	3E	35
Feldbach, Austria.	47N	15¾E	33
Feldberg, Mt., Ger.	47¾N	8E	30
Feldkirch, Austria.	47¼N	10E	33
Felixstowe, England.	52N	1¼E	23
Felletin, France.	45¾N	2¼E	32
Feltre, Italy.	46N	11¾E	31
Fenelon Falls, Ontario.	44½N	78¾W	69
Fenestrelle, Italy.	45N	7E	31
Fenghsien, China.	35N	116E	48
Fenghwang, China.	28N	110E	48
Fengkieh, China.	31¼N	109½E	48
Fengning, China.	42N	117E	48
Fengsiang, China.	34½N	107½E	49
Feni Is., Pacific (inset).	4S	154E	60
Fenit, Ireland.	52¼N	9¾W	26
Fenny Stratford, Eng.	52N	¾W	23
Fens, The, England.	52¾N	½E	23
Fenyang, China.	37½N	111E	48
Feodosiya, U.S.S.R.	45N	35½E	38
Feolin, Scotland.	55¾N	6W	25
Ferbane, Ireland.	53¼N	8W	26
Fere-Champenoise, Fr.	48¾N	4E	30
Ferfer, Somali Rep.	5N	45E	56
Fergana, U.S.S.R.	40½N	71¾E	39
Fergus, Ontario, Can.	43¾N	80¼W	68
Fergusson I., Pac. (ins.).	9S	151E	60
Feriana, Tunisia.	35N	8½E	35
FERMANAGH, N. Ire.	54¼N	7½W	23
Fermo, Italy.	43¼N	13¾E	36
Fermoy, Eire.	52¼N	8¼W	26
Fernan Vaz, Gabon.	1½S	9E	56
Fernando De Noronha Is., Brazil.	4S	33W	78
Fernando Po, Africa.	3½N	8¾E	57
Fernie, Br. Col., Can.	49½N	115W	73
Fernley, Nev., U.S.A.	39½N	119¼W	74
Ferns, Eire.	52½N	6½W	22
Ferozepore, India.	31N	74¾E	44
Ferrai, Greece.	41N	26½E	37
Ferrara, Italy.	44¾N	11¾E	36
Ferrat, C., Algeria.	36N	¼W	35
Ferrette, France.	47½N	7¼E	31
Ferrycarrig, Eire.	52¼N	6½W	26
Fetesti, Romania.	45N	27E	38
Fethaland, Pt. of, Scot.	61N	1¼W	24
Fethiye, Turkey.	37N	28½E	41
Fetlar I., Scotland (ins.).	60½N	1W	24
Fettercairn, Scotland.	56¾N	2½W	24
Fez, Morocco.	34N	5W	35
Fianarantsoa, Malagasy.	22S	47E	56
Fianga, Cent. Afr. Rep.	10N	15E	56
Fichtel Mts., Germany.	50N	11½E	33
Fidenza, Italy.	44¾N	10E	31
Field, Br. Col., Can.	51½N	116½W	73
Fier, Albania.	40¾N	19½E	37
Fier, R., France.	46¼N	6¼E	31
Fiera Di Primiero, It.	46¼N	11¾E	31

Fife—Galveston [103]

Place	Lat.	Long.	No.
FIFE, Scotland.	56¼N	3W	24
Fife Ness, Scotland.	56¼N	2½W	25
Figeac, France.	44¾N	2E	32
Figueras, Spain.	42¼N	2¾E	35
Figueiria da Foz, Port.	40N	9W	35
Figuig, Morocco.	32N	1¼W	35
FIJI ISLANDS, Pacific.	17½S	179E	64
Filabusi, Rhodesia.	20½S	29¼E	51
Filey, England.	54¼N	¼W	25
Filiasi, Romania.	44½N	23½E	37
Filiatra, Greece.	37N	21½E	37
Filicudi I., Mediterran.	38½N	14¾E	36
Filisur, Switzerland.	46½N	9¾E	31
Fillmore, Sask., Can.	49¾N	103½W	70
Finale, Italy.	44¾N	11¼E	31
Findhorn, Scotland.	57¾N	3½W	24
Fingal, Tas., Aust. (ins.).	41¾S	148E	59
Fingwe, Mozambique.	15S	32E	31
Finike, Turkey.	36¼N	30¼E	40
FINISTERE, France.	48¼N	4W	31
Finisterre, C., Spain.	43N	9¼W	35
Finke, The, Riv., Aust.	26S	135E	60
FINLAND. Europe.	63N	25E	29
Finland, G. of, Balt. S.	60N	26E	29
Finlay R., Br. Col., Can.	56¼N	124W	66
FINMARK, Norway.	69N	22E	29
Finn, R., Eire.	54¾N	7¾W	26
Finsteraarhorn, Mt., Switzerland.	46½N	8¼E	31
Finstown, Scotland.	59N	3W	24
Fintona, Ireland.	54½N	7½W	26
Fiordland, S.I., N.Z.	45½S	167E	63
Florenzuola d'Arda, It.	45N	9½E	31
Firdaus, Iran.	34N	58E	40
Firuzabad, Iran.	29N	53E	40
Fish Riv., C. Pr., S. Afr.	32S	25¼E	53
Fisher Bay, Man., Can.	51½N	97¼W	71
Fisher Str., N.W. Can.	63½N	85W	66
Fishguard, Wales.	52N	5W	22
Fishwater, C.Pr., S.Afr.	31¾S	18¼E	52
Fismes, France.	49¼N	3¾E	30
Fitchburg, Mass., U.S.	42½N	71¾W	69
Fitful Head, Scotland.	60N	1½W	24
Fitzroy, W. Aust. (ins.).	18S	126E	61
Fitzroy Riv., Queens.	23½S	151E	60
Fitzroy, R., W. Aust.	17½S	123½E	58
Fiume, Yugoslavia.	45½N	14¼E	37
Flagstaff, Ariz., U.S.A.	35N	112W	74
Flagstaff, C.Pr., S.Afr.	31S	29½E	53
Flamboin, France.	48½N	3¼E	30
Flamborough Hd., Eng.	54¼N	0	23
Flanders, Belgium.	51N	3½E	30
Flathead, L., Mont., U.S.	47¾N	114¼W	74
Flattery, C., Queens.	15S	145½E	60
Flattery, C., Wash., U.S.	48¼N	124¾W	74
Fleetwood, England.	53¾N	3W	25
Flekkefiord, Norway.	58¼N	6E	29
Fleming, Sask., Can.	50N	101½W	70
Flensburg, Germany.	54½N	9E	33
Flers, France.	48¾N	½W	31
Flesa, Libya.	28½N	14E	34
Fleurus, Belgium.	50½N	4½E	30
Fleury, France.	49¼N	1¼E	31
Flinders Bay, W. Aust.	34¼S	115E	61
Flinders I., Tas., Aust.	40S	148E	59
Flinders Ra., S. Aust.	32S	138E	58
Flinders Reef, Aust.	17½S	148E	60
Flinders Riv., Queens.	20½S	141E	60
Flinflon, Man., Can.	54¾N	101¾W	70
Flint, Mich., U.S.A.	43N	83¾W	75
Flint I., Pacific.	11S	151W	64
FLINT, & T., Wales.	53¼N	3¼W	22
Flize, France.	49¾N	4¾E	30
Flora Reef, Australia.	17S	148E	60
Florence, Ala., U.S.A.	34¾N	87¾W	75
Florence, Italy.	43¾N	11¼E	36
Florence, S.Car., U.S.A.	34¼N	79¾W	75
Florencia, Colombia.	1½N	77W	78
Florennes, Belgium.	50¼N	4½E	30
Flores I., Azores (ins.).	39¾N	31W	35
Flores I., Br. Col., Can.	49¼N	126W	72
Flores I., Indonesia.	8½S	121E	47
Flores Sea, E. Indies.	7S	123E	47
Floresti, U.S.S.R.	48N	28½E	37
Florianopolis, Brazil.	27½S	48¼W	79
Florida, Can. Is. (ins.).	28¼N	14W	35
Florida City, Fla., U.S.	26N	81W	77
FLORIDA, U.S.A.	27½N	82W	75
Florida, Uruguay.	34¼S	56¼W	79
Florida Keys, Fla., U.S.	24¾N	81W	75
Florina, Greece.	41N	21E	37
Florina, N. Terr., Aust.	14S	132E	60
Floro I., Norway.	61¾N	5E	29
Flumendosa R., Sard.	39¼N	9¼E	36
Flushing, Nether.	51½N	3½E	30
Fly, R., N. Guinea (ins.).	8½S	143½E	60
Foam Lake, Sask., Can.	51¾N	103½W	70
Foca, Turkey.	38½N	26¾E	37
Foca, Yugoslavia.	43½N	19E	37
Fochabers, Scotland.	57¾N	3¼W	24
Fochville, T'vaal, S. Afr.	26½S	27½E	55
Foel, Wales.	52½N	3¾W	22
Foesani, Romania.	46N	27E	38
Foggia, Italy.	41½N	15½E	36
Foinaven, Mt., Scot.	58½N	4¾W	24
Foix, France.	43N	1½E	32
FOIX, France (inset).	42¾N	2E	32
Folden Fiord, Norway.	64N	11¾E	29
Folden Fiord, Norway.	68N	15½E	26
Foligno, Italy.	43N	12¾E	36
Folkestone, England.	51¼N	1¼E	23
Follonica, Italy.	43N	10¾E	36
Fond du Lac, Wis., U.S.	43¾N	88½W	75
Fondi, Italy.	41¼N	13¼E	36
Fondo, Italy.	46½N	11E	31
Fontainebleau, Fr.	48¼N	2¾E	30
Fontenay le Comte, Fr	46½N	¾W	32
Foochow, China.	26N	119E	48
Forbach, France.	49¼N	6¾E	30
Forbes, N.S.W. Aust.	33½S	148E	55
Forbes Reet, Swazi.	26½S	31¼E	59
Forcados, Nigeria.	5¼N	5½E	57
Forcalquier, France.	43¾N	5¾E	32
Forchheim, Germany.	49¾N	11E	33
Fordingbridge, Eng.	50¾N	1¾W	23
Forelands, The, Eng.	51½N	1½E	23
Forest, Ontario, Can.	43¼N	82W	68
Forest of Dean, Eng.	51¾N	2½W	22
Forestburg, Alb., Can.	52¾N	112W	73
Forestier Pen., Aust.	43S	148E	59
Forfar, Scotland.	56¾N	2¾W	24
Forges-les-Eaux, Fr.	49½N	1½E	31
Forget, Sask., Can.	49¾N	102¾W	70
Forli, Italy.	44¼N	12E	36
Formby, England.	53½N	3W	22
Formentera I., Spain.	38¾N	1½E	35
Formerie, France.	49¾N	1¾E	31
Formosa, Argentina.	26¼S	58W	79
FORMOSA, China.	23½N	121E	48
Formosa B., Tanzania.	2½S	40E	56
Formosa Strait, China.	24½N	119½E	48
Fornova di Toro, Italy.	44¾N	10E	31
Forres, Scotland.	57½N	3½W	24
Forrest, Vict. Aust.	38½S	143¾E	59
Forrest River, W. Aust.	15S	128E	61
Forsayth, Queens., Aust.	18½S	143½E	60
Forsinard, Scotland.	58¼N	4W	24
Forst, Germany.	51¾N	14¾E	33
Forsyth Is., Queens.	16½S	138E	60
Forsyth, L., S.I., N.Z.	(inset C).		63
Forsyth, Mon., U.S.A.	47N	106¾W	74
Fort Albany, Ont. (ins.).	52¼N	81¾W	71
Fortaleza, Brazil.	3¾S	38¾W	79
Fort Archambault, Cent. Afr. Rep.	9¼N	18½E	56
Fort Assiniboine, Can.	54¼N	114¾W	73
Fort Augustus, Scot.	57¼N	4¾W	24
Fort Beaufort, C. Pr.	32¾S	26¾E	53
Fort Bragg, Cal., U.S.A.	39¾N	124W	74
Fort Brown, C. Pr.	33¼S	26½E	53
Fort Crampel, C.Afr.Rep.	7N	19½E	56
Fort Dauphin, Malag.	25S	47E	56
Fort de France, Martinique.	14½N	61W	77
Fort de Posel, C.Afr.Rep.	5N	19E	56
Fort Dodge, Ia., U.S.A.	42½N	94¼W	75
Fort Edward, T'vaal.	23¼S	30E	54
Fortescue & R., W. Aust.	21S	116E	61
Fortezza, Italy.	46¾N	11½E	31
Fort Flatters, Algeria.	28N	7E	34
Fort Frances, Ont., Can.	48¾N	93¼W	71
Fort Fraser, Br. Col.	54N	124½W	72
Fort George, Canada.	53¾N	78¾W	66
Fort George, Scotland.	57½N	4W	24
Fort Henrique Couceiro, S.W. Africa (inset).	17½S	15E	51
Forth, Firth of, Scot.	56N	3W	25
Forth, R., Scotland.	56¼N	4½W	25
Fort Hertz, Burma.	27¼N	97½E	43
Fort Jameson. see CHIPATA.			
Fort Johnston, Malawi.	14½S	35¼E	51
Fort Lallemand, Alg.	31½N	6½E	34
Fort Lamy, Chad.	12¼N	15E	56
Fort Lauderdale, U.S.	26¼N	80¼W	75
Fort Manning. see MCHINJI.			
Fort Matachewan, Can.	48N	80¾W	68
Fort Miribel. Algeria.	29½N	3E	34
Fort Morgan, U.S.A.	40N	104W	74
Fort Munro, Pakistan.	30N	70E	46
Fort Myers, Fla., U.S.A.	27N	82W	75
Fort Nelson, Br. Col.	58¾N	122½W	66
Fort Peck, Mon., U.S.A	48N	106½W	74
Fort Polignac, Algeria.	27N	8E	34
Fort Portal, Uganda.	¾N	30¼E	56
Fort Qu'Appelle, Sask.	50¾N	103¾W	70
Fort Rosebery. see MANSA.			
Fort Rousset, Congo (B.)	½S	16E	56
Fort Saint, Tunisia.	30N	10E	34
Fort St. James, Br. Col.	54½N	124¼W	72
Fort St. John, Br. Col.	56¼N	120¾W	66
Fort Sandeman, W. Pakistan.	31¼N	69½E	43
Fort Saskatchewan, Alberta, Canada.	53¾N	113W	73
Fort Scott, Kan., U.S.A.	37½N	95W	75
Fort Severn, Ont., Can.	56N	87½W	66
Fort Sibut, C. Afr. Rep.	5¾N	19E	56
Fort Smith, Ark., U.S.A.	35¼N	94¼W	75
Fort Sumner, U.S.A.	34½N	104W	74
Fort Vermilion, Alb.	58¼N	116W	66
Fort Wayne, Ind., U.S.A.	41N	85¼W	75
Fort William, Ontario.	48¼N	89¼W	71
Fort William, Queens.	22½S	140E	60
Fort William, Scot.	56¾N	5¼W	24
Fort Worth, Tex., U.S.	32¾N	97¼W	75
Fort Yukon, Alaska.	66N	145W	74
Fortrose, Scotland.	57½N	4¼W	24
Foshan, China.	23N	113E	48
Fossano, Italy.	44½N	7¾E	31
Fossato Di Vico, Italy.	43¼N	12½E	36
Fosse, Belgium.	50½N	4¾E	30
Fossombrone, Italy.	43¾N	12½E	36
Fougeres, France.	48¼N	1¼W	31
Foula I., Scot. (inset).	60¼N	2¼W	34
Foulwind, C., S.I., N.Z.	41¾S	171½E	26
Foumban, Cameroon.	6N	11E	56
Fountainhall, Scot.	55¾N	3W	25
Fourchu, C. Breton I.	45¾N	60¼W	67
Fouriesburg, O.F.S.	28½S	28E	53
Fourka, Greece.	40N	23½E	37
Fourteen Streams, C.Pr.	28S	24¾E	51
Foveaux Str., S.I., N.Z.	46¾S	168E	63
Foveran, Scotland.	57½N	2W	24
Fow River, China.	30N	106E	48
Fowey, England.	50¼N	4¾W	22
Fowler's Bay, S. Aust.	32S	132½E	58
Fowling, China.	30N	107E	48
Fowning, China.	34N	120E	48
Fowyang, China.	33N	116E	48
Fox Valley, Sask., Can.	50½N	109¼W	70
Foxe Basin, N.W. Can.	68N	78W	66
Foxe Channel, N.W.T.	65N	80W	66
Foxe Pen., N.W. Canada.	65N	77W	66
Foxton, N.I., N.Z.	40½S	175¼E	62
Foxwarren, Man., Can.	50½N	101W	70
Foyers, Scotland.	57¼N	4½W	24
Foyle, L. & R, Ireland.	55¼N	7W	26
Foynes, Ireland.	52½N	9¼W	26
Fraize, France.	48¼N	7E	30
Framlingham, Eng.	52¼N	1¼E	23
Francavilla Fontana, Italy.	40½N	17¾E	36
FRANCE. Europe.	47N	2E	32
Frances, L., Yukon, Can.	61N	129W	66
Franceville, Congo (B.)	1¾S	13½E	56
FRANCHE COMTE, Fr.	47N	6¼E	32
Francistown, Botswana.	21F	27½E	51
Franc's Pk., Wyo., U.S.A.	44N	109½W	74
Franeker, Nether.	53N	5½E	30
Frankenberg, Germany.	51N	9E	30
Frankfield, Jamaica.	18¼N	77½W	77
Frankfort, C.Pr., S.Afr.	32¾S	27½E	53
Frankfort, O.F.S.	27¼S	28½E	55
Frankfort, Ky., U.S.A.	38¼N	85W	75
Frankfurt-on-Main, Ger.	50N	8¾E	33
Frankfurt-on-Oder, Germany.	52¼N	14½E	33
Franklin, C.Pr., S.Afr.	30½S	29½E	53
Franklin B., N.W. Can.	70N	126W	66
Franklin D. Roosevelt L., Wash., U.S.A.	48N	118W	74
Franklin, Pa., U.S.A.	41½N	79¾W	68
Franz, Ontario, Can.	48½N	84½W	68
Franz Josef Land Is., U.S.S.R.	80N	50E	39
Frascati, Italy.	41¾N	13E	36
Fraser I., Queens., Aust.	25¼S	153¼E	60
Fraser, Mt., W. Aust.	26S	118E	61
Fraser Riv., Br. Col.	49N	123W	72
Fraserburg, Cape Pr.	32S	21½E	52
Fraserburg Rd., C. Pr.	32¾S	22E	52
Fraserburgh, Scotland.	57¾N	2W	24
Fraserdale, Ont., Can.	49¾N	81½W	71
Fraser Range, W. Aust.	32¼S	122¾E	61
Fraser R., Br. Col., Can.	50¾N	121½W	65
Frasne, France.	47N	6E	31
Frater, Ontario, Can.	47½N	84½W	68
Frauenfeld, Switz.	47¾N	8¾E	31
Fray Bentos, Uruguay.	33S	58¼W	79
Frazer, Riv., W. Aust.	17S	123E	61
Fred. Hendrik I., N.Guin.	8S	138½E	47
Fredericia, Denmark.	55½N	9½E	33
Fredericton, New Bruns.	46N	66¾W	67
Frederiksdal, Green.	60N	45W	66
Frederikshaab, Green.	62N	50W	66
Frederikshavn, Den.	57½N	10¾E	29
Frederikstad, T'vaal.	26½S	27¼E	55
Fredrikstad, Norway.	59N	11½E	29
Fredriksvaern, Nor.	59N	10E	29
Freetown, Sierra Leone.	8½N	13¼W	57
Fregenal, Spain.	38¼N	6¾W	35
Frehel, C., France.	48¾N	2¼W	31
Freiberg, Germany.	51N	13¼E	33
Freiburg, Germany.	48N	7¾E	33
Freising, Germany.	48¼N	11¾E	33
Frejus, France.	43½N	6¾E	32
Frejus Tunnel, France-Switz.	45¼N	6¾E	31
Fremantle, W. Aust.	32S	115¾E	61
Fremont, Neb., U.S.A.	42N	96½W	75
Fremont Peak, U.S.A.	43¼N	110W	74
French Hoek, C. Pr.	34S	19E	52
French I., Vict., Aust.	38¼S	145½E	59
Frenchpark, Ireland.	53¾N	8½W	26
FRENCH SOMALILAND, see AFARS & ISSAS.			
Freshfield, C., Antarc.	68½S	151¼E	80
Freshwater, I. of W.	50¾N	1½W	23
Fresnillo, Mexico.	23¼N	103W	76
Fresno, Calif., U.S.A.	36¾N	119¾W	74
Freudenburg, Ger.	50¾N	7¼E	30
Frevent, France.	50¼N	2¼E	30
Freycinet, C., W. Aust.	34S	115E	61
Freycinet Pen., Aust.	42¼S	148¼E	59
Freystadt, Austria.	48½N	14½E	33
Frias, Argentina.	28S	65W	79
Fribourg, Switz.	46¾N	7¼E	31
Friedburg, Germany.	50½N	8¾E	30
Friedland, U.S.S.R.	54½N	21E	33
Friedrichshafen, Ger.	47¾N	9½E	33
FRIESLAND, Nether.	53N	5¾E	30
FRIESOYTHE, Germany.	53N	8E	30
Frinton, England.	51¾N	1¼E	23
Friockheim, Scotland.	56¾N	2¾W	24
Frisian Is., Nether.	53¾N	6E	33
FRIULI-VENEZIA GIULIA, Italy	46½N	13E	36
Fro Is., Norway.	64N	8½E	29
Frobisher B., N.W. Can.	62N	66W	66
Frohaket, Norway.	64N	9E	29
Froien I., Norway.	63¾N	8½E	29
Frolovo, U.S.S.R.	49½N	44E	38
Frome, England.	51¼N	2½W	22
Frome, L., S. Aust.	30¾S	139¾E	59
Frome, Riv. S. Aust.	30¾S	137¾E	59
Frosinone, Italy.	41¾N	13¼E	36
Fruges, France.	50½N	2¼E	30
Frunze, U.S.S.R.	42¾N	74½E	39
Fryatt, Ont., Can. (ins.).	49¾N	83½W	71
Fryvaldov, Czecho.	50¼N	17¼E	33
Fuchin, China.	48N	131E	39
Fuchow, China.	28N	116¼E	48
Fudai, Japan.	40N	142E	49
Fuenterrabia, Spain.	43¼N	1¾W	35
Fuerteventura I., Canary Islands.	28½N	14W	35
Fuga I., Luzon, P.I.	19N	121E	47
Fuhsien, China.	39¾N	122E	48
Fuji Yama, Japan.	35¼N	138¾E	49
FUKIEN, China.	26N	118E	49
Fukuchiyama, Japan.	35½N	135E	49
Fukue, Japan	32¾N	128¾E	49
Fukui, Japan.	36N	136¼E	49
Fukuoka, Japan.	33½N	130½E	49
Fukushima, Japan.	37¾N	140½E	49
Fukuyama, Japan.	34½N	133E	49
Fulda, Riv., Germany.	51N	9½E	33
Fulda, Germany.	50½N	9¾E	33
Fumay, France.	50N	4¾E	30
Fumbwe, Ghana.	8¾N	2W	57
Funafuti, Pacific.	9¾S	180E	64
Funchal, Madeira I.	32¾N	17W	35
Fundacion, Colombia.	10½N	74¾W	77
Fundy, B. of, Canada.	45N	66W	66
Funen, Denmark.	55½N	10½E	29
Furnace, Scotland.	56¼N	5¼W	25
Furneaux Grp., Aust.	40¼S	148¼E	59
Furnes, Belgium.	51N	2½E	30
Furstenau, Germany.	52½N	7½E	30
Furstenfeld, Austria.	47N	16E	33
Furth, Germany.	49½N	11E	33
Furu Fiord, Ice. (ins.).	66½N	22W	29
Furukawa, Japan.	38½N	141E	49
Furumbala, C. Afr. Rep.	5N	22E	56
Fury & Hecla Str., N.W. Canada.	70N	84W	66
Fushih, China.	37N	109¾E	48
Fushun, China.	42N	124E	48
Fusin, China.	42N	123E	48
Fussen, Germany.	47¾N	10¾E	33
Fuwa, U.A.R. (inset).	31½N	30½E	50
Fuyu, China.	46N	125E	49
Fyne, L., Scotland.	56N	5¼W	25
Fyvie, Scotland.	57½N	2½W	24
GABELA, Angola.	10¾S	14¼E	56
Gaberones, Botswana.	24½S	25¾E	54
Gabes & G., Tunisia.	33¾N	10¼E	35
GABON, Africa.	1S	12E	56
Gabredarre, Ethiopia.	7N	43¾E	56
Gabrovo, Bulgaria.	42¾N	25¼E	37
Gace, France.	48¾N	¼E	31
Gach-Saran, Iran.	30¼N	51E	40
Gacko, Yugoslavia.	43N	18½E	36
Gadag, India.	15¼N	75¾E	45
Gadsden, Ala., U.S.A.	34N	86W	75
Gaeta, Italy.	41¼N	13½E	36
Gaferut, Pacific.	10N	145E	64
Gafsa, Tunisia.	34½N	8½E	35
Gaghara, R., India.	26N	83E	44
Gagliano, Italy.	39¾N	18½E	36
Gago Kotinyi, Angola.	14½S	21½E	56
Gaillac, France.	43¾N	1¾E	32
Gaillon, France.	49¼N	1¼E	31
Gainab, Riv., S.W. Afr.	28S	19E	51
Gainesville, Fla., U.S.A.	29½N	82½W	75
Gainesville, Ga., U.S.A.	34N	84W	75
Gainsborough, Eng.	53½N	¾W	23
Gainsborough, Sask., C.	49¼N	101½W	70
Gainy, U.S.S.R.	60½N	54E	38
Gairdner Riv., W. Aust.	34½S	119¾F	61
Gairdner, L., S. Aust.	31½S	135¾E	59
Gairloch, Scotland.	57¾N	5¾W	24
Gairlochy, Scotland.	57N	5W	24
Gakuch, Kash. (ins.).	36N	73¾E	44
Galag, Iran.	25½N	59¾E	40
Galana Riv., Tanzania.	3S	40E	56
Galapagos Is., Pacific.	0N	90W	18
Galashiels, Scotland.	55¾N	2¾W	25
Galatina, Italy.	40¼N	18¼E	36
Galatz, Romania.	45½N	28E	37
Galdar, Can. Is. (ins.).	28¼N	15½W	35
Galdhopiggen, Mt., Norway.	61½N	8½E	29
Galeana, Mexico.	24¾N	100W	76
Galesburg, Ill., U.S.A.	41N	90¼W	75
Galgate, England.	54N	2¾W	22
Galich, U.S.S.R.	58½N	42¼E	38
GALICIA, Spain.	42¾N	8W	35
GALILEE, Israel (inset).	33N	35E	40
Galilee, L., Queens.	22½S	14E	60
Galilee, Sea of, Israel.	32¾N	35½E	40
Galisteo, Spain.	40N	6¼W	35
Gallarate, Italy.	45¾N	8¾E	31
Galle, Ceylon.	6N	80¼E	45
Gallego Riv., Spain.	41¾N	1W	35
Gallegos, Argentina.	51¾S	69¼W	78
Galley Head, Eire.	51½N	8¾W	26
Gallipoli, see GELIBOLU.			
Gallipoli, Italy.	40N	18E	36
Gallivare, Sweden.	67¼N	20½E	29
Gallo, C. of, Sicily.	38¼N	13¼E	36
Galloway, Mull of, Scot.	55N	5W	25
Gallup, N. Mex., U.S.A.	36N	108W	74
Galston, Scotland.	55¾N	4½W	25
Galt, Ontario, Canada.	43¼N	80¼W	68
Galtee Mts., Eire.	52¼N	8W	26
Galtur, Austria.	47N	10¼E	31
Galveston, Tex., U.S.A.	29¼N	94¾W	75

Place	Lat.	Long.	No.
Galway Bay, Ireland.	53¼N	9¼W	26
GALWAY & T., Eire.	53¼N	9¼W	26
Gam, Riv., China.	21N	105E	48
Gambaga, Ghana.	10½N	½W	57
Gambela, Ethiopia.	8N	35E	56
GAMBIA, Africa.	13½N	15W	57
Gambier Is., S. Aust.	35½S	136¼E	59
Gamboma, Congo (B.)	2S	16E	56
Gamlakarleby, Fin.	64N	23½E	29
Gamtoos, C.Pr., S.Afr.	34S	25E	53
Gan, Riv., China.	50N	120E	39
Ganale Darya Riv., Eth.	4½N	42E	56
Gananoque, Ont., Can.	44½N	76¼W	69
Gandak, R., India.	26½N	84½E	44
Gander, Newf., Can.	49N	54¼W	67
Gandi, Nigeria.	12½N	5¼E	75
Gandia, Spain.	39N	0	35
Gangaw, Burma.	22½N	94¼E	46
Ganges, R., Ind.-Pak.	22N	89E	44
Gangtok, Sikkim, Ind.	27½N	88¼E	44
Ganjam, India.	19¼N	85E	45
Gans B., C.Pr., S.Afr.	34½S	19¼E	52
Ganyushkino, U.S.S.R.	47N	49E	38
Gao, Mali.	16½N	0	50
Gap, France.	44½N	6E	31
Gara, L., Ireland.	54N	8¼W	26
Garachine, Panama.	8N	78W	77
Garah, N.S.W., Aust.	29S	149½E	59
GARD, France.	44N	4½E	32
Garda, Italy.	45½N	10½E	31
Garda, Lake, Italy.	45½N	10½E	36
Garden City, U.S.A.	38N	100½W	74
Gardez, Afghanistan.	33N	69E	43
Gardner I., Pacific.	26N	169W	64
Gardner I., Pacific.	5S	175W	64
Garelochhead, Scot.	56½N	4¾W	25
Gargano, Mt., Italy.	41¾N	15½E	36
Gargnano, Italy.	45½N	10½E	31
Garian, Libya.	32¼N	13E	34
Garibaldi Park, Br. Col.	50N	123W	72
Garies, C.Pr., S.Afr.	30½S	18E	52
Garissa, Kenya.	1S	40E	56
Garm, U.S.S.R.	39N	70E	38
Garmisch-Parten- kirchen, Germany.	47½N	11E	31
Garoe, Somali Republic.	8N	48E	56
Garonne, R., France.	44½N	0	32
Garoua, Cameroon.	9¼N	13½E	56
Garove I., Pacific (inset).	5S	150E	60
Garron Pt., Ireland.	55N	6W	26
Garry, L., N.W. Can.	67N	100W	66
Garry, L., Scotland.	57N	5W	24
Garstang, England.	53¾N	2¾W	25
Gartok, China.	30N	99E	43
Gartok, Tibet.	31¼N	81E	43
Garvagh, Ireland.	55N	6¾W	26
Garwolin, Poland.	52N	21¼E	33
Gary, Indiana, U.S.A.	41¼N	87¼W	75
GASCONY, France.	44N	0	32
Gascoyne, Mt., W.Aust.	25S	116½E	61
Gascoyne, R., W.Aust.	25S	116½E	61
Gash, Riv., Sudan.	15N	35E	56
Gashaka, Nigeria.	7½N	11½E	56
Gasmata, New Britain, Pacific (inset).	6½S	150E	60
Gaspe & Pen., Canada.	48½N	64¼W	67
Gassino, Italy.	45¼N	7¾E	31
Gassol, Nigeria.	8½N	10½E	57
Gata, C., Cyprus.	34¼N	33E	41
Gata, C. de, Spain.	36¼N	2W	35
Gatehouse, Scotland.	54¾N	4¼W	25
Gateshead, England.	55N	1½W	25
Gatooma, Rhodesia.	18½S	30E	51
Gatton, Queens., Aust.	27½S	152¼E	59
Gaud-i-Zirreh, Afghan.	30N	65E	43
Gauhati, India.	26¼N	91¼E	46
Gavdhos, I. of, Crete.	35N	24E	37
Gavle, Sweden.	60½N	17¼E	29
Gavoi, Sardinia.	40¼N	9E	36
Gavray, France.	49N	1¼W	30
Gawler, S. Australia.	34¼S	138¼E	59
Gaya, Niger.	12N	3½E	57
Gaya, India.	24¼N	85E	44
Gayndah, Queen., Aust.	25½S	151¼E	60
GAZA, Mozambique.	23½S	33E	51
Gaza, U.A.R.	31¼N	34¼E	41
Gaziantep, Turkey.	37N	37¼E	41
Gdansk, Poland.	54½N	19E	29
Gdynia, Poland.	54½N	18½E	33
Geba, Port. Guin.(ins.).	12½N	14¼W	57
Gebeit, Sudan.	21N	36½E	40
Gedaref, Sudan.	14N	35½E	56
Gediz, Riv., Turkey.	38½N	27E	37
Geelong, Vict., Aust.	38½S	144½E	59
Geelvink B., N. Guinea.	3S	135½E	47
Geertruidenberg, Neth.	51½N	5E	30
Geeveston, Tas., Aust.	43½S	147E	59
Geh, Iran.	26N	60E	40
Geidam, Nigeria.	12½N	12E	57
Geita, Tanzania.	3S	32E	56
Gela, Sicily.	37N	14E	36
GELDERLAND, Nether.	52N	6E	30
Geldern, Germany.	51½N	6½E	30
Gelibolu, Turkey.	40½N	26½E	41
Gelligaer, Wales.	51½N	3¼W	22
Gelsenkirchen, Ger.	51½N	7E	33
Gemas, Malaysia (inset).	2½N	102½E	47
Gemunden, Germany.	51N	9E	30
Genadendal, Cape Pr.	34S	19½E	52
Genesee, Idaho, U.S.A.	46½N	117W	74
Genesee, R., N.Y., U.S.	43¼N	77¼W	69
Geneva, Switzerland.	46½N	6½E	31
Geneva, L., Switz.-Fr.	46½N	6½E	31
Genil Riv., Spain.	37¼N	4¼W	35
Gennargentu, Mt., It.	40N	9½E	36
Genoa, Italy.	44¼N	9E	36
Gensan, see WONSAN.			
Geographe B., W.Aust.	33½S	115¼E	61
Geographe Ch., W.Aust.	25S	114E	61
George, C.Pr., S. Africa.	34S	22½E	52
George Riv., Que., Can.	58N	67W	66
George, L., N.S.W.	35S	149¼E	59
George Sd., S.I., N.Z.	44½S	167¼E	63
George Tn., Tas. (inset).	41S	146¼E	59
Georgetown, Guyana.	7N	58W	78
Georgetown, Del., U.S.	38¼N	75¼W	75
Georgetown, Ken., U.S.	38¼N	84¼W	75
Georgetown, Malaysia.	5½N	100¼E	47
Georgetown, Ont., Can.	13¼N	79¾W	68
Georgetown, Pr.Ed.I.	46¼N	62¼W	67
Georgetown, Queens.	18½S	143¼E	60
Georgetown, U.S.A.	33½N	79¼W	75
GEORGIA, U.S.A.	33N	84W	75
GEORGIA, U.S.S.R.	42N	44E	38
Georgia, Str. of, Can.	49¼N	124W	66
Georgian B., Ont., Can.	45¼N	81W	68
Georgida, C.Pr., S.Afr.	33½S	23½E	52
Georgievsk, U.S.S.R.	44N	43½E	38
Georgina Riv., Queens.	23S	139½E	60
Gera, Germany.	50½N	12E	33
Geraldine, S.I., N.Z.	44S	171¼E	63
Geraldine Mine, W.Aus.	27½S	115E	61
Geraldton, W. Aust.	28½S	114¼E	61
Geraldtown, Ont. (ins.).	49¼N	87W	71
Gerdau, T'vaal, S. Afr.	26½S	26E	55
Gerdauen, U.S.S.R.	54¼N	21¼E	33
Gerlogubi, Ethiopia.	6½N	45E	56
GERMANY, Europe.			
Germersheim, Ger.	49¼N	8¼E	30
Germiston, T'vaal.	26¼S	28¼E	55
Gernsheim, Germany.	49½N	8¼E	30
Gerolstein, Germany.	50¼N	6½E	32
Gerona, Spain.	42N	2½E	35
Gerrard, Br. Col., Can.	50½N	117¼W	73
GERS, France.	43½N	½E	32
Gers, R., France.	44½N	½E	32
Gex, France.	46¼N	6E	31
Geysdorp, T'vaal,S.Afr.	26½S	25½E	55
Gezira Canal, Sudan.	14½N	33E	56
Ghadames, Libya.	30¼N	9¼E	34
Ghail, Saudi Arabia.	22½N	46E	40
GHANA, Africa.	6N	1W	50
Ghara, R., see SUTLEJ. R.			
Ghardaia, Algeria.	32½N	3½E	35
Ghat, Libya.	25N	10¼E	50
Ghats, Eastern, India.	16N	80E	45
Ghats, Western, India.	15N	75E	45
Ghazipur, India.	25¼N	83½E	44
Ghazni, Afghanistan.	33½N	68¼E	42
Ghazza R., U.A.R. (ins).31½N		34½E	40
Ghedi, Italy.	45¼N	10¼E	31
Gheel, Belgium.	51¼N	5E	30
Ghent, Belgium.	51¼N	3½E	30
Gherla, Romania.	47N	24E	37
Ghizar, Kashmir (ins.).	36N	73E	44
Ghorband, Afghan.	35N	68E	43
Ghurian, Afghan.	34¼N	61¼E	43
Giado, Libya.	32N	12E	34
Giant's Castle, Mt., Natal.	29¼S	29½E	53
Giant's Causeway, N.Ir.	55¼N	6½W	26
Giarabub, Libya.	30N	25E	34
Giarra, Sicily.	37¼N	15¼E	36
Gibara, Cuba.	21N	76¼W	77
Gibeon, S.W. Africa.	25¼S	17¾E	51
Gibihi, Queens., Aust.	24S	150E	60
Gibraltar & Str., Med.	36¼N	5¼W	35
Gibson Desert, W.Aust.	24¼S	125E	61
Gibson, W. Australia.	33½S	122E	61
Gien, France.	47¼N	2¼E	32
Giessen, Germany.	50½N	8½E	33
Gifford, Scotland.	55½N	2¾W	25
Gifu, Japan.	35½N	136¾E	49
Gigha, I. of, Scotland.	55½N	5¾W	25
Giglio, I., Italy.	42¼N	10¼E	36
Gijon, Spain.	43½N	5½W	35
Gila Bend, Ariz., U.S.A.	33N	113W	74
Gila, R., Ariz., U.S.A.	32¾N	114¼W	74
Gilbert Is., Pacific.	0	175E	64
Gilbert Plains, Canada.	51¼N	100¼W	70
Gilbert Riv., Queens.	18½S	141E	60
Gilberton, Queens., Aust.	19S	143E	60
Giles, L., W. Aust.	29S	120E	61
Gilgai, W. Australia.	31¼S	120E	61
Gilgandra, N.S.W.	31½S	148¼E	59
Gilgil, Tanzania.	1S	36E	56
Gil Gil Riv., N.S.W.	29¼S	148¼E	59
Gilgit & Riv., India.	35¼N	74¼E	44
Gill, L., Ireland.	54¼N	8¼W	26
Gillam, Man., Can.	56¼N	94¾W	71
Gillen, L., W. Aust.	26¼S	125E	61
Gilles, L., S. Aust.	32¼S	136¼E	59
Gillespie Pt., S.I., N.Z.	43½S	169¼E	63
Gillette, Wyo., U.S.A.	44N	105¼W	74
Gilley, France.	47N	6¼E	31
Gilliat, Queens., Aust.	20½S	141¼E	60
Gillingham, England.	51¼N	2½E	23
Gilsland, England.	55N	2¼W	25
Gilyui, Riv., U.S.S.R.	56N	125E	39
Gimli, Manitoba, Can.	50½N	97W	71
Gimembip, Papua (ins.).	6S	141E	60
Gingin, W. Australia.	31½S	115¼E	61
Gingindlovu, Natal.	29S	31¼E	55
Ginir, Ethiopia.	7¼N	40¼E	56
Ginosa, Italy.	40½N	16¼E	31
Ginzo, Spain.	42N	7¼W	35
Gioia, G. of, Italy.	38¼N	15¼E	36
Gioisa Ionica, Italy.	38¼N	16¼E	36
Gioja, Italy.	40½N	17E	36
Gippsland Vict., Aust.	37½S	147½E	56
Giresun, Turkey.	41N	38E	41
Girga, U.A.R.	26¼N	32E	41
Girishk, Afghanistan.	31½N	64¼E	43
GIRONDE & R., France.	45N	1W	32
Girvan, Scotland.	55N	4¾W	25
Gisburn, England.	54N	2¼W	22
Gisors, France.	49¼N	1¾E	30
Giulianova, Italy.	42¼N	14E	36
Giurgiu, Romania.	44N	26E	37
Givet, France.	50¼N	4¾E	32
Gizhiga, U.S.S.R.	62N	160E	39
Glace Bay, C. Breton I.	46¼N	60W	67
Glacier, Br. Col., Can.	51¼N	117¼W	73
Glacier Park, Br. Col.	51¼N	117¼W	73
Gladbeck, Germany.	51¼N	7E	30
Gladstone, Man., Can.	50¼N	99W	71
Gladstone, N.S.W.	31S	153E	59
Gladstone, Queensland.	23¾S	151¼E	60
Gladstone, S., Aust.	33¼S	138¼E	59
Gladstone, W. Aust.	25¼S	114¼E	61
Glamis, Scotland.	56½N	3W	24
Glamoc, Yugoslavia.	44N	17E	37
GLAMORGAN, Wales.	51½N	3¼W	27
Glandorf, Germany.	52¼N	8E	30
Glarus, Switzerland.	47N	9E	31
Glasgow, Scotland.	55¾N	4¼W	25
Glasgow, Mon., U.S.A.	48¼N	106¾W	74
Glas Maol, Mt., Scot.	56¾N	3¼W	24
Glass, R., Scotland.	57¼N	4¾W	24
Glastonbury, Eng.	51¼N	2¾W	22
Glazov, U.S.S.R.	58N	53E	38
Gleichen, Alb., Can.	51N	113W	73
GLEIWITZ, see GLIWICE.			
Glen, O.F.S., S. Africa.	29S	26¼E	55
Glen Affric, Scotland.	57¼N	5W	24
Glen Afton, N.I., N.Z.	37½S	175E	62
Glenarm, Ireland.	55N	5¾E	25
Glenbarr, Scotland.	55½N	5¾W	24
Glencoe, Natal.	28¼S	30¼E	55
Glencoe, Scotland.	56¾N	4¾W	24
Glen Cove, U.S. (ins.).	41N	74W	75
Glendale, Calif., U.S.A.	34N	118¼W	74
Glendive, Mon., U.S.A.	47¼N	104¾W	74
Glenelg, S. Australia.	35S	138¼E	59
Glenelg, Scotland.	57¼N	5¾W	24
Glenelg, R., Vict., Aust.	38S	141E	59
Glenfinnan, Scotland.	56¾N	5¼W	24
Glen Florry, W. Aust.	22¼S	116E	61
Glengad Head, Ire.	55¼N	7W	26
Glengarriff, Eire.	51¾N	9¾W	26
Glen Harry, Cape Pr.	32¼S	24¼E	52
Glenhope, S.I., N.Z.	41¼S	172¾E	63
Glen Innes, N.S.W.	29¼S	151¼E	59
Glenluce, Scotland.	54¼N	4¾W	24
Glenmorgan, Aust.	27S	149¼E	59
Glen Orrin, Scotland.	57¼N	4¾W	24
Glenreagh, N.S.W.	30S	153E	59
Glen Ross, W. Aust.	24S	118E	61
Glenrothes, Scotland.	56¼N	3W	25
Glenroy, W. Aust. (ins.).	17S	126½E	61
Glenthorn, S. Africa.	32½S	26¼E	53
Glenties, Eire.	54¾N	8¼W	26
Glenwood Springs, U.S.	40N	107¼W	74
Gliwice, Poland.	50¼N	18¼E	33
Glogow, Poland.	51¼N	16E	33
Glommen, Riv., Nor.	59N	11¼E	29
Glorenza, Italy.	46½N	10¼E	31
Glossop, England.	53¼N	1¾W	22
GLOUCESTER, England.	51¼N	2¼W	22
Gloucester, U.S.A.	42½N	70¾W	69
Gloucester, Australia.	32S	152E	59
Glubczyce, Poland.	50¼N	17¾E	33
Glubokoe, U.S.S.R.	55N	27E	29
Gluckstadt, Germany.	53¾N	9¼E	30
Glukhov, U.S.S.R.	52N	34E	38
Glynn, Eire.	52¼N	6¾W	22
Gmund, Austria.	48¼N	15E	33
Gmund Spittal, Austria.	47N	13¼E	33
Gmunden, Austria.	48N	13¼E	33
Gniew, Poland.	53¾N	18¼E	33
Gniezno, Poland.	52½N	17¼E	33
Gnowangerup, W.Aust.	34S	118E	61
Goa, India.	15¼N	74E	45
Goalpara, India.	26¼N	90¼E	46
Goaso, Ghana.	6N	2¼W	57
Goat Fell Mt., Scot.	55½N	5¼W	25
Goba, Mozambique.	26S	31¼E	51
Gobabis, S.W. Africa.	22¼S	19E	51
Gobi Desert, Mongolia.	45N	105E	42
Goch, Germany.	51¼N	6¼E	30
Godai, Kashmir (inset).	35N	75E	44
Godalming, England.	51¼N	¾W	23
Godavari, R., India.	16½N	82E	45
Goddard R., W. Aust.	31½S	124E	61
Goderich, Ont., Can.	43¾N	81¾W	68
Goderville, France.	49¼N	¼E	31
Godhavn, Greenland.	69¼N	52¼W	66
Godhra, India.	22¼N	73¼E	44
Godmanchester, Eng.	52¼N	¼W	23
Godstone, England.	51¼N	0	23
Godthaab, Greenland.	62N	53W	80
Godwane R., T'vaal.	25¼S	30¼E	54
Godwin Austen, Mt., India.	35¼N	76¼E	44
Godya, U.S.S.R.	61N	57E	38
Goeree, Netherlands.	51¾N	3¾E	30
Gogra, R., see GAGHARA, R.			
Gogrial, Sudan.	8¼N	28E	56
Goiania, Brazil.	16½S	49W	79
GOIAS, Brazil.	12S	49W	78
Goias, Brazil.	16S	50W	78
Gojome, Japan.	40N	140E	49
Gokwe, Rhodesia.	18S	29E	51
Golchikha, U.S.S.R.	71N	83¼E	39
Golcondda India.	17¼N	78¼E	43
GOLD COAST, see GHANA.			
Goldap, Poland.	54¼N	22¼E	33
Golden, Br. Col., Can.	51¼N	116¾W	73
Golden Bay, S.I., N.Z.	40¼S	172¾E	63
Golden Grove, Costa R.	10N	83¾W	77
Golden Ridge, W. Aust.	31S	122E	61
Golden Vale, Eire.	52¼N	8¼W	26
Golfito, Costa Rica.	9N	83¾W	77
Golfo Aranci, Sardinia.	41N	9½E	36
Gollel, Swaziland.	27¼S	32E	55
Golo, Riv., Corsica.	42¼N	9½E	36
Golodnaya, Steppe, U.S.S.R.	46N	70E	39
Golspie, Scotland.	58N	4W	24
Gombe, Nigeria.	10¼N	11E	75
Gomel, U.S.S.R.	52¼N	31E	38
Gomera I., Canary Is.	28N	17W	35
Gonaives, Haiti.	19N	73W	77
Gonave, I. de la, Haiti.	18¼N	72¼W	77
Gonda, India.	27¼N	82E	44
Gondar, Ethiopia.	12¼N	37¼E	56
Gondrecourt, France.	48½N	5¼E	30
Gongola, Riv., Nigeria.	9½N	12E	57
Goniadz, Poland.	53½N	22¼E	33
Good Hope, N.W. Can.	66¼N	128¼W	66
Goodenough I., Pacific.	9S	151E	60
Goodenough, C., Antarc.	66S	127E	80
Goodeve, Sask., Can.	51½N	103¼W	70
Goodhouse, C.Pr., S.Afr.	29S	18½E	52
Gooding, Idaho, U.S.A.	43N	115W	74
Goodingnow, W. Aust.	29S	118E	61
Goodna, Queens., Aust.	27½S	153E	59
Goodooga, N.S.W.	29¼S	147¼E	59
Goodrich, England.	51¼N	2¾W	22
Goodwick, Wales.	52N	5W	22
Goodwood, England.	50¼N	2W	23
Goole, England.	53¾N	¾W	23
Goomalling, W. Aust.	31¼S	116¾E	61
Goondiwindi, Aust.	28¼S	150¼E	60
Goondoon, Queens.	25S	152E	60
Goongarrie & L., W.Aust.	30S	121¼E	61
Goose Bay, Labrador.	53¼N	60¼W	67
Goose, L., Calif., U.S.A.	42N	120W	74
Goplo, L. of, Poland.	52¼N	18¼E	33
Gora, Poland.	50¼N	16E	33
Goraas, C.Pr., S. Afr.	31¼S	21¼E	52
Gorakhpur, India.	26¼N	83¼E	44
Gorda I., W. Indies.	18N	63W	77
Gordon Downs, Aust.	18S	129E	60
Gordon, R., Tas., Aust.	42¼S	145¼E	59
Gordonvale, Queens.	17S	145¼E	60
Gore, Ethiopia.	8N	35E	56
Gore, S.I., N.Z.	46S	169E	63
Gore Bay, Ont., Can.	46N	82¼W	68
Gorey, Eire.	52¼N	6¼W	26
Gorgoram, Nigeria.	12¼N	10¼E	57
Gori, U.S.S.R.	42N	44E	38
Gorinchem, Nether.	52N	5E	30
Gorizia, Italy.	46N	13¼E	36
Gorkha, Nepal.	28N	84¼E	44
Gorki, U.S.S.R.	56¼N	44E	38
Gorlitz, Germany.	51¼N	15E	33
Gorlovka, U.S.S.R.	48¼N	38E	38
Gorno Altaisk, U.S.S.R.	52N	86E	39
Gorodok, U.S.S.R.	50N	102E	39
Goroke, Vict., Aust.	36¼S	141¼E	59
Gorong Is., Indonesia.	4S	131¼E	47
Gorontalo, Celebes, E.I.	1N	123E	47
Gor. Orehovitsa, Bulg.	43N	25¼E	37
Gort, Ireland.	53¼N	8¾W	26
Gorumna I., Ireland.	53¼N	9¼W	26
Gorzow Wlkp., Poland.	52½N	15E	33
Goschenen, Switz.	46½N	8¼E	31
Goslar, Germany.	52N	10¼E	33
Gospic, Yugoslavia.	44¼N	15¼E	36
Gosport, England.	50¼N	1¼W	23
Gossen I., Norway.	62¼N	7E	29
Gostivar, Yugoslavia.	41¼N	21E	37
Gostynin, Poland.	52¼N	19¼E	33
Gota, Riv., Sweden.	57¼N	12E	29
Goteborg, Sweden.	57¼N	12E	29
Gotha, Germany.	51N	10¼E	33
Gotland, Baltic Sea.	57¼N	18¼E	29
Goto Is., Japan.	33N	129E	49
Gotska Sandon I., Swe.	58¼N	19E	29
Gottingen, Germany.	51½N	10E	33
Gottwaldov, Czecho.	49¼N	17¼E	33
Gouarec, France.	48¼N	3¼W	32
Gouda, C. Pr., S. Afr.	33¼S	19E	52
Gouin Resr., Que., Can.	48½N	75¾W	66
Goulburn Is., N. Terr.	11¼S	133E	60
Goulburn, Riv., Aust.	36S	144½E	59
Goulburn, N.S.W.	34¼S	149¼E	59
Goundam, Mali.	16N	4W	57
Gourdon, France.	44¼N	1¼E	32
Goure, Nigeria.	13¼N	10E	56
Gourin, France.	48N	3¾W	32
Gourits, R., C.Pr., S.Afr.	34¼S	22E	52
Gournay, France.	49¼N	1¼E	30
Gourock, Scotland.	55¼N	4¾W	25
Govan, Sask., Canada.	51¼N	105W	70
Govelsberg, Ger.(ins.).	51¼N	7¼W	30
Govena, C., U.S.S.R.	60N	165E	39
Govenlock, Sask., Can.	49¼N	109¼W	70
Governors Bay, S.I., N.Z. (inset C).			63
Gowganda, Ont., Can.	47¼N	80¼W	68
Gowna, L., Ireland.	53¼N	7¼W	26
Goya, Argentina.	29S	59W	79
Goyder's Lagoon, S. Australia.	26¼S	139¼E	59
Goz Beida, Chad.	12¼N	21¼E	56
Gozo I., Malta.	36N	14¼E	34
Graaff-Reinet, C. Pr.	32¼S	24¼E	52
Graafwater, C.Pr., Afr.	32S	18¼E	52
Grabouw, C.Pr., S.Afr.	34¼S	19E	52

Place	Lat.	Long.	No.
Grabow, Germany.	53¼N	11½E	33
Gracac, Yugoslavia.	44¼N	15½E	36
Gracay, France.	47¼N	1½E	31
Gracias a Dios, Pt. & C., Nicaragua.	15N	83¼w	77
Graciosa, Azores (ins.).	39N	28w	35
Graciosa I., Canary Is.	29¼N	13½w	35
Grafton, N.S.W., Aust.	29½s	153E	59
Grafton, N.D., U.S.A.	48¼N	97¼w	74
Graham, Ontario, Can.	49½N	90¼w	71
Graham I., Br. Col.	53½N	132¼w	66
Graham Land, see ANTARCTIC PENINSULA			
Grahamstown, C. Pr.	33½s	26½E	53
Graian Alps, Fr.-Switz.	45½N	7E	31
Graiba, Tunisia.	34½N	10E	35
Grajewo, Poland.	53½N	22½E	33
Gral Pico, Argentina.	35½s	63½w	79
Grammont, Belgium.	50¾N	4E	30
Grampian Mts., Scot.	57N	4w	24
Grampound, England.	50¼N	5w	22
Granada, Nicaragua.	12N	86w	77
GRANADA & Tn., Sp.	37¼N	3½w	35
Granard, Ireland.	53¾N	7¼w	26
Granby, Quebec, Can.	45¼N	72¾w	69
Gran Canaria, Can. Is.	28N	15½w	35
Grand Bahama I., W.I.	27N	77½w	77
Grand Canal, China.	35N	117E	48
Grand Canal, Eire.	53¼N	7w	26
Grand Canyon, U.S.A.	36¼N	113w	74
Grand Comore, Indian Ocean (inset).	12s	43½E	56
Grand Coulee Dam, U.S.	48N	119w	74
Grand Falls, Labrador.	53¾N	64¼w	66
Grand Falls, Canada.	47N	67¾w	67
Grand Falls, Newf., Can.	49N	55¼w	67
Grand Forks, Br. Col.	49N	118¼w	72
Grand Forks, U.S.A.	48N	97¼w	75
Grand I., Neb., U.S.A.	41N	98¼w	74
Grand Junction, U.S.A.	39N	108¼w	74
Grand Marais, U.S.A.	47½N	90¼w	75
Grand Mere, Que., Can.	46½N	72½w	69
Grandola, Portugal.	38N	8½w	35
Grand Popo, Dahomey.	6¼N	2E	57
Grand Rapids, Can.	53¼N	99½w	70
Grand Rapids, Minnesota, U.S.A.	47¼N	93w	75
Grand Rapids, Michigan, U.S.A.	42¼N	85½w	68
Grand Teton Mt., U.S.	43½N	111w	74
Grande B., Argentina.	51s	68w	78
Grande Luce, Le, Fr.	47½N	½E	31
Grande Prairie, Can.	55¼N	118¼w	75
Grande, Riv., Brazil.	20s	51¼w	79
Grande Terre, Guadaloupe, W.I.	16N	62w	77
Grandview, Man., Can.	51¼N	100½w	70
Grandvilliers, France.	49½N	2E	30
Grange, England.	54¼N	3w	25
Grange, Ireland.	54¼N	8¼w	26
Grangemouth, Scot.	56N	3¾w	24
Grangeville, Id., U.S.A.	46N	116w	74
Granite Pk., Mont., U.S.	45N	110w	74
Granitola, C. of, Sicily.	37¼N	12¾E	36
Granollers, Spain.	41½N	2½E	35
Gran Paradiso, Mt., It.	45½N	7¼E	31
Gran Sasso, Italy.	42¼N	13½E	36
Grantham, England.	52¾N	¾w	23
Grantown-on-Spey, Scotland.	57¼N	3¾w	24
Grants, N. Mex., U.S.A.	35N	108w	74
Granum, Alb., Can.	49¾N	113¼w	73
Granville, France.	48¾N	1¾w	31
Granville, L., Canada.	56N	100w	66
Graskop, T'vaal, S. Afr.	25s	30¾E	54
Grasmere, England.	54¼N	3w	25
Grasse, France.	43½N	6½E	32
Grassington, Eng.	54¼N	2w	25
Grass Patch, W. Aust.	33s	122½E	61
GRAUBUNDEN, Switz.	46¼N	9½E	31
Grave, Netherlands.	51¾N	5½E	30
Gravedona, Italy.	46¼N	9½E	31
Gravelbourg, Sask.	49¾N	106¾w	70
Gravelines, France.	51N	2E	30
Gravelotte, France.	49N	6E	30
Gravenhurst, Ont., Can.	45N	79¼w	68
Gravesend, England.	51¼N	¼E	23
Gravina, Italy.	40¾N	16¼E	36
Gray, France.	47¼N	5½E	31
Gray, C., Antarc.	67s	142E	80
Grayson, Sask., Can.	50¾N	102¼w	70
Graz, Austria.	47N	15¼E	33
Great Abaco I., W.I.	26¼N	77¼w	77
Gt. Anyuy R., U.S.S.R.	69N	161E	39
Gt. Australian Bight.	33s	130E	58
Gt. Barrier I., N.I., N.Z.	36¼s	175½E	62
Gt. Barrier Reef, Aust.	17s	146½E	60
Gt. Bear L., N.W. Can.	66N	120w	66
Gt. Beeren, Germany.	52¼N	13½E	33
Gt. Belt, Denmark.	55¼N	11E	33
Gt. Berg Riv., C. P.	32½s	18E	52
Gt. Bitter, L., U.A.R.	30¼N	32½E	41
Gt. Blasket Is., Ireland.	52N	10½w	26
Gt. BrakR., C.Pr.,S.Afr.	34s	22½E	52
Gt. Crosby, England.	53¼N	3w	22
Gt. Dividing Ra., Aust.	25s	150E	58
Gt. Driffield, England.	54N	¼w	25
Gt. Dunmow, Eng.	51¾N	½E	23
Gt. Exuma I., W.I.	23¼N	76w	77
Gt. Falls, Man., Can.	50¼N	96w	71
Gt. Falls, Mon., U.S.A.	47¼N	111½w	74
Gt. Fish R., S.W. Africa.	28s	17E	51
Gt. Fish R., C. Pr.	33s	27E	53
Gt. Gerau Germany.	50N	8½E	30
Gt. Inagua, I., Baham.	21N	73¼w	77
Gt. Kei R., C.Pr., S.Afr.	32½s	27¼E	53

G.A.

Place	Lat.	Long.	No.
Gt. Lake, Tas. (ins.).	42s	146½E	59
Gt. Lyakhov I., U.S.S.R.	73N	142E	39
Gt. Makarikari L., Bots.	21s	26E	51
Gt. Malvern, England.	52¼N	2¼w	22
Gt. Mercury I., N.Z.	36½s	175½E	62
Gt. Nama Ld., S.W.Afr.	25s	17E	51
Gt. Natuna I., Indon.	4N	108E	47
Gt. Ormes Hd., Wales.	53¼N	3¾w	22
Gt. Ruaha River, Tanz.	8s	38E	56
Gt. St. Bernard Pass, Switzerland.	45½N	7½E	31
Gt. Salt L., Ut., U.S.A.	41N	112¼w	74
Gt. Slave L., Canada.	62N	114w	66
Gt. Victoria Des., W.Aust.	29s	125E	61
Gt. Whale R., Que., Can.	55N	76w	66
Gt. Whernside Mt., England.	54¼N	2w	25
Gt. Yarmouth, Eng.	52¼N	1¾E	23
Greco, C., Cyprus.	35N	34E	41
GREECE, Europe.	40N	22E	19
Greeley, Col., U.S.A.	40¼N	104¾w	74
Green, C., N.S.W.Aust.	37¼s	150E	59
Green Head, W. Aust.	30s	115E	61
Green I., Pacific (inset).	5s	155E	60
Green B., Wis., U.S.A.	44½N	88w	75
Green Lake, Sask., Can.	54½N	107½w	70
Green Island, S.I., N.Z.	46s	170½E	63
Green Mts., U.S.A.	44N	73w	69
Green Riv., Col., U.S.A.	40¼N	109w	74
Green Riv., Ut., U.S.A.	38N	110w	74
Greenbushes, W. Aust.	33½s	116E	61
GREENLAND, N. Amer.	70N	40w	65
Greenlaw, Scotland.	55¾N	2¼w	25
Greenock, Scotland.	56N	4¾w	25
Greenore, Eire.	54N	6¼w	26
Greenore Pt., Eire.	52¼N	6¼w	26
Greenough, W. Aust.	28¾s	115E	61
Greensboro, U.S.A.	36¼N	79¾w	75
Greenville, Ala., U.S.A.	32N	87w	75
Greenville, Miss., U.S.	33¼N	91w	75
Greenville, S.C., U.S.A.	34¼N	82¼w	75
Greenwich, U.S.A.(ins.)	41N	74w	75
Greenwood, Br. Col.	49¼N	118¼w	72
Greetsiel, Germany.	53¾N	7¼E	30
Gregory Salt S., W.Aust.	20s	128E	61
Gregory, L., W. Aust.	26s	120E	61
Gregory, L., S. Aust.	29s	139¼E	59
Gregory Ra., Aust.	19s	143E	60
Gregory, Riv., Queens.	17¼s	139E	60
Greifswald, Germany.	54¼N	13½E	33
Greiz, Germany.	50¾N	12¼E	33
Gremikha, U.S.S.R.	68N	39½E	38
Grenaa, Denmark.	56½N	10½E	29
Grenada, Miss., U.S.A.	33½N	90w	75
Grenada I., W.I.	12¼N	61¼w	77
Grenadines Is., W.I.	12¼N	61¼w	77
Grenchen, Switz.	47¼N	7¼E	31
Grenfell, N.S.W., Aust.	34s	148E	59
Grenfell, Sask., Can.	50½N	103w	70
Grenoble, France.	45¼N	5½E	32
Grenville, C., Queens.	12s	143E	60
Gressoney la Trinite, Italy.	45¾N	7¾E	31
Gretna Green, Scot.	55N	3¼w	25
Greve, Italy.	43½N	11½E	36
Grevenbroich, Ger.	51N	6½E	30
Grevesmuhlen, Ger.	53¾N	11¼E	33
Grey, C., N. Terr., Aust.	12½s	136½E	60
Grey Abbey, N. Ire.	54¼N	5¼w	26
Greybull, Wyo., U.S.A.	44N	108w	74
Greylingstad, T'vaal.	26½s	28¾E	55
Greymouth, S.I., N.Z.	42½s	171½E	63
Grey Range, Australia.	29s	142E	59
Greys Pk., Col., U.S.A.	40N	106w	74
Greystone, C.Pr.,S.Afr.	33½s	25E	53
Greystones, Eire.	53N	6w	26
Greytown, Natal.	29s	30½E	55
Greytown, N.I., N.Z.	41s	175½E	62
Grezzana, Italy.	45½N	11E	36
Gribingi, R., C. Afr. R.	8¼N	19E	56
Griffith, N.S.W., Aust.	34¼s	146E	59
Grik, Malaysia (inset).	5¼N	100¼E	47
Grim, C., Tas., Aust.	40½s	144¾E	59
Grimari, Cen. Afr. Rep.	5½N	20E	56
Grimsby, England.	53¾N	0	23
Grimsey I., Iceland.	66¼N	18w	29
Grimstad, Norway.	58¼N	8½E	29
Grindelwald, Switz.	46½N	8E	31
Grindsted, Denmark.	55¾N	9E	33
Grinnell Pen., N.W.Can.	77N	92w	66
Griquatown, S. Africa.	28½s	23½E	52
Gris Nez, C., France.	51N	1½E	30
Grodek Jagiellonski, U.S.S.R.	49¾N	23¾E	33
Grodkow, Poland.	50½N	17¼E	33
Grodno, U.S.S.R.	53¼N	23¾E	38
Grodzisk, Poland.	52¼N	16¼E	33
Groenlo, Netherlands.	52¼N	6½E	30
Groix, I. de, France.	47¼N	3¼w	32
Grojec, Poland.	51¾N	20¾E	33
Grombalia, Tunisia.	36¼N	10½E	36
Groningen, Nether.	53¼N	6½E	30
Groom, Ireland.	52¼N	8½w	26
Groot Marico, T'vaal.	25½s	26¼E	54
Grootdoring, C. Pr.	30s	23E	52
Groot Drink, C. Pr.	28¼s	21¼E	52
Groote Eylandt, Aust.	14s	136¼E	60
Groote R., C. Pr., S. Afr.	34s	25E	52
Grootfontein, C. Pr.	33s	21¼E	51
Grootfontein, S.W.Afr.	19¼s	18E	52
Grootvlei, Transvaal.	26½s	28¾E	55
Gros Bois, France.	47¼N	6¼E	31
Gr. Glockner, Austria.	47¼N	12¼E	31
Grossenhain, Ger.	51¼N	13½E	33

Place	Lat.	Long.	No.
Grosseto, Italy.	42¼N	11E	36
Grouard, Alb., Can.	55¼N	116¼w	73
Growl, R., N.S.W., Australia.	32s	146E	59
Grozny, U.S.S.R.	43¼N	45½E	38
Grudziadz, Poland.	53½N	18½E	33
Gruinard B., Scotland.	58N	5¼w	24
Grunstadt, Germany.	49¼N	8½E	30
Gruyeres, Switzerland.	46½N	7E	31
Gryazi, U.S.S.R.	52N	40E	38
Gryfice, Poland.	54N	15½E	33
Guadalajara, Mexico.	20¼N	103¼w	76
Guadalajara, Spain.	40¾N	3¼w	35
Guadalcanal I., Pacific.	9¼s	160E	64
Guadalquivir, R., Sp.	38N	5w	35
Guadalupe, Mexico.	26¼N	101w	76
Guadalupe, Mexico.	29¼N	110¼w	76
Guadalupe I., Mexico.	28¼N	118¼w	65
Guadarrama, Sierra de, Spain.	41N	3¾w	35
Guadeloupe I., W.I.	16¼N	61½w	77
Guadiana, Riv., Spain.	37N	7¼w	35
Guadix, Spain.	37¼N	3w	35
Guadalope, R., Spain.	37¼N	0	35
Guaimaca, Honduras.	15N	84w	76
Gualeguaychu, Arg.	33s	58¼w	79
Guam I., Pacific.	13¼N	144½E	64
Gua Musang, Malaysia.	4¼N	102½E	47
Guanajay, Cuba, W.I.	22¾N	82¾w	77
Guanajuato, Mexico.	21¼N	102w	76
GUANAJUATO, Mexico.	21N	101¼w	76
Guanare, R., Venez.	8N	67¾w	77
Guane, Cuba.	22N	84w	77
Guanta, Venezuela.	10N	64¾w	77
Guantanamo, Cuba.	20¼N	75¼w	77
Guapore, Riv., Brazil.	10s	65w	78
Guarda, Portugal.	40¼N	7¼w	35
Guardafui, C., Africa.	12N	51½E	50
Guasipati, Venezuela.	7¼N	62w	77
Guastalla, Italy.	45N	10½E	31
Guata, La, Honduras.	15N	86w	77
GUATEMALA, C. Amer.	16N	90w	76
Guatemala, Guat.	14½N	90¼w	76
Guaviare, R., Colombia.	4N	68w	78
Guayama, Puerto Rico.	18N	66w	77
Guayaquil, Ecuador.	2s	80w	78
Guaymas, Mexico.	28N	111w	76
Guazapares, Mexico.	27¼N	108w	76
Gubere, Cent. Afr. Rep.	6N	26¼E	56
Gubin, Poland.	52N	15E	33
Guchin, Mongolia.	46N	103E	39
Gudermes, U.S.S.R.	43N	47E	38
Guebwiller, France.	48N	7¼E	30
Guelph, Ontario, Can.	43¼N	80¼w	68
Guenca, Spain.	40N	2w	35
Guenrouet, France.	47¼N	2w	32
Guer, France.	48N	2w	31
Guerande, France.	47¼N	2¼w	32
Guerche, La, France.	48N	1¼w	31
Gueret, France.	46¼N	1¾E	32
Guernsey, Chan. Is.	49N	2½w	32
Guerrara, Algeria.	32¼N	4¼E	35
GUERRERO, Mexico.	17¼N	100w	76
Guerrero, Mexico.	28¼N	107¼w	76
GUIANIA, BR. see GUYANA.			
GUIANA, DUTCH., see SURINAM.			
GUIANA, FRENCH, S. Amer.	4N	53w	78
Guider, Cameroon.	10N	14E	56
GUIENE, France (inset).	45N	1E	32
Guil, R., France.	44½N	6¾E	31
Guildford, England.	51¼N	½w	23
Guildford, W. Aust.	32s	116E	61
Guimar, Can. Is. (ins.).	28¼N	16¼w	35
GUINEA, W. Africa.	10N	10w	50
GUINEA, PORT., W. Afr.	12N	15w	50
Guines, Cuba.	22¾N	82w	77
Guingamp, France.	48¾N	3¼w	31
Guira de Melina, Cuba.	22¾N	82¼w	77
Guiria, Venezuela.	11N	62¼w	77
Guisborough, Eng.	54¼N	1w	25
Guise, France.	49¾N	3½E	30
Gujranwala, Pakistan.	32¼N	74¼E	44
Gujrat, Pakistan.	33N	74E	44
Gula, Uganda.	2¼N	32E	56
Gulbarga, India.	17¼N	76¼E	45
Gulfport, Miss., U.S.A.	30¼N	89¼w	75
Gulgong, N.S.W., Australia.	32¼s	149¼E	59
Gull Lake, Sask., Can.	50¼N	108¼w	70
Gullane, Scotland.	56N	2¾w	25
Gullera, Spain.	39¼N	¼w	35
Gulpaigan, Iran.	33¼N	51E	41
Guma, China.	37¼N	79E	43
Gumbi, Nigeria.	13N	5E	57
Gumbinnen, U.S.S.R.	54¼N	22¼E	33
Gummersbach, Ger.	51N	7½E	30
Gummi, Nigeria.	12N	5½E	57
Gumusane, Turkey.	40¼N	39E	41
Gundagai, N.S.W., Aust.	35s	148E	59
Gundelsheim, Ger.	49¼N	9¼E	33
Gunnedah, N.S.W., Aust.	31s	150¼E	59
Guntakal, India.	15¼N	77¼E	45
Guntur, India.	16¼N	80¼E	45
Gunyidi, W. Aust.	30¼s	116E	61
Gunzenhausen, Ger.	49N	11E	33
Gurgan, Iran.	36¼N	54¼E	40
Gurkha, Nepal.	28¼N	84¼E	44
Gurley, N.S.W., Aust.	29½s	150¼E	59
Guryev, U.S.S.R.	47N	52E	38
Gusinje, Yugoslavia.	42½N	20E	37
Guspini, Sardinia.	39¼N	8½E	36
Gustrow, Germany.	53¾N	12¼E	33
Gutha, W. Australia.	28½s	116E	61
GUYANA, S. America.	(inset),		77
Guymon, Okl., U.S.A.	37N	101¼w	74
Guyra, N.S.W., Aust.	30¼s	151¼E	59

Place	Lat.	Long.	No.
Guysborough, Canada.	45¼N	61¼w	67
Guzman, Mexico.	19¼N	103¾w	76
Gwaai & R., Rhodesia.	19¼s	27¼E	51
Gwabegar, N.S.W.	30¼s	149E	59
Gwadar, Pakistan.	25¼N	62¼E	46
Gwalior, India.	26¼N	78¼E	44
Gwanda, Rhodesia.	21s	29E	54
Gwatar, Iran.	25¼N	61½E	40
Gweebarra B., Ireland.	54¾N	8¼w	26
Gwelo, R., Rhodesia.	18s	28E	51
Gwelo, Rhodesia.	19¼s	30E	51
Gwydir, R., N.S.W.	29¼s	149¼E	59
Gyamda, China.	30N	93E	43
Gyantse, Tibet.	29N	90E	43
Gydanski Pen., U.S.S.R.	70N	75E	39
Gympie, Queens., Aust.	26¼s	152¼E	60
Gyor, Hungary.	47¼N	17¼E	37
Gypsumville, Canada.	51¾N	98¼w	71
Gyula, Hungary.	46¼N	21¼E	37
H			
HAABAI GROUP, Pacific.	20s	176w	64
Haan, Germany (inset).	51N	7E	33
Haarlem, Netherlands.	52¼N	4½E	30
Haarlem, C.Pr., S.Afr.	33¼s	23¼E	52
Haast & R., S.I., N.Z.	43¼s	169E	63
Habaswein, Kenya.	2N	39E	56
Habbaniya, Iraq.	33N	44E	41
Haboro, Japan.	44¼N	141¾E	49
Hachenburg, Germany.	50¼N	7¾E	30
Hachinohe, Japan.	40¼N	141E	49
Hachioji, Japan.	35¼N	139¼E	49
Haddington, Scotland.	56N	2¾w	25
Haddon Corner, S.Aust.	26¼s	141E	60
Hadejia & R., Nigeria.	12¼N	10E	57
Hadele Gubo, Ethiopia.	11¼N	42E	56
Hadera, Israel (inset).	2¼N	35E	40
HADHRAMAUT (inset).	16N	48E	40
Haditha, Iraq.	33¼N	42½E	41
Hadleigh, England.	52N	1E	23
Ha Dong, China.	21N	105¼E	48
Hadraniya, Iraq.	36N	43E	41
Haecht, Belgium.	51N	4½E	30
Haeju, Korea.	38N	125¼E	49
Haenam, Korea.	34¼N	126¼E	49
Haenertsburg, T'vaal.	24s	30E	54
Hafar Al Batin, Saudi Arabia.	28N	46E	41
Haft Kel, Iran.	32N	49½E	41
Hafun, C., Somali Rep.	10N	51E	56
Hagen, Germany.	51¼N	7½E	33
Hagenow, Germany.	53¼N	11¼E	33
Hagerstown, Md., U.S.	39½N	77¾w	75
Hagersville, Ont., Can.	43N	80w	68
Ha Giang, China.	22¼N	105E	48
Hags Head, Ireland.	53N	9¼w	26
Hagu, Japan.	34¼N	131¼E	49
Hague, Sask., Canada.	52¼N	106¼w	70
Hague, C. de la, France.	49¼N	2w	31
Hague, The, Nether.	52¼N	4¼E	30
Haguenau, France.	49N	7¾E	30
Hahn, Germany.	50¼N	7¾E	30
Haib, S.W. Africa.	28¼s	18¼E	52
Haicheng, China.	41N	122¼E	48
Haifa, Israel (inset).	32¼N	35E	40
Haig, W. Australia.	31s	126E	61
Haikow, China.	20N	110¼E	48
Hail, Saudi Arabia.	27¼N	42¼E	40
Hailar, Riv., China.	49N	120E	39
Haileybury, Ont., Can.	47¼N	79¼w	68
Hailsham, England.	50¾N	¼E	23
Hailun, China.	47N	128E	39
Hailung, China.	43N	126E	49
Hainan L. & Str. China.	21¼N	111E	48
HAINAUT, Belgium.	50¼N	3¾E	33
Haiphong, Vietnam.	21N	106¾E	47
Haitan I., China.	26N	120E	48
HAITI, W. Indies.	19¼N	72¼w	77
Hajnowka, Poland.	52¾N	23¾E	33
Hakodate, Japan.	41¾N	140¾E	49
Hal, Belgium.	50¾N	4¼E	30
Halaib, Sudan.	22¼N	36¼E	40
Halberstadt, Germany.	52N	11¼E	33
Halden, Norway.	59N	11¼E	29
Hale, R., N. Terr., Aust.	24s	136E	60
Halesowen, England.	52¼N	2w	22
Halesowen, Cape Pr.	32¼s	25¾E	53
Halesworth, England.	52¼N	1½E	23
Halfway House, T'vaal.	26s	28E	51
Halfway Tree, Jamaica.	18N	77w	77
Hali, Saudi Arabia.	19¼N	41¼E	40
Halifax, England.	53¾N	1¾w	25
Halifax, N.S., Canada.	44¼N	63¾w	67
Halifax, Queens., Aust.	18¼s	146¼E	60
Haliri, Riv., Iran.	28N	57E	40
Halkirk, Alb., Can.	52¼N	112¼w	73
Halkirk, Scotland.	58¼N	3¼w	24
Hall, Germany.	49¼N	9½E	33
Hall Is., Pacific.	9N	152E	64
Hall Pen., N.W. Can.	63N	65w	66
Halle on Saale, Ger.	51¼N	12E	33
Hallein, Austria.	47¾N	13E	33
Hallerberg, Germany.	51¼N	9½E	30
Hall's Creek, W. Aust.	18¼s	127¼E	61
Hallstadhammar, Swe.	60N	16¼E	29
Halmahera I., Indon.	1N	128E	47
Halmstad, Sweden.	56¾N	13E	29
Halsingborg, Sweden.	56N	12¾E	29
Halstead, England.	52N	½E	23
Haltwhistle, England.	54¾N	2¼w	25
Halven, Germany (ins.).	51N	7½E	33
Ham, France.	49¾N	3E	30
Ham, Syria.	35N	36E	41
Hamada, Japan.	35N	132E	49
Hamadan, Iran.	34¼N	48¼E	40

C

[106] Hamamatsu—Holbrook

Place	Lat.	Long.	No.
Hamamatsu, Japan.	34¾N	137¾E	49
Hamanskraal, T'vaal.	25½S	28¼E	54
Hamar, Norway.	61N	11E	29
Hambantota, Ceylon.	6¼N	81¼E	45
Hambecourt, France.	48½N	4¾E	30
Hamburg, C.Pr., S.Afr.	33¼S	27½E	53
Hamburg, Germany.	53½N	10E	33
Hameenlinna, Finland.	61N	24½E	29
Hamersley Ra., W. Aust.	22S	117½E	61
Hamhung, Korea.	40N	127½E	49
Hami, see QOMUL.			
Hamilton, N.I., N.Z.	37¾S	175¼E	62
Hamilton, Oh., U.S.A.	39¼N	84¾W	75
Hamilton, Ont., Can.	43¼N	80W	68
Hamilton, Scotland.	55¾N	4W	25
Hamilton, Vict., Aust.	37¾S	142E	59
Hamilton Inlet, Newfoundland (ins.)	54N	58W	67
Hamilton Riv., S.Aust.	27½S	136E	60
Hamilton Riv., Queens.	23½S	140E	60
Hamina, Finland.	60½N	27¼E	29
Hamley Bridge, S.Aust.	34¼S	138¾E	59
Hamm, Germany.	51¾N	7¾E	33
Hammamet, G., Tunis.	36N	10½E	35
Hammelin Pool & Tn., W. Australia.	26S	114E	61
Hammerfest, Norway.	70¾N	24E	29
Hammonia, O.F.S.	28¾S	27¾E	55
Hampden, S.I., N.Z.	45¼S	170¾E	63
HAMPSHIRE, England.	51N	1¼W	23
Hamun-i-Jaz Murian, Iran.	27½N	59E	40
Hamun-i-Mashkel, Pak.	28N	62½E	46
Hamun-i-Zambul Helmand, Afghan.	30½N	61E	43
Han Pijesak, Yugo.	44N	19E	37
Han River, China.	30½N	114E	48
Han River, Korea.	37½N	127E	49
Hana, Hawaii, U.S.A.	20N	155E	72
Hanalt, Austria.	47N	11½E	31
Hanamaki, Japan.	39N	141E	49
Hanamkonda, India.	18N	79½E	45
Hanau, Germany.	50¼N	9E	33
Hanceville, Br. Col.	52N	123W	79
Hanchung, China.	33N	107E	48
Hangchow, China.	30¼N	120¼E	48
Hankey, C. Pr., S. Afr.	33¾S	24¾E	53
Hanko, Finland.	60¼N	23E	29
Hankong, China.	25¼N	119E	48
Hankow, China.	30¾N	114¼E	48
Hanle, Kashmir (inset).	32½N	79E	44
Hanley, England.	53N	2¼W	22
Hanley, Sask., Can.	51¾N	106½W	70
Hanmer, S.I., N.Z.	42½S	172¾E	63
Hanna, Alberta, Can.	51¾N	111¾W	73
Hannaford, Queensland.	27S	150E	53
Hannibal, Mo., U.S.A.	39¾N	91¼W	75
Hanoi, Viet Nam.	21¼N	105½E	48
Hanover, C. Pr., S. Afr.	31S	24½E	53
Hanover, Germany.	52½N	9¾E	33
Hanover, Ont., Can.	44¼N	80¾W	68
Hanover I., Chile.	50¾S	75½W	78
Hanover Rd., Cape Pr.	31S	24½E	57
Hantsport, N.S., Can.	45N	64¼W	67
Hanyang, China.	30¾N	114¼E	48
Haohsien, China.	34N	115½E	48
Hao I., Pacific.	19S	140W	64
Haparanda, Sweden.	65¾N	24E	29
Haradera, Somali Rep.	5N	47E	56
Harar, Ethiopia.	9¼N	42E	56
Harbin, China.	45¾N	126¾E	49
Harburg, Ger. (inset).	53½N	10E	30
Harcourt, New Bruns.	46¾N	65¼W	67
Harda, India.	22½N	77E	44
Hardanger Field, Nor.	60¼N	7½E	29
Hardanger Fiord, Nor.	60¼N	6E	29
Harden, N.S.W., Aust.	34¾S	148½E	59
Hardenburt, Nether.	52½N	6½E	30
Harderwijk, Nether.	52¼N	5½E	30
Hardey, R., W. Aust.	22½S	116E	61
Hardin, Mon., U.S.A.	46N	107½W	74
Harding, Natal.	30½S	30E	55
Hardisty, Alb., Can.	52¾N	111¼W	73
Hardwar, India.	30N	78¼E	44
Hardwicke B., S. Aust.	35S	137¼E	59
Hardy, Algeria.	35½N	2E	35
Hareidland, Norway.	62½N	5¾E	29
Harewood Airport, S.I., N.Z. (ins. C).			63
Harfleur, France.	49½N	¼E	31
Harg, Sweden.	60¼N	18¼E	29
Hargeisa, Somali Rep.	9½N	44E	56
Haringvliet, Nether.	51¾N	4¼E	30
Hari, Riv., Sumatra.	1½S	104E	47
Hari Rud, Riv., Afghan.	34N	62½E	43
Harlech, Wales.	52¾N	4¼W	22
Harleston, England.	52½N	1¼E	23
Harlingen, Nether.	53¼N	5½E	30
Harlingen, Tex., U.S.A.	26N	97W	75
Harlow, England.	51¾N	¼E	23
Harmon Field, Newf.	48N	58W	66
Harnai, Pakistan.	30N	68E	46
Harnosand, Sweden.	62¾N	18E	29
Haro, Spain.	42½N	3W	35
Harper Springs, Aust.	22½S	133½E	60
Harris, Sask., Can.	51¾N	107½W	70
Harris I., Scotland.	57¾N	7W	24
Harrisburg, Penn., U.S.	40¼N	76¾W	75
Harrismith, O.F.S.	28¼S	29¼E	55
Harrismith, W. Aust.	33S	117¾E	61
Harrison, Ark., U.S.A.	36½N	93W	75
Harriston, Ont., Can.	44N	81W	68
Harrogate England.	54N	1½W	25
Harrow, England.	51½N	¼W	23
Harsova, Romania.	44¾N	28E	37
Hart, R., N. Terr., Aust.	14S	136E	60
Hartberg, Austria.	47¼N	16E	33
Hartebeest, R., C. Pr.	28S	21E	51
Hartfontein, Cape Pr.	31¾S	26¼E	53
Hartford, Conn., U.S.A.	41¾N	72¾W	69
Hartland, England.	51N	4½W	22
Hartland, Canada.	46½N	67½W	67
Hartland Pt., England.	51N	4½W	22
Hartlepool, England.	54¾N	1¼W	25
Hartley, Rhodesia.	18¼S	30¼E	51
Hartney, Man., Can.	49½N	100½W	70
Harvey, W. Australia.	33S	116E	61
Harwich, England.	52N	1½E	23
HARYANA, India.	29N	77E	44
Harz Mts., Germany.	51½N	10½E	33
Hase, Riv., Germany.	52¾N	7¼E	30
Haslemere, England.	51¼N	¾W	23
Haspe, Germany (ins.).	51¼N	7½E	33
Hassan, India.	13N	76¼E	45
Hasselt, Belgium.	51N	5¼E	30
Hastings, England.	50¾N	¾E	23
Hastings, Minn., U.S.A.	44¾N	92¾W	75
Hastings, Nebr., U.S.A.	40½N	98½W	74
Hastings, N.I., N.Z.	39¾S	176¾E	62
Hastings, Ont., Can.	44¼N	78W	69
Hateg, Romania.	45½N	23E	37
Hatfield, England.	51¾N	¼W	23
Hatherleigh, England.	50¾N	4W	22
Hatherley, Transvaal.	25¾S	28½E	54
Hathras, India.	27½N	78¼E	44
Hatteras, C., U.S.A.	35¼N	75½W	75
Hattiesburg, Miss. U.S.	31¼N	89¼W	75
Hattingen, Ger. (ins.).	51¼N	7¼E	33
Hattingspruit, Natal.	28¼S	30¼E	55
Hatton, Ceylon, (ins.).	7N	80½E	45
Hatven, Hungary.	47½N	19½E	33
Haugesund, Norway.	59½N	5E	29
Haura, S. Yemen. (ins.).	14¾N	47½E	40
Hauraki G., N.I., N.Z.	36½S	175E	62
Hauroko, L., S.I., N.Z.	46S	167¼E	63
Hauta, S. Yemen. (ins.).	14¼N	47E	40
Hauta, Saudi Arabia.	23½N	47E	40
HAUTE GARONNE, Fr.	43½N	1½E	32
HAUTE LOIRE, France.	45N	4E	32
HAUTE MARNE, France.	48N	5¼E	32
HAUTE RHIN, France.	48N	7½E	32
HAUTE SAONE, France.	47¾N	6E	32
HAUTE SAVOIE, France.	46N	6¼E	32
HAUTE VIENNE, France.	46N	1¼E	32
HAUTES ALPES, France.	44¾N	6E	32
HAUTES PYRENEES, Fr.	43N	0	32
Havana, Cuba.	23N	82½W	77
Havant, England.	50¾N	1W	23
Havel, R., Germany.	52¾N	12E	33
Havelock, Ont., Can.	44½N	77¾W	69
Havelock, S.I., N.Z.	41¼S	173¾E	63
Havelock, N., N.I., N.Z.	39¾S	177E	62
Haverfordwest, Wales.	51¾N	5W	22
Haverhill, England.	52¼N	½E	23
Haverhill, Mass., U.S.	42¾N	71W	69
Haverstraw, N.Y., U.S.	41¼N	74W	69
Havre, Mon., U.S.A.	48N	110W	74
Havre, Le, France.	49½N	0	31
HAWAIIAN IS., Pacific.	21N	157W	64
Hawarden, Sask., Can.	51½N	106½W	70
Hawdon, L., S. Aust.	37S	140E	54
Hawea, L., S.I., N.Z.	44½S	169E	63
Hawera, N.I., N.Z.	39½S	174¼E	62
Hawes, England.	54¼N	2¼W	25
Hawi, Hawaii, U.S.A.	20N	155E	74
Hawick, Scotland.	55½N	2¾W	25
Hawke, C., Australia.	32¼S	152½E	59
Hawke Bay, N.I., N.Z.	39¼S	177½E	62
Hawker, S. Australia.	32S	138½E	59
Hawkesbury, N.S.W.	33½S	151½E	59
Hawkesbury, Ont., Can.	45¾N	74¾W	69
Hawkhurst, England.	51N	½E	23
Hawng Sawn, Thai.	19N	98E	43
Hawston, C.Pr., S.Afr.	34¼S	19¼E	52
Hawthorne, U.S.A.	38N	119W	74
Hay, N.S.W., Aust.	34½S	144¾E	59
Hay, Wales.	52N	3W	22
Hay River, N.W. Can.	61N	117W	66
Hay, R., N. Terr., Aust.	22½S	137E	60
Hay R., N.W.T., Can.	60¾N	115¾W	65
Hayange, France.	49¼N	6E	30
Haydon, Queens., Aust.	18S	141½E	60
Hayes Pen., Greenland.	76½N	65W	65
Hayes R., Man., Can.	56¾N	92¼W	71
Hayle, England.	50¼N	5½W	22
Hayling I., England.	50¾N	1W	23
Hays, Kansas, U.S.A.	38¾N	100W	74
Haywards Heath, Eng.	51N	0	23
Hazaribagh, India.	24N	85½E	44
Hazelton, Br. Col., Can.	55¼N	127¾W	72
Hazleton, Penn., U.S.A.	41N	76W	69
Hazlett, L., Australia.	22S	129¼E	60
Heacham, England.	53N	½E	23
Healdtown, Cape Pr.	32¾S	26¾E	53
Healesville, Vict., Aust.	37¾S	145½E	59
Heanor, England.	53N	1¼W	23
Heany Junc., Rhodesia.	20S	28¾E	54
Hearst, Ontario, Can.	49¾N	83¾W	71
Hebbronville, Tex., U.S.	27N	99W	74
Hebel, Queens., Aust.	29S	147¾E	60
Hebrides, Is., Scotland.	57N	7W	24
Hebron, Jordan.	32¼N	35¼E	41
Hebron, Canada (ins.).	58N	63W	67
Hecate Str., Canada.	53N	131W	66
Hechingen, Germany.	48½N	9E	32
Hectorspruit, T'vaal.	25½S	31¾E	54
Hede, France.	48¼N	1¾W	31
Hedesunda, Sweden.	60½N	17¼E	29
Hedgehope, S.I., N.Z.	46¼S	168½E	66
Hedon, England.	53¾N	¼W	23
Heerenveen, Nether.	52¾N	5¾E	30
Heerlen, Netherlands.	50¾N	6E	30
Heide, Germany.	54¼N	9E	33
Heidelberg, Germany.	49½N	8¾E	33
Heidelberg, Cape Pr.	34¼S	21E	52
Heidelberg, T'vaal.	26½S	28¼E	55
Heilbron, O.F.S., S.Afr.	27¼S	28E	55
Heilbronn, Germany.	49¼N	9¼E	33
HEILUNGKIANG, China.	47N	128E	49
Heinsburg, Alb., Can.	53¾N	110½W	73
Heinsburg, Germany.	51N	6E	30
Heis, Somali Rep.	11N	46E	56
HEJAZ, Saudi Arabia.	24N	38E	40
Heklo, Mt., Ice. (ins.).	64N	19W	29
Hekpoort, T'vaal, S.Afr.	26S	27½E	54
Hel, Poland.	54½N	18¾E	33
Helder, Netherlands.	52¾N	4¾E	30
Helen Reef, Pacific.	3N	131¼E	64
Helena, Mon., U.S.A.	46¾N	112W	74
Helensburgh, Scotland.	56N	4¾W	25
Helen Springs, Aust.	18S	133½E	60
Helensville, N.I., N.Z.	36¾S	174½E	62
Helgafell, Ice. (inset).	65N	22W	29
Heligoland, N. Sea.	54¼N	8E	33
Hell Ville, Malagasy.	13½S	48¼E	56
Helmand, R., Afghan.	30N	63E	43
Helmand Des., Afghan.	31N	65E	24
Helmond, Nether.	51½N	5½E	30
Helmsdale, Scotland.	58¼N	3¾W	24
Helmsley, England.	54¼N	1W	25
Helpmekaar, Natal.	28½S	30½E	55
Helsingfors, see HELSINKI.			
Helsingor, Denmark.	56N	12½E	29
Helsinki, Finland.	60¼N	25E	29
Helston, England.	50¼N	5¼W	22
Helvellyn, Mt., Eng.	54½N	3W	25
Helvetia, O.F.S., S.Afr.	29¾S	26½E	55
Helwan, U.A.R.	30N	31½E	41
Hemel Hempstead, Eng.	51¾N	½W	23
Henares, Riv., Spain.	40N	5W	35
Hendaye, France.	43N	1¾W	35
Henderson, N.I., N.Z. (inset A).			62
Hendrina, T'vaal, S.Afr.	26¼S	29¾E	55
Hengchow, see HENGYANG.			
Hengelo, Nether.	52¼N	6¾E	30
Henghsien, China.	22½N	109E	48
Hengshan, China.	27N	112½E	48
Hengyang, China.	27N	112½E	48
Henley, S.I., N.Z. (inset D).			63
Henley, T'vaal (ins.).	26½S	28E	51
Henley-in-Arden, Eng.	52¼N	2W	23
Henley-on-Thames, England.	51½N	¾W	23
Hennebont, France.	47¾N	3W	31
Henrietta Maria, C., Ontario, Canada.	55N	82¼W	66
Henry, Riv., W. Aust.	22½S	116E	61
Henty, N.S.W., Aust.	35½S	147E	59
Henzada, Burma.	17¾N	95½E	43
Heppenheim, Germany.	49½N	8¾E	30
Heppner, Ore., U.S.A.	45N	119¾W	74
Herat, Afghanistan.	34½N	62¼E	43
HERAULT, France.	43½N	3½E	32
Herbault, France.	47½N	1¼E	31
Herbede, Ger. (inset).	51¼N	7¼E	33
Herbert, Sask., Can.	50½N	107¼W	70
Herbert, Mt., S.I., N.Z. (inset C).			63
Herbert Pk., Mt., S.I., N.Z. (inset C).			63
Herberton, Australia.	17¼S	145½E	60
Herbertsdale, C. Pr.	34S	21¾E	52
Herborn, Germany.	50¾N	8¼E	30
Herceg Novi, Yugo.	42½N	18½E	36
Herchmer, Man., Can.	57¼N	94¼W	71
Hercules, T'vaal, S.Afr.	25¾S	28¼E	54
Heredia, Costa Rica.	10N	84W	77
HEREFORD & Tn., Eng.	52¼N	2¾W	22
Hereheretue I., Pacific.	20S	146W	64
Herford, Germany.	52¼N	8¾E	33
Herisau, Switzerland.	47½N	9¼E	31
Herisson, France.	46½N	3E	32
Herm, Channel Islands.	49½N	2½W	31
Herma Ness, Scotland.	61N	1W	24
Hermansburg, Aust.	24S	132¾E	60
Hermanus, Cape Pr.	34½S	19¼E	52
Hermidale, N.S.W.	31½S	146¾E	59
Hermitage, S.I., N.Z.	43¾S	170½E	63
Hermon, C. Pr., S. Afr.	33½S	19E	52
Hermon, Mt., Syria.	33¼N	35¾E	40
Hermosillo, Mexico.	28½N	111W	76
Hernad, R., Hungary.	48½N	21E	33
Herne Bay, England.	51½N	1¼E	23
Herne, Germany (ins.).	51½N	7¼E	33
Heron Bay, Ont., Can.	48¾N	86¼W	68
Herrenburg, Germany.	48½N	8¾E	30
Herrick, Tas., Aust.	41S	148E	59
Herschel, C. Pr., S. Afr.	30½S	27¼E	53
Herseliya, Israel (ins.).	32¼N	35E	40
Hersfeld, Germany.	51N	9½E	33
Herta, U.S.S.R.	48¼N	26¼E	37
HERTFORD & Tn., Eng.	51¾N	¼W	23
Hertogenbosch, Neth.	51¾N	5¼E	30
Hertzog, C. Pr., S. Afr.	32½S	26¾E	53
Hertzogville, O.F.S.	28¼S	25½E	55
Hervas, Spain.	40¼N	6W	35
Herve, Belgium.	50¾N	5¾E	30
Hervey B., Queens., Aust.	25S	153E	60
Hesdigneul, France.	50½N	1¾E	30
Hesdin, France.	50¼N	2E	30
Hesi, R., Israel (inset).	31½N	34½E	40
HESSEN, Germany.	50½N	8½E	30
Hessle, England.	53¾N	½W	23
Hesso, S. Australia.	32S	137½E	59
Hetton-le-Hole, Eng.	54¾N	1½W	25
Heuningneskloof, C.Pr.	29½S	24½E	53
Hexham, England.	55N	2¼W	25
Heysham, England.	54¼N	3W	25
Heytesbury, England.	51¼N	2¼W	22
High River, Alb., Can.	50½N	113¾W	73
Heywood, England.	53½N	2¼W	25
Heywood, Vict., Aust.	38¼S	141¾E	59
Hialeah, Fla., U.S.A.	26N	80W	75
Hibaka, Saudi Arabia.	30N	42E	41
Hibbs Pt., Tas., Aust.	42½S	145E	59
Hicks Bay, N.I., N.Z.	37½S	178¼E	62
HIDALGO, Mexico.	21N	98W	76
Hierro I., Can. Is. (ins.).	27¾N	18W	35
Higginsville, W. Aust.	32S	122E	61
Higham Ferrers, Eng.	52½N	½W	23
Highbridge, England.	51¼N	3W	22
Highflats, Natal.	30¼S	30¼E	55
High Pt., N.C., U.S.A.	36N	80W	75
High Prairie, Alb., Can.	55½N	116½W	73
High Rocky Pt., Tas., Australia (inset).	42¾S	145E	59
High Tatra, Poland-Czechoslovakia	49¼N	20E	33
Highworth, England.	51½N	1½W	23
High Wycombe, Eng.	51½N	¾W	23
Hiiumaa I., U.S.S.R.	59N	22½E	29
Hikone, Japan (ins.).	35¼N	136¼E	49
Hikueru I., Pacific.	17S	142W	64
Hikurangi, N.I., N.Z.	35½S	174¼E	62
Hilden, Germany.	51¼N	7E	30
Hildesheim, Germany.	52¼N	10E	33
Hill River, W. Aust.	30½S	115E	61
Hilla, Iraq.	32½N	44½E	41
Hillston, N.S.W., Aust.	33½S	145½E	59
Hilo, Hawaii, U.S.A.	20N	155E	74
Hilversum, Nether.	52¼N	5¼E	30
HIMACHAL-PRADESH, India.	31N	77E	44
	33N	76½E	44
Himalaya Mts., Asia.	30N	80E	43
Himare, Albania.	40N	19½E	37
Himeji, Japan.	35N	135E	49
Hinchinbrook I., Aust.	18¼S	146¼E	60
Hinckley, England.	52½N	1½W	23
Hindhead, England.	51¼N	¾W	23
Hindmarsh, L., Aust.	36S	142E	59
Hindon, S.I., N.Z. (inset D).			63
Hindu Kush Mts., Afgh.	36N	70E	43
Hindupur, India.	14N	77½E	45
Hingham, England.	52½N	1E	23
Hinghwa, China.	33N	120E	48
Hingi, China.	25N	105E	48
Hingol, Riv., Pakistan.	25N	65E	43
Hingoli, India.	19¾N	77¼E	45
Hinno I., Norway.	68¼N	16E	29
Hinojosa, Spain.	38½N	5W	35
Hiratsuki, Japan.	35N	139½E	49
Hirosaki, Japan.	40½N	140½E	49
Hiroshima, Japan.	34½N	132½E	49
Hirson, France.	50N	4¼E	30
HISPANIOLA, W. Indies.	19N	74W	77
Hissar, India.	29¼N	75¾E	44
Hit, Iraq.	33½N	42¾E	41
Hitachi, Japan.	37N	141E	49
Hitchin, England.	51¾N	¼W	23
Hitra I., Norway.	63¾N	8½E	29
Hivaoa I., Pacific.	10S	139W	64
Hjalmar, L. of, Sweden.	59N	16E	29
Hlabisa, Natal.	28¼S	31¾E	55
Hlatikulu, Swaziland.	27S	31¼E	55
Hlobane, Natal.	27¾S	31E	55
Hoa Binh, China.	21N	105E	48
Hobart, Tas., Aust.	42¾S	147¼E	59
Hobbs, N. Mex., U.S.A.	32¾N	103W	74
Hobbs Coast, Antarc.	75S	140W	80
Hobhouse, O.F.S.	29½S	27E	55
Hoboken, Belgium.	51¼N	4¼E	30
Hoboken, N.J., U.S.A.	40¾N	74W	75
Hoburgen, Sweden.	57N	19E	29
Hochow, China.	35½N	103E	43
Hochst, Germany.	50N	8¾E	30
Hochwan, China.	30N	106E	48
Hockenheim, Germany.	49¼N	8½E	30
Hodeida, Yemen (ins.).	14¾N	43E	40
Hodgson, Man., Can.	51¼N	97½W	71
Hodmezo-Vasarhely, Hungary.	46½N	20¼E	37
Hodnet, England.	52¾N	2½W	22
Hodonin, Czecho.	48¾N	17E	33
Hoedic, I., France.	47¼N	3W	31
Hoedjies, C. Pr., S. Afr.	31½S	20½E	52
Hoekschewaard I., Neth.	51¾N	4½E	30
Hof, Germany.	50½N	12E	33
Hof, Iceland (inset).	64N	17W	29
Hofei, China.	32N	117½E	48
Hofeng, China.	30N	110E	48
Hofmeyr, C. Pr., S. Afr.	31¾S	25¾E	53
Hofn, Iceland (inset).	64¼N	15W	29
Hofsjokull, Iceland.	64¾N	19W	29
Hofuf, Saudi Arabia.	25½N	49¾E	40
Hogs Back Mt., C. Pr.	32¾S	27¼E	53
Hohenau, Austria.	48¾N	16¾E	33
Hohenlimburg, Germany (inset).	51½N	7½E	33
Hohenlinden, Germany.	48N	12E	33
Hohenwestedt, Germany (inset).	54¼N	9½E	33
Hohe Tauern, Austria.	47N	12E	33
Hohneck, Mt., France.	48N	7E	30
Hokianga Harbour, N.I., N.Z.	35½S	173½E	62
Hokitika, S.I., N.Z.	42¾S	171E	63
HOKKAIDO, Japan.	43N	142E	49
Hokow, China.	23N	112¾E	48
Hokshan, China.	22½N	113E	48
Holbeach, England.	52¾N	0	23
Holbrook, Ariz., U.S.A.	34¾N	110¼W	74
Holbrook, N.S.W.	35¾S	147¼E	59

Place	Lat.	Long.	No.
Holguin, *Cuba.*	21N	76¼w	77
HOLLAND. see NETHERLANDS.			
Holland, *England.*	52½N	¼w	23
Hollywood, *Calif., U.S.*	34N	118w	74
Holmfirth, *England.*	53½N	1¾w	23
Holoog, *S.W. Africa.*	27½s	18E	51
Holroyd, *Riv., Queens.*	14s	141½E	60
Holseno I., *Norway.*	60½N	4½E	29
Holstebro, *Denmark.*	56N	8E	29
Holsworthy, *England.*	50½N	4¼w	22
Holt, *England.*	52½N	1½E	23
Holt, *Wales.*	53¼N	2¾w	23
Holy I., *England.*	55½N	1¾w	25
Holy I., *Wales.*	53¼N	4½w	22
Holyhead, *Wales.*	53¼N	4½w	22
Holyoke, *Mass., U.S.A.*	42¼N	72½w	69
Holywell, *Wales.*	53¼N	3¼w	22
Holzminden, *Ger.*	51¾N	9½E	33
Home Hill, *Queens., Aust.*	20s	148E	60
Homer, *Alaska, U.S.A.*	60N	150w	74
Homs, *Syria.*	34½N	36½E	41
Homs, *Libya.*	32½N	14½E	34
HONAN, *China.*	34N	113E	48
Honavar, *India.*	14¼N	74½E	45
Honda, *Colombia.*	5N	74¾w	77
Hondeklip B., *C. Pr.*	30¼s	17½E	52
Hondewater, *C. Pr.*	33¼s	20½E	52
HONDURAS, *C. America.*	15N	87¼w	77
Honfleur, *France.*	49¼N	¼E	31
Hongkong, *China.*	22¼N	114½E	48
Hongsong, *Korea.*	37N	127E	49
Honiton, *England.*	50¾N	3¼w	22
Honjo, *Japan.*	39N	140E	49
Honolulu, *Hawaii, Pac.*	21¼N	158½w	74
HONSHU, *Japan.*	38N	140E	49
Hontrop, *Ger. (inset).*	51¼N	7½E	33
Hood, Mt., *Ore., U.S.A.*	45¼N	122w	74
Hood Point, *W. Aust.*	34s	119E	61
Hooghly & R., *India.*	23N	88¼E	44
Hoogstraeten, *Belg.*	51¼N	4½E	30
Hook of Holland, *Neth.*	52N	4¼E	30
Hook Head, *Ireland.*	52¼N	6½w	26
Hook I., *Queens., Aust.*	20s	149E	63
Hoopstad *O.F.S.*	27¼s	26E	55
Hoorn, *Netherlands.*	52¼N	4½E	30
Hoorn Is., *Pacific.*	14s	179w	64
Hoover Dam, *Ariz.,U.S.*	36N	115w	74
Hope, *Br. Col., Can.*	49¼N	121¼w	72
Hope, L., *W. Aust.*	32¼s	120½E	61
Hopedale, *Newf., Can.*	55N	60w	67
Hopefield, *C. Pr., S. Afr.*	33s	18½E	52
HOPEH, *China.*	38N	115E	48
Hopetoun, *Vict., Aust.*	35¼s	142½E	59
Hopetoun, *W. Aust.*	34s	120½E	61
Hopetown, *C.Pr.,S.Afr.*	29¼s	24E	53
Hopkins, L., *Aust.*	24s	129E	60
Hopo, *China.*	23N	116E	48
Hoppo, *China.*	22N	109E	48
Hoquiam, *Wash., U.S.A.*	47N	124w	74
Horb, *Germany.*	48¼N	8½E	30
Horde, *Germany (ins.).*	51N	7½E	33
Horgen, *Switzerland.*	47¼N	8½E	31
Horley, *England.*	51¼N	¼w	23
Hormuz, Str. of, *Pers.G.*	26N	56E	40
Horn, *Austria.*	48¾N	15½E	33
Horn, C., *Chile.*	56s	67¼w	78
Hornavan Afvan, L. of, *Sweden.*	66N	18E	29
Hornby, *S.I., N.Z.*	43¼s	172½E	63
Horncastle, *England.*	53¼N	¼w	23
Horndean, *England.*	51N	1w	23
Hornindal, *Norway.*	62N	7E	29
Hornsby, *N.S.W., Aust.*	33¼s	151E	59
Hornsea, *England.*	53¼N	¼w	23
Horonobe, *Japan.*	45¼N	142E	49
Horrelville, *S.I., N.Z.*	43¼s	172½E	63
Horrigan, *W. Aust.*	23¼s	118E	61
Horsens, *Denmark.*	55¼N	10E	33
Horseshoe, *W. Aust.*	26s	118½E	61
Horsham, *England.*	51¼N	¼w	23
Horsham, *Vict., Aust.*	36¼s	142½E	59
Horsovsky Tyn, *Czech.*	49¼N	13E	33
Horta, *Azores (inset).*	38¼N	28¼w	35
Horten, *Norway.*	59¼N	10E	29
Horton, *C. Pr., S. Afr.*	33s	27E	53
Horwich, *England.*	53½N	2¼w	23
Hoshangabad, *India.*	22¼N	77¾E	44
Hoshiarpur, *India.*	31½N	76E	44
Hospitalet, L', *France.*	42¼N	1½E	32
Hot Springs, *Ark.,U.S.*	34½N	93w	75
Hotseh, *China.*	35N	115½E	48
Houat, I., *France.*	47¼N	3w	31
Houdan, *France.*	48¾N	1½E	30
Houghton-le-Spring, *England.*	54¼N	1¼w	25
Houston, *Br. Col., Can.*	54¼N	126½w	72
Houston, *Tex., U.S.A.*	29¼N	95¼w	75
Hout Bay, *C. Pr., S. Afr.*	34s	18¼E	52
Houtkraal, *C.Pr.,S.Afr.*	30¼s	24¼E	53
Houwater, *C.Pr.,S.Afr.*	30¼s	23¼E	52
Houhoek, *C.Pr.,S.Afr.*	34¼s	19¼E	52
Hove, *England.*	50¾N	¼w	23
Howden, *England.*	53½N	¾w	25
Howe, C., *N.S.W., Aust.*	37¼s	150E	59
Howick, *Natal.*	29¼s	30½E	55
Howick, *N.I., N.Z.*		(inset A).	62
Howland I., *Pacific.*	1N	178w	64
Howley, *Newf., Can.*	49¼N	57w	67
Howrah, *India.*	22¼N	88¼E	44
Howth & Head, *Eire.*	53¼N	6w	26
Hoy, I., *Scotland.*	59N	3¼w	24
Hoy Sound, *Scotland.*	59N	3¼w	24
Hoya, *Germany.*	52¾N	9½E	30
Hoylake, *England.*	53¼N	3¼w	22
Hoyun, *China.*	23½N	115E	48
Hradec Kralove, *Czech.*	50¼N	15½E	33
Hron, *Riv., Czecho.*	48¾N	18½E	33
Hrubieszow, *Poland.*	50¼N	24E	33
Hsiamen, *China.*	24¼N	118E	48
Hsiangfan, *China.*	32N	112E	48
Hsiapachen, *China.*	41¼N	107E	48
Hsinchu, *Formosa.*	24¾N	121E	48
Hsinking, see CHANGCHUN.			
Hsuchang, *China.*	34¼N	114E	48
Hsuchow, *China.*	34¼N	117¼E	48
Hualienkang, *Formosa.*	24N	121½E	48
Huancavelica, *Peru.*	13s	75w	78
Huancayo, *Peru.*	12¼s	75w	78
Huanuco, *Peru.*	9½s	76w	78
Huaras, *Peru.*	9½s	77¼w	78
Huascaran, Mt., *Peru.*	9s	77¼w	78
Huasco, *Chile.*	28¼s	71¼w	79
Hubli, *India.*	15¼N	75½E	45
Huchow, see WUHING.			
Huckingen, *Ger. (ins.).*	51¼N	6½E	33
Huckitta, *N. Terr.,Aust.*	22¼s	136E	60
Hucknall Torkard, *Eng.*	53N	1¼w	23
Huddersfield, *England.*	53½N	1¾w	23
Hude, *Germany.*	53¼N	8¼E	30
Hudiksvall, *Sweden.*	61¼N	17¼E	29
Hudson Bay, *Canada.*	60N	86w	66
Hudson Bay Junction, *Sask., Canada.*	53N	102½w	70
Hudson R., *N.Y., U.S.A.*	41N	73¾w	69
Hudson Strait, *Canada.*	62N	71w	66
Hue, *Vietnam.*	16¼N	107¼E	47
Huedin, *Romania.*	47N	23E	37
Huehuetenango, *Guat.*	15N	92w	76
Huelgoat, *France.*	48¼N	3¾w	31
Huelva, *Spain.*	37¼N	6¾w	35
Huercalovera, *Spain.*	37¼N	2w	35
HUESCA, *Spain.*	42¼N	¼w	35
Hughenden, *Queens.*	20¾s	144½E	60
Hugh, The River, *Aust.*	25s	134E	60
Hugh Town, *Scilly Is., England (inset).*	49¼N	6¼w	22
Huhehot, *China.*	41N	111¼E	48
Huia, *N.I., N.Z.*		(inset A).	62
Huichon, *Korea.*	40N	126¼E	49
Huila, Mt., *Colombia.*	3N	78w	78
Huirau Ra., *N.I., N.Z.*	38¼s	177E	62
Huisne, R., *France.*	48N	¼E	31
Hukow, *China.*	30N	116E	48
Hula, L., *Israel (inset).*	33N	35½E	40
Hulan, *China.*	46N	126½E	49
Hull, *England.*	53¾N	¼w	23
Hull, *Quebec, Canada.*	45¼N	75¾w	69
Hull I., *Pacific.*	5s	173w	64
Huls, *Germany (inset).*	51¼N	7¼E	33
Hulst, *Netherlands.*	51¼N	4E	30
Hulun, *China.*	49N	120E	39
Huma, *China.*	52N	127E	39
Humacao, *Puerto Rico.*	18N	66w	77
Humansdorp, *C. Pr.*	34s	24¼E	53
Humber, R., *England.*	53¼N	¼w	23
Humboldt R., *U.S.A.*	41N	117w	74
Humenne, *Czecho.*	49N	22E	33
Hun, River, *China.*	40N	124E	48
HUNAN, *China.*	28N	112E	48
Hunchun, *China.*	43N	130E	49
Hung River, *China.*	33N	115E	48
HUNGARY, *Europe.*	47N	19E	37
Hungerford, *England.*	51¼N	1½w	23
Hungerford, *Australia.*	29s	144¼E	60
Hungnam, *Korea.*	40N	128E	49
Hungshui Riv., *China.*	24N	110E	48
Hungtze, L., *China.*	33N	118E	48
Hunmanby, *England.*	54¼N	¼w	25
Hunna, *N.I., N.Z.*		(inset A).	62
Hunstanton, *England.*	52¾N	½E	23
Hunte, *Riv., Germany.*	53¼N	8½E	30
Hunter I., *Br. Col., Can.*	52N	128¼w	72
Hunter Is., *Tas., Aust.*	40¼s	144¼E	59
Hunter, I., *N.S.W.*	33s	151½E	59
HUNTINGDON, *England.*	52¼N	¼w	23
Huntington, *U.S.A.*	38N	82¼w	75
Huntly, *N.I., N.Z.*	37¼s	175¼E	62
Huntly, *Scotland.*	57¼N	2¾w	24
Huntsville, *Ont., Can.*	45¼N	79¼w	68
Hunyani, R., *Rhodesia.*	17s	30½E	51
Huon, G., *N. Gui. (ins.).*	7s	147¼E	60
Huon Is., *Pacific.*	18s	16½E	64
Huon, R., *Tas., Aust.*	43¼s	146¾E	59
HUPEH, *China.*	31N	112E	49
Hurghada, *U.A.R.*	27N	33½E	41
Huron, *S. Dak., U.S.A.*	44¼N	98w	74
Huron, L., *U.S.A.-Can.*	45N	82w	68
Hurunui R., *S.I., N.Z.*	42¼s	173½E	63
Husi, *Romania.*	46¼N	28E	37
Husum, *Germany.*	54¼N	9E	33
Hutchinson, *C. Pr.*	31¼s	23½E	52
Hutchinson, *Kan., U.S.*	38N	98w	74
Huto River, *China.*	38N	116E	48
Hutou, *China.*	47N	133E	39
Hutt, *Riv., N.I., N.Z. (inset B).*			62
Hutte, La, *France.*	48¼N	0E	31
Huttwil, *Switzerland.*	47¼N	7¾E	31
Huy, *Belgium.*	50½N	5¼E	30
Hvammstangi, *Iceland.*	65¼N	21w	29
Hvar & I., *Yugoslavia.*	43¼N	16½E	37
Hvit I., *Antarctica.*	67s	50E	80
Hwaian, *China.*	33¼N	119E	48
Hwaiyang, *China.*	34¼N	115E	48
Hwang Hai, see YELLOW SEA.			
Hwang-Ho, R., *China.*	37¼N	119E	48
Hwangchwan, *China.*	32N	115E	48
Hwanghsien, *China.*	37½N	120½E	48
Hwayuan, *China.*	28½N	109½E	48
Hweichang, *China.*	25¼N	115½E	48
Hweimin, *China.*	37¼N	117½E	48
Hweitseh, *China.*	27N	103½E	48
Hwohsien, *China.*	37N	111E	48
Hyden, *W. Australia.*	32¼s	119E	61
Hyde Park, *Guyana.*	7N	57w	77
Hyderabad, *India.*	17¼N	78½E	45
Hyderabad, *Pakistan.*	25¼N	68E	43
Hyeres Is., *France.*	43¼N	6¼E	32
Hyesanjin, *Korea.*	41¼N	128½E	49
Hyndman Pk., *U.S.A.*	44N	114w	74
Hythe, *England.*	51¼N	1½E	23

I

Place	Lat.	Long.	No.
IALPUG, L., *U.S.S.R.*	45¼N	28½E	37
Iasi, see JASSY.			
Ibadan, *Nigeria.*	7¼N	4E	57
Ibague, *Colombia.*	4¼N	75¼w	78
Ibarra, *Ecuador.*	¼N	78¼w	78
Iberville, *Que., Can.*	45¼N	73¼w	69
Ibeto, *Nigeria.*	10¼N	5½E	57
Ibi, *Yemen (inset).*	14¼N	44½E	40
Ibi, *Nigeria.*	8¼N	9½E	57
Ibiza & I., *Balearic Is.*	39N	1E	35
Ibo, *Mozambique.*	12s	40½E	56
Ibri, *Muscat & Oman.*	23¼N	56E	40
Ica, *Peru.*	14s	75¼w	78
ICELAND, *N. Atlantic.*	65N	18w	29
Icha, *U.S.S.R.*	56N	157E	39
Ichang, *China.*	30¼N	111¼E	48
Icheng, *China.*	32N	112E	48
Ichinoseki, *Japan.*	39N	141E	49
Ichow, see LINI.			
Ida, Mt., *W. Aust.*	28¼s	121E	61
Idah, *Nigeria.*	7N	6½E	57
IDAHO, *U.S.A.*	44N	114w	74
Idaho Falls, *Id., U.S.A.*	43¼N	112w	74
Idar-Oberstein, *Ger.*	49¼N	7¼E	33
Ideles, *Algeria.*	24N	7E	50
Idfu, *U.A.R.*	25N	32¼E	40
Idi, *Sumatra.*	5N	97¾E	47
Idice, *Riv., Italy.*	44¼N	11¼E	36
Idlofa, *Congo (K.).*	5s	19¼E	56
Idlewild, *N.Y., U.S.A.*	40¼N	74w	75
Idrigill Point, *Scot.*	57¼N	6¾w	24
Idstein, *Germany.*	50N	8¼E	30
Idutywa, *C. Pr., S. Afr.*	32¼s	28¼E	53
Ierapetra, *Crete.*	35N	25¼E	37
Iesi, *Italy.*	43¼N	13¼E	36
Ifakara, *Tanzania.*	8s	37E	56
Ife, *Nigeria.*	7¼N	4½E	57
Iffene, *Sudan.*	12¼N	22E	56
Ifni, *Morocco.*	29¼N	10w	50
Ifon, *Nigeria.*	6¼N	5½E	57
Igarka, *U.S.S.R.*	67¼N	86½E	39
Iglesias, *Sardinia.*	39¼N	8E	36
Ignace, *Ontario, Can.*	49¼N	91¼w	71
Igneada, *Turkey.*	41¼N	28E	37
Iguala, *Mexico.*	18¼N	99¾w	76
Igualada, *Spain.*	41¼N	1½E	35
Iguape, *Brazil.*	24¼s	48w	79
Iguatu, *Brazil (inset).*	6¼s	39¼w	79
Ihasy, *Riv., Malagasy.*	22s	45¼E	56
Ihosy, *Malagasy. (ins.).*	23s	46E	56
Ihsien, *China.*	41¼N	121¼E	48
Ihtiman, *Bulgaria.*	42¼N	23¼E	37
Iida, *Japan.*	35¼N	138E	49
Iisalmi, *Finland.*	63N	27E	38
Ijebu-Igbo, *Nigeria.*	7N	4½E	57
IJmuiden, *Nether.*	52¼N	4½E	30
IJssel, R., *Nether.*	52¼N	6E	30
IJzendijke, *Nether.*	51¼N	3½E	30
Ikaria I., *Greece.*	37¼N	26¼E	37
Ikeda, *Japan.*	43N	143½E	49
Ikirun, *Nigeria.*	8N	4½E	57
Ikom, *Nigeria.*	6¼N	8½E	57
Ikopa R., *Malagasy.*	16¼s	46E	56
Ikot Ekpene, *Nigeria.*	5¼N	7½E	57
Ilagan, *Luzon, P.I.*	17N	121¼E	47
Ilan, *China.*	47N	129¼E	49
Ilanz, *Switzerland.*	46¼N	9½E	31
Ilaro, *Nigeria.*	7N	3E	57
Ilawa, *Poland.*	53¼N	19½E	33
Ilchester, *England.*	51N	2¾w	22
ILE DE FRANCE, *France.*	49N	2E	32
Ilek, *Riv., U.S.S.R.*	52N	54E	38
Iles de Glenan, *France.*	47¼N	4w	31
Ilford, *England.*	51¼N	0	23
Ilfracombe, *Queens.*	23¼s	144E	60
Ilfracombe, *England.*	51¼N	4½w	22
Ilheos, *Brazil.*	15s	39w	79
Ili, *U.S.S.R.*	44N	78E	39
Ili, River, *U.S.S.R.*	46N	75E	39
Iliamna, L., *Alaska, U.S.*	60N	158w	74
Ilkeston, *England.*	53N	1¼w	23
Ilkley, *England.*	54N	1¾w	23
Ill, Riv., *U.S.S.R.*	47¼N	9¼E	31
Illampu, Mt., *Bolivia.*	16s	68w	79
Illapel, *Chile.*	31¼s	71w	79
ILLE ET VILAINE, *France.*	48N	1¾w	31
Iller, *Riv., Germany.*	48¼N	10E	33
Illiers, *France.*	48¼N	1¼E	31
Illimani, Mt., *Bolivia.*	17s	67¼w	79
ILLINOIS, *U.S.A.*	40N	89w	75
Ilmen, L., *U.S.S.R.*	58¼N	31¼E	38
Ilminster, *England.*	51N	3w	22
Ilo, *Peru.*	17¼s	71¼w	78
Iloilo, *Panay, P.I.*	10¼N	122½E	47
Ilorin, *Nigeria.*	8¼N	4½E	57
Imabari, *Japan.*	34N	133½E	49
Iman & Riv., *U.S.S.R.*	46¼N	134E	49
Imandra, L., *U.S.S.R.*	68N	33E	38
Imanombo, *Malagasy.*	24¼s	45½E	56
Imbaimadad, *Guyana (inset).*	6N	60w	77
Imbros I., *Turkey.*	40¼N	26E	37
Imei, *Ethiopia.*	6¼N	42½E	56
Imjin River, *Korea.*	38N	126½E	49
Immenstadt, *Germany.*	47¼N	10¼E	33
Immigrant, *O.F.S.*	29s	25½E	55
Inmingham, *Eng.*	53¼N	¼w	23
Imola, *Italy.*	44¼N	11½E	36
Imotski, *Yugoslavia.*	43¼N	17½E	37
Impendle, *Natal.*	29¼s	29½E	55
Imperia, *Italy.*	44N	8E	32
Imperial, *Calif., U.S.A.*	32½N	116w	74
Imperial, *Sask., Can.*	51¼N	105¼w	70
Imperial Dam, *U.S.A.*	33N	114¼w	74
Imphal, *India.*	24¼N	94E	46
Imrali I., *Turkey.*	40¼N	28¼E	37
Imst, *Austria.*	47¼N	10¾E	33
Inangahua R., *S.I., N.Z.*	41¼s	171¼E	63
Inari & L., *Finland.*	69N	28E	29
Inca, *Balearic Is.*	39¼s	3E	35
Ince, C., *Turkey.*	42N	35E	41
Inchnadamff, *Scotland.*	58¼N	5w	24
Inchon, *Korea.*	37¼N	126½E	49
Indals, *Riv., Sweden.*	63N	17E	29
Indarra, *W. Australia.*	28¼s	115¼E	61
Indaw, *Burma.*	24¼N	96E	46
Independence, *Mo.,U.S.*	39¼N	94¼w	75
Indian Desert, see THAR DESERT.			
Indian Hd., *Sask., Can.*	50¼N	103¾w	70
INDIANA, *U.S.A.*	40N	86w	75
Indianapolis, *U.S.A.*	39¼N	86¼w	75
Indiga, *U.S.S.R.*	68N	49E	38
Indigirka, R., *U.S.S.R.*	71¼N	150E	39
Indonesia, *Pacific.*	0	115E	47
Indore, *India.*	22¼N	75½E	44
Indragiri, R., *Sumatra.*	0	103½E	47
INDRE & Riv., *France.*	46¼N	1½E	32
INDRE ET LOIRE, *France.*	47¼N	¼E	32
Indre Sulen I., *Norway.*	61N	4¼E	29
Indus, R., *Pakistan.*	24N	67½E	46
Indwe, *C. Pr., S. Afr.*	31¼s	27¼E	53
Inebolu, *Turkey.*	42N	33½E	41
Infantas, *Colombia.*	7¼N	74w	77
In Gall, *Nigeria.*	17N	7E	50
Ingersoll, *Ont., Can.*	43N	81w	68
Ingham, *Queens., Aust.*	18¼s	146¼E	60
Ingleborough, Mt., *England.*	54¼N	2¼w	25
Ingleton, *England.*	54¼N	2¼w	25
Inglewood, *N.I., N.Z.*	39¼s	174¼E	62
Inglewood, *Queens.*	28¼s	151E	60
Inglewood, *Vict., Aust.*	36¼s	143¼E	59
Ingolstadt, *Germany.*	48¼N	11½E	33
Ingonish, *C. Breton I.*	46¼N	60¼w	67
Ingre, *France.*	48N	1½E	30
In Guezzam, *Algeria.*	20N	7E	50
Ingwavuma, *Natal.*	27¼s	32E	55
Inhambane, *Moz.*	23¼s	35¼E	51
Inharrime, *Moz.*	24¼s	35E	51
Inishbofin, I., *Ireland.*	53¼N	10¼w	26
Inisheer, *Ireland.*	53N	9¼w	26
Inishkea Is., *Ireland.*	54¼N	10w	26
Inishmaan I., *Ireland.*	53N	9¼w	26
Inishmurray I., *Ireland.*	54¼N	8¼w	26
Inishowen Hd., *N. Ire.*	55¼N	7¼w	26
Inishtrahull I., *Ireland.*	55¼N	7¼w	26
Inishturk I., *Ireland.*	53¼N	10¼w	26
Injune, *Queens., Aust.*	25¼s	148½E	60
Inland Sea, *Japan.*	34N	133E	49
Inn, R., *Austria.*	47¼N	11¼E	33
Inn, R., *Germany.*	48¼N	13E	33
Innamincka, *S. Aust.*	27¼s	140½E	59
Inner Sound, *Scotland.*	57¼N	6w	24
Innerleithen, *Scotland.*	55¼N	3w	24
Innisfail, *Alb., Can.*	52N	114w	73
Innisfail, *Queens., Aust.*	17¼s	146E	60
Innsbruck, *Austria.*	47¼N	11½E	33
Inny, R., *Ireland.*	53¼N	7¾w	26
Inowroclaw, *Poland.*	52¼N	18½E	33
Insch, *Scotland.*	57¼N	2¾w	24
Inscription, C., *W.Aust.*	25¼s	112¼E	61
Insterburg, see CHERNYAKHOVSK.			
Interlaken, *Switz.*	46¼N	7¾E	31
Inveraray, *Scotland.*	56¼N	5¼w	24
Inverbervie, *Scotland.*	56¼N	2¼w	24
Invercargill, *S.I., N.Z.*	46¼s	168¼E	63
Inverell, *N.S.W., Aust.*	29¼s	151E	59
Inverey, *Scotland.*	57N	3¼w	24
Invergarry, *Scotland.*	57¼N	4¾w	24
Invergordon, *Scotland.*	57¼N	4w	24
Invermoriston, *Scot.*	57¼N	4½w	24
Inverness, *C. Breton I.*	46¼N	61¼w	67
INVERNESS & Tn., *Scot.*	57¼N	4¼w	24
Inverurie, *Scotland.*	57¼N	2¼w	24
Inyandge, R., *Moz.*	20s	35E	51
Inza, *U.S.S.R.*	53¼N	46E	38
Iona, I., *Scotland.*	56¼N	6¼w	24
Ionian Is., *Greece.*	38¼N	20½E	37
Ionian Sea, *Med.*	38N	19E	37
Ios, I. of, *Greece.*	36¼N	25¼E	37
IOWA, *U.S.A.*	42N	93w	75
Iowa City, *Iowa, U.S.A.*	41¼N	91¼w	75
Ipel' River, *Hungary.*	47¼N	19E	33
Ipin, *China.*	28¼N	104¼E	48
Ipoh, *Malaysia (inset).*	4¼N	101¼E	47
Ippi, *Cen. Afr. Rep.*	6N	21E	56
Ipsala, *Turkey.*	40¼N	26¼E	37
Ipswich, *England.*	52¼N	1¼E	23
Ipswich, *Queens., Aust.*	27¼s	153E	60
Iquique, *Chile.*	20¼s	70w	79
Iquitos, *Peru.*	3¼s	73w	78
Iraklion, *Crete.*	35¼N	25E	37
IRAN, *Asia.*	33N	53E	41
Irapuato, *Mexico.*	20¼N	101¼w	76
IRAQ, *Asia.*	33N	44E	41

Place	Lat.	Long.	No.
Irbid, *Jordan* (inset).	32½N	35½E	40
Irbit, *U.S.S.R.*	57¾N	63E	38
Irene, *T'vaal, S. Africa.*	25¾S	28¼E	55
Iri, *Korea.*	36N	127E	49
Iringa, *Tanzania.*	7¾S	35¾E	56
Iriona, *Honduras.*	16N	85W	77
Irkutsk, *U.S.S.R.*	52¼N	104¼E	39
Irma, *Alberta, Can.*	52¾N	111¼W	73
Iron Baron, *S. Aust.*	33S	137¼E	59
Iron Knob, *S. Aust.*	32¾S	137¼E	59
Iron Mt., *Mich., U.S.A.*	46N	88W	75
Ironbridge, *England.*	52¾N	2½W	22
Ironwood, *Mich., U.S.*	46½N	90W	75
Iroquois Falls, *Ontario, Canada* (inset).	49N	80W	71
Irrawaddy R., *Burma.*	16N	95E	43
Irthing, R., *England.*	55N	2¾W	25
Irtysh, R., *U.S.S.R.*	61N	69E	39
Irumu, *Congo (K.).*	1½N	29¾E	56
Irun, *France.*	43¼N	1¾W	32
Irvine, *Alberta, Can.*	50N	110¼W	73
Irvine, *Scotland.*	55¾N	4¾W	25
Irvine Bank, *Queens.*	17½S	145E	60
Irwin, *W. Australia.*	29¼S	115E	61
Isaacs, R., *Queens., Aust.*	24S	150E	60
Isafjordlur, *Ice.* (ins.).	66N	23W	29
Isandlwana, *Natal.*	28¼S	30¾E	55
Isar, Riv., *Germany.*	49N	13E	33
Isarco, Riv., *Italy.*	46½N	11½E	31
Isari, *Greece.*	37½N	22E	37
Ischia, *Italy.*	40¾N	13¾E	36
Ischl, *Austria.*	47¾N	13½E	33
Isdell, R., *W. Aust.*(ins.).	16½S	125E	61
Isdud, *Israel* (inset).	31¾N	34½E	40
Ise & B., *Japan.*	35N	137E	49
Iseo, & L. *Italy.*	45½N	10E	31
ISERE & R., *France.*	45¼N	6½E	32
Iserlohn, *Ger.* (inset).	51¼N	7¾E	33
Iseyin, *Nigeria.*	8N	3¾E	57
Isfahan, *Iran.*	32½N	51E	40
Isha Baidoa, *Somalia.*	3N	44E	56
Ishan, *China.*	24½N	109E	48
Ishikari & Riv., *Japan.*	43N	141E	49
Ishim, *U.S.S.R.*	56N	69½E	39
Ishim, Riv., *U.S.S.R.*	51N	68E	39
Ishimbayeva, *U.S.S.R.*	53½N	56E	38
Ishinomaki, *Japan.*	38½N	141¼E	48
Ishkuman, *Kash.*(ins.).	36¾N	74E	44
Isigny, *France.*	49¼N	1W	31
Isili, *Sardinia.*	39¾N	9E	36
Isipingo, *Natal.*	30S	31E	55
Isiro, *Congo (K.).*	3N	27½E	56
Isisford, *Queens., Aust.*	24¼S	144½E	60
Iskenderon, *Turkey.*	36½N	36¼E	41
Iskilip, *Turkey.*	40¾N	34½E	41
Islamabad, *Kash.* (ins.).	34N	75¼E	44
Island Lagoon, *S. Aust.*	31½S	137E	59
Islands, B. of, *N.I., N.Z.*	35¼S	174¼E	62
Islands, B. of, *Newf., Can.*	49N	58W	67
Islay Is., *Scotland.*	55¾N	6¼W	25
Isle, R., *France.*	45N	¼E	32
Isle Royale, *Mich., U.S.A.*	48N	89W	68
Isle of Ely, *England.*	52½N	0	23
I. de Groix, *France.*	47¾N	3½W	31
I. d'Ouessant Lampaul, *France.*	48½N	5W	31
I. d'Yeu, *France.*	46¾N	2¼W	32
Islington, *S.I., N.Z.* (inset C)			63
Ismail, *U.S.S.R.*	45¼N	28¾E	38
Ismailia, *Egypt*	30¾N	32¼E	50
Isna, *Egypt.*	25N	32½E	40
Isoka, *Zambia.*	10¼S	32¾E	51
Isoladella Scala, *Italy.*	45¼N	11E	31
Isolato, *Italy.*	46½N	9½E	31
Ispagnac, *France.*	44¼N	3¾E	32
Isparta, *Turkey.*	37½N	30½E	41
Ispica, *Sicily.*	36¾N	15E	36
ISRAEL.	32N	35E	41
Israelite Bay, *W. Aust.*	33½S	123½E	61
Issano, *Br. Guiana* (ins.).	6N	59W	77
Issigeac, *France.*	45N	½E	32
Issik Kol, *U.S.S.R.*	42N	76E	39
Issoudun, *France.*	47N	2E	32
Istanbul, *Turkey.*	41N	29E	41
Istiaia, *Greece.*	39N	23½E	37
Istonio, *Italy.*	42N	15E	36
Istria Pen., *Yugoslavia.*	45½N	14E	37
Itabira, *Brazil.*	19½S	43W	79
Itala, *Somalia.*	2¾N	46¼E	56
ITALY, *S. Europe.*			36
Itarsi, *India.*	22¾N	77¾E	44
Itatiaya, Mt., *Brazil.*	22S	45W	78
Itea, *Greece.*	38½N	22½E	37
Ithaca, *N.Y., U.S.A.*	42¼N	76½W	69
Ithake, *Greece.*	38¼N	20¾E	37
Itu, *Nigeria.*	5½N	8E	57
Ituna, *Sask., Canada.*	51¼N	103½W	70
Itzehoe, *Germany* (ins.).	54N	9½E	30
Ivalo, *Finland.*	68N	28E	38
Ivanhoe, *N.S.W., Aust.*	32¾S	144¼E	59
Ivanhoe, *W. Aust.*	15½S	128½E	60
Ivano-Frankovsk, *U.S.S.R.*	49N	24¾E	83
Ivanovo, *U.S.S.R.*	57N	41E	38
Ivdel, *U.S.S.R.*	61N	60E	38
Ivigtut, *Greenland.*	61¾N	47¾W	66
Iviza & Is., *Med.*	39N	1¾E	34
IVORY COAST, *Africa.*	5N	5W	50
Ivrea, *Italy.*	45½N	7¾E	31
Ivry, *France.*	48¾N	1½E	31
Ivybridge, *England.*	50¼N	3¾W	22
Iwakuni, *Japan.*	34N	132E	49
Iwamizawa, *Japan.*	43N	142E	49
Iwo, *Nigeria.*	7½N	4¼E	57
Ixopo, *Natal.*	30¼S	30E	55
Izabal, L. de, *Guat.*	15½N	89W	76
Izhevsk, *U.S.S.R.*	56¾N	53¼E	38
Izhma & R., *U.S.S.R.*	65N	54E	38
Izmir, *Turkey.*	38½N	27E	41
Izmit, *Turkey.*	40¾N	30E	41
JABALPUR, *India.*	23¼N	80E	44
Jablonec, *Czecho.*	50¾N	15¼E	33
Jablonica, *Czecho.*	48½N	17½E	33
Jablunovske, *Czecho.*	49½N	18¾E	33
Jabrin Oasis, *S. Arabia.*	23N	48½E	40
Jaca, *Spain.*	42½N	½W	32
Jacaleapa, *Nicaragua.*	14N	86W	77
Jachal, *Argentina.*	30¼S	69W	79
Jackman, *Maine, U.S.A.*	46N	70W	75
Jackson, *Mich., U.S.A.*	42¼N	84½W	68
Jackson, *Miss., U.S.A.*	32¼N	90¼W	75
Jackson, Mt., *W. Aust.*	30S	119E	61
Jackson, *Tenn., U.S.A.*	36N	89W	75
Jackson, *Wyo., U.S.A.*	43½N	110¾W	74
Jacksonville, *U.S.A.*	30¼N	81¾W	75
Jacksonville, *Ill., U.S.A.*	39¾N	90¼W	75
Jacmel, *Haiti.*	18¼N	73½W	77
Jacobabad, *Pakistan.*	28N	68E	43
Jacobs, *Ontario, Can.*	50¼N	90W	71
Jacobsdal, *O.F.S., S. Afr.*	29S	24¾E	55
Jacobshavn, *Green.*	69¼N	51¼W	66
Jade B., *Germany.*	53½N	8¼E	30
Jaen, *Spain.*	37¾N	3¾W	35
Jaffa-Tel Aviv, *Israel.*	32N	34¾E	41
Jaffa, C., *S. Australia.*	37S	139½E	59
Jaffna Pen. & Lagoon, *Ceylon.*	9¾N	80E	45
Jagdalpur, *India.*	19N	82E	45
Jagersfontein, *O.F.S.*	29¾S	25½E	55
Jaguey Grande, *Cuba.*	22½N	81W	77
Jahashi, *Arabia.*	22½N	51½E	40
Jahrum, *Iran.*	28N	53½E	40
Jaipur, *India.*	27N	75¾E	44
Jaisalmer, *India.*	27N	70¾E	46
Jakarta, *Java.*	6¼S	106¾E	47
Jakkalspruit, *O.F.S.*	28¼S	29½E	55
Jalalabad, *Afghan.*	34¼N	70½E	43
Jalapa, *Nicaragua.*	13¾N	86W	77
Jalapa, *Mexico.*	19½N	97W	76
Jaleswar, *Nepal.*	26½N	86E	44
Jalgaon, *India.*	21N	75¾E	45
Jalingo, *Nigeria.*	8¾N	11¼E	57
JALISCO, *Mexico.*	21N	103W	76
Jalk, *Iran.*	27¾N	62¾E	46
Jalna, *India.*	19¾N	75¾E	45
Jalon, Riv., *Spain*	41½N	2W	35
Jalor, *India.*	25½N	72½E	44
Jalpa, *Mexico.*	22N	103W	76
Jalpaiguri, *India.*	26½N	89E	44
Jaluit Is., *Pacific.*	6N	169E	64
JAMAICA I., *W. Indies.*	18N	78W	77
Jambi, *Sumatra.*	1¾S	103¾E	47
James B., *Canada.*	53N	80W	66
James R., *S. Dak., U.S.A.*	43N	97½W	74
James R., *Virg., U.S.A.*	37N	76W	75
James Ross I., *Antarc.*	64¼S	58W	80
Jamestown, *C. Pr.*	31¼S	26¾E	53
Jamestown, *N.Y., U.S.*	42¼N	79¼W	68
Jamestown, *S. Aust.*	33¼S	138¾E	59
Jamestown, *N.D., U.S.*	47¾N	98W	74
James W. Ellsworth Ld., *Antarctica.*	76S	100W	80
Jammer B., *Denmark.*	57¼N	9E	29
Jammersdrift, *O.F.S.*	29¾S	27E	55
Jammu, *Kashmir.*	32¾N	75E	44
JAMMU & KASHMIR, *Ind.*	35N	75E	42
Jamnagar, *India.*	22½N	70E	46
Jamshedpur, *India.*	23N	86¼E	44
Jamwala, *India.*	21N	71E	43
Jandia Pta., *Can. Is.* (ins.).	28N	14½W	35
Jan Mayen I., *Arctic.*	71N	8W	80
Janow, *Poland.*	52¼N	23¼E	33
Jansenville, *C. Pr., S. Afr.*	33S	24¾E	53
Januaria, *Brazil.*	15¾S	44½W	79
Janville, *France.*	48¼N	1¾E	31
Janze, *France.*	48N	1½W	31
Jaora, *India.*	23¾N	75¼E	44
JAPAN.	36N	138E	49
Japen I., *New Guinea.*	1¾S	136E	47
Japura, R., *Brazil.*	1¾S	67W	78
Jaral, *Honduras.*	15N	87W	76
Jardee, *W. Australia.*	34¼S	116¼E	61
Jardine R., *Queens., Aust.*	10½S	142E	60
Jardines de la Reina Is., *Cuba, W. Indies.*	21N	78W	77
Jargeau, *France.*	47¾N	2¼E	31
Jarlarpet, *India.*	12½N	78½E	45
Jarocin, *Poland.*	52N	17½E	33
Jaromer, *Czecho.*	50¼N	15¾E	33
Jaroslaw, *Poland.*	50N	22¾E	33
Jarrow, *England.*	55N	1½W	25
Jarvis I., *Pacific.*	½S	159¾W	64
Jary, Riv., *Brazil.*	1S	52W	78
Jashpurnagar, *India.*	23N	84E	44
Jasikan, *Ghana.*	7½N	½E	57
Jasina, *U.S.S.R.*	48½N	24½E	37
Jask, *Iran.*	25¾N	57¾E	40
Jaslo, *Poland.*	49¾N	21½E	33
Jason Pen., *Antarctica.*	66¼S	61W	80
Jasper & Nat. Park, *Alberta, Canada.*	52¾N	118W	73
Jassy, *Romania.*	47¼N	27½E	37
Jaszbereny, *Hungary.*	47½N	20E	37
Jath, *India.*	17N	75¼E	45
Jativa, *Spain.*	39N	½W	35
Jauf, *Saudi Arabia.*	29¾N	39¾E	41
Jauja, *Peru* (inset).	11¾S	75¼W	78
Jaunpur, *India.*	25¾N	82¾E	44
JAVA I., *Indonesia.*	7S	110E	47
Javary, Riv., *Brazil.*	4S	70W	78
Java Sea, *Indonesia.*	5S	111E	47
Javron, *France.*	48½N	¾W	31
Jazir, *Arabia.*	18N	56E	40
Jebba, *Nigeria.*	9N	4¾E	57
JEBEL SHAMMAR, *Arab.*	27½N	41E	40
Jedburgh, *Scotland.*	55½N	2½W	25
Jedrzejow, *Poland.*	50¾N	20½E	33
Jefferson City, *U.S.A.*	38½N	92¼W	75
Jefferson, Mt., *U.S.A.*	38¾N	117½W	74
Jeffreys B., *C. Pr., S. Afr.*	34S	25E	53
Jega, *Nigeria.*	12¼N	4¼E	57
Jelai, R., *Malaysia* (inset).	4N	102¼E	47
Jelec, *Yugoslavia.*	43½N	18½E	36
Jelenia Gora, *Poland.*	51N	15¾E	33
Jelgava, *U.S.S.R.*	56¾N	23¾E	38
Jelib, *Somalia.*	½N	42¾E	56
Jellicoe, *Ont., Can.* (ins.).	49¾N	87¾W	71
Jema, *Cent. Afr. Rep.*	6¼N	25E	56
Jemaa, *Nigeria.*	9½N	8¼E	57
Jena, *Germany.*	51N	11½E	33
Jenbach, *Austria.*	47½N	11¾E	31
Jenin, *Jordan* (inset).	32½N	35¼E	40
Jeparit, *Vict., Aust.*	36¼S	142E	59
Jerash, *Jordan* (inset).	32¼N	35½E	40
Jeremie, *Haiti.*	18½N	74¼W	77
Jerez, *Spain.*	36¾N	6W	35
Jericho, *Jordan* (ins.).	31¾N	35½E	40
Jericho, *Queens., Aust.*	23½S	146E	60
Jerilderie, *N.S.W., Aust.*	35¼S	145¾E	59
Jersey, *Channel Is.*	49¼N	2¼W	31
Jersey City, *U.S.* (ins.).	40¾N	74W	75
Jerusalem, *Isr.-Jordan.*	31¾N	35¼E	40
Jervis B., *N.S.W., Aust.*	35S	150¾E	59
Jerzu, *Sardinia.*	39¾N	9½E	36
Jessains, *France.*	48¼N	4½E	30
Jesselton, see KOTA KINABALU.			
Jessore, *Pakistan* (ins.).	23¼N	89¼E	46
Jesup, *Geo., U.S.A.*	32N	82W	75
Jever, *Germany.*	53½N	7¾E	30
JEWISH A.P., *U.S.S.R.*	49N	131E	39
Jeypore, *India.*	18¾N	82¾E	45
Jhansi, *India.*	25½N	78½E	44
Jhawani, *Nepal.*	27½N	84½E	44
Jhelum & R., *Pakistan.*	33N	73¾E	46
Jhunjhunu, *India.*	28¼N	75¼E	44
Jibuti, *Fr. Somaliland.*	11½N	43¼E	56
Jidda, *Saudi Arabia.*	21½N	39½E	40
Jiggalong, *W. Aust.*	23½S	121E	61
Jihlava, *Czecho.*	49½N	15½E	33
Jijiga, *Ethiopia.*	9¼N	42¾E	56
Jiloca, Riv., *Spain.*	40N	0	35
Jimenez, *Mexico.*	27½N	105W	76
Jindabyne, *N.S.W.*	36¼S	148½E	59
Jindrichuv Hradec, *Czechoslovakia.*	49¼N	15E	33
Jinja, *Uganda.*	½N	33¼E	56
Jiran, *Ethiopia.*	7¾N	37E	56
Jitarning, *W. Aust.*	32¾S	118E	61
Joao Pessoa, *Brazil* (ins.).	7S	35W	79
Joazeiro, *Brazil.*	10S	41W	78
Joban, *Japan.*	37N	141E	49
Jobwe, *Ghana.*	8¼N	2W	57
Jodhpur, *India.*	26½N	73E	44
Jodoigne, *Belgium.*	50¾N	4¾E	30
Joensuu, *Finland.*	62½N	29½E	29
Joggins, *No. Scot., Can.*	45¾N	64½W	67
Johannesburg, *T'vaal.*	26S	28E	55
John Day, *Ore., U.S.A.*	44½N	119W	74
John Day R., *Ore., U.S.A.*	46N	121W	74
John o' Groats, *Scot.*	58¾N	3W	24
Johnshaven, *Scotland.*	56¾N	2¼W	24
Johnsonville, *N.I., N.Z.* (inset B).			62
Johnston Lakes, The, *W. Australia.*	32½S	121E	61
Johnston I., *Pacific.*	17N	170W	64
Johnstone Strait, *Can.*	50½N	126W	72
Johnstone, *Scotland.*	55¾N	4½W	25
Johnstown, *Pa., U.S.A.*	40½N	78¾W	75
JOHORE, *Malaysia.*	2N	103E	47
Johore Bahru, *Malaysia.*	1½N	103¾E	47
Joigny, *France.*	48N	3½E	32
Joinville, *Brazil.*	26½S	48¾W	79
Joinville, *France.*	48½N	5¼E	30
Joinville I., *Antarctica.*	63½S	53W	80
Jokea, *Papua* (inset).	8S	146½E	60
Jokelen, *Norway.*	60½N	6¼E	29
Jokjakarta, *Java.*	7¾S	110½E	47
Jokkmokk, *Sweden.*	66½N	20E	29
Jol Buri, *Thailand.*	13N	101E	43
Joliet, *Illinois, U.S.A.*	41½N	88W	75
Joliette, *Quebec, Can.*	46¼N	73½W	69
Jolo, *Sulu Arch., P.I.*	6N	121E	47
Jonaya, *Lith., U.S.S.R.*	55N	24E	33
Jones Sd., *N.W.T., Can.*	76N	85W	66
Jonesville, *Alaska, U.S.*	61½N	150W	74
Jonkoping, *Sweden.*	57¾N	14¼E	29
Jonzac, *France.*	45½N	½W	32
Joplin, *Missouri, U.S.A.*	37N	94½W	75
Jordaan, *O.F.S., S. Afr.*	27½S	27¼E	55
JORDAN, *Asia.*	32N	36E	41
Jordan, R., *Jordan.*	32N	35½E	40
Jordan Valley, *Ore., U.S.*	43N	117½W	74
Jorhat, *India.*	27½N	94E	43
Jos, *Nigeria.*	10N	9E	57
Josselin, *France.*	48N	2½W	31
Joubertina, *C.Pr., S.Afr.*	33¾S	24E	53
Joubertstroon, *T'vaal.*	23¾S	30E	54
Jouvellanos, *Cuba.*	22¾N	81¼W	77
Juan de Fuca Strait, *Canada-U.S.A.*	48¼N	124W	72
Juan Fernandez Is., *Pac.*	33S	80W	78
Juarez, *Mexico.*	18N	93W	76
Juaso, *Ghana.*	6½N	1W	57
Juba, *Sudan.*	5N	31E	56
Juba, Riv., *Somali. Rep.*	0	42½E	56
Jubba, *Arabia.*	28N	41½E	40
Jucar, Riv., *Spain.*	39¼N	¼W	35
Jucaro, *Cuba.*	21½N	79W	77
Juchitan, *Mexico.*	16½N	95W	76
Judaea, *Jordan* (ins.).	31¾N	35¼E	40
Judah, Wilderness of, *Israel* (inset).	31½N	35¼E	40
Judenburg, *Austria.*	47N	15E	37
Juggernaut, see PURI.			
Juian, *China.*	28N	121½E	48
Juigalpa, *Nicaragua.*	12N	85W	77
Juikin, *China.*	26N	116E	48
Juist, I., *Germany.*	53¾N	7E	30
Juiz de Fora, *Brazil.*	21½S	43¾W	79
Jujuy, *Argentina.*	24S	65½W	79
Jukao, *China.*	32½N	121E	48
Juliaca, *Peru* (inset).	15½S	70¼W	78
Julia Crk., *Queens., Aust.*	20½S	141½E	60
Julianehaab, *Green.*	60¾N	46W	66
Julich, *Germany.*	50¾N	7½E	30
Julimes, *Mexico.*	28N	105¾W	76
JULLUNDUR, *India.*	31¼N	75½E	44
Jumilla, *Spain.*	38½N	1W	35
Jumla, *Nepal.*	29¼N	82E	44
Jumme, R., *Germany.*	53½N	7½E	30
Jumna, R., *India.*	25¼N	81¾E	44
Junagadh, *India.*	21½N	70½E	46
Jundah, *Queens., Aust.*	24¾S	143E	60
Juneau, *Alaska, U.S.A.*	58½N	134¾W	66
Junee, *N.S.W., Aust.*	34¾S	147½E	59
Jungfrau, *Switz.*	46½N	8E	31
Jungkiang, *China.*	26N	109E	48
Junin, *Argentina.*	34½S	61W	79
Jur, R., *Sudan.*	8½N	28¼E	56
Jura, I. & Sound, *Scot.*	56N	6W	25
JURA, *France.*	46¾N	6E	32
Jura Mts., *France.*	47N	6½E	32
Jurado, *Colombia.*	7¼N	77½W	77
Jurbarkas, *U.S.S.R.*	55N	22¾E	33
Jurby, *England.*	54¼N	4½W	25
Jurien Bay, *W. Aust.*	30¼S	115E	61
Jurua, R., *Brazil.*	3S	67W	78
Juruena, R., *Brazil.*	7S	58W	78
Jusan, *Japan.*	41N	140½E	49
Jussey, *France.*	47¾N	6E	30
Juterbog, *Germany.*	52N	13E	33
Juticalpa, *Honduras.*	14¾N	86W	77
JUTLAND, *Denmark.*	56N	9E	29
Juwain, *Afghanistan.*	32N	62E	43
Juwara, *Arabia.*	19N	57E	40
Jyvaskyla, *Finland.*	62N	26E	38
Jyekundo, *China.*	33N	97E	43
K2, MT., see GODWIN AUSTEN.			
Kaafiord, *Norway.*	70N	23½E	29
Kaal Spruit, *O.F.S.*	29¼S	26E	55
Kaap Muiden, *T'vaal.*	25½S	31¼E	54
Kabaena I., *E. Indies.*	6S	122E	47
Kabala, *S. Leone* (ins.).	9½N	11½W	57
Kabale, *Uganda.*	2S	30E	56
Kabalo, *Congo.*	6S	27E	56
Kabansk, *U.S.S.R.*	52N	108E	39
KABARDINO BALK A.S.S.R., *U.S.S.R.*	43N	43E	38
Kabba, *Nigeria.*	7¾N	6E	57
Kabel, *Germany* (ins.).	51¼N	7½E	33
Kabi, *Nigeria.*	13N	12½E	56
Kabinda, *Angola.*	5½S	12¼E	56
Kabinda, *Congo.*	6¼S	24¼E	56
Kabo, *Cen. Afr. Rep.*	7½N	18½E	56
Kabompo R., *Zambia.*	13½S	23½E	51
Kabul & R., *Afghan.*	34½N	69E	43
Kachia, *Nigeria.*	9¾N	7¾E	57
Kachuga, *U.S.S.R.*	54N	106E	39
Kadasaka, *Nigeria.*	14N	5½E	57
Kadi, *India.*	23¼N	72¼E	44
Kadina, *S. Australia.*	34S	137¾E	59
Kadugli, *Sudan.*	11N	29¾E	56
Kaduna, *Nigeria.*	10½N	7½E	57
Kadur, *India.*	13½N	76E	45
Kaesong, *Korea.*	38N	126¾E	59
Kafanchan, *Nigeria.*	9½N	8¼E	47
Kaffir R., *O.F.S., S.Afr.*	29½S	26E	55
Kafia Kingi, *Sudan.*	9¾N	24¾E	56
Kafr El Dauwar *Egypt.*	31½N	30E	50
Kafue, *Zambia.*	15¾S	28½E	51
Kafue, R., *Zambia.*	16S	28½E	51
Kagan, *U.S.S.R.*	40N	65E	50
Kagoshima, *Japan.*	31½N	130½E	48
Kahama, *Angola.*	16½S	14E	46
Kahama, *Tanzania.*	3¾S	32½E	56
Kahemba, *Congo.*	7¼S	18½E	56
Kahnsien, *China.*	25½N	115E	48
Kahoku, *Japan.*	38½N	140E	49
Kahoolawe I., *Pacific.*	20N	158W	64
Kahsing, *China.*	31N	121E	48
Kaiama, *Nigeria.*	9½N	4E	57
Kaianda, *Angola.*	11S	23E	56
Kaiapoi, *S.I., N.Z.*	43¼S	172¾E	63
Kaieteur Falls, *British Guiana* (inset).	5N	59½W	77
Kaifeng, *China.*	34¾N	114½E	48
Kaikohe, *N.I., N.Z.*	35½S	173¾E	62
Kaikoura, *S.I., N.Z.*	42½S	173¾E	63
Kailu, *China.*	43N	120½E	39
Kailua, *Hawaii, U.S.A.*	20N	155E	74
Kaimanawa Ra., *N.Z.*	39S	176E	62
Kaipara Har., *N.I., N.Z.*	36¼S	174¼E	62
Kaira, *India.*	22¾N	72¾E	44
Kairouan, see QAIRWAN.			
Kairuku, *Papua* (ins.).	8S	147E	60
Kaisersesch, *Germany.*	50¼N	7¼E	30
Kaiserslautern, *Ger.*	49½N	7¾E	33

Place	Lat.	Long.	No.
Kaisiadorys, Lithuania, U.S.S.R.	55N	24½E	33
Kaitaia, N.I., N.Z.	35S	173½E	62
Kaitangata, S.I., N.Z.	46½S	169¾E	63
Kaitoke I., N.I., N.Z. (inset B).			62
Kaitum Riv., Sweden.	67N	21E	29
Kajaani, Finland.	64¼N	27¾E	29
Kaka, Cent. Afr. Rep.	6N	26E	56
Kakamas, C. Pr., S. Afr.	28¾S	20½E	52
Kakhovka, U.S.S.R.	47N	33E	38
Kakia, Bech. Prot.	25S	23E	51
Kakinada, India.	17N	82¼E	45
Kalabaka, Greece.	39½N	21½E	37
Kalabo, Zambia.	15S	22½E	51
Kaladan, R., Burma.	20N	93E	43
Kalahari Desert, Bech.	23S	22E	51
Kalakan, U.S.S.R.	54N	118E	39
Kalamai, Greece.	37N	22¼E	37
Kalamazoo, Mich., U.S.A.	42¼N	85½W	68
Kalannie, W. Aust.	30½S	117E	61
Kalaotoa I., Indon.	7½S	122E	47
Kalat, Pakistan.	29N	66½E	46
Kalgan, see WANCHUAN.			
Kalgoorlie, W. Aust.	30½S	121½E	61
Kalimantan, Indon.	0	114E	47
Kalimnos, I. of, Greece.	37N	27E	37
Kalinin, U.S.S.R.	56½N	36E	38
Kaliningrad, U.S.S.R.	54½N	20½E	29
Kalisz, Poland.	51¾N	18E	33
Kalix River, Sweden.	66½N	23E	29
Kalkfontein, Bots.	22½S	21E	51
Kalkrand, S.W. Africa.	24S	17E	51
Kall, L. of, Sweden.	63N	13E	29
Kallista, Tas., Aust. (ins.)	43S	146½E	59
Kalmalo, Nigeria.	13½N	5½E	57
Kalmar, Sweden.	56¾N	16½E	29
Kalmar Sound, Sweden.	57N	17E	29
Kalmunai, Ceyl. (ins.).	7½N	81¾E	45
Kalmykovo, U.S.S.R.	48½N	52E	38
Kalpitiya, Ceyl. (ins.).	8¼N	79¾E	45
Kalocsa, Hungary.	46½N	19E	37
Kalomo, Zambia.	17S	26½E	51
Kaluga, U.S.S.R.	54½N	36¼E	38
Kalunga Kameia, Ang.	12S	21E	56
Kalutara, Ceylon.	6½N	80E	45
Kalvarija, U.S.S.R.	54½N	23½E	33
Kalyazin, U.S.S.R.	57N	37½E	38
Kama, R., U.S.S.R.	55½N	49½E	38
Kamabai, S. Leone (ins.).	9½N	12W	51
Kamaishi, Japan.	39N	142E	49
Kamashilu, Angola.	8S	19E	56
Kamba, Nigeria.	12N	3½E	57
Kamberg, Germany.	50½N	8½E	30
Kambia, S. Leone (ins.).	9N	12½W	57
Kambove, Congo (K.).	11S	26¾E	56
Kamchatka, U.S.S.R.	56N	160E	39
Kamen, Germany (ins.).	51½N	7½E	33
Kamen, U.S.S.R.	53½N	81½E	39
Kamenets Podolsk, U.S.S.R.	48½N	26½E	38
Kamensk, U.S.S.R.	48½N	40½E	38
Kamensk Uralsky, U.S.S.R.	56½N	62¾E	38
Kamenskoe, U.S.S.R.	63N	167E	39
Kamet, Mt., Himalayas.	30¾N	79½E	44
Kamien Pomoski, Pol.	54N	14½E	33
Kamishin, U.S.S.R.	50N	45½E	38
Kamloops, Br. Col., Can.	50¾N	120½W	72
Kamo, N.I., N.Z.	35½S	174½E	62
Kampala, Uganda.	½N	32½E	56
Kampar R., Sumatra.	½N	103½E	47
Kampen, Netherlands.	52½N	6E	30
Kamptee, India.	21½N	79½E	44
Kamsack, Sask., Can.	51½N	101½W	70
Kan River, China.	29N	116E	48
Kan River, China.	49½N	125E	39
Kana, T'vaal, S. Africa.	25½S	27½E	54
Kanab, Utah, U.S.A.	37N	113½W	74
Kanash, U.S.S.R.	56N	47½E	38
Kanazawa, Japan.	36½N	136½E	49
Kanchow, China.	26N	115E	48
Kanda Kanda, Congo (K.)	7S	23½E	56
Kandagach, U.S.S.R.	49N	57½E	38
Kandahar, Afghan.	31½N	65½E	43
Kandalaksha, U.S.S.R.	67½N	32½E	38
Kandalakskaya B., U.S.S.R.	66¾N	33E	38
Kandangan, Indon.	3S	115½E	47
Kandavu I., Fiji, Pac.	19S	178½E	64
Kandersteg, Switz.	46½N	7½E	31
Kandi, Dahomey.	11N	2¾E	57
Kandla, India.	23N	70½E	46
Kandos, N.S.W., Aust.	32½S	150E	59
Kandreho, Malagasy.	17½S	46E	56
Kandy, Ceylon.	7½N	80¾E	45
Kane, Penn., U.S.A.	41½N	79W	68
Kangamba, Angola.	13½S	20E	56
Kangar, Malay. (inset).	6½N	100½E	47
Kangaroo I., S. Aust.	35¾S	137½E	59
Kangaruma, Guyana. (inset).	5N	59W	77
Kangean Is., Indonesia.	7S	115½E	47
Kanggye, Korea.	41N	127E	49
Kanggyong, Korea.	36N	127E	49
Kangnung, Korea.	38N	129E	49
Kangombe, Angola.	14S	20E	56
Kangsar, Malay. (inset).	4¾N	100½E	47
Kaniapiskau, R. & L., Quebec, Canada.	58½N	68W	66
Kanin, C., U.S.S.R.	68¾N	43½E	38
Kanin Pen., U.S.S.R.	68N	45E	38
Kankakee, Ill., U.S.A.	41½N	87¾W	75
Kankan, Guinea.	10N	9W	50
Kanker, India.	20½N	81½E	45
Kankesanturai, Ceylon.	9¾N	80E	45

Place	Lat.	Long.	No.
Kannapolis, U.S.A.	35N	81W	75
Kano, Nigeria.	12N	8½E	57
Kanowana, S. Aust.	27½S	139E	60
Kanowna, W. Aust.	30½S	121½E	61
Kanoya, Japan.	31N	131E	49
Kanpur, India.	26½N	80½E	44
KANSAS, U.S.A.	39N	99W	74
Kansas City, U.S.A.	39½N	94½W	75
Kansas R., Kan., U.S.A.	39N	95W	75
Kansk, U.S.S.R.	56N	95E	39
KANSU, China.	35½N	102E	48
Kantang, Thailand.	7½N	99E	47
Kanturk, Ireland.	52¼N	8¾W	26
Kantzehs, China.	32N	100E	43
Kanukov, U.S.S.R.	47N	47½E	38
Kanye, Botswana.	25S	25½E	54
Kao Bang, Indo-China.	23N	106½E	47
Kaochow, China.	21¾N	111E	48
Kao-Lan, China.	36N	104E	43
Kaohsuing, Formosa.	22½N	120E	48
Kaolack, Senegal (inset).	14N	16W	57
Kaomi, China.	37N	119½E	48
Kaoyu & L., China.	33N	118E	48
Kapingamarangi I., Pac.	1N	154E	64
Kapiri Mposhi, Zambia.	14S	28½E	51
Kapiti I., N.I., N.Z.	40½S	175E	62
Kapoeas R., Kal. Indon.	0	109½E	47
Kapoeta, Sudan.	5N	33E	56
Kapompa, Ghana.	8N	1¼W	57
Kaposvar, Hungary.	46½N	17½E	37
Kapsan, Korea.	41½N	128E	49
Kapunda, S. Aust.	34½S	139E	59
Kapuskasing, Ont., Can.	49½N	82½W	71
Kara, U.S.S.R.	69¼N	65E	39
KARA-KALPAK A.S.S.R., U.S.S.R.	43N	57E	38
Karachev, U.S.S.R.	53N	35E	38
Karachi, Pakistan.	24¾N	67E	46
Karafuto, see SAKHALIN.			
Karaga, U.S.S.R.	59½N	163E	39
Karaganda, U.S.S.R.	49¾N	73½E	39
Karaginski I., U.S.S.R.	59½N	163E	39
Karakash, China.	37½N	79E	43
Karakash, R., China.	38N	80E	43
Karakoram Mts., India.	36N	77E	43
Karakoram Pass, Kashmir (inset).	35½N	78E	44
Karakose, Turkey.	39½N	43E	41
Karaman, Turkey.	37½N	33½E	41
Karamea, S.I., N.Z.	41½S	172E	63
Karamea B., S.I., N.Z	41½S	171¾E	63
Karamechen, Bots.	21½S	27½E	54
Karanghutagh, China.	36½N	80E	43
Karanjie, W. Aust. (ins.).	16½S	127½E	61
Karapiro, N.I., N.Z.	38S	175½E	62
Karasburg, S.W. Africa.	28S	18E	51
Karasjok, Norway.	69½N	24E	29
Karatagh Pass, Kashmir (inset).	35½N	78½E	44
Karatsu, Japan.	33½N	130E	49
Karbach, Germany.	51N	9E	33
Karbala, Iraq.	32½N	44E	41
Karbar, W. Australia.	26½S	116½E	61
Karcag, Hungary.	47½N	21E	37
Kardhitsa, Greece.	39½N	22E	37
Karee, O.F.S., S. Africa.	29S	26½E	55
Kareima, Sudan.	18N	32E	40
KARENNI, Burma.	19N	97½E	43
Karesuando, Sweden.	68N	23E	38
Kargat, U.S.S.R.	55N	80E	39
Kargil, Kash. (inset).	34½N	76E	44
Kargya, Kash. (inset).	33½N	77½E	44
Kariba Gorge, Zambia.	17S	28E	51
Karibib, S.W. Afr. (ins.).	22S	16E	51
Karikal, India.	11N	79½E	45
Karimata Is. Indonesia.	1½S	109E	47
Karimundjawa Is., Java.	6S	110E	47
Karisimbi, Mt., Congo (K.).	1½S	29½E	56
Karistos, Greece.	38N	24½E	37
Karitane, S.I., N.Z. (inset D).			63
Karkaralinsk, U.S.S.R.	49N	75E	39
Karlgarin, W. Aust.	32½S	118E	61
Karlo I., Finland.	65N	25E	29
Karlovac, Yugoslavia.	45½N	15½E	37
Karlovci, Yugoslavia.	45N	20E	37
Karlovo, Bulgaria.	42½N	24½E	37
Karlovy Vary, Czecho.	50½N	13E	33
Karlshamn, Sweden.	56N	15E	29
Karlskrona, Sweden.	56½N	15½E	29
Karlsruhe, Germany.	49N	8½E	33
Karlstad, Sweden.	59½N	13½E	29
Karnal, India.	29½N	77E	44
Karnali, R., Nepal.	29N	81E	44
Karnobat, Bulgaria.	42½N	27E	37
Karonga, Malawi.	10S	34E	51
Karonie, W. Aust.	31½S	122½E	61
Karoo, The Great, C. Pr., S. Africa.	32½S	23E	52
Karoonda, S. Aust.	35S	140E	59
Karora, Sudan.	18N	38E	40
Karpenision, Greece.	39N	22E	37
Karperon, Greece.	40N	21½E	37
Karpinsk, U.S.S.R.	60N	60E	38
Karragullen, W. Aust.	32S	116E	61
Karreedouw, C. Pr.	34S	24½E	53
Karreekloof, C. Pr.	29½S	23½E	52
Karri, W. Australia.	29½S	122½E	61
Kars, Turkey.	40½N	43½E	41
Karsakpay, U.S.S.R.	48N	67E	39
Karshi, U.S.S.R.	39N	66E	40
Kartaly, U.S.S.R.	53N	61E	38
Karumba, Queens., Aust.	17½S	140½E	60
Karumbu, Angola.	8S	20E	56
Karwar, India.	14¾N	74½E	45

Place	Lat.	Long.	No.
Kasai, R., Congo (K.).	3½S	19½E	56
Kasama, Zambia.	10½S	31½E	51
Kasaragod, India.	12½N	75E	45
Kasba, L., N.W. Can.	60N	101W	66
Kasempa, Zambia.	13½S	25½E	51
Kashan, Iran.	34½N	51½E	40
Kashgar, Sinkiang, Chi.	39½N	76E	39
Kashin, U.S.S.R.	57½N	37E	38
Kashiwazaki, Japan.	37N	138½E	49
Kashmar, Iran.	35½N	58E	40
Kashmir (inset)	35N	76E	44
Kashmor, Pakistan.	28½N	69½E	46
Kasimov, U.S.S.R.	55N	42E	38
Kasinka, Botswana.	18S	24E	51
Kasko, Finland.	62½N	21½E	29
Kaslo, Br. Col., Can.	49½N	116½W	73
Kasoma, Zambia.	11½S	29½E	51
Kasos, I. of, Greece.	35½N	27E	37
Kassala, Sudan.	15½N	36E	56
Kassel, Germany.	51½N	9E	33
Kastamonu, Turkey.	41½N	33¾E	41
Kastelli, Crete, Greece.	35½N	23½E	37
Kastellion, Crete, Gr.	35½N	25½E	37
Kastoria, Greece.	40½N	21½E	37
Kastornoe, U.S.S.R.	52N	38E	38
Kastrop-Rauxel, Germany (inset).	51½N	7½E	33
Kastrosikia, Greece.	39N	20½E	37
Kasungu, Malawi.	13S	33E	56
Kasur, Pakistan.	31½N	74½E	46
Kata, U.S.S.R.	59N	102E	39
Kataba, Zambia.	16S	25E	51
Katagum, Nigeria.	12½N	10½E	57
Katakolon, Greece.	37¾N	21½E	37
Kataku-Kombe, Con. (K.)	3½S	24½E	56
Katanning, W. Aust.	33½S	117E	61
KATCHIN STATE, Burma.	26N	97½E	43
Katerini, Greece.	40½N	22½E	37
Katha, Burma.	24½N	96½E	43
Katherine, Australia.	14½S	132½E	60
Kathua, Kashmir (ins.).	32N	75½E	44
Katiraveli, Ceylon (ins).	8½N	81½E	45
Katkop, C. Pr., S. Afr.	30½S	20E	52
Katkop, C. Pr., S. Afr.	31S	28½E	53
Katmandu, Nepal.	27¾N	85½E	44
Katokhi, Greece.	38½N	21E	37
Katoomba, N.S.W.	33½S	150½E	59
Katowice, Poland	50N	19E	33
Katrine, Loch, Scot.	56¼N	4½W	25
Katsena, R., Nigeria.	7½N	9E	57
Katsina, Nigeria.	13N	7½E	57
Kattavia, Rhodes Is., Gr.	36N	27½E	41
Kattegat Str., Den.-Swe.	57N	11E	29
Katun, R., U.S.S.R.	53N	86E	39
Katwijk, Netherlands.	52¼N	4½E	30
Kau, Moluccas Indon.	1N	127¾E	47
Kauai I., Hawaii, U.S.	20½N	154½E	74
Kaunas, U.S.S.R.	55N	24E	29
Kaura Namoda, Nig.	12½N	6½E	57
Kautokeino, Norway.	68½N	23E	29
Kavaje, Albania.	41N	19½E	37
Kavak, Turkey.	41N	27E	41
Kavali, India.	15N	80E	45
Kavalla, Greece.	41N	24¾E	37
Kavieng, New Ireland, Pacific (inset).	2½S	151E	60
Kawagoe, Japan.	36N	139½E	49
Kawakawa, N.I., N.Z.	35½S	174E	62
Kawambwa, Zambia.	9½S	29½E	51
Kawardha, India.	22N	81½E	44
Kawasaki, Japan.	35½N	139½E	48
Kawerau, N.I., N.Z.	38S	176½E	62
Kawhia Har., N.I., N.Z.	38S	174½E	62
Kaydale, T'vaal, S. Afr.	26½S	28½E	55
Kayes, Mali.	14½N	11W	50
Kayseri, Turkey.	38½N	35½E	41
Kazachye, U.S.S.R.	70½N	136½E	39
Kazakh, U.S.S.R.	41½N	45½E	38
KAZAKH S.S.R. U.S.S.R.	48N	65E	39
Kazan, U.S.S.R.	55½N	49E	38
Kazan Retto I., Pacific.	25N	141E	64
Kazanlik, Bulgaria.	42½N	25½E	37
Kazatin, U.S.S.R.	50N	29E	38
Kazhim, U.S.S.R.	60½N	51½E	38
Kazombo, Angola.	11½S	23E	56
Kaztalovka, U.S.S.R.	50N	49E	38
Kazvin, Iran.	36½N	50E	40
Kazym, R., U.S.S.R.	64N	66E	39
Kazymskaya, U.S.S.R.	64N	68E	39
Kea, I. of, Greece.	37½N	24½E	37
Keady, Ireland.	54½N	6½W	26
Kebili, Tunisia.	33½N	9E	35
Kechno, Poland.	51½N	18E	33
Kecskemet, Hungary.	47N	19½E	37
KEDAH, Malaysia.	6N	100½E	47
Kedainiai, U.S.S.R.	55½N	24E	33
Keelung, Formosa.	25N	121½E	48
Keer-Weer, C., Aust.	13½S	142E	60
Keetmanshoop, S.W. Africa.	26½S	18½E	51
KEEWATIN, N.W. Can.	63N	90W	66
Keewatin, Ont., Can.	49¾N	94½W	71
Keffi, Nigeria.	9N	7½E	57
Keflavick, Iceland (ins.).	64N	22½W	29
Kegali, U.S.S.R.	64N	161E	39
Kegalla, Ceylon (inset).	7½N	80½E	45
Kegaska, Quebec, Can.	50½N	61½W	67
Kehl, Germany.	48½N	7½E	30
Kei Is., Indonesia.	5½S	132½E	47
Kei Road, C. Pr., S. Afr.	32½S	27½E	53
Keighley, England.	53½N	1¾W	25
Keimoes, C. Pr., S. Afr.	28½S	21E	52
Kei Mouth, C. Pr., S. Afr.	32½S	28½E	53
Keiskammahoek, C. Pr., S. Africa.	32½S	27½E	53

Place	Lat.	Long.	No.
Keitele, L. of, Finland.	63N	25E	29
Keith, Scotland.	57½N	3W	24
Keith, S. Australia.	36S	140½E	59
Keithley Creek, Can.	52½N	121½W	72
Kekirawa, Ceylon (ins.).	8N	80½E	45
KELANTAN, Malaysia.	5N	102E	47
Kelcyre, Albania.	40½N	20½E	37
Keld, England.	54½N	2W	25
Kelibia, Tunisia.	37N	11E	35
Kelkit River, Turkey.	41N	36½E	41
Kellerberrin, W. Aust.	31½S	117½E	61
Kellett, C., N.W. Can.	73N	125W	66
Kelliher, Sask., Can.	51½N	103¾W	70
Kellogg, Idaho, U.S.A.	47N	116W	74
Kells, see CEANANNUS MOR.			
Kelowna, Br. Col., Can.	49½N	119½W	72
Kelrzyn, Poland.	54N	21½E	33
Kelso, Natal.	30½S	30½E	55
Kelso, Scotland.	55½N	2½W	25
Kelvington, Sask., Can.	52½N	103½W	70
Kem & River, U.S.S.R.	65N	34½E	38
Kemaman, Malay (ins.)	4½N	103½E	47
Kemboma, Gabon.	1N	13E	56
Kemerovo, U.S.S.R.	55½N	86E	39
Kemi, Finland.	66N	25E	38
Kemi, L., Finland.	66½N	27½E	29
Kemmerer, Wyo., U.S.A.	42N	110½W	74
Kemp Land, Antarc.	67½S	57E	80
Kempsey, N.S.W., Aust.	31S	152½E	59
Kempten, Germany.	47¾N	10½E	33
Kempton, Tasmania, Australia (inset).	42½S	147½E	59
Kempville, Ont., Can.	45N	75½W	69
Kenadsa, Algeria.	31½N	2½W	34
Kenai Pen., Alaska, U.S.	60N	150W	74
Kenaston, Sask., Can.	51½N	106½W	70
Kendal, England.	54½N	2¾W	25
Kendal, T'vaal, S. Afr.	26S	29E	55
Kendal R., Queens., Aust.	14S	141½E	60
Kendenup, W. Aust.	34½S	117½E	61
Kendrew, C. Pr., S. Afr.	32½S	24½E	53
Kenema, S. Leone (inset).	8N	11¼W	57
Kengtung, Burma.	21½N	99½E	43
Kenhardt, C. Pr., S. Afr.	29½S	21½E	52
Kenifra, Morocco.	33N	6W	34
Kenilworth, England.	52½N	1½W	23
Kenmare, Ireland.	51½N	10W	26
Kenmore, Scotland.	56½N	4W	25
Kennecott, Alaska, U.S.	61½N	142¾W	66
Kennedy, Sask., Can.	50N	102½W	70
Kennedy, C. Fla., U.S.A.	28N	81W	75
Kenogami, Que., Can.	48½N	71W	69
Kenora, Ont., Can.	49¾N	94½W	71
Kenosha, Wis., U.S.A.	42½N	87¾W	75
Kensington, Pr. Ed. I.	46½N	63½W	66
KENT, England.	51½N	½E	27
Kent Pen., N.W. Can.	68N	108W	66
Kentani, C. Pr., S. Afr.	32½S	28½E	53
KENTUCKY, U.S.A.	38N	85W	75
Kentville, Canada.	45½N	64½W	67
KENYA, E. Africa.	1N	38E	56
Kenya, Mt., Kenya.	0	37½E	56
Keppel B., Queens., Aust.	23½S	151E	60
KERALA, India.	10N	77E	45
Kerang, Vict., Aust.	35½S	143¾E	59
Keraudren, C., W. Aust.	20S	120E	61
Kerch, U.S.S.R.	45½N	36½E	38
Kerema, Papua (inset).	8S	146E	60
Keremeos, Br. Col., Can.	49½N	119¾W	72
Keren, Ethiopia.	16N	38½E	56
Kerguelen I., Ind. Oc.	50S	70E	19
Keri Keri, N.I., N.Z.	35½S	174E	62
Kerintji, Mt., Sumatra.	2S	101½E	47
Keriya, China.	37N	82E	43
Kerki, U.S.S.R.	37½N	65E	40
Kerkrade, Netherlands.	50¾N	6E	30
Kermadec Is., S. Pacific.	30S	178W	64
Kerman, Iran.	30½N	57E	40
Kermanshah, Iran.	34½N	47E	40
Kerme, G. of, Turkey.	37N	28E	37
Kermine, U.S.S.R.	40N	65E	40
Kerrobert, Sask., Can.	52N	109½W	70
KERRY, Eire.	52¼N	9½W	26
Kerry Head, Eire.	52½N	10W	26
Kerulen, R., China.	49N	119E	39
Kesan, Turkey.	40¾N	26½E	41
Kesh, Ireland.	54½N	7½W	26
Kestell, O.F.S., S. Afr.	28½S	28½E	55
Kestenga, U.S.S.R.	66N	32E	29
KESTEVEN, England.	53N	½W	23
Keswick, England.	54½N	3½W	25
Keszthely, Hungary.	46¾N	17½E	36
Ket, R., U.S.S.R.	58N	83E	39
Keta, Ghana.	6N	1E	57
Ketapang, Kal., Indon.	1½S	110E	47
Ketchikan, Alaska, U.S.	55½N	131½W	66
Kete Krachi, Ghana.	7½N	0	57
Keton, U.S.S.R.	50N	144E	39
Kettering, England.	52½N	¾W	23
Ketting, C. Pr., S. Afr.	33S	21½E	52
Kettwig, Ger. (inset).	51½N	7E	33
Keweenaw B., U.S.A.	47½N	88½W	68
Key Harb., Ont., Can.	46N	80½W	69
Key, L., Ireland.	54N	8½W	26
Key West, Fla., U.S.A.	24½N	81½W	75
Keynsham, England.	51½N	2½W	22
Khabarovo, U.S.S.R.	70N	60E	38
Khabarovsk, U.S.S.R.	48½N	135E	39
Khachmas, U.S.S.R.	41½N	48E	38
Khadkal, Mongolia.	50N	100E	39
Khaibar, Saudi Arabia.	25½N	40E	40
Khairpur, Pakistan.	27½N	68½E	43
Khairwan, Yem. (ins.).	15½N	44½E	40
KHAKASS A.P., U.S.S.R.	53N	90E	39
Khalaf, Muscat & Oman.	21N	58E	40

[110] Khalka River—Konosha

Place	Lat.	Long.	No.
Khalka River, *China.*	49½N	119E	39
Khalkis, *Greece.*	38½N	23½E	37
Khalmer-Yu, *U.S.S.R.*	68N	64½E	38
Khami, *Rhodesia.*	20½S	28½E	54
Khamir, *Yemen* (ins.).	15½N	44E	40
Khamis Mushait, *Saudi Arabia.*	18N	42½E	40
Khamsara, *U.S.S.R.*	52½N	96E	39
Khana Abasa, *China.*	44N	114½E	39
Khanabad, *Afghan.*	36½N	69E	43
Khanaqin, *Iraq.*	34½N	45½E	41
Khandpara, *India.*	20½N	85½E	45
Khandwa, *India.*	21½N	76½E	44
Khanfur, *S. Yem.* (ins.)	14½N	45E	40
Khanka, L., *U.S.S.R.*	45N	132E	39
Khanty Mansisk, *U.S.S.R.*	62N	69E	39
Khanu, *Iran.*	28N	57½E	40
Khan Yunis, *U.A.R.*	31½N	34½E	40
Khara Usu Nur, L., *Mongolia.*	48N	92E	39
Kharagpur, *India.*	22½N	87½E	44
Kharan Kalat, *Pak.*	28½N	65½E	46
Kharga Oasis, *U.A.R.*	25N	30E	40
Kharit, *Saudi Arabia.*	23½N	51E	40
Kharkov, *U.S.S.R.*	50N	36½E	38
Kharmanli, *Bulgaria.*	42N	26E	37
Kharovsk, *U.S.S.R.*	60N	40E	38
Khartaksha, *Kash.* (ins.).	35N	76½E	44
Khartoum, *Sudan.*	15½N	32½E	56
Khasab, *Mus. & Oman.*	25½N	55½E	40
Khasi Hills, Mts., *India.*	26N	91E	43
Khaskovo, *Bulgaria.*	42N	25½E	37
Khatanga, R. & B., *U.S.S.R.*	73N	106E	39
Kherson, *U.S.S.R.*	46½N	32½E	38
Kheta & R., *U.S.S.R.*	71½N	101½E	39
Khilok, *U.S.S.R.*	51N	110E	39
Khingan Mts., *China.*	50N	121E	39
Khios I., see CHIOS I.			
Khirgis Nur, L., *Mong.*	49N	93E	39
Khiva, *U.S.S.R.*	41½N	60½E	42
Khmelnitskiy, *U.S.S.R.*	49½N	27E	38
Khoi, *Iran.*	38½N	45E	40
Kholm, *U.S.S.R.*	57½N	31½E	38
Khong, *Cambodia.*	14N	106E	47
Khor & R., *U.S.S.R.*	48N	134E	39
Khorog, *U.S.S.R.*	38N	72E	39
Khorramshahr, *Iran.*	30½N	48½E	41
Khoseda Khard, *U.S.S.R.*	67N	59E	38
Khotan, *China.*	37N	80E	43
Khroma, R., *U.S.S.R.*	72N	145E	39
Khulna, *Pakistan.*	22½N	89½E	44
Khur, *Iran.*	33½N	55½E	40
Khurda, *India.*	20½N	85½E	45
Khurma, *S. Arabia.*	21½N	42½E	40
Khurramabad, *Iran.*	33N	48E	41
Khushab, *Pakistan.*	32½N	72½E	46
Khuzdar, *Pakistan.*	27½N	66½E	46
Khvalinsk, *U.S.S.R.*	52½N	48E	38
Khyber Pass, *Pakistan.*	34½N	71½E	46
Kiakhta, *U.S.S.R.*	50½N	106½E	39
Kialing, *China.*	30N	106E	48
Kiama, *N.S.W., Aust.*	34½S	151E	59
Kiamusze, *China.*	46½N	130E	39
Kian, *China.*	27N	115E	48
Kiangling, *China.*	30N	112½E	48
Kiangpeh, *China.*	29½N	106½E	48
KIANGSI, *China.*	27½N	115E	48
KIANGSU, *China.*	33N	120E	48
Kiangtu, *China.*	32½N	119E	48
Kiaohsien, *China.*	37N	120E	48
Kiaokia, *China.*	27N	103E	43
Kiating, *China.*	29N	103½E	43
Kiberg, *Norway.*	71N	31E	29
Kibi, *Ghana.*	6N	½W	57
Kicevo, *Yugoslavia.*	41½N	21½E	37
KickingHorsePass, *Can.*	51½N	116½W	73
Kidderminster, *Eng.*	52½N	2½W	22
Kidnappers, C., *N.Z.*	39½S	177E	62
Kidston, *Queens., Aust.*	19S	144½E	60
Kidwelly, *Wales.*	51½N	4½W	22
Kiel & Canal, *Ger.*	54½N	10½E	33
Kielce, *Poland.*	51N	20½E	33
Kienchwanchow, *Chi.*	26½N	100E	43
Kienko, *China.*	32N	105½E	48
Kienning, *China.*	27N	117½E	48
Kienow, *China.*	27N	118E	48
Kienping, *China.*	42N	120E	48
Kienteh, *China.*	29½N	119½E	48
Kienyang, *China.*	27½N	110E	48
Kienyang, *China.*	27½N	117½E	48
Kiev, *U.S.S.R.*	50½N	30½E	38
Kiewietskuil, *C. Pr.*	32½S	23½E	52
Kieta, *Pacific* (inset).	6S	155E	60
Kifisia, *Greece.*	38N	24E	37
Kigoma, *Tanzania.*	4½S	29½E	56
Kikinda, *Yugoslavia.*	45½N	20½E	37
Kikonai, *Japan.*	41½N	140½E	49
Kikori, R., *Papua* (ins.).	7½S	144E	60
Kikwit, *Congo (K.).*	5½S	18½E	56
Kila Drasan, *Pakistan.*	36N	72E	43
Kila Panja, *Afghan.*	36½N	72E	43
Kilbeggan, *Ireland.*	53½N	7½W	26
Kilchoan, *Scotland.*	56½N	6½W	24
Kilchu, *Korea.*	41N	129½E	49
Kilcoole, *Ireland.*	53½N	6W	26
Kilcullen, *Ireland.*	53N	6¾W	26
KILDARE & Tn., *Ire.*	53½N	7W	26
Kildonan, *Scotland.*	58½N	3¾W	24
Kildonan, *Rhodesia.*	17S	31E	51
Kilfenora, *Ireland.*	53N	9W	26
Kilif, *Afghanistan.*	37½N	66E	43
Kilimanjaro, Mt., *Tanz.*	3S	37½E	56
Kil Kaur, R., *Pakistan.*	25½N	62½E	43
Kilkee, *Ireland.*	52½N	9½W	26
Kilkeel, *Ireland.*	54N	6W	25
Kilkelly, *Ireland.*	53½N	8¾W	26
KILKENNY & Tn., *Ire.*	52½N	7½W	26
Kilkhampton, *Eng.*	50½N	4½W	22
Kilkieran B., *Ireland.*	53½N	9¾W	26
Killadysert, *Ireland.*	52½N	9W	26
Killala & B., *Ireland.*	54½N	9½W	26
Killaloe, *Ireland.*	52½N	8½W	26
Killaloe, *Ontario, Can.*	45½N	77½W	69
Killam, *Alberta, Can.*	52½N	111½W	73
Killarney, *Ireland.*	52N	9½W	26
Killarney, *Man., Can.*	49½N	99½W	70
Killarney, *Ont., Can.*	46N	81½W	68
Killarney, *Queens., Aust.*	28½S	152E	60
Killary Harb., *Ireland.*	53½N	10W	26
Killean, *Scotland.*	55½N	5¾W	22
Killeshandra, *Ireland.*	54N	7½W	25
Killimar, *Ireland.*	53½N	8¼W	66
Killiecrankie, Pass of, *Scotland.*	56½N	3¾W	24
Killin, *Scotland.*	56½N	4¼W	25
Killini, *Greece.*	38N	21E	37
Killybegs, *Ireland.*	54½N	8½W	26
Kilmacthomas, *Ire.*	52½N	7½W	26
Kilmallock, *Ireland.*	52½N	8½W	26
Kilmaluag, *Scotland.*	57½N	6¼W	24
Kilmarnock, *Scotland.*	55½N	4½W	25
Kilmelfort, *Scotland.*	56½N	5½W	25
Kilmichael Pt., *Eire.*	52½N	6W	26
Kilmore, *Eire.*	52½N	6¼W	26
Kilmorie, *Scotland.*	55½N	5¼W	25
Kilmore, *Vict., Aust.*	37½S	145E	59
Kilninian, *Scotland.*	56½N	6¼W	24
Kilninver, *Scotland.*	56½N	5½W	25
Kilombero, R., *Tanzania.*	8S	37½E	56
Kilosa, *Tanzania.*	6½S	37E	56
Kilrea, *Ireland.*	55N	6½W	25
Kilrush, *Ireland.*	52½N	9½W	26
Kilsheelan, *Ireland.*	52½N	7½W	26
Kilsyth, *Scotland.*	56N	4W	25
Kilwa Kivinje, *Tanz.*	8½S	39½E	56
Kilwinning, *Scotland.*	55½N	4¾W	25
Kimberley, *Canada.*	49½N	116W	73
Kimberley, *C.Pr., S.Afr.*	28½S	24½E	53
Kimberley Downs, *W. Aust.* (inset).	17S	125E	61
Kimbolton, *England.*	52½N	¼W	23
Kimbolton, *N.I., N.Z.*	40S	175½E	62
Kimi, Tn. & C., *Gr.*	38½N	24E	37
Kimry, *U.S.S.R.*	57N	37E	38
Kimsquit, *Br. Col., Can.*	52½N	127W	72
Kinabalu, Mt., *E. Mal.*	6N	116½E	47
Kinbrace, *Scotland.*	58½N	4W	24
Kincaid, *Sask., Can.*	49½N	107W	70
KINCARDINE & Tn., *Scot.*	57N	2½W	24
Kinchinjunga, Mt., *Nepal-Sikkim.*	27½N	88½E	44
Kinderscout, Mt., *Eng.*	53½N	2W	23
Kindersley, *Sask., Can.*	51½N	109W	70
Kindu, *Congo (K.).*	3S	26E	56
Kinel, *U.S.S.R.*	53N	51E	38
Kineshma, *U.S.S.R.*	57½N	42½E	38
King George Sound, *W. Australia.*	35S	118E	61
King I., *Br. Col., Can.*	52½N	127½W	72
King I., *Burma.*	12½N	98½E	43
King I., *Tas., Aust.*	40S	144E	58
King Leopold Ra., *Aust.*	17S	126E	61
King Sd., *W. Aust.* (ins.).	17S	123E	61
King William I., *Can.*	69N	98W	66
King William's Town, *C. Pr., S. Africa.*	33S	27½E	53
Kingairloch, *Scotland.*	56½N	5¾W	24
Kingaroy, *Queens., Aust.*	26½S	151½E	60
Kingcome Inlet, *Can.*	50½N	126½W	72
Kingisepp, *U.S.S.R.*	58½N	22½E	38
Kingman, *Ariz., U.S.A.*	35½N	114W	74
Kingmen, *China.*	31N	112E	48
Kingsbridge, *Eng.*	50½N	3¾W	22
Kingsclere, *England.*	51½N	1¼W	23
Kingscote, *S. Aust.*	35½S	137½E	59
Kingscourt, *Eire.*	53½N	6¾W	26
Kingsley, *Natal.*	28S	30½E	55
Kings Lynn, *England.*	52½N	½E	23
Kingston, *England.*	51½N	¼W	23
Kingston, *Jamaica.*	18N	76¾W	77
Kingston, *N.Y., U.S.A.*	41½N	74W	69
Kingston, *Ont., Can.*	44½N	76½W	69
Kingston, *S. Aust.*	36½S	139½E	59
Kingston, *S.I., N.Z.*	45½S	168½E	63
Kingstown, *Wind. Is.*	13½N	61¼W	77
Kingsville, *Ont., Can.*	42N	82½W	68
Kingswood, *T'vaal.*	27½S	25½E	55
Kington, *England.*	52½N	3W	22
Kingtungting, *China.*	24½N	101E	43
Kingussie, *Scotland.*	57½N	4W	24
Kingwilliamstown, *Ireland.*	52½N	9¼W	26
Kingyang, *China.*	36N	107½E	48
Kinhsien, *China.*	39N	121½E	48
Kinhwa, *China.*	29½N	119½E	48
Kinistino, *Sask., Can.*	53N	105W	70
Kinleith, *N.I., N.Z.*	38½S	176E	62
Kinloch Rannoch, *Scot.*	56½N	4¼W	24
Kinlochewe, *Scotland.*	57½N	5¼W	24
Kinlochleven, *Scot.*	56½N	5W	24
Kinnairds Hd., *Scot.*	57½N	2W	24
Kinnegad, *Ireland.*	53½N	7¼W	26
Kinross, *Scotland.*	56½N	3½W	25
Kinross, *T'vaal, S. Afr.*	26½S	29E	55
Kinsale & Harb., *Ire.*	51½N	8½W	26
Kinshasa, *Congo (K.).*	4½S	15½E	56
Kintampo, *Ghana.*	8N	1¾W	57
Kintyre Pen., *Scotland.*	55½N	5½W	25
Kinuso, *Alberta, Can.*	55½N	115½W	73
Kinvarra, *Ireland.*	53½N	8¾W	26
Kinyangiri, *Tanzania.*	4½S	34½E	56
Kinzig, R., *Germany.*	48½N	7½E	30
Kioga, L., *Uganda.*	1½N	33E	56
Kiolen Mts., *Norway.*	68N	16E	29
Kiparissia & G., *Gr.*	37½N	21½E	37
Kipling, *Sask., Can.*	50½N	102½W	70
Kipungo, *Angola.*	15S	14E	56
Kirchdorf, *Germany.*	52½N	8½E	30
Kirchhain, *Germany.*	50½N	9E	30
Kircubbin, *Ireland.*	54½N	5½W	25
Kirensk, *U.S.S.R.*	58N	108E	39
Kirgiz Steppe, *U.S.S.R.*	50N	65E	39
KIRGIZ, *U.S.S.R.*	41N	75E	39
KIRIN, *China.*	43N	127E	49
Kirkbean, *Scotland.*	54½N	3½W	25
Kirkby Lonsdale, *Eng.*	54½N	2½W	25
Kirkby Moorside, *Eng.*	54½N	¾W	25
Kirkby Stephen, *Eng.*	54½N	2½W	25
Kirkcaldy, *Scotland.*	56½N	3¼W	25
Kirkconnel, *Scotland.*	55½N	4W	25
Kirkcudbright, *Scot.*	54½N	4W	25
Kirkenes, *Norway.*	69½N	30E	29
Kirkham, *England.*	53½N	3W	22
Kirkinner, *Scotland.*	54½N	4½W	25
Kirkintilloch, *Scot.*	56N	4¼W	25
Kirkland, L., *Ont., Can.*	48½N	80W	68
Kirklareli, *Turkey.*	41½N	27½E	37
Kirkmichael, *England.*	54½N	4½W	25
Kirkmichael, *Scotland.*	56½N	3½W	24
Kirkoswald, *England.*	54½N	2¾W	25
Kirkoswald, *Scotland.*	55½N	4¾W	25
Kirkstile, *Scotland.*	55½N	3W	25
Kirkuk, *Iraq.*	35½N	44½E	41
Kirkwall, *Scotland.*	59N	3W	24
Kirkwood, *C. Pr., S. Afr.*	33½S	25½E	53
Kirn, *Germany.*	49½N	7½E	30
Kirov, *U.S.S.R.*	54N	35E	38
Kirov, *U.S.S.R.*	58½N	49½E	38
Kirovabad, *U.S.S.R.*	40½N	46½E	38
Kirovakan, *U.S.S.R.*	41½N	44E	38
Kirovograd, *U.S.S.R.*	48½N	32½E	38
Kirovsk, *U.S.S.R.*	67½N	33½E	38
Kirriemuir, *Scotland.*	56½N	3W	24
Kirsanov, *U.S.S.R.*	52½N	42½E	38
Kirsehir, *Turkey.*	38½N	34E	41
Kirton-in-Lindsey, *Eng*	53½N	½W	23
Kiruna, *Sweden.*	67½N	20E	29
Kiryu, *Japan.*	36½N	139½E	49
Kisangani, *Congo (K.).*	½N	25½E	56
Kisbey, *Sask., Canada.*	49½N	102½W	70
Kishangarh, *India.*	26½N	74½E	44
Kishinev, *U.S.S.R.*	47N	28½E	38
Kishiwada, *Japan.*	34½N	135½E	49
Kishtwar, *Kashmir.*	33½N	75½E	44
Kisii, *Kenya.*	1S	35E	56
Kiskunfelegyhaza, *Hungary.*	46½N	19½E	37
Kiskunhalas, *Hung.*	46½N	19½E	37
Kislovodsk, *U.S.S.R.*	44N	42½E	38
Kismayu, *Somali Rep.*	½S	42½E	56
Kiso, Riv., *Japan.*	35N	137E	49
Kispest, *Hungary.*	47½N	19½E	37
Kisumu, *Kenya.*	0	34½E	56
Kitakyushu, *Japan.*	34N	131E	49
Kitale, *Kenya.*	31½N	35E	56
Kitami, *Japan.*	44N	144E	49
Kitangari, *Tanzania.*	10½S	39E	56
Kitchener, *Ont., Can.*	43½N	80½W	68
Kitchener, *W. Aust.*	31S	124½E	61
Kitchioh, *China.*	23N	116E	48
Kitega, *Congo (K.).*	3½S	30E	56
Kithira, I., *Greece.*	36½N	23E	37
Kithnos, I. of, *Greece.*	37½N	24½E	37
Kitimat & R., *Can.*	54N	128½W	72
Kitty Hawk, *U.S.A.*	36N	76W	75
Kitui, *Kenya.*	1½S	38E	56
Kitwe, *Zambia.*	13S	28E	51
Kityang, *China.*	23½N	116E	48
Kitzbuhel, *Austria.*	47½N	12½E	31
Kitzingen, *Germany.*	49½N	10½E	33
Kiuchow, *China.*	25N	106E	48
Kiukiang, *China.*	29½N	116½E	48
Kizel, *U.S.S.R.*	58½N	58E	38
Kizil Irmak, R., *Turkey*	41½N	34E	41
Kizlyar, *U.S.S.R.*	44N	47E	38
Klaarstroom, *C. Pr.*	33½S	22½E	52
Kladanj, *Yugoslavia.*	44½N	18½E	36
Kladno, *Czecho.*	50½N	14E	33
Klagenfurt, *Austria.*	46½N	14½E	33
Klaipeda, *U.S.S.R.*	55½N	21½E	38
Klamath Falls, *U.S.A.*	42½N	121½W	74
Klang, *Malaysia* (inset).	3N	101½E	47
Klar River, *Sweden.*	59N	14E	29
Klawer, *C. Pr., S. Afr.*	31½S	18½E	52
Kleena Kleene, *Canada.*	52N	124½W	72
Kleinbegin, *Cape Pr.*	28½S	21½E	52
Kleinpoort, *Cape Pr.*	33½S	24½E	53
Klerksdorp, *T'vaal, South Africa.*	27S	26½E	55
Kleve, *Germany.*	51½N	6E	33
Klintehamn, *Sweden.*	57N	19E	29
Klip River, *Transvaal.*	26½S	28E	51
Klipbak, *C. Pr., S. Afr.*	29½S	22½E	52
Klipbank, *C. Pr., S. Afr.*	32½S	22½E	52
Klipdale, *C. Pr., S. Afr.*	34½S	20E	52
Klipheuwel, *Cape Pr.*	33½S	18½E	52
Kliphoek, *C. Pr., S. Afr.*	31½S	18½E	52
Klipplaat, *C. Pr., S. Afr.*	33S	24½E	53
Kljuc, *Yugoslavia.*	44½N	16½E	36
Klodawa, *Poland.*	52½N	19E	33
Klodzka, *Poland.*	50½N	16½E	33
Klondike R., *Yukon.*	64N	139W	66
Klosters, *Switzerland.*	46½N	9½E	31
Klouto, *Togo.*	7N	½E	57
Kluang, *Malaysia* (inset).	2N	103½E	47
Kluczborek, *Poland.*	51N	18½E	33
K. Mbre, *Cent. Afr. Rep.*	7N	20E	56
Knapdaar, *C. Pr., S. Afr.*	30½S	26½E	53
Knaresborough, *Eng.*	54N	1½W	25
Knight Inlet, *Canada.*	51N	125½W	72
Knighton, *Wales.*	52½N	3W	22
Knin, *Yugoslavia.*	44N	16E	36
Knittelfeld, *Austria.*	47½N	14½E	33
Knjazevac, *Yugoslavia.*	43½N	22½E	37
Knob, C., *W. Aust.*	34½S	119E	61
Knockmealdown Mts., *Ireland.*	52½N	8W	26
Knox Coast, *Antarc.*	66½S	105E	80
Knoxville, *Tenn., U.S.A.*	36N	84W	75
Knutsford, *England.*	53½N	2½W	22
Knyazhpogos, *U.S.S.R.*	62½N	51E	38
Knysna, *C. Pr., S. Afr.*	34S	23E	52
Knyszyn, *Poland.*	53½N	23E	33
Ko Pa Ngan I., *Thai.*	10N	100E	43
Ko Samui I., *Thailand.*	9N	100E	43
Kobayashi, *Japan.*	32N	131E	49
Kobe, *Japan.*	34½N	135½E	49
Koblenz, *Germany.*	50½N	7½E	33
Kobryn, *U.S.S.R.*	52½N	24½E	38
Koburg, *Germany.*	50½N	11E	33
Kocaeli, see IZMIT.			
Kocane, *Yugoslavia.*	41½N	22½E	37
Kocevje, *Yugoslavia.*	45½N	15E	37
Kochechuma, R., *U.S.S.R.*	65N	100E	39
Kocher, Riv., *Germany.*	49N	9E	33
Kochi, *Japan.*	33½N	133½E	49
Kochumdek, *U.S.S.R.*	65N	92E	39
Kock, *Poland.*	51½N	22½E	33
Kodiak, *Alaska, U.S.A.*	57N	151W	74
Kodima, *U.S.S.R.*	62½N	44½E	38
Koekemoer, *T'vaal.*	26½S	26½E	55
Koekenaap, *Cape Pr.*	31½S	18½E	52
Koffifontein, *O.F.S.*	29½S	25E	55
Koforidua, *Ghana.*	6½N	½W	57
Kofu, *Japan.*	35½N	138½E	49
Koge, *Denmark.*	55½N	12½E	33
Kohat, *Pakistan.*	33½N	72E	43
Koivisto, *U.S.S.R.*	60½N	28½E	38
Kojonup, *W. Aust.*	34S	117½E	61
Kokand, *U.S.S.R.*	40½N	71E	39
Kokanee Glacier, *Can.*	49½N	117½W	73
Kokchetav, *U.S.S.R.*	53½N	69½E	39
Kokeby, Mt., *W. Aust.*	32S	117E	61
Kokerit, *Guyana* (ins.).	8N	59W	77
Kokkola, *Finland.*	64N	23E	36
Koko, *Nigeria.*	11½N	4½E	57
Koko Nor, L., *China.*	37N	100E	43
Kokpekty, *U.S.S.R.*	49N	82E	39
Kokstad, *C. Pr., S. Afr.*	30½S	29½E	53
Kokumbi, *Angola.*	10S	19E	56
Kola & R., *U.S.S.R.*	69N	33E	38
Kola Pen., *U.S.S.R.*	67N	38E	38
Kolan, *China.*	39N	111½E	48
Kolar, *India.*	13½N	78½E	45
Kolarovgrad, *Bulgaria.*	43N	27E	37
Kolda, *Senegal* (inset).	13N	15W	57
Kolding, *Denmark.*	55½N	9½E	33
Kolguev I., *U.S.S.R.*	69N	49E	38
Kolhapur, *India.*	16½N	74½E	45
Kolin, *Czechoslovakia.*	50N	15½E	33
Koln, see COLOGNE.			
Kolo, *Poland.*	52½N	18½E	33
Kolobrzeg, *Poland.*	54½N	15½E	33
Kolomiya, *U.S.S.R.*	48½N	25E	38
Kolomna, *U.S.S.R.*	55N	38½E	38
Kolpakovo, *U.S.S.R.*	55N	155E	39
Kolpashevo, *U.S.S.R.*	58½N	82½E	39
Kolyma, R., *U.S.S.R.*	69N	160E	39
Kolymski B., *U.S.S.R.*	70N	160E	39
Komadugu, R., *Nigeria.*	13N	13E	57
Komarno, *Czecho.*	47½N	18E	33
Komatipoort, *T'vaal.*	25½S	32E	54
Komboti, *Greece.*	39N	21E	37
Komga, *C. Pr., S. Afr.*	32½S	27½E	53
KOMI A.S.S.R., *U.S.S.R.*	63N	55E	38
Komotini, *Greece.*	41N	25½E	37
Kompanjiesdrif, *C. Pr.*	33½S	24E	53
Komsomolets B., *U.S.S.R.*	45N	53E	38
Komsomolets I., *Arc.*	80½N	98E	39
Komsomolsk, *U.S.S.R.*	50½N	137E	39
Konakri, *Guinea.*	9½N	13½W	50
Konch, *India.*	26N	79E	44
Kondakovo, *U.S.S.R.*	70N	152E	39
Kondinin, *W. Aust.*	32½S	118½E	61
Kondinskoe, *U.S.S.R.*	62½N	66E	38
Kondoa Irangi, *Tanzania.*	5S	35½E	56
Kondopoga, *U.S.S.R.*	62½N	34½E	38
Konduka, *Papua* (inset).	9S	142E	60
Kondut, *W. Aust.*	30½S	116E	61
Kong, *Ivory Coast.*	9N	4½W	50
Kongka Dzong, *Tibet.*	29N	91E	43
Kongmoon, *China.*	22½N	112½E	48
Kongolo, *Congo (K.).*	5½S	27E	56
Kongsberg, *Norway.*	60N	9E	29
Kongsvinger, *Norway.*	60N	12E	29
Kongwa, *Tanzania.*	6S	36½E	56
Konigsberg, see KALININGRAD.			
Konigshofen, *Ger.*	49½N	9½E	33
Konigshutte, see KROLEWSKA HUTA.			
Konigswinter, *Ger.*	50½N	7½E	30
Konin, *Poland.*	52½N	18½E	33
Konispol, *Albania.*	39½N	20E	37
Konjic, *Yugoslavia.*	43½N	18E	37
Konkib, R., *S.W. Africa.*	28S	17E	51
Konosha, *U.S.S.R.*	61½N	40E	38

Konotop-Lacapelle [111]

Place	Lat.	Long.	No.
Konotop, U.S.S.R.	51½N	33E	38
Konskie, Poland.	51¼N	20½E	33
Konstantinovka, U.S.S.R.	48N	37¾E	38
Konstanz, Germany.	47¾N	9¼E	31
Kontagora, Nigeria.	10¼N	5½E	57
Konya, Turkey.	37¾N	32½E	41
Konza, Kenya.	1¾S	37E	56
Kookynie, W. Aust.	29¼S	121½E	51
Koolamarra, Queens.	20¼S	140¼E	60
Koopmansfontein, C. Pr., S. Africa.	28¼S	24E	53
Koorawatha, N.S.W.	34S	148¾E	59
Koorda, W. Aust.	30¾S	117½E	61
Kootenay L. & R., Can.	49½N	116¾W	73
Kootenay Park, Can.	51N	116W	73
Kootjieskolk, C. Pr.	31¼S	20¼E	52
Kopperamanna, S. Aust.	28¾S	138¾E	59
Koppies, O.F.S., S. Afr.	27¼S	27½E	55
Koprivnica, Yugo.	46¼N	16¾E	36
Korat, see NAKHON RATCHASIMA.			
Korbu, Mt., Mal. (ins.).	4¾N	101½E	47
Korcula & I., Yugo.	43N	17E	37
Korczyn, Poland.	50¼N	20¾E	33
KOREA, Asia.	38N	127E	49
Korea Strait, Korea.	35N	129E	49
Koritsa, Albania.	40¾N	20¾E	37
Koriyama, Japan.	37½N	140½E	48
Korkodon, U.S.S.R.	65½N	153E	39
Korku, Kashmir (ins.).	35½N	76½E	44
Kormakiti, C., Cyprus.	35½N	32½E	41
Kormend, Hungary.	47N	16½E	37
Kornik, Poland.	52¼N	17E	33
Korogwe, Tanzania.	5¼S	38½E	56
Koroit, Victoria, Aust.	38¼S	142¼E	59
Koronowo, Poland.	53¼N	18E	33
Korosten, U.S.S.R.	51½N	28E	38
Korotoyak, U.S.S.R.	51N	39½E	38
Korsakov, U.S.S.R.	47N	144E	39
Korsor, Denmark.	55¼N	11¼E	33
Korumburra, Victoria.	38½S	145¾E	59
Kos I., Aegean Sea.	36¾N	27¼E	37
Kosaka, Japan.	40½N	140½E	49
Koscian, Poland.	52N	16¾E	33
Koscierzyna, Poland.	54¼N	18E	33
Kosciusko, Mt., Aust.	36S	149E	59
Kosh Agach, U.S.S.R.	50N	89E	39
Koshan, China.	48N	125E	39
Kosi, Riv., India.	25½N	87E	44
Kosice, Czechoslovakia.	48¾N	21¼E	33
KOSMET, Yugoslavia.	42½N	21E	37
Koso Gol, Mongolia.	52N	99E	39
KOSOVO-METOHIJA, Yugoslavia.	42½N	21E	37
Kostajnica, Yugo.	45¼N	16½E	36
Koster, T'vaal, S. Afr.	25¾S	27E	55
Kosti, Sudan.	13¼N	32¾E	56
Kostroma, U.S.S.R.	57¾N	41E	38
Kostrzyn, Poland.	52½N	17¼E	33
Kostrzyn, Poland.	52½N	14¾E	33
Kosyavon, U.S.S.R.	66½N	60E	38
Koszalin, Poland.	54¼N	16¼E	33
Kota Bharu, Malaysia.	6N	102¼E	47
Kota Kinabalu, E. Malaysia.	6N	116E	47
Kota Kota, see NKHOTAKOTA.			
Kota Tinggi, Malaysia.	1¾N	103¾E	47
Kotaagung, Sumatra.	5½S	105E	47
Kotabaru, Indon.	3¼S	116¼E	47
Kotah, India.	25¼N	75¾E	44
Kotelnich, U.S.S.R.	58N	48E	38
Kotelnikovo, U.S.S.R.	47¾N	43¼E	38
Kotelny I., U.S.S.R.	75N	138E	39
Kothen, Germany.	51¾N	12E	33
Kotka, Finland.	60½N	27E	29
Kotlas, U.S.S.R.	61N	46½E	38
Kotli, Kashmir (ins.).	33¾N	74E	44
Koton Karifi, Nigeria.	8N	6¾E	57
Kotonu, Dahomey.	6¼N	2½E	57
Kotor, Yugoslavia.	42½N	18¾E	37
Kotovsk, U.S.S.R.	47¾N	29¾E	38
Kotri, Pakistan.	25¼N	68E	43
Kottbus, Germany.	51¾N	14¼E	33
Kotuy, Riv., U.S.S.R.	68N	104E	39
Kotzebue, Alaska, U.S.	66N	161W	74
Kouande, Dahomey.	10¼N	1½E	57
Koudekraal, O.F.S.	30½S	26½E	55
Koudougou, Up. Volta.	12¼N	2¼W	57
Koulikoro, Mali.	13N	7½W	50
Koumala, Queens., Australia.	21¾S	149¼E	60
Kounradski, U.S.S.R.	47N	75E	39
Kouvola, Finland.	61N	27E	38
Kovin, Yugoslavia.	44¾N	21E	37
Kovno, see KAUNAS.			
Kovrov, U.S.S.R.	56½N	41¼E	38
Kowal, Poland.	52½N	19¼E	33
Kowel, U.S.S.R.	51¼N	24¾E	38
Kowloon, China.	22½N	114¾E	48
Koyiu, China.	22½N	112½E	48
Kozani, Greece.	40¼N	22E	37
Kozhikode, India.	11¼N	75¾E	45
Kozienice, Poland.	51½N	21½E	33
Kozle, Poland.	50¼N	18E	33
Kpandu, Ghana.	7N	¼E	57
Kpong, Ghana.	6¼N	0	57
Kra Isthmus, Thailand.	10N	99E	43
Kraankuil, C.Pr., S.Afr.	29¾S	24¼E	53
Krabi, Thailand.	8N	99E	43
Krabin, Thailand.	14N	102E	43
KRACHI, Ghana.	8N	0	57
Kragero, Norway.	59N	9½E	29
Kragujevac, Yugoslavia	44N	21E	37
Krajnfors, Sweden.	63N	17E	29
Krakatau I., Indonesia.	6¼S	105½E	47
Krakeel River, C. Pr.	33¾S	23¼E	53
Krakow, see CRACOW.			
Kraljevo, Yugoslavia.	43¾N	20¾E	37
Kralovany, Czecho.	49¼N	19E	33
Kramatorska, U.S.S.R.	48½N	37E	38
Kranj, Yugoslavia.	46¼N	14¼E	36
Kranskop, Natal.	29S	30¾E	55
Krantz Berg, T'vaal.	24½S	27½E	54
Kraskino, U.S.S.R.	42½N	131E	49
Kraslice, Czecho.	50¼N	12½E	33
Krasnaya Sloboda, U.S.S.R.	48½N	45E	38
Krasnik, Poland.	51N	22¼E	33
Krasnodar, U.S.S.R.	45N	39E	38
Krasnoselkupsk, U.S.S.R.	65N	82E	39
Krasnoturinsk, U.S.S.R.	59¾N	60½E	38
Krasnoufimsk, U.S.S.R.	56½N	57¾E	38
Krasnouralsk, U.S.S.R.	58½N	60E	39
Krasnovishersk, U.S.S.R.	60½N	57E	38
Krasnovodsk, U.S.S.R.	40N	53E	38
Krasnoyarsk, U.S.S.R.	56N	93E	39
Krasny Yar, U.S.S.R.	46½N	49E	38
Krasnystaw, Poland.	51N	23¼E	33
Kratie, Cambodia.	12½N	106E	47
Kratovice, Czecho.	49½N	15E	33
Kratovo, Yugoslavia.	42N	22E	37
Krefeld-Urdingen, Germany.	51¼N	6½E	33
Krekenava, U.S.S.R.	55½N	24¼E	33
Kremenchug, U.S.S.R.	49N	33½E	38
Kremnica, Czecho.	48¾N	19E	33
Krems, Austria.	48½N	15½E	33
Kresevo, Yugoslavia.	43¾N	18E	36
Kresta B., U.S.S.R.	66N	180E	39
Kribi, Cameroon.	3N	10E	56
Krige, C. Pr., S. Afr.	34¼S	19½E	52
Krilon, C., U.S.S.R.	46N	142E	49
Krimml, Austria.	47¼N	12E	31
Krioneri, Greece.	38¼N	21½E	37
Krios, C., Crete.	35N	23½E	37
Krishna, Riv., India.	16N	81E	45
Kristiansand, Norway.	58¼N	8E	29
Kristianstad, Sweden.	56N	14E	29
Kristiansund, Norway.	63¼N	7¾E	29
Kristiinankaupunki, Finland.	62¼N	21¼E	29
Kristinehamn, Sweden.	59N	14E	29
Krivoi Rog, U.S.S.R.	48N	33¼E	38
Krk, Yugoslavia.	45N	14½E	36
Krolewska Huta, Pol.	50¼N	19E	33
Krom R., C. Pr., S. Afr.	32S	23E	52
Kromeriz, Czecho.	49¼N	17½E	33
Kronstad, U.S.S.R.	60N	29¾E	38
Kroonstad, O.F.S.	27¾S	27¼E	55
Kropotkin, U.S.S.R.	45¼N	40½E	38
Krosno, Poland.	49¾N	21¾E	33
Krosno, Poland.	52N	15E	33
Krotoszyn, Poland.	51¾N	17½E	33
Krsko, Yugoslavia.	46N	15½E	36
Kruger Park, S. Africa.	24S	31½E	54
Krugers, O.F.S., S. Afr.	30S	25¾E	55
Krugersdorp, T'vaal.	26S	27¾E	55
Kruidfontein, C. Pr.	32¾S	22E	52
Kruisfontein, C. Pr.	34S	24¾E	53
Kruje, Albania.	41½N	19¾E	37
Krusevac, Yugoslavia.	43½N	21¼E	37
Krustpils, U.S.S.R.	56½N	25¾E	29
Kruszwica, Poland.	52¾N	18¼E	33
Krumlov, Czecho.	48¾N	14¼E	33
Krzyz, Poland.	53N	16½E	33
Ksar Smeidi, Mali.	22N	4W	50
Kuala Besut, Malaysia.	5¾N	102¾E	47
Kuala Brang, Malaysia.	5N	103E	47
Kuala Dungun, Malay.	4¾N	103¼E	47
Kuala Krai, Malaysia.	5¾N	102E	47
Kuala Lipis, Malaysia.	4¼N	102E	47
KUALA LUMPUR, Malay.	3½N	101¾E	47
Kuala Selangor, Malay.	3¼N	101¼E	47
Kuala Tembeling, Mal.	4N	102¼E	47
Kuala Trengganu, Mal.	5¼N	103¼E	47
Kuango, Cent. Afr. Rep.	5N	20E	56
Kuantan, Malaysia.	3¾N	103¼E	47
Kuba, U.S.S.R.	41½N	48E	38
Kuban, R., U.S.S.R.	45¼N	38E	38
Kubango, Angola.	14S	16E	56
Kubenskoe, L., U.S.S.R.	59¾N	39¼E	38
Kuberle, U.S.S.R.	47N	42E	38
Kubia, Angola.	16½S	22E	56
Kubusie, C. Pr., S. Afr.	32½S	27½E	53
Kucha, China.	42N	83E	39
Kuchengtze, China.	44N	89½E	39
Kuching, E. Malaysia.	1½N	110¼E	47
Kudat, E. Malaysia.	7N	116¾E	47
Kufstein, Austria.	47½N	12¼E	33
Kugaly, U.S.S.R.	44N	79E	39
Kuhak, Iran.	27¼N	63¼E	40
Kui, Thailand.	12½N	100E	43
Kuibis, S.W. Africa.	26¾S	16¾E	51
Kuibyshev, U.S.S.R.	53¼N	50E	38
Kuizeb, R., S.W. Africa.	23S	14E	51
Kukawa, Nigeria.	13N	13½E	57
Kukerin, W. Aust.	33¼S	118E	61
Kukes, Albania.	42N	20½E	37
Kula, Bulgaria.	44N	22½E	37
Kulaly I., U.S.S.R.	45N	50E	38
Kulanuldi, Kash. (ins.).	36½N	77½E	44
Kulay, U.S.S.R.	58N	75E	39
Kulebaki, U.S.S.R.	55½N	42½E	38
Kulin, W. Australia.	32¾S	118¼E	61
Kulja, Sinkiang, China.	44N	81¼E	39
Kullen, Sweden.	56½N	13E	29
Kulmbach, Germany.	50N	11½E	33
Kululli, Ethiopia.	14¼N	40E	56
Kulun-Nor, China.	49N	116½E	39
Kulunda, U.S.S.R.	53N	79E	39
Kulwin, Vict., Aust.	35S	142¾E	59
Kum, Riv., Korea.	35N	129E	49
Kuma Riv., U.S.S.R.	45N	46E	38
Kumagaya, Japan.	36N	139E	49
Kumai B., Indonesia.	3S	111¾E	47
Kumamoto, Japan.	32¾N	130¾E	48
Kumanovo, Yugo.	42¼N	21½E	37
Kumara, S.I., N.Z.	42¾S	171¼E	63
Kumara River, China.	52N	126E	39
Kumarl, W. Australia.	32½S	122E	61
Kumasi, Ghana.	6¾N	1¾W	57
Kumawu, Ghana.	7N	1¼W	57
Kumba, Nigeria.	4½N	9½E	57
Kumbakonam, India.	12N	79E	43
Kumbher, Nepal.	28N	81½E	43
Kumbungu, Ghana.	9½N	1W	57
Kumchon, Korea.	36N	128E	49
Kumea, N.I., N.Z. (inset A).			62
Kumhae, Korea.	35N	129E	49
Kumta, India.	14¼N	74¼E	45
Kunduz Riv., Afghan.	37N	67½E	43
Kunene, Riv., Angola.	17S	12E	56
Kunga, Angola.	9S	14E	56
Kunhsien, China.	32½N	111E	48
Kums, S.W. Africa.	28S	19½E	52
Kun Lun Mts., China.	37N	80E	43
Kunama, N.S.W.	35½S	149E	60
Kundip, W. Australia.	33¾S	120¼E	61
Kungrad, U.S.S.R.	43N	59E	40
Kungur, U.S.S.R.	57½N	57E	38
Kungurri, Queens., Aust.	21½S	148E	60
Kunming, China.	25¼N	102½E	43
Kunmunyah, W. Aust.	16S	125E	61
Kunsan, Korea.	36N	126¾E	48
Kuolayarvi, U.S.S.R.	67N	29E	38
Kuopio, Finland.	63N	27¾E	29
Kupa Riv., Yugoslavia.	45½N	16½E	36
Kupang, Timor, Indon.	10¼S	123½E	47
Kupyansk, U.S.S.R.	50N	38E	38
Kura River, U.S.S.R.	39N	49E	38
Kurasai, China.	37N	84E	43
Kurashiki, Japan.	35N	134E	49
KURDISTAN, Turkey.	37½N	43½E	41
Kurdzhali, Bulgaria.	41½N	25¼E	37
Kure, Japan.	34¼N	132½E	48
Kure I., Pacific.	29N	179W	64
Kureyka, Riv., U.S.S.R.	66N	88E	39
Kurgan, U.S.S.R.	55½N	65¼E	39
Kuria I., Pacific.	0	172E	64
Kuria Muria Is., Muscat & Oman.	16N	56E	40
Kuridala, Queens., Aust.	21½S	140½E	60
Kuril Is., U.S.S.R.	45N	150E	39
Kurkliai, U.S.S.R.	55¼N	25E	33
Kurisches Haff, U.S.S.R.	55N	21E	33
Kurnalpi, W. Aust.	31S	122¼E	61
Kurnool, India.	15¾N	78E	45
Kurow, S.I., N.Z.	44¾S	170½E	63
Kurrajong, W. Aust.	28S	121E	61
Kursk, U.S.S.R.	51¾N	36¼E	38
Kuruman, C. Pr., S. Afr.	27½S	23½E	51
Kurume, Japan.	33¼N	130½E	48
Kurunegala, Ceylon.	7½N	80½E	45
Kusaie I., Pacific.	5N	164E	64
Kushaka, Nigeria.	10½N	6¾E	57
Kushchevsk, U.S.S.R.	47N	40E	38
Kusheriki, Nigeria.	10½N	6½E	57
Kushevat, U.S.S.R.	65N	65E	38
Kushih, China.	32¼N	116E	48
Kushikino, Japan.	32N	131E	49
Kushk, Afghanistan.	35N	62½E	43
Kushka, U.S.S.R.	35¼N	62½E	43
Kushiro, Japan.	43N	144¼E	49
Kushva, U.S.S.R.	58¼N	59¾E	38
Kusong, Korea.	40N	125E	49
Kustanay, U.S.S.R.	53¼N	63½E	39
Kut Al Imara, Iraq.	32¼N	46E	41
Kutahya, Turkey.	39½N	30E	41
Kutaisi, U.S.S.R.	42¼N	42¾E	38
Kutchan, Japan.	43N	141E	49
Kutina, Yugoslavia.	45¼N	16¾E	36
Kutno, Poland.	52¼N	19¼E	33
Kutsing, China.	25½N	104E	48
Kutum, Sudan.	14¾N	24¾E	56
Kuusamo, Finland.	66N	29E	38
Kuvandi, U.S.S.R.	51½N	57E	38
KUWAIT & B., Arabia.	29N	47½E	41
Kuyeh, China.	35¼N	115½E	48
Kuznetsk, U.S.S.R.	53N	46½E	38
Kvalo, Norway.	71N	24E	29
Kvalo I., Norway.	70½N	19E	29
Kwaiping, China.	23½N	110E	48
Kwajalein, Pacific.	9N	162E	64
Kwale, Nigeria.	5¾N	6½E	57
Kwamba, Mozambique.	15S	37E	51
Kwangchang, China.	27N	116¼E	48
Kwangchow, China	23¼N	113¼N	48
Kwanghwa, China.	32¼N	111½E	48
Kwangju, Korea.	35¼N	127E	49
Kwangnan, China.	24N	105E	48
Kwangsi-Chuang, Chi.	24N	108E	48
KWANGTUNG, China.	23½N	112½E	48
Kwanhsien, China.	31N	103E	48
Kwantung Pen., China.	39N	121E	48
Kwatarkwashi, Nigeria.	12N	6¾E	57
Kwe Not, R., Thailand.	18N	100E	43
Kweekwa, C. Pr., S. Afr.	31¼S	22¾E	52
Kweichin, China.	31N	117½E	48
KWEICHOW, China.	27N	106E	48
Kweiki, China.	28N	117½E	48
Kweilin, China.	25¼N	110¼E	48
Kweisui, see HUHEHOT.			
Kweiyang, China.	26½N	106½E	48
Kweiyang, China.	25¾N	112¾E	48
Kwinana, W. Aust.	32S	115¾E	61
Kwito Kwanavale, Angola.	15½S	19E	56
Kyabram, Vict., Aust.	36½S	145E	59
Kyangin, Burma.	18¼N	95¼E	43
Kyaring Tso, L., China.	35N	97E	43
Kyaukpadaung, Burma.	21N	95E	43
Kyaukpyu, Burma.	19½N	93½E	43
Kyaukse, Burma.	22N	96¼E	43
Kyi Chu, R., Tibet.	29N	90E	43
Kyleakin, Scotland.	57¼N	5¾W	24
Kyle of Durness, Scot.	58½N	4¾W	24
Kyle of Lochalsh, Scot.	57¼N	5½W	24
Kyle of Tongue, Scot.	58½N	4½W	24
Kyles of Bute, Scot.	55¾N	5¼W	25
Kyll, R., Germany.	49¾N	6¾E	38
Kyllburg, Germany.	50N	6½E	38
Kyneton, Vict., Aust.	37¼S	144½E	59
Kynuna, Queens., Aust.	21¾S	142E	60
Kyogle, N.S.W., Aust.	28½S	153E	59
Kyongju, Korea.	36N	129E	49
Kyoto, Japan.	35N	135¾E	48
Kyrenia, Cyprus.	35½N	33½E	41
Kyritz, Germany.	53N	12½E	33
Kyshtym, U.S.S.R.	56N	60½E	38
Kytakh, U.S.S.R.	73N	125E	39
Kytlym, U.S.S.R.	59N	59E	38
KYUSHU, Japan.	33N	131E	48
Kyustendil, Bulgaria.	42¼N	22¾E	37
Kyzyl, U.S.S.R.	51½N	94E	39
Kyzyl Arvat, U.S.S.R.	39N	56E	38
Kyzyl Kum, D., U.S.S.R.	42N	65E	40
Kzyl Orda, U.S.S.R.	44¾N	65½E	39
LA ALBUERA, Spain.	38¾N	6¾W	35
La Baneza, Spain.	42¼N	6W	35
La Barca, Mexico.	20½N	102¾W	76
La Bassee, France.	50½N	3E	30
La Baule, France.	47¼N	2½W	31
Labazhskoye, U.S.S.R.	67½N	52E	38
La Bisbal, Spain.	42N	3E	32
La Brae, Trin. (ins.).	10½N	61½W	77
La Calle, Algeria.	37N	8½E	35
La Capelle, France.	50N	3¾E	30
La Ceiba, Honduras.	15¾N	87W	77
La Charite, France.	47N	3E	32
La Chatre, France.	46¾N	2E	32
La Chartre-s-Loir, Fr.	47¾N	½E	31
La Chevre, C. de, Fr.	48¼N	4½W	31
La Chorrea, Panama.	8½N	80W	77
La Crosse, Wis., U.S.A.	43¾N	91¼W	75
La Dorada, Colombia.	5¼N	75W	77
La Escala, Spain.	42N	3E	32
La Fayette, Ind., U.S.A.	40½N	86¾W	75
La Ferte Bernard, Fr.	48¼N	¾E	31
La Ferte St. Aubin, Fr.	47¾N	2E	31
La Ferte-s-Jouarre, Fr.	49N	3½E	30
La Ferte Vidame, Fr.	48¾N	½E	31
La Fleche, France.	47¾N	¼W	31
La Fleche, Sask., Can.	49¾N	106½W	70
La Galite, I., Med. Sea.	37½N	8¾E	36
La Grande, Ore., U.S.A.	45¼N	118¾W	74
La Grange, Geo., U.S.A.	33N	85W	75
La Grange, W. Aust.	18¾S	121¾E	61
La Guaira, Venezuela.	10½N	67W	77
La Guardia, N.Y., U.S.A. (inset).	41N	74W	75
La Haye du Puits, Fr.	49½N	1½W	31
La Haye Pesnel, Fr.	48¾N	1¼W	31
La Heve, C. de, France.	49½N	0	31
La Hutte, France.	48½N	0	35
La Junta, Colo., U.S.A.	38N	103½W	71
La Laguna, Canary Is.	28¾N	16¼W	34
La Linea, Spain.	36¼N	5¼W	35
La Loupe, France.	48½N	1E	31
La Marsa, Tunisia.	37N	10E	36
La Martre, L., N.W. Can.	63N	119W	66
La Monta, France.	44¾N	7E	31
La Mure, France.	45N	5¾E	31
La Nouvelle, France.	43N	3E	32
La Panne, Belgium.	51¼N	2½E	30
La Paragua, Venezuela.	7N	63W	77
La Paz, Bolivia.	16½S	68W	79
La Paz, Mexico.	24¼N	110½W	76
La Plata, Argentina.	35S	58W	79
La Quiaca, Argentina.	22S	66W	79
La Reole, France.	44½N	0	32
La Rioja, Argentina.	29½S	67W	79
La Roche Bernard, Fr.	47½N	2¼W	31
La Rochelle, France.	46¼N	1W	32
La Roche-s-Yon, Fr.	46½N	1½W	32
La Roda, Spain.	39¼N	2¼W	35
La Serena, Chile.	30S	71W	78
La Soledad, Mexico.	25N	105W	76
La Souterraine, Fr.	46¾N	1½E	32
La Suze, France.	47¾N	0	31
La Trinite, France.	48¼N	3W	32
La Tuque, Que., Can.	47½N	72¾W	69
La Union, Salvador.	13N	87½W	76
La Union, Spain.	37¾N	1W	35
La Urbana, Venezuela.	7½N	67W	77
Laa, Austria.	48¾N	16½E	33
Laasphe, Germany.	51N	8½E	30
Labelle, Quebec, Can.	46½N	74¾W	69
Labiau, U.S.S.R.	54¾N	21E	33
LABRADOR, Canada.	54N	62W	66
Labuan I., E. Malaysia.	5¼N	115½E	47
Lac la Biche, Alb., Can.	54¾N	111¾W	73
Lac la Hache, Br. Col.	51¾N	121¼W	72
Lac la Plonge, Can.	55¼N	107¾W	70
Lac Leman, see GENEVA.			
Lac Seul, Ont., Can.	50½N	92½W	71
Lacanau Ocean, France.	45N	1¼W	32
Lacapelle Marival, Fr.	44¾N	2E	32

Place	Lat.	Long.	No.
Laccadive Is., *Arab. S.*	10½N	73E	43
Lacepede B., *S. Aust.*	37S	139½E	59
Lacepede Is., *W. Aust.*	17S	122E	61
Lachine, *Quebec, Can.*	45½N	73¾W	69
Lachlan, R., *N.S.W.*	34¼S	144E	59
Lachute, *Quebec, Can.*	45¾N	74½W	69
Lacombe, *Alb., Can.*	52½N	113¾W	73
Laconi, *Sardinia, Italy.*	39¾N	9E	36
Laconia, *U.S.A.*	43N	72W	75
Ladismith, *C.Pr., S.Afr.*	33½S	21¼E	52
Ladoga, L., *U.S.S.R.*	61N	31E	38
Lady Frere, *C.Pr., S.Afr.*	31¾S	27¼E	53
Lady Grey, *C.Pr., S.Afr.*	30¾S	27¼E	53
Ladybrand, *O.F.S.*	29¼S	27½E	55
Ladysmith, *Br. Col., Can.*	49N	123¾W	72
Ladysmith, *Natal.*	28½S	29¾E	55
Lae,, *New Guinea.*	7S	147E	64
Laeken, *Belgium.*	51N	4¼E	30
Lafayette, *La., U.S.A.*	30¼N	92W	75
Lafia, *Nigeria.*	8½N	8½E	57
Lafiagi, *Nigeria.*	9N	5¼E	57
Lagan, *U.S.S.R.*	45½N	47½E	38
Lagan, R., *Ireland.*	54¾N	5¾W	25
Lagan, R., *Sweden.*	56½N	13E	29
Lage, *Germany.*	52N	8¾E	30
Lagen, R., *Norway.*	59½N	10E	29
Lagens, *Azores* (inset).	38¼N	28¼E	35
Lagg, *Scotland.*	56N	6W	25
Laghouat, *Algeria.*	34N	2¾E	35
Lagny, *France.*	49N	2¾E	30
Lagoa, *Azores* (inset).	37¾N	25¾W	35
Lagonegro, *Italy.*	40¼N	15¾E	36
Lagos, *Nigeria.*	6½N	3½E	57
Lagos, *Portugal.*	37N	8¾W	35
Lagos de Moreno, *Mex.*	21½N	102W	76
Lahat, *Sumatra Indon.*	4S	104E	47
Lahej, *S. Yemen.* (ins.).	14¼N	45E	40
Lahijan, *Iran.*	37N	50E	41
Lahinch, *Ireland.*	52¾N	9½W	26
Lahn, Riv., *Germany.*	50¼N	7½E	30
Lahnstein, *Germany.*	50¼N	7½E	30
Lahore, *Pakistan.*	31½N	74¼E	44
Lahr, *Germany.*	48½N	7¾E	30
Lahti, *Finland.*	61N	25¾E	29
Lai, *Cen. Afr. Rep.*	9½N	16¼E	56
Laigle, *France.*	48¾N	½E	31
Laignes, *France.*	47¾N	4½E	30
Laila, *Saudi Arabia.*	22½N	46½E	40
Laingsburg, *Cape Pr.*	33¼S	21E	52
Laings Nek, *Natal.*	27½S	29¾E	55
Lainio, Riv., *Sweden.*	67N	25E	29
Laipin, *China.*	24N	109E	48
Lairg, *Scotland.*	58N	4½W	24
Laiyang, *China.*	37N	121E	48
Lake Brown, *W. Aust.*	30¾S	118E	61
Lake Cargelligo, *Aust.*	33¼S	146¼E	59
Lake Charles, *U.S.A.*	30¼N	93¼W	75
Lake City, *Flor., U.S.A.*	30N	82½W	75
Lake Grace, *W. Aust.*	33S	118E	61
Lake Louise, *Alb., Can.*	51½N	116¼W	73
Lake Success, *N.Y., U.S.A.* (inset).	41N	74W	75
Lakefield, *Ont., Can.*	44½N	78¼W	69
Lakeland, *Flor., U.S.A.*	28N	81¾W	75
Lake's Entrance, *Vict.*	37¾S	148E	59
Lakeside, *W. Aust.*	31S	122E	61
Lakhnau, *India.*	26¾N	81E	44
Lakhpat, *India.*	23¾N	68¾E	46
Lakonia, G. of, *Greece.*	36¾N	22¾E	37
Lakse Fiord, *Norway.*	71N	27E	29
Lalapasa, *Turkey.*	41¾N	26¾E	37
Lalla Rookh, *W. Aust.*	20½S	119E	61
Lamar, *Colo., U.S.A.*	37½N	104W	74
Lamarche, *France.*	48N	5¾E	30
Lamayuru, *Kash.*(ins.).	34½N	77E	44
Lamballe, *France.*	48½N	2½W	31
Lambarene, *Gabon.*	1S	10E	56
Lambay I., *Eire.*	53½N	6W	22
Lambert, C., *W. Aust.*	20½S	117½E	61
Lambert's Bay, *C. Pr.*	32¼S	18¼E	52
Lambourn, *England.*	51½N	1½W	23
Lamego, *Portugal.*	41¼N	7¾W	35
Lamesa, *Texas, U.S.A.*	33N	102½W	74
Lamia, *Greece.*	39N	22½E	37
Lamington, *Queens.*	28¼S	153E	60
Lamitan, *Basilan, P.I.*	7N	122E	47
Lamlash, *Scotland.*	55½N	5¼W	25
Lammermuir Hills, *Scotland.*	55¾N	2¾W	25
Lamotrek I., *Pacific.*	9N	150E	64
Lamotte Beuvron, *Fr.*	47½N	2E	31
Lampedusa I., *Med.*	36N	12½E	34
Lampertheim, *Ger.*	49½N	8½E	30
Lampeter, *Wales.*	52¼N	4¼W	22
Lampi, I., *Burma.*	10¾N	98¼E	43
Lampman, *Sask., Can.*	49¼N	102¾W	70
Lamu, *Kenya.*	2¼S	41E	56
Lana, *Italy.*	46½N	11¼E	31
Lanai, *Hawaii, U.S.A.*	20¾N	156W	74
Lanark, *Ontario, Can.*	45N	76½W	69
LANARK & Tn., *Scot.*	55¾N	3¾W	25
LANCASHIRE, *England.*	53¾N	2½W	25
Lancaster, *England.*	54¼N	2¾W	25
Lancelot Mt., *W. Aust.*	26½S	123½E	61
Lanchester, *England.*	54¾N	1¾W	25
Lanchi, *China.*	29N	119E	48
Lanchow, *China.*	36N	104E	48
Lanchung, *China.*	32N	106E	48
Landau, *Germany.*	49¼N	8¼E	33
Landau-a-d-Isar, *Ger.*	48¾N	12¾E	33
Landeck, *Austria.*	47¼N	10½E	31
Landen, *Belgium.*	50¾N	5E	30
Landerneau, *France.*	48½N	4½W	31
Landes, *France.*	44¼N	1¼W	32
LANDES, *France.*	44N	¾W	32
Landis, *Sask., Canada.*	52¼N	108¼W	70
Landivisiau, *France.*	48½N	4W	31
Land's End, *England.*	50N	5¾W	22
Land's End, *N.W. Can.*	77N	123W	66
Landsberg, *Germany.*	48N	11E	33
Landsborough, Riv., *Queensland, Aust.*	22¼S	144E	60
Landshut, *Germany.*	48½N	12¼E	33
Landskrona, *Sweden.*	56N	12¾E	29
Landwarow, *U.S.S.R.*	54¾N	25E	33
Lanesboro, *Ireland.*	53¾N	8W	26
Lang, *Sask., Canada.*	49¾N	104¼W	70
Langeais, *France.*	47½N	½E	31
Langebaan, *C.Pr., S.Afr.*	33S	18E	52
Langeberg, Mt., *C. Pr.*	34S	21½E	52
Langeland, *Denmark.*	55N	11E	33
Langenberg, *Ger.*(ins.).	51¼N	7¼E	33
Langenburg, *Canada.*	50¾N	101¾W	70
Langensalza, *Germany.*	51N	10¾E	33
Langenthal, *Switz.*	47¼N	7¾E	31
Langeoog, I., *Germany.*	53¾N	7½E	30
Langham, *Sask., Can.*	52¼N	106¾W	70
Langholm, *Scotland.*	55¼N	3W	25
Langkawi, *Malay.* (ins.)	6¼N	100E	47
Lango, I., *Norway.*	68¾N	15E	29
Langport, *England.*	51N	2¾W	22
Langres, *France.*	47¾N	5¼E	32
Langres Plateau, *Fr.*	47¾N	5E	32
Langsa, *Sumatra.*	4½N	98E	47
Langsele, *Sweden.*	63N	17E	29
Langsuan, *Thailand.*	10N	99E	43
Langtry, *Texas, U.S.A.*	30N	102W	76
LANGUEDOC, *France.*	44N	3E	32
Lanigan, *Sask., Can.*	51¾N	105W	70
Lannilis, *France.*	48½N	4½W	31
Lannion, *France.*	48¾N	3½W	31
Lanquin, *Guatemala.*	16N	90W	76
Lansing, *Mich., U.S.A.*	42¾N	84½W	68
Lanslebourg, *France.*	45¼N	6¾E	31
Lantsang, *China.*	22½N	100E	47
Lanusei, *Sardinia.*	39¾N	9½E	36
Lan Yu Is., *Formosa.*	22N	121E	48
Lanzarote I., *Canary Is.*	29N	13½W	35
Lao Kay, *China.*	22½N	104E	48
Laoag, *Luzon, P.I.*	18¼N	120½E	47
Laodicea, *Turkey.*	37½N	28E	41
Laoha, Riv., *China.*	42N	119E	39
LAOIGHIS, *Ireland.*	53N	7¼W	26
Laokai, *Vietnam.*	22½N	104E	47
Laon, *France.*	49½N	3½E	32
LAONING, *China.*	42½N	122½E	48
LAOS, *East Asia.*	19N	104E	47
Lapage, L., *W. Aust.*	31S	122½E	61
LAPLAND, *Swed.-Fin.*	68¼N	25E	29
Lapleau, *France.*	45½N	2¼E	32
Lapovo, *Yugoslavia.*	44¼N	21E	37
Laprairie, *Que., Can.*	45½N	73½W	69
Lapseki, *Turkey.*	40½N	26¾E	37
Laptev Sea, *U.S.S.R.*	75N	125E	39
Lapy, *Poland.*	53N	23E	33
Laqiya, *Sudan.*	20N	28E	40
Lar, *Iran.*	28N	54¼E	40
Larache, *Morocco.*	35¼N	6¼W	35
Laramie, *Wyo., U.S.A.*	42N	105W	74
Larbert, *Scotland.*	56N	4W	25
Larche, *France.*	45N	2E	32
Lardo, *Br. Col., Can.*	50¼N	117W	73
Laredo, *Texas, U.S.A.*	27½N	99½W	74
Largo, *Scotland.*	56¼N	2¾W	25
Largs, *Scotland.*	55¾N	4¾W	25
Larino, *Italy.*	41¾N	15E	36
Larissa, *Greece.*	39½N	22½E	37
Larkana, *Pakistan.*	27½N	68¼E	46
Larnaca, *Cyprus.*	35N	33¾E	41
Larne & L., *N. Ireland.*	54¾N	5¾W	26
Laroche, *Belgium.*	50¼N	5½E	30
Larochette, *Lux.*	49¾N	6¼E	30
Larvik, *Norway.*	59N	10E	29
Laryak, *U.S.S.R.*	62N	80E	39
Las Anod, *Somali Rep.*	8N	47E	56
Las Cruces, *N.Mex, U.S.*	31¾N	107W	74
Las Cruces, *Venezuela.*	8N	72½W	77
Las Khoreh, *Som. Rep.*	11N	47½E	56
Las Palmas, *Canary Is.*	28¼N	15½W	35
Las Perlas, *Nicaragua.*	12N	84W	77
Las Tablas, *Panama.*	8N	80W	77
Las Vegas, *Nev., U.S.A.*	36¼N	115¼W	74
Las Vegas, *N.M., U.S.A.*	35¾N	105W	74
Lasdehnen, *U.S.S.R.*	55N	22½E	33
Lashio, *Burma.*	22¾N	97¾E	43
Lashkar, *India.*	26¼N	78¼E	44
L'Assomption, *Can.*	45¾N	73¾W	69
Lastourville, *Gabon.*	1S	13E	56
Lastovo I., *Yugoslavia.*	42¾N	16¾E	37
Lat, River, *France.*	44¼N	½E	32
Latakia, *Syria.*	35½N	35¾E	41
Latchford, *Ont., Can.*	47¼N	79¾W	68
Lathen, *Germany.*	52¾N	7½E	30
Latheron, *Scotland.*	58¼N	3½W	24
LATIUM, *Italy.*	42N	13E	36
Latrun, *Israel* (inset).	31¾N	35E	40
Latur, *India.*	18¼N	76¾E	45
LATVIA, *U.S.S.R.*	57N	24E	38
Lau, *Nigeria.*	9¼N	11½E	57
Lau Is., *Pacific.*	19S	179W	64
Lauder, *Scotland.*	55¾N	2¾W	25
Lauenburg, *Germany.*	53½N	10½E	33
Laugharne, *Wales.*	51¾N	4½W	22
Launceston, *England.*	50¾N	4½W	22
Launceston, *Tasmania.*	41½S	147¼E	59
Launois, *France.*	49¾N	4½E	30
Laura, *Queens., Aust.*	15½S	144½E	60
Laurel, *Miss., U.S.A.*	31¾N	89¼W	75
Laurencekirk, *Scot.*	56¾N	2½W	24
Laurentide Park, *Can.*	47½N	71½W	69
Lauria, *Italy.*	40N	16E	37
Lausanne, *Switz.*	46½N	6¾E	31
Laut I., *Indonesia.*	3¾S	116¼E	47
Lauter, Riv., *Germany.*	49N	8¼E	30
Lauterburg, *Germany.*	49N	8¼E	30
Lauterecken, *Germany.*	49½N	7½E	30
Lauwers Zee *Nether.*	53½N	6¼E	30
Laval, *France.*	48¼N	¾W	31
Lavamund, *Austria.*	46¾N	15E	37
Lavaur, *France.*	43¾N	1¾E	32
Laveno, *Italy.*	45¾N	8¾E	31
Laverton, *W. Aust.*	28½S	122½E	61
Lavis, *Italy.*	46¼N	11E	31
Lavrion, *Greece.*	37¾N	24E	37
Lawagan, *New Ireland, Pacific* (inset).	3S	152E	60
Lawlers, *W. Australia.*	28S	120½E	61
Lawra, *Ghana.*	10½N	3W	57
Lawrence, *Kan., U.S.A.*	39N	95W	75
Lawrence, *Mass., U.S.A.*	42¾N	71W	69
Lawrence, *S.I., N.Z.*	45¾S	169¾E	63
Lawton, *Okla., U.S.A.*	34¾N	98¼W	74
Laxey, *England.*	54¼N	4½W	25
Laxfield, *England.*	52¼N	1¼E	23
Laxford Bridge, *Scot.*	58½N	5W	24
Laysan I., *Pacific.*	28N	171W	64
Le Biot, *France.*	46¼N	6¾E	31
Le Blanc, *France.*	46¾N	1E	32
Le Bourg d'Oisans, *Fr.*	45N	6E	31
Le Brassus, *Switz.*	46½N	6¼E	31
Le Cateau, *France.*	50N	3½E	30
Le Creusot, *France.*	46¾N	4½E	32
Le Croisic, *France.*	47¼N	2¾W	31
Le Crotoy, *France.*	50¼N	1½E	30
Le Faouet, *France.*	48N	3½W	31
Le Grand, C., *W. Aust.*	34S	122E	63
Le Gd. Fougeray, *Fr.*	47¾N	1¾W	31
Le Grande Luce, *Fr.*	47¾N	½E	31
Le Havre, *France.*	49¾N	¼E	31
Le Kef, *Tunisia.*	36N	8½E	35
Le Lion d'Angers, *Fr.*	47½N	¾W	31
Le Locle, *Switzerland.*	47¼N	6¾E	31
Le Mans, *France.*	48N	¼E	31
Le Mele, *France.*	48½N	¼E	31
Le Palais, *France.*	47¼N	3¼W	31
Le Petit Quevilly, *Fr.*	49½N	1E	31
Le Puy, *France.*	45N	3¾E	32
Le Quesnoy, *France.*	50¼N	3½E	30
Le Teste de Buch, *Fr.*	44¾N	1¼W	32
Le Touquet, *France.*	50½N	1½E	23
Le Treport, *France.*	50N	1½E	32
Le Verdon, *France.*	45½N	1W	32
Le Vigan, *France.*	44N	3¾E	32
Leadenham, *England.*	53¼N	½W	23
Leader, *Sask., Canada.*	51N	109½W	70
Leadhills, *Scotland.*	55½N	3¾W	25
Leadville, *Colo., U.S.A.*	39N	106W	74
Leah, *Ont., Can.* (ins.).	50½N	81¾W	71
Leamington, *England.*	52¼N	1½W	23
Leamington, *Ont., Can.*	42N	82½W	68
Leane, L., *Ireland.*	52N	9½W	26
Learmonth, *W. Aust.*	22½S	114E	61
Leatherhead, *England.*	51¼N	¼W	23
Leavenworth, *Kansas.*	39¼N	95W	75
Leba, *Poland.*	54¾N	17½E	33
Lebach, *Germany.*	49½N	7E	30
Lebanon, *N.H., U.S.A.*	43¾N	72¼W	69
LEBANON, *Asia.*	34N	35½E	41
Lebrija, *Spain.*	36¾N	6W	35
Lebskie, *Poland.*	54¾N	17½E	33
Lebu, *Chile.*	37½S	73½W	79
Lebyazhe, *U.S.S.R.*	52N	78E	39
Lecce, *Italy.*	40¼N	18¼E	36
Lecco & L., *Italy.*	45¾N	9½E	31
Lech, Riv., *Germany.*	49N	11E	33
Lechlade, *England.*	51¾N	1¾W	23
Lectoure, *France.*	43¾N	¾E	32
Leczyca, *Poland.*	52N	19¼E	33
Leczna, *Poland.*	51¼N	23E	33
Ledbury, *England.*	52N	2½W	22
Ledesma, *Argentina.*	23½S	65W	79
Leduc, *Alberta, Can.*	53¼N	113½W	73
Lee, River, *Ireland.*	52N	8¼W	26
Lee Stream Riv., *S.I., N.Z.* (inset D).			63
Leeds, *England.*	53¾N	1½W	25
Leek, *England.*	53¼N	2W	22
Leer, *Germany.*	53½N	7½E	33
Leerdam, *Netherlands.*	52N	5¼E	30
Leese, *Germany.*	52½N	9¼E	30
Leeton, *N.S.W., Aust.*	34½S	146½E	59
Leeudoringstad, *S.Afr.*	27¼S	26¼E	55
Leeuwarden, *Nether.*	53¼N	5¾E	30
Leeward Is., *W. Indies.*	17N	63W	77
Lefka, *Cyprus.*	35N	33E	41
Lefkoniko, *Cyprus.*	35½N	33½E	41
Lefroy, L., *W. Aust.*	31¼S	122E	61
Legaspi, *Luzon, P.I.*	13¼N	123¾E	47
Lege, *France.*	46¾N	1¼W	32
Legge, Mt., *Tasmania.*	41½S	147¾E	59
Leghorn, *Italy.*	43½N	10¼E	36
Legnago, *Italy.*	45¼N	11½E	31
Legnano, *Italy.*	45½N	8¾E	31
Legnica, *Poland.*	51¼N	16¼E	33
Leh, *Kashmir.*	34N	77½E	43
Lehe, *Germany.*	53½N	8½E	30
Leiah, *Pakistan.*	31N	71E	46
Leibnitz, *Austria.*	46¾N	15½E	33
LEICESTER & Tn., *Eng.*	52¾N	1¼W	23
Leiden, *Netherlands.*	52¼N	4½E	30
Leigh, *England*(*Lancs.*).	53½N	2½W	25
Leigh, *Eng.* (*Essex*).	51½N	¾E	23
Leighton Buzzard, *Eng.*	51¾N	¾W	23
Leine, Riv., *Germany.*	52¾N	9½E	33
LEINSTER, *Eire.*	53N	7W	26
Leiptig, *U.S.S.R.*	46¼N	29E	37
Leipzig, *Germany.*	51¼N	12½E	33
Leiria, *Portugal.*	39¾N	9W	35
Leith, *Scotland.*	56N	3¼W	25
Leith Hill, *England.*	51¼N	½W	23
LEITRIM, *Eire.*	54N	8W	26
Leiyang, *China.*	26½N	112½E	48
Lek, Riv., *Nether.*	52N	5E	30
Lekhaina, *Greece.*	38N	21½E	37
Leksand, *Sweden.*	61N	15E	29
Leliefontein, *Cape Pr.*	30¼S	18¼E	52
Lemberg, *Sask., Can.*	50¾N	103¼W	70
Lemgo, *Germany.*	52N	9E	30
Lemmer, *Nether.*	53N	5¾E	30
Lemnos I., *Greece.*	40N	25¼E	37
Lena, *Spain.*	43¼N	6W	35
Lena, Riv., *U.S.S.R.*	73N	126E	39
Lenak Pass, *China.*	34N	80E	43
Lengerich, *Germany.*	52¼N	7¾E	30
Leninabad, *U.S.S.R.*	40N	70E	39
Leninakan, *U.S.S.R.*	40¾N	43¾E	38
Leningrad, *U.S.S.R.*	60N	30¼E	38
Leninogorsk, *U.S.S.R.*	50¼N	84E	39
Leninsk-Kuznetski, *U.S.S.R.*	54¾N	86¼E	39
Lenk, *Switzerland.*	46½N	7½E	31
Lenkoran, *U.S.S.R.*	39N	48E	38
Lenne, Riv., *Germany.*	51½N	6¾E	30
Lennonville, *W. Aust.*	28S	118E	61
Lennoxton, *Natal.*	27¾S	30E	55
Lens, *France.*	50½N	2¾E	23
Lentini, *Sicily.*	37¼N	15E	36
Leoben, *Austria.*	47½N	15E	33
Leogane, *Haiti, W.I.*	18N	73W	77
Leoi, *Thailand.*	17½N	102E	43
Leominster, *England.*	52¼N	2¾W	22
Leominster, *U.S.A.*	42½N	71¾W	69
Leon, *Mexico.*	21N	101¾W	76
Leon, *Nicaragua.*	12½N	86½W	77
LEON, *Spain.*	42N	6W	35
Leongatha, *Vict., Aust.*	38½S	146E	59
Leonora, *W. Aust.*	29S	121¼E	61
Leopold II, L., *Congo*(*K.*)	2¼S	18½E	56
Leopold Downs, *W.Aust.*	18S	126E	61
Leopoldina, *Brazil.*	15S	51W	79
Leopoldville, see KINSHASA.			
Lepel, *U.S.S.R.*	55N	28E	38
Lepontine Alps, *Switz.*	46½N	8½E	31
Lercara Friddi, *Sicily.*	37¾N	13¾E	36
Lerdo, *Mexico.*	25½N	103¾W	76
Lere, *Cent. Afr. Rep.*	10N	14E	56
Leribe, *Lesotho.*	28½S	28E	53
Lerida, *Spain.*	41¾N	¾E	35
Lerins, Is. de, *France.*	43½N	7E	32
Lerno, Mt., *Sardinia.*	40¾N	9½E	36
Leros, I. of, *Greece.*	37N	27E	37
Lerwick, *Scot.* (inset).	60¼N	1¼W	24
Les Andelys, *France.*	49¼N	1½E	31
Les Bordes, *France.*	47¾N	2½E	30
Les Cayes, *Haiti, W.I.*	18N	74W	77
Les Ecrehou Is., *Chan.I.*	49¼N	2W	31
Les Ponts de Ce, *Fr.*	47½N	½W	31
Les Sept Iles, *France.*	48¾N	3½W	32
Lesina, L. of, *Italy.*	42N	15½E	36
Leskovac, *Yugoslavia.*	43N	22E	37
Leskovik, *Albania.*	40¼N	20½E	37
Leslie, *T'vaal, S. Afr.*	26¼S	29E	55
Leslie, *Scotland.*	56¼N	3¼W	25
Lesmont, *France.*	48½N	4¼E	30
Lesvos, I., *Agean Sea.*	39¼N	26½E	37
Lesozavodsk, *U.S.S.R.*	45N	133E	39
Lesparre, *France.*	45¼N	1W	32
Lessay, *France.*	49¼N	1½W	31
Lesse, Riv., *Belgium.*	50¼N	4¾E	30
Lesser Slave L., *Can.*	55½N	115½W	73
Lesseyton, *C.Pr., S.Afr.*	31¾S	26¾E	53
Lessines, *Belgium.*	50¾N	3½E	30
Lestock, *Sask., Canada.*	51½N	104½W	70
Lesueur I., W. *Aust.*	13½S	128E	61
LESOTHO, *Africa.*	31½S	28½E	53
Leszno, *Poland.*	51¾N	16½E	33
Letaba, R., *T'vaal, S.Afr.*	23¾S	31½E	54
Lethbridge, *Alb., Can.*	49¾N	112¾W	73
Lethem, *Guyana.* (ins.)	3N	60W	77
Leticia, *Colombia.*	4¼S	70W	78
Letjiesbosch, *C. Pr.*	32½S	22¼E	52
Letmath, *Ger.* (inset).	51¼N	7½E	33
Letskraal, *C.Pr., S. Afr.*	32¼S	24¾E	53
Lette, *N.S.W., Aust.*	34¼S	143¼E	59
Letterkenny, *Ireland.*	55N	7¾W	26
Leuk, *Switzerland.*	46½N	7½E	31
Levack, *Ontario, Can.*	46¾N	81½W	68
Levadhia, *Greece.*	38½N	23E	37
Levanger, *Norway.*	64N	11¾E	29
Levanna, Mt., *Italy.*	45½N	7¼E	31
Levant Coast, *E. Med.*	34N	35E	34
Leven, *Scotland.*	56¼N	3W	25
Leveque, C., *W. Aust.*	16½S	123E	61
Levice, *Czechoslovakia.*	48¼N	18½E	33
Levin, *N.I., N.Z.*	40½S	175¼E	62
Levis, *Quebec, Canada.*	46¾N	71W	69
Levkas I., *Greece.*	38¾N	20¾E	37
Levoka, *Czecho.*	49N	20½E	33
Lewes, *England.*	50¾N	0	23
Lewes, R., *Yukon, Can.*	62N	136W	66
Lewis, I. of, *Scotland.*	58N	6½W	24
Lewis Pass, *S.I., N.Z.*	42½S	172½E	63
Lewiston, *Id., U.S.A.*	46½N	117W	74
Lewiston, *Me, U.S.A.*	44¼N	70¼W	69
Lewistown, *U.S.A.*	47½N	110W	74
Lexington, *Ky., U.S.A.*	38N	84½W	75
Leyburn, *England.*	54¼N	1¾W	25
Leyden, see LEIDEN.			
Leydsdorp, *T'vaal.*	24S	30½E	54
Leyte I., *Philippines.*	11N	124¾E	47
Lhasa, *Tibet.*	29¾N	91E	43

Lhatse—Lowther [113]

Place	Lat.	Long.	No.
Lhatse Dzong, *Tibet.*	29N	86E	43
Lhokseumawe, *Sumatra.*	5¼N	97¼E	47
Lhontse Dzong, *Tibet.*	28N	92¼E	43
Liangyang, *China.*	21¼N	112E	48
Lianoso, *Can. Is.* (ins.).	28¼N	18W	35
Liao, River, *China.*	41N	121E	39
Liaocheng, *China.*	37N	116E	48
Liaohsien, *China.*	37N	112¼E	48
Liaotung, G. of, *China.*	40N	121E	48
Liaoyang, *China.*	41¼N	123E	48
Liaoyuan, *China.*	42¾N	124E	39
Liard & R., *Canada.*	60¼N	123¼W	66
Liari, *Pakistan.*	25¼N	66E	43
Liart, *France.*	49¾N	4¼E	30
Libau, see LIEPAJA.			
Libenge, *Congo (K.).*	3¾N	18¾E	56
Liberec, *Czecho.*	50¾N	15E	33
Liberia, *Costa Rica.*	10½N	85½W	77
LIBERIA, *W. Africa.*	6N	9W	50
Libertas, *O.F.S., S. Afr.*	28¼S	27¼E	55
Libode, *C. Pr., S. Afr.*	31½S	29E	53
Libourne, *France.*	45N	¼W	32
Libramont, *Belgium.*	50N	5½E	30
Libreville, *Gabon.*	½N	9½E	56
Libyan Desert, *Libya.*	28N	23E	34
Licata, *Sicily.*	37N	14E	36
Lichfield, *England.*	52¾N	1¾W	23
Lichtenburg, *T'vaal.*	26¼S	26¼E	55
Licosa Pt., *Italy.*	40¼N	15E	36
Lida, *U.S.S.R.*	53¾N	25¼E	38
Liddel, Riv., *Scotland.*	55N	3W	25
Lidkoping, *Sweden.*	58½N	13E	29
Lido Di Roma, *Italy.*	41¾N	12¼E	36
Lidzbark, *Poland.*	54N	20¼E	33
LIECHTENSTEIN, *Europe.*	47N	9½E	31
LIEGE & Tn., *Belgium.*	50¾N	5½E	30
Lieksa, *Finland.*	63N	30E	38
Lienyang, *China.*	24½N	112¼E	48
Lienyunkang, *China.*	35N	120E	48
Lienz, *Austria.*	46¾N	12¾E	33
Liepaja, *U.S.S.R.*	56½N	21E	38
Lierre, *Belgium.*	51¼N	4½E	30
Liestal, *Switzerland.*	47½N	7¾E	31
Lievin, *France.*	50½N	2¾E	30
Liezen, *Austria.*	47½N	14¼E	33
Liffey, Riv., *Eire.*	53¼N	6½W	26
Lifford, *Eire.*	54¾N	7½W	26
Liffre, *France.*	48¼N	1½W	31
Lifu I., *Loyalty Is., Pac.*	21S	167¼E	64
Ligny-en-Barrois, *Fr.*	48½N	5¼E	30
Ligonha, Riv., *Moz.*	16½S	39E	56
LIGURIA, *Italy.*	44½N	9E	36
Ligurian Sea, *Italy.*	43½N	9E	36
Lihir I., *Pacific* (inset).	3S	153E	60
Lihsien, *China.*	30N	111E	48
Lihue, *Hawaii, U.S.A.*	20½N	154½W	74
Likasi, *Congo (K.).*	11S	26½E	51
Likely, *Br. Col., Can.*	52¾N	121¼W	72
Likiang, *China.*	27N	100E	43
Likiep I., *Pacific.*	10N	166E	64
Likungo, Riv., *Moz.*	17½S	38E	51
Liling, *China.*	28N	113E	48
Lille, *France.*	50¾N	3¼E	32
Lillehammer, *Norway.*	61N	10½E	29
Lillers, *France.*	50½N	2½E	30
Lillesand, *Norway.*	58¼N	8½E	29
Lillhardal, *Sweden.*	62N	14E	29
Lilliput, *T'vaal, S. Afr.*	22½S	29¼E	54
Lillo, *Belgium.*	51¼N	4¼E	30
Lillooet, *Br. Col., Can.*	50¾N	122W	72
Lilongwe, *Malawi.*	14S	33¾E	51
Lilydale, *Tas. Aust.* (ins.)	41½S	147¼E	59
Limfjorden, *Denmark.*	57N	9E	29
Lim, Riv., *Yugoslavia.*	43¼N	19½E	37
Lima, *Ohio, U.S.A.*	40¾N	84¼W	75
Lima, *Peru.*	12S	77W	78
Lima, Riv., *Portugal.*	41¾N	8¾W	35
Limanowa, *Poland.*	49¾N	20¼E	33
Limassol, *Cyprus.*	34¾N	33¼E	41
Limavady, *N. Ireland.*	55N	7W	26
Limbara, Mt., *Sardinia.*	40¾N	9¼E	36
LIMBOURG, *Belgium.*	51N	5½E	30
Limburg, *Germany.*	50¼N	8E	30
LIMBURG, *Netherlands.*	51¼N	6E	30
LIMERICK, & Tn., *Ir.*	52½N	9W	26
Limerick, *Sask., Can.*	49¾N	106¼W	70
Limmen Bight, *Aust.*	15S	136E	60
Limni, *Greece.*	38¾N	23¼E	37
Limoges, *France.*	45¾N	1¼E	32
Limon, *Colo., U.S.A.*	39N	103¾W	74
Limon, *Costa Rica.*	10N	83W	77
LIMOUSIN, *France.*	45N	1½E	32
Limoux, *France.*	43¼N	2¼E	32
Limpopo, Riv., *Moz.*	25S	33E	51
Lin, *Albania.*	41N	20¾E	37
Lina, *Saudi Arabia.*	28¾N	43¾E	41
Linares, *Chile.*	36S	71¾W	79
Linares, *Mexico.*	24¾N	99¼W	76
Linares, *Spain.*	38¼N	3¾W	35
Lincoln, *Argentina.*	35S	61¼W	79
LINCOLN, *England.*	53¼N	½W	23
Lincoln, *Neb., U.S.A.*	40¾N	96¾W	75
Lincoln, *S.I., N.Z.* (inset C).			63
Lindau, *Germany.*	47½N	9¾E	33
Linden, *W. Aust.*	29S	122¼E	61
Linden, *Germany.*	52¼N	9¾E	33
Lindesnes, *Norway.*	58N	7E	29
Lindi, *Tanzania.*	10S	39¾E	56
Lindley, *O.F.S., S. Afr.*	27¾S	28E	55
Lindsay, *Ont., Can.*	44¼N	78¾W	69
LINDSEY, *England.*	53¼N	½W	23
Lindya, Riv., *U.S.S.R.*	65N	126E	39
Line Islands, *Pacific.*	0	157W	64
Linfen, *China.*	36N	111¼E	48
Lingakok, *Tibet.*	30N	87¼E	43
Lingayen, *Luzon, P.I.*	16N	120¼E	47
Lingeh, *Iran.*	26½N	55E	40
Lingen, *Germany.*	52½N	7¼E	33
Lingga Arch., *Indonesia.*	½S	104¾E	47
Linghsien, *China.*	26½N	113½E	48
Lingling, *China.*	26N	111E	48
Linglo, *China.*	24½N	106E	48
Linguaglossa, *Sicily.*	37¾N	15¼E	36
Lingyuan, *China.*	41¼N	119E	48
Linhai, *China.*	28¾N	121E	48
Lini, *China.*	35½N	118¼E	48
Linkoping, *Sweden.*	58½N	15¾E	29
Linkow, *China.*	45¼N	130E	49
Linlithgow, *Scotland.*	56N	3½W	25
Linnhe, Loch, *Scot.*	56½N	5¼W	24
Linosa I., *Med. Sea.*	36½N	12E	34
Linping, *China.*	24¾N	114E	48
Linsell, *Sweden.*	62¼N	14E	29
Linslade, *England.*	52N	¾W	23
Linstead, *Jamaica,* (ins).	18N	77W	77
Lintan, *China.*	34¾N	104E	48
Linthal, *Switzerland.*	46¾N	9E	31
Linton, *England.*	52¼N	¼E	23
Linton, *N. Dak., U.S.A.*	47N	100W	74
Lintsing, *China.*	37N	116E	48
Linz, *Austria.*	48¼N	14¼E	33
Lionhead, *Ont., Can.*	45N	81¼W	68
Lions, G. of, *France.*	43N	4E	32
Lipari Is., *Italy.*	38½N	15E	36
Lipcani, *U.S.S.R.*	48¼N	26¾E	37
Lipetsk, *U.S.S.R.*	52¾N	39½E	38
Liphook, *England.*	51N	¾W	23
Liping, *China.*	26N	109E	48
Lipno, *Poland.*	52¾N	19¼E	33
Lippe, Riv., *Germany.*	51½N	6¾E	30
Lippstadt, *Germany.*	51¾N	8¼E	30
Lipton, *Sask., Canada.*	51N	104W	70
Liptrap, C., *Vict., Aust.*	39S	146E	59
Lipuchi, *Mozambique.*	13S	35E	56
Lira, *Uganda.*	2¼N	32¾E	56
Liria, *Spain.*	39¾N	¾W	35
Lisbon, *Portugal.*	38¾N	8¾W	35
Lisburn, *N. Ireland.*	54½N	6W	26
Liscannor B., *Ireland.*	53N	9W	26
Lisdoonvarna, *Ireland.*	53N	9¼W	26
Lishan, *China.*	37¾N	111E	48
Lishui, *China.*	32N	119E	48
Lishui, *China.*	28N	120E	48
Lisianski I., *Pacific.*	26N	174W	64
Lisieux, *France.*	49¼N	¼E	31
Liskeard, *England.*	50½N	4½W	22
Lismore, *Eire.*	52¼N	8W	26
Lismore, *N.S.W., Aust.*	28¾S	153¼E	59
Lismore I., *Scotland.*	56½N	5½W	24
Listowel, *Eire.*	52½N	9½W	26
Listowel, *Ont., Can.*	43¾N	81W	68
Litang, *China.*	22¾N	109E	48
Litang, Riv., *China.*	28N	102E	43
Lithgow, *N.S.W., Aust.*	33½S	150¼E	59
LITHUANIA, *U.S.S.R.*	56N	23E	38
Litokhoron, *Greece.*	40N	22¼E	37
Litomerice, *Czecho.*	50½N	14¼E	33
Little Akaloa, *S.I., N.Z.* (inset C).			63
Little Belt, *Denmark.*	55½N	10E	33
Little L. Broom, *Scot.*	57¾N	5¼W	24
Little River, *S.I., N.Z.* (inset C).			63
Little Rock, *Ark., U.S.*	34¾N	92¼W	75
Little St. Bernard Pass, *France-Switz.*	45¾N	7E	31
Littlehampton, *Eng.*	50¾N	½W	23
Littleton, *Ireland.*	52¾N	7¾W	26
Littoria, *Italy.*	41½N	13E	36
Litunde, *Mozambique.*	13S	36¾E	51
Liu River, *China.*	24N	109E	48
Liuan, *China.*	32N	116¼E	48
Liuchow, *China.*	24N	109E	48
Liverpool, *England.*	53½N	2¾W	22
Liverpool, *N.S.W., Aust.*	34S	151E	59
Liverpool, *Canada.*	44N	64¾W	67
Liverpool B., *N.W. Can.*	70N	129W	66
Liverpool River, *Aust.*	12S	134E	60
Livingston, *Guatemala.*	15½N	89W	76
Livingstone, *U.S.A.*	45¾N	110¼W	74
Livingstone, *Zambia.*	17¾S	25¾E	51
Livingstone Memorial, *Zambia.*	12S	31E	51
Livingstonia, *Malawi.*	10½S	34E	51
Livno, *Yugoslavia.*	43¾N	17E	36
Livny, *U.S.S.R.*	52½N	37½E	38
Livorno, see LEGHORN.			
Liwale, *Tanzania.*	9¾S	38E	56
Lizala, *Congo (K.).*	2¼N	21½E	56
Lizard Pt., *England.*	50N	5¼W	22
Ljubinje, *Yugoslavia.*	43N	18E	36
Ljubljana, *Yugoslavia.*	46N	14¼E	37
Ljubuski, *Yugoslavia.*	43¼N	17½E	36
Ljusdal, *Sweden.*	61¾N	16E	29
Ljusne, Riv., *Sweden.*	61N	16E	29
Llanarth, *Wales.*	52¼N	4¼W	22
Llanberis, *Wales.*	53¼N	4¼W	22
Llandaff, *Wales.*	51½N	3¼W	22
Llandilo, *Wales.*	51¾N	4W	22
Llandovery, *Wales.*	52N	3¾W	22
Llandrindod Wells, *Wales.*	52¼N	3¼W	22
Llandudno, *Wales.*	53¼N	3¾W	22
Llandyssul, *Wales.*	52N	4¼W	22
Llanelly, *Wales.*	51¾N	4¼W	22
Llanerchymedd, *Eng.*	53¼N	4¼W	22
Llanes, *Spain.*	43½N	5W	35
Llanfair, *Wales.*	52¾N	3¼W	22
Llanfihangel-Ystrad, *Wales.*	52¼N	4¼W	22
Llanfyllin, *Wales.*	52¾N	3¼W	22
Llangadock, *Wales.*	25N	3W¾	22
Llangefni, *England.*	53¼N	4¼W	22
Llangollen, *Wales.*	53N	3¼W	22
Llangurig, *Wales.*	52½N	3½W	22
Llanidloes, *Wales.*	52½N	3½W	22
Llanrhystyd, *Wales.*	52¼N	4W	22
Llanrwst, *Wales.*	53¼N	3¾W	22
Llantrisant, *Wales.*	51½N	3¼W	22
Llanwrtyd Wells, *Wales.*	52¼N	3¾W	22
Llanymynech, *Wales.*	52¾N	3W	22
Llerena, *Spain.*	38¼N	6W	35
Lloyd B., *Queens., Aust.*	12½S	143¼E	60
Lloydminster, *Canada.*	53¼N	110W	70
Loanda, *Angola.*	9S	13¼E	56
Loango, *Congo (B.).*	4½S	12E	56
Loanja, *Zambia.*	16½S	25E	51
Lobatsi, *Botswana.*	25½S	25¾E	54
Lobei, R., *Congo (B.).*	3¼N	18¼E	56
Lobito, *Angola.*	12¼S	13¾E	56
Lobos, *Argentina.*	35¼S	59W	79
Lobos I., *Can. Is.* (ins.).	28¾N	13¾W	35
Locarno, *Switzerland.*	46¼N	8¾E	31
Lochaber, *Scotland.*	57N	4¼W	24
Lochaline, *Scotland.*	56½N	5¾W	25
Loch Arkaig, *Scotland*	57N	5W	24
Loch Assynt, *Scotland.*	58¼N	5W	24
Loch Boisdale, *Scot.*	57¼N	7¼W	24
Loch Broom, *Scotland.*	58N	5¼W	24
Loch Caolisport, *Scot.*	55¾N	5¾W	25
Loch Carron, *Scotland.*	57½N	5½W	24
Loch Duich, *Scotland.*	57¼N	5½W	24
Lochearnhead, *Scot.*	56½N	4¼W	25
Lochem, *Netherlands.*	52¼N	6½E	30
Loches, *France.*	47¼N	1E	31
Loch Fionn, *Scotland.*	57¾N	5¼W	24
Lochgilphead, *Scot.*	56N	5½W	25
Loch Goil, *Scotland.*	56N	5W	25
Loch Hourn, *Scotland.*	57¼N	5½W	24
Lochinver, *Scotland.*	58¼N	5¼W	24
Loch Laggan, *Scotland.*	57N	4¼W	24
Loch Leven, *Scotland.*	56¾N	5W	24
Loch Lochy, *Scotland.*	57N	4¾W	24
Lochluichart, *Scotland.*	57½N	5W	24
Lochmaben, *Scotland.*	55¼N	3¼W	25
Loch Mhor, *Scotland.*	57¼N	4½W	24
Loch Morar, *Scotland.*	56¾N	5¾W	24
Loch More, *Scotland.*	58¼N	5W	24
Lochnagar, Mt., *Scot.*	57N	3¼W	24
Loch Na Keal, *Scot.*	56½N	6W	24
Loch Naver, *Scotland.*	58¼N	4¼W	24
Loch Quoich, *Scotland.*	57N	5¼W	24
Loch Rannoch, *Scot.*	56¾N	4¼W	24
Lochranza, *Scotland.*	55¾N	5¼W	25
Loch Scridain, *Scot.*	56½N	6W	25
Loch Seaforth, *Scot.*	57¾N	6¾W	24
Loch Shell, *Scotland.*	58N	6½W	24
Loch Shiel, *Scotland.*	56¾N	5½W	24
Loch Snizort, *Scot.*	57½N	6½W	24
Loch Sunart, *Scotland.*	56¾N	5¾W	24
Loch Sween, *Scotland.*	56N	5½W	25
Loch Treig, *Scotland.*	56¾N	4¾W	24
Lockeport, *Canada.*	43¾N	65¼W	67
Lockerbie, *Scotland.*	55¼N	3¼W	25
Lockhart, *N.S.W., Aust.*	35½S	146¾E	59
Lockport, *N.Y., U.S.A.*	43¼N	78¾W	69
Locmine, *France.*	47¾N	2¾W	31
Locri, *Italy.*	38¼N	16¼E	36
Locronan, *France.*	48¼N	4W	31
Loddon, *England.*	52½N	1½E	23
Lodeve, *France.*	43¾N	3¼E	32
Lodge Grass, *U.S.A.*	45N	107W	74
Lodi, *Italy.*	45¼N	9½E	36
Lods, *France.*	47N	6¼E	31
Lodwar, *Kenya.*	3¼N	35¼E	56
Lodz, *Poland.*	51¾N	19½E	33
Loeriesfontein, *C. Pr.*	31S	19¼E	52
Lofoten Is., *Norway.*	68½N	14E	29
Lofsla, B. of, *Sweden.*	60¼N	18E	29
Lofter, *O.F.S., S. Afr.*	30¼S	25¼E	55
Loftus, *England.*	54½N	¾W	25
Lofu Riv., *Zambia.*	8S	31E	51
Logan, *Utah, U.S.A.*	41¾N	111¾W	74
Logan, Mt., *Yukon.*	60½N	140¼W	66
Logone, R., *Cameroon.*	13N	14E	56
Logrono, *Spain.*	42½N	2½W	35
Loguno, C., *Moz.*	14S	41E	56
Loharu, *India.*	28½N	76E	44
Lohathla, *C. Pr., S. Afr.*	28S	23E	51
Lohne, *Germany.*	52¾N	8¼E	30
Loing, Riv., *France.*	48¼N	2¾E	30
Loire, Riv., *France.*	47¼N	¼W	31
LOIRE, *France.*	45¾N	4E	32
LOIRE ATLANTIQUE, *Fr.*	47¼N	2W	32
LOIRET, *France.*	48N	2¼E	32
LOIR ET CHER, *France.*	47¼N	1¼E	32
Loja, *Ecuador.*	4S	79W	78
Loja, *Spain.*	37¼N	4¼W	35
Lokeren, *Belgium.*	51N	4E	30
Loko, *Nigeria.*	8¼N	8E	57
Lokoja, *Nigeria.*	7¾N	6¾E	57
Lolland, *Denmark.*	54¾N	11¼E	33
Lollar, *Germany.*	50½N	8¾E	30
Lom, *Bulgaria.*	43¾N	23¼E	37
Lom, Riv., *Cameroon.*	5N	13E	56
Loma Mts., *S. Leone*	9N	11¼W	57
LOMBARDY, *Italy.*	45½N	10E	36
Lombez, *France.*	43¼N	¾E	32
Lombok I., *Indonesia.*	8½S	116¼E	47
Lome, *Togo.*	6¼N	1¼E	57
Lomela, *Congo (K.).*	2½S	23¼E	56
Lomello, *Italy.*	45¼N	8¾E	31
Lomond, L., *Scotland.*	56¼N	4½W	25
Lomsak, *Thailand.*	17N	102E	43
Lomza, *Poland.*	53¼N	22¼E	33
London, *England.*	51½N	0	23
London, *Ont., Can.*	43N	81¼W	68
LONDONDERRY & Tn., *N. Ireland.*	55N	7¼W	26
Long Beach, *U.S.A.*	33¾N	118¼W	74
Long Eaton, *England.*	52¾N	1¼W	23
Long I., *Bahamas, W.I.*	23¼N	75W	77
Long I., *N.Y., U.S.A.*	41N	73W	69
Long I., *Pacific* (inset).	5S	147E	60
Long, Loch, *Scotland.*	56N	4¾W	25
Longarone, *Italy.*	46¼N	12¼E	31
LONGFORD, *Eire.*	53¾N	7¾W	26
Long's Peak, *U.S.A.*	40¼N	105¾W	74
Longlac, *Ont., Can.*	49¾N	86¾W	71
Longpre, *France.*	50N	2E	30
Long Preston, *Eng.*	54N	2¼W	22
Longreach, *Australia.*	23¼S	144¼E	60
Long Stratton, *Eng.*	52½N	1¼E	23
Long Sutton, *Eng.*	52¾N	¼E	23
Longton, *England.*	53N	2¼W	22
Longtown, *England.*	55N	2¾W	25
Longue, *France.*	47½N	0	31
Longuyon, *France.*	49½N	5½E	30
Longview, *Tex., U.S.A.*	32½N	94W	75
Longview, *Wash., U.S.*	46N	123¼W	74
Longwy, *France.*	49½N	5¾E	30
Long-Xuyen, *Vietnam.*	10½N	105½E	47
Lonigo, *Italy.*	45¼N	11¼E	31
Loningen, *Germany.*	52¾N	7¾E	30
Lons-le-Saunier, *Fr.*	46¾N	5¾E	31
Looe, *England.*	50¼N	4¼W	22
Lookout Pt., *W. Aust.*	35S	118E	61
Loongana, *W. Aust.*	31S	127E	58
Lopatin, *U.S.S.R.*	44N	48E	38
Lopatka, *U.S.S.R.*	52N	157E	39
Lopatka, C., *U.S.S.R.*	71¼N	150E	39
Lopei, *China.*	48N	131E	39
Lopez, C., *Gabon.*	½S	8¾E	56
Lop Nor, L., *China.*	40N	90E	42
Lora Creek, R., *S. Aust.*	28S	135E	60
Lorain, *Ohio, U.S.A.*	41½N	82W	75
Loralai, *Pakistan.*	30¼N	69E	43
Lorca, *Spain.*	37¾N	1¾W	35
Lorch, *Germany.*	50N	7¾E	30
Lord Howe Is., *S. Pac.*	31½S	159E	64
Lordsburg, *U.S.A.*	32½N	109W	74
Lorenzago, *Italy.*	46½N	12½E	31
Loreo, *Italy.*	45N	12¼E	31
Lorica, *Columbia.*	9N	76W	77
Lorient, *France.*	47¾N	3¼W	31
Lorrach, *Germany.*	47½N	7¾E	33
LORRAINE, *France.*	49N	6E	32
Lorris, *France.*	48N	2½E	30
Lort, Riv., *W. Aust.*	33½S	121¼E	61
Los Alamos, *U.S.A.*	35¾N	106¼W	74
Los Angeles, *Cal., U.S.*	34N	118W	74
Los Angeles, *Chile.*	37½S	72¼W	79
Los Mochis, *Mexico.*	26N	109¼W	76
Los Roques Is., *Venez.*	12N	67W	77
Los Santos, *Spain.*	38½N	6¼W	35
Los Toques, *Venezuela.*	10½N	67W	77
Losap I., *Pacific.*	7N	151E	64
Loshan, *China.*	29½N	104E	48
Losinj Is., *Yugoslavia.*	44½N	14¼E	36
Loskop, *Natal.*	29S	29½E	55
Lossiemouth, *Scot.*	57¾N	3¼W	24
Lostwithiel, *England.*	50½N	4¾W	22
LOT, *France.*	44½N	1¾E	32
LOT ET GARONNE, *Fr.*	44½N	½E	32
Lota, *Chile.*	37S	73¼W	78
Lothair, *T'vaal, S. Afr.*	26½S	30¼E	59
Lothbeg, *Scotland.*	58¼N	3¾W	25
Loting, *China.*	22½N	110½E	44
Lottigna, *Switzerland.*	46½N	9E	31
Loudeac, *France.*	48¼N	2¾W	31
Loudun, *France.*	47N	0	32
Loughborough, *Eng.*	52¾N	1¼W	23
Loughor, *Wales.*	51¾N	4W	22
Loughrea, *Eire.*	3¾N	8¼W	26
Louis Trichardt, *T'vaal, S. Africa.*	23S	30E	54
Louisburg, *C. Breton I.*	46N	60W	67
Louisburgh, *Ireland.*	53¾N	9¾W	26
Louisiade Arch., *Pac.*	11S	153E	64
LOUISIANA, *U.S.A.*	32N	92W	75
Louisville, *Ky., U.S.A.*	38N	85¾W	75
Louisville, *Que., Can.*	46¼N	72¾W	69
Loukhi, *U.S.S.R.*	66N	33E	29
Loule, *Portugal.*	37¼N	8W	35
Louny, *Czechoslovakia.*	50¼N	13¾E	33
Lourdes, *France.*	43N	0	32
Lourenco Marques, *Mozambique.*	526S	32½E	54
LOUTH & Tn., *Eire.*	53¾N	6½W	26
Louth, *England.*	53¼N	0	23
Louvain, *Belgium.*	50¾N	4¾E	30
Louviers, *France.*	49¼N	1E	31
Louvigne, *France.*	48¼N	1W	31
Louwsburg, *Natal.*	27S	31¼E	55
Lovanger, *Sweden.*	64¼N	21¼E	29
Lovat Riv., *U.S.S.R.*	58¼N	32E	38
Lovech, *Bulgaria.*	43N	24¾E	37
Lovell, *Wyo., U.S.A.*	44¾N	108¼W	74
Lovelock, *Nev., U.S.A.*	40N	118W	74
Lovere, *Italy.*	45¾N	10E	31
Loverna, *Sask., Can.*	51¾N	110W	70
Lovett, *Alberta, Can.*	53N	116¾W	73
Lovisa, *Finland.*	60¼N	26¼E	29
Lowell, *Mass., U.S.A.*	42¾N	71¼W	69
Lower Adamson, *S. Afr.*	31S	26¼E	53
Lower Arrow Lake, *Can.*	49¾N	118W	73
Lower Hutt, *N.I., N.Z.*	41½S	175E	62
LOWER SAXONY, *Ger.*	52¾N	8E	30
Lowestoft, *England.*	52½N	1¾E	23
Lowicz, *Poland.*	52¼N	20E	33
Lowther, *England.*	54½N	2¼W	25

Place	Lat.	Long.	No.
Loxton, *C. Pr., S. Afr.*	31½S	22¾E	52
Loxton, *S. Australia.*	34½S	140½E	59
Loyal, L., *Scotland.*	58½N	4½W	24
Loyalty Is., *Pacific.*	21S	167½E	64
Loyang, *China.*	35N	112½E	48
Loyuan, *China.*	26½N	120E	48
LOZERE, *France.*	44½N	3¾E	32
Loznica, *Yugoslavia.*	44½N	19E	37
Lualua, Riv., *Moz.*	18S	37E	51
Luambala, *Moz.*	13½S	36¼E	56
Luang Prabang, *Laos.*	19¾N	102E	47
Luanginga, R., *Zambia.*	15S	22½E	51
Luangwa, R., *Zambia.*	9S	28½E	51
Luangwa, R., *Zambia.*	16S	30½E	51
Luangwebungu, R., *Zambia.*	14S	23E	51
Luanshya, *Zambia.*	13¼S	28½E	51
Luapula, R., *Congo (K.)*	12S	28¾E	56
Luarca, *Spain.*	43¾N	6½W	35
Luban, *Poland.*	51N	15¼E	33
Lubang Is., *Phil. Is.*	13¾N	120¼E	47
Lubango, *Angola.*	15S	13½E	56
Lubartow, *Poland.*	51½N	22¾E	33
Lubawa, *Poland.*	53½N	19½E	33
Lubben, *Germany.*	52N	14E	33
Lubbock, *Tex., U.S.A.*	33½N	102W	74
Lubeck, *Germany.*	53¾N	10¾E	33
Lubin, *Poland.*	51½N	16¼E	33
Lublin, *Poland.*	51¼N	22½E	33
Lubliniec, *Poland.*	50¾N	19E	33
Lubny, *U.S.S.R.*	50N	33E	38
Lubumbashi, *Congo (K.)*	11½S	26½E	56
Lucan,, *Eire*	53½N	6½W	22
Lucca, *Italy.*	43¾N	10½E	36
Luce Bay, *Scotland.*	54¾N	4¾W	25
Lucea, *Jamaica*, (ins.).	18¼N	78W	77
Lucena, *Spain.*	37¼N	4½W	35
Lucenec, *Czecho.*	48¼N	19½E	37
Lucera, *Italy.*	41½N	15½E	36
Lucerne, see LUZERN.			
Luchow, *China.*	28¾N	105½E	48
Luchow, *Germany.*	53N	11E	33
Luchulingo, R., *Moz.*	12S	37E	51
Luckau, *Germany.*	51½N	13½E	33
Luckenwadle, *Germany.*	52N	13¼E	33
Luckhoff, *O.F. S.Afr.*	29¾S	24¾E	55
Lucknow, see LAKHNAU.			
Lucknow, *Ont., Can.*	44N	81½W	68
Lucky Lake, *Sask., Can.*	51N	107¼W	70
Lucon, *France.*	46½N	1¼W	32
Ludenscheid, *Ger.* (ins.).	51N	7¾E	33
Luderitz, *S.W. Africa.*	26¾S	15¼E	51
Ludgershall, *England.*	51¼N	1½W	23
Ludhiana, *India.*	30¾N	75¾E	44
Ludlow, *England.*	52¼N	2¾W	22
Ludwigsburg, *Ger.*	48¾N	9¼E	33
Ludwigshafen, *Ger.*	49½N	8½E	33
Ludwigslust, *Germany.*	53½N	11½E	33
Luebo, *Congo (K.).*	5¼S	21½E	56
Luena, Riv., *Zambia.*	14½S	24E	51
Luepa, *Venezuela.*	6N	61W	77
Lufkin, *Texas, U.S.A.*	31½N	95W	75
Luga, *U.S.S.R.*	58¾N	29¾E	38
Lugagnano, *Italy.*	44¾N	9¾E	31
Lugano & L., *Switz.*	46N	9E	31
Lugansk, *U.S.S.R.*	48¾N	39¼E	38
Lugela, Riv., *Moz.*	17S	37E	51
Lugg, Riv., *Wales.*	52N	2¾W	22
Lugh Ferrandi, *Som. R.*	3¾N	42½E	56
Lugnaquillia, *Eire.*	53N	6½W	22
Lugo, *Spain.*	43¼N	7½W	35
Lugoj, *Romania.*	45¾N	22E	37
Lugovoy, *U.S.S.R.*	42N	72E	39
Luhaiya, *Yemen.*	15¾N	42¾E	56
Luho, *China.*	32½N	119E	48
Luichow Penin., *China.*	21N	110E	48
Luimbale, *Angola.*	12S	152E	56
Luing, I. of, *Scotland.*	56¼N	5¾W	25
Luino, *Italy.*	46N	8¾E	31
Luisa *Congo (K.).*	7¼S	22½E	56
Lujenda, Riv., *Moz.*	11½S	38E	56
Lukovit, *Bulgaria.*	43¼N	24E	37
Lukow, *Poland.*	52N	22½E	33
Lulea, *Sweden.*	65¾N	22E	29
Luleburgaz, *Turkey.*	41¼N	27¼E	37
Luling, *China.*	40N	119E	48
Luluabourg, *Congo (K.)*	6S	22½E	56
Lumbres, *France.*	50¾N	2E	30
Lumby, *Br. Col., Can.*	50¼N	119W	72
Lumphanan, *Scotland.*	57¼N	2½W	24
Lumsden, *Sask., Can.*	50¾N	104¾W	70
Lumsden, *S.I., N.Z.*	45¾S	168½E	63
Lumut, *Malaysia* (inset).	4¼N	100½E	47
Lunan B., *Scotland.*	56½N	2½W	24
Lund, *Sweden.*	55¾N	13E	29
Lundazi, *Zambia.*	12¼S	33½E	51
Lundi, Riv., *Rhodesia.*	21S	32E	51
Lundy I., *England.*	51¼N	4¾W	22
Luneburg, *Germany.*	53¼N	10½E	33
Lunel, *France.*	43¾N	3¾E	32
Lunen, *Germany* (ins.).	51¾N	7½E	33
Lunenburg, *Canada.*	44¼N	6½E	67
Luneville, *France.*	48¾N	6½E	32
Lung, *Mongolia.*	48N	105E	35
Lunga, Riv., *Zambia.*	14S	27E	59
Lungan, *China.*	32¼N	104¼E	41
Lunghwa, *China.*	42N	117½E	43
Lungi, *S. Leone* (ins.).	8¼N	13W	58
Lungki, *China.*	24¾N	118E	47
Lungkiang, *China.*	47N	126E	38
Lungling, *China.*	24½N	98½E	49
Lungmoon, *China.*	23¾N	114E	43
Lungna, *China.*	25N	115E	48
Lungsi, *China.*	35N	105E	48
Luninets, *U.S.S.R.*	52½N	27E	38
Lunn River, *India.*	24N	68E	48
Lunsemfwa R., *Zambia.*	15S	30E	53
Lunsklip, *T'vaal, S. Afr.*	24S	29E	51
Lupar, *Batang* (R.). *Indon.*	1½N	111E	47
Lupeh, *China.*	44N	120¾E	37
Lupi, *China.*	50N	119E	39
Lure, *France.*	47¾N	6½E	39
Lurena, *Luzon, P.I.*	14N	122E	40
Lurgan, *N. Ireland.*	54½N	6¼W	27
Luri, *Corsica.*	43N	9¼E	36
Lurio, *Mozambique.*	13½S	40½E	56
Lusaka, *Zambia.*	15½S	28¼E	56
Lusambo, *Congo (K.).*	5S	23½E	56
Lushiku, *Angola.*	7S	20E	56
Lushoto, *Tanzania.*	4¾S	38¼E	56
Lüshun, *China.*	38¾N	121¼E	48
Lusikisiki, *C. Pr., S. Afr.*	31¼S	29¾E	53
Lusk, *Eire.*	53½N	6¼W	26
Lusk, *Wyo., U.S.A.*	43N	104¾W	74
Lus la Croix Haute, *Fr.*	44¾N	6E	31
Lüta, *China.*	39N	122E	48
Lut Desert, *Iran.*	31N	58E	40
Luton, *England.*	51¾N	¼W	23
Lutsk, *U.S.S.R.*	50¾N	25¼E	38
Lutterworth, *England.*	52½N	1W	23
Luttig, *C. Pr., S. Afr.*	32½S	22¼E	52
Luttringhausen, *Germany* (inset).	51N	7¼E	33
Lutzerath, *Germany.*	50¼N	7E	30
Lutzputs, *C. Pr., S. Afr.*	28½S	20¾E	52
Luwingu, *Zambia.*	10¼S	30E	51
Luwiya, Riv., *Moz.*	16S	33E	51
LUXEMBOURG, *Europe.*	49¾N	6¼E	30
LUXEMBOURG, *Belgium.*	50N	5¼E	30
Luxembourg, *Lux.*	49¾N	6¼E	30
Luxeuil, *France.*	47¾N	6½E	30
Luxor, *U.A.R.*	25¾N	32¾E	50
Luz, *France.*	42¾N	¼W	32
Luzern & L., *Switz.*	47N	8¼E	31
Luzon I., *Philippines.*	15N	121E	47
Lvov, *U.S.S.R.*	49¾N	24E	38
Lwanping, *China.*	41½N	117½E	48
Lyallpur, *Pakistan.*	31½N	73E	46
Lybster, *Scotland.*	58¼N	3¼W	24
Lycksele, *Sweden.*	64½N	18E	38
Lydd, *England.*	51N	1E	23
Lydda, *Israel* (inset).	32N	35E	40
Lydenburg, *T'vaal.*	25S	30½E	54
Lydney, *England.*	51¾N	2½W	22
Lyell Mine, Mt., *Tas.*	42S	145¾E	59
Lyme Bay, *England.*	50½N	3W	22
Lyme Regis, *England.*	50¾N	3W	22
Lymington, *England.*	50¾N	1½W	23
Lympne, *England.*	51¼N	1E	23
Lynchburg, *U.S.A.*	37¼N	79W	75
Lynd R., *Queens., Aust.*	15½S	142½E	60
Lyndbrook, *Queens.*	17¾S	144½E	60
Lyndhurst, *England.*	51N	1½W	23
Lyndhurst, *S. Aust.*	30¼S	138½E	59
Lyndon, R., *W. Aust.*	23½S	114E	61
Lynmouth, *England.*	51¼N	4W	22
Lynn, *Mass., U.S.A.*	42½N	70¾W	69
Lynton, *England.*	51¼N	3¾W	22
Lynton, *W. Australia.*	28S	114½E	61
LYONNAIS, *France.*	45¾N	4¼E	32
Lyons, *France.*	45¾N	4¾E	32
Lyons, R., *W. Aust.*	25S	116E	61
Lys, R., *Belgium.*	51¼N	3¼E	30
Lystra, *Turkey.*	37½N	32½E	41
Lysva, *U.S.S.R.*	57¾N	57¾E	38
Lytham St. Annes, *Eng.*	53¾N	3W	25
Lyttelton, *S.I., N.Z.*	43½S	172¾E	63
Lytton, *Br. Col., Can.*	50¼N	121½W	72
MA'AD, *Jordan* (ins.).	32¾N	35½E	40
Ma'an, *Jordan.*	30¼N	35½E	41
Maas, Riv., *Nether.*	51¾N	5E	30
Maastricht, *Nether.*	50¾N	5¾E	30
Mabber, C., *Som. Rep.*	9N	51E	56
Mablethorpe, *England.*	53¼N	¼E	23
Mabonto, *S. Leone* (ins.).	8¾N	11¾W	57
Mabote, *Mozambique.*	22S	34E	51
Mabuli, *C. Pr., S. Afr.*	26S	24E	51
McAlester, *Okl., U.S.A.*	35N	96W	75
McAllen, *Texas, U.S.A.*	26N	98W	74
Macala, *Brazil.*	0	51W	78
Macassar, *Celebes.*	5¼S	119½E	47
Macau (Port), *China.*	22¼N	113½E	48
McBride, *Br. Col., Can.*	53¼N	120¼W	72
MacCarthy, *Gamb.* (ins.)	13½N	14¾W	57
Macclesfield, *England.*	53¼N	2¼W	22
McClintock Channel, *N.W.T., Canada.*	72N	103W	66
McClure Str., *N.W. Can.*	74N	120W	66
McCook, *Neb., U.S.A.*	40½N	101W	74
MacDonald, L., *Aust.*	23½S	129E	60
MacDonnell Ra., *Aust.*	23¾S	133E	60
MacDuff, *Scotland.*	57¾N	2½W	24
Macedonia, *Yugo.-Gr.*	41N	22E	37
Macaeio, *Brazil* (ins.).	9½S	36W	79
Macerata, *Italy.*	43¼N	13½E	36
MacFarlane, L., *S. Aust.*	32S	137E	59
Macgillycuddy's Reeks, *Eire.*	52N	9¾W	26
McGregor, *C. Pr., S. Afr.*	34S	19¾E	52
McGrath, *Alaska, U.S.A.*	62N	158½W	74
Machache, Mt., *Leso.*	29¼S	28E	53
Machadodorp, *T'vaal.*	25¾S	30¼E	54
Macha, *U.S.S.R.*	60N	118E	39
Machico, *Madeira,*	32¾N	16¾W	35
Machiques, *Venezuela.*	10N	72½W	77
Machrihanish, *Scot.*	55½N	5¾W	25
Machynlleth, *Wales.*	52¾N	3¾W	22
Macin, *Romania.*	45¼N	28¼E	37
MacIntyre, R., *N.S.W.*	29¼S	148½E	59
MacKay, *Queens., Aust.*	21¼S	149E	60
MacKay, L., *Australia.*	22½S	129E	60
McKean I., *Pacific.*	2S	176W	64
MacKenzie, *N.W.T. Can.*	63N	115W	66
MacKenzie Mts., *Can.*	64N	130W	66
MacKenzie R., *N.W.T., Canada.*	69N	125W	66
MacKenzie S., *Antarc.*	68S	70E	80
MacKies, *Ont., Can.*	48¼N	90W	71
MacKinaw City, *U.S.A.*	46N	85W	75
McKinlay, *Queensland.*	21¼S	141¼E	60
McKinley, Mt., *Alaska.*	63N	150W	74
MacKinnon Rd., *Kenya.*	4S	38¾E	56
Macklin, *Sask., Can.*	52¼N	110W	70
Macksville, *N.S.W.*	30¾S	153E	59
Maclean, *N.S.W., Aust.*	29½S	153¼E	59
MacLeantown, *C. Pr.*	32¾S	27¾E	53
MacLear, *C. Pr., S. Afr.*	31S	28¼E	53
MacLeay R., *Australia.*	31S	153E	59
McLennan, *Alb., Can.*	55¾N	116¾W	73
MacLeod, *Alb., Can.*	49¾N	113¼W	73
Macloutsie R., *Bots.*	22S	28½E	51
McMurdo Sd., *Antarc.*	77S	165E	80
McMurray, *Alb., Can.*	56¾N	111¼W	66
Macomer, *Sardinia.*	40¼N	8¾E	36
Macon, *France.*	46¼N	4¾E	32
Macon, *Georgia, U.S.A.*	32¾N	83¾W	75
Macoun, *Sask., Can.*	49¼N	103¼W	70
Macovane, *Moz.*	21½S	35E	51
MacQuarie Harbour, *Tas., Aust.* (inset).	42¼S	145½E	59
McRae, Mt., *W. Aust.*	22½S	117½E	61
Macroom, *Eire.*	51¾N	9W	26
Macumba R., *S. Aust.*	28S	137¼E	59
MADAGASCAR. see MALAGASY REPUBLIC.			
Madalena, *Azores* (ins.).	38½N	28¼W	35
Madang, *N. Guin.* (ins.).	5¼S	145¾E	60
Maddalena, *Sardinia.*	41¼N	9¼E	36
Madeba, *Jordan* (ins.).	31¾N	35½E	40
Madeira Is., *Atlantic.*	32¾N	17W	35
Madeira R., *Brazil.*	5½S	61¼W	78
Madhya Pradesh, *India.*	23N	80E	44
Madiagoune, *Up. Volta*	11¼N	¾E	57
Madinet al Faiyum, see EL FAIYUM.			
Madison, *Wis., U.S.A.*	43N	89¼W	75
Madley, Mt., *W. Aust.*	24S	124E	61
Madoc, *Ontario, Can.*	44½N	77½W	69
Madona, *U.S.S.R.*	56¾N	26¼E	38
Madonela, *C.Pr., S. Afr.*	30¼S	30E	53
Madonie, Mt., *Sicily.*	38N	14E	36
MADRAS & Tn., *India.*	13N	80¼E	45
Madre, Sierra, *Mexico.*	25N	106W	76
Madrid, *Spain.*	40½N	3¾W	35
Madridejos, *Spain.*	39½N	3¾W	35
Madura I., *Indonesia.*	7S	113½E	47
Madurai, *India.*	10N	78¼E	45
Maebashi, *Japan.*	36½N	139E	49
Mael, *France.*	48½N	3¼W	31
Maeseyck, *Belgium.*	51¼N	5¾E	30
Maesteg, *Wales.*	51½N	3¾W	22
Maevatanana, *Malagasy.*	17S	46¾E	56
Maewo I., *Pacific.*	14S	169E	64
Mafeking, *C. Pr., S. Afr.*	25¾S	25¾E	51
Mafeking, *Man., Can.*	52¾N	101W	70
Mafeteng, *Lesotho.*	29½S	27½E	53
Maffra, *Vict., Aust.*	38S	147E	59
Mafia I., *Tanzania.*	7¾S	39¾E	56
Mafra, *Portugal.*	39N	9¼W	35
Magadan, *U.S.S.R.*	59½N	150¾E	39
Magadi, *Kenya.*	1¾S	37¼E	56
Magaliesburg, *T'vaal.*	26S	27½E	55
Magangue, *Colombia.*	9¼N	74¾W	77
Magaria, *Niger. Rep.*	13N	9E	57
Magas, *Iran.*	27N	61½E	40
Magato Mts., *T'vaal.*	22½S	30¼E	54
Magdala, *Ethiopia.*	11¼N	39½E	56
Magdala, Mt., *Isr.* (ins.).	33N	36E	40
Magdalen Is., *Canada.*	47½N	61¾W	67
Magdalena R., *Col.*	11N	74¾W	77
Magdalena, *Mexico.*	30½N	111W	76
Magdalena R., *Mexico.*	30½N	113W	76
Magdeburg, *Germany.*	52¼N	11¾E	33
Magee I., *Ireland.*	54¾N	5¾W	25
Magelang, *Java, Ind.*	7½S	110¼E	47
Magellan, Str. of, *Chile.*	52S	75W	78
Magenta, *Italy.*	45½N	9E	31
Mageroen I., *Norway.*	72N	24E	29
Maggiore, L., *Italy.*	46N	8¾E	36
Maghera, *N. Ireland.*	54¾N	6¾W	26
Magherafelt, *Ireland.*	54¾N	6½W	26
Maglaj, *Yugoslavia.*	44½N	18E	36
Maglie, *Italy.*	40N	18½E	37
Magnitogorsk, *U.S.S.R.*	53½N	59E	38
Magog, *Quebec, Can.*	45¼N	72W	69
Magrath, *Alb., Can.*	49½N	112¾W	73
Magusheni, *S. Africa.*	31¾S	29½E	53
Magwe, *Burma.*	20¼N	95E	43
Mahabaleshvar, *India.*	18N	73½E	45
Mahaddie Wein, *Som. R.*	3N	45½E	56
Mahajamba B., *Malag.*	15S	46E	56
Mahajan, *India.*	28½N	73¾E	44
Mahajilo, R., *Malagasy.*	20S	45E	56
Mahakam, R., *Indon.*	½S	117½E	47
Mahalapye, *Botswana.*	23S	26¾E	51
Mahalla El Kubra, *U.A.R.*	30¾N	31E	50
Mahanadi, R., *India.*	21N	87E	44
Mahanoro, *Malagasy.*	20S	48¾E	56
Mahaoya, *Ceylon* (ins.).	7½N	81¼E	45
Mahaweli R., *Cey.* (ins.)	8½N	81¼E	45
Mahdia, *Tunisia.*	35½N	11E	35
Mahe, *India.*	11¾N	75½E	45
Mahia Pen., *N.I., N.Z.*	39¼S	178E	62
Maho, *Ceylon,* (ins.).	7¾N	80¼E	45
Mahon. *Minorca, Med.*	40N	4¼E	35
Mahosi, *Mozambique.*	24S	32E	51
Mahua, *Mozambique.*	13¾S	37½E	56
Mahuva, *India.*	21¼N	71¾E	46
Maiche, *France.*	47½N	6¾E	31
Maidan-i-Naftun, *Iran.*	32N	49E	41
Maiden Newton, *Eng.*	50¾N	2½W	22
Maidenhead, *England.*	51½N	¾W	23
Maidi, *Yemen.*	16¼N	42½E	46
Maidstone, *England.*	51¼N	½E	23
Maiduguri, *Nigeria.*	12N	13E	57
Maijuju, *Nigeria.*	9¾N	9¼E	57
Maikop, *U.S.S.R.*	44½N	40E	38
Main, R., *Germany.*	50N	8½E	33
Mainana I., *Pacific.*	1N	173E	64
MAINE, *France.*	48N	0	32
MAINE, *U.S.A.*	45N	69W	75
MAINE ET LOIRE, *Fr.*	47¼N	1¾W	32
Maine, Riv., *France.*	47¼N	1W	32
Maine, Riv., *Ireland.*	52¼N	9¾W	26
Mainland, *Orkneys.*	59N	3W	24
Mainland, *Shet.*, (ins.).	60½N	1¼W	24
Mainpuri, *India.*	27¼N	79½E	44
Maintenon, *France.*	48¾N	1½E	31
Maintirano, *Malagasy.*	18S	44E	56
Mainz, *Germany.*	50N	8¼E	33
Mairhofen, *Austria.*	47¼N	12E	31
Maisi, C., *Cuba, W.I.*	20N	74W	77
Maitland, *N.S.W., Aust.*	32¾S	151½E	59
Maitland, L., *W. Aust.*	27S	121½E	61
Maizuru, *Japan.*	35½N	135¼E	49
Majaguel, *Colombia.*	8¾N	75W	77
Maji, *Ethiopia.*	6¼N	35¾E	56
Majma'a *Saudi Arabia.*	26N	45E	40
Majorca, *Balearic Is.*	39¾N	3E	35
Majunga, *Malagasy.*	15¾S	46¼E	56
Majuro I., *Pacific.*	8N	171E	64
Makale, *Ethiopia.*	13½N	39½E	56
Makamik, *Que., Can.*	48¾N	79W	69
Makar, *U.S.S.R.*	48N	53E	38
Makara, *N.I., N.Z.*	(Inset B)		62
Makarska, *Yugoslavia.*	43¼N	17E	36
Makemo I., *Pacific.*	15S	145W	64
Makeni, *Sierra Leone.*	9N	12¼W	57
Makeyevka, *U.S.S.R.*	48N	38E	38
Makhachkala, *U.S.S.R.*	43N	47½E	38
Makhaola, *Lesotho.*	30S	28¾E	53
Makin I., *Pacific.*	4N	172E	64
Makindu, *Kenya.*	2½S	36¼E	56
Makokou, *Gabon.*	½N	12¾E	56
Makokskraal, *T'vaal.*	26¼S	26¾E	55
Makoua, *Congo (B.).*	0	15¾E	56
Makow, *Poland.*	49¾N	19¾E	33
Makow, *Poland.*	53N	21E	33
Makowe, *Natal.*	28S	32E	55
Makri, *Greece.*	41N	25½E	37
Makumbi, *Congo (K.).*	5¾S	20¾E	56
Makurazaki, *Japan.*	31N	130½E	49
Makurdi, *Nigeria.*	7¾N	8½E	57
Makwassie, T'vaal, *S.A.*	27¼S	26E	55
Malabar Coast, *India.*	10N	75¾E	45
MALACCA & Tn., *Malay.*	2¼N	102¼E	47
Malacca Str., *Indonesia.*	4N	100E	47
Malad City, *Id., U.S.A.*	42¼N	112¼W	74
Maladeta, Mt., *Spain.*	42¾N	¾E	35
Malaga, *Spain.*	36¾N	4½W	35
Malagarasi, *Tanzania.*	5S	30¾E	56
MALAGASY REBUBLIC, (inset).			56
Malahide, *Eire.*	53½N	6W	22
Malaita I., *Pacific.*	9S	161E	64
Malakand, *Pakistan.*	34½N	72E	46
Malang, *Java Indon.*	8S	112½E	47
Malange, *Angola.*	9½S	16¼E	56
Malar, L., *Sweden.*	59½N	17E	29
Malatya, *Turkey.*	38¼N	38¼E	4
MALAYSIA, *S.E. Asia.*	4N	110E	4
MALAWI, *Africa.*	12½S	34½E	5
MALAYA, see WEST MALAYSIA			
Malaya Vishera, *U.S.S.R.*	58¾N	32¼E	3
Malaybalay, *Mind., P.I.*	7½N	125E	4
Mal Bay, *Ireland.*	52¾N	9½W	2
Malbon, *Queens., Aust.*	21S	140½E	6
Malbork, *Poland.*	54N	19E	3
Malcolm, *W. Aust.*	29S	121½E	6
Malcolm Pt., *W. Aust.*	33½S	123½E	6
Malden, *Mass., U.S.A.*	42½N	71W	6
Malden I., *Pacific.*	4S	155W	6
Maldive Is., *Indian Oc.*	5N	74E	4
Maldon, *England.*	51¾N	¾E	2
Maldonado, *Uruguay.*	35S	55W	7
Malea, C., *Greece.*	36½N	23¼E	3
Male, *Italy.*	46¼N	10¾E	3
Malekula I., *Pacific.*	17S	166E	6
Malelane, *T'vaal, S.Afr.*	25½S	31½E	5
Malembe, *Congo, (B.).*	3S	12E	5
Maler Kotla, *India.*	30½N	76E	4
Malestroit, *France.*	47¾N	2½W	3
Malgas, *C. Pr., S. Afr.*	34¼S	20½E	5
Malhada, *Brazil.*	14S	43W	7
MALI, *West Africa.*	19N	2W	5
Malia, *India.*	23N	70½E	4
Malin, *Ukr., U.S.S.R.*	51N	29E	3
Malin Head, *Eire.*	55¼N	7½W	2
Malindi, *Kenya.*	3¼S	40E	5
Malines, *Belgium.*	51N	4½E	3
Malkara, *Turkey.*	41N	26¾E	3
Malkinia, *Poland.*	52¾N	22E	3
Malko Trnovo, *Bulg.*	42N	27½E	3
Mallacoota, *Vict., Aust.*	37½S	149¾E	5
Mallaig, *Scotland.*	57N	5¾W	2
Mallaranny, *Ireland.*	53¾N	9¾W	2
Malles, *Italy.*	46¾N	10½E	3
Mallina, *W. Aust.*	21S	117½E	6
Mallnitz, *Austria.*	47N	13E	3
Mallow, *Eire.*	52¼N	8¾W	2

Place	Lat.	Long.	No.
Mallwyd, Wales.	52½N	3¾W	22
Malmberget, Sweden.	67¼N	21E	29
Malmedy, Belgium.	50¼N	6E	30
Malmesbury, C. Pr.	33⅓S	18¼E	52
Malmesbury, Eng.	51¼N	2W	22
Malmo, Sweden.	55¾N	13E	29
Maloelap I., Pacific.	9N	171E	64
Malombe, L., Malawi.	14⅓S	35½E	51
Malona. Rhodes, Gr.	36N	27¼E	41
Malonga, Congo (K.).	10⅓S	23¼E	56
Maloyaroslavets, U.S.S.R.	55N	36½E	38
Malpas, England.	53N	2¾W	22
Malpelo I., Colombia.	4N	82W	78
Malstrom Whirlpool, Norway.	68N	12E	29
MALTA, Mediterranean.	35¾N	14E	36
Malta, Mont., U.S.A.	48¼N	107¼W	74
Maltahohe, S.W. Afr.	24⅓S	17E	51
Malton, England.	54¼N	¾W	22
Malung, Sweden.	60¼N	13¼E	29
Malvan, India.	16N	73¼E	45
Malvern Hills, Eng.	52¼N	2¼W	22
Mama, U.S.S.R.	58N	111E	39
Mambere R., Congo (B.)	3N	17E	56
Mambone, Moz.	21S	35E	51
Mamers, France.	48¼N	¼E	31
Mamfe, Nigeria.	5¼N	9¼E	57
Mampong, Ghana.	7N	1¼W	57
Mamore, R., Brazil.	11S	65W	78
Mamou, Guinea, (ins.).	10¼N	12¼W	57
Mampawah, Kal., Indon.	½N	109E	47
Mamyklan, U.S.S.R.	61N	122E	39
Man, Isle of, England.	54¼N	4¼W	25
Manaar & G. of, Ceylon.	9N	79E	45
Manacor, Majorca I.	39¼N	3¼E	35
Managua, Nicaragua.	12N	86¼W	77
Manah, Saudi Arabia.	23N	57E	40
Manaia, N.I., N.Z.	39¼S	174E	62
Manakara, Malagasy.	22S	48E	56
Manakau,Mt.,S.I.,N.Z.	42¼S	173¼E	63
Manakha, Yemen (ins.).	15N	44E	40
Manama, Bahrain I.	26¼N	50E	40
Manana, Panama.	9N	78W	77
Mananjary, Malagasy.	21¼S	48¼E	56
Manaos, Brazil.	3S	60W	78
Manapouri,L.,S.I.,N.Z.	45¼S	167¼E	63
Manass & R., China.	45N	85E	39
Manatif, Saudi Arabia.	20N	57E	40
Manawatu,N.I.,N.Z.	40¼S	175E	62
MANCHE, France.	49N	1W	31
Manchester, England.	53¼N	2¼W	22
Manchester, U.S.A.	43N	71¼W	69
MANCHURIA, China.	44N	127E	49
Mand, Riv., Iran.	28N	52E	40
Manda, Tanzania.	10¼S	34¼E	56
Mandal, Norway.	58N	7¼E	29
Mandalay, Burma.	22N	96E	43
Mandal Gobi, Mong.	45N	108E	39
Mandar, G. of, Celebes, E.I.	3S	119E	47
Mandas, Sardinia.	39¼N	9¼E	36
Mandeville, Jam.(ins.).	18N	77¼W	77
Mandimba, Moz.	14S	36¼E	51
Mandinga, Panama.	9N	79W	77
Mandla, India.	22¼N	80¼E	44
Mandra, Pakistan.	73¼N	33¼E	46
Mandritsara, Malagasy.	16S	49E	56
Mandsaur, India.	24N	75E	44
Manduria, Italy.	40¼N	17¼E	36
Mandvi, India.	22¼N	69¼E	44
Manfredonia, Italy.	41¼N	16E	36
Mangaia I., Pacific.	22S	159W	64
Mangahao,R,N.I.,N.Z.	40¼S	175E	62
Mangakino, N.I., N.Z.	38¼S	176E	62
Mangalia, Romania.	43¼N	28¼E	37
Mangalore, India.	12¼N	74¼E	45
Manganore, C. Pr.	28S	23E	52
Mangareva I., Pacific.	23¼S	135W	64
Mangaroa, N.I., N.Z. (inset B).			62
Mangere, N.I., N.Z. (inset A).			62
Mangkalihat, C., Borneo.	1N	119E	47
MANGO, Togo.	10¼N	¼E	57
Mangoky R., Malagasy.	21S	44¼E	56
Mangoli, Sula Is., Indon.	1⅓S	125¼E	47
Mangonui, N.I., N.Z.	35S	173¼E	62
Mangrol, India.	21¼N	70¼E	46
Manhattan, Kansas, U.S.A.	39N	96¼W	75
Manhattan, N.Y., U.S.A. (inset).	40¼N	74W	75
Mani, Tibet.	35N	87¼E	43
Manihiki Is., Pacific.	11S	162¼W	64
Manila, Luzon, P.I.	14¼N	121E	47
Manilla, N.S.W., Aust.	30¼S	150¼E	59
Maninga R., Zambia.	13S	24E	51
Manipur, see IMPHAL.			
Manipur Riv., Burma.	23¼N	94E	43
Manisa, Turkey.	38¼N	27¼E	41
Manistee, Mich., U.S.A.	44N	86W	75
MANITOBA, Canada.	54N	98W	71
Manitoba, L., Man., Can.	51N	98¼W	71
Manitou, Man., Can.	49¼N	98¼W	71
Manitoulin I., Canada.	45¼N	82W	68
Manizales, Colombia.	5N	75¼W	75
Manja, Malagasy (ins.)	21¼S	44¼E	76
Manjafa, Chad.	11N	15E	56
Mankaiana, Swazi.	26¼S	31E	55
Mankato, Minn., U.S.A.	44N	94W	75
Mankial, Kash. (ins.).	35¼N	73¼E	44
Mankoya, Zambia.	15S	25E	51
Manly, N.S.W., Aust.	33¼S	151¼E	59
Mannheim, Germany.	49¼N	8¼E	33
Mannin B., Ireland.	53¼N	10¼W	26
Manning-tree, Eng.	52N	1E	23
Mannu, C., Sardinia.	40N	8¼E	36
Mano, Sierra Leone.	8N	12¼W	57
Manokwari, N. Guinea.	½S	134E	47
Manono, Congo (K.).	7¼S	27¼E	56
Manor Hamilton, Ire.	54¼N	8¼W	26
Manresa, Spain.	41¼N	1¼E	35
Mansa, Zambia.	11S	29E	51
Mansel I., N.W.T, Can.	62N	80W	66
Mansfield, England.	53¼N	1¼W	23
Mansfield, Oh., U.S.A.	40¼N	82¼W	75
Mansfield, Vict., Aust.	37S	146E	59
Mansilla, Spain.	42¼N	5¼W	35
Mansura, U.A.R.	31N	31¼E	50
Manta, Nigeria.	10N	6¼E	57
Mantes-Gassicourt, Fr.	49N	1¼E	30
Mantua, Cuba, W.I.	21¼N	84¼W	77
Mantua, Italy.	45¼N	10¼E	36
Manua Is., Samoa, Pac.	14¼S	168¼W	64
Manuherikia R., N.Z.	45¼S	169¼E	63
Manukau Harb., N.Z.	37S	174¼E	62
Manurewa, N.I., N.Z.	37S	175E	62
Manus I., Pacific (inset).	2S	147E	60
Manville, Alb., Can.	53¼N	111¼W	73
Manyas, Turkey.	40N	28E	37
Manyas Golu, L., Turk.	40¼N	28E	37
Manyara, L., Tanzania.	3¼S	35¼E	56
Manyberries, Alb., Can.	49¼N	110¼W	73
Manych, L., U.S.S.R.	47N	42¼E	38
Manzai, Pakistan.	32¼N	70¼E	43
Manzanares, Spain.	39N	3¼W	35
Manzanillo, Mexico.	19N	104¼W	76
Manzanillo, Cuba, W.I.	20¼N	77¼W	77
Manzini, Swaziland.	26¼S	31¼E	55
Mao, Chad.	14N	15¼E	56
Mapanza, Zambia.	16¼S	27E	51
Mapela, T'vaal, S. Afr.	24S	28¼E	54
Mapinhane, Moz.	22¼S	35E	51
Mapire, Venezuela.	7¼N	64¼W	77
Maple Creek, Sask.	49¼N	109¼W	70
Mapumulo, Natal.	29¼S	31E	55
Maqdaha, S. Yemen.	14¼N	49E	40
Maqna, Saudi Arabia.	28N	35E	41
Mara, T'vaal, S. Africa.	23S	29¼E	54
Maraca, I. de, Brazil.	3N	50W	78
Maracaibo, Venezuela.	10¼N	71¼W	77
Maracay, Venezuela.	10¼N	67¼W	77
Marada, Libya.	29N	19E	34
Maraeti, N.I., N.Z. (inset A).			62
Maragheh, Iran.	37¼N	46E	41
Marais, C. Pr., S. Afr.	32¼S	24¼E	53
Maraisburg, T'vaal.	26S	28E	51
Marajo I., Brazil.	1S	49¼W	78
Marakei I., Pacific.	2N	173E	64
Maralal, Kenya.	2N	37E	56
Maralbashi, China.	40N	78E	39
Marali, Cent. Afr. Rep.	6N	18E	56
Marampa, Sa. Le. (ins.)	8¼N	12¼W	57
MARAMURESH, Rom.	46¼N	24E	37
Marandellas, Rhodesia.	18¼S	31¼E	51
Maranello, Italy.	44¼N	10¼E	31
MARANHAO, Brazil.	5S	45W	78
Maranon, R., Peru.	4S	74W	78
Marargia, C., Sardinia.	40¼N	8¼E	36
Maras, Turkey.	37¼N	37E	41
Marathon, Queens., Aust.	21S	143E	60
Maratua I., Indonesia.	2¼N	118¼E	47
Marazion, England.	50N	5¼W	22
Marbella, Spain.	36¼N	5W	35
Marble Bar, W. Aust.	20¼S	119¼E	61
Marble Canyon, U.S.A.	36¼N	112W	74
Marble Hall, T'vaal.	25S	29¼E	54
Marburg, Germany.	50¼N	8¼E	30
Marcali, Hungary.	46¼N	17¼E	37
Marcelin, Sask., Can.	53N	106¼W	70
March, England.	52¼N	0	23
Marchand, Man., Can.	49¼N	96¼W	71
Marchand, Morocco.	33¼N	6¼W	35
MARCHE, France, (ins.).	46N	1¼E	32
Marchena, Spain.	37¼N	5¼W	35
MARCHES, Italy.	43¼N	13¼E	36
Mar Chiquita L., Arg.	30¼S	62¼W	79
Marcus I., Pacific.	25N	153E	64
Mardie, W. Aust.	21S	116E	61
Mar del Plata, Arg.	38S	57¼W	79
Mardin, Turkey.	37¼N	40¼E	41
Mare I., Pacific.	21¼S	168E	64
Mareb, R., Ethiopia.	15N	37E	56
Maree, L., Scotland.	57¼N	5¼W	24
Mareeba, Queens., Aust.	17S	145¼E	60
Marengo, Algeria.	36¼N	2¼E	35
Marennes, France.	45¼N	1¼W	32
Maretimo I., Sicily.	38N	12E	36
Margaree Harb., Can.	46¼N	61¼W	67
Maragret Bay, Can.	51¼N	127¼W	72
Margaret Riv., W. Aust.	34S	115E	61
Margarita, I. de, Venez.	11N	64¼W	77
Margate, England.	51¼N	1¼E	23
Margelan, U.S.S.R.	40¼N	71¼E	40
Marhoum, Algeria.	34¼N	¼W	35
MARI A.S.S.R., U.S.S.R.	57N	47E	38
Maria Is., N. Terr., Aust.	15S	136E	60
Maria I., Tas. (ins.).	42¼S	148E	59
Maria Madre I., Mex.	22N	107W	76
Maria Madgalena I., Mexico.	22N	106W	76
Maria V. Diemen, C., N.I., N.Z.	34¼S	172¼E	62
Mariampole, U.S.S.R.	54¼N	23¼E	33
Marianas Is., Pacific.	15N	145E	64
Marianao, Cuba, W.I.	23N	82¼W	77
Marianna, Fla., U.S.A.	30¼N	85¼W	75
Marianské Lázně, Czecho.	50N	12¼E	33
Mariato Pta., Panama.	7¼N	81W	77
Mariazell, Austria.	47¼N	15¼E	33
Maribor, Yugoslavia.	46¼N	15¼E	36
Maridi, Sudan.	5N	29¼E	56
Marie Galante I., W.I.	16N	61¼W	77
Mariehamn, Sweden.	60¼N	20E	29
Mariembourg, Belg.	50¼N	4¼E	30
Marienbad, see MARIANSKE LAZNE.			
Mariental, S.W. Africa.	24S	17¼E	51
Mariestad, Sweden.	58¼N	13¾E	21
Marietta, Ga., U.S.A.	34N	84¾W	75
Marigny, France.	48¼N	3¼E	30
Mariinsk, U.S.S.R.	56¼N	87¼E	39
Marikana, T'vaal.	25¼S	27¼E	54
Marilana, W. Aust.	22¼S	119E	61
Marin, Martin., W.I.	14¼N	61W	77
Marion Reef, Aust.	19S	153E	60
Maripa, Venezuela.	7¼N	65W	77
Maritime Alps, Italy.	44N	7¼E	36
Maritsa, R., Bulgaria.	42¼N	25E	37
Mariupol, see ZHDANOV.			
Market Bosworth, Eng.	52¼N	1¼W	23
Market Deeping, Eng.	52¼N	¼W	23
Market Drayton, Eng.	53N	2¼W	22
Market Harborough, England.	52¼N	1W	23
Market Hill, N.Ireland.	54¼N	6¼W	26
Market Rasen, Eng.	53¼N	¼W	23
Market Weighton, Eng.	54N	¾W	22
Markha, R., U.S.S.R.	64N	116E	39
Markham Mt., Antarc.	83S	163E	80
Markinch, Scotland.	56¼N	3W	25
Markovo, U.S.S.R.	64N	170E	39
Marlborough, Guyana. (inset).	8N	58W	77
Marlborough, Eng.	51¼N	1¾W	23
MARLBOROUGH, N.Z.	42S	173¼E	63
Marle, France.	49¾N	3¾E	30
Marlenburg, N. Guinea	3¼S	144E	60
Marlo, Victoria, Aust.	37¼S	148¼E	59
Marlow, C. Pr., S. Afr.	32S	25¼E	53
Marlow, England.	51¼N	¾W	23
Marmande, France.	44¼N	¼E	32
Marmara, S. of, Turk.	40¼N	28E	41
Marmaris, Turkey.	36¼N	28¼E	41
Mar Menor, Spain.	37¼N	¾W	35
Marmolada, Mt., Italy.	46¼N	11¼E	31
Marmora, Ont., Can.	44¼N	77¼W	69
Marmugao, Goa.	15N	74E	45
Marnay, France.	47¼N	5¼E	32
MARNER. & DEP., Fr.	49N	4E	32
Maroona, Vict., Aust.	37¼S	143E	59
Marovody, Malagasy.	16S	46¼E	56
Marquard, O.F.S.	28¼S	27¼E	55
Marquesas Is., Pacific.	10S	140W	64
Marquette, U.S.A.	46¼N	87¼W	68
Marrakesh, Morocco.	31¼N	8W	35
Marrara, Italy.	44¼N	11¼E	31
Marrawah, Tas., Aust.	41S	144¼E	59
Marree, S. Australia.	29¼S	138E	59
Marromeu, Moz.	18¼S	36E	51
Marsa Fatma, Ethiopia.	15N	40E	56
Marsa Sha'ab, Sudan.	23N	36E	40
Marsabit, Kenya.	2¼N	37¼E	56
Marsala, Sicily.	37¼N	12¼E	36
Marseilles, France.	43¼N	5¼E	32
Marseilles, O.F.S.	29¼S	27¼E	55
Marshall Is., Pacific.	10N	170E	64
Marshfield, England.	51¼N	2¼W	22
Mars-la-Tour, France.	49N	5¼E	30
Martaban, G. of, Burma.	16N	97E	43
Martelange, Belgium.	49¾N	5¼E	30
Martha's Vineyard I., Mass.	41¼N	70¼W	69
Martigne Ferchaud, France.	47¾N	1¼W	31
Martigny, Switz.	46N	7E	31
Martigues, France.	43¼N	5E	32
Martina Franca, Italy.	40¼N	17¼E	36
Martinboro, N.I.,N.Z.	41¼S	175¼E	62
Martindale, C. Pr.	33¼S	26¼E	53
Martinique I., W.I.	14¼N	61W	77
Martinsburg, Austria.	48¼N	15E	33
Marton, N.I., N.Z.	40S	175¼E	62
Marton, Queens., Aust.	15¼S	145E	60
Martorell, Spain.	41¼N	2E	35
Maru, Kashmir (ins.).	33¼N	75¼E	44
Marua, Cameroon.	10¼N	14¼E	56
Marudi, Guyana. (ins.).	2S	59W	77
Marula, Rhodesia.	20¼S	28E	54
Marveloes, France.	44¼N	3¼E	32
Marvel Loch, W. Aust.	32S	119E	61
Mary, U.S.S.R.	37¼N	61¼E	40
Maryborough, Queens.	25¼S	152¼E	60
Maryborough, Vict.	37S	143¼E	59
Marydale, C. Pr., S. Afr.	29¼S	22E	52
Maryfield, N. Terr., Australia.	15¼S	134E	60
Maryfield, Sask., Can.	49¼N	101¼W	70
Maryland, Rhodesia.	17¼S	31E	51
MARYLAND, U.S.A.	39N	77W	75
Maryport, England.	54¼N	3¼W	25
Marysville, Ut., U.S.A.	38N	112¼W	74
Marysville, Canada.	46N	66¼W	67
Mas Afuera Is., Chile.	34S	81W	78
Mas Atierra Is., Chile.	34S	79W	78
Masan, Korea.	35¼N	128¼E	49
Masangena, Moz.	22S	33E	51
Masara, Sicily.	37¼N	12¼E	36
Masasi, Tanzania.	10¼S	38¼E	56
Masaya, Nicaragua.	12N	86¼W	77
Masbate, Luzon, P.I.	12N	123E	47
Masbate I., P.I.	12¼N	123¼E	47
Mascara, Algeria.	35¼N	¼E	35
Maselspoort, O.F.S.	29S	26¼E	55
Maseru, Lesotho.	29¼S	27¼E	55
Masham, England.	54¼N	1¾E	23
MASHONALAND, Rhod.	18S	31¼E	51
Masia, Mozambique.	25S	32¼E	51
Masindi, Kenya.	2N	32E	56
Masinga, Mozambique.	23¼S	35¼E	51
Masira I., Saudi Arabia.	21N	58E	40
Mask, Lough, Eire.	53¼N	9¼W	26
Mason City, Io., U.S.A.	43¼N	93¼W	75
Mason, L., W. Aust.	27¼S	119E	61
Massa, Italy.	44N	10¼E	36
Massa Marittima, Italy.	43N	11E	36
MASSACHUSETTS, U.S.	42¼N	72W	75
Massakori, Chad.	13N	15¼E	56
Massawa, Ethiopia.	15¼N	39¼E	56
Massena, N.Y., U.S.A.	45N	75W	69
Massenya, Chad.	11¼N	16E	56
Massevaux, France.	47¾N	7E	30
Massey, Ont., Can.	46¼N	82W	68
Massulipatnam, see BANDAR.			
MATABELELAND, Rhod.	19S	28E	51
Matadi, Congo (K.).	5¼S	13¼E	56
Matagalpa, Nicaragua.	13¼N	85¼W	77
Matakana, N.S.W., Aust.	33S	146E	59
Matakana, N.I., N.Z.	37¼S	176¼E	62
Mataki, Mus. & Oman.	20N	55E	40
Matala, Zambia.	15S	27E	51
Matale, Ceylon, (ins.).	7¼N	80¼E	45
Matam, Senegal.	15N	13W	50
Matamata, N.I., N.Z.	37¼S	175¼E	62
Matamoros, Mexico.	25¼N	97¼W	76
Matane, Quebec, Can.	48¼N	67¼W	67
Matanzas, Cuba, W.I.	23N	81¼W	77
Matape, Mexico.	28¼N	110W	76
Matapala, C., C. Rica.	8¼N	83¼W	77
Matapan, C., Greece.	36¼N	22¼E	37
Matapedia, Que., Can.	48N	67W	67
Matara, Ceylon, (ins.).	6N	80¼E	45
Mataranka, N. Terr., Australia.	15S	133E	60
Matarka, Morocco.	33N	3W	34
Matatiele, C. Pr.,S.Afr.	30¼S	28¼E	53
Mataura & R., S.I., New Zealand.	46¼S	168¼E	63
Mateadira, Lesotho.	29S	27¼E	53
Matehuala, Mexico.	23¼N	100¼W	76
Matelot, Trinidad, W.I. (inset).	11¼N	61W	77
Matera, Italy.	40¼N	16¼E	36
Matetsi, Rhodesia.	18S	26E	51
Mateur, Tunisia.	37N	9¼E	36
Mathews, Mt., N.I., N.Z. (inset B).			62
Mathura, India.	27¼N	77¼E	44
Matjesfontein, C. Pr.	33¼S	20¼E	52
Matlock, England.	53¼N	1¼W	23
Matochkin Shar, U.S.S.R.	73¼N	56¼E	39
Matopo Hills, Rhodesia.	21S	28E	51
Matrah, Mus. & Oman.	23¼N	58¼E	40
Matruh, U.A.R.	31¼N	27¼E	34
Matsu I., China.	26N	120E	48
Matsuda, Japan.	35N	132E	49
Matsue, Japan.	35¼N	133E	49
Matsumae, Japan.	41N	140E	49
Matsumoto, Japan.	36¼N	138E	49
Matsuyama, Japan.	33¼N	132¼E	49
Mattawa, Ont., Can.	46¼N	78¼W	69
Matterhorn, Switz.	46N	7¼E	31
MATO GROSSO, Brazil.	15S	54W	78
Matun, Afghanistan.	33¼N	70E	43
Maturin, Venezuela.	9¼N	63W	77
Maubeuge, France.	50¼N	4E	30
Mauchline, Scotland.	55¼N	4¼W	25
Maui I., Hawaii, U.S.A.	20¼N	154¼W	64
Mauke I., Pacific.	20S	156W	64
Mauleon Lichane, Fr.	43¼N	1W	32
Maun, Botswana.	20S	23E	51
Maunda, Mozambique.	12S	39E	51
Maure, France.	48N	2W	31
Mauriac, France.	45¼N	2¼E	32
MAURITANIA, Africa.	19N	13W	50
Mauritius I., Ind. Oc.	20¼S	57¼E	19
Mauron, France.	48¼N	2¼W	31
Maushij, Yemen (inset)	14N	44E	40
Mawarena, Bougainville, Pacific (inset).	6¼S	155E	60
Mawlaik, Burma.	23¼N	94E	43
Maxwelltown, Scot.	55N	3¼W	25
Maxwelton, Queens.	20¼S	142E	60
May, I. of, Scotland.	56¼N	2¼W	25
May Pen, Jamaica, W. Indies (inset).	18N	77¼W	77
Maya, R., U.S.S.R.	60N	134E	39
Mayaguana I., Bah. Is.	22¼N	73W	77
Mayaguez, Puerto Rico.	18¼N	67¼W	77
Mayama, Congo (B.).	3¼S	15E	56
Maybole, Scotland.	55N	4¼W	25
Mayenne, France.	48¼N	¾W	31
MAYENNE, R. & DEP., Fr.	48N	2¾W	32
Mayford, C. Pr., S. Afr.	32¼S	25¼E	53
Mayn, R., U.S.S.R.	64N	178E	39
Maynooth, Eire.	53¼N	6¼W	26
MAYO, Co., Eire.	54N	9W	26
Mayor I., N.I., N.Z.	37¼S	176¼E	62
Mayor Krest, U.S.S.R.	67N	144E	39
Mayotte I., Africa.	13S	45E	56
Maytown, Queens., Aust.	16S	144¼E	60
Mayoumba, Gabon.	3¼S	10¼E	56
Mazabuka, Zambia.	15¼S	27¼E	51
Mazar-i-Sharif, Afghanistan.	36¼N	67¼E	43

Place	Lat.	Long.	No.
Mazarron, *Spain.*	37½N	1¼W	35
Mazaruni, R., *Guyana.* (inset).	7N	58W	77
Mazatenango, *Guat.*	14½N	91½W	76
Mazatlan, *Mexico.*	23N	106¼W	76
Mazinan, *Iran.*	37N	56E	40
Mazoe, Riv., *Moz.*	17S	34E	51
Mbabane, *Swaziland.*	26¼S	31¼E	55
M'Baiki, *Congo (B.).*	4N	18E	56
Mbala, *Zambia.*	9S	31E	51
Mbale, *Uganda.*	1N	34E	56
Mbam, R., *Cameroon.*	4N	11½E	56
Mbandaka, *Congo (K.).*	0	18¼E	56
Mbanga, *Cameroon.*	4½N	10E	56
Mbari, R., *Cent. Afr. Rep.*	5N	23E	56
Mbere, R., *Cent. Afr. Rep.*	9N	16½E	56
Mbeya, *Tanzania.*	8¾S	33½E	56
M'Bigou, *Gabon.*	2S	12E	56
Mbuji Mayi, *Congo (K.).*	6S	23¾E	56
Mbulu, *Tanzania.*	4S	35E	56
Mchinji, *Malawi.*	13¾S	32¾E	51
Me Yon, R., *Thailand.*	17N	101E	43
Mead, L., *Nev., U.S.A.*	36¼N	115W	74
Meadow L., *Sask., Can.*	54¼N	108½W	70
Meadows, *O.F.S., S. Afr.*	29½S	26¾E	55
Meaford, *Ont., Can.*	44¾N	80¾W	68
Meakan, Mt., *Japan.*	43N	144E	49
Meandarra, *Queensland.*	27¼S	150E	60
MEATH, *Eire.*	53½N	6¾W	26
Meaux, *France.*	49N	3E	32
Mecca, *Saudi Arabia.*	21¼N	40E	40
Mecheria, *Algeria.*	33½N	¼W	35
Mechlin, see MALINES.			
Mecome, *Moz.*	22S	32E	51
Medan, *Sumatra.*	3½N	98¾E	47
Medawachchiya, *Cey.*	8½N	80½E	45
Medellin, *Colombia.*	6N	75½W	77
Medemblik, *Nether.*	52¾N	5E	30
Medenine, *Tunisia.*	33½N	10½E	35
Medford, *Ore., U.S.A.*	42¼N	122¾W	74
Medgidia, *Romania.*	44¼N	28¼E	37
Medias, *Romania.*	46N	24¼E	37
Medicine Hat, *Alberta.*	50N	110¾W	73
Medina, *N.Y., U.S.A.*	43¼N	78½W	69
Medina, *Saudi Arabia.*	24½N	39¾E	40
Medina de Rioseco, *Sp.*	42N	5W	35
Medina del Campo, *Sp.*	41¼N	5W	35
Medina Sidonia, *Sp.*	36½N	6W	35
Mediterranean Sea.	37½N	12½E	34
Medo, *Mozambique.*	13S	39E	56
Medstead, *Sask., Can.*	53¼N	108W	70
Medvezhegorsk, *U.S.S.R.*	63N	34½E	38
Medway, R., *England.*	51¼N	½E	23
Meeberrie, *W. Aust.*	27S	116E	61
Meekatharra, *W. Aust.*	26½S	118½E	61
Meerut, *India.*	29N	77¾E	44
Mega, *Ethiopia.*	4N	38¼E	56
Megantic, *Que., Can.*	45¾N	71W	69
Megara, *Greece.*	38N	23½E	37
Megen, *Netherlands.*	51¾N	5½E	30
Megiddo, Mt., *Israel.*	32½N	35¼E	40
Mehadia, *Romania.*	45N	22½E	37
Mehdia, *Morocco.*	34¼N	6¾W	35
Mehsana, *India.*	23½N	72½E	44
Meihsien, *China.*	24¼N	116E	48
Mein, *Queens., Aust.*	12½S	142½E	60
Meiningen, *Germany.*	50½N	10½E	33
Meiringen, *Switz.*	46¾N	8¼E	31
Meissen, *Germany.*	51¼N	13¼E	33
Mekambo, *Gabon.*	1N	13½E	56
Meknes, *Morocco.*	34N	5½W	35
Meko, *Nigeria.*	7½N	2¾E	57
Mekong R., *Vietnam.*	8N	105E	47
Melanesia, *Pacific.*	2½S	160E	64
Melbourn, *England.*	52N	0	23
Melbourne, *England.*	52¾N	1½W	23
MELBOURNE, *Vict., Aust.*	37¾S	145E	59
Meldorf, *Ger.* (inset).	54N	9E	30
Melekess, *U.S.S.R.*	54¼N	49½E	38
Melfi, *Chad.*	11N	18E	56
Melfi, *Italy.*	41N	15¾E	36
Melfort, *Sask., Can.*	53N	104¾W	70
Melilla, *Morocco.*	35¼N	3W	35
Melita, *Manitoba, Can.*	49¼N	101W	70
Melito, *Italy.*	38N	16E	37
Melitopol, *U.S.S.R.*	46¾N	35½E	38
Melk, *Austria.*	48¼N	15¼E	33
Melksham, *England.*	51¼N	2W	22
Melle, *France.*	46¼N	¼W	32
Melmoth, *Natal.*	28½S	31½E	55
Melness, *Scotland.*	58½N	4½W	24
Melnik, *Czecho.*	50½N	14½E	33
Melo, *Uruguay.*	32½S	54W	79
Melrose, *N. Scot., Can.*	45½N	62W	67
Melrose, *Scotland.*	55½N	2¾W	25
Melsetter, *Rhodesia.*	19½S	32¾E	51
Melton Mowbray, *Eng.*	52¾N	¾W	23
Meltonwold, *C. Pr.*	31½S	22½E	52
Melun, *France.*	48½N	2¾E	32
Melville, *Sask., Can.*	51N	102¾W	70
Melville B., *Greenland.*	75N	62W	66
Melville I., *Australia.*	11½S	131E	60
Melville I., *Canada.*	75N	111W	66
Melville, L., *Can.* (ins.).	54N	59W	67
Melville Pen., *N.W. Can.*	68N	84W	64
Melvin, L., *Ireland.*	54½N	8¼W	26
Memba, *Mozambique.*	14¼S	40¼E	56
Memel, *O.F.S., S. Afr.*	27½S	29½E	55
Memel, see KLAIPEDA.			
Memmingen, *Germany.*	48N	10¼E	33
Memphis, *U.A.R.*	29¾N	32E	40
Memphis, *Tenn., U.S.A.*	35¼N	90W	75
Memphis, *Tex., U.S.A.*	35N	100½W	74
Menado, *Celebes, Indon.*	1½N	125E	47
Menaggio, *Italy.*	46N	9¼E	31
Menai Strait, *Wales.*	53¼N	4¼W	22
Menaka, *Mali.*	16N	3E	50
Menam, Riv., *Thailand.*	17N	100E	43
Mende, *France.*	44½N	3½E	32
Menderes, R., *Turkey.*	37½N	27¼E	37
Mendip Hills, *England.*	51¼N	2¾W	22
Mendocino, C., *U.S.A.*	40½N	124¼W	74
Mendoza, *Argentina.*	32¾S	68¾W	79
Menggala, *Sumatra.*	4S	106E	47
Mengtsz, *China.*	23½N	103¼E	48
Menin, *Belgium.*	50¾N	3¼E	30
Menominee, R., *U.S.A.*	45N	88W	76
Mens, *France.*	44¾N	5¾E	31
Mentakab, *Malay.* (ins.)	3½N	102¼E	47
Mentawai Is., *Sumatra.*	2S	99E	42
Mentone, *France.*	43¾N	7½E	32
Menzel-Bourguiba, *Tunisia.*	37¼N	9¾E	35
Menzel-Temini, *Tun.*	36¾N	10¾E	36
Menzies, *W. Australia.*	29¾S	121E	61
Meppel, *Netherlands.*	52¾N	6¼E	30
Meppen, *Germany.*	52¾N	7¼E	33
Mer, *France.*	47¾N	1½E	31
Mera, R., *Italy.*	46¼N	9E	31
Merabello, G. of, *Crete.*	35¼N	26E	37
Merano, *Italy.*	46¾N	11¼E	36
Mercara, *India.*	12½N	75¾E	45
Merced, *Calif., U.S.A.*	37¼N	120½W	74
Mercedes, *Argentina.*	29¼S	58W	79
Mercedes, *Uruguay.*	33¼S	58W	79
Mercer, *N.I., N.Z.*	37¼S	175E	62
Mercoeur, *France.*	45¼N	2E	32
Mercy, C., *N.W. Can.*	66N	65W	66
Mere, *England.*	51N	2¼W	22
Mereg, *Somali Rep.*	4N	47E	56
Mergenevski, *U.S.S.R.*	50N	51E	38
Mergui, *Burma.*	12½N	98¾E	43
Mergui Arch., *Burma.*	11½N	98E	43
Merida, *Mexico.*	20¾N	89¾W	76
Merida, *Spain.*	39N	6½W	35
Merida, *Venezuela.*	8¾N	71¼W	77
Meriden, *Conn., U.S.A.*	41½N	72¾W	69
Meridian, *Miss., U.S.A.*	32¼N	88¾W	75
Merinda, *Queens., Aust.*	20S	148E	60
Merino, *C. Pr., S. Afr.*	32¼S	25½E	53
MERIONETH, *Wales.*	52¾N	4W	22
Merowe, *Sudan.*	18½N	31¾E	50
Merredin, *W. Aust.*	31½S	118¼E	61
Merrick, Mt., *Scotland.*	55¼N	4½W	25
Merriman, *C.Pr., S. Afr.*	31½S	23½E	53
Merritt, *Br. Col., Can.*	50N	120¾W	72
Merriwa, *N.S.W., Aust.*	32S	150¼E	59
Merrygoen, *N.S.W.*	32S	149E	59
Mersa Matruh, *U.A.R.*	31¾N	27¼E	34
Merseburg, *Germany.*	51¼N	12E	33
Mersey, R., *England.*	53¼N	2¾W	22
Mersin, *Turkey.*	36¾N	34¾E	41
Mersing, *Malaysia* (ins.).	2¼N	103¾E	47
Merta, *India.*	26½N	74E	44
Mertajam, *Malay* (ins.)	5½N	100¼E	47
Merthyr Tydfil, *Wales.*	51¾N	3½W	22
Meru, Mt., *Tanzania.*	3¼S	36¾E	56
Merv, see MARY.			
Merweville, *C. Pr.*	32¾S	21½E	52
Merzig, *Germany.*	49½N	6¾E	30
Mesagne, *Italy.*	40½N	18E	36
Meschede, *Germany.*	51½N	8¼E	30
Meshed, *Iran.*	36¼N	59½E	40
Meshra er Req, *Sudan.*	8N	29E	56
Meslay du Maine, *Fr.*	48N	½W	31
Mesocco, *Switzerland.*	46½N	9¼E	31
Mesolongion, *Greece.*	38½N	21½E	37
MESOPOTAMIA, *Iraq.*	34N	43E	41
Messac, *France.*	47¾N	1¾W	31
Messancy, *Belgium.*	49½N	5¾E	30
Messina, *Italy.*	38¼N	15½E	36
Messina, *T'vaal, S. Afr.*	22¼S	30E	54
Messines, *Belgium.*	50¾N	2¾E	30
Messinia, G. of, *Greece.*	37N	22E	37
Messini, *Greece.*	37N	22E	37
Mestre, *Italy.*	45½N	12¼E	31
Meta, Riv., *Colombia.*	6N	67½W	77
Metaponto, *Italy.*	40½N	16¾E	36
Methven, *S.I., N.Z.*	43¾S	171¾E	63
Methwold, *England.*	52½N	½E	23
Metkovic, *Yugoslavia.*	43N	17¾E	37
Metsovon, *Greece.*	39½N	21¼E	37
Metz, *France.*	49½N	6¼E	32
Meulaboh, *Sumatra.*	4¼N	96¼E	47
MEURTHE ET MOSELLE, *France.*	49N	6E	32
Meuse, R., *Belgium.*	50½N	5E	30
MEUSE, R. & DEP., *Fr.*	49N	5½E	32
Mevagissey, *England.*	50¼N	4¾W	22
Mexborough, *Eng.*	53½N	1¼W	23
Mexcala, *Mexico.*	18N	99¾W	76
Mexicali, *Mexico.*	32½N	115½W	76
MEXICO, *S. America.*	19N	100W	76
Mexico City, *Mexico.*	19½N	99W	76
Mexico, G. of, *Mexico.*	25N	92½W	76
Mezen & R., *U.S.S.R.*	65¾N	44E	38
Mezen B., *U.S.S.R.*	66N	44E	38
Mezenc, Mt., *France.*	44¾N	4¼E	32
Mezidon, *France.*	49N	0	31
Mezieres, *France.*	49¾N	4¾E	32
M. Het, *Laos.*	21N	104E	47
Mhow, *India.*	22½N	75¾E	44
M. Hun Sieng Hung, *Laos.*	22N	103E	43
Miahuatlan, *Mexico.*	16½N	96½W	76
Miami, *Rhodesia.*	17S	29¾E	51
Miami, *Florida, U.S.A.*	25¾N	80¼W	75
Miandrivazo, *Malag.*	19½S	45½E	56
Mianwali, *Pakistan.*	32½N	71¾E	44
Miarinarivo, *Malagasy.*	19S	47E	56
Mica, *T'vaal, S. Africa.*	24¼S	30¾E	54
MICHIGAN, *U.S.A.*	44N	85W	75
Michigan, L., *U.S.A.-Canada.*	43N	87W	75
Michikamau, L., *Can.*	54N	64W	67
Michipicoten I., *Can.*	48N	85½W	68
Michoacan, *Mexico.*	19N	102W	76
Michurin, *Bulgaria.*	42¼N	27¾E	37
Michurinsk, *U.S.S.R.*	52¾N	40½E	38
Micronesia, *Pacific.*	10N	150E	64
Mid Illovo, *Natal.*	30S	30½E	55
Midale, *Sask., Can.*	49½N	103¼W	70
Middelburg, *T'vaal.*	25¾S	29½E	55
Middelkerke, *Belgium.*	51¼N	2¾E	30
Middelpos, *C. Pr.*	32S	20¼E	52
Middelwit, *T'vaal.*	24¾S	27¼E	54
Middleburg, *C. Pr.*	31½S	25E	53
Middleburg, *Nether.*	51½N	3½E	30
Middlebury, *Vt., U.S.A.*	44N	73¼W	69
Middleham, *England.*	54¼N	1¾W	25
Middle Is., *W. Aust.*	34S	123E	61
Middlesbrough, *Eng.*	54½N	1¼W	25
Middleton, *C. Pr., S. Afr.*	33S	25¾E	53
Middleton, *England.*	53½N	2¼W	22
Middleton, *Canada.*	45N	65¼W	67
Middleton, *Queens., Australia.*	22½S	141½E	60
Middleton-in-Teesdale, *England.*	54¾N	2W	25
Middletown, *Conn. U.S.*	41½N	72¾W	69
Middletown, *N.Y., U.S.*	41½N	74½W	69
Middlewich, *England.*	53¼N	2½W	23
Midhurst, *England.*	51N	¾W	22
Midland, *Ont., Can.*	44¾N	80W	68
Midland, *Tex., U.S.A.*	32N	102W	74
Midland Junc., *W. Aust*	31¾S	116E	61
Midleton, *Ireland.*	52N	8¼W	26
MIDLOTHIAN, *Scotland.*	55¾N	3¼W	25
Midnapore, *India.*	22½N	87½E	44
Midongy Sud, *Malag.*	23½S	46E	56
Midway, *Br. Col., Can.*	49N	118¾W	72
Midway I., *Pacific.*	28N	178W	64
Midye, *Turkey.*	41¾N	28E	41
Miedzychod, *Poland.*	52½N	16E	33
Miedzyrzec, *Poland.*	52N	22¾E	33
Miedzyrzecz, *Poland.*	52½N	15½E	33
Mienningting, *China.*	24N	100E	43
Mienyang, *China.*	32N	105E	48
Mier, *Mexico.*	26½N	99¼W	76
Migdol, *T'vaal, S. Afr.*	27S	25½E	55
Mikhailovka, *U.S.S.R.*	47¾N	46¾E	38
Mikhailovka, *U.S.S.R.*	50N	43E	38
Mikindani, *Tanzania.*	10½S	40E	56
Mikkeli, *Finland.*	61¾N	27¼E	29
Mikonos, I. of, *Greece.*	37½N	25½E	37
Mikulov, *Czecho.*	48¾N	16¾E	33
Milan, *Italy.*	45½N	9¼E	36
Milange, *Mozambique.*	16½S	36E	51
Milas, *Turkey.*	37½N	27½E	37
Milazzo, *Sicily.*	38¼N	15¼E	36
Mildenhall, *England.*	52¼N	½E	23
Mildura, *Vict., Aust.*	34S	142E	59
Mileai, *Greece.*	39¼N	23¼E	37
Miles, *Queens., Aust.*	26¾S	150¼E	60
Miles City, *U.S.A.*	46½N	105¾W	74
Milestone, *Sask., Can.*	50N	104½W	70
Mileura, *W. Aust.*	26½S	117½E	61
Milevsko, *Czecho.*	49½N	14¼E	33
Milford, *England.*	51¼N	¾W	23
Milford, *England.*	55½N	2W	25
Milford, *Mass., U.S.A.*	42¼N	71½W	69
Milford Haven, *Wales.*	51¾N	5W	22
Milford Sd., *S.I., N.Z.*	44½S	167¾E	63
Milgarra, *Queens., Aust.*	17½S	141E	60
Mili I., *Pacific.*	6N	172E	64
Miliane, R., *Tunisia.*	36¾N	10¼E	36
Miling, *W. Australia.*	30½S	116¼E	61
Milkovo, *U.S.S.R.*	56N	159E	39
Milk Riv., *Alb., Can.*	49N	112W	73
Millas, *France.*	42½N	3E	32
Millau, *France.*	44N	3E	32
Miller, *C. Pr., S. Afr.*	33S	24E	53
Millerovo, *U.S.S.R.*	48N	40½E	38
Millet, *Alberta, Can.*	53¼N	113½W	73
Millford, *Ireland.*	55N	7¾W	26
Mill I., *Antarctica.*	65¾S	100E	80
Millicent, *S. Aust.*	37½S	140¼E	59
Millinocket, *U.S.A.*	46N	69W	75
Millmerran, *Queens.*	28S	151¼E	60
Millom, *England.*	54¼N	3¼W	25
Millport, *Scotland.*	55¾N	5W	25
Mill Stream, *W. Aust.*	21½S	116½E	61
Millstreet, *Ireland.*	52N	9W	26
Milltown Malbay, *Ire.*	52¾N	9½W	26
Millwood, *C. Pr., S. Afr.*	34S	23E	52
Milly Milly, *W. Aust.*	26½S	117E	61
Milnet, *Ontario, Can.*	46¾N	81W	68
Milos, I. of, *Greece.*	36¾N	24½E	37
Milparinka, *N.S.W.*	29¾S	142E	59
Milton, *Ontario, Can.*	43½N	80W	68
Milton, *S.I., N.Z.*	46¼S	170E	63
Milverton, *England.*	51N	3¼W	22
Milwaukee, *Wis., U.S.A.*	43N	88W	68
Mimico, *Ont., Can.*	43¾N	79½W	68
Mimizan, *France.*	44¼N	1¼W	32
Min, River, *China.*	28¼N	104½E	48
Minab, *Iran.*	27N	57E	40
Minas, *Uruguay.*	34½S	55½W	79
Minas Basin, *Canada.*	45¼N	64W	67
Minas de Pis Pis, *Nicar.*	14½N	84¾W	77
MINAS GERAIS, *Brazil.*	18½S	54W	79
Minatitlan, *Mexico.*	17¾N	94½W	76
Minch, The, *Scotland.*	58N	6W	24
Mindanao I., *P.I.*	8N	125E	47
Minden, *Germany.*	52¼N	9E	33
Minderoo, *W. Aust.*	22S	115E	61
Mindoro I., *P.I.*	13N	121E	47
Mindoro Strait, *P.I.*	12¼N	121E	47
Minehead, *England.*	51¼N	3½W	22
Mine Head, *Ireland.*	52N	7½W	26
Mineralnye Vody, *U.S.S.R.*	44N	43E	38
Mineral Wells, *U.S.A.*	32¾N	98¼W	74
Minervnio Murge, *It.*	41N	16¼E	36
Mingan *W. Aust.*	29½S	117½E	16
Mingan, *Quebec, Can.*	50¼N	64W	67
Mingenew, *W. Aust.*	29¼S	115½E	61
Minginoo, *W. Aust.*	25¼S	115¼E	61
Mingshui, *China.*	42N	96E	39
Mingulay I., *Scotland.*	56¾N	7½W	24
Mingunna Sk., *W. Aust.*	22½S	120E	61
Minho, *Jamaica.* (ins.)	17¾N	77W	77
Minho, R., *Portugal.*	42N	8¾W	35
Minhow, see FOOCHOW.			
Minigwal, L., *W. Aust.*	29S	123E	61
Minilya & R., *W. Aust.*	24S	114E	61
Minmarg, *Kash.* (ins.).	34¾N	75¼E	44
Minna, *Nigeria.*	9½N	6½E	57
Minneapolis, *U.S.A.*	45N	93¼W	75
Minnedosa, *Man., Can.*	50¼N	100W	70
MINNESOTA, *U.S.A.*	46N	95W	75
Minorca I., *Balearic Is.*	40N	4¼E	35
Minsk, *U.S.S.R.*	54N	27½E	38
Minsk Mazowiecki, *Poland.*	52¼N	21½E	33
Minton, *Sask., Can.*	49¼N	104½W	70
Minturno, *Italy.*	41¼N	13¾E	36
Minusinsk, *U.S.S.R.*	53¾N	91½E	39
Minvoul, *Gabon.*	2N	12E	56
Miosen, L., *Norway.*	60½N	10½E	29
Miquelon Is., *Atlantic.*	47N	56¼W	67
Mira, *Italy.*	45½N	12E	31
Miraj, *India.*	16¾N	74¾E	45
Miranda de Ebro, *Sp.*	42¾N	3W	35
Miranda do Douro, *Portugal.*	41½N	6¼W	35
Mirande, *France.*	43½N	¼E	32
Mirandela, *Portugal.*	41½N	7¼W	35
Mirandola, *Italy.*	44¾N	11E	31
Mirani, *Queens., Aust.*	21¼S	149E	60
Mirano, *Italy.*	45½N	12E	31
Mirecourt, *France.*	48¼N	6E	30
Miri, *East Malaysia.*	4¼N	114E	47
Miriam Vale, *Aust.*	24¼S	151½E	60
Mirjawa, *Iran.*	29N	61E	40
Mirosi, *Romania.*	44½N	25E	37
Mirpur, *Kashmir.*	33¼N	73¾E	44
Mirror, *Alberta, Can.*	52½N	113W	73
Miryang, *Korea.*	35½N	128½E	49
Mirzapur, *India.*	25¼N	82¾E	44
Misgar, *Kash.* (inset).	36¾N	74¾E	44
Mishan, *China.*	46N	132E	49
Mishawaka, *Ind., U.S.*	41¾N	86W	68
Misilmeri, *Sicily.*	38N	13½E	36
Misiones, *Argentina.*	27S	55W	79
Miskito Cayos, *W.I.*	14½N	82½W	77
Miskolc, *Hungary.*	48N	20¾E	37
Misool I., *Indonesia.*	2S	130E	47
Missinaib, R., *Ont., Can.*	52N	80W	66
Mission *Br. Col., Can.*	49¼N	122¼W	72
MISSISSIPPI, *U.S.A.*	33N	90W	75
Mississippi R., *U.S.A.*	30N	90W	75
Missoula, *Mont., U.S.A.*	46¾N	114W	74
MISSOURI, *U.S.A.*	38N	92½W	75
Mistassini, L., *Que., Can.*	51N	73½W	66
Mistretta, *Sicily.*	38N	14½E	36
Misurata, *Libya.*	32½N	15E	34
Mitau, see JELGAVA.			
Mitcheldean, *Eng.*	51¾N	2½W	22
Mitchell, *S. Dak. U.S.A.*	44N	98½W	74
Mitchell R., *Queens.*	15¼S	141½E	60
Mitchell R., *Vict., Aust.*	38S	147¾E	59
Mitchelstown, *Eire.*	52¼N	8¼W	26
Mitiaro I., *Pacific.*	20S	158W	64
Mitrovica, *Yugoslavia.*	45N	19½E	37
Mitrovica, *Yugoslavia.*	43N	20¾E	37
Mitsda, *Libya.*	31½N	13E	34
Mitta Mitta R., *Aust.*	36¼S	147E	59
Mittelland Can., *Ger.*	52½N	8½E	30
Mittenwald, *Austria.*	47¾N	11¼E	31
Mitu, *Colombia.*	1N	70W	78
Mitzic, *Gabon.*	1N	12E	56
Miyako, *Japan.*	39¾N	142E	49
Miyakonojo, *Japan.*	31¾N	131E	49
Miyazaki, *Japan.*	32N	131½E	49
Miyun, *China.*	41N	117E	48
Mizen Head, *Eire.*	51½N	9¾W	26
Mizen Head, *Eire.*	52¾N	6W	26
Mizil, *Romania.*	45N	26½E	37
Mkushi, *Zambia.*	14S	29E	51
Mkwava, *Tanzania.*	10S	38E	56
Mlada Boleslav, *Czech.*	50½N	15E	33
Mladenovac, *Yugo.*	44½N	20½E	37
Mlawa, *Poland.*	53N	20¼E	33
Mljet I., *Yugoslavia.*	42¾N	17½E	37
Mo, *Norway.*	66½N	14E	38
Moab, *Utah, U.S.A.*	38½N	109½W	74
Moama, *N.S.W., Aust.*	36S	144¾E	59
Moamba, *Moz.*	25½S	32½E	51
Mobie, *Cent. Afr. Rep.*	5N	21½E	56
Mobile, *Ala., U.S.A.*	30¾N	88W	75
Mobridge, *U.S.A.*	45½N	100W	74
Moc. da Praia, *Mozam.*	11¼S	40¼E	56
Moc. do Rovuma, *Moz.*	11½S	39E	56
Mocha, *Yemen* (inset).	13¾N	44E	40
Mochlos, *Crete.*	35N	26E	41
Mocorito, *Mexico.*	25½N	108W	76
Moctezuma, *Mexico.*	30¼N	106½W	76
Modane, *France.*	45¼N	6½E	31

Modbury—Multan [117]

Place	Lat.	Long.	No.
Modbury, *England.*	50½N	4W	22
Modderfontein, *T'vaal.*	26S	28E	55
Modderpoort, *O.F.S.*	29¼S	27½E	55
Modder R., *C. Pr.*	29¼S	24½E	53
Modena, *Italy.*	44½N	11E	36
Modica, *Sicily.*	36¾N	14¾E	36
Modlin, *Poland.*	52½N	20½E	33
Moembaze, *Moz.*	17S	38½E	56
Moen, *Denmark.*	55N	12½E	33
Moffat, *Scotland.*	55½N	3½W	25
Mogadishu, *Som. Rep.*	2N	45½E	56
Mogador, *Morocco.*	31½N	9¾W	50
Mogan, *Can. Is.* (ins.).	27¾N	15¾W	35
Mogilev, *U.S.S.R.*	54N	30½E	38
Mogilev, *U.S.S.R.*	48½N	27¾E	38
Mogocha, *U.S.S.R.*	53¾N	119¾E	39
Mogok, *Burma.*	23N	96½E	43
Mogumba, *W. Aust.*	31S	116E	61
Mogzon, *U.S.S.R.*	52N	111E	39
Mohacs, *Hungary.*	46N	18¾E	37
Mohaka R., *N.I., N.Z.*	39¼S	177¼E	62
Mohales Hoek, *Lesotho.*	30S	27½E	55
Mohammadia, *Algeria.*	35¾N	0	35
Mohammerah, see KHORRAMSHAHR.			
Mohawk R., *N.Y., U.S.*	42¾N	73¾W	69
Moheli, *Indian Ocean.*	12¼S	43¾E	56
Mohill, *Ireland.*	54N	7¾W	26
Mohne, R., *Germany.*	51½N	6½E	30
Moho, *China.*	53½N	121E	39
Mointy, *U.S.S.R.*	48N	73E	39
Moira, *Ireland.*	54½N	6¼W	26
Moisie B. & R., *Quebec, Canada.*	50½N	66W	67
Moissala, *Cent. Afr. Rep.*	8N	17½E	56
Mojave, *Calif., U.S.A.*	35N	118¼W	74
Mokau, *N.I., N.Z.*	38¾S	174½E	62
Mokeetsi, *T'vaal, S. Afr.*	23¾S	30¼E	54
Mokolo, *Cameroon.*	10¾N	14E	56
Mokpo, *Korea.*	34¾N	126½E	49
Mokwa, *Nigeria.*	9½N	5E	57
Mold, *Wales.*	53¼N	3¼W	22
MOLDAVIA, *U.S.S.R.*	47N	29E	38
Molde, *Norway.*	62¾N	7¼E	29
Mole Creek, *Tas., Aust.*	41½S	146½E	59
Mole de Nicolas, Le, *Haiti.*	20N	73W	77
Molen River, *C.Pr., South Africa.*	33¾S	22¾E	52
Molepolole, *Botswana.*	24¼S	25½E	51
Molfetta, *Italy.*	41¼N	16½E	36
Molina, *Spain.*	40¾N	2W	35
Moline, *Ill., U.S.A.*	42N	90W	75
Molise, *Italy.*	41½N	14½E	36
Moll, *Belgium.*	51¼N	5¼E	30
Mollendo, *Peru.*	17S	72W	78
Mollerin, *W. Aust.*	30¼S	117½E	61
Molokai, *Hawaii.*	20½N	154¾W	74
Molong, *N.S.W., Aust.*	33S	148¾E	59
Molopo R., *S.W. Africa.*	28S	20E	51
Molotova, C., *U.S.S.R.*	82N	95E	39
Molsheim, *France.*	48½N	7½E	30
Molteno, *C. Pr., S. Afr.*	31¼S	26½E	53
MOLUCCA IS., *Indonesia.*	2½S	127½E	47
Moma, R., *U.S.S.R.*	66N	142E	39
Mombasa, *Kenya.*	4S	39½E	56
Mombetsu, *Japan.*	44½N	143½E	49
Momchilgrad, *Bulg.*	41½N	25½E	37
Mompos, *Colombia.*	9½N	74½W	77
Mona I., *Puerto R., W.I.*	18N	68W	77
MONACO, *Europe.*	43¾N	7½E	32
Monadhliath Mts., *Scotland.*	57¼N	4¼W	24
Monaghan & T., *Eire.*	54¼N	7W	26
Monashee Mts., *Can.*	51N	118¼W	37
Monasterace, *Italy.*	38½N	16½E	37
Monastir, *Sardinia.*	39½N	9¼E	36
Monastir, see BITOLJ.			
Monastir, *Tunisia.*	35¾N	10¾E	35
Monawhanna, *Guyana.* (inset).	9N	60W	77
Moncalieri, *Italy.*	45N	7¾E	31
Monchegorsk, *U.S.S.R.*	67¾N	32½E	38
Monchiero, *Italy.*	44½N	8E	31
Moncontour, *France.*	48¼N	2¾W	31
Moncton, *Canada.*	46¼N	64¾W	67
Mondego R., *Portugal.*	40N	9W	35
Mondoneda, *Spain.*	43¼N	7¼W	35
Mondovi, *Italy.*	44¼N	7¾E	36
Mondragone, *Italy.*	41¼N	14E	36
Mondu, *Cen. Afr. Rep.*	8½N	16E	56
Monemvasia, *Greece.*	36¾N	23E	37
Monet, *Quebec, Can.*	48½N	75¼W	69
Monforte, *Spain.*	42½N	7¼W	35
Monger, L., *W. Aust.*	29S	117E	61
Monghyr, *India.*	25¼N	86½E	44
MONGOLIA, *Asia.*	45N	105E	39
Mongolia, In., *China.*	45N	118E	48
Mongrando, *Italy.*	45½N	8E	31
Mongu, *Zambia.*	15¼S	23E	51
Moniaive, *Scotland.*	55¼N	4W	25
Monkey R., *Br. Hond.*	16½N	89W	77
Monkira, *Queens., Aust.*	25S	140½E	60
MONMOUTH & Tn., *Eng.*	51¾N	3W	22
Monopoli, *Italy.*	41N	17½E	36
Mono. Pta. del, *Nicarag.*	12N	84W	77
Monroe, *La., U.S.A.*	32½N	92W	75
Monrovia, *Liberia.*	6¼N	10¾W	50
Mons, *Belgium.*	50½N	4E	30
Monschau, *Germany.*	50½N	6¼E	30
Mont aux Sources, *Natal, O.F.S.*	28¾S	28¾E	55
Mont Blanc, *France.*	45¾N	6¾E	31
Mont Cenis, *France.*	45¼N	6¾E	31
Mont de Marsan, *Fr.*	44N	½W	32
Mont Joli, *Que., Can.*	48½N	68¼W	67
Mt. Pelvoux, *France.*	45N	6½E	31
Mt. St. Michel, *Fr.*	48½N	1½W	31
Montagnana, *Italy.*	45¼N	11½E	31
Montagrier, *France.*	45¼N	½E	32
Montagu, *C. Pr., S. Afr.*	33¾S	20¼E	52
Montague, *Canada.*	46¼N	62¾W	67
Montague Sound, *W. Aust.* (inset).	14S	126E	61
Montalban, *Spain.*	40¾N	¾W	35
Montalto, Mt., *Italy.*	38N	16E	36
MONTANA, *U.S.A.*	47N	110W	74
Montargis, *France.*	48N	2¾E	32
Montauban, *France.*	44N	1¼E	32
Montauk Pt., *N.Y., U.S.A.*	41N	72W	69
Montbazon, *France.*	47¼N	¾E	31
Montbeliard, *France.*	47½N	6¾E	32
Montbrison, *France.*	45½N	4E	32
Montcornet, *France.*	49¾N	4E	30
Montdidier, *France.*	49½N	2½E	30
Monte Bello Is., *W. Aust.*	20½S	115E	61
Montebelluna, *Italy.*	45¾N	12E	31
Montebourg, *France.*	49½N	1½W	31
Monte Carlo, *France.*	43¾N	7½E	32
Monte Cristi, *Dom. Rep.*	20N	72W	77
Monte Cristo I., *Italy.*	42¼N	10½E	36
Montego B., *Jamaica.*	18½N	77¾W	77
Montelimar, *France.*	44½N	4¾E	32
Montello, *Nev., U.S.A.*	41½N	114¼W	74
Montemagno, *Italy.*	45N	8½E	31
Monte Morelos, *Mex.*	25N	100W	76
MONTENEGRO, *Yugo.*	43N	19E	37
Montepulciano, *Italy.*	43N	11¾E	36
Montereau, *France.*	48½N	3E	30
Monterey, *Cal., U.S.A.*	36½N	122W	74
Monteria, *Colombia.*	9N	75¾W	77
Monterrey, *Mexico.*	25¾N	100¼W	76
Monte Sant Angelo, *Italy.*	41¾N	16E	36
Montes Claros, *Brazil.*	16½S	43¾W	79
Montevideo, *Uruguay.*	35S	56¼W	79
Montfort-sur-Meu, *France.*	48¼N	2W	31
Montgomery, *Alabama, U.S.A.*	32½N	86¼W	75
Monticelli, *Italy.*	45N	10E	31
Monticello, *Ut., U.S.A.*	37¾N	109¼W	74
Montier-en-Der, *Fr.*	48½N	4¾E	30
Montiglio, *Italy.*	45N	8¼E	31
Montijo, *Portugal.*	38¾N	9W	35
Montilla, *Spain.*	37½N	4¾W	35
Montlhery, *France.*	48½N	2¼E	30
Montlucon, *France.*	46¼N	2½E	32
Montmagny, *Que., Can.*	47N	70½W	69
Montmartre, *Canada.*	50¼N	103¼W	70
Montmedy, *France.*	49½N	5¼E	30
Montmelian, *France.*	45½N	6E	31
Montmirail, *France.*	48¾N	3½E	30
Monto, *Queens., Aust.*	25S	151½E	60
Montoire, *France.*	47¾N	1E	31
Montoro, *Spain.*	38N	4¼W	35
Montpelier, *Id., U.S.A.*	42N	111¼W	74
Montpelier, *Vt., U.S.A.*	44¼N	72¾W	69
Montpellier, *France.*	43½N	3¾E	32
Montreal, *Que., Can.*	45½N	73½W	69
Montreuil, *France.*	50½N	1¾E	32
Montreuil Bellay, *Fr.*	47¼N	0	31
Montreux, *Switz.*	46½N	7E	31
Montrichard, *France.*	47½N	1¼E	31
Montrose, *Colo., U.S.A.*	38½N	107¾W	74
Montrose, *Scotland.*	56¾N	2½W	24
Montserrat I., *W.I.*	16N	62W	77
Monza, *Italy.*	45½N	9¼E	36
Monze, C., *Pakistan.*	25N	67E	43
Monzon, *Spain.*	42N	¼E	32
Mooiplaas, *C. Pr.*	32¾S	28E	53
Mooi River, *Natal.*	29¼S	30E	55
Moonta, *S. Australia.*	34S	137½E	59
Moora, *W. Australia.*	30½S	116E	61
Moore, L., *W. Aust.*	30S	117½E	61
Moore R., *W. Aust.*	31¼S	115½E	61
Moorea, *Pacific.*	18S	150W	64
Moorreesburg, *C. Pr., South Africa.*	33¼S	18¾E	52
Moose Factory, (ins.) *Ontario, Canada.*	51¼N	80½W	71
Moose Jaw, *Sask., Can.*	50½N	105½W	70
Moose R., *Ont., Can.*	51½N	80½W	71
Moosomin, *Sask., Can.*	50N	101½W	70
Moosonee, *Ont., Can.*	51¼N	80¾W	71
Mora, *Cameroon.*	11½N	14E	56
Mora, *Portugal.*	39N	8¼W	35
Mora, *Spain.*	40¼N	¾W	35
Mora, *Sweden.*	61N	14E	29
Moradabad, *India.*	29N	78¾E	44
Moramanga, *Malagasy.*	19S	48¼E	56
Morane I., *Pacific.*	23S	138W	64
Morant B., & Pt., *Jam., W. Indies* (inset).	18N	77W	77
Morar, L., *Scotland.*	57N	5¾W	24
Morari Tso, L., *Kashmir* (inset).	33N	78¼E	44
Morava, R., *Czecho.*	48N	17E	33
Morava, R., *Yugo.*	44¾N	21E	37
MORAVIA, *Czecho.*	49¼N	17E	33
Morawa, *W. Australia.*	29¼S	116E	61
Moray, *Scotland.*	57½N	3¼W	24
Moray Firth, *Scot.*	57½N	3¾W	24
Morbach, *Germany.*	49¾N	7¼E	30
Morbegno, *Italy.*	46¼N	9½E	31
Morbihan, B. de, *Fr.*	47½N	3W	32
Morbihan, G. de, *Fr.*	47½N	2¾W	31
MORBIHAN, *France.*	48N	3W	32
Morcone, *Italy.*	41¼N	15E	36
Morden, *Man., Can.*	49¼N	98W	71
MORDOV A.S.S.R., *U.S.S.R.*	54N	44E	38
Morea, *Greece.*	37½N	22E	37
Morecambe & B., *Eng.*	54N	3W	2
Moree, *N.S.W., Aust.*	29½S	149¾E	59
Morel, *Switzerland.*	46½N	8E	31
Morelia, *Mexico.*	19¾N	101¼W	76
Morella, *Spain.*	40½N	0	35
Morella, *Queens., Aust.*	23S	143½E	60
Morena, Sierra, *Spain.*	38½N	5W	35
Moresby I., *Br. Col., Can.*	53N	132W	66
Moret, *France.*	48½N	2¾E	30
Moreton, *England.*	50¾N	3¾W	22
Moreton I. & B., *Aust.*	27S	153½E	59
Moreton in the Marsh, *England.*	52N	1¾W	23
Moreuil, *France.*	49¾N	2½E	30
Morez, *France.*	46½N	6E	31
Morgan, *S. Australia.*	34S	139½E	59
Morgans, *W. Aust.*	28¾S	122E	61
Morgenzon, *T'vaal.*	26¾S	29½E	55
Morges, *Switzerland.*	46½N	6½E	31
Mori, *Japan.*	42N	141E	49
Morija, *Lesotho.*	29¾S	27½E	55
Morinville, *Alb., Can.*	53¾N	113¾W	73
Morioka, *Japan.*	39¾N	141¼E	49
Morisset, *N.S.W., Aust.*	33S	151½E	59
Moriston, R., *Scot.*	57¼N	4¾W	24
Morkalla, *Vict., Aust.*	34¼S	141E	59
Morkokha, R., *U.S.S.R.*	63N	119E	39
Morlaix, *France.*	48½N	3¾W	32
Morley, *England.*	53¾N	1½W	23
Mornington I., *Queens., Australia.*	16½S	138E	60
Morobe, *N. Guin.* (inset).	8S	148E	60
MOROCCO, *N. Africa.*	33N	5W	50
Moro, G. of, *Philippines.*	7N	122½E	47
Morogoro, *Tanzania.*	6¾S	37¾E	56
Moron, *Cuba.*	22N	78½W	77
Moron, *Spain.*	37N	5½W	35
Morondava, *Malagasy.*	20¼S	44¼E	56
Moroto, *Uganda.*	3N	35E	56
Morotai I., *Indonesia.*	2½N	128½E	47
Morpeth, *England.*	55½N	1¾W	25
Morphou, *Cyprus.*	35N	33E	41
Morrinsville, *N.I., N.Z.*	37¾S	175½E	62
Morris, *Man., Can.*	49½N	97¼W	71
Morrumbene, *Moz.*	23¾S	35½E	51
Morse, *Sask., Can.*	50½N	107W	70
Morshansk, *U.S.S.R.*	53½N	42E	38
Mortagne, *France.*	48½N	½E	31
Mortain, *France.*	48½N	1W	30
Mortara, *Italy.*	45¼N	8¾E	31
Mortlach, *Sask., Can.*	50½N	106W	70
Mortlake, *Vict., Aust.*	38S	142¾E	59
Moruba, *Cent. Afr. Rep.*	6½N	20E	56
Morundah, *N.S.W., Aust.*	35S	146½E	59
Moruya, *N.S.W., Aust.*	36S	150E	59
Morven, *Queens., Aust.*	26½S	147E	60
Morven, *Scotland.*	56½N	5¾W	24
Morven, Mt., *Scotland.*	58½N	3¾W	24
Morwell, *Vict., Aust.*	38¼S	146½E	59
Moscow, *U.S.S.R.*	55¾N	37½E	38
MOSELLE, *France.*	49N	6½E	32
Moselle, R., *Fr.-Ger.*	50½N	7½E	32
Moses Pt., *Alaska.*	64½N	160¼W	74
Mosgiel, *S.I., N.Z.*	46S	170½E	63
Moshi, *Tanzania.*	3¼S	37½E	56
Moshupa, *Botswana.*	24¾S	25½E	54
Mosjoen, *Norway.*	66N	14E	38
Moss, *Norway.*	59½N	10½E	29
Mossamedes, *Angola.*	15¼S	12½E	50
Mossbank, *Sask., Can.*	50N	106W	70
Mossburn, *S.I., N.Z.*	45¼S	168½E	63
Mossel B., *C. Pr., S. Afr.*	34S	22E	52
MOSSGIEL, *N.S.W., Aust.*	33¼S	144½E	59
Mossman, *Queens., Aust.*	16½S	146E	60
Mossoro, *Brazil.*	5S	37¼W	79
Mosso, S. Maria, *Italy.*	45¾N	8¼E	31
Moss Vale, *N.S.W., Aust.*	34¼S	150½E	59
Mostaganem, *Algeria.*	36N	0	35
Mostar, *Yugoslavia.*	43½N	17¾E	37
Mosteiros, *Azores* (ins.).	38N	26W	35
Mosucize, *Moz.*	21S	33E	51
Mosul, *Iraq.*	36½N	43½E	41
Motherwell, *Scotland.*	55¾N	4W	25
Motilla, *Spain.*	39½N	2W	35
Motiti I., *N.I., N.Z.*	37¾S	176½E	62
Motril, *Spain.*	36¾N	3½W	35
Motta di Lavenza, *It.*	45¾N	12½E	36
Motteville, *France.*	49½N	1E	32
Motueka, *S.I., N.Z.*	41S	173E	63
Motuhora, *N.I., N.Z.*	38¼S	177½E	62
Motutapu I., *N.I., N.Z.* (inset A).			62
Mouchard, *France.*	47N	5¾E	31
Moudon, *Switzerland.*	46½N	6¾E	31
Moukani, *Congo (B.).*	2S	12½E	56
Mouila, *Gabon.*	1¾S	11E	56
Moukden, see SHENYANG.			
Moulamein, *Australia.*	35S	144E	59
Moulins, *France.*	46½N	3½E	32
Moulmein, *Burma.*	16½N	97½E	43
Moulouya R., *Morocco.*	35½N	2½W	35
Mountain Ash, *Wales.*	51¾N	3½W	22
Mt. Ayliff, *C.Pr., S.Afr.*	30¾S	29½E	53
Mt. Barker, *W. Aust.*	34¾S	117½E	61
Mt. Barker, *S. Aust.*	35S	138¾E	59
Mt. Bellew, *Br., Ire.*	53½N	8¼W	26
Mt. Burrell Sta., *Aust.*	24S	133½E	60
Mt. Cook, *S.I., N.Z.*	43½S	170½E	63
Mt. Cuthbert, *Queens.*	20S	140E	60
Mt. Edgar, *W. Aust.*	20¾S	120E	61
Mt. Fletcher, *C. Pr.*	30¾S	28½E	53
Mt. Forest, *Ont., Can.*	44N	80¾W	68
Mt. Frere, *C. Pr., S. Afr.*	31S	29E	53
Mt. Gambier, *S. Aust.*	37¾S	140¾E	59
Mt. Garnet, *Queens*	17¾S	145½E	60
Mt. Hope, *S. Aust.*	34¼S	135½E	58
Mt. Isa, *Queens., Aust.*	20¾S	139½E	60
Mt. Keen, *Scotland.*	57N	3W	24
Mt. Lavinia, *Ceylon.*	6¾N	80E	45
Mt. Leinster, *Eire.*	52½N	6¾W	22
Mt. Magnet, *W. Aust.*	28S	117½E	61
Mt. Margaret, *W. Aust.*	22S	118½E	61
Mountmellick, *Ireland.*	53N	7¼W	26
Mt. Morgan, *Queens.*	24S	150E	60
Mt. Mulligan, *Queens.*	16¾S	144¾E	60
Mt. Perry, *Queens.*	25¼S	151½E	60
Mt. Robson Park, *Can.*	53N	118¼W	73
Mt. Stewart, *C. Pr., South Africa.*	33¼S	24½E	53
Mt. Vernon, *Ill., U.S.A.*	38N	89W	75
Mt. Vernon, *N.Y., U.S.A.* (inset).	41N	74W	75
Mounts Bay, *England.*	50N	5½W	22
Moura, *Portugal.*	38N	7½W	35
Mouri, *Ghana.*	5¼N	1W	57
Mourilyan, *Queens.*	17½S	146E	60
Mourne Mts., *Ireland.*	54¼N	6W	26
Mouscron, *Belgium.*	50¾N	3¼E	30
Mts. Noires, *France.*	48¼N	3¾W	31
Moutier, *Switzerland.*	47¼N	7½E	31
Moutiers, *France.*	45½N	6½E	31
Mouzon, *France.*	49½N	5¼E	30
Moville, *Ireland.*	55N	87W	26
Moy, *Scotland.*	57N	4¼W	24
Moy, R., *Ireland.*	54¼N	9¼W	26
Moyale, *Kenya.*	4N	38½E	56
Moyasta, *Ireland.*	52¾N	9¾W	26
Moyagee, *W. Aust.*	27¾S	118E	61
Moyero, R., *U.S.S.R.*	69N	103E	39
Moyie Range, *Can.*	49½N	116¼W	73
Moyobamba, *Peru.*	6S	77W	78
MOZAMBIQUE, *E. Africa.*	20S	35E	51
Mozambique Channel.	20S	40E	50
Mozambique, *Moz.*	15S	41E	56
Mozdok, *U.S.S.R.*	43½N	45E	38
Mozhga, *U.S.S.R.*	56½N	52½E	38
Mozyr, *U.S.S.R.*	52N	29E	38
Mpaha, *Ghana.*	8½N	1½W	57
Mpanda, *Tanz.* (ins.).	6¼S	31E	56
Mpika, *Zambia.*	11¾S	31½E	51
Mporokoso, *Zambia.*	9¼S	30E	51
Mpraeso, *Ghana.*	6½N	¾W	57
Mpulungu, *Zambia.*	8¾S	31E	56
M'Puze, *Mozambique.*	23S	32E	51
Mqanduli, *C. Pr., S. Afr.*	31¾S	28¾E	53
M. Sing, *Laos.*	21N	101E	43
Mtengula, *Moz.*	12¼S	34¾E	51
Mtensk, *U.S.S.R.*	53N	37E	38
Mtunzini, *Natal.*	29S	31½E	55
Mtwalume, *Natal.*	30¼S	30½E	55
Mtwara, *Tanzania.*	10¼S	40½E	56
Muar & R., *Mal.* (ins.).	2N	102½E	47
Muaraenim, *Sumatra.*	4S	103½E	47
Mubi, *Nigeria.*	10½N	13½E	57
Muccanoo, *W. Aust.*	21S	120E	61
Muchalls, *Scotland.*	57N	2¼W	24
Muchea, *W. Aust.*	31¼S	116E	61
Much Wenlock, *Wales.*	52½N	2½W	22
Muck I., *Scotland.*	56¾N	6¼W	24
Muckle Roe I., *Scot.*	60½N	1½W	24
Mucoque, *Mozambique.*	22S	35½E	51
Mudanya, *Turkey.*	40½N	29E	37
Mudgee, *N.S.W., Aust.*	32¾S	149½E	59
Muff, *Ireland.*	55N	7¼W	26
Mufulira, *Zambia.*	12¼S	28½E	51
Mugla, *Turkey.*	37¼N	28¼E	37
Muglad, *Sudan.*	11N	27E	56
Muhammad Qol, *Sudan.*	21N	37E	40
Muhlberg, *Germany.*	51½N	13E	33
Muhldorf, *Germany.*	48¼N	12½E	33
Muhlhausen, *Ger.*	51¼N	10½E	33
Muine Bheag, *Eire.*	52¾N	7W	26
Muirkirk, *Scotland.*	55½N	4W	25
Muiskraal, *C. Pr., S. Afr.*	34S	21½E	52
Muizenberg, *C. Pr.*	34S	18½E	52
Muka, *Cent. Afr. Rep.*	7½N	22E	56
Mukacevo, *U.S.S.R.*	48½N	22¾E	38
Mukalla, *S. Yem.* (ins.).	14½N	49½E	40
Mukuba, *Mozambique.*	17S	37¼E	51
Mukubella, *Moz.*	16¼S	38E	56
Mukusu, *Angola.*	18S	21½E	56
Mulde, Riv., *Germany.*	51¾N	12½E	33
Muldersvlei, *C. Pr.*	33¾S	18¾E	52
Mulege, *Mexico.*	27N	112W	76
Mulga Downs, *W. Aust.*	22S	118E	61
Mulgrave, *Canada.*	45¾N	61¼W	67
Mulhacen, Mt., *Spain.*	37N	3¼W	35
Mulheim, *Germany.*	51½N	7E	30
Mulhouse, *France.*	47¾N	7¼E	32
Muliama, *New Ireland, Pacific* (inset).	4S	153E	66
Muling, Riv., *China.*	46N	133E	49
Mull, *Scotland.*	56½N	6W	25
Mull Head, *Scotland.*	59½N	3W	24
Mull of Galloway, *Scotland.*	54¾N	5W	55
Mull of Kintyre, *Scot.*	55¼N	5¾W	25
Mull, Sound of, *Scot.*	56½N	6W	25
Mullaittivu, *Ceylon.*	9¼N	80¾E	24
Mullen, *Nebr., U.S.A.*	42N	101W	74
Mullewa, *W. Aust.*	28½S	115½E	61
Mullheim, *Germany.*	47¾N	7½E	30
Mulligan R., *S. Aust.*	27S	138½E	60
Mullinahone, *Ireland.*	52½N	7½W	26
Mullingar, *Ireland.*	53½N	7¼W	26
Mullion, *England.*	50N	5¼W	22
Mulobezi, *Zambia.*	17S	25E	51
Multan, *Pakistan.*	30¼N	71½E	44

[118] Mumbles—Neustadt

Place	Lat.	Long.	No.
Mumbles, *Wales*.	51½N	4W	22
Mumbwa, *Zambia*.	15S	27E	51
Muna, Riv., *U.S.S.R.*	68N	123E	39
Munbinia, *W. Aust.*	28S	118E	61
Munchen, see MUNICH.			
Munchen-Gladbach, *Germany*.	51¼N	6½E	30
Muncie, *Ind., U.S.A.*	40¼N	85½W	75
Mundabullangana *W. Australia*.	20½S	118E	61
Mundare, *Alb., Can.*	53¾N	112¼W	73
Munden, *Germany*.	51¼N	9½E	33
Mundesley, *England*.	52¾N	1½E	23
Mundford, *England*.	52½N	½E	23
Mundiwindi, *W. Aust.*	24S	120E	61
Mundubbera, *Aust.*	25½S	151E	60
Mungallala, R., *Aust.*	28S	147E	59
Mungana, *Queens., Aust.*	17¼S	144½E	60
Mungari, *Moz.*	17½S	33¾E	51
Mungbere, *Congo (K.)*.	2½N	28E	56
Mungina, *W. Aust.*	22½S	119E	61
Mungindi, *Queens., Aust.*	29S	149E	60
Munich, *Germany*.	48¼N	11½E	33
Munising, *U.S.A.*	46½N	86¾W	68
Munja, *W. Aust.* (ins.).	16½S	125E	61
Munnik, *T'vaal, S.'fr.*	23¾S	30E	54
Munster, *Eire*.	52N	9W	26
Munster, *Germany*.	52N	7¾E	33
Munster, *France*.	48N	7E	30
Muntadgin, *W. Aust.*	32S	118¼E	61
Muntok, *Banka, Indon.*	2¼S	105E	47
Munyango, *Angola*.	12S	18½E	56
Muonio Riv., *Sweden*.	67N	23E	29
Mupyong-ni, *Korea*.	40½N	127E	49
Mur, *France*.	48¼N	3W	31
Murashi, *U.S.S.R.*	59N	49E	38
Murat, *France*.	45¼N	3E	32
Muratli, *Turkey*.	41¼N	27¼E	37
Muravera, *Sardinia*.	39¼N	9½E	36
Murbat, *Mus. & Oman*.	17N	54¾E	40
Murchison, Mt., *S.I., N.Z.*	43S	171½E	63
Murchison R., *W. Aust.*	27½S	115E	61
Murchison, W., *W. Aust.*	26S	119½E	61
MURCIA & Town, *Sp.*	38¼N	1½W	35
Murdanna, *W. Aust.*	31½S	122½E	61
Murdine, *W. Aust.*	28½S	118E	61
Muren, *Mongolia*.	50N	100E	39
Muresul Riv., *Hung.*	46¼N	20½E	37
Muret, *France*.	43½N	¼E	32
Murgab, *U.S.S.R.*	39N	73E	39
Murghab Riv., *Afghan.*	35N	62½E	43
Murgo, *Kash.* (inset).	35N	78E	44
Murgon, *Queens., Aust.*	26¼S	152E	60
Murgoo, *W. Aust.*	27½S	116½E	61
Muri, *Nigeria*.	9¼N	10¾E	57
Murion Is., *W. Aust.*	22S	114E	61
Muritz See, *Germany*.	53¼N	13E	33
Murmansk, *U.S.S.R.*	69N	33¼E	38
Murnau, *Germany*.	47½N	11E	33
Muro, C., *Corsica*.	41½N	8¾E	36
Murom, *U.S.S.R.*	55½N	42E	38
Muroran, *Japan*.	42½N	141E	49
Muros, *Spain*.	42¾N	9W	35
Murra-Munda, *W. Aust.*	24S	120E	61
Murrabit, *Vict., Aust.*	35½S	144E	59
Murray Bridge, *S. Aust.*	35S	139¼E	59
Murray Harb., *Canada*.	46N	62½W	67
Murray, R., *S. Aust.*	35½S	139½E	59
Murraysburg, *C. Pr.*	32S	23¾E	53
Murree, *W. Pakistan*.	33¾N	73¼E	46
Murren, *Switzerland*.	46½N	7¾E	31
Mur River, *Austria*.	47½N	15E	33
Murrumbidgee, R., *N.S.W., Australia*.	34¾S	145¼E	59
Murrurundi, *N.S.W.*	31¾S	150¾E	59
Murshidabad, *India*.	24½N	88¼E	44
Murten, *Switzerland*.	47N	7E	31
Murtoa, *Vict., Aust.*	36½S	142½E	59
Murupara, *N.I., N.Z.*	38½S	176¾E	62
Mururoa I., *Pacific*.	21S	139W	64
Murwara, *India*.	24N	80½E	43
Murwillumbah, *Aust.*	28¼S	153½E	59
Murzuq, *Libya*.	26N	14¼E	50
Murzzuschlag, *Austria*.	47½N	15¾E	33
Mus, *Turkey*.	38¾N	41¾E	41
Musawa, *Nigeria*.	12¼N	7¼E	57
Muscat, *Mus. & Oman*.	23½N	58E	40
MUSCAT & OMAN, *Asia*.	20N	57E	40
Musgrave, *Queens.*	14¾S	143½E	60
Musgrave I., *Queens.*	10S	142E	60
Musi, Riv., *Sumatra*.	2S	105E	47
Muskegon, *U.S.A.*	43¼N	86½W	75
Muskogee, *Okl., U.S.A.*	35¾N	95½W	75
Musoma, *Tanzania*.	1½S	33½E	56
Musselburgh, *Scot.*	56N	3W	25
Musselshell R., *U.S.A.*	48N	108W	74
Mustajidda, *S. Arabia*.	27N	42E	40
Muswellbrook, *Aust.*	32¼S	151E	59
Mut, *U.A.R.*	25½N	28¾E	40
Mutankiang, *China*.	44½N	129½E	49
Mutarara, *Moz.*	17½S	35E	51
Muthukuru, *India*.	14¼N	80E	45
Mutsu B., *Japan*.	41N	141E	49
Muttaburra, *Queens.*	22½S	144½E	60
Muttra, *India*.	27½N	77½E	43
Muya, *U.S.S.R.*	56N	116E	39
Muzaffarabad, *India*.	34¼N	73½E	43
Muzaffargarh, *Pak.*	30N	71¼E	46
Muzaffarnagar, *India*.	29½N	77¾E	44
Muzart, Riv., *China*.	40N	90E	39
Muzhi, *U.S.S.R.*	66N	65E	38
Mwanza, *Tanzania*.	2½S	32¾E	56
Mweelrea, Mt., *Ire.*	53½N	9¾W	26
Mweka, *Congo (K.)*.	4¾S	21½E	56
Mwenzo, *Zambia*.	9S	33E	51
Mweru, L., *Congo (K.)*.	9S	28E	56
Mwinilunga, *Zambia*.	11¾S	24E	51
Myingyan, *Burma*.	21½N	95½E	43
Myitkyina, *Burma*.	25¼N	97½E	43
Myjava, *Czecho.*	48¾N	17½E	33
Mymensingh, *Pak.*	24¾N	90½E	46
Mynfontein, *C. Pr.*	31S	24E	53
MynyddPrescelly, *Wales*.	52N	5W	22
Myrtle Beach, *U.S.A.*	33½N	79W	75
Mysliborz, *Poland*.	53N	15E	33
MYSORE, *India*.	14¾N	76E	45
Mysore, *India*.	12¼N	76¾E	45
Myszyniec, *Poland*.	53¼N	21¼E	33
Mytho, *Vietnam*.	10½N	106¼E	47
Mytilene, *Lesvos I. Agean Sea*.	39¼N	26½E	37
Mzimba, *Malawi*.	11¾S	33½E	51
Mzinja, Riv., *Moz.*	12S	35½E	51
NAAB, Riv., *Germany*.	49N	12½E	33
Naantali, *Finland*.	60½N	22E	29
Naarden, *Netherlands*.	52¼N	5E	30
Naas, *Eire*.	53¼N	6¾W	26
Nababeep, *C. Pr., S. Afr.*	29½S	17¾E	52
Naband, *Iran*.	27½N	52½E	40
Nabeul, *Tunisia*.	36½N	10½E	35
Nabha, *India*.	30¼N	76¼E	44
Nablus, *Jordan*.	32¼N	35¼E	41
Naboomspruit, *T'vaal, South Africa*.	24½S	28¾E	54
Nachingweg, *Tanzania*.	10½S	38E	56
Nachod, *Czecho.*	50½N	61E	33
Nachvak Fj., *Lab.* (ins.).	59N	63¾W	67
Nacozari, *Mexico*.	30¼N	110W	76
Nadiad, *India*.	23N	73E	44
Nadym, Riv., *U.S.S.R.*	66N	72E	39
Naestved, *Denmark*.	55¼N	12E	33
Nafada, *Nigeria*.	11N	11¼E	57
Naga, *Luzon, P.I.*	14N	123½E	47
NAGALAND, *India*.	26N	95E	46
Nagano, *Japan*.	36¾N	138¼E	49
Nagaoka, *Japan*.	37½N	138¾E	49
Nagapattinam, *India*.	10¾N	79¾E	45
Nagar Parkar, *Pakistan*.	24¼N	70¾E	46
Nagasaki, *Japan*.	32¾N	130E	49
Nagaur, *India*.	27¼N	73¾E	44
Nagda, *India*.	23½N	75½E	44
Nagina, *India*.	29½N	78¼E	44
Nagorny, *U.S.S.R.*	56N	124E	39
Nagoya, *Japan*.	35¼N	136¾E	49
Nagpur, *India*.	21¼N	79E	44
Nagrong, *Tibet*.	32½N	84E	43
Nagykanizsa, *Hung.*	46½N	17E	37
Nahe, Riv., *Germany*.	49¾N	7¾E	30
Naibandan, *Iran*.	32½N	57E	40
Nailsworth, *England*.	51¾N	2¼W	22
Nain, *Labrador*, (ins.).	56½N	61¾W	67
Nain, *Iran*.	32½N	53E	40
Naini Tal, *India*.	29¼N	79½E	44
NAIRN & Tn., *Scotland*.	57¾N	3¾W	24
Nairn, Riv., *Scotland*.	57¾N	3¾W	24
Nairobi, *Kenya*.	1¼S	36¾E	56
Naistenyarvi, *U.S.S.R.*	62½N	32½E	38
Naivasha, *Kenya*.	¾S	36½E	56
Najin, *Korea*.	42½N	131E	49
Naju, *Korea*.	35N	127E	49
Nakatsu, *Japan*.	33½N	131¼E	49
Nakawn Lampong, *Thailand*.	18N	100E	43
Nakawn Patom, *Thai.*	14N	100E	43
Nakawn Sawan, *Thai.*	16N	101E	43
Nakawn Sritamarat, *Thai.*	8N	100E	43
Nakhichevan, *U.S.S.R.*	39N	45E	41
Nakhodka, *U.S.S.R.*	43N	133E	49
Nakhon Ratchasima, *Thai.*	15N	102¼E	47
Nakina, *Ontario, Can.*	50¼N	86¾W	71
Naklo, *Poland*.	53¼N	17½E	33
Nakop, *S.W. Africa*.	28S	20E	52
Naktong, Riv., *Korea*.	35N	129E	49
Nakuru, *Kenya*.	¼S	36E	56
Na Kusp, *Br. Col., Can.*	50¼N	117¾W	73
Nal, *Pakistan*.	27¾N	66¼E	46
Nalchik, *U.S.S.R.*	43N	43E	38
Nalgonda, *India*.	17N	79¼E	45
Nam Dinh, *Vietnam*.	20¼N	106E	48
Nam Tso, L., *China*.	31N	91E	43
Namakzar, L., *Iran*.	31N	57½E	40
Namanga, *Tanzania*.	2½S	36½E	56
Namangan, *U.S.S.R.*	41N	71¾E	39
Namapa, *Moz.*	13½S	39¾E	56
NAMAQUALAND, *S. Afr.*	30S	18E	52
Namasagali, *Uganda*.	1N	33E	56
Namatanai, *New Ireland, Pac.* (ins.).	3½S	152½E	60
Nambour, *Queens., Aust.*	26¾S	153E	60
Namhoi, see FOSHAN.			
Namoi, Riv., *N.S.W.*	38S	148E	59
Namonuito I., *Pacific*.	9N	150E	64
Nampa, *Idaho, U.S.A.*	43¾N	116½W	74
Nampo, *Korea*.	39N	125E	49
Nampula, *Moz.*	15S	39¼E	56
Namsos, *Norway*.	64¾N	11½E	29
Namu, *Br. Col., Can.*	51¾N	127¾W	72
NAMUR & Tn., *Belg.*	50½N	4¾E	30
Namwala, *Zambia*.	15¾S	26¼E	51
Namwon, *Korea*.	35½N	127½E	49
Namyslow, *Poland*.	51N	17½E	33
Nan, *Thailand*.	18½N	101E	43
Nana Kandundu, *Ang.*	11½S	23E	56
Nanaimo, *Canada*.	49¼N	124W	72
Nanam, *Korea*.	41¾N	129¾E	49
Nanango, *Queens., Aust.*	26¾S	152½E	60
Nanao, *Japan*.	37N	137E	49
Nanchang, *China*.	28¾N	115¾E	48
Nancheng, *China*.	27½N	116E	48
Nanchung, *China*.	30¾N	106E	48
Nancy, *France*.	48¾N	6¼E	30
Nanda Devi, Mt., *Ind.*	30¼N	80E	44
Nander, *India*.	19¼N	77¼E	45
Nandgaon, *India*.	21N	81E	44
Nandi, *Rhodesia*.	21S	31½E	54
Nandod, *India*.	22N	73½E	45
Nanga-Eboko, *Camer.*	4¾N	12½E	56
Nanga Parbat, Mt. *Kashmir* (inset).	35¼N	74¼E	44
Nangkartse Dzong, *Tibet*.	29N	91E	43
Nanguare, *Moz.*	12½S	37¾E	56
Nanhsiung, *China*.	25¼N	114¾E	48
Nanking, *China*.	32¼N	118¾E	48
Nanling Mts., *China*.	25N	108E	48
Nannine, *W. Aust.*	27S	118¼E	61
Nanning, *China*.	22½N	108¼E	48
Nannup, *W. Aust.*	34S	115¾E	61
Nanpan Riv., *China*.	25N	106E	48
Nansen, Mt., *Antarc.*	85½S	165W	80
Nanson, *W. Australia*.	28½S	114½E	61
Nantes, *France*.	47¼N	1½W	31
Nanton, *Alb., Can.*	50¼N	113¾W	73
Nantua, *France*.	46¼N	5¾E	32
Nantung, *China*.	32N	121E	48
Nantwich, *England*.	53N	2½W	22
Nanumanga I., *Pacific*.	7S	175E	64
Nanumea I., *Pacific*.	6S	176E	64
Nanutarra, *W. Aust.*	22½S	115½E	61
Nanyang, *China*.	33N	112E	48
Nanyuki, *Kenya*.	0	37E	56
Nao, C., *Spain*.	38¾N	¼W	35
Naoetsu, *Japan*.	37N	138E	49
Napanee, *Ont., Can.*	44¼N	77W	69
Napas, *U.S.S.R.*	60N	82E	39
Napier, *C. Pr., S. Afr.*	34½S	20E	52
Napier, *N.I., N.Z.*	39½S	177E	62
Napinka, *Man., Can.*	49¼N	100¾W	70
Naples & B., *Italy*.	40¾N	14¼E	36
Napo, R., *Peru*.	½S	76W	78
Napperby Sta., *Aust.*	22½S	132½E	60
Nara, R., *Pakistan*.	24N	69E	69
Naracoorte, *S. Aust.*	37S	140¾E	45
Naradhan, *N.S.W.*	33½S	146¼E	59
Narasapatnam, *India*.	17½N	82½E	45
Narbada R., see Narmada.			
Narbonne, *France*	43¼N	3E	32
Narembeen, *W. Aust.*	32S	118E	61
Naretha, *W. Aust.*	31S	125E	61
Narew, *Poland*.	52¾N	23½E	33
Narmada R., *India*.	21¾N	74E	44
Narngulu, *W. Aust.*	28¾S	114¾E	61
Narob, Rjv., *S.W. Afr.*	26S	17½E	51
Narok, *Kenya*.	1S	36E	56
Narrabri, *N.S.W., Aust.*	30½S	149¾E	59
Narran R., *N.S.W.*	29¾S	147½E	59
Narrandera, *N.S.W.*	34¾S	146½E	59
Narrikup, *W. Aust.*	35S	117½E	61
Narrogin, *W. Aust.*	33S	117¼E	61
Narromine, *N.S.W.*	32¼S	148¼E	59
Narsarssuak, *Greenland*.	61N	45W	66
Narsinghpur, *India*.	23N	79¼E	44
Narva, *U.S.S.R.*	59½N	28¼E	38
Narvega, C., *Antarc.*	71S	10W	80
Narvik, *Norway*.	68¾N	17¼E	29
Naryan-Mar, *U.S.S.R.*	67½N	53E	38
Nary Kary, *U.S.S.R.*	63N	65E	38
Narym, *U.S.S.R.*	58¾N	81½E	39
Naryn, *U.S.S.R.*	41½N	76E	39
Nasarawa, *Nigeria*.	8½N	7¾E	57
Naseby, *S.I., N.Z.*	45S	170¼E	63
Nashua, *N.H., U.S.A.*	42¾N	71½W	69
Nashville, *Tenn., U.S.A.*	36¼N	86¾W	75
Nasi, L. of, *Finland*.	62N	24E	29
Nasia, *Ghana*.	10¼N	¾W	57
Nasice, *Yugoslavia*.	45½N	18E	36
Nasik, *India*.	20N	73¾E	45
Nasir, *Sudan*.	8½N	33¾E	56
Nasirabad, *India*.	26¼N	74¾E	45
Nassau I., *Bahama Is.*	25N	77½W	77
Nassau, *Germany*.	50½N	7½E	30
Nassau I., *Pacific*.	11S	167W	64
Nassau Ra., *New Guinea*.	4S	137E	47
Nassau R., *Queens., Aust.*	15¾S	141½E	60
Nasser, L., *U.A.R.*	23N	32E	40
Nassjo, *Sweden*.	57¾N	15E	29
Nata, *Saudi Arabia*.	27N	48E	41
Natal, *Brazil*.	6S	35¼W	78
NATAL, *S. Africa*.	29S	30½E	55
Natanz, *Iran*.	34N	52E	40
Natashkwan, *Que., Can.*	50N	62W	67
Natchez, *Miss., U.S.A.*	31½N	91¼W	69
Nathanya, *Isr.* (inset).	32¼N	35E	40
National City, *U.S.A.*	32½N	117½W	74
Natitingou, *Dahomey*.	10¼N	1½E	57
Natron, L., *Tanzania*.	2½S	36¼E	56
Natsmia, *W. Aust.*	27½S	114E	61
Natuna Is., *Indonesia*.	4N	108E	47
Naturaliste, C., *W. Aust.*	33½S	115E	61
Nauders, *Austria*.	46¾N	10½E	31
Naumburg, *Germany*.	51¼N	11¾E	33
Nauplia, *Greece*.	37½N	23E	37
Nauru I., *Pacific*.	½S	166½E	64
Nautla, *Mexico*.	20N	97W	76
Nava, *W. Australia*.	26½S	114E	61
Nava del Rey, *Spain*.	41¼N	5¼W	35
Navarin, C., *U.S.S.R.*	62¼N	179¼E	39
NAVARRA, *Spain*.	42¾N	2W	35
Navarre, *Vict., Aust.*	37S	143¼E	59
Navassa I., *Carib. Sea*	18N	76W	77
Naver, R. & L., *Scot.*	58¾N	4½W	24
Navojoa, *Mexico*.	27N	109½W	76
Navrongo, *Ghana*.	10¾N	1¼W	57
Nawabshah, *Pakistan*.	27½N	68E	43
Nawalapitiya, *Ceylon*.	7N	80½E	45
Naxos I., *Aegean Sea*.	37N	25½E	37
NAYARIT, *Mexico*.	22N	105W	76
Nayoro, *Japan*.	44½N	142½E	49
Nazareth, *Israel* (ins.).	32¾N	35¼E	40
Nazko, *Br. Col., Can.*	52¾N	123¼W	72
Nchanga, *Zambia*.	12½S	28E	51
Ncheu, *Malawi*.	15S	35E	56
Ncoha, *C. Pr., S. Afr.*	31¾S	27¾E	53
Ndele, *Cen. Afr. Rep.*	8½N	20¾E	56
Ndeni I., *Pacific*.	10½S	165E	64
N'Djole, *Gabon*.	0	11E	51
Ndola, *Zambia*.	13S	28¾E	56
Neagh, L., *N. Ireland*.	54¾N	6½W	26
Neales, The, *S. Aust.*	28¼S	136¾E	59
Neail, L., *N. Terr., Aust.*	24S	130E	60
Neapolis, *Crete*.	35¼N	25½E	37
Neapolis, *Greece*.	40½N	21½E	37
Neath, *Wales*.	51¾N	3¾W	22
Nebine R., *N.S.W., Aust.*	29¼S	146¾E	59
Nebit Dag, *U.S.S.R.*	39¾N	54½E	40
NEBRASKA, *U.S.A.*	42N	100W	74
Neckar, R., *Germany*.	49½N	8¾E	33
Necker I., *Pacific*.	25N	165W	64
Necochea, *Argentina*.	38¾S	58¾W	79
Needham Market, *Eng.*	52¼N	1E	23
Needles, *Calif., U.S.A.*	35N	115W	74
Neepawa, *Man., Can.*	50¼N	99¾W	70
Neftegorsk, *U.S.S.R.*	44N	40E	38
Negaunee, *Mich., U.S.A.*	46½N	87¾W	68
Negombo, *Ceylon*.	7¼N	79¾E	45
Negotin, *Yugoslavia*.	44¼N	22½E	37
Negrais, C., *Burma*.	16N	94¼E	43
NEGRI-SEMBILAN, *Malay*.	2½N	102E	47
Negro B., *Somali Rep.*	8N	50E	56
Negro R., *Argentina*.	40S	64W	78
Negro R., *Brazil*.	¾S	65W	78
Negros I., *Phil. I.*	10N	123E	47
Neh, *Iran*.	32N	60E	40
Neilersdrif, *C. Pr.*	28¾S	21E	52
Neisse, R., *Ger.-Poland*.	52N	15E	33
Neiva, *Colombia*.	3N	75¼W	78
Nejd Desert, *S. Arabia*.	25N	45E	40
Nelgekhe, R., *U.S.S.R.*	67N	136E	39
Nelia, *Queens., Aust.*	20¾S	142¼E	60
Nelkan, *U.S.S.R.*	58N	138E	39
Nellore, *India*.	14½N	80E	45
Nelma, *U.S.S.R.*	48N	139E	39
Nelskop, *C. Pr., S. Afr.*	30½S	20½E	52
Nelson, *Br. Col., Can.*	49½N	117¼W	73
Nelson, *England*.	53¾N	2¼W	22
NELSON, *S.I., N.Z.*	41½S	172½E	63
Nelson, C., *Vict., Aust.*	38¼S	141½E	59
Nelson Head, *N.W. Can.*	72N	122W	66
Nelson R., *Man., Can.*	56¾N	93W	71
Nelspoort, *C. Pr., S. Afr.*	32S	23E	52
Nelspruit, *T'vaal*.	25½S	31E	54
Nemecky Brod, *Czechoslovakia*.	49½N	15½E	33
Nemours, *France*.	48¼N	2¾E	32
Nemuro, *Japan*.	43¼N	145½E	48
Nemuro Str. *Japan*.	43¾N	145¼E	48
Nen, Riv., *England*.	52¾N	¼E	23
Nenagh, *Eire*.	52¾N	8¼W	26
Nenana, *Alaska, U.S.A.*	64¾N	150W	74
Neno, *Malawi*.	15S	35E	56
Nepa & Riv., *U.S.S.R.*	59N	109E	39
NEPAL, *Asia*.	28N	85E	44
Nepalganj, *Nepal*.	28N	81¾E	44
Nephin, Mt., *Eire*.	54N	9¼W	26
Nerac, *France*.	44¼N	¼E	32
Nerchinsk, *U.S.S.R.*	51¾N	116¾E	39
Neretvar Riv., *Yugo.*	43N	17½E	36
Neris Riv., *U.S.S.R.*	55¼N	21¼E	33
Nero River, *Italy*.	42½N	12½E	36
Nes, *Netherlands*.	53½N	5¾E	30
Nes, *U.S.S.R.*	66½N	45E	38
Ness, Loch, *Scotland*.	57¼N	4½W	24
Nesslau, *Switzerland*.	47¼N	9½E	31
Netherdale, *Australia*.	21½S	148½E	60
NETHERLANDS, *Europe*.	53N	5E	30
Nethybridge, *Scotland*.	57½N	3¾W	24
Nettancourt, *France*.	49N	5E	30
Nettuno, *Italy*.	41¾N	12½E	36
Neu Ulm, *Germany*.	48½N	10E	33
Neubrandenburg, *Ger.*	53½N	13¼E	33
Neuchatel & L., *Switz.*	47N	6¾E	31
Neudorf, *Sask., Can.*	50¾N	103W	70
Neuenberg, *Germany*.	48¾N	8½E	30
Neuenberg, *Germany*.	53½N	8E	30
Neuenhaus, *Germany*.	52½N	7E	30
Neuenkirchen, *Ger.*	52½N	8E	30
Neuenrade, *Germany*.	51¼N	7¾E	30
Neufchateau, *Belgium*.	49¾N	5½E	30
Neufchateau, *France*.	48½N	5¾E	30
Neuhaus, *Ger.* (inset).	53¾N	9E	30
Neumunster, *Germany*.	54N	10E	33
Neung-s-Beuvron, *Fr.*	47½N	2E	31
Neunkirchen, *Austria*.	47¾N	16E	33
Neunkirchen, *Ger.*	49¼N	7¼E	33
NEUQUEN & Tn. & R., *Argentina*.	39S	68W	79
Neuruppin, *Germany*.	53N	12¾E	33
Neuse, R., *N.C., U.S.A.*	35N	77W	75
Neusiedler, L. of, *Austria*.	47¾N	16¾E	33
Neuss, *Germany*.	51¼N	6¾E	30
Neustadt, *Schles-Holst. Germany*.	54N	10¾E	33
Neustadt, *Bavaria. Germany*.	49½N	10½E	33

Neustadt—Novi [119]

Place	Lat.	Long.	No.
Neustadt (a-d-Wald-Naab), *Germany*.	49¾N	12¼E	33
Neustadt, *Rhine. Ger.*	49½N	8¼E	30
Neustadt, L. Sax. *Ger.*	52½N	9½E	33
Neustrelitz, *Germany*.	53¼N	13E	33
Neuville, *France*.	46¾N	½E	32
Neuville aux Bois, *Fr.*	48N	2E	30
Neuvy le Roi, *France*.	47½N	½E	31
Neuwied, *Germany*.	50½N	7½E	30
NEVADA, *U.S.A.*	39N	117W	74
Nevada Sierra, *Spain*.	37N	3W	35
Nevel, *U.S.S.R.*	56N	30E	38
Nevers, *France*.	47N	3¼E	32
Nevertire, *N.S.W.*	31¾S	147¾E	59
Nevesinje, *Yugoslavia*.	43¼N	18E	36
Nevin, *Wales*.	52¾N	4½W	22
Nevinnomyssk, *U.S.S.R.*	44½N	42E	38
Nevis, Ben, *Scotland*.	56¾N	5W	24
Nevis I., *Lee. Is, W.I.*	17¼N	62½W	77
Nevis, L., *Scotland*.	57N	5¾W	24
Nevyanski, *U.S.S.R.*	57½N	60E	38
New Abbey, *Scotland*.	55N	3½W	25
New Albany, *U.S.A.*	38¼N	86W	75
New Alresford, *Eng.*	51¼N	1¼W	23
New Amsterdam, *Guy.*	6½N	57¼W	78
New Bedford, *U.S.A.*	41¾N	71W	74
New Bern, *N.C., U.S.A.*	35¼N	77W	75
New Bethesda, *C. Pr.*	31¾S	24½E	53
New Birmingham, *Ire.*	52½N	7½W	26
New Brighton, *N.Z.*	43½S	172¾E	63
New Britain, *U.S.A.*	41¾N	72¾W	69
New Britain I., *Pacific*.	6S	151E	60
NEW BRUNSWICK, *Can.*	46½N	66½W	67
New Brunswick, *New Jers., U.S.A.* (ins.).	40¾N	74W	75
New Buckenham, *Eng.*	52½N	1¼E	23
NEW CALEDONIA, *Pac.*	21¾S	163E	18
New Carlisle, *Que., Can.*	48N	65½W	67
New Castle, *Pa., U.S.A.*	41N	80¼W	74
New Cumnock, *Scot.*	55½N	4¼W	25
New Deer, *Scotland*.	57½N	2¼W	24
New Denver, *Br. Col.*	50N	117¼W	73
New England, *C. Pr.*	31S	27½E	53
New England Ra., *Aust.*	30S	152E	59
New Forest, *England*.	50¾N	1½W	23
New Galloway, *Scot.*	55N	4¼W	25
New Georgia Group, *Pacific*.	8¼S	157¼E	64
New Glasgow, *Canada*.	45¾N	62¾W	67
NEW GUINEA, *Pacific*.	8S	142E	64
NEW HAMPSHIRE, *U.S.*	43½N	71½W	69
New Hanover, *Natal*.	29¼S	30½E	55
New Hanover I., *Pacific*.	2½S	150E	60
New Haven, *Conn., U.S.*	41¼N	73W	75
New Hazelton, *Can.*	55¼N	127½W	72
NEW HEBRIDES IS., *Pac.*	16S	167E	19
New Holland, *Eng.*	53¾N	¼W	23
New Hunstanton, *Eng.*	53N	½E	23
New Ireland I., *Pac.* (ins.).	3S	152E	60
NEW JERSEY, *U.S.A.*	40N	74½W	75
New Liskeard, *Ontario*.	47½N	79¾W	68
New London, *U.S.A.*	41¼N	72¼W	75
New Lynn, *N.I., N.Z.* (inset A).			62
NEW MEXICO, *U.S.A.*	35N	106W	74
New Norfolk, *Tas., Australia*.	42¾S	147E	59
New Orleans, *La., U.S.A.*	30N	90W	75
New Pitsligo, *Scot.*	57½N	2¼W	24
New Plymouth, *N.Z.*	39S	174E	62
New Providence I., *Bahamas, W.I.*	25N	77½W	75
New Quay, *Wales*.	52¼N	4¼W	22
New Radnor, *Wales*.	52¼N	3¼W	22
New Richmond, *Can.*	48¼N	65¾W	67
New River Harbour, *S.I., N.Z.*	46¾S	168E	63
New Rochelle, *N.Y., U.S.A.*	40¾N	73¾W	69
New Romney, *England*.	51N	1E	23
New Ross, *Eire*.	52¼N	7W	26
New Siberia Is., *U.S.S.R.*	75N	140E	39
NEW SOUTH WALES, *Aust.*	32S	147E	59
New Toronto, *Ontario*.	43½N	79½W	68
New Waterford, *C. Breton I., Can.*	46¼N	60¼W	67
New Westminster, *Can.*	49¼N	122¾W	72
New York, *U.S.A.*	40¾N	74W	75
NEW YORK, *U.S.A.*	43N	75W	75
NEW ZEALAND, *Pacific*.	41S	174E	62
Newala, *Tanzania*.	11S	39¼E	56
Newark, *England*.	53¼N	¾W	23
Newark, *N.J., U.S.A.*	40¾N	74¼W	75
Newbiggin, *England*.	55¼N	1½W	25
Newburgh, *N.Y., U.S.*	41½N	74W	69
Newburgh, *Scotland*.	56¼N	3¼W	25
Newbury, *England*.	51¼N	1¼W	23
Newcastle, *Ireland*.	52½N	9W	26
Newcastle, *N. Ireland*.	54¼N	5¾W	25
Newcastle, *Natal*.	27¾S	30E	55
Newcastle, *Canada*.	47N	65¾W	67
Newcastle, *N.S.W., Aust.*	33S	151¾E	59
Newcastle, *U.S.A.*	43¾N	104½W	74
Newcastle-on-Tyne, *England*.	55N	1½W	25
Newcastle-under-Lyme, *England*.	53N	2¼W	22
Newcastle Emlyn, *Wales*.	52N	4½W	22
Newcastle Waters, *N. Terr., Aust.*	17½S	133½E	60
Newdegate, *W. Aust.*	33S	119E	61
Newent, *England*.	52N	2½W	22
NEWFOUNDLAND, *Can.*	55N	60W	66
Newgate, *Br. Col., Can.*	49N	115W	73
Newhaven, *England*.	50¾N	0	23
Newington, *T'vaal.*	24¾S	31¼E	54
Newmarket, *Eire*.	52¼N	9W	26
Newmarket, *England*.	52¼N	½E	23
Newmarket, *Ont., Can.*	44N	79½W	68
Newmarket-on-Fergus, *Ireland*.	52¾N	8¾W	26
Newnham, *England*.	51¾N	2¼W	22
Newport, *Ark., U.S.A.*	36N	91W	75
Newport, *Eire*.	53¾N	9½W	26
Newport, *Mon., Eng.*	51½N	3W	22
Newport, *Essex, Eng.*	52N	¼E	23
Newport, *Salop, Eng.*	52¾N	2½W	22
Newport, *Wales*.	52N	4¾W	22
Newport, *Que., Can.*	48¼N	64¾W	67
Newport, *R.I., U.S.A.*	41½N	71½W	69
Newport, *Scotland*.	56½N	3W	25
Newport, *I. of Wight*.	50¾N	1¼W	23
Newport News, *U.S.A.*	37N	76½W	75
Newport Pagnell, *Eng.*	52¼N	¾W	23
Newquay, *England*.	50½N	5W	22
Newry, *N. Ireland*.	54¼N	6¼W	26
Newton, *Mass., U.S.A.*	42¼N	71¼W	69
Newton Abbot, *Eng.*	50½N	3½W	22
Newton Stewart, *Scot.*	55N	4½W	25
Newton-upon-Trent, *England*.	53¼N	1W	23
Newtondale, *C. Pr., South Africa*.	33½S	27E	53
Newtonmore, *Scotland*.	57N	4W	24
Newtown, *Wales*.	52½N	3¼W	22
Newtownards, *N. Ire.*	54½N	5¾W	26
Newtownbarry, *Ire.*	52½N	6½W	22
Newtownbutler, *Ire.*	54¼N	7¼W	26
Newtown Hamilton, *Ireland*.	54¼N	6½W	26
Newtown Mt. Kennedy, *Ireland*.	53¼N	6¼W	26
Newtownstewart, *Ire.*	54¾N	7¼W	26
Nezhin, see NYEZHIN.			
Ngamakwe, *C. Pr.*	32¼S	27¾E	53
Ngami, L., *Botswana*.	20½S	22½E	51
Ngaoundere, *Camer.*	7¼N	13½E	56
Ngapara, *S.I., N.Z.*	45S	170¾E	63
Ngaring Tso, L., *China*.	35N	97½E	43
Ngaruawahia, *N.Z.*	37¾S	175¼E	62
Ngaruroro R., *N.I., N.Z.*	39½S	176¾E	62
N'Gaski, *Nigeria*.	10½N	4¾E	57
Ngatik, *Pacific*.	5N	158E	64
Ngauruhoe, Mt., *N.Z.*	39S	175½E	62
Ngoga, Riv., *Botswana*.	19S	23E	51
N'Gombe Pt., *Gabon*.	0	10E	56
N'Goume, Riv., *Gabon*.	1S	11E	56
Ngouri, *Chad*.	13¼N	15E	56
Ngqeleni, *C. Pr., S. Afr.*	31¾S	29E	53
Nguigmi, *Niger*.	14N	13E	56
Ngulu I., *Pacific*.	9N	138E	64
Nguru, *Nigeria*.	13N	10¾E	57
Nha Trang, *Vietnam*.	12¼N	109¼E	47
Nhill, *Victoria, Aust.*	36¼S	141½E	59
Niagara F., *N.Y.-Ont.*	43¼N	79W	68
Niagra, *W. Aust.*	29¼S	121½E	61
Niamey, *Niger*.	13¾N	2E	50
Niangara, *Congo (K.).*	3¾N	27½E	56
Niari Riv., *Congo (B.).*	4S	11½E	56
Nias I., *Sumatra*.	1N	97½E	47
NIASSA, *Mozambique*.	13S	37½E	51
Nibbiano, *Italy*.	44¾N	9¼E	31
NICARAGUA, *C. America*.	13N	85½W	77
Nicaragua, L., *Nicar.*	11½N	85½W	77
Nicastro, *Italy*.	39N	16¼E	36
Nice, *France*.	43¾N	7¼E	32
Nickol B., *W. Aust.*	20¾S	117E	61
Nicobar Is., *Ind. Oc.*	7N	93E	19
Nicosia, *Cyprus*.	35¼N	33¼E	41
Nicosia, *Sicily*.	37¾N	14½E	36
Nicoya, Pen. of, *C. Rica*.	10N	85¾W	77
Nidd, Riv., *England*.	54¼N	1¾W	25
Nidda, Riv., *Germany*.	50N	8¾E	30
Nidzica, *Poland*.	53¼N	20½E	33
Niekerkshoop, *C Pr.*	29¼S	22¾E	52
Niemen, R., *U.S.S.R.*	55¼N	22½E	38
Nienburg, *Germany*.	52½N	9¼E	30
Nietta, *Tas., Aust.*	41½S	146E	59
Nieuport, *Belgium*.	51¼N	2¾E	30
Nieuwoudtville, *C. Pr.*	31½S	19¼E	52
Nieuwport, *Nether.*	52N	5E	30
NIEVRE, *France*.	47¼N	3½E	32
Nigde, *Turkey*.	37¾N	34¾E	41
Nigel, *T'vaal, S. Afr.*	26½S	28½E	55
NIGER, *Africa*.	19N	9E	50
Niger River, *Nigeria*.	4¼N	6E	50
NIGERIA, *W. Africa*.	9N	8E	57
Nigg, *Scotland*.	57¾N	4W	24
Nigrita, *Greece*.	41N	23½E	37
Nihoa I., *Pacific*.	23N	162W	64
Nihotupu, *N.I., N.Z.* (inset A).			62
Niigata, *Japan*.	37½N	139E	49
Niihau I., *Pacific*.	21N	160W	64
Niihou I., *Hawaii*.	20½N	154¼W	74
Nijkerk, *Netherlands*.	52¼N	5½E	30
Nijmegen, *Nether.*	51¾N	5¾E	30
Nikaweratiya, *Ceylon*.	7¾N	80¼E	45
Nikki, *Dahomey*.	10N	3¼E	57
Nikolaev, *U.S.S.R.*	47N	32E	38
Nikolaevskiy, *U.S.S.R.*	50N	45E	38
Nikolayevsk, *U.S.S.R.*	53¼N	140¾E	39
Nikolsk, *U.S.S.R.*	59N	45½E	38
Nikopol, *Bulgaria*.	43¾N	24¾E	37
Nikopol, *U.S.S.R.*	47½N	34E	38
Niksic, *Yugoslavia*.	42¾N	19E	37
Nikunau I., *Pacific*.	1S	176E	64
Nile Delta, *U.A.R.*	31N	31E	40
Nile Riv., *U.A.R.*	23N	31½E	50
Nilgiri Hills, *India*.	11¼N	76¾E	45
Nimbiri, *Ghana*.	10N	¼E	57
Nimes, *France*.	43¾N	4½E	32
Nimmitabel, *N.S.W.*	36½S	149¼E	59
Nimule, *Sudan*.	3¾N	32¼E	56
Nindigully, *Queens., Australia*.	28¼S	149E	59
Ninety Mile Beach, *Victoria, Aust.*	38½S	147½E	59
Ninety-Mile Beach, *N.Z.*	35S	173E	62
Nineveh, *Iraq*.	36¾N	43E	41
Ningan, *China*.	44½N	130E	39
Ningko, *China*.	31N	119E	48
Ningpo, *China*.	30N	121½E	48
Ningsia, see YINCHUAN.			
Ningsiang, *China*.	28N	112½E	48
Ningteh, *China*.	27N	119¾E	48
Ningtu, *China*.	26¼N	115½E	48
Ningwu, *China*.	39N	112¼E	48
Ningyuan, *China*.	27½N	103E	43
Ninove, *Belgium*.	50¾N	4E	30
Niobrara R., *U.S.A.*	42¾N	98W	74
Niort, *France*.	46¼N	½W	32
Nipawin, *Sask., Can.*	53¼N	104W	70
Nipigon, *Ont., Can.*	49N	88¼W	66
Nipigon, L., *Ont., Can.*	50N	88½W	66
Nipissing, L., *Ont., Can.*	46¼N	80W	68
Niriz, *Iran*.	29N	54¾E	40
Nirmal, *India*.	19N	78¼E	45
Nis, *Yugoslavia*.	43¼N	21¾E	37
Nishapur, *Persia*.	36N	58½E	40
Nissan I., *Pacific*.	5S	154E	64
Niteroi, *Brazil*.	23S	43W	78
Nith, Riv., *Scotland*.	55N	3¾W	25
Nithsdale, *Scotland*.	55¼N	3¾W	25
Nitra, *Czecho.*	48¼N	18E	33
Nitra Riv., *Czecho.*	47½N	18¼E	33
Niuafoo I., *Pacific*.	15S	178W	64
Niuatobutabu I., *Pacific*.	15S	174W	64
Niue I., *Pacific*.	19S	170W	64
Niulakita I., *Pacific*.	11S	179E	64
Niutao I., *Pacific*.	7S	178E	64
Nivelles, *Belgium*.	50½N	4½E	30
NIVERNAIS, *Fr.*, (ins.).	47¼N	3½E	32
Nizamabad, *India*.	18½N	78E	45
Nizh Zolotitsa, *U.S.S.R.*	66N	40E	38
Nizhne Angarsk, *U.S.S.R.*	56N	110E	39
Nizhne Kolymsk, *U.S.S.R.*	68½N	161E	39
Nizhne Udinsk, *U.S.S.R.*	55N	99E	39
Nizhni Baskunchak, *U.S.S.R.*	48N	47E	38
Nizhni Lomov, *U.S.S.R.*	54N	43E	38
Nizhni Sergi, *U.S.S.R.*	57N	59E	38
Nizhni Tagil, *U.S.S.R.*	58N	60E	39
Nizza, *Italy*.	44¾N	8¼E	31
Njombe, *Tanzania*.	9¼S	34¾E	56
Nkala, *Zambia*.	16S	26E	51
Nkandla, *Natal, S. Afr.*	28¾S	31¼E	55
Nkhotakota, *Malawi*.	13S	34¼E	51
Nkongsamba, *Camer.*	5N	10E	56
Nkwalini, *Natal, S. Afr.*	28¾S	31½E	55
Nkwanta, *Ghana*.	6½N	2W	57
Noailles, *France*.	49¼N	2¼E	30
Noasca, *Italy*.	45½N	7½E	31
Noazanabiz, *S.W. Afr.*	23½S	18½E	51
Nobber, *Ireland*.	53¾N	6¾W	26
Nobelsfontein, *C. Pr.*	31¾S	23E	52
Nobeoka, *Japan*.	33½N	131¾E	49
Noce, Riv., *Italy*.	46¼N	11¼E	31
Noci, *Italy*.	40¾N	17¼E	36
Nocundra, *Queens.*	27½S	142½E	60
Noerbo, *Norway*.	58¾N	5¼E	29
Nogales, *Ariz., U.S.A.*	31½N	111W	74
Nogara, *Italy*.	45¼N	11E	31
Nogata, *Japan*.	33¾N	130¾E	00
Nogayty, *U.S.S.R.*	48½N	55½E	38
Nogent-le-Rotrou, *Fr.*	48¼N	¾E	32
Nogent-s-Seine, *Fr.*	48½N	3½E	30
Nogliki, *U.S.S.R.*	51½N	143E	39
Nogoya, *Argentina*.	32½S	60W	79
Noirmoutier, I. de, *Fr.*	47N	2¼W	32
Nokomis, *Sask., Can.*	51½N	105W	70
Nokoue, L., *Dahomey*.	6½N	2½E	57
Nola, *Italy*.	41N	14½E	36
Nolinsk, *U.S.S.R.*	57½N	50E	38
Nome, *Alaska, U.S.A.*	64½N	165W	65
Nomeny, *France*.	49N	6¼E	30
Nomoi I., *Pacific*.	5N	152E	64
Nonant, *France*.	48¾N	¼E	31
Nonda, *Queens., Aust.*	20¾S	141¾E	60
Nongoma, *Natal*.	27¾S	31½E	55
Nonno, *Ethiopia*.	8N	37½E	56
Nonouti I., *Pacific*.	½S	174E	64
Noodsberg, *Natal*.	29½S	30¾E	55
Noojee, *Vict., Aust.*	37¾S	146¼E	59
Nookawarra, *W. Aust.*	26½S	117E	61
Noonkanbah, *W. Aust.*	18S	125E	61
Noordwolde, *Nether.*	53N	6E	30
NORD, *France*.	50¾N	3E	32
Nord Fiord, *Norway*.	62N	4¾E	29
Norddeich, *Germany*.	53¾N	7¼E	30
Norden, *Germany*.	53¾N	7¼E	33
Nordenham, *Germany*.	53½N	8½E	30
Norderney I., *Germany*.	53¾N	7½E	30
Nordeste, *Azores* (ins.).	38N	25½W	35
Nordhausen, *Germany*.	51½N	10¾E	33
Nordhorn, *Germany*.	52½N	7E	30
Nordkyn Pen., *Norway*	71N	28E	29
Nordlingen, *Germany*.	ʻ8¾N	10½E	33
Nordvik, *U.S.S.R.*	3½N	110E	39
Nore, Riv., *Eire*.	52¾N	7¼W	26
NORFOLK, *England*.	52¾N	1E	23
Norfolk, *Va., U.S.A.*	36¾N	76½W	75
Norfolk Is., *S. Pacific*.	29S	168E	18
Norfolk, *Nebr., U.S.A.*	42N	97W	75
Norg, *Holland*.	53N	6½E	30
Norham, *England*.	55¾N	2¼W	25
Norilsk, *U.S.S.R.*	69½N	88E	39
Norman, *Okla., U.S.A.*	35N	97½W	75
Norman Wells, *Canada*.	65N	125¼W	66
Normanby I., *Pac.* (insert).	10S	151E	60
Normanby R., *Queens.*	14½S	144E	60
NORMANDY, *France*.	49½N	0	31
Normanton, *Queens.*	17¾S	141E	60
Nornalup, *W. Aust.*	35S	116¾E	61
Norrkoping, *Sweden*.	58¾N	16¼E	29
NORRLAND, *Sweden*.	64N	16E	29
Norseman, *W. Aust.*	32¼S	121¾E	61
Norsk, *U.S.S.R.*	52N	130E	39
Nort, *France*.	47½N	1½W	31
N. Battleford, *Canada*.	52¾N	108¼W	70
N. Bay, *Ontario, Can.*	46¼N	79½W	68
N. Berwick, *Scotland*.	56N	2¾W	25
N. Canadian R., *U.S.A.*	35½N	95½W	75
N. Cape, *N.I., N.Z.*	34½S	173E	62
N. Cape, *Norway*.	71½N	25¾E	29
N. CAROLINA, *U.S.A.*	35½N	78W	75
N. Channel, *Ont., Can.*	46N	83W	68
N. DAKOTA, *U.S.A.*	47N	100W	74
N. & S. Esk, R., *Scot.*	56¾N	2½W	24
N. Foreland, *England*.	51¼N	1½E	23
N. Frisian Is., *North S.*	54¾N	8½E	27
NORTH ISLAND, *N.Z.*	38S	176E	62
N. Kennedy, *Queens., Australia*.	19S	146E	60
N. Platte, *Nebr., U.S.A.*	41¼N	100¾W	74
N. OSETIAN A.S.S.R., *U.S.S.R.*	43N	44E	38
N. Portal, *Sask., Can.*	49N	102½W	70
NORTH RHINE-WESTPHALIA, *Germany*.	52N	8E	30
N. Riding, *England*.	54½N	1½W	25
N. Ronaldsay I., *Scot.*	59¼N	2½W	24
North Sea, *N. Europe*.	55½N	3E	28
N. Sydney, *Canada*.	46¼N	60¼W	67
N. Taranaki Bight, *N.I., N.Z.*	39S	174¼E	62
N. TERRITORY, *Aust.*	20S	133E	58
N. Triglia, *Greece*.	40¼N	23¼E	37
N. Uist, *Scotland*.	57½N	7¼W	24
N. Vancouver, *Br. Col., Canada*.	49¼N	122¾W	72
N. Walsham, *England*.	52¾N	1½E	23
N.W. Cape, *W. Aust.*	21½S	114E	61
N.W. TERRITORIES, *Can.*	66N	100W	66
Northallerton, *Eng.*	54½N	1½W	25
Northam, *T'vaal, S.Afr.*	25S	27¼E	54
Northam, *W. Aust.*	31¾S	116¾E	61
NORTHAMPTON & Tn., *England*.	52¼N	¾W	23
Northampton, *Mass., U.S.A.*	42¼N	72½W	69
Northampton, *W. Aust.*	28¼S	114½E	61
Northcliffe, *W. Aust.*	34¾S	116E	61
Northern Sporades Is., *Aegean Sea*.	39N	25E	37
Northiam, *England*.	51N	¾E	23
Northland, *N.I., N.Z.*	35½S	173½E	62
Northleach, *England*.	51¾N	1¾W	23
NORTHUMBERLAND, *England*.	55¼N	2W	25
Northumberland, C., *S. Australia*.	38S	140½E	59
Northumberland Str., *Canada*.	46N	63W	67
Northwest River, *Newf., Can.* (ins.).	53½N	60W	67
Northwich, *England*.	53¼N	2½W	22
Norton, *England*.	54¼N	¾W	25
Norton Sound, *Alaska*.	63N	162W	74
Norvalspont, *C. Pr.*	30¾S	25½E	53
Norwalk, *Conn., U.S.A.*	41¼N	73½W	69
NORWAY, *Europe*.	63N	10E	29
Norway House, *Can.*	54N	97¾W	71
Norwich, *Conn., U.S.A.*	41½N	72W	69
Norwich, *England*.	52¾N	1½E	23
Norwood, *N.Y., U.S.A.*	44¾N	75W	69
Norwood, *Ont., Can.*	44½N	78W	69
Noshiro, *Japan*.	40¼N	140E	49
Nosop, R., *S.W. Africa*.	27S	21E	51
Noss Head, *Scotland*.	58½N	3W	24
Nosy Be I., *Malagasy*.	13½S	48¼E	56
Notec, Riv., *Poland*.	52½N	16E	33
Noto, *Sicily*.	37N	15E	36
Notre Dame B., *Newf.*	49½N	55W	67
NOTTINGHAM & Tn., *England*.	53N	1¼W	23
Nottingham Rd., *Nat.*	29¼S	30E	55
Nouakchott, *Mauritania*	18N	16W	50
Noumea, *New Cal., Pac.*	22¼S	166½E	64
Noupoort. *C. Pr., South Africa*.	31¼S	25E	53
Nova Chaves, *Angola*.	10½S	21¼E	56
Nova Friburgo, *Brazil*.	22¼S	42¼W	79
Nova Lisboa, *Angola*.	12¾S	15¾E	56
Nova Lusitania, *Moz.*	20S	34½E	51
NOVA SCOTIA, *Canada*.	45N	64W	67
Nova Zagora, *Bulg.*	42½N	26E	37
Novara, *Italy*.	45½N	8½E	36
Novaya Ladoga, *U.S.S.R.*	60N	32¼E	38
Novaya Lyalya, *U.S.S.R.*	58½N	61E	38
Novaya Sibir I., *U.S.S.R.*	75N	150E	39
Novaya Zemlya I., *U.S.S.R.*	73N	55E	38
Nove Zamky, *Czecho.*	48N	18¼E	33
Novgorod, *U.S.S.R.*	58½N	31¼E	38
Novi Ligure, *Italy*.	44¾N	8¾E	36

[120] Novi Pazar—Ortonville

Place	Lat.	Long.	No.
Novi Pazar, Bulgaria.	43¼N	27E	37
Novi Pazar, Yugoslavia.	43N	20½E	37
Novi Sad, Yugoslavia.	45¼N	19¾E	37
Novo Bogatinski, U.S.S.R.	47N	52E	38
Novocherkassk, U.S.S.R.	47½N	40E	38
Novogrudok, U.S.S.R.	53½N	25¾E	38
Novokazalinsk, U.S.S.R.	47N	62E	39
Novokuznetsk, U.S.S.R.	54N	87E	39
Novomoskovsk, U.S.S.R.	54N	38¼E	38
Novo Redondo, Ang.	11½s	13¾E	56
Novorossiysk, U.S.S.R.	44¾N	37¾E	38
Novosergievka, U.S.S.R.	52N	54E	38
Novosibirsk, U.S.S.R.	55N	83E	39
Novouzensk, U.S.S.R.	51N	48E	38
Novy Port, U.S.S.R.	67¾N	73E	39
Nowa Sol, Poland.	51¾N	15¾E	33
Nowe, Poland.	53½N	18¾E	33
Nowendoc, N.S.W.	31½s	151¼E	59
Nowgong, India.	26¼N	92¾E	43
Nowingi, Vict., Aust.	34½s	142¼E	59
Nowra, N.S.W., Aust.	34¾s	150¾E	59
Nowshera, Pakistan.	34N	72E	43
Nowy Ruda Poland.	50½N	16½E	33
Nowy Sacz, Poland.	49¾N	20¾E	33
Nowy Targ, Poland.	49½N	20E	33
Noyant, France.	47½N	½E	31
Noyers, France.	47¾N	4E	32
Nqutu, Natal.	28¼s	30¾E	55
Nsanje, Malawi.	17s	35¼E	51
Nsawam, Ghana.	5¾N	¼W	57
Nsukka, Nigeria.	7N	7½E	57
N'Tima, Congo (B.).	4s	12E	56
Ntywenka, C.Pr., S.Afr.	31¼s	28½E	53
Nuanetsi, Rhodesia.	21½s	30¾E	51
Nubian Desert, Sudan.	21N	33E	40
Nubra, R., Kash. (ins.).	34N	78E	44
Nueces, R., Tex., U.S.A.	28N	99W	74
Nueltin, L., N.W. Can.	61N	99W	66
Nueva Rosita, Mexico.	27¾N	101½W	76
Nuevitas, Cuba, W.I.	21½N	77½W	77
Nuevo Laredo, Mexico.	27½N	99½W	76
NUEVO LEON, Mexico.	25N	100W	76
Nugget Pt., S.I., N.Z.	46½s	169¾E	63
Nui I., Pacific.	9s	178E	64
Nuits-s-Armancon, Fr.	47¾N	4E	30
Nukufetau I., Pacific.	9s	179E	64
Nukuhiva I., Pacific.	9s	141W	64
Nukunono I., Pacific.	10s	172W	64
Nukuoro I., Pacific.	4N	155E	64
Nukus, U.S.S.R.	42½N	60E	40
Nullagine, W. Aust.	21½s	120½E	61
Nullarbor Plain, S. Aust.	31s	130E	58
Numan, Nigeria.	9½N	12E	57
Numurkah, Vict., Aust.	36s	145½E	59
Nun River, China.	47N	124E	39
Nuneaton, England.	52½N	1½W	23
Nunivak I., Alaska, U.S.A. (inset).	60N	169W	74
Nunkiang, China.	49¾N	125E	39
Nunlochy, Scotland.	57½N	4½W	24
Nunnery Pool, W. Aust.	26½s	116E	61
Nuoro, Sardinia.	40¼N	9¼E	36
Nuqui, Colombia.	5½N	77W	77
Nura, Riv., U.S.S.R.	50N	70E	39
Nure, River, Italy.	45N	9¾E	31
Nurmes, Finland.	63½N	29E	29
Nurnberg, Germany.	49½N	11E	33
Nurri, Sardinia.	39¾N	9¼E	36
Nusaybin, Syria.	37N	41½E	41
Nushki, Pakistan.	29¾N	66E	43
Nutts Corner, N. Ire.	54¾N	6¼W	26
Nutwood Downs, Aust.	16s	133½E	60
Nuwara Eliya, Ceylon.	7N	80¾E	45
Nuwefontein, S.W.Af.	28s	19E	52
Nuwerus, C. Pr.	31¼s	18¼E	52
Nuweveld Range, C. Pr., S. Africa.	32½s	22E	52
Nuy, C. Pr., S. Africa.	33¾s	19½E	52
Nuyts Pt., W. Aust.	35s	116¾E	61
Nya Chu River, China.	30N	101E	43
Nyabing, W. Aust.	33½s	118¼E	61
Nyaksimvol, U.S.S.R.	62N	61E	38
Nyala, Sudan.	12N	25E	56
Nyamaroi, Mozam.	16½s	37E	51
Nyandoma, U.S.S.R.	61¾N	40¼E	38
Nyasa, L., Malawi.	12s	34½E	51
Nyborg, Norway.	70N	28E	29
Nyda & Riv., U.S.S.R.	66½N	72E	39
Nyenchintangla Range, Tibet.	30N	90E	43
Nyeri, Kenya.	½s	37E	56
Nyezhin, U.S.S.R.	51¼N	31¾E	38
Nyiregyhaza, Hung.	48N	21¾E	37
Nykobing, Denmark.	54¾N	12E	33
Nykoping, Sweden.	58¾N	17E	29
Nylstroom, T'vaal.	24¾s	28¼E	54
Nymagee, N.S.W., Aust.	32s	146¼E	56
Nymburk, Czecho.	50¼N	15E	33
Nyngan, N.S.W., Aust.	31½s	147¼E	59
Nyon, Switzerland.	46½N	6¼E	31
Nyong, R., Cameroon.	3N	10E	56
Nysa, Poland.	50½N	17¼E	33
Nyurba, U.S.S.R.	62N	119E	39
Nyuya, Riv., U.S.S.R.	61N	115E	39
OAHU I., Hawaii, Pac.	21½N	158W	64
Oak Lake, Man., Can.	49¾N	101W	70
Oak Ridge, U.S.A.	36½N	84W	75
Oakengates, England.	52¾N	2½W	22
Oakey, Queens., Aust.	27½s	151¾E	59
Oakham, England.	52¾N	¾W	23
Oakland, Calif., U.S.A.	37¾N	122¼W	74
Oaklands, .S.W., Aust.	35½s	146¼E	59
Oakover Riv., W. Aust.	20¾s	120E	61
Oakville, Ont., Can.	43½N	79¾W	68
Oamaru, S.I., N.Z.	45s	171E	63
Oarusib, R., S.W. Africa.	19s	13E	51
Oates Land, Antarctica.	70s	160E	80
Oatlands, C. Pr., S.Afr.	32¾s	24¼E	53
Oatlands, Tas., Aust.	42¼s	147¼E	59
OAXACA, & Tn., Mex.	17N	97W	76
Ob, Gulf of, U.S.S.R.	70N	73E	39
Ob, River, U.S.S.R.	66¾N	69E	39
Oba, Ontario, Canada.	49N	84W	71
Oban, Scotland.	56½N	5½W	25
Oban, Stewart I., N.Z.	47s	168E	63
Obbia, Somali Rep.	5¼N	48½E	50
Oberammergau, Ger.	47½N	11E	31
Oberhausen, Ger. (ins.).	51½N	6¾E	33
OBERLAND, Switz.	46½N	7½E	31
Oberndorf, Germany.	48¼N	8½E	30
Oberon, N.S.W., Aust.	34s	150E	58
Obersdorf, Germany.	47½N	10¼E	31
Oberstein, Germany.	49½N	7¾E	30
Oberwald, Switz.	46½N	8¼E	31
Obi Is., Moluccas.	1½s	127¾E	47
Obidos, Brazil.	2s	55½W	78
Obihiro, Japan.	43N	143¼E	49
Obisfelde, Germany.	52½N	11E	33
Obluche, U.S.S.R.	49¾N	131E	39
Obo, Cent. Afr. Rep.	5N	26½E	56
Obokh, Afars & Issas.	12N	43¼E	56
Oborniki, Poland.	52¾N	16¾E	33
Oboue, River, Gabon.	0	12E	56
Obozerskaya, U.S.S.R.	63½N	40½E	38
Obra Can. & R., Poland.	52N	16E	33
Obuasi, Ghana.	6¼N	1¾W	57
Obyachevo, U.S.S.R.	60N	50E	38
Ocana, Colombia.	8N	73½W	77
Ocean, C., Alaska, U.S.A.	60N	140W	66
Ocean Falls, Br. Col., Canada.	52¼N	127¾W	72
Ocean I., Pacific.	1s	169E	64
Ochemchiri, U.S.S.R.	43N	41½E	38
Ochil Hills, Scotland.	56¼N	3¾W	25
Ockelbo, Sweden.	61N	17E	29
Ocos, Guatemala.	14½N	92½W	76
Ocotal, Nicaragua.	13¾N	86½W	77
Ocotepeque, Honduras.	14½N	89W	76
Ocotlan, Mexico.	20¼N	103W	76
October Revolution Is., U.S.S.R.	79½N	96E	39
Ocumare, Venezuela.	10N	67W	77
Oda, Ghana.	6N	1W	57
Odaejin, Korea.	41½N	130E	49
Odate, Japan.	40N	140½E	49
Oddur, Somali Rep.	4N	43E	56
Odemis, Turkey.	38¼N	28E	37
Odendaalsrus, O.F.S.	27¾s	26¾E	55
Odemira, Portugal.	37¾N	8½W	35
Odense, Denmark.	55¼N	10¼E	29
Oder, R., Ger.-Poland.	53½N	14¾E	33
Oderzo, Italy.	45¾N	12½E	31
Odessa, Texas, U.S.A.	32N	102½W	74
Odessa, U.S.S.R.	46½N	30¾E	38
Odiham, England.	51¼N	1W	23
Odorhei, Romania.	46½N	25¼E	37
Odzala, Congo (B.).	1N	15E	56
Odzi River, Rhodesia.	20s	32E	51
Oenpilli, N. Terr., Aust.	12½s	132½E	60
Oetz R., Austria.	47¼N	10¾E	31
Ofanto River, Italy.	41¼N	16¼E	36
OFFALY, Eire.	53¼N	7½W	26
Offenbach, Germany.	50N	8¾E	33
Offenburg, Germany.	48½N	8E	30
Offranville, France.	49¾N	1E	31
Ogaki, Japan.	35¼N	136½E	49
Ogbomosho, Nigeria.	8¼N	4¼E	57
Ogden, Utah, U.S.A.	41¼N	112W	74
Ogema, Sask., Can.	49¾N	104¾W	70
Oglio R., Italy.	45N	10¾E	31
Ognon, Riv., France.	47½N	6E	31
Ogoja, Nigeria.	6½N	8¾E	57
Ogowe R., Gabon.	0	11E	50
Ogudu, Nigeria.	9N	5E	57
Oguta, Nigeria.	5½N	6½E	57
Ohakune, N.I., N.Z.	39½s	175½E	62
Ohau, L., S.I., N.Z.	44¼s	170E	63
OHIO, U.S.A.	40N	83W	75
Ohio River, U.S.A.	37N	88W	75
Ohligs, Germany (ins.).	51N	7E	33
Ohrid, Yugoslavia.	41¼N	20¾E	37
Ohrid, L. of, Albania.	41N	20½E	37
Ohrigstad, T'vaal.	24¾s	30½E	54
Ohura, N.I., N.Z.	38¾s	175E	62
Oil City, Penn., U.S.A.	41¼N	79¾W	68
Oilgate, Eire.	52½N	6½W	22
Oimyakon, U.S.S.R.	64N	142¾E	39
Oirot Tura, U.S.S.R.	52N	86E	39
OISE, R. & DEP., France.	49¼N	2¾E	32
Oita, Japan.	33¼N	131½E	48
Ojinaga, Mexico.	29½N	104½W	76
Oka River, U.S.S.R.	57N	103E	39
Okahandja, S.W. Afr.	22s	17E	51
Okaihau, N.I., N.Z.	35¼s	173¾E	62
Okanagan, L., Br. Col.	450N	119½W	72
Okanogan R., U.S.A.	8¼N	119½W	74
Okaya, Japan.	36N	138E	49
Okayama, Japan.	34¾N	134E	48
Okazaki, Japan.	35N	137E	49
Oke-Odde, Nigeria.	8½N	5E	57
Okeechobee, L., U.S.A.	27N	81W	75
Okehampton, Eng.	50¾N	4W	22
Okene, Nigeria.	7½N	6¼E	57
Okha, U.S.S.R.	53½N	143E	39
Okhotsk, U.S.S.R.	59¼N	143¼E	39
Okhotsk Sea, E. Asia.	55N	147E	39
Oki Islands, Japan.	36N	133E	49
Okiep, C. Pr., S. Afr.	29¾s	18E	52
Okigwi, Nigeria.	5¾N	7½E	57
Okitipupa, Nigeria.	6½N	5E	57
OKLAHOMA, U.S.A.	36N	98W	74
Oklahoma City, U.S.A.	35½N	97½W	74
Okondja, Congo (B.).	1s	13½E	56
Okotoks, Alb., Can.	50¾N	114W	73
Okovango R., Angola.	17s	18E	56
Okoyo, Congo (B.).	1½s	15E	56
Okpari, Nigeria.	5½N	6E	57
Okujiri I., Japan.	42N	139½E	49
Okwa Riv., Botswana.	22½s	22E	51
Oland I., Sweden.	56¾N	16¾E	29
Olary, S. Australia.	32¼s	140¼E	59
Olavarria, Argentina.	37s	60½W	79
Olawa, Poland.	51N	17½E	33
Olbia, Sardinia.	41N	9½E	36
Old Castile, Spain.	42N	3½W	35
Oldcastle, Ireland.	53¾N	7¼W	26
Oldenburg, Germany.	53¼N	8¼E	33
Oldenburg, Germany.	54¼N	10¾E	33
Oldenzaal, Nether.	52¼N	6½E	30
Oldesloe, Ger. (inset).	53¾N	10E	30
Oldham, England.	53½N	2¼W	22
Old Head of Kinsale, Eire.	51½N	8¼W	26
Oldman R., Alb., Can.	49¾N	112W	73
Old Meldrum, Scot.	57¼N	2¼W	24
Olds, Alberta, Canada.	51¾N	114¼W	73
Olean, N.Y., U.S.A.	42¼N	78½W	69
Oleggio, Italy.	45½N	8½E	31
Olekma Riv., U.S.S.R.	61N	121E	39
Olekminsk, U.S.S.R.	60¼N	120½E	39
Olenek, U.S.S.R.	68N	112E	39
Olenek Riv., U.S.S.R.	73N	120E	39
Oleron, Ile d', France.	46N	1¼W	32
Olesnica, Poland.	51¼N	17½E	33
Olga, U.S.S.R.	44N	135E	39
Olga, Mt., Australia.	25½	131E	60
Olifants Deift, T'vaal.	24¼s	26¾E	54
Olifants R., T'vaal.	24s	31¼E	54
Olivenza, Spain.	39N	7W	35
Olives, Mt. of, Jordan (inset).	31¾N	35¼E	40
Oliwa, Poland.	54½N	18½E	33
Ollague, Chile.	21¼s	68¼W	79
Ollerton, England.	53¼N	1W	23
Olney, England.	52¼N	¾W	23
Olomouc, Czecho.	49½N	17¼E	33
Olonets, U.S.S.R.	61N	33E	38
Oloron-Ste-Marie, Fr.	43¼N	¾W	32
Olot, Spain.	42¼N	2½E	32
Olovyannaya, U.S.S.R.	51N	115½E	39
Olpe, Germany.	51N	8E	30
Olsztyn, Poland.	53¾N	20½E	33
Olten, Switzerland.	47¼N	8E	31
Oltenita, Romania.	44N	26½E	37
Oltul, Riv., Romania.	43¾N	25E	37
Olympia, Wash., U.S.A.	47N	123W	74
Olympos, Mt., Greece.	40N	22½E	34
Olympus, Mt., Cyprus.	35N	33E	41
Olyutorski, C., U.S.S.R.	60N	170E	39
Omagh, N. Ireland.	54½N	7¼W	26
Omaha, Nebr., U.S.A.	41¼N	96W	75
Omaha Beach, France.	49¼N	1W	31
Omakhta, U.S.S.R.	57N	131E	39
OMAN, see MUSCAT & OMAN.			
Oman, G. of, Asia.	24N	58E	40
Omarama, S.I., N.Z.	44½s	170E	63
Omaruru, S. W. Afr.	21½s	16E	51
Ombrone R., Italy.	42½N	11E	36
Omdraaisvlei, C. Pr.	30s	23¼E	52
Omdurman, Sudan.	15½N	32¼E	50
Ometepec, Mexico.	16½N	98¼W	76
Omis, Yugoslavia.	43¼N	16½E	36
Omo River, Ethiopia.	4¾N	35¼E	56
Omolon Riv., U.S.S.R.	68N	159E	39
Omoloy Riv., U.S.S.R.	72N	131E	39
Omsk, U.S.S.R.	55N	73¼E	39
Omu, Japan.	45N	143E	49
Omura, Japan.	33N	130E	49
Omuta, Japan.	33N	130½E	49
Omutninsk, U.S.S.R.	58N	52½E	38
Onderstedoring, S.Afr.	30½s	20½E	52
Ondo, Nigeria.	7¼N	5¼E	57
Onega & R., U.S.S.R.	64N	38E	38
Onega, G. of, U.S.S.R.	64N	37E	38
Onega, L., U.S.S.R.	61½N	36E	38
Onehunga, N.I., N.Z.	37s	174¾E	62
O'Neill, Neb., U.S.A.	42N	99W	74
Oneida, L., N.Y., U.S.	43¼N	76W	69
Ongar, England.	51¾N	¼E	23
Ongeluksfontein, S.Afr.	32½s	21½E	52
Ongerup, W. Aust.	34s	118½E	61
Ongjin, Korea.	38N	125E	49
Ongole, India.	15½N	80E	45
Onilahy R. Malagasy.	23½s	44¾E	56
Onitsha, Nigeria.	6¼N	7E	57
Ono, Japan.	36N	136½E	49
Ono I., Pacific.	21s	180E	64
Onoke, L., N.I., N.Z. (inset B).			62
Onon River, U.S.S.R.	51N	114E	39
Onotoa I., Pacific.	2s	175E	64
Onoway, Alb., Can.	53¾N	114¼W	73
Onpo, China.	22N	110E	48
Onrust R., C. Pr., S.Af.	34½s	19E	52
Onseepkans, C. Pr.	28¾s	19¼E	52
Onslow, W. Aust.	21½s	115E	61
ONTARIO, Canada.	52N	88W	66
Ontario, L., U.S.A.-Canada.	43½N	78W	69
Oodnodatta, S. Aust.	27½s	136E	60
Ooldea, S. Australia.	30½s	131¾E	58
Oontoo, Queens., Aust.	27½s	141½E	60
Oostburg, Netherlands.	51½N	3½E	30
Oosterhout, Nether.	51¾N	5E	30
Oosterland, Nether.	53N	5E	30
Oostmalle, Belgium.	51¼N	4¾E	30
Oostvlieland, Nether.	53¼N	5E	30
Ootacamund, India.	11½N	76½E	45
Ootsa L., Br. Col., Can.	53¾N	126¼W	72
Opalenica, Poland.	52¼N	16½E	33
Opalton, Queens., Aust.	23s	142½E	60
Opalville, Queens., Aust.	24¾s	142¾E	60
Opanake, Ceylon.	6¾N	80¾E	43
Opatow, Poland.	50¾N	21½E	33
Opava, Czecho.	50N	18E	33
Opeinde, Netherlands.	53N	6¼E	30
Ophthalmia Range, W. Australia.	22½s	120E	61
Opihi Riv., S.I., N.Z.	44¼s	171½E	63
Opobo, Nigeria.	4½N	7¾E	57
Opochka, U.S.S.R.	56¾N	28¾E	38
Opoczno, Poland.	51½N	20¼E	33
Opole, Poland.	50¾N	18E	33
Oporto, Portugal.	41¼N	8¾W	35
Opotiki, N.I., N.Z.	38s	177¼E	62
Oppeln, see OPOLE.			
Oppenheim, Germany.	49¾N	8¼E	30
Oprang, Kash. (ins.).	37¼N	75¾E	44
Opua, N.I., N.Z.	35¼s	174E	62
Opunake, N.I., N.Z.	39½s	173¾E	62
Oqair, Saudi Arabia.	25½N	50E	41
Ora, Italy.	46¼N	11¼E	31
Ora Banda, W. Aust.	30¼s	121E	61
Oradea, Romania.	47N	22E	37
Orallo, Queens., Aust.	26½s	148½E	60
Oran, Argentina.	23s	64W	79
Oran, Algeria.	35¾N	¾W	35
Orange, France.	44¼N	4¾E	32
Orange, N.S.W., Aust.	33¼s	149E	59
ORANGE FREE STATE, South Africa.	28s	27E	53
Orange R., C. Pr.	28½s	16½E	51
Orangeburg, U.S.A.	33½N	81W	75
Orangeriver, C. Pr	29¾s	24¼E	53
Orangeville, ,Ont., Can.	43¾N	80W	68
Orangorongo R., N.I., N.Z. (inset B).			62
Oranjefontein, T'vaal.	23½s	27¾E	54
Oranjeville, O.F.S.	27s	28¼E	54
Oranmore, Ireland.	53½N	9W	26
Orany, U.S.S.R.	54¼N	24¼E	33
Orastie, Romania.	45¾N	23½E	37
Oravita, Romania.	45N	21¾E	37
Orawia, S.I., N.Z.	46s	167¾E	63
Orba River, Italy.	45N	8¾E	31
Orbost, Vict., Aust.	37¾s	148½E	59
Orchies, France.	50½N	3¼E	37
Orchila I., Venezuela.	12N	66W	71
Orcieres, France.	44½N	6¼E	31
Orco, Riv., Italy.	45¼N	7¾E	31
Ord, Mt., W. Aust. (ins.).	17s	126E	69
Ord River, W. Aust.	17s	129E	69
Ordu, Turkey.	41N	38E	41
Ordubad, U.S.S.R.	39N	46E	38
Orduna, Spain.	43N	3W	35
Ordzhonikidze, U.S.S.R.	43N	44E	38
Orebro, Sweden.	59¼N	15¼E	29
OREGON, U.S.A.	44N	120W	74
Oregrund, Sweden.	60½N	18¾E	29
Orekhovo, Bulgaria.	43½N	24E	37
Orekhovo-Zuyevo, U.S.S.R.	56N	39E	38
Orel, U.S.S.R.	53N	36E	38
Oren, Turkey.	37N	28E	37
Orenburg, U.S.S.R.	51¾N	55¼E	38
Orense, Spain.	42¼N	8W	35
Oreti Riv., S.I., N.Z.	46¾s	168E	63
Orford, England.	52¼N	1¾E	23
Orford Ness, Queens.	11½s	142½E	60
Orhei, U.S.S.R.	47¼N	28½E	37
Orialla, Guyana (ins.).	5N	56W	77
Orihuela, Spain.	38N	¾W	35
Orillia, Ontario, Can.	44¾N	79½W	68
Orinoco R., Venezuela.	9N	61W	78
ORISSA, India.	20N	84E	43
Oristano, & G., Sard.	39¾N	8½E	36
Orizaba, Mexico.	18¾N	97¼W	76
Orkhon, R., Mongolia.	50N	106E	39
Orkney Is., Scotland.	59N	3W	24
Orlando, Fa., U.S.A.	28½N	81½W	75
ORLEANAIS, France.	48N	2E	32
Orleans, France.	48N	1¾E	32
Ormara, Pakistan.	25N	64¾E	43
Ormskirk, England.	53½N	2¾W	22
ORNE, R. & DEP., Fr.	48¾N	¼W	32
Ornskoldsvik, Sweden.	63N	19E	29
Orochen, U.S.S.R.	58N	125E	39
Orooluk I., Pacific.	8¾N	155E	64
Orosei, & G., Sardinia.	40¼N	9¾E	36
Orosei, Sardinia.	40¼N	9¾E	36
Orotava, La & G., Canary Is.	28½N	16½W	35
Orotuk, U.S.S.R.	62N	148E	39
Orrefors, Sweden.	57N	15E	29
Orroroo, S. Australia.	32¾s	138½E	59
Orsha, U.S.S.R.	54½N	30¼E	38
Orsieres, Switzerland.	46N	7¼E	31
Orsk, U.S.S.R.	51¼N	58½E	38
Orsova, Romania.	44¾N	22½E	37
Ortegal, C., Spain.	43¾N	8W	35
Orthez, France.	43¼N	¾W	32
Ortigueia, Spain.	43¾N	8W	35
Ortiz, Mexico.	28N	111W	76
Ortles, Mt., Italy.	46½N	10½E	31
Ortona, Italy.	42¼N	14½E	36
Ortonville, Minn. U.S.	45½N	96W	78

Orunia—Peiserton [121]

Place	Lat.	Long.	No.
Orunia, Poland.	54½N	18¾E	37
Oruro, Bolivia.	18S	67W	38
Orvieto, Italy.	42¾N	12¼E	36
Osa, Pen. de, Costa Rica.	11N	84W	77
Osage R., Miss., U.S.A.	38N	94W	75
Osaka, Japan.	34¾N	135½E	49
Osede, Germany.	52¼N	8E	30
Osh, U.S.S.R.	40½N	72¾E	39
Oshawa, Ontario Can.	43¾N	78¾W	69
Oshkosh, Wis., U.S.A.	44N	88½W	75
Oshoek, Transvaal.	26½S	31E	55
Oshogbo, Nigeria.	7¾N	4½E	57
Osijek, Yugoslavia.	45½N	18¾E	37
Oslo & Fiord, Norway.	60N	10¾E	29
Osmanabad, India.	18¼N	76E	45
Osnabruck, Germany.	52¼N	8E	33
Osowiec, Poland.	53½N	22¼E	33
Osoyoos, Br. Col., Can.	49N	119½W	72
Oss, Netherlands.	51¾N	5½E	30
Oste, Riv., Germany.	53¾N	9E	30
Ostend, Belgium.	51¼N	3E	30
Ostend, N.I., N.Z. (inset A).			62
Oster Dal R., Sweden.	61N	15E	29
Ostero, Faeroe Is. (ins.).	62N	7W	29
Ostersund, Sweden.	63¼N	14¾E	29
Osthofen, Germany.	49¾N	8½E	30
Ostia, Italy.	41¾N	12¼E	36
Ostiglia, Italy.	45N	11¼E	31
Ostrand, Sweden.	62½N	17E	29
Ostrava, Czecho.	49¾N	18¼E	33
Ostrod, Poland.	53¾N	20E	33
Ostroleka, Poland.	53N	21½E	33
Ostrov, Romania.	44N	27¼E	37
Ostrov, U.S.S.R.	57½N	28¼E	38
Ostrow, Poland.	52¾N	22E	33
Ostrow, Poland.	51¾N	17¾E	33
Ostrowiec, Poland.	51N	21½E	33
Osumi Is. & Str., Jap.	30½N	130½E	49
Osuna, Spain.	37¼N	5¼W	35
Oswego, N.Y., U.S.A.	43½N	76½W	74
Oswestry, England.	52¾N	3W	22
Oswiecim, Poland.	50N	19¼E	33
Ota, Japan.	35N	133E	49
OTAGO, S.I., N.Z.	45S	169½E	63
Otago, S.I., N.Z.	45¾S	170¾E	63
Otahuhu, N.I., N.Z. (inset A).			62
Otaki, N.I., N.Z.	40¾S	175¼E	62
Otaru, Japan.	43¼N	141E	49
Otavi, S.W. Africa.	20S	17¾E	50
Othery, England.	51N	3W	22
Otira, S.I., N.Z.	42¾S	171½E	63
Otjiwarongo, S.W.Afr.	20½S	16¾E	51
Otley, England.	53¾N	1¾W	23
Otorohanga, N.I.,N.Z.	38¼S	175¼E	62
Otranto, Italy.	40½N	18½E	36
Otranto, Str. of, Italy.	40N	19E	37
Otrokovice, Czecho.	49¼N	17½E	33
Otsu, Japan.	43N	143½E	49
Ottawa, Ontario, Can.	45½N	75¾W	66
Ottawa Riv., Ont., Can.	45½N	74W	69
Otter Ferry, Scotland.	56N	5¼W	25
Otterburn, England.	55¼N	2¼W	25
Otterndorf, Germany.	53¾N	8¾E	30
Ottery St. Mary, Eng.	50¾N	3¼W	22
Ottignies, Belgium.	50¾N	4½E	30
Ottosdal, T'vaal, S.Afr.	26¾S	26E	55
Ottoshoop, T'vaal, S.Af.	25¾S	26E	55
Ottumwa, Iowa, U.S.A.	41N	92½W	75
Otur Kyuyel, U.S.S.R.	70N	140E	39
Otway, C., Vict., Aust.	39S	143½E	59
Otwock, Poland.	52¼N	21¼E	33
Ouadda, Cen. Afr. Rep.	8N	22¼E	56
Ouagadougou, Upper Volta.	12¼N	1½W	57
Ouahigouya, U. Volta.	13¾N	2W	57
Oualata, Mauritania.	17N	7W	50
Ouam R., C. Afr. Rep.	7½N	18E	56
Ouargla, Algeria.	31½N	5E	35
Ouberg, C. Pr., S. Afr.	32¼S	24½E	53
Oudjda, Morocco.	34½N	2W	35
Oudon, Riv., France.	47¾N	1W	31
Oudtshoorn, C. Pr., South Africa.	33½S	22¼E	52
Oued Zem, Morocco.	32¾N	6½W	35
Ouesso, Congo (B.).	2N	16E	56
Oufrane, Algeria.	28½N	0	34
Oughterard, Ireland.	53½N	9½W	26
Ouidah, Dahomey.	6½N	2E	57
Ouistreham, France.	49¼N	¼W	31
Oujda, Morocco.	34¾N	2W	35
Oulchy le Chateau, Fr.	49¼N	3½E	30
Ouled Djella, Algeria.	34½N	5E	35
Oulu, Finland.	65N	25½E	29
Oulu, L. of, Finland.	64½N	27E	29
Oulx, Italy.	45N	7E	31
Oumuur, C. Pr., S. Afr.	31S	20¼E	52
Ounas River, Finland.	66½N	25½E	29
Oundle, England.	52½N	½W	23
Oup, Riv., S.W. Africa.	27S	21E	51
Ouplaas, C. Pr., S. Afr.	32¼S	23¾E	53
Our, Riv., Germany.	49¾N	6½E	30
Ourique, Portugal.	37¾N	8¼W	35
Ouro Preto, Brazil.	20½S	43½W	78
Ourthe, R., Belgium.	50¼N	5¾E	30
Ouse, Riv., England.	52¾N	¼E	23
Oust, Riv., France.	47¾N	2W	31
Outlook, Sask., Can.	51½N	107W	70
Outram, S.I., N.Z. (inset D).			63
Ouyen, Vict., Aust.	35S	142¼E	59
Ouzouer le Marche, Fr.	48N	1½E	31
Ovada, Italy.	44½N	8¾E	31
Ovalle, Chile.	30½S	71¼W	79
Ovar, Portugal.	40¾N	8½W	35
Overath, Germany.	51N	7½E	30
Overflakkee Is., Neth.	51¾N	4E	30
OVERIJSSEL, Nether.	52½N	6½E	30
Overton, England.	53N	3W	22
Oviedo, Spain.	43½N	5¾W	35
Ovruch, U.S.S.R.	51¼N	28½E	38
Owel, L., Ireland.	53½N	7½W	26
Owen Sd., Ont., Can.	44½N	81W	68
Owen Stanley Range, Mts., Papua (inset).	9S	149E	60
Owensboro, U.S.A.	37¾N	87½W	75
Owerri, Nigeria.	5½N	7E	57
Owo, Nigeria.	7¼N	5½E	57
Ox Mts., Eire.	54¼N	9W	26
Oxelosund, Sweden.	59N	17E	29
OXFORD & Tn., Eng.	51¾N	1¼W	23
Oxford, No. Scot., Can.	45¾N	63¾W	67
Oxford, S.I., N.Z.	43½S	172½E	63
Oxley, N.S.W., Aust.	34½S	144E	59
Oyem, Gabon.	2N	12E	56
Oykell Bridge, Scotland.	58N	4¾W	24
Oyo, Nigeria.	8N	4E	57
Oyo, Sudan.	22N	36E	40
Oyonnax, France.	46¼N	5¾E	31
Oyster Bay, Tasmania.	42S	148E	59
Oyun Kyuyel, U.S.S.R.	69N	138E	39
Ozarks, L. of the, U.S.A.	37N	93W	75
Ozieri, Sardinia.	40½N	9E	36
Ozorkow, Poland.	52N	19¼E	33
PA'AN, China.	30N	99½E	42
Paarl, C. Pr., S. Africa.	33¾S	19E	52
Pabbay, Scotland.	57¾N	7¼W	24
Pabjanice, Poland.	51¾N	19½E	33
Pabna, Pakistan.	24N	89¼E	44
Pacaltsdorp, C.Pr., Afr.	34S	22½E	52
Pachbhadra, India.	26N	72¼E	44
Pachino, Sicily.	36¾N	15E	36
Pachmarhi, India.	22½N	78½E	44
Pachuca, Mexico.	20½N	98¾W	76
Pacific, Br. Col., Can.	54¾N	128¼W	72
PACIFIC OCEAN.	0	160W	18
Pacy, France.	49N	1½E	31
Padang, Sumatra.	1S	100¼E	47
Padang-Sidimpuan, Sumatra, Indon.	1½N	99E	47
Padani, U.S.S.R.	63½N	33½E	38
Paderborn, Germany.	51¾N	8¾E	33
Padiham, England.	53¾N	2¼W	22
Padron, Spain.	42¾N	8¾W	35
Padstow, England.	50½N	5W	22
Padua, Italy.	45½N	11¾E	36
Paducah, Kent., U.S.A.	37½N	88¾W	75
Paeroa, N.I., N.Z.	37½S	175¾E	62
Paesano, Italy.	44¾N	7¼E	31
Pafuri, Mozambique.	22½S	31½E	51
Pag Is., Yugoslavia.	44½N	14¾E	36
Pagai Is., Sumatra.	3S	100E	47
Pagan I., Pacific.	18N	146E	64
Pagny, France.	49N	6E	30
Pago Pago, Samoa, Pac.	14½S	170¾W	64
Pagona, Papua (inset).	8S	143E	60
PAHANG, Malaysia.	3½N	103½E	47
Pahiatua, N.I., N.Z.	40½S	175¾E	62
Pahlevi, Iran.	37½N	49½E	40
Paiakumbu, Sumatra.	¼S	101½E	47
Paignton, England.	50½N	3½W	22
Paiho, China.	32½N	110E	48
Pailingmiao, China.	43N	111E	48
Pailung River, China.	32½N	106E	48
Paimboeuf, France.	47¼N	2W	31
Paimpol, France.	48¾N	3W	31
Paisley, Ontario, Can.	44½N	81¼W	68
Paisley, Scotland.	55¾N	4½W	25
Pak Lei, Laos.	18N	102E	47
Pakhoi, see PEIHAI.			
PAKISTAN, EAST.	24N	90E	43
PAKISTAN, WEST.	30N	67E	43
Pakokku, Burma.	21¼N	95E	43
Pakrac, Yugoslavia.	45½N	17¼E	36
Paks, Hungary.	46½N	19E	37
Pakse, Laos.	15N	105¾E	47
Pal, China.	34N	80E	43
Pala, Cen. Afr. Rep.	9½N	15E	56
Palamcottah, India.	8¾N	77¾E	45
Palamos, Spain.	42N	3E	35
Palana, U.S.S.R.	59N	160E	39
Palanpur, India.	24¼N	72½E	44
Palapye Rd., Botswana.	22½S	27½E	51
Palar, Riv., India.	12½N	80E	45
PALATINATE, Germany.	49¾N	7½E	30
Palau Is., Pacific.	7¾N	134¾E	18
Palau, Sardinia.	41¼N	9½E	36
Palawan I., P.I.	9N	118E	47
Palazzolo Acreide, Sicily.	36¾N	15¼E	36
Paleisheuwel, C. Pr.	32½S	18¾E	52
Palembang, Sumatra.	3S	104¾E	47
Palencia, Spain.	42N	4½W	35
Palenque, Mexico.	17½N	92W	76
Palenque, Panama.	9N	79W	77
Palermo, Sicily.	38¼N	13½E	36
Palestine, Tex., U.S.A.	32N	96W	75
Palestrina, Italy.	42N	13E	36
Paletwa, Burma.	21¼N	92½E	43
Palghat, India.	10¾N	76¾E	45
Palgrave, Mt., W. Aust.	23S	116E	61
Pali, India.	25¾N	73¼E	44
Palinuro, C., Italy.	40N	15¼E	36
Palisadoes Airport, Jamaica, W.I. (ins.).	18N	77W	77
Palk Strait, India.	10N	80E	45
Pallinup Riv., W. Aust.	34¾S	119E	61
Palliser Bay, N.I., N.Z.	41½S	175E	62
Palliser, C., N.I., N.Z.	41½S	175¼E	62
Palm Beach, Fla., U.S.A.	26¾N	80¼W	75
Palm Is., Queens., Aust.	18S	146½E	60
Palm Springs, U.S.A.	33¾N	116½W	74
Palma, Majorca I., Med.	39½N	2¾E	34
Palma, Mozambique.	10¾S	40½E	56
Palma I., Can. Is. (ins.).	28¾N	18W	35
Palmas, C., Liberia.	4½N	7¾W	50
Palmer R., Queens., Aust.	16S	142½E	60
Palmerston N., N.Z.	40½S	175½E	62
Palmerston, Ont., Can.	43¾N	80¾W	68
Palmerston, S.I., N.Z.	45½S	170¾E	63
Palmerville, Queens., Australia.	16S	144E	60
Palmi, Italy.	38½N	15¾E	36
Palmmicken, U.S.S.R.	54¾N	20E	33
Palmyra, Syria.	34½N	38E	41
Palmyra I., Pacific.	6N	162W	64
Palmyras Pt., India.	20¾N	87E	44
Palos, Spain.	37¼N	7W	35
Palos, C. de, Spain.	37½N	½W	35
Palu, Celebes, Indon.	1S	119¾E	47
Pamiers, France.	43¼N	1½E	32
Pamir Plateau, U.S.S.R.	39N	73E	42
Pamlico Sd., U.S.A.	35¼N	76W	75
Pampas, The, Arg.	37S	60W	78
Pamplona, Spain.	43N	1¾W	35
Pampoenpoort, C. Pr.	31S	22¾E	52
Panama City, Florida.	30N	86W	75
PANAMA, & G., Panama	8½N	79½W	77
Panama Canal, Panama.	8½N	80W	77
Panaria Is., Med.	38½N	15E	36
Panaro River, Italy.	44¾N	11½E	31
Panay I., P.I.	11¼N	122½E	47
Panbula, N.S.W., Aust.	37S	150E	59
Panbult, T'vaal, S. Afr.	26¾S	30½E	55
Pancevo, Yugoslavia.	44¾N	20¾E	37
Pandara, W. Aust.	25½S	116E	61
Panevezys, U.S.S.R.	55¾N	24¼E	38
Panfilov, U.S.S.R.	45N	80E	39
Pangala, Congo (B.).	3½S	14½E	56
Pangani, R., Tanzania.	5S	38E	56
Pangani, Tanzania. (ins.).	6S	39E	50
Pangkiang, China.	43N	112E	39
Pangkor Pt., Mal. (ins.).	4¼N	100½E	47
Pangong Tso, L., Kashmir (inset).	34N	78½E	44
Panipat, India.	29½N	77E	44
Panjim, India.	15½N	73¾E	45
Pankshin, Nigeria.	9½N	9½E	57
Panmunjom, Korea.	38N	126½E	49
Panna, India	24¾N	80¼E	44
Panne, La, Belgium.	51N	2½E	30
Pantelleria I., Medit.	36¾N	12E	34
Paoki, China.	34½N	107E	48
Paola, Italy.	39½N	16E	36
Paoshan, China.	31½N	122E	48
Paoting, China.	38N	115½E	48
Paotow, China.	41N	110E	48
Paoying, China.	33N	119E	48
Papa, Hungary.	47½N	17½E	37
Papakura, N.I., N.Z. (inset A).			62
Papa Stour I., Scotland.	60½N	1¾W	24
Papas, C. Greece.	38¼N	21½E	37
Papatoetoe, N.I N.Z., (insetA).			62
Papa Westray I., Scot.	59½N	2¾W	24
Papeete I., Pacific.	18S	149W	64
Papenburg, Germany.	53N	7½E	33
Papey I., Iceland (ins.).	65N	15W	29
Paphos, Cyprus.	35N	32½E	41
PAPUA, New Guinea.	7½S	145E	64
Papun, Burma.	18N	97½E	43
PARA, Brazil.	4S	52W	78
Para, see BELEM.			
Para River, Brazil.	½S	48W	78
Parachilna, S. Aust.	31S	138½E	59
Paracin, Yugoslavia.	43¾N	21½E	37
Paragua, R., Venezuela.	7N	63W	77
Paraguana Pen., Venez.	12N	70W	77
Paraguari, Paraguay.	25½S	57W	79
PARAGUAY, S. America.	22½S	57W	79
Paraguay R., Paraguay.	23S	58W	79
PARAIBA, Brazil.	7S	37W	78
Paraiba, see JOAO PESSOA.			
Paraiso, Mexico.	18½N	93¼W	76
Parakhino Poddube, U.S.S.R.	58N	33E	38
Parakou, Dahomey.	9½N	2½E	57
Paramaribo, Surinam.	6N	55W	78
Paramushir I., U.S.S.R.	50N	156E	39
Parana, Argentina.	32S	60½W	78
PARANA, Brazil.	24½S	52W	78
Parana River, Brazil.	27¼S	55W	78
Paranagua, Brazil.	25½S	48¼W	78
Paranthan, Ceylon.	9½N	80½E	45
Parattah, Tas. (ins.).	42¼S	147½E	59
Paray-le-Monial, Fr.	46½N	4¼E	32
Parchim, Germany.	53¾N	11¾E	33
Parczew, Poland.	51½N	23E	33
Pardubice, Czecho.	50N	15¾E	33
Parengarenga Harb, N.I., N.Z.	34½S	173E	62
Paria, G. of, Venezuela.	10½N	62½W	77
Parika, Guyana (ins.).	7N	58W	77
Paris, France.	48¾N	2¼E	32
Paris, Ontario, Canada.	43¼N	80½W	68
Park Rynie, Natal.	30½S	30¾E	55
Parker Pt., Queens.	16½S	139E	60
Parkersburg, U.S.A.	39¼N	81½W	75
Parkes, N.S.W., Aust.	33¼S	148¼E	59
Parkeston, W. Aust.	31S	122E	61
Parkhill, Ont., Can.	43¼N	81¾W	68
Parknasilla, Ireland.	51¾N	9¾W	26
Parma, Italy.	44¾N	10¼E	31
Parnahyba, Brazil.	3S	42W	78
Parnahyba R., Brazil.	4S	45W	78
Parnassus, S.I., N.Z.	42¾S	173¼E	63
Parnu & B., U.S.S.R.	58½N	24½E	38
Paroo, W. Australia.	26½S	119E	61
Paroo R., N.S.W., Aust.	34S	142E	59
Paros I., Aegean Sea.	37N	25¼E	37
Parral, Mexico.	27N	105½W	76
Parramatta, N.S.W.	33¾S	151E	59
Parras, Mexico.	25½N	102½W	76
Parrsboro, No. Scotia.	45½N	64½W	67
Parry, C., N.W. Canada.	70N	125W	66
Parry Is., N.W. Canada.	76N	105W	66
Parry Sound, Ont., Can.	45½N	80W	68
Parsnip R., Br. Col.	55¼N	123¾W	68
Partabgarh, India.	24N	74¾E	44
Parthenay, France.	46¾N	¼W	32
Partinico, Sicily.	38N	13E	36
Parvatipuram, India.	18N	83½E	43
Parys, O.F.S., S. Afr.	27S	27½E	55
Pasadena, Calif., U.S.A.	34N	118W	74
Pasadena, Texas, U.S.A.	30N	95W	75
Pasak, Riv., Thailand.	14N	101E	43
Pascani, Romania.	47¼N	26½E	37
PAS DE CALAIS, France.	50½N	2¼E	32
Pasewalk, Germany.	53½N	14E	33
Pasig, Luzon, P.I.	15N	121E	47
Pasing, Germany.	48¼N	11½E	33
Pasir Mas, Malay (ins.).	6N	102E	47
Pasir Puteh, Malay (ins.)	5¾N	102E	47
Pasley, C., W. Aust.	34S	123E	61
Pasni, Pakistan.	25¼N	63E	47
Paso, El, Mexico.	32N	106½W	76
Passau, Germany.	48½N	13½E	33
Passero, C., Sicily.	36¾N	15E	36
Passmore Riv., S. Aust.	31S	139¾E	59
Pasto, Colombia.	1½N	77¼W	78
PATAGONIA, Argentina.	44S	68W	78
Patan, India.	23¾N	72¼E	44
Patan, Nepal.	27¾N	85¼E	44
Patani, Thailand.	6¾N	101¼E	47
Patay, France.	48N	1¾E	31
Patchewollock, Aust.	35½S	142E	59
Patea, N.I., N.Z.	39¾S	174½E	62
Pategi, Nigeria.	8¾N	5¾E	57
Pateley Bridge, Eng.	54¼N	1¾W	23
Patensie, C.Pr., S.Afr.	33¾S	24¾E	53
Paterno, Sicily.	37½N	15E	36
Paternoster, C. Pr.	32¾S	18E	52
Paterson, N.J., U.S.A.	41N	74¼W	74
Pathankot, India.	32½N	75½E	44
Patiala, India.	30¼N	76½E	44
Patmos, I. of, Greece.	37¼N	26½E	37
Patna, India.	25¾N	85¼E	44
Patras, & G. of, Gr.	38¼N	21¾E	37
Patrington, England.	53¾N	0	23
Patrocinio, Brazil.	19S	47W	79
Patterdale, England.	54½N	3W	25
Patti, Sicily.	38¼N	15E	36
Patuca Pta., Honduras.	16N	84W	77
Patuca Riv., Honduras.	16N	85W	77
Pau, France.	43¼N	½W	32
Pauillac, France.	45¼N	¾W	32
Pauking, see SHAOYANG.			
Pauktaw, Burma.	20N	93E	43
Paul Roux, O.F.S.	28¼S	28E	55
Paullo, Italy.	45½N	9½E	31
Paulpietersburg, Nat.	27½S	30¾E	55
Pavia, Italy.	45¼N	9¼E	36
Pavlodar, U.S.S.R.	52½N	77E	39
Pavlovsk, U.S.S.R.	50½N	40E	38
Pavullo, Italy.	44¼N	11E	36
Pawtucket, U.S.A.	41¾N	71¼W	69
Payne River, Que., Can.	60N	70W	66
Paynesville, W. Aust.	28S	118E	61
Paysandu, Uruguay.	32¼S	58W	79
Paz, La, Honduras.	14N	87W	77
Pazardzik, Bulgaria.	42¼N	24¼E	37
P. Condore I., Indo-Chi.	8½N	107E	47
Peace River, Alb., Can.	56½N	117W	73
Peak Hill, N.S.W., Aust.	32¾S	148¼E	59
Peak Hill, W. Aust.	25½S	118¾E	61
Peake Creek, S. Aust.	28S	136E	60
Pearl Harbour, Hawaii, U.S.A. (inset).	20½N	155¼W	74
Pearl Riv., Miss., U.S.A.	30N	90W	75
Pearston, C. Pr., S. Afr.	32½S	24¼E	53
Peary Land, Greenland.	82¾N	34W	80
Pec, Yugoslavia.	42½N	20½E	37
Pecha Buri, Thailand.	13N	100E	43
Pechabun, Thailand.	16½N	101E	47
Pechenga, U.S.S.R.	69½N	31¼E	38
Pechora, U.S.S.R.	65¼N	57E	38
Pechora Riv. & Est. & Sea, U.S.S.R.	68N	53½E	38
Pecora, C., Sardinia.	39¼N	8¼E	36
Pecos Riv., Texas, U.S.A.	30N	101W	74
Pecos, Texas, U.S.A.	31½N	103½W	74
Pecs, Hungary.	46N	18¼E	37
Pedro Bank, Carib. Sea.	17N	78W	78
Peebinga, S. Aust.	35S	141E	59
Peebles, Sask., Canada.	50½N	103W	70
PEEBLES & Tn., Scot.	55¾N	3¼W	25
Peekskill, U.S. (inset).	41¼N	74W	75
Peel, I. of Man, Eng.	54¼N	4¾W	25
Peel Fell, Mt., Scotland.	55¼N	2½W	25
Peel River, Canada.	67¾N	134¾W	66
Peene, Riv., Germany.	53¾N	14E	33
Peery, L., N.S.W., Aust.	31S	143½E	59
Pegasus Bay, S.I., N.Z.	43¼S	172¾E	63
Pegu, Burma.	17½N	96½E	43
Pegwell B., England.	51¼N	1½E	23
Pegwill, T'vaal (inset).	26S	28¼E	52
Pehanchen, China.	48N	127E	39
Peihai, China.	21½N	109E	48
Peine, Germany.	52¼N	10¼E	33
Peipus, L., U.S.S.R.	58½N	27½E	38
Peiserton, C.Pr., S.Afr.	28½S	23½E	52

Place	Lat.	Long.	No.
Pekalongan, *Java.*	7s	109½E	47
Pekan, *Malaysia.*	3½N	103½E	47
Peking, *China.*	40N	116½E	48
Pelee, Mt., *Martinique.*	15N	61W	77
Peleng I., *Celebes, Indon.*	1½s	123¼E	47
Pelhrimov, *Czecho.*	49½N	15¼E	33
Peljesac Pen., *Yugo.*	43N	17½E	36
Pella, *C.Pr., S. Africa.*	29s	19E	52
Pella Gozzano, *Italy.*	45¾N	8¼E	31
Pellston, *Mich., U.S.A.*	45½N	84¾W	75
Pelly, *Sask., Canada.*	51¾N	101¾W	70
Pelly River, *Yukon.*	62¾N	136½W	66
Pelly, L., *N.W. Canada.*	65N	101W	66
Peloponnesus Pen., *Gr.*	37N	21E	37
Pelotas, *Brazil.*	32s	52½W	79
Pemba, *Zambia.*	17s	27E	51
Pemba I., *Zanzibar I.*	5¼s	39¾E	56
Pemberton, *W. Aust.*	34½s	116E	61
Pembina R., *Alb., Can.*	54¾N	114¼W	73
Pembroke, *Ont., Can.*	45¾N	77¼W	69
PEMBROKE & T., *Wales.*	51¾N	5W	21
Pena Golosa Mt., *Spain*	40½N	0	35
Penang, *Malaysia.*	5½N	100¼E	47
Penas, C., *Spain.*	43½N	6W	35
Penas, G. de, *Chile.*	47s	75W	78
Pendembu, *Sierra Leone.*	8¼N	10¾W	57
Pender B., *W. Aust.*	17s	123E	61
Pendine, *Wales.*	51¾N	4½W	22
Pendleton, *Ore., U.S.A.*	46N	119W	74
Penganga Riv., *India.*	20N	76¾E	44
Penglai, *China.*	37¾N	120¾E	48
Pengpu, *China.*	33N	117E	48
Penguin, *Tas., Aust.*	41¼s	146E	59
Penicuik, *Scotland.*	55¾N	3¼W	25
Peniscola, *Spain.*	40½N	¼E	35
Penistone, *England.*	53½N	1¾W	23
Penki, *China.*	41N	123E	48
Penmaenmawr, *Wales.*	53¼N	4W	22
Penmarch, Pte. de, *Fr.*	47¾N	4¼W	32
Pennant, *Sask., Can.*	50½N	108¼W	70
Penne, *Italy.*	42½N	14E	36
Penner River, *India.*	14½N	80E	45
Pennine Alps, *Switz.-It.*	46N	7¾E	31
Pennine Chain, *Eng.*	54N	2¼W	25
PENNSYLVANIA, *U.S.A.*	41N	78W	75
Penobscot, R., *U.S.A.*	44½N	68¾W	67
Penola, *S. Australia.*	37½s	140¾E	59
Penonome, *Panama.*	8½N	80W	77
Penrhyndeudraeth, *Wales.*	53N	4W	22
Penrith, *England.*	54¾N	2¾W	25
Penrith, *N.S.W.* (inset).	34s	150½E	58
Penryn, *England.*	50¼N	5W	22
Pensacola, *Fla., U.S.A.*	30½N	87¼W	75
Pensford, *England.*	51½N	2½W	22
Pentecost I., *Pacific.*	15s	169E	64
Penticton, *Br. Col.*	49½N	119½W	72
Pentland, *Queens., Aust.*	20½s	145½E	60
Pentland Firth, *Scot.*	58¾N	3W	24
Pentland Hills, *Scot.*	55¾N	3¼W	25
Pentre Foelas, *Wales.*	53N	3½W	22
Penza, *U.S.S.R.*	53¼N	45E	38
Penzance, *England.*	50¼N	5½W	22
Penzhina Riv., *U.S.S.R.*	62N	165E	39
Penzhinskaya, G. of, *U.S.S.R.*	60N	161E	39
Peoria, *Illinois, U.S.A.*	40¾N	89¾W	75
Pepan River, *China.*	25N	106E	48
Peqin, *Albania.*	41N	19½E	37
Pera Hd., *Queens., Aust.*	12½s	142E	60
Peradeniya, *Ceylon.*	7¼N	80¾E	45
PERAK & R., *Malay.* (ins.).	4½N	101E	47
Perce, *Quebec, Canada.*	48½N	64¼W	67
Percyville, *Queens.*	18½s	143½E	60
Perdeberg, *O.F.S.*	29s	25¼E	55
Perdekop, *T'vaal, S.Afr.*	27¼s	29¾E	55
Perdu, Mt., *Spain.*	42¾N	¼E	35
Perdue, *Sask., Canada.*	52N	107½W	70
Perekop, *U.S.S.R.*	46¼N	33¾E	38
Perenjori, *W. Aust.*	29½s	116½E	61
Pergamino, *Argentina.*	34s	60½W	79
Pergola, *Italy.*	43¾N	13E	36
Periers, *France.*	49¼N	1½W	31
Perigueux, *France.*	45½N	¾E	32
Perim I., *S. Yemen* (ins.)	14N	44E	40
PERLIS, *Malaysia* (inset).	6½N	100¼E	47
Perm, *U.S.S.R.*	58N	56¼E	38
Pernambuco, see RECIFE.			
PERNAMBUCO, *Brazil.*	8s	38W	78
Peron, C., *W. Aust.*	32½s	115½E	61
Peronne, *France.*	49¾N	2¾E	32
Peron Pen. & C. *W. Aust.*	25½s	114E	61
Perosa, *Italy.*	45N	7¼E	31
Perovsk, see KZYL ORDA.			
Perpignan, *France.*	42¾N	2¾E	32
Perros-Guirec, *France.*	48¾N	3½W	31
Pershore, *England.*	52¼N	2W	22
Persian Gulf, *Asia.*	26N	53E	49
Perth, *N. Bruns., Can.*	46¾N	67¾W	67
Perth, *Ontario, Can.*	45N	76¼W	69
PERTH & CO., *Scotland.*	56½N	3½W	25
Perth, *W. Australia.*	32s	115¾E	61
Perth Amboy, *N.J., U.S.A.* (inset).	40¾N	74W	75
PERU, *S. America.*	11s	74W	78
Perugia, *Italy.*	43N	12½E	36
Perwez, *Belgium.*	50½N	4¾E	30
Pesaro, *Italy.*	44N	13E	36
Pescadores Is., *China.*	23½N	119E	48
Pescara & Riv., *Italy.*	42½N	14¼E	36
Peschany, C., *U.S.S.R.*	43N	52E	38
Peschici, *Italy.*	42N	16E	36
Peschiera, *Italy.*	45½N	10½E	31
Pescia, *Italy.*	44N	10¾E	36
Peshawar, *Pakistan.*	34N	71½E	46
Peshkopije, *Albania.*	41½N	20½E	37
Petah Tiqva, *Israel.*	32N	35E	41
Petauke, *Zambia.*	14s	31½E	51
Peter Ist I., *Antarctica.*	69s	90¾W	80
Peterborough, *Eng.*	52½N	¼W	23
Peterborough, *Ontario.*	44½N	78¼W	69
Peterborough, *S. Aust.*	33s	138¾E	59
Peterhead, *Scotland.*	57½N	1¾W	24
Peterlee, *England.*	54¾N	1¼W	25
Petersburg, *Alas.* (inset).	58N	133W	74
Petersburg, *C.Pr., S.Af.*	32¼s	25E	53
Petersburg, *Va., U.S.A.*	37¼N	77½W	75
Petersfield, *England.*	51N	1W	23
Peterswald Hill, Mt., *W. Australia.*	26½s	124E	61
Peto, *Mexico.*	20¼N	89W	76
Petone, *N.I., N.Z.*	41½s	174¾E	62
Petra Is., *U.S.S.R.*	77N	112E	39
Petras, Mt., *Antarc.*	76½s	130W	80
Petrich, *Bulgaria.*	41½N	23¼E	37
Petrolia, *Ontario, Can.*	43N	82¼W	68
Petrolina, *Brazil* (ins.).	10s	41W	79
Petropavlovsk, *U.S.S.R.*	53N	158¾E	39
Petropavlovsk, *U.S.S.R.*	55N	69¼E	39
Petropolis, *Brazil.*	22½s	43W	79
Petrosani, *Romania.*	45½N	23¼E	37
Petrovac, *Yugoslavia.*	44½N	16¼E	36
Petrovac, *Yugoslavia.*	44½N	21½E	37
Petrovsk, *U.S.S.R.*	52N	45E	38
Petrovsk, *U.S.S.R.*	51N	109E	39
Petrovskoe, *U.S.S.R.*	45½N	43E	38
Petrozavodsk, *U.S.S.R.*	61¾N	34½E	38
Petrusburg, *O.F.S. S.Afr.*	29s	25½E	53
Petrus Steyn, *O.F.S.*	27¾s	28E	55
Petrusville, *C.Pr., S.Afr.*	30s	24¾E	51
Petsamo, see PECHENGA.			
Pettigoe, *Ireland.*	54½N	7¾W	26
Pettorano, *Italy.*	42N	14E	36
Petworth, *England.*	51N	½W	23
Pevensey, *England.*	50¾N	¼E	23
Pezenas, *France.*	43½N	3½E	32
Pforzheim, *Germany.*	48¾N	8¾E	30
Pfungstadt, *Germany.*	49¾N	8½E	33
Pha Nga, *Thailand.*	8N	98E	43
Phalodi, *India.*	27¼N	72¼E	44
Phan Rang, *Vietnam.*	11¾N	109E	47
Phan Thiet, *Vietnam.*	11N	108E	47
Phe, *Kashmir* (inset).	33½N	76¾E	44
Phenix City, *Ala., U.S.*	32½N	85W	75
Philadelphia, *C. Pr.*	33¾s	18½E	52
Philadelphia, *U.S.A.*	40N	75W	75
Philippeville, see SKIKDA.			
Philippi, L., *Queens.*	24½s	138½E	60
PHILIPPINE IS., *Pacific.*	12N	123E	47
Philippolis, *O.F.S.*	30½s	25¼E	55
Philippsburg, *Ger.*	49¼N	8½E	30
Philipstown, *C. Pr.*	30½s	24½E	53
Philippopolis, see PLOVDIV.			
Phillip I., *Vict., Aust.*	38½s	145E	59
Phillips, *W. Australia.*	33½s	120E	61
Phoenix, *Ariz., U.S.A.*	33½N	112W	74
Phoenix I., *Pacific.*	4s	170W	64
Phu Lang Thuong, *Chi.*	21N	106E	48
Phu Quoc I., *Cambodia.*	10N	104E	47
Piacenza, *Italy.*	45N	9¾E	36
Piadena, *Italy.*	45¼N	10½E	31
Pialba, *Queens., Aust.*	25¼s	152¾E	60
Pianosa, I. of, *Italy.*	42¾N	10E	36
Piashti, *Quebec, Can.*	50¼N	62¾W	67
Piatra-Neamt, *Rom.*	47N	26½E	37
PIAUHY, *Brazil.*	8s	42W	78
Piaui River, *Brazil.*	7s	43W	79
Piawaning, *W. Aust.*	30¾s	116¼E	61
Piazza Armerina, *Sic.*	37½N	14½E	36
Pibor River, *Sudan.*	8N	32E	56
PICARDY, *France.*	50N	2E	32
Pichieh, *China.*	28N	105E	48
Pickering, *England.*	54¼N	¾W	25
Pico I., *Azores* (inset).	38½N	28¼W	35
Pico de Teide, Mt., *Canary Is.* (inset).	28¼N	16½W	35
Picola, *Victoria, Aust.*	36s	145E	59
Picton, *N.S.W., Aust.*	34¼s	150½E	59
Picton, *S.I., N.Z.*	41¼s	174E	63
Pictou, *No. Scot., Can.*	45¾N	62¾W	67
Piedad, La, *Mexico.*	20½N	102W	76
Piedimulera, *Italy.*	46N	8¼E	31
PIEDMONT, *Italy.*	45N	8E	36
Piedras Negras, *Mex.*	28¾N	100½W	76
Pieirasanta, *Italy.*	44N	10E	36
Pieksamaki, *Finland.*	62½N	27E	29
Pielinen, L., *Finland.*	63N	30E	38
Pielis, L. of, *Finland.*	63½N	30E	29
Pieman River, *Tas.*	41¾s	145E	59
Pienaar's Riv. *T'vaal.*	25¼s	28¼E	54
Pienaarspoort, *T'vaal, S. Africa* (inset).	25¾s	28½E	51
Pierre, *S. D., U.S.A.*	44½N	100½W	74
Piestany, *Czecho.*	48¾N	17¾E	33
Pietarsaari, *Finland.*	63¾N	22½E	29
Pietermaritzburg, *Nat.*	29½s	30¼E	55
Pietersburg, *T'vaal.*	24s	29½E	54
Piet Retief, *T'vaal, S.Af.*	27s	30¾E	55
Pieve di Cadore, *Italy.*	46½N	12½E	38
Pigeon Bay, *S.I., N.Z.* (inset C).			63
Piggs Peak, *Swaziland.*	26s	31¼E	55
Piketberg, *C.Pr., S.Afr.*	33s	18¾E	52
Pila, *Poland.*	53¼N	16¾E	33
Pilane, *Botswana.*	24½s	26E	54
Pilar, *Paraguay.*	27s	58¼W	79
Pilbara, *W. Australia.*	21¼s	118E	61
Pilcomayo R., *Parag.*	21s	64W	79
Pilgrim's Rest, *T'vaal.*	24¾s	30¼E	54
Pilibhit, *India.*	28½N	80E	44
Pilica River, *Poland.*	51¾N	21½E	33
Pillau, see BALTISK.			
Pilliga, *N.S.W., Aust.*	30¼s	149E	59
Pilos, *Greece.*	37N	21½E	37
Pilsen, see PLZEN.			
Pimba, *S. Australia.*	31¼s	136¾E	59
Pinaki I., *Pacific.*	19s	139W	64
Pinar Del Rio, *Cuba.*	22½N	83½W	77
Pincher Creek, *Alb., Canada.*	49½N	114W	73
Pinczow, *Poland.*	50½N	20½E	33
Pindar, *W. Australia.*	28½s	115¾E	61
Pindarrara, *W. Aust.*	23s	115E	61
Pindus Mts., *Greece.*	40N	21E	37
Pine Bluff, *Ark., U.S.A.*	34¼N	92W	75
Pine Creek, *N. Terr.*	13¾s	131¾E	60
Pine Point, *N.W. Can.*	61N	114W	66
Pine Ridge, *S.D., U.S.A.*	43N	102½W	74
Pinega River, *U.S.S.R.*	64¼N	42E	38
Pinehill, *Queens., Aust.*	23¾s	147E	60
Pinerolo, *Italy.*	44¾N	7¼E	31
Pines, I. of, *Pacific.*	23½s	165E	64
Pinetown, *Natal.*	29¾s	30¾E	55
Piney, *France.*	48¼N	4¼E	30
Ping, Riv., *Thailand.*	14N	101E	43
Pingchuan, *China.*	41N	119E	48
Pingelap I., *Pacific.*	7N	161E	64
Pingelly, *W. Australia.*	32½s	117E	61
Pingin, *W. Australia.*	30s	123E	61
Pingliang, *China.*	35½N	107E	48
Pinglo, *China.*	38N	106E	48
Pinglo, *China.*	25N	110¼E	48
Pingrup, *W. Australia.*	33½s	118½E	61
Pingting, *China.*	38N	113½E	48
Pingtung, *Formosa.*	22½N	120E	48
Pingwu, *China.*	32½N	104¾E	48
Pingyang, see LINFEN.			
Pinhel, *Portugal.*	40¾N	7¼W	35
Pini I., *Sumatra, Indon.*	0	98E	47
Pininoa, *N.I., N.Z.*, (inset B).			62
Pinjarra, *W. Australia.*	32½s	116E	61
Pinkiang, *China*	29N	113E	48
Pilgrim's Rest, *T'vaal*	24¾s	30¾E	54
Pinkilla, *Queens., Aust.*	27s	144E	60
Pinnarro, *S. Australia.*	35¼s	141E	59
Pinos, I. de, *Cuba.*	21¾N	82¾W	77
Pinsk, *U.S.S.R.*	52¼N	26E	38
Piobesi, *Italy.*	45N	7½E	31
Piombino, *Italy.*	43N	10½E	36
Pioneer I., *U.S.S.R.*	80N	90E	39
Piotrkow, *Poland.*	51½N	19¾E	33
Piove, *Italy.*	45¼N	12E	31
Piraeus, *Greece.*	38N	23½E	37
Pirapora, *Brazil.*	17½s	45W	79
Pirgos, *Greece.*	36½N	22½E	37
Pirgos, *Crete.*	35N	25E	37
Pirmasens, *Germany.*	49¼N	7½E	33
Pirna, *Germany.*	51N	14E	33
Pirot, *Yugoslavia.*	43¼N	22½E	37
Piru, *Serang, Indonesia.*	3s	128¼E	47
Pisa, *Italy.*	43¾N	10½E	36
Pisco, *Peru.*	13¾s	76¼W	78
Pisek, *Czechoslovakia.*	49½N	14¼E	33
Pishin, *Pakistan.*	30¾N	67E	46
Pishpek, see FRUNZE.			
Pistoia, *Italy.*	44N	11E	36
Pisuerga Riv., *Spain.*	41¾N	5W	35
Pitcairn I., *Pacific.*	25s	130W	64
Pite, Riv., *Sweden.*	65N	21½E	29
Pitea, *Sweden.*	65½N	21¼E	29
Pitesti, *Romania.*	44¾N	24¾E	37
Pithara, *W. Australia.*	30½s	117E	61
Pithiviers, *France.*	48¼N	2¼E	30
Pitlochry, *Scotland.*	56¾N	3¾W	24
Pitlyar, *U.S.S.R.*	66N	66E	38
Pito, *Panama.*	8N	77½W	77
Pitsani, *Botswana.*	25¾s	25E	54
Pitsanulok, *Thailand.*	17N	101E	43
Pitt I., *Br. Col., Can.*	53½N	130W	72
Pittsburgh, *Pa., U.S.A.*	40½N	80W	75
Pittsfield, *Mass., U.S.A.*	42½N	73¼W	69
Pittsworth, *Queens.*	27¾s	152E	60
Piura, *Peru.*	5¼s	80½W	78
P. Kesch, Mt., *Switz.*	46½N	9¾E	31
Placentia & B., *Newf.*	47¼N	54W	67
Plainfield, *U.S.* (inset).	40¾N	74W	75
Plainview, *Tex., U.S.A.*	34¼N	102W	74
Plana Cays, *Bahamas.*	22½N	73½W	77
Plancoet, *France.*	48½N	2¼W	31
Plasencia, *Spain.*	40N	6W	35
Plaston, *T'vaal, S. Afr.*	25¼s	31E	54
Plateau des Minquiers, *English Channel.*	49N	2W	31
Plati, *Greece.*	40½N	22½E	37
Platinum, *Alaska.* (ins.)	59¾N	161W	74
Platte, R., *Nebr., U.S.A.*	41N	98W	74
Plauen, *Germany.*	50½N	12¼E	33
Plav, *Yugoslavia.*	42½N	20E	37
Plelan, *France.*	48N	2W	31
Plenty, B. of, *N.I., N.Z.*	37¾s	177E	62
Plentywood, *U.S.A.*	48N	105W	74
Plesetsk, *U.S.S.R.*	63N	40E	38
Plesivec, *Czecho.*	48½N	20½E	33
Pleszew, *Poland.*	51¾N	17½E	33
Plettenberg B., *C. Pr.*	34s	23½E	52
Pleven, *Bulgaria.*	43½N	24½E	37
Pljevlja, *Yugoslavia.*	43½N	19¼E	37
Plock, *Poland.*	52½N	19¾E	33
Ploermel, *France.*	48N	2¼W	31
Ploesti, *Romania.*	45N	26E	37
Plombieres, *France.*	48N	6½E	32
Plon, *Germany.*	54¼N	10½E	33
Plonsk, *Poland.*	52½N	20½E	33
Plouaret, *France.*	48½N	3½W	31
Plovdiv, *Bulgaria.*	42¼N	24¾E	37
Plum Coulee, *Canada.*	49¼N	97¾W	71
Plumtree, *Rhodesia.*	20½s	27¾E	51
Plymouth, *England.*	50½N	4¼W	22
Plymouth, *Mass., U.S.A.*	42N	70¾W	69
Plymouth, *N.H., U.S.A.*	43¾N	71¾W	69
Plymouth, *Tobago* (ins.).	12N	60W	77
Plympton, *England.*	50½N	4W	22
Plynlimon, *Wales.*	52½N	3¾W	22
Plzen, *Czechoslovakia.*	49¾N	13½E	33
Pnom Penh, *Cambodia.*	11½N	105E	47
Po River, *Italy.*	45N	12¼E	36
Pocatello, *Id., U.S.A.*	42¾N	112½W	74
Pochutla, *Mexico*	15¾N	96½W	76
Pocklington, *England.*	54N	¾W	23
Poctun, *Guatemala.*	17N	89W	76
Podebrady, *Czecho.*	50¼N	15¼E	33
Podgorica, see TITOGRAD.			
Podkamennaya, *U.S.S.R.*	62N	90E	39
Podporozhye, *U.S.S.R.*	60¾N	33¾E	38
Podolsk, *U.S.S.R.*	55½N	37½E	38
Poggibonsi, *Italy.*	43½N	11¼E	36
Pogradec, *Albania.*	40¾N	20¾E	37
Pohang, *Korea.*	36N	129E	49
Poinsett, C., *Antarc.*	65½s	112½E	80
Point Pedro, *Ceylon.*	9¾N	80¼E	45
Pointe-a-Pitre, *W. In.*	16¼N	61½W	77
Pointe Noire, *Congo (B.)*	4¾s	11¾E	56
Poirino, *Italy.*	45N	7¾E	31
Poissy, *France.*	49N	2¼E	30
Poitiers, *France.*	46½N	½E	32
POITOU *France.*	46½N	1W	32
Poix, *France.*	49¾N	2E	30
Pokaakku I., *Pacific.*	15N	169E	64
Pokataroo, *N.S.W.*	29½s	148½E	59
Pokotu, *China.*	49N	121E	39
Pokrovsk, *U.S.S.R.*	61½N	129¼E	39
Pola, see PULA.			
POLAND, *Europe.*			33
Polatli, *Turkey.*	39¾N	32½E	41
Polgar, *Hungary.*	47¾N	21E	37
Poli, *Cameroon.*	8½N	13½E	56
Poli, *China.*	46N	130½E	49
Policastro & G. of, *It.*	40N	15¾E	36
Poligny, *France.*	46¾N	5¾E	31
Polillo Is., *Luzon, P.I.*	15N	122E	47
Polis, *Cyprus.*	35N	32E	41
Polla, *Italy.*	40½N	15¼E	36
Pollensa, *Balearic Is.*	40N	3E	35
Polnovat, *U.S.S.R.*	63½N	66E	38
Polonnaruwa, *Ceylon.*	8N	81E	45
Polotsk, *U.S.S.R.*	55½N	28¾E	38
Poltava, *U.S.S.R.*	49½N	34½E	38
Polui River, *U.S.S.R.*	66½N	67E	38
Polwysep Hel, *Poland.*	55N	19E	33
Polyarny, *U.S.S.R.*	69N	33E	29
POLYNESIA, *Pacific.*	0	170W	64
Pombal, *Portugal.*	40N	8¾W	35
Pomene, *Mozambique.*	22½s	36E	51
Pomeranian B., *Ger.*	54½N	14¼E	33
Pomeroy, *W. Aust.*	22½s	117½E	61
Pomona, *Calif., U.S.A.*	34N	118W	74
Pomorie, *Bulgaria.*	42½N	27½E	37
Pompeii, *Italy.*	40¾N	14¾E	36
Ponape I., *Pacific.*	7N	158E	64
Ponca City, *Okla., U.S.A.*	36¾N	97W	75
Ponce, *Puerto Rico.*	18N	66¾W	77
Pond Inlet, *Canada.*	72½N	77W	66
Pondicherry, *India.*	12N	79¾E	45
Pondoland, *C.Pr., S.Af.*	31½s	29½E	53
Ponferrada, *Spain.*	42½N	6¾W	35
Ponnaiyar Riv., *India.*	11¾N	79½E	45
Ponoi, *U.S.S.R.*	67N	41E	38
Ponoka, *Alberta, Can.*	52½N	113½W	73
Pont Aven, *France.*	48N	3¾W	31
Pont Canavese, *Italy.*	45½N	7½E	31
Pont Erwyd, *Wales.*	52½N	4W	22
Pont L'Abbe, *France.*	48N	4¼W	31
Pont Leccia, *Corsica.*	42½N	9¼E	36
Pont L'Eveque, *France.*	49¼N	¼E	32
Ponta Delgada, *Azores.*	37¾N	26W	35
Ponta Grossa, *Brazil.*	25s	50¼W	79
Pont-a-Mousson, *Fr.*	49N	6¼E	30
Pontardawe, *Wales.*	51¾N	3¾W	22
Pontarlier, *France.*	46¾N	6¼E	32
Pontaubault, *France.*	48½N	1¼W	31
Pontchateau, *France.*	47½N	2W	31
Pontchartrain, L., *U.S.*	30N	90W	75
Ponte, *Italy.*	46¼N	10E	31
Pontedera, *Italy.*	43½N	10½E	36
Pontefract, *England.*	53¾N	1¼W	23
Ponte San Pietro, *Italy.*	45¾N	9½E	31
Pontevedra, *Spain.*	42½N	8¾W	35
Ponthierville, *Congo (K.)*	½s	25½E	56
Pontianak, *Kal., Indon.*	½s	109E	47
Ponti Di Piave, *Italy.*	45¾N	12½E	31
Pontine Is., *Italy.*	40¾N	13E	36
Pontivy, *France.*	48N	3W	31
Pontoise, *France.*	49¼N	2E	32
Ponto Tolle, *Italy.*	45N	12¼E	31
Pontorson, *France.*	48½N	1½W	31
Pontremoli, *Italy.*	44½N	9¾E	36
Pontresina, *Switz.*	46½N	9¾E	31
Pontrieux, *France.*	48¾N	3W	31
Pontrilas, *Wales.*	52N	3W	22
Pont St. Vincent, *Fr.*	48½N	6E	30
Pontville, *Tasmania.*	42¾s	147½E	59
Pontypool, *England.*	51¾N	3W	22
Pontypridd, *Wales.*	51½N	3¼W	22
Ponza, I. of, *Italy.*	41N	13E	36
Poole, *England.*	50¾N	2W	23
Poolewe, *Scotland.*	57¾N	5¾W	24
Poonboon, *N.S.W., Aust.*	35s	143½E	59
Poona, *India.*	18½N	74E	45
Pooncarie, *N.S.W.*	33½s	142½E	59

Place	Lat.	Long.	No.
Poopelloe, L., N.S.W.	31½s	144E	59
Poopo, L., Bolivia.	19s	67w	79
Poortje, C. Pr., S. Afr.	30¼s	22½E	52
Popayan, Colombia.	2¼N	76¼w	78
Poperinghe, Belgium.	50¾N	2¾E	30
Poplar Bluff, Missouri.	37N	90w	75
Poplar, Mon., U.S.A.	48N	105w	74
Popocatepetl, Mt.,Mex.	18½N	98½w	76
Popoli, Italy.	42¼N	14E	36
Poprad, Czechoslovakia.	49N	20¼E	33
Populonia, Italy.	43N	10¼E	36
Porali Riv., Pakistan.	25¼N	65½E	43
Porbandar, India.	21½N	69¾E	43
Porcher I., Br. Col., Can.	54N	130¼w	72
Porcupine R., Alaska.	66¼N	145w	66
Porec, Yugoslavia.	45¼N	13½E	36
Porhoet, France.	48¼N	2¼w	32
Pori, Finland.	61¼N	21½E	29
Porjus, Sweden.	67N	20E	38
Porkhov, U.S.S.R.	57¼N	29½E	38
Porkkala, Finland.	60N	25E	29
Porlamar, Venezuela.	11¼N	64w	77
Porlock, England.	51¼N	3½w	22
Pornic, France.	47¼N	2¼w	32
Porpoise B., Antarctica.	67s	128E	80
Porrentruy, Switz.	47¼N	7E	31
Porsanger Fjord, Nor.	71N	26E	29
Port Adelaide, S. Aust.	34¾s	138½E	59
Porta Dell Alice, Italy.	39¼N	17E	36
Portadown, N. Ire.	54¼N	6¼w	26
Portaferry, N Ireland	54¼N	5¼w	26
Portage la Prairie, Can.	50N	98¼w	71
Portal, N. Dak., U.S.A.	49N	103w	74
Port Alberni, Br. Col.	49¼N	124¾w	72
Port Albert, Vict., Aust.	38¾s	146¾E	59
Portalegre, Portugal.	39¼N	7¼w	35
Port Alexandre, Angola.	16s	12E	56
Port Alfred, C. Pr.	33¼s	27E	53
Port Alice, Br. Col.	50¼N	127¼w	72
Port Alma, Queens.	23¼s	151E	60
Port Amielia, Mozam.	13s	40½E	56
Port Angeles, U.S.A.	48¼N	123½w	74
Port Antonio, Jam.	18¼N	76¼w	77
Portarlington, Ire.	53¼N	7¼w	26
Port Arthur, see LÜSHUN			
Port Arthur,Ont.,Can.	48¼N	89¼w	68
Port Arthur, Tas., Aust.	43¼s	148E	59
Port Askaig, Scotland.	55¼N	6¼w	25
Port Augusta, S. Aust.	32¼s	137¾E	59
Port au Prince, Haiti.	18¼N	72¼w	77
Port-aux-Basques,Can.	47¼N	59¼w	67
Port Beaufort, C. Pr.	34¼s	20¾E	52
Port Blair, Andaman Is.	11¼N	92¾E	43
Port Bradshaw, Aust.	12s	137¼E	60
Port Burwell, Newf.	60N	64w	66
Port Chalmers, N.Z.	45¾s	170¾E	63
Port Charles, Australia.	12s	131E	60
Port Chester, U.S.A.	41N	74w	70
Port Clinton, Queens.	22¼s	151E	60
Port Cloates, W. Aust.	22¼s	113¾E	61
Port Colborne, Ont.	42¾N	79¼w	68
Port Coquitlam, Can.	49¼N	122¾w	72
Port Curtis, Queens.	23¼s	151¼E	60
Port Danger, Queens.	28s	154E	60
Port Darwin, N. Terr.	12s	131E	60
Port Davey, Tas., Aust.	43¼s	146E	59
Port de Paix, Haiti, W.I.	20N	72¼w	77
Port Dickson, Malaysia.	2¼N	101¾E	47
Port Douglas, Queens.	16¼s	145½E	60
Port Dover, Ont., Can.	42¾N	80¼w	68
Port Elgin, Ont., Can.	44¼N	81¼w	68
Port Elizabeth, C. Pr.	34s	25¾E	53
Port Ellen, Scotland.	55¼N	6¼w	25
Port Erin, I. of M., Eng.	54¼N	4¾w	25
Porterville, C. Pr., S. Af.	33s	19E	52
Port Essington, Can.	54¼N	130w	72
Port Essington, Aust.	11s	132E	60
Port Etienne, Mauritania.	20¾N	17w	50
Port Fairy, Vict., Aust.	38¼s	142¼E	59
Port Francqui, Congo (K.).	4¼s	20¼E	56
Port Gentil, Gabon.	1s	8¼E	56
Port Glasgow, Scot.	56N	4¾w	25
Port Hardy, Br. Col.	50¼N	127¼w	72
Port Harcourt, Nigeria.	4¼N	7E	57
Port Hassan II,Morocco.	34¼N	6¼w	35
Port Hawkesbury, Can.	45¼N	61¼w	67
Porthcawl, Wales.	51¼N	3¾w	22
Port Headland, W. Aust.	20¼s	118¼E	61
Port Herald, see NSANJE			
Port Hood, C. Breton I.	46N	61¼w	67
Port Hope, Ont., Can.	44N	78¼w	69
Port Huron, Michigan.	43N	82¼w	68
Portimao, Portugal.	37¼N	8¼w	35
Portishead, England.	51¼N	2¾w	22
Port Kembla, N.S.W.	34¼s	150¾E	59
Portland England.	50¼N	2¼w	22
Portland, Me., U.S.A.	43¾N	70¼w	69
Portland, N.S.W., Aust.	33¼s	150E	59
Portland, Ore., U.S.A.	45¼N	122¾w	74
Portland B., Vict., Aust.	38¼s	141¾E	59
Portland, C., Tas., Aust.	40¼s	148E	59
Portland Promontory, Quebec, Canada.	59N	78w	66
Portland Pt., Jamaica, W.I. (inset).	17¼N	77w	77
Portlaoighise, Eire.	53N	7¼w	26
Portlethen, Scotland.	57N	2w	24
Port Lincoln, S. Aust.	34¼s	136E	59
Port Logan, Scotland.	54¼N	5w	25
Port Louis, France.	47¼N	3¼w	31
Port Lyttelton,S.I.,N.Z. (inset C).			
Port McArthur, Aust.	16s	136E	60
Port Macquarie, Aust.	31¼s	153E	59
Portmadoc, Wales.	52¾N	4¼w	22
Portmahomack, Scot.	57¾N	3¾w	24
Port Maria, Jamaica, W.I. (inset).	18¼N	77¼w	77
Port Martin, Antarc.	67s	142E	80
Port Maud, W. Aust.	23s	114E	61
Port Menier, Que., Can.	49¼N	64¼w	67
Port Moody, Br. Col.	49¼N	122¾w	72
Port Moresby, N. Guin.	9½s	147½E	60
Port Musgrave, Aust.	11s	142E	60
Portnacroish, Scot.	56¼N	5¼w	24
Port Nelson, Man., Can.	57N	92¼w	71
Portneuf, Que., Can.	46¾N	72w	69
Port Nicholson, N.I., N.Z. (inset B).			62
Port Nolloth, C. Pr.	29¼s	16¾E	52
Porto, Corsica.	42¼N	8¾E	36
Porto Alegre, Brazil.	30s	51w	79
Porto Amboim, Angola.	11s	13¼E	56
Porto Bello, Moz.	17s	37E	56
Portobello, Scotland.	56N	3w	25
Portobello, Panama.	9¼N	79¾w	77
Porto Civitanova, It.	43¼N	13¾E	36
Porto de Santa Maria, Spain.	36¼N	6¼w	35
Porto Empedocle, It.	37¼N	13¾E	36
Porto Esperanca, Braz.	19¼s	57¼w	79
Port Franco, Para.	22s	59w	78
Port of Ness, Scotland.	58¼N	6¼w	24
Port of Spain, Trin.	10¼N	61¼w	77
Portogandi, Panama.	9N	78w	77
Porto Garibaldi, Italy.	44¼N	12¼E	31
Port Okha, India.	22¼N	68E	43
Porto Lago, Greece.	41N	25E	37
Porto Maurizio, Italy.	43¼N	8E	36
Porto Montt, Chile.	41¼s	73w	78
Porto Novo, India.	11¼N	79¾E	43
Porto Novo, Dahomey.	6¼N	2½E	57
Porto Santo I., Madeira Islands (inset).	33N	16w	35
Porto Suarez, Bolivia.	19s	59w	78
Porto Torres, Sardinia.	40¾N	8¼E	36
Porto Vecchio, Corsica.	41¼N	9¼E	36
Porto Velho, Brazil.	8¼s	64w	78
Portpatrick, Scotland.	54¼N	5w	25
Port Pedro, Ceylon.	9¼N	80¼E	45
Port Perry, Ont., Can.	44¼N	79w	68
Port Petrovsk, see MAKHACH-KALA.			
Port Phillip Bay, Aust.	38s	144¾E	59
Port Pirie, S. Aust.	33¼s	138E	59
Port Radium, N.W.Can.	66N	117w	66
Portree, Scotland.	57¼N	6¼w	24
Port Renfrew, Br. Col.	48¼N	124¾w	72
Port Rowan, Ont., Can.	42¾N	80¼w	68
Port Royal, Jamaica.	17¾N	77w	77
Portrush, N. Ireland.	55¼N	6¾w	26
Port Safaga, U.A.R.	26¼N	33¾E	41
Port Said, U.A.R.	31¼N	32¼E	50
Port St. Johns, C. Pr.	31¼s	29¼E	53
Portsall, France.	48¼N	4¾w	31
Port Shepstone, Natal.	30¼s	30¼E	55
Port Simpson, Br. Col.	54¼N	130¼w	72
Portsmouth, Dominica.	15¼N	61¼w	77
Portsmouth, England.	50¾N	1w	23
Portsmouth, U.S.A.	43N	70¼w	69
Portsmouth, Ohio, U.S.	38½N	82¾w	75
Portsmouth, Va., U.S.A.	36¾N	76¼w	75
Portsoy, Scotland.	57¾N	2¾w	24
Port Stanley, Falk. Is.	51¼s	58w	78
Port Stanley, Ont., Can.	42¾N	81¼w	68
Port Stephens, N.S.W.	32¾s	152E	59
Port Stewart, Queens.	14s	143¼E	60
Port Sudan, Sudan.	19¼N	37E	50
Port Sunlight, Eng.	53¼N	3w	22
Port Swettenham, Malaysia.	3N	101¼E	47
Port Talbot, Wales.	51¼N	3¾w	22
Port Townsend, U.S.A.	48N	122¾w	72
PORTUGAL, Europe.			35
Portugalete, Spain.	43¼N	3w	35
Portugalia, Angola.	7s	21E	56
Portuguesa R., Venez.	8¼N	68w	77
Portumna, Eire.	53¼N	8¼w	26
Port Vendres, France.	42¼N	3¼E	32
Port Wakefield, S.Aust.	34¼s	138¼E	59
Portway, England.	52N	3w	22
Port Weld, Malay (ins.).	5N	100¼E	47
Posadas, Argentina.	27¼s	56w	79
Posen, see POZNAN.			
Postmasburg, C. P.	28¼s	23E	52
Potchefstroom, T'vaal.	26¼s	27E	55
Potenza, Italy.	40¾N	15¼E	36
Poteriteri, L., S.I., N.Z.	46s	167E	63
Potfontein, C. Pr.	30¼s	24¼E	52
Potgietersrus, T'vaal.	24¼s	29E	54
Poti, U.S.S.R.	42¼N	41¾E	38
Potiskum, Nigeria.	11¼N	11¼E	57
Potomac R., Va., U.S.A.	39N	77w	74
Potosi, Bolivia.	19¼s	65¾w	79
Potrerillos, Chile.	26¼s	69¼w	79
Potrerillos, Honduras.	15N	88w	77
Potsdam, Germany.	52¼N	13E	33
Pottuvil, Ceylon.	6¾N	81¾E	45
Pouce Coupe, Br. Col.	55¼N	120¼w	72
Poughkeepsie, U.S.A.	41¾N	74w	69
Poulton-le-Fylde, Eng.	53¾N	3w	22
Poupan, C. Pr., S. Afr.	30s	24¼E	53
Poverty Bay., N.I., N.Z.	38¼s	178F	62
Povoa de Varzim, Port.	41¼N	9w	35
Povoacao, Azores (ins.).	38N	25¼w	35
Powassan, Ontario, Can.	46¼N	79¼w	68
Powder R., Mon., U.S.A.	47N	105¼w	74
Powell R., Br. Col., Can.	49¾N	124¼w	72
Powell's Creek, Aust.	17¼s	133E	60
Poyang, L., China.	29N	116¼E	48
Povarkovo, U.S.S.R.	50N	130E	39
Poza Grande, Mexico.	26N	112w	76
Pozega, Yugoslavia.	45¼N	17¼E	36
Poznan, Poland.	52¼N	17E	33
Pozoblanco, Spain.	38¼N	5w	35
Pozzuoli, Italy.	40¼N	14¼E	36
Prachin Buri, Thailand.	14N	102E	43
Prachuabkirikhan, Thailand.	12N	100E	43
Prades, France.	42¼N	2¼E	32
Prague, Czecho.	50N	14¼E	33
Prairie, Queens., Aust.	21s	144¼E	60
Prairie R., Sask., Can.	53N	103w	70
Prampram, Ghana.	5¾N	¼E	57
Pran Kao, Thailand.	12¼N	100E	43
Prato, Italy.	43¾N	11E	36
Pratt, Kansas, U.S.A.	37¼N	99w	74
Pre, Thailand.	18N	100E	43
Prebbleton, S.I., N.Z.		(inset C).	
Precenicco, Italy.	46N	13E	36
Predazzo, Italy.	46¼N	11¼E	31
Predoi, Italy.	47N	12E	31
Preeceville, Sask., Can.	52	102¼w	70
Pre-en-Pail, France.	48¼N	¼w	31
Pregel, R. U.S.S.R.	54¼N	20¼E	33
Premeno, Italy.	46N	8¼E	31
Premier Mine, T'vaal.	25¼s	28¼E	51
Prenzlau, Germany.	53¼N	13¼E	33
Prerov, Czecho.	49¼N	17¼E	33
Prespa, L. of Yugo.	41N	21E	37
Presque I., Me., U.S.A.	46¾N	68w	67
Presov, Czecho.	49N	21¼E	33
Pre St. Didier, Italy.	45¼N	7E	31
Prescott, Ariz., U.S.A.	34¼N	112¼w	74
Prescott, Ont., Can.	44¼N	75¼w	69
Presevo, Yugoslavia.	42¼N	21¼E	37
Prestatyn, England.	53¼N	3¼w	22
Preston, England.	53¼N	2¾w	22
Preston, C., W. Aust.	21s	116E	61
Preston, Ontario, Can.	43¼N	80¼w	68
Prestonpans, Scotland.	56N	3w	25
Prestwick, Scotland.	55¼N	4¼w	25
Pretoria, T'vaal, S.Afr.	25¼s	28¼E	54
Prevesa, Greece.	39N	20¾E	37
Pribor, Czecho.	49¼N	18¼E	33
Pribram, Czecho.	49¼N	14E	33
Price, Utah, U.S.A.	39¼N	111w	74
Priekule, U.S.S.R.	55¼N	21¼E	33
Prieska, C., Pr., S. Afr.	29¼s	22¼E	52
Prijedor, Yugoslavia.	45N	16¼E	36
Prijepolje, Yugoslavia.	43¼N	19¼E	37
Prilep, Yugoslavia.	41¼N	21¼E	37
Priluki, U.S.S.R.	51N	32¼E	38
Primorsko Akhtarskaya, U.S.S.R.	46N	38E	38
PRIMORYE, U.S.S.R.	46N	136E	39
Prince Albert, C. Pr.	33¼s	22E	52
Prince Albert, Sask.	53¼N	105¼w	70
Prince Albert National Park, Sask., Can.	54N	106w	70
Prince Albert, Pen. & Sound, N.W.Can.	72N	115w	66
Pr. Albert Rd., C. Pr.	33s	21¾E	52
Pr. Alfred, C., N.W.Can.	73N	125w	66
Pr. Charles I., N.W.T.	67¼N	75¾w	66
Pr. Charles Mts., Antarc.	71s	68E	80
PRINCE EDWARD I., Can.	46¼N	63w	67
Prince George, Br. Col.	53¾N	122¾w	72
Pr. Harald Co., Antarc.	69s	36E	80
Prince of Wales I., Alaska, U.S.A.	55¼N	133w	65
Pr. of Wales I., N.W.T.	73N	99w	66
Pr. of Wales I., Queens.	10¼s	142E	60
Prince of Wales Strait, N.W. Canada.	73N	119w	66
Pr. Patrick I., N.W.Can.	75N	120w	66
Prince Rupert, Br. Col.	54¼N	130¼w	72
Princes Risborough, England.	51¾N	¾w	23
Princess Astridld, Antarctic.	70¼s	15E	80
Princess Charlotte B., Queensland, Aust.	14¼s	144E	60
Princess Eliz. Ld., Antarctic.	70s	75E	80
Princess Royal I., Can.	53N	129w	72
Prince's Town, Trinidad, W. Indies (inset).	10¼N	61w	77
Princeton, Br. Col.	49¼N	120¼w	72
Principe I., W. Africa.	1¼N	7¼E	57
Priors, C. Pr., S. Afr.	30¼s	25¼E	55
Priorzersk, U.S.S.R.	61¼N	30E	38
Prinzapolca, Nicarag.	13N	84w	77
Pripet Riv., U.S.S.R.	51¼N	31E	38
Pristina, Yugoslavia.	42¼N	21¼E	37
Privas, France.	44¼N	4¼E	32
Prizren, Yugoslavia.	42¼N	20¾E	37
Prizzi, Sicily.	37¾N	13¼E	36
Progreso, Mexico.	21¼N	89¾w	76
Progreso, El, Hond.	15N	88w	77
Prokopevsk, U.S.S.R.	54N	86¾E	39
Prome, Burma.	18¼N	95¼E	43
Promontorio, Mexico.	25N	105w	76
Proserpine, Queens.	20¼s	148¼E	60
Prosna Riv., Poland.	51¼N	17¾E	33
Prostejov, Czecho.	49¼N	17¼E	33
Proston, Queens., Aust.	26¼s	151¼E	60
Protem, C. Pr., S. Afr.	34¼s	20E	52
Protivin, Czecho.	49¼N	14¼E	33
Provadiya, Bulgaria.	43N	27¼E	37
PROVENCE, France.		43E	32
Providence, N.W.T.	61¼N	117¼w	66
Providence Cha., W.I.	26N	76¾w	77
Providence, C., S.I., N.Z.	46s	166¾E	63
Providence, R.I.,U.S.A.	41¾N	71¼w	69
Providencia, I. de., W.I.	13N	82w	77
Providenciales, Baham.	22N	72¼w	77
Provins, France.	48¼N	3¼E	32
Provo, Utah, U.S.A.	40¼N	111½w	74
Provost, Alberta, Can.	52¼N	110¼w	73
Prozor, Yugoslavia.	43¾N	17¼E	36
Prudnik, Poland.	50¼N	17¾E	33
Prum, Germany.	50¼N	6¼E	30
Pruszkow, Poland.	52¼N	20¾E	33
Prut Riv., Romania.	45N	28E	37
Pruzana, U.S.S.R.	52¼N	24¾E	33
Prydz B., Antarctica.	69¼s	75¼E	80
Przemysl, Poland.	49¾N	22¾E	33
Przhevalsk, U.S.S.R.	42N	78¼E	39
Pskov, U.S.S.R.	57¼N	28¼E	38
Proskuro, U.S.S.R.	49N	27E	38
Ptuj, Yugoslavia.	46¼N	16E	36
Puchov, Czecho.	49¼N	18¼E	33
Puck, Poland.	54¼N	18¼E	33
Puckford, Mt., W. Aust.	25s	116E	61
Pudimoe, C. Pr., S.Afr.	27¼s	25E	51
Pudukkottai, India.	10¼N	79E	45
PUEBLA, Mexico.	18N	98w	76
Puebla de Treves, Sp.	42¼N	7¼w	35
Pueblo, Colo., U.S.A.	38¼N	104¾w	74
Pueblo Nuevo, Panama.	8N	82w	77
Pueblo Nuevo, Venez.	12N	70w	77
Puentedeume, Spain.	43¼N	8¼w	35
Puerh, China.	23N	101¼E	43
Puerta Angel, Mexico.	15¼N	96¼w	76
Pto. Armuelles, Panama.	8N	83w	77
Pto. Ayacucho, Colombia.	6N	67¼w	77
Puerto Barrios, Guate.	15¼N	88¼w	76
Puerto Berrio, Colom.	6¼N	74¼w	77
Puerto Cabello, Venez.	10¼N	68w	77
Pto. Cabezas, Nicarag.	14¼N	84w	77
Pto. Carreno, Colombia.	6N	67¼w	77
Puerto Castillo, Honduras.	16N	86w	77
Pto. Cortes, Costa Rica.	9¼N	84w	77
Puerto Cortez, Hond.	15¼N	88w	77
Puerto Deseado, Arg.	47¼s	66w	78
Pto. Esperanca, Brazil.	19¼s	57¼w	79
Pto. Estrella, Colombia.	12¼N	72w	77
Pta. Gallinas,Colombia.	12¼N	72w	77
Pta. Gorda, Br. Hond.	16N	88w	76
Pto. Maldonado, Peru.	12¼s	69w	79
Puerto Mexico, see COATZACOALCOS.			
Puerto Montt, Chile.	41¼s	73w	78
Puerto Plata, Dominica.	20N	70¼w	77
Puerto Princesa, P.I.	9¼N	118¾E	47
PUERTO RICO I., W.I.	18N	66w	77
Puerto Wilches, Colom.	7¼N	73¾w	77
Pugachev, U.S.S.R.	52N	49E	38
Puget Sound, U.S.A.	47¼N	123w	72
Puianne, L. of, Fin.	61N	25E	29
Pukaki, L., S.I., N.Z.	44s	170¼E	63
Pukapuka I., Pacific.	14s	139w	64
Pukekohe, N.I., N.Z.	37¼s	175E	62
Puket, Thailand.	7¾N	98¼E	47
Pukow, China.	32N	118E	48
Pula, Sardinia.	39N	9E	36
Pula, Yugoslavia.	45N	13¾E	36
Pulap I., Pacific.	9N	149E	64
Pulaski, Tenn., U.S.A.	35N	87w	75
Pulawy, Poland.	51¼N	22E	33
Pulicat, & L., India.	13¼N	80¼E	45
Pullman, Wash., U.S.A.	47N	117¼w	74
Pultusk, Poland.	53N	21E	33
Pulusuk I., Pacific.	8N	145E	64
Pumbridge, L's, W.Aust.	29s	125E	61
Pumpsaint, Wales.	52N	4w	22
Punaka, Bhutan.	27¼N	90E	44
Punch, India.	33¼N	74E	44
Puneh, Kash. (inset).	34N	74E	44
Punganuru, India.	13¼N	78¼E	45
Punge, Riv., Mozam.	20s	35E	51
Pungsan, Korea.	41N	128E	49
Punia, Lith., U.S.S.R.	54¼N	24E	33
PUNJAB, India.	31N	77E	43
Puno, Peru.	15s	70w	79
Punta Arenas, Chile.	53s	71w	78
Puntarenas, Costa Rica.	10N	85w	77
Pur River, U.S.S.R.	67N	78E	39
Purari R., Papua (inset).	8s	145E	60
Purchena, Spain.	37¼N	2¼w	35
Puri, India.	19¾N	85¾E	45
Purley, England.	51¼N	0	23
Purnea, India.	25¼N	87¼E	44
Purus, Riv., Brazil.	4s	61w	78
Purulia, India.	23¼N	86¼E	44
Pusan, Korea.	35¼N	129E	49
Pushkino, U.S.S.R.	51¼N	47E	38
Pusht-i-Badam, Iran.	33N	56E	40
Putaruru, N.I., N.Z.	38s	175¾E	62
Putien, China.	25¼N	119E	48
Puting, C., Borneo, E.I.	3s	112E	47
Putla, Mexico.	17N	97¼w	76
Putsonderwater, C.Pr.	29¼s	21¼E	52
Puttalam, Ceylon.	8N	79¾E	45
Puttelange, France.	49N	6¾E	30
Putumayo R., Colombia.	4s	70w	78
PUY DE DOME, France.	45¼N	3E	32
Pwllheli, Wales.	52¾N	4¾w	22
Pyandzh R., Afghan.	37N	70¾E	43
Pyapon, Burma.	16¼N	95¾E	43
Pyasina Riv., U.S.S.R.	73¼N	85¼E	39
Pyasinski B., U.S.S.R.	73N	85E	39
Pyatigorsk, U.S.S.R.	44N	43E	38
Pyinmana, Burma.	19¾N	96¼E	43
Pyongyang, Korea.	39N	125¾E	49
Pyrenees Mts., Fr.-Sp.		43E	32
PYRENEES ORIENTALES, France.	42¼N	2¼E	32
Pyrgos, Greece.	37¼N	21¼E	37
Pyrzyce, Poland.	53¼N	15E	33

[124] Qacha's Nek—Rimatara

Place	Lat.	Long.	No.
QACHA'S NEK, *Lesotho*	30s	28½E	35
Qaf, *Saudi Arabia.*	31½N	37½E	41
Qain, *Iran.*	34N	60E	40
Qairwan, see KAIROUAN.			
Qais, *Iran.*	26N	54E	40
Qaisuma, *Saudi Arabia.*	29N	43E	41
Qal'at Al Akhdar, *Sa. Ar.*	28N	37½E	41
Qal'at Al Mu'adhdham, *Saudi Arabia.*	27½N	37½E	41
Qal'at Sura, *Sa. Arabia.*	26½N	38½E	40
Qalqilya, *Israel* (ins.).	32¼N	34¾E	40
Qamata, *C. Pr., S. Afr.*	32s	27½E	53
Qana, *Saudi Arabia.*	28N	42E	40
Qara, *U.A.R.*	29½N	26½E	40
Qara Boghaz, G. of, *U.S.S.R.*	41N	53½E	38
Qara Qum *U.S.S.R.*	39N	60E	40
Qaraghan, *Iraq.*	34N	44E	41
Qasr Farafra, *U.A.R.*	26½N	27½E	41
Qasrqand, *Iran.*	27N	60½E	40
Qatar Pen., *Arabia.*	25½N	51½E	40
Qatif, *Saudi Arabia.*	26½N	50E	40
Qattara Dep., *U.A.R.*	30N	27½E	41
Qena, *U.A.R.*	26½N	32½E	50
Qila Saifullah, *Paki.*	30½N	68½E	46
Qishm & I., *Iran.*	26N	56E	40
Qishn, *S. Yemen.* (ins.).	15½N	51½E	40
Qizan, *Saudi Arabia.*	17N	42½E	40
Qizil Uzun R., *Iran.*	37N	49E	41
Qomul, *China.*	42½N	93½E	39
Qoqodala, *C. Pr.*	31½s	27E	53
Quairading, *W. Aust.*	32s	117½E	61
Quang Ngai, *Vietnam.*	15N	108½E	47
Quang Tri, *Vietnam.*	16½N	107½E	47
Qu'Appelle, *Sask. Can.*	50½N	104w	70
Quartu S. Elena, *Sard.*	39½N	9E	36
Quatre Bras, *Belgium.*	50½N	4½E	30
Quatsino, *Canada.*	50½N	127½w	72
Quchan, *Iran*	37N	58E	40
Que Que, *Rhodesia.*	19s	30E	51
Queanbeyan, *N.S.W.*	35½s	149E	59
QUEBEC, *Canada.*	54N	70w	66
Quebec, *Quebec, Can.*	46½N	71¼w	69
Qn. Charlotte Is., *Can.*	53N	132w	66
Qn. Elizabeth Cape, *Tasmania* (inset).	43½s	148E	59
Qn. Elizabeth Is., *N.W. Canada.*	77N	100w	66
Qn. Mary Ld., *Antarc.*	68s	95E	80
Qn. Maud G., *N.W.Can.*	68N	101w	66
Qn. Maud Ld., *Antarc.*	75s	15E	80
Qn. Maud Ra., *Antarc.*	85½s	165w	80
Queens, *N.Y., U.S.A.*	41N	74w	75
Queensberry, Mt., *Scot.*	55½N	3½w	25
Queenscliff, *Victoria.*	38½s	144½E	59
Queensferry, *Scotland.*	56N	3½w	25
QUEENSLAND, *Aust.*	23s	146E	58
Queenstown, *C. Pr.*	31½s	27E	53
Queenstown, *Eire*, see COBH.			
Queenstown, *S.I., N.Z.*	45s	168½E	63
Queenstown, *Tasmania.*	42s	145½E	59
Quedlinburg, *Ger.*	51½N	11E	33
Quelimane, *Mozam.*	17½s	37E	51
Quelite, *Mexico.*	23½N	106½w	76
Quelpart I., *Korea.*	33N	127E	49
Quemoy, I., *China.*	24½N	118E	48
Quentin, *France.*	48½N	3w	31
QUERETARO, *Mexico.*	20½N	100½w	76
Querobabi, *Mexico.*	30N	111w	76
Quesnel & R., *Canada.*	53N	122½w	72
Quesnel, L., *Br. Col.*	52½N	121w	72
Quetico, *Ont., Can.*	48½N	91w	71
Quetta, *Pakistan.*	30N	66½E	43
Quezaltenango, *Guat.*	15N	92w	76
Quezon, *Luzon, P.I.*	15N	121E	47
Quibdo, *Colombia.*	5½N	76½w	77
Quiberon, *France.*	47½N	3w	32
Quiberon & B., *France.*	47½N	3w	31
Quigley, *Alberta, Can.*	56½N	111w	73
Quill Lakes, *Sask.*	51½N	104½w	70
Quilon, *India.*	9N	76½E	45
Quilpie, *Queens., Aust.*	27s	144½E	60
Quimper, *France.*	48N	4w	31
Quimperle, *France.*	48N	3½w	31
Quincy, *Ill., U.S.A.*	40N	91½w	75
Qui Nhon, *Vietnam.*	13½N	109E	47
Quintanar de la Orden, *Spain.*	39½N	3w	35
QUINTANA ROO, *Mexico.*	20N	88w	76
Quirindi, *N.S.W., Aust.*	31½s	150½E	59
Quisico, *Mozambique.*	25s	35E	51
Quito, *Ecuador.*	¼s	78½w	78
Quita Sueno Bank, *W.I.*	14N	81w	77
Qum, *Iran.*	34½N	51E	40
Qumbu, *C. Pr., S. Afr.*	31½s	28½E	53
Quorn, *S. Australia.*	32½s	138E	59
Quryat, *Mus. & Oman.*	23½N	59E	40
Qusaiyir, *S. Yemen.*	15N	50E	40
Quseir, *U.A.R.*	25½N	34E	41
Quthing, *Lesotho.*	30½s	27½E	53
RAAHE, *Finland.*	64½N	25E	29
Raasay, I. *Scotland.*	57½N	6w	24
Rab Is., *Yugoslavia.*	44½N	14½E	36
Raba Riv., *Hungary.*	47½N	17½E	37
Rabat, *Morocco.*	34N	7w	35
Rabaul, *N. Brit., Pac.*	4½s	152½E	64
Rabigh, *Saudi Arabia.*	22½N	39E	40
Racconigi, *Italy.*	44½N	7½E	31
Race, C., *Newf., Can.*	46½N	53¼w	67
Rachov, *U.S.S.R.*	48N	24½E	37
Raciborz, *Poland.*	50N	18½E	33
Racine, *Wis., U.S.A.*	42½N	87½w	75
Rada, *Yemen* (inset).	15N	45E	40
Radisson, *Sask., Can.*	52½N	107½w	70
RADNOR, *Wales.*	52½N	3¼w	22
Radolfzell, *Germany.*	47½N	9E	31
Radom, *Poland.*	51½N	21½E	33
Radomir, *Bulgaria.*	42½N	23E	37
Radomsko, *Poland.*	51N	19½E	33
Radstadt, *Austria.*	47½N	13½E	33
Radstock, *England.*	51½N	2½w	22
Radville, *Sask., Can.*	49½N	104½w	70
Radziejow, *Poland.*	52½N	18½E	33
Radzymin, *Poland.*	52½N	21½E	33
Radzyn, *Poland.*	51½N	22½E	33
Rae Isthmus, *N.W.Can.*	67N	88w	66
Raesfeld, *Germany.*	51½N	7E	30
Raeside, L., *W. Aust.*	29s	122E	61
Raetihi, *N.I., N.Z.*	39½s	175½E	62
Rafaela, *Argentina.*	31½s	61½w	79
Rafai, *Cen. Afr. Rep.*	5N	24E	56
Raga, *Sudan.*	8N	25½E	56
Ragalla, *Ceylon.*	7N	81E	45
Ragged Mt., *W. Aust.*	33s	123E	61
Raglan, *N.I., N.Z.*	37½s	174½E	62
Ragusa, see DUBROVNIK.			
Ragusa, *Sicily.*	36½N	14½E	36
Rahad Riv., *Sudan.*	14N	34E	56
Raheng, *Thailand.*	17N	99E	43
Raiatea I., *Pacific.*	16s	151w	64
Raichur, *India.*	16½N	77½E	45
Raida, *S. Yemen* (ins.).	15N	47½E	40
Raigarh, *India.*	21½N	83½E	44
Raikot, *India.*	22½N	70E	43
Rainier, Mt., *U.S.A.*	46½N	122w	74
Raipur, *India.*	21½N	81½E	44
Raivavae I., *Pacific.*	23s	148w	64
Raj Nandgaon, *India.*	21½N	81E	44
Rajahmundry, *India.*	17N	81½E	45
Rajang, R., *E. Malaysia.*	2½N	111½E	47
Rajapalaiyam, *India.*	9½N	77½E	45
RAJASTHAN, *India.*	27½N	73E	44
Rajburi, *Thailand.*	13N	100E	43
Rajshahi, *Pakistan.*	24½N	88½E	44
Rakahanga I., *Pacific.*	10s	161w	64
Rakaia Riv., *S.I., N.Z.*	43½s	172½E	63
Rakas, L., *Tibet.*	30½N	81½E	44
Rakhyut, *Mus. & Oman.*	16N	53E	40
Rakops, *Botswana.*	21½s	24E	51
Rakhshan R., *Pakistan.*	27½N	63E	43
Rakvere, *U.S.S.R.*	59½N	26½E	38
Raleigh, *N.C., U.S.A.*	35½N	78½w	75
Rama, *Nicaragua.*	12N	84½w	77
Ramah, *Labrador, Can.*	59N	63½w	67
Ramallah, *Jord.* (ins.).	32N	35½E	40
Ramaquabane, *Bots.*	20½s	27½E	54
Ramathlabama, *Bots.*	25½s	25½E	54
Ramban, *Kash.* (ins.).	33N	75½E	44
Rambervillers, *Fr.*	48½N	6½E	30
Rambouillet, *France.*	48½N	2E	30
Rambutyo I., *Pac.* (ins.).	2s	147½E	60
Ramgarh, *India.*	22½N	81E	44
Ramle, *Israel* (inset).	32N	35E	40
Ramnad, *India.*	9½N	78½E	45
Ramnicul-Valcea, *Romania.*	45½N	24½E	37
Rampart, *Alaska, U.S.A.*	65N	150w	74
Rampur, *India.*	28½N	79E	44
Rampur Rajaori, *Kashmir* (inset).	33½N	74E	44
Ramree I., *Burma.*	19½N	93½E	43
Ramsay, *Ont., Can.*	47½N	82½w	68
Ramsey, *England.*	52½N	¼w	23
Ramsey, *I. of M., Eng.*	54½N	4½w	25
Ramsey I., *Wales.*	51½N	5½w	22
Ramsgate, *England.*	51½N	1½E	23
Ramso Fiord, *Norway.*	63½N	8E	29
Ramu R., *N. Guin.* (ins.).	4s	145E	60
Rancagua, *Chile.*	34½s	70½w	79
Rance, Riv., *France.*	48½N	2w	31
Ranchi, *India.*	23½N	85½E	44
Randazzo, *Sicily.*	37½N	14½E	36
Randers, *Denmark.*	56½N	10E	29
Randfontein, *T'vaal.*	26½s	27½E	51
Rands, L., *Norway.*	60½N	10E	29
Ranea, *Sweden.*	66N	23E	29
Ran Fiord, *Norway.*	66N	12½E	29
Rangamata, *Pakistan.*	22½N	92E	43
RangaunuB., *N.I., N.Z.*	34½s	173½E	62
Rangia, *India.*	26½N	92E	43
Rangiora, *S.I., N.Z.*	43½s	172½E	63
Rangiroa I., *Pacific.*	15s	148w	64
Rangitikei, R., *N.Z.*	40½s	175½E	62
Rangitoto I., *N.I., N.Z.* (inset A).			62
Rangoon, *Burma.*	16½N	96½E	43
Rangpur, *Pakistan.*	25½N	89E	44
Raniganj, *India.*	26N	88E	44
Rankine, *N. Terr.*	19½s	136½E	60
Rankin's Springs, *Aust.*	33½s	146½E	59
Rann of Cutch, *India.*	24N	70E	43
Rannes, *Queens., Aust.*	24s	150½E	60
Ranong, *Thailand.*	10N	98E	43
Rapallo, *Italy.*	44½N	9½E	36
Rapid City, *Man., Can.*	50½N	100w	70
Rapid City, *S.D., U.S.A.*	44N	103½w	74
Raqqa, *Syria.*	36N	39E	41
Rariega, *C. Pr., S. Afr.*	33½s	25½E	53
Rarotonga I., *Pacific.*	21s	160w	64
Ras Abu Madd, *Saudi Aeabia.*	25N	37E	40
Ras Banas, *U.A.R.*	24N	36E	40
Ras el Hadd, *Mus & Om.*	23N	59E	40
Ras Madraka, *Mus & Om.*	19N	56½E	40
Ras Tanura, *Saudi Ar.*	26½N	50E	40
Raseiniai, *U.S.S.R.*	55½N	23E	33
Rashad, *Sudan.*	12N	31E	56
Raska, *Yugoslavia.*	43½N	20½E	37
Rasna, *U.S.S.R.*	52½N	23½E	33
Rason, L., *W. Aust.*	28½s	124E	61
Rastatt, *Germany.*	48½N	8½E	30
Ratangarh, *India.*	28N	74½E	44
Ratanpur, *India.*	22½N	82½E	44
Ratcliffe B., *W. Aust.*	35s	117½E	61
Rath, *Germany* (inset).	51½N	6½E	33
Rathdrum, *Eire.*	53N	6½w	26
Rathenow, *Germany.*	52½N	12½E	33
Rathkeale, *Eire.*	52½N	9w	26
Rathlin I., *N. Ireland.*	55½N	6½w	26
Rathmelton *Ireland.*	55N	7½w	26
Rathfryland, *Ireland.*	54½N	6½w	25
Ratibon, see RACIBORZ.			
Ratingen, *Ger.* (inset).	51½N	6½E	33
Ratisbon, *Germany.*	49N	12E	33
Ratlam, *India.*	23½N	75E	44
Ratnagiri, *India.*	17N	73½E	45
Ratnapura, *Ceylon.*	6½N	80½E	45
Ratno, *U.S.S.R.*	51½N	24½E	38
Raton, *N.M., U.S.A.*	37N	105w	74
Rattenberg, *Austria.*	47½N	11½E	31
Rattray, *Scotland.*	56½N	3½w	25
Raurkela, *India.*	22½N	84½E	44
Raukumara Ra., *N.Z.*	38s	178E	62
Rauma, *Finland.*	61½N	21½E	29
Ravenglass, *England.*	54½N	3½w	25
Ravenna, *Italy.*	44½N	12½E	36
Ravenshoe, *Queens.*	17½s	145½E	60
Ravensthorpe, *W. Aust.*	33½s	120E	61
Ravenswood, *Queens.*	20s	147E	60
Ravi Riv., *Pakistan.*	31N	72E	44
Rawa Ruska, *U.S.S.R.*	50½N	23½E	38
Rawalpindi, *Pakistan.*	33½N	73½E	46
Rawlinna, *W. Aust.*	31s	125½E	61
Rawlins, *Wyo., U.S.A.*	41½N	107½w	74
Rawson, *Argentina.*	43½s	65w	78
Rawsonville, *C. Pr.*	33½s	19½E	52
Rawtenstall, *England.*	53½N	2½w	22
Rayleigh, *England.*	51½N	½E	23
Raymond, *Alb., Can.*	49½N	112½w	73
Raymore, *Sask., Can.*	51½N	104½w	70
Rayon, *Mexico.*	21½N	99½w	76
Rayong, *Thailand.*	13N	101E	43
Raz, Pte. du, *France.*	48N	4½w	32
Razgrad, *Bulgaria.*	43½N	26½E	37
Re, I. de, *France.*	46½N	1½w	32
Reading, *England.*	51½N	1w	23
Reading, *Pa., U.S.A.*	40½N	76w	75
Reads Drift, *C. Pr.*	29½s	23½E	52
Reay, *Scotland.*	58½N	3½w	24
Reay Forest, *Scotland.*	58½N	5w	24
Rebecca, L., *W. Aust.*	30s	122½E	61
Rebecca, Mt., *W. Aust.*	26½s	116½E	61
Rebun I., *Japan.*	46N	141E	49
Recanati & Pt., *Italy.*	43½N	13½E	36
Recherche Arch., *W.Aust.*	34s	122½E	61
Recife, *Brazil.*	8s	35w	79
Recita, *Romania.*	45½N	22E	37
Recklinghausen, *Ger.*	51½N	7½E	30
Recoaro, *Italy.*	45½N	11½E	31
Redang Pt., *Malaysia* (ins.).	5½N	103E	47
Red Basin, *China.*	30N	106E	48
Red Bluff, *Cal., U.S.A.*	40½N	122½w	74
Red Bluff, *W. Aust.*	24s	114E	61
Redcar, *England.*	54½N	1w	25
Redcliff, *Alberta, Can.*	50N	110½w	73
Red Cliffs, *Vict., Aust.*	34½s	142½E	59
Redcliffe, *Queens., Aust.*	27s	153E	59
Red Deer & R., *Alberta.*	52½N	114w	73
Reddersburg, *O.F.S.*	29½s	26½E	55
Redding, *Calif., U.S.A.*	40½N	122½w	74
Redditch, *England.*	52½N	2w	23
Redditt, *Ontario, Can.*	50N	94½w	71
Redhill, *England.*	51½N	½w	23
Red Hill, *Vict., Aust.*	38½s	145E	59
Red Hill, *W. Aust.*	22s	116E	61
Red, L., *Minn., U.S.A.*	48N	95w	75
Red Lake, *W. Aust.*	33s	122E	61
Redmond, *Ore., U.S.A.*	44N	121w	74
Redon, *France.*	47½N	2½w	32
Redonda I., *W.I.*	17N	62½w	77
Redondela, *Spain.*	42½N	8½w	35
Red River, *China.*	20N	106E	48
Red River, *Queensland.*	16½s	141½E	60
Red River, *La., U.S.A.*	31N	91½w	75
Red Sea, *Asia.*	20N	40E	50
Redruth, *England.*	50½N	5½w	22
Redvers, *Sask., Can.*	49½N	101½w	70
Ree, L., *Ireland.*	53½N	8w	26
Reefton, *S.I., N.Z.*	42s	172E	63
Reepham, *England.*	52½N	1E	23
Reeth, *England.*	54½N	2w	25
Refugio, *Texas, U.S.A.*	28N	97w	75
Reggio, *Italy.*	38½N	15½E	36
Reggio, *Italy*	44½N	10½E	36
Regina, *Sask., Can.*	50½N	104½w	70
Regneville, *France.*	49N	1½w	31
Reguengos, *Portugal.*	38½N	7½w	35
Rehoboth, *S.W. Africa.*	23½s	17E	55
Rehovot, *Israel* (inset).	31½N	34¾E	40
Reichenberg, see LIBEREC.			
Reims, *France.*	49½N	4E	32
Reindeer L., *Man., Can.*	52½N	98w	71
Reindeer L., *Sask., Can.*	57½N	103w	66
Reinheim, *Germany.*	49½N	8½E	30
Reinosa, *Spain.*	43N	4½w	35
Reisholz, *Ger.* (inset).	51N	6½E	33
Reitz, *O.F.S., S. Afr.*	27½s	28½E	55
Rembang, *Java.*	6½s	111½E	47
Remedios, *Mexico.*	24½N	106½w	76
Remedios, *Panama.*	8N	82w	77
Remiremont, *France.*	48N	6½E	30
Remscheid, *Germany.*	51½N	7½E	33
Rendsburg, *Germany.*	54½N	9½E	33
Renfrew, *Ontario, Can.*	45½N	76½w	69
RENFREW, *Scotland.*	55½N	4½w	25
Rengat, *Sum. Indon.*	1s	103E	47
Reni, *U.S.S.R.*	45½N	28½E	3
Renigunta, *India.*	13½N	80E	4
Renish Pt., *Scotland.*	57½N	7w	24
Renk, *Sudan.*	11½N	32½E	56
Renmark, *S. Australia.*	34½s	140½E	59
Rennell I., *Solomons.*	11½s	160½E	64
Rennes, *France.*	48½N	1½w	3
Reno, *Nevada, U.S.A.*	39½N	119½w	74
Reno River, *Italy.*	44½N	12½E	3
Renosterkop, *C. Pr.*	32½s	23E	52
Repulse B., *Queensland.*	21s	148½E	60
Requena, *Spain.*	39½N	1w	35
Resht, *Iran.*	37½N	49½E	40
Resistencia, *Argentina.*	27½s	59w	79
Resko, *Poland.*	53½N	15½E	33
Resolution, *N.W.T.*	61½N	113½w	6
Resolution I., *N.W.T.*	61½N	65w	6
Resolution I., *S.I., N.Z.*	45½s	166½E	63
Reston, *Scotland.*	55½N	2½w	25
Rethel, *France.*	49½N	4½E	32
Rethimnon, *Crete.*	35½N	24½E	37
Rethy, *Belgium.*	51½N	5E	30
Retina, *W. Australia.*	27s	116½E	61
Reunion I., *Ind. Oc.*	21s	55½E	1
Reus, *Spain.*	41½N	1E	35
Reutlinger, *Germany.*	48½N	9E	32
Revel, see TALLINN.			
Revelstoke, *Br.Col., Can.*	51N	118w	72
Revigny, *France.*	48½N	5E	30
Rewa, *India.*	24½N	81½E	44
Rey, I. del, *Panama.*	8N	78w	77
Reykjavik, *Iceland.*	64N	22w	28
Rezekne, *U.S.S.R.*	56½N	27½E	38
Rezina, *U.S.S.R.*	47½N	28½E	37
Rhaetian Alps, *Europe.*	46½N	10E	31
Rhayader, *Wales.*	52½N	3½w	22
Rheda, *Germany.*	51½N	8½E	30
Rhein, *Sask., Canada.*	51½N	102½w	70
Rheinan, *France.*	48½N	7½E	30
Rheinbach, *Germany.*	50½N	7E	30
Rheine, *Germany.*	52½N	7½E	30
Rheinhausen, *Ger.* (ins.)	51½N	6½E	33
Rheinwaldhorn, Mt., *Switzerland.*	46½N	9½E	31
Rhenen, *Netherlands.*	52N	5½E	30
Rheydt, *Germany.*	51½N	6½E	30
Rhiconich, *Scotland.*	58½N	5w	24
RHINELAND, *Germany.*	50N	7E	30
Rhinelander, *U.S.A.*	46N	89½w	75
Rhine, Riv., *Germany.*	50½N	7½E	33
Rhio Arch., see RIOUW Arch.			
Rho, *Italy.*	45½N	9E	31
RHODE ISLAND, *U.S.A.*	41½N	71½w	75
Rhodes, *C. Pr., S. Afr.*	30½s	28E	53
Rhodes & Is., *Aegean S.*	36½N	30E	37
RHODESIA, *Africa.*	20s	25E	5
Rhodope Hlds., *Bulg.*	41½N	24E	37
Rhondda, *Wales.*	51½N	3½w	22
RHONE, *France.*	46N	4½E	3
Rhum, I. & Sd. of, *Scot.*	57N	6½w	24
Rhyl, *Wales.*	53½N	3½w	22
Rhynie, *Scotland.*	57½N	2½w	24
Rians, *France.*	43½N	5½E	3
Riasi, *Kashmir* (ins.).	33½N	75E	44
Ribadeo, *Spain.*	43½N	7w	35
Ribble, Riv., *England.*	53½N	2½w	22
Ribe, *Denmark.*	55½N	8½E	29
Ribeira Grande, *Azores*	37½N	25½E	3
Ribeirao Preto, *Brazil.*	21½s	47½w	79
Ribera, *Sicily.*	37½N	13½E	36
Riberalta, *Bolivia.*	10½s	65w	78
Ribi, *N. Guinea* (inset).	6s	146E	60
Rich, *Morocco.*	32N	4w	34
Riche, C., *W. Aust.*	34½s	118½E	61
Richford, *Vt., U.S.A.*	45N	72½w	69
Richibucto, *N. Bruns.*	46½N	65w	67
Richland, *Wash., U.S.A.*	47N	119w	7
Richmond, *C.Pr., S.Af.*	31½s	24E	5
Richmond, *Ind., U.S.A.*	39½N	85w	7
Richmond, *Nat., S.Af.*	29½s	30½E	5
Richmond, *Qu., Aust.*	20½s	143½E	6
Richmond, *S.I., N.Z.*	41½s	173½E	6
Richmond, *Surrey, Eng.*	51½N	½w	2
Richmond, *Tas.* (ins.).	42½s	147½E	5
Richmond, *Va., U.S.A.*	37½N	77½w	7
Richmond, *Yorks., Eng.*	54½N	1½w	2
Richtersveld, *C.Pr.S.Af.*	28½s	17E	5
Ridgelands, *Queensland.*	23s	150E	6
Ridgetown, *Ont., Can.*	42½N	82w	6
Ridley Riv., *W. Aust.*	20s	118½E	6
Riebeek, E. *C.Pr., S.Af.*	33½s	26½E	5
Riebeek Kasteel, *C.Pr.*	33½s	19E	5
Riebeek, W., *C. Pr.*	33½s	18½E	5
Ried, *Austria.*	48½N	13½E	3
Riegel, *Germany.*	48½N	7½E	3
Rienz Riv., *Italy.*	46½N	11½E	3
Riesa, *Germany.*	51½N	13½E	3
Riet, *C. Pr., S. Africa.*	30½s	24½E	5
Rietbron, *C. Pr., S. Afr.*	33s	23½E	5
Rietfontein, *C. Pr.*	31½s	24E	5
Rieti, *Italy.*	42½N	13E	3
Rietpoel, *C. Pr., S. Afr.*	34½s	20E	5
Rietvlei, *C. Pr., S. Afr.*	30½s	29½E	5
Riga, *U.S.S.R.*	57N	24E	3
Riga, G. of, *U.S.S.R.*	57½N	23E	3
Rigan, *Iran.*	28N	59E	4
Rigo, *Papua* (inset).	10s	147E	6
Rigolet, *Labrador.*	54½N	58½w	6
Riihimaki, *Finland.*	60½N	24½E	2
Rijeka, *Yugoslavia.*	45½N	14½E	3
Rimatara I., *Pacific.*	23s	154w	6

Place	Lat.	Long.	No.
Rimaucourt, *France.*	48¼N	5¼E	30
Rimbey, *Alberta, Can.*	52¾N	114¼W	73
Rimini, *Italy.*	44N	12½E	36
Rimogne, *France.*	49¾N	4½E	30
Rimouski, *Que., Can.*	48½N	68½W	67
Rimutaka Ra. *N.Z.*	(inset B).		62
Rincon Pk., *U.S.A.*	36N	105¾W	74
Ringkjobing, *Denmark.*	56N	8E	29
Ringmer, *England.*	50¾N	0	23
Ringwood, *England.*	50¾N	1¾W	23
Ringvasso, *Norway.*	70N	18½E	29
Riobamba, *Ecuador.*	2S	78½W	78
Rio Branca, *Brazil.*	10S	67¾W	78
Rio Bravo del Norte, *Mex.*	30N	105W	76
Rio Caribe, *Venezuela.*	11N	63½W	77
Rio Chico, *Venezuela.*	10N	66W	77
Rio Claro, *Trinidad.*	10½N	61W	77
Rio Cuarto, *Arg.*	33¼S	64¼W	79
RIO DE JANEIRO, *Brazil.*	23S	43W	79
Rio de Oro, *Colombia.*	8¾N	73½W	77
Rio de Oro, see SPANISH SAHARA.			
Rio del Rey, *Nigeria.*	4¾N	8¾E	57
Rio Diablo, *Panama.*	9N	78W	77
Rio Grande, *Brazil.*	32S	52W	79
Rio Grande, *Nicarag.*	12½N	83½W	77
Rio Grande, *U.S.A.-Mexico.*	26N	97¼W	65
RIO GRANDE DO NORTE, *Brazil.*	5½S	36W	78
RIO GRANDE DO SUL, *Bra.*	32S	55W	78
Riohacha, *Colombia.*	12N	73W	77
RIO MUNI, *Africa.*	1½N	10½E	57
Rio Tinto, *Spain.*	37½N	6½W	35
Rionero, *Italy.*	41N	15¾E	36
Riosucio, *Colombia.*	7½N	77W	77
Riouw Arch., *Indonesia.*	¾N	104E	47
Ripley, *England.*	54N	1½W	25
Ripon, *C. Pr., S. Africa.*	33S	26E	53
Ripon, *England.*	54¼N	1½W	25
Rishon Le Siyon, *Israel* (inset).	32N	35E	40
Risle, Riv., *France.*	49½N	½E	31
Risor, *Norway.*	58¾N	9E	29
Risut, *Mus. & Oman.*	16N	54E	40
Riva, *Italy.*	45¾N	10¾E	31
Rivarolo, *Italy.*	45¼N	7¾E	31
Rivera, *Uruguay.*	31S	55¾W	79
Rivera, *Venezuela.*	8½N	72W	77
Riverhead, *N.I., N.Z.* (inset A).			62
Riverhurst, *Sask., Can.*	51N	106¾W	70
Rivers, *Manitoba, Can.*	50N	100¼W	70
Rivers Inlet, *Br. Col.*	51¾N	127¼W	72
Riversdale, *C.Pr., S. Afr.*	34¼S	21¼E	52
Riverside, *C. Pr., S. Afr.*	30S	29¾E	53
Riverton, *C.Pr., S. Afr.*	28½S	24¾E	53
Riverton, *Man., Can.*	51N	97W	71
Riverton, *S. Aust.*	34S	138¾E	59
Riverton, *S.I., N.Z.*	46½S	168E	63
Riverton, *Wyo., U.S.A.*	43¼N	108W	74
Riviera Coast, *France.*	43¾N	8E	32
Riviere-du-Loup, *Que.*	47¾N	69½W	69
Rivoli, *Italy.*	45N	7½E	31
Riyadh, *Saudi Arabia.*	24¾N	46½E	40
Rizaiyeh, *Iran.*	37½N	45E	40
Rize, *Turkey.*	41N	41E	41
Rizzuto, C. of, *Italy.*	38¾N	17E	36
Roan Antelope, see LUANSHYA.			
Roanne, *France.*	46N	4¼E	32
Roanoke, *Va., U.S.A.*	37¼N	80W	75
Roaringwater B., *Ire.*	51½N	9½W	26
Robben I., *C.Pr., S.Afr.*	33¾S	18¼E	52
Robbin I., *Tas.* (ins.).	40½S	145E	59
Robe, *S. Australia.*	37¼S	139¾E	59
Robe River, *W. Aust.*	22S	115¾E	61
Robert Pt., *W. Aust.*	32½S	115E	61
Robertson, *C.Pr. S.Afr.*	33¾S	20E	52
Robertstown, *Ireland.*	53¼N	6¾W	26
Roberval, *Quebec, Can.*	48½N	72¼W	69
Robinson & R., *Aust.*	16S	136½E	60
Roblin, *Manitoba, Can.*	51¼N	101¼W	70
Robsart, *Sask., Can.*	49½N	109¼W	70
Robson, Mt., *Br. Col.*	53¼N	119W	72
Roca, C., *Portugal.*	38¾N	9½W	35
Rocadas, *Angola.*	17S	15E	56
Rocanville, *Sask., Can.*	50½N	101¾W	70
Rocca, S., Casciano, *It.*	44N	12E	36
Rocha, *Uruguay.*	34½S	54½W	79
Rochdale, *England.*	53½N	2¼W	22
Rocheachic, *Mexico.*	27N	107W	76
Roche Bernard, La, *Fr.*	47½N	2¼W	31
Rochechouart, *France.*	45¾N	¾E	32
Rochefort, *Belgium.*	50¼N	5¼E	30
Rochefort, *France.*	46N	¾W	32
Roches Douvres, *Fr.*	49¼N	3W	31
Rochester, *England.*	55¼N	2½W	25
Rochester, *England.*	51¼N	½E	23
Rochester, *Minn., U.S.A.*	44N	92½W	75
Rochester, *N.H., U.S.A.*	43¼N	71W	69
Rochester, *N.Y., U.S.A.*	43¼N	77¾W	69
Rochester, *Vict., Aust.*	36½S	144¾E	59
Rock I., *Ill., U.S.A.*	41½N	90½W	75
Rockford, *Ill., U.S.A.*	42¼N	89W	75
Rockhampton, *Queens.*	23½S	150½E	60
Rockingham, *W. Aust.*	32½S	115¾E	61
Rockingham B., *Queens.*	18S	146E	60
Rockland, *Me., U.S.A.*	44N	69W	75
Rock Riv., *Ill., U.S.A.*	42N	90W	75
Rock Springs, *Wyo., U.S.*	42N	109W	74
Rockstone, *Guy.* (ins.).	6N	58W	77
Rocky Mount, *U.S.A.*	36N	77¾W	75
Rocky Mts., *N. Amer.*	50N	110W	20
Rocky Pt., *W. Aust.*	33½S	124E	61
Rocroi, *France.*	50N	4½E	30
Rodenkirchen, *Ger.*	53½N	8½E	30
Rodez, *France.*	44½N	2½E	32
Rodna Veche, *Rom.*	47½N	24¾E	37
Rodosto, see TEKIRDAG.			
Rodvig, *Denmark.*	55¼N	12¼E	33
Roebourne, *W. Aust.*	20¾S	117E	61
Roebuck, *W. Australia.*	18S	122E	61
Roer, Riv., *Germany.*	51¼N	6E	30
Roermond, *Nether.*	51¼N	6E	30
Rogachev, *U.S.S.R.*	53N	30E	38
Roggeveld Mts., *C.Pr.*	32¼S	20¼E	52
Rohan, *France.*	48N	2¾W	31
Rohrbach, *France.*	49N	7¼E	30
Rohri, *Pakistan.*	27½N	68E	43
Rohtak, *India.*	29N	76½E	44
Rois Bheinn, *Scotland.*	56¾N	5¾W	24
Roisel, *France.*	50N	3E	30
Rokan, R., *Sum. Indon.*	2½N	101E	47
Roland, *Tas.* (inset).	41½S	146½E	59
Roldal, *Norway.*	60N	7½E	29
Rolla, *Br. Col., Can.*	56N	120W	72
Rolla, *Missouri, U.S.A.*	38N	92W	75
Rolleston, *Queens., Aust.*	24½S	148½E	60
Rolleston, *S.I., N.Z.* (inset C).			63
Roma, *Queens., Aust.*	26½S	148¾E	60
Romagnano, *Italy.*	45¾N	8¾E	31
Roman, *Romania.*	47N	27E	37
Romana, La, *Dom. Rep.*	18N	69W	77
ROMANIA, *Europe.*			37
Romanovski, see KROPOTKIN.			
Romans, *France.*	45N	5E	32
Romblon, *Luzon, P.I.*	12½N	122½E	47
Rome, *Georgia, U.S.A.*	34¼N	85W	75
Rome, *Italy.*	42N	12½E	36
Rome, *N.Y., U.S.A.*	43¼N	75½W	69
Romford, *England.*	51½N	¼E	23
Romilly, *France.*	48¾N	3¾E	32
Romorantin, *France.*	47¼N	1¾E	32
Rompin R., *Malay* (ins.)	2½N	103¾E	47
Romsdal Is., *Norway.*	62½N	6E	29
Romsey, *England.*	51N	1½W	23
Rona I., *Scotland.*	57½N	6W	24
Ronaldsay, N., *Scot.*	59½N	2½W	24
Ronaldsay, S., *Scot.*	58¾N	3W	24
Roncador Cay, *W.I.*	14N	80W	77
Ronco, *Italy.*	44½N	9E	31
Ronda, *Spain.*	36¾N	5W	35
Rondeau, *Ont., Can.*	42½N	82W	68
Rongelap I., *Pacific.*	11N	165E	64
Rongotai Airport, *N.I., N.Z.* (ins. B)			62
Ronne, *Bornholm, Den.*	55N	14¾E	29
Roodepoort, *T'vaal.*	26¼S	28E	51
Roosendaal, *Nether.*	51½N	4½E	30
Roossenekal, *T'vaal.*	25¼S	30E	54
Roosevelt I., *Antarc.*	79S	163W	80
Roper R., *N. Terr., Aust.*	15S	136E	60
Roquefort, *France.*	44¼N	¼W	32
Rora Head, *Scotland.*	58¾N	3½W	24
Roraima, Mt., *Venezuela.*	6N	60W	77
Rorkes Drift, *Natal.*	28¼S	30½E	55
Rorketon, *Man., Can.*	51½N	99½W	70
Rorschach, *Switz.*	47½N	9½E	31
Ros L., *Norway.*	65¾N	14E	29
Rosa, Monte, *Switz.*	46N	7¾E	31
Rosalind Bank, *Carib. S.*	17N	81W	77
Rosario, *Argentina.*	33S	60¾W	79
Rosario, *Mexico.*	23N	106W	76
Rosario, *Mexico.*	30N	116W	76
Rosario Bank, *Carib. S.*	18N	84W	77
Rosario, Is. del, *Colom.*	10¼N	75¼W	77
Rosarno, *Italy.*	38½N	16E	36
Rosas & G. of, *Spain.*	42¼N	3¼E	35
Roscoff, *France.*	48¾N	4W	31
ROSCOMMON, *Eire.*	53¾N	8¼W	26
Roscrea, *Eire.*	53N	7¾W	26
Rose I., *Pacific.*	15S	168W	64
Roseau, *Dominica I.*	15¼N	61½W	77
Roseau, *Minn., U.S.A.*	48¾N	95¾W	71
Rosebery, *Tasmania.*	41¾S	145½E	59
Roseburg, *Ore., U.S.A.*	43N	124W	74
Rosedale, *Queens., Aust.*	24¾S	152E	60
Roseires, *Sudan.*	11¾N	34½E	56
Rosendal, *O.F.S. S. Afr.*	28½S	28E	55
Rosenheim, *Germany.*	47¾N	12¼E	33
Rosetown, *Sask., Can.*	51½N	108W	70
Rosetta, *U.A.R.*	31½N	30½E	50
Rosewood, *N. Terr., Au.*	16¾S	129E	60
Rosewood, *Queens., Au.*	27½S	152¾E	59
Rosignol, *Guyana* (ins.)	6½N	57W	77
Rosiori de Vede, *Rom.*	44N	25E	37
Roskilde, *Denmark.*	55½N	12E	33
Roslavl, *U.S.S.R.*	54N	33E	38
Rosmead, *C. Pr. S. Afr.*	31½S	25¼E	53
Rosporden, *France.*	48N	3¾W	31
Ross, *England.*	52N	2½W	22
Ross, *S.I., N.Z.*	43S	170¾E	63
Ross, *Tasmania, Aust.*	42S	147½E	59
ROSS & CROMARTY, *Scotland.*	57¾N	5W	24
Ross I., *Antarctica.*	77½S	168E	80
Ross I., *Manitoba, Can.*	54½N	98W	71
Ross Sea, *Antarctica.*	75S	180W	80
Rossan Pt., *Eire.*	54¾N	8¾W	26
Rossano, *Italy.*	39½N	16¾E	36
Rossash, *U.S.S.R.*	50N	39½E	38
Rossburn, *Man., Can.*	50¾N	101W	70
Rossel I., *Pacific* (ins.).	11S	154E	60
Rossland, *Br. Col., Can.*	49N	117¾W	72
Rosslare, *Eire.*	52¼N	6¼W	26
Rosso, C., *Sardinia.*	42¼N	8½E	36
Rosthern, *Sask., Can.*	52¾N	106¼W	70
Rostock, *Germany.*	54N	12¼E	33
Rostov, *U.S.S.R.*	57¼N	39½E	38
Rostov-on-Don, *U.S.S.R.*	47¼N	39¾E	38
Rostrenen, *France.*	48¼N	3¼W	31
Roswell, *N.M., U.S.A.*	33¾N	104¾W	74
Rota I., *Pacific.*	13N	145E	64
Rothbury, *England.*	55¼N	2W	25
Rother, Riv., *England.*	51N	¾E	23
Rotherham, *England.*	53½N	1¼W	23
Rothes, *Scotland.*	57½N	3¼W	24
Rothesay, *N. Brun. Can.*	45¼N	66W	67
Rothesay, *Scotland.*	55¾N	5W	25
Rothwell, *England.*	52½N	1W	23
Roti I., *Timor, Indon.*	10¾S	123¼E	47
Roto, *N.S.W., Aust.*	33S	145¼E	59
Rotondella, *Italy.*	40¼N	16½E	36
Rotondo, Mt., *Corsica.*	42¼N	9E	32
Rotoroa, L., *S.I., N.Z.*	41¾S	172½E	63
Rotorua, *N.I., N.Z.*	38¼S	176¼E	62
Rotterdam, *Nether.*	52N	4½E	30
Rotuma I., *Pacific.*	12S	176E	64
Rottumeroog, I., *Neth.*	53½N	6½E	30
Roubaix, *France.*	50¾N	3¼E	32
Rouen, *France.*	49½N	1¼E	32
Rouleau, *Sask., Can.*	50¼N	104¾W	70
Roulers, *Belgium.*	51N	3E	30
Rousay, *Scotland.*	59¼N	3W	24
ROUSSILLON, *France.*	42½N	2½E	32
Rouxville, *O.F.S. S.Af.*	30½S	26¾E	53
Rouyn, *Quebec, Can.*	48¼N	79¼W	68
Rovaniemi, *Finland.*	66½N	25E	29
Rovato, *Italy.*	45½N	10E	31
Rovereto, *Italy.*	45¾N	11E	31
Rovigo, *Italy.*	45N	11¾E	36
Rovinj, *Yugoslavia.*	45N	13¾E	36
Rovno, *U.S.S.R.*	50¾N	26½E	38
Rovuma, Riv., *Moz.*	11S	40E	56
Rowardennan, *Scot.*	56¼N	4¾W	25
Rowena, *N.S.W., Aust.*	29¾S	149E	59
Rowicz, *Poland.*	51½N	17E	33
ROXBURGH, CO., *Scot.*	55½N	2¾W	25
Roxburgh, *S.I., N.Z.*	45½S	169¼E	63
Royal Canal, *Eire.*	53½N	6½W	26
Royal Oak, *U.S.A.*	42½N	83¼W	68
Royan, *France.*	45½N	1¼W	32
Roye, *France.*	49¾N	2¾E	30
Roy Hill, *W. Aust.*	22½S	120E	61
Royston, *England.*	52N	0	23
Rozan, *Poland.*	53N	21½E	33
Rozana, *U.S.S.R.*	53N	25E	33
Rozanka, *U.S.S.R.*	53½N	24¾E	33
Roznava, *Czecho.*	48¾N	20½E	33
Rozwadow, *Poland.*	50½N	22E	33
Ruahine Ra., *N.I., N.Z.*	40S	176E	62
Ruamahanga R., *N.I., N.Z.* (ins. B).			62
Ruapehu, Mt., *N.Z.*	39¼S	175½E	62
Ruapuke I., *S.I., N.Z.*	47S	168E	63
Rub Al Khali Desert, *Arabia.*	20N	50E	40
Rubbervale, *T'vaal, S.Af.*	24S	30½E	54
Rubicon, Riv., *Italy.*	44¼N	12¼E	36
Rubtsovsk, *U.S.S.R.*	51½N	81E	39
Rudesheim, *Germany.*	50N	7¾E	30
Rudnichny, *U.S.S.R.*	60N	52½E	38
Rudnitza, *U.S.S.R.*	48¼N	29E	37
Rudok, *China.*	34N	80E	43
Rudolf, L., *Kenya.*	4N	36E	56
Rudolstadt, *Germany.*	50½N	11½E	33
Rue, *France.*	50¼N	1¾E	30
Ruenya Riv., *Moz.*	17S	33½E	51
Ruette, *Austria.*	47½N	10¾E	33
Rufa'a, *Sudan.*	15N	33½E	56
Ruffec, *France.*	46N	¼E	32
Rufiji, Riv., *Tanzania.*	8S	39E	56
Rufunsa, *Zambia.*	15S	29½E	51
Rugby, *England.*	52½N	1¼W	23
Rugeley, *England.*	52¾N	2W	23
Rugen I., *Germany.*	54½N	13½E	33
Rugles, *France.*	48¾N	¾E	31
Ruhr, R., *Germany.*	52N	8E	33
Ruka, *Afghanistan.*	35N	70E	43
Rukuku, *Botswana.*	19½S	23½E	51
Rukwa, L., *Tanzania.*	8S	33E	56
Rum Cay, *Bahamas.*	23½N	75W	77
Ruma, *Yugoslavia.*	45N	20E	37
Rumah, *Saudi Arabia.*	26N	47E	40
Rumbalara, *N. Terr.*	25¼S	134½E	60
Rumbek, *Sudan.*	7N	29¾E	56
Rumilly, *France.*	45¾N	6¼E	31
Rum Jungle, *N. Terr.*	13S	130E	60
Rumoi, *Japan.*	44N	141E	49
Rumula, *Queens., Aust.*	16S	145E	60
Runanga, *S.I., N.Z.*	42½S	171¼E	63
Runaway, C., *N.I., N.Z.*	37½S	178E	62
Runcorn, *England.*	53¼N	2¾W	22
Rungwa, *Tanzania.*	7S	33E	56
Rupert House, *Quebec.*	51½N	78¾W	71
Rupert R., *Que., Can.*	51½N	78½W	71
Rurutu I., *Pacific.*	21S	150W	64
Rusapi, *Rhodesia.*	18½S	32¼E	51
Ruschevo, *U.S.S.R.*	52½N	44E	38
Ruschuk, see RUSSE.			
Rushden, *England.*	52¼N	½W	23
Rushiri I., *Japan.*	46N	141E	49
Russe, *Bulgaria.*	43¾N	26E	37
Russell, *Manitoba, Can.*	50¾N	101¼W	70
Russellville, *U.S.A.*	35½N	93W	75
Russian Mission, *Alaska, U.S.A.* (inset).	61N	161W	74
RUSSIAN S.F.S. REPUBLIC.			38, 39
Russkaya Harb., *U.S.S.R.*	76N	62E	39
Russki Zavorot, C., *U.S.S.R.*	69N	54½E	38
Rustak, *Afghanistan.*	37½N	70E	43
Rustenburg, *T'vaal.*	25¾S	27¼E	54
Rustig, *O.F.S., S. Afr.*	27½S	27E	55
Ruston, *La., U.S.A.*	32N	92½W	75
Rutba, *Iraq.*	33N	40E	40
Ruthin, *Wales.*	53¼N	3¼W	22
RUTLAND, *England.*	52¾N	¾W	23
Rutland, *Vt., U.S.A.*	43½N	73W	69
Ruwenzori, Mt., *Uganda.*	½N	30E	56
Ruzaevka, *U.S.S.R.*	53½N	45E	38
RWANDA, *C. Africa*	2S	30E	56
Ryazan, *U.S.S.R.*	54½N	39¾E	38
Ryazhsk, *U.S.S.R.*	53N	40E	38
Rybachi Pen., *U.S.S.R.*	69¾N	32½E	39
Rybinsk, *U.S.S.R.*	58N	38¾E	38
Rybinskoe Res., *U.S.S.R.*	58N	38E	38
Ryde, *I. of W., Eng.*	50¾N	1¼W	23
Rye, *England.*	51N	¾E	23
Ryechitsa, *U.S.S.R.*	52½N	30E	38
Rylstone, *N.S.W., Aust.*	33S	150E	59
Ryno, *C. Pr., S. Afr.*	31¼S	28E	53
Rypin, *Poland.*	53N	19½E	33
Rzeszow, *Poland.*	50N	22E	33
Rzhev, *U.S.S.R.*	56¼N	34¼E	38
SAALE, RIV., *Germany.*	51¼N	12E	33
Saales, *France.*	48¼N	7E	30
Saalfeld, *Germany.*	50½N	11¼E	33
Saanen, *Switzerland.*	46½N	7¼E	31
SAAR, *Germany.*	49¼N	7E	30
Saarbrucken, *Ger.*	49¼N	7E	30
Saarburg, *Germany.*	49½N	6½E	30
Saaremaa, *U.S.S.R.*	58N	22½E	38
Saarguemund, see SARREGUEMINES.			
Saari Selka, *Finland.*	68N	28E	29
Saarlautern, *Saar., Ger.*	49¼N	7E	33
SABAH, see EAST MALAYSIA.			47
Saba I., *W. Indies.*	17½N	63W	77
Sabac, *Yugoslavia.*	44¾N	19¾E	37
Sabadell, *Spain.*	41½N	2E	35
Sabana de la Mar, *W.I.*	18½N	69W	77
Sabanalarga, *Colombia.*	10¾N	75W	77
Sabi Riv., *Rhodesia.*	22S	32E	51
Sabie, *Mozambique.*	25½S	32½E	51
Sabie & R., *T'vaal.*	25S	30¾E	54
Sabieburg, *T'vaal.*	25S	31½E	54
Sabinas, *Mexico.*	28N	101W	76
Sabine Mt., *Antarctica.*	72S	167E	80
Sabine R., *Tex., U.S.A.*	29¾N	93¾W	75
Sabirabad, *U.S.S.R.*	40N	48E	38
Sable, *France.*	47¾N	¼W	31
Sable I., *Canada.*	44N	60W	66
Sabor, Riv., *Portugal.*	41¼N	7¼W	35
Sabres, *France.*	44¼N	1W	32
Sabrina Ld., *Antarc.*	66S	115E	80
Sabzawar, *Afghan.*	33½N	62E	43
Sabzawar, *Iran.*	36¼N	57½E	40
Sacile, *Italy.*	46N	12½E	31
Sackingen, *Germany.*	47½N	8E	30
Sackville, *N. Bruns., Can.*	46N	64¼W	64
Sacramento, *Cal., U.S.*	38½N	121½W	77
Sacramento R. *Cal. US.*	38N	122W	74
Sacueni, *Romania.*	47¼N	22¼E	37
Sa'da, *Yemen.*	16¾N	43½E	40
Sadaba, *Spain.*	42½N	1¼W	35
Sadiya, *India.*	27¾N	95¾E	43
Sado I., *Japan.*	38N	138½E	49
Sado River, *Portugal.*	38¼N	9W	35
Safad, *Israel* (inset).	33N	35½E	40
Safford, *Ariz., U.S.A.*	33N	110W	74
Saffron Walden, *Eng.*	52N	¼E	23
Saga, *Japan.*	33N	130E	49
Sagaing, *Burma.*	22N	96E	43
Saginaw, *Mich., U.S.A.*	43½N	84W	68
Sagsag, *New Britain, Pacific* (inset).	6S	149E	60
Saguenay R., *Quebec.*	48¼N	69¾W	69
Sagunto, *Spain.*	39½N	0	35
Sahagur, *Spain.*	42½N	5W	35
Sahara, Desert, *N. Afr.*	20N	5E	50
Saharanpur, *India.*	30N	77½E	43
Saida, *Lebanon.*	33½N	35½E	41
Saidabad, *Iran.*	29½N	56E	40
Saigon, *Vietnam.*	11N	107E	47
Saihut, *S. Yemen.*	15¼N	51¼E	40
Sailan, *S. Yem.* (ins.)	15N	46E	40
Saimaa, L. of, *Finland.*	61½N	29E	29
Sain Shanda, *Mongolia.*	43N	108E	39
St. Abb's Head, *Scot.*	56N	2¼W	25
St. Affrique, *France.*	44N	2¾E	32
St. Agnes, *England.*	50¼N	5¼W	22
St. Aignan, *France.*	47¼N	1¼E	31
St. Albans, *England.*	51¾N	¼W	23
St. Albans Head, *Eng.*	50½N	2W	22
St. Albert, *Alb. Can.*	53¾N	113¾W	73
St. Andre, C., *Malagasy.*	16S	44E	56
St. Andrews, *Scotland.*	56¼N	2¾W	25
St. Anne, *Channel Is.*	49¾N	2¼W	31
St. Ann's B., *Jamaica.*	18½N	77¼W	77
St. Ann's Head, *Wales.*	51¾N	5¼W	22
St. Anthony, *Id., U.S.A.*	44¾N	111¼W	74
St. Arnaud, *Vict., Aust.*	36½S	143¼E	59
St. Asaph, *Wales.*	53¼N	3½W	22
St. Aubin du Cormier, *France.*	48½N	1¼W	31
St. Austell, *England.*	50¼N	4¾W	22
St. Avold, *France.*	49¼N	6½E	30
St. Barthelemy I., *W.I.*	17¾N	62¾W	77
St. Bees Head, *Eng.*	54½N	3¾W	25
St. Blasien, *Germany.*	47¾N	8¼E	32
St. Blazey, *England.*	50½N	4½W	22
St. Boniface, *Man. Can.*	49¾N	97W	71
St. Brides Bay, *Wales.*	51¾N	5W	22
St. Brieuc, & B., *Fr.*	48½N	2¾W	32
St. Calais, *France.*	48N	¾E	31
St. Catherines, *Ontario.*	43¼N	79¼W	68
St. Catharine's Pt., *Eng.*	50½N	1¼W	23
St. Cere, *France.*	44¾N	2E	32
St. Chely, *France.*	45N	3¼E	32
St. Ciers, *France.*	45¼N	¾W	32
St. Clair, L., *U.S.-Can.*	42½N	82¾W	68
St. Claud, *France.*	45¾N	½E	32

[126] St. Claude—Sandray

Place	Lat.	Long.	No.
St. Claude, *France.*	46½N	5¾E	31
St. Clears, *Wales.*	51¾N	4½W	22
St. Cloud, *Minn., U.S.A.*	45¾N	94W	75
St. Columb, *England.*	50½N	5W	20
St. Croix I., *W. Indies.*	17½N	64¾W	72
St. Cuthbert's, *C. Pr.*	31½S	28¾E	52
St. Cyr, *France.*	48¾N	2E	37
St. David's, *Wales.*	51¾N	5¼W	23
St. Denis, *France.*	49N	3E	32
St. Die, *France.*	48¼N	7E	32
St. Dizier, *France.*	48½N	5E	30
St. Elias, Mt., *Yukon.*	60¼N	141W	66
St. Etienne, *France.*	45½N	4½E	32
St. Eustatius I., *Lee. Is.*	17½N	63W	77
St. Evariste, *Que., Can.*	46N	71W	69
St. Fillans, *Scotland.*	56½N	4W	25
St. Finan's B., *Ireland.*	52N	10¼W	26
St. Firmin, *France.*	44¾N	6E	31
St. Florent, *Corsica.*	42¾N	9E	32
St. Florentin, *France.*	48N	3½E	30
St. Flour, *France.*	45N	3¼E	32
St. Francis, *Me., U.S.A.*	47¼N	68¾W	67
St. Francis, C., *C. Pr.*	34¼S	25E	53
St. Fulgent, *France.*	46¾N	1¼W	32
St. Gallen, *Switz.*	47½N	9½E	31
St. Gaudens, *France.*	43N	¾E	32
St. George, *New B. Can.*	45N	67W	67
St. George, *Ut., U.S.A.*	37N	114W	74
St. George, *Que., Can.*	46¼N	70¾W	69
St. Georges, *Belgium.*	50½N	5¼E	30
St. George's, *Gren. W.I.*	12N	62W	77
St. George's, *Newf. Can.*	48¼N	58½W	67
St. George's Chan., *U.K.*	52N	6W	22
St. Germain, *France.*	48¾N	2E	32
St. Gervais, *France.*	45¾N	6¾E	31
St. Giers-s-Gironde, *Fr.*	45¼N	1W	32
St. Gildas, Pte. de, *Fr.*	47N	2¾W	31
St. Gilles, *France.*	43¾N	4¼E	32
St. Girons, *France.*	43N	1¼E	32
St. Goar, *Germany.*	50¼N	7¾E	30
St. Gotthard Tunnel, *Switzerland.*	46½N	8½E	31
St. Gowan's Hd., *Wales*	51½N	5W	22
St. Helena, *Atlantic Oc.*	16S	5W	19
St. Helena B., *C. Pr.*	32¾S	18¼E	52
St. Helens, *England.*	53½N	2¾W	22
St. Helens, *Tasmania.*	41¼S	148¼E	59
St. Helier, *Channel Is.*	49¼N	2¼W	32
St. Hilaire, *France.*	48½N	1W	31
St. Hilaire-au-Temple, *France.*	49N	4½E	30
St. Hippolyte, *France.*	47¼N	6¾E	31
St. Hubert, *Belgium.*	50N	5½E	30
St. Hyacinthe, *Que. Can.*	45¾N	73W	69
St. Ingbert, *Germany.*	49¼N	7¼E	30
St. Ives, *England.*	52¼N	0	23
St. Ives, *England.*	50¼N	5½W	22
St. Jean, *Quebec, Can.*	45¼N	73¼W	69
St. Jean d'Angely, *Fr.*	46N	¼W	32
St. Jean-de-Luz, *Fr.*	43¼N	1¾W	32
St. Jean de Maurienne, *France.*	45¼N	6¼E	31
St. Jerome, *Que., Can.*	45¾N	74W	69
St. Johann, *Austria.*	47¾N	12½E	31
St. Johann, *Austria.*	47¼N	13E	33
St. John, *New B., Can.*	45¼N	66W	67
St. John I., *W. Indies.*	18N	65W	77
St. John, L., *Que., Can.*	48¾N	72W	69
St. John R., *N. Bruns.*	45¼N	66W	67
St. Johns, *Antigua, W.I.*	17N	62W	77
St. John's, *Newf., Can.*	47½N	52¾W	67
St. John's Pt., *Ireland.*	54¼N	5¾W	26
St. John's Pt., *Ireland.*	54½N	8½W	26
St. Johnstone, *Ireland.*	55N	7½W	26
St. Joseph, *Mo., U.S.A.*	40N	95W	75
St. Joseph, *Que., Can.*	46¼N	71W	69
St. Joseph, L., *Ontario.*	51N	91W	71
St. Julien, *France.*	46N	6E	32
St. Julien la Roche, *Fr.*	46N	6E	31
St. Just, *England.*	50N	5½W	22
St. Kilda, *S.I., N.Z.*	(inset	D).	63
St. Kilda I., *Scotland.*	58N	8W	28
St. Kitts, *Lee. Is., W.I.*	17¼N	62¾W	77
St. Lambert, *Que., Can.*	45½N	73½W	69
St. Laurent, *France.*	46½N	6E	31
St. Lawrence, *Queens.*	22¼S	149½E	60
St. Lawrence I., *Alaska.*	62N	170W	74
St. Lawrence R., *Can.*	49N	66W	66
St. Leonard, *N. Bruns.*	47¼N	68W	67
St. Leonards, *England.*	50¾N	½E	23
St. Lo, *France.*	49¼N	1¼W	32
St. Louis, *Senegal*	16N	16½W	50
St. Louis, *Mo., U.S.A.*	38¾N	90¼W	75
St. Lucia B., *Natal.*	28¼S	32½E	54
St. Lucia, *Wind. Is., W.I.*	14N	61W	77
St. Maixent, *France.*	46¼N	0	32
St. Malo, *France.*	48¾N	2W	32
St. Marc, *Haiti, W.I.*	19¼N	73W	77
St. Marks, *C. Pr., S.Afr.*	32S	27½E	53
St. Martin I., *Lee. Is.*	18N	63W	77
St. Mary R., *Alb., Can.*	49½N	113W	73
St. Marys, *Ont., Can.*	43¼N	81¼W	68
St. Mary's, *Scilly Is. Eng.*	50N	6¼W	22
St. Mary's, *Scotland.*	58¾N	2¾W	24
St. Mary's, *Tasmania.*	41½S	148¼E	59
St. Mathieu, Pte. de, *Fr.*	48¼N	4¾W	32
St. Matthew I., *Burma.*	10N	98E	43
St. Matthias Group, *Pac.*	2S	150E	60
St. Matthew Island, *N. Pac.* (inset).	60¼N	172W	42
St. Maurice, *Switz.*	46¼N	7E	31
St. Maurice R., *Quebec.*	46¼N	72¾W	69
St. Mawes, *England.*	50¼N	5W	22
St. Meen, *France.*	48¼N	2W	31
St. Michel, *France.*	45¼N	6½E	31

Place	Lat.	Long.	No.
St. Mihiel, *France.*	49N	5½E	30
St. Moritz, *Switz.*	46½N	9¾E	31
St. Nazaire, *France.*	47¼N	2¼W	32
St. Neots, *England.*	52¼N	¼W	23
St. Nicolas, *Belgium.*	51¼N	4E	30
St. Nicolas du Port, *Fr.*	48½N	6¼E	30
St. Niklaus, *Switz.*	46¼N	7¾E	31
St. Omer, *France.*	50¾N	2¼E	32
St. Paul, *France.*	42¾N	2¾E	32
St. Paul, *Minn., U.S.A.*	45N	93¼W	75
St. Paul des Metis, *Can.*	54N	111¼W	73
St. Pere en Retz, *Fr.*	47N	2W	31
St. Peter Port, *Chan. Is.*	49½N	2¾W	31
St. Petersburg, *U.S.A.*	27¾N	82¾W	75
St. Pierre, *Wind. Is.*	14¾N	61¼W	77
St. Pierre d'Albigny, *France.*	45½N	6¼E	31
St. Pierre-Eglise, *Fr.*	49¾N	1½W	31
St. Pol, *France.*	50¼N	2¼E	32
St. Pol de Leon, *Fr.*	48¾N	4W	31
St. Polten, *Austria.*	48¼N	15½E	33
St. Pons, *France.*	43½N	2¾E	32
St. Quentin, *France.*	49¾N	3¼E	32
St. Raymond, *Que. Can.*	47N	72W	69
St. Rhemy, *Italy.*	45¾N	7¼E	31
St. Saens, *France.*	49¾N	1¼E	31
St. Sartoro Is., *Norway.*	60¼N	5E	29
St. Sebastien, C., *Malag.*	13S	49E	56
St. Servan, *France.*	48¾N	2W	32
St. Sever, *France.*	43¾N	¾W	32
St. Thomas, *Ont., Can.*	42¾N	81¼W	68
St. Thomas I., *W.I.*	18¼N	65W	77
St. Trond, *Belgium.*	50¾N	5½E	30
St. Tuna, *Sweden.*	61N	15E	29
St. Valery, *France.*	50¼N	1¾E	32
St. Valery-en-Caux, *Fr.*	49¾N	¾E	30
St. Vincent, C., *Port.*	37N	9W	35
St. Vincent, G. of, *S.Aus.*	35S	138E	59
St. Vincent I., *W. Ind.*	13¼N	61¼W	77
St. Vith, *Belgium.*	50¼N	6¼E	30
St. Walburg, *Sask. Can.*	53¾N	109¼W	70
St. Wendel, *Germany.*	49½N	7¼E	30
St. Yrieux, *France.*	45½N	1¼E	32
Ste. Croix, *Switz.*	46¾N	6½E	31
Ste. Marie, *Que., Can.*	46½N	71W	69
Ste. Marie, C., *Malag.*	26½S	45E	56
Ste. Menehould, *Fr.*	49N	5E	30
Ste. Thecle, *Que., Can.*	47N	72½W	69
Saintes, *France.*	45¾N	¾W	32
SAINTONGE, *Fr.* (ins.).	45N	1W	32
Saio, *Ethiopia.*	8N	34¾E	56
Saipan I., *Pacific.*	15N	145E	64
Saishu Strait, *Korea.*	34N	127E	49
Saiun, *S. Yemen.* (ins.)	16N	49E	40
Sajama, Mt., *Bolivia.*	18S	69W	79
Sak Riv., *C. Pr., S. Afr.*	30S	20½E	52
Saka Dzong, *Tibet.*	29N	85E	43
Sakai, *Japan.*	34½N	135E	49
Sakaka, *Saudi Arabia.*	30N	40E	41
Sakambunli, *Angola.*	10S	22E	56
Sakania, *Congo* (*K.*).	12¾S	28½E	56
Sakarya, R., *Turkey.*	40N	31E	41
Sakata, *Japan.*	39N	140E	49
Sakhalin I., *U.S.S.R.*	50N	143E	39
Sakhalinski B., *U.S.S.R.*	54N	141E	39
Sakota, *Ethiopia.*	12½N	39E	56
Sakr, *S. Yemen.* (ins.).	15¼N	51E	40
Salado R., *Argentina.*	32S	61W	79
Salado R., *Argentina.*	38S	65W	79
Salado Riv., *Mexico.*	27N	99W	76
Salaga, *Ghana.*	8½N	½W	57
Salahuddin, *Iraq.*	36½N	44E	41
Salajar I., *Indon.*	6S	121E	47
Salama, *Israel* (inset).	32N	35E	40
Salama, *Guatemala.*	15N	90W	76
Salamanca, *Spain.*	41N	5½W	35
Salamanca, *U.S.A.*	42¼N	78¾W	69
Salamaua, *N. Guin.* (ins.).	7S	147½E	60
Salangen, *Norway.*	68½N	17½E	38
Salazar, *Angola.*	9S	15E	56
Salbris, *France.*	47½N	2E	31
Salcombe, *England.*	50¼N	3¾W	22
Saldanha & B., *C. Pr.*	33S	18E	52
Salde, *Senegal.*	16N	13W	50
Saldus, *U.S.S.R.*	56¾N	22½E	38
Sale, *England.*	53½N	2¼W	22
Sale, *Italy.*	45N	8¾E	31
Sale, *Victoria, Aust.*	38S	147E	59
Salekhard, *U.S.S.R.*	66½N	66½E	38
Salem, *C. Pr., S. Afr.*	33½S	26½E	53
Salem, *India.*	11¾N	78¼E	45
Salem, *Mass., U.S.A.*	42½N	70¾W	69
Salem, *Oregon, U.S.A.*	45N	123W	74
Salemi, *Sicily.*	37¾N	13E	36
Salen, *Scotland.*	56½N	6W	25
Salen, *Scotland.*	56¾N	5¾W	24
Salerno & G., *Italy.*	40¾N	14¾E	36
Salford, *England.*	53½N	2¼W	22
Salida, *Colorado, U.S.A.*	38N	106W	74
Salignac, *France.*	45N	1½E	32
Salima, *Malawi.*	14S	34¼E	51
Salina, *Kansas, U.S.A.*	38¾N	97¾W	74
Salina Is., *Medit.*	38½N	15E	36
Salina, *Utah, U.S.A.*	39N	111¾W	74
Salina Cruz, *Mexico.*	16N	95½W	76
Salinas, *Calif., U.S.A.*	36¾N	121¾W	74
Salinas, *Mexico.*	26N	100½W	76
Saline R., *Kan., U.S.A.*	38½N	97W	75
Salins, *France.*	47N	6E	31
Salisbury, *England.*	51N	1¾W	23
Salisbury I., *N.W. Can.*	63N	78W	66
Salisbury, *Me., U.S.A.*	38N	75W	75
Salisbury, *N.Bruns. Can.*	46N	65W	67
Salisbury, *Rhodesia.*	17¾S	31E	51
Salisbury Plain, *Eng.*	51¼N	1¾W	23

Place	Lat.	Long.	No.
Sallyana, *India.*	28½N	82¼E	44
Salmon, *Idaho, U.S.A.*	45N	114W	74
Salmon Arm, *Canada.*	50¾N	119¼W	72
Salmon Gums, *W. Aust.*	33S	121½E	61
Salo, *Italy.*	45½N	10½E	31
Salonika, see THESSALONIKI.			
Salonta, *Romania.*	46¾N	21¾E	37
Salorno, *Italy.*	46¼N	11¼E	31
Salsette I., *India.*	19N	72¾E	45
Salsk, *U.S.S.R.*	47N	42E	38
Salta, *Argentina.*	25S	65¼W	79
Saltaire, *C. Pr., S. Afr.*	33¾S	26E	53
Saltash, *England.*	50½N	4¼W	22
Saltburn-by-the-Sea, *England.*	54½N	1W	25
Saltcoats, *Sask., Can.*	51¼N	102W	70
Saltcoats, *Scotland.*	55½N	4¾W	25
Saltee Is., *Eire.*	52¼N	6½W	22
Saltfleet, *England.*	53½N	¼E	23
Saltillo, *Mexico.*	25½N	101W	76
Salt Lake, *Kash.* (ins.).	35N	80E	44
Salt Lake City, *U.S.A.*	40¾N	112W	74
Salt Riv., *C. Pr., S.Afr.*	33½S	24¼E	53
Salt R., *Ariz., U.S.A.*	33N	112½W	74
Salto, *Uruguay.*	31¾S	58W	79
Salto, Riv., *Italy.*	42¾N	12½E	36
Salton Sea, *Cal., U.S.A.*	33¼N	116W	74
Saltpan, *O.F.S., S. Afr.*	28¾S	26E	55
Saltpond, *Ghana.*	5N	1W	57
Saltrou, *Haiti, W.I.*	18N	72½W	77
Saluzzo, *Italy.*	44½N	7½E	31
SALVADOR, *C. America.*	13¾N	89W	76
Salvador, *Sask., Can.*	52¼N	109½W	70
Salvador, *Brazil.*	12¾S	38½W	78
Salvatierra, *Mexico.*	20N	101W	76
Salwa, *Qatar.*	25N	51E	40
Salween Riv., *Burma.*	17N	97E	43
Salyany, *U.S.S.R.*	39½N	49E	38
Salzach, R., *Germany.*	48¼N	13E	33
Salzbrunn, *S.W. Africa.*	24S	17½E	51
Salzburg, *Austria.*	47¾N	13E	33
Salzwedel, *Germany.*	52¾N	11¼E	33
Samakh, *Israel,* (Ins.).	32¾N	35½E	40
Samalayuca, *Mexico.*	32N	106½W	76
Samana Cay, *Bahamas.*	23N	73½W	77
Samar I., *P.I.*	12N	125E	47
Samara, see KUIBYSHEV.			
Samari, *Papua* (inset).	10S	151E	60
SAMARIA, *Jord.* (ins.).	32¼N	35¼E	40
Samarinda, *Kal., Indon.*	½S	117¼E	47
Samarkand, *U.S.S.R.*	40N	67E	40
Samarra, *Iraq.*	34¼N	44E	40
Samawa, *Iraq.*	31¼N	45¼E	40
Sambalpur, *India.*	21½N	84E	44
Sambas, *Kal., Indon.*	1¼N	109E	47
Sambor, *U.S.S.R.*	49½N	23¼E	38
Sambre, Riv., *France.*	50¼N	4E	30
Samchok, *Korea.*	37½N	129E	49
Same, *Tanzania.*	4S	37¾E	56
Samer, *France.*	50½N	1¾E	30
Samnan, *Iran.*	35¾N	53½E	40
SAMOA IS., *Pacific.*	14S	171W	64
Samokov, *Bulgaria.*	42¼N	23½E	37
Samos I., *Aegean Sea.*	37¾N	26¾E	37
Samothrace, I., *Aegean*	40½N	25½E	37
Samso, *Denmark.*	55¾N	11E	33
Samson, Mt., *W. Aust.*	22½S	117½E	61
Samsun, *Turkey.*	41¼N	36¼E	41
Samtredi, *U.S.S.R.*	42½N	42E	38
Samzumling, *Kashmir.*	34¾N	78½E	44
San River, *Poland.*	50¾N	22E	33
San Ambrogio, *Italy.*	45½N	10¾E	31
San Ambrosia, *Chile.*	26S	80W	78
San Andres, *Guatemala.*	17N	90W	76
San Andres Tuxtla, *Mexico.*	18¼N	95½W	76
San Andres, I. de, *W.I.*	12½N	82W	77
San Angelo, *Italy.*	45¼N	9¼E	31
San Angelo, *Tex., U.S.A.*	31½N	100½W	74
San Antioco, *Sardinia.*	39N	8½E	36
San Antonio, C., *Cuba.*	22N	85W	77
San Antonio de los Cobres, *Argentine.*	24S	66W	79
San Antonio, *Texas, U.S.A.*	29½N	98½W	74
San Augustin, *Mexico.*	32½N	106W	76
San Augustin, C., *P.I.*	6½N	126½E	47
San Aurdal, *Norway.*	61N	9¾E	29
San Benedetto, *Italy.*	43N	13¾E	36
San Bernardino, *Cal., U.S.A.*	34½N	117¼W	74
San Blas, *Mexico.*	21½N	105½W	76
San Blas, *Mexico.*	26¼N	108¾W	76
San Blas, C., *Fla., U.S.A.*	30N	85W	75
San Candido, *Italy.*	46¾N	12¼E	31
San Carlos, *Nicaragua.*	11N	85W	77
San Carlos, *Venezuela.*	9½N	68½W	77
San Caterina, *Italy.*	46½N	10½E	31
San Cristobal, *Venez.*	7¾N	72¼W	78
San Cristobal I., *Pac.*	10½S	162E	64
San Croce, C. of, *Sicily.*	37N	15¼E	36
San Diego, *Cal., U.S.A.*	32¾N	117¼W	74
San Dimas, *Mexico.*	24¼N	106W	76
San Domingo, *Mexico.*	30¾N	116W	76
San Eugenia Pt., *Mex.*	27¾N	115¼W	76
San Felipe, *Chile.*	32¾S	70¾W	79
San Felipe, *Mexico.*	22N	88W	76
San Felipe, *Mexico.*	31N	115W	76
San Felipe, *Venezuela.*	10¼N	68¾W	77
San Feliu de Guixols, *Sp.*	41¾N	3E	35
San Felix, *Venezuela.*	8N	62½W	77
San Felix I., *Chile.*	26S	80W	78
San Fernando, *Chile.*	35S	71W	79
S. Fernando, *Luzon, P.I.*	16N	120E	47
San Fernando, *Mexico.*	24¾N	98W	76

Place	Lat.	Long.	No.
San Fernando, *Mexico.*	30N	115¼W	76
San Fernando, *Spain.*	36½N	6¼W	35
San Fernando, *Trinid.*	10¼N	61½W	77
San Fernando, *Venez.*	7N	68W	77
San Francisco, *Nic.*	11N	84W	77
San Francisco, *Arg.*	32S	62½W	79
San Francisco, *Cal., U.S.A.*	37¾N	122½W	74
San Francisco, *Dom. R.*	19½N	70W	77
San Francisco del Oro, *Mexico.*	26¾N	106W	76
San Gavino, *Sardinia.*	39½N	8¾E	36
S. German, *Puerto Rico.*	18N	67W	77
S. Giorgio, Pt. of, *Italy.*	43N	13¾E	36
S. Giovanni in Fiore, *Italy.*	39¼N	16¾E	36
San Ilario, *Italy.*	44¾N	10½E	31
San Joaquin R., *U.S.A.*	38N	122W	74
San Jorge, *Nicaragua.*	11N	86W	77
San Jorge, G., *Arg.*	48S	68W	78
S. Jorge, G. of, *Spain.*	41N	1E	35
S. Jorge I., *Azores*(ins.).	38¾N	28W	35
San Jose, *Calif., U.S.A.*	37¼N	122W	74
San Jose, *Costa Rica.*	10N	84¼W	77
San Jose, *Guatemala.*	14N	91W	76
S. Jose, *Panay, P.I.*	10½N	122E	47
San Jose, *Uruguay.*	34½S	57W	79
S. Juan Del Norte, *Nic.*	11N	83¾W	77
San Jose Del Cabo, *Mex.*	23N	109¾W	76
San Juan, *Argentina.*	31½S	68¼W	79
San Juan, *Puerto Rico.*	18N	66W	77
San Juan, *Venezuela.*	11½N	68½W	77
S. Juan R., *Ut., U.S.A.*	36¾N	111W	74
S. Juan Del Norte, *Nic.*	11N	83¾W	77
San Juan Del Rio, *Mex.*	24¾N	104½W	76
S. Juan Del Sur, *Nicar.*	11¼N	87W	77
S. Juan Ixcoy, *Guat.*	15½N	91W	76
San Julian, *Argentina.*	49¼S	68W	78
S. Kvalo I., *Norway.*	70N	18E	29
San Leonardo, *Italy.*	46¾N	11½E	31
San Luis, *Argentina.*	33½S	66¼W	79
San Luis, *Cuba, W.I.*	20N	76W	77
S. Luis de la Paz, *Mex.*	21¼N	100¾W	76
San Luis Obispo, *U.S.*	35¼N	120¾W	74
San Luis Potosi, *Mex.*	22¼N	101W	76
San Marcial, *Mexico.*	28½N	110¼W	76
San Marcos, *Guatemala.*	15N	92W	76
San Marcos, *Mexico.*	20¾N	104¼W	76
S. Marcos, *Tex., U.S.A.*	30N	97½W	74
San Marino, *Italy.*	44N	12½E	36
S. Martino de Calvi, *It.*	46N	9¾E	31
San Mateo, *Cal., U.S.A.*	37½N	122¼W	74
San Mateo, *Venezuela.*	10N	64¼W	77
S. Matias, G. de, *Arg.*	41¾S	64W	78
San Miguel, *Salvador.*	13¼N	88¼W	77
San Nazzaro, *Italy.*	45¼N	9E	31
San Nicandro, *Italy.*	41¾N	15½E	36
San Pedro, *Br. Hond.*	17½N	89W	77
San Pedro, *Paraguay.*	24S	57W	79
San Pedro, *Venezuela.*	7N	63W	77
San Pedro de las Colonias, *Mexico.*	25½N	103W	76
S. Pedro Sula, *Hond.*	15½N	88W	77
San Pietro, *Sardinia.*	39N	8¼E	36
S. Polo D'Enza, *Italy.*	44½N	10½E	31
San Quintin, *Mexico.*	30½N	116W	76
S. Rafael de Atamaica, *Venezuela.*	7½N	67½W	77
San Rafael, *Argentina.*	34½S	68½W	79
San Remo, *Italy.*	43¾N	7¾E	36
San Roque, *Spain.*	36¼N	5¼W	35
S. Roque, *Azores* (ins.).	38¼N	28½W	35
San Roque, C. de, *Brazil.*	5½S	35W	78
San Salvador, *Angola.*	6½S	14E	56
S. Salvador I., *Bahamas.*	24N	74½W	77
San Salvador, *Salvador.*	13¾N	89¼W	76
San Sebastian, *Spain.*	43¼N	2W	35
S. Sebastian, C., *Moz.*	22½S	36E	51
San Sebastien, *Canarys.*	28N	17W	35
S. Stefano, Pt. of, *Italy.*	42½N	11E	36
San Valentin, *Chile.*	48S	75W	78
S. Vicente, *Madeira.*	32¾N	17W	35
San Vicente, *Spain.*	43¼N	4½W	35
S. Victor, *Guyana* (ins.)	8N	60W	77
San Vincenzo, *Italy.*	43N	10½E	36
S. Vito Chietino, *Italy.*	42¼N	14½E	36
S. Vito, C. of, *Sicily.*	38¼N	12¾E	36
Sana, Riv., *Yugoslavia.*	45N	16½E	36
Sana, *Yemen.*	15¼N	44¼E	40
Sanaga Riv., *Cameroon.*	4N	10E	56
Sanana I., *Sulas, Indon.*	2½S	126E	47
Sanaro, Riv., *Italy.*	42¼N	14½E	36
Sancerre, *France.*	47¼N	2¾E	37
Sanchez, *Dom. Rep.*	19N	69¾W	77
Sancti Spiritus, *Cuba.*	22N	79½W	77
Sand, *Italy.*	47N	12E	31
Sand, *Norway.*	59½N	6½E	29
Sand Flats, *C. Pr. S.Afr.*	33½S	26E	53
Sandakan, *E. Malaysia.*	5¾N	118¼E	47
Sanday I., *Scotland.*	59¼N	2½W	24
Sandbach, *England.*	53N	2½W	22
Sandberg, *C. Pr., S.Afr.*	32½S	18½E	52
Sanderson, *Tex., U.S.A.*	30N	102½W	74
Sandfontein, *S.W. Afr.*	22½S	20E	51
Sandgate, *England.*	51N	1¼E	23
Sandgate, *Queens.*	27¼S	153E	60
Sandhead, *Scotland.*	54¾N	5W	25
Sandnes, *Norway.*	59N	5¾E	29
Sando, *Faeroe Is.* (ins.).	62N	7W	29
Sandoa, *Congo* (*K.*).	9¾S	23E	56
Sandomierz, *Poland.*	50¾N	21¾E	33
Sandover River, *Aust.*	21S	137½E	60
Sandoway, *Burma.*	18½N	94¼E	4
Sandown, *England.*	50¾N	1¼W	2
Sandray, *Scotland.*	57N	7¼W	2

Place	Lat.	Long.	No.
Sandusky, Ohio, U.S.A.	42N	83w	75
Sandvik, Iceland (ins.).	63½N	23w	29
Sandwich, England.	51¼N	1¼E	23
Sandy Bight, W. Aust.	34s	123E	61
Sandy, C., Tas. (ins.).	41¼s	144½E	59
Sandy,C., Queens. Aust.	24½s	153¼E	60
Sangamner, India.	19N	74E	43
Sangatolon, U.S.S.R.	62N	150E	39
Sangcharak, Afghan.	36N	66½E	43
Sangha C., Congo (B.).	1s	17E	56
Sangihe Is., Indonesia.	3½N	125¼E	47
Sangju, Korea.	36½N	128E	49
Sangre Grande, Trin.	11N	61w	77
Sangwala, Ghana.	9¼N	1w	57
Sanji Pass, China.	32N	92½E	43
Sanjo, Japan.	38N	139E	49
Sanlucar, Spain.	36¼N	6¼w	35
Sanluri, Sardinia.	39¼N	8¾E	36
Sanmen, China.	34¼N	111E	48
Sannieshof, T'vaal.	26¼s	25¼E	55
Sanok, Poland.	49¼N	22¼E	33
Sanquhar, Scotland.	55¼N	4w	25
Sansane-Mangu, Togo.	10¼N	¼E	57
Santa Ana, Cal., U.S.A.	33¾N	117¾w	74
Sta. Ana, Madeira Is.	32¼N	17w	35
Santa Ana, Salvador.	14N	89¼w	76
Santa Barbara, Hond.	15¼N	87w	77
Santa Barbara, Hond.	15N	88w	77
Santa Barbara, Mexico.	26¼N	106w	76
Santa Barbara, U.S.A.	34¼N	119¾w	74
Santa Barbara, Venez.	8N	71¼w	77
Santa Barbara, Venez.	7N	61w	77
STA. CATARINA, Brazil.	27s	51w	79
Santa Clara, Cuba.	22¼N	80w	77
Santa Cruz, Argentina.	50s	69w	78
Sta. Cruz, Azores (ins.).	39N	28w	35
Sta. Cruz, Azores (ins.).	39¼N	31w	35
Santa Cruz, Bolivia.	17¼s	63¼w	79
Sta. Cruz, Calif., U.S.A.	37N	122¼w	74
Santa Cruz, Canary Is.	28¼N	16¼w	50
Sta. Cruz, Luzon, P.I.	14¼N	122¼E	47
Sta. Cruz, Madeira Is.	32¼N	17w	35
Santa Cruz, Venezuela.	8N	64¼w	77
Santa Cruz Is., Pacific.	11s	166E	64
Sta. Cruz de la Palma, Canary Is. (inset).	28¼N	17¾w	35
Sta. Cruz de Tenerife, Canary Is. (inset).	28¼N	16¼w	35
Sta. Cruz del Sar, Cuba.	21N	78w	77
Sta. Dorotea, Panama.	7¼N	78w	77
Sta. Elena, Costa Rica.	11N	85¼w	77
Sta. da Estrela, Port.	40¼N	7¼w	35
Sta. Eufemia, G. of, It.	38¼N	16E	36
Santa Fe, Argentina.	31¼s	61w	79
Santa Fe, Cuba, W.I.	22N	82w	77
Sta. Fe, N.M., U.S.A.	35¼N	106w	74
Sta. Genoveva, Mexico.	23N	110w	76
Santa Ines I., Chile.	54s	73w	78
Sta. Isabel, Fernando Po.	3¼N	8¼E	57
Sta. Isabel, Uruguay.	32¼s	56¼w	79
Santa Isabel I., Pacific.	7¼s	159E	64
Sta. Maria, Brazil.	29¼s	54w	79
Sta. Maria, Calif.,U.S.A.	35N	120¼w	74
Santa Maria, Switz.	46¼N	10¼E	31
Santa Maria di Leuca, C., Italy.	39¼N	18¼E	36
Santa Maria, Venezuela.	6¼N	67¼w	77
Sta. Maria Delpire, Ven.	8N	65¼w	77
Sta. Maria, I., Azores.	37¼N	25¼w	35
Sta. Marta, Colombia.	11N	74w	77
Santa Rita, Honduras.	8¼N	87¼w	76
Santa Rosa, Argentina.	36¼s	64¼w	79
Santa Rosa, Honduras.	14¼N	89w	77
Sta. Rosa, N.Mex.,U.S.A.	35N	104¾w	74
Santa Teresa, Mexico.	25¼N	97¼w	76
Santadi, Sardinia.	39N	8¼E	36
Santai, China.	31¼N	105E	48
Santander, Spain.	43¼N	3¾w	35
Santany, Balearic Is.	39¼N	3¼E	35
Santarem, Portugal.	39¼N	8¾w	35
Santhia, Italy.	45¼N	8E	31
Santiago, Chile.	33¼s	70¾w	78
Santiago, Dom. Rep.	19¼N	70¼w	77
Santiago, Honduras.	15¼N	87¼w	76
Santiago de Cuba.	20N	76w	77
Santiago, Spain.	43N	8¼w	35
Santiago Del Estero, Argentina.	28s	64¼w	79
Santillana, Spain.	43¼N	4w	35
Santipur, India.	23¼N	88½E	44
Santo Domingo, Dominican Rep.	18¼N	70w	77
Santona, Spain.	43¼N	3¼w	35
Santos, Brazil.	24s	46¼w	79
Sanyati Riv., Rhodesia.	16s	28E	51
Sanyuan, China.	34½N	109E	48
Sao Borja, Brazil.	28¼s	56w	79
Sao Francisco R., Brazil.	9s	40w	78
Sao Hill, Tanzania.	8s	35E	56
Sao Luiz, Brazil.	2¼s	44¼w	78
Sao Miguel I., Azores.	38N	25¼w	35
SAO PAULO & Tn., Braz.	23¼s	46¼w	79
Sao Thome I.,G.of Guinea.	¼N	6¼E	50
Saona, I. de, Dom. Rep.	18N	68w	77
SAONE ET LOIRE, Fr.	46¼N	4¼E	32
Sapientza, I. of, Greece.	36¼N	21¼E	37
Sapporo, Japan.	43N	141¼E	49
Sapri, Italy.	40N	15¼E	36
Saqqiz, Iran.	36¼N	46E	40
Sara Buri, Thailand.	14¼N	101E	43
Saragossa, Spain.	41¼N	1w	35
Sarajevo, Yugoslavia.	43¼N	18¼E	37
Saran Paul, U.S.S.R.	64N	61E	38
Sarangani Is., P.I.	5¼N	125¼E	47
Saransk, U.S.S.R.	54¼N	45E	38
Sarapul, U.S.S.R.	56¼N	54E	38
Saratov, U.S.S.R.	51¼N	46E	38
SARAWAK, see EAST MALAYSIA.			
Saray, Turkey.	41¼N	28E	37
Sarbaz, Iran.	27N	61E	40
Sarca, Riv., Italy.	45¼N	11E	31
Sardarshahr, India.	28¼N	74¼E	44
SARDINIA, Mediter.	40N	9E	34
Sarentino, Italy.	46¼N	11¼E	31
Sargans, Switzerland.	47N	9¼E	31
Sargodha, Pakistan.	32N	72¼E	44
Sari, Iran.	36¼N	53E	40
Sarikamis, Turkey.	40¼N	42¼E	41
Sarina, Queens., Aust.	21¼s	149¼E	60
Sar-i-Pul, Afghanistan.	36N	66E	43
Sariwan, Korea.	38¼N	126E	49
Sariz, Iran.	31N	55¼E	40
Sark, Channel Islands.	49¼N	2¼w	31
Sarlat, France.	44¼N	1¼E	32
Sarna, Sweden.	61¼N	13E	29
Sarnia, Ontario, Can.	43N	82¼w	68
Saronno, Italy.	45¼N	9E	31
Saros, G. of, Turkey.	40¼N	26¼E	37
Sarra, Libya.	22N	22E	50
Sarralbe, France.	49N	7E	30
Sarre, England.	51¼N	1¼E	23
Sarrebourg, France.	48¼N	7E	30
Sarreguemines, Fr.	49¼N	7E	30
Sarreunion, France.	49N	7E	30
Sarria, Spain.	43N	7¼w	35
Sartas, U.S.S.R.	42N	53E	38
Sartene, Corsica.	41¼N	9E	36
SARTHE, R. & DEP., Fr.	48N	0	32
Sarur, Mus. & Oman.	23¼N	57¼E	40
Sartynya, U.S.S.R.	63N	63E	38
Sarvar, Hungary.	47¼N	17E	37
Sarysu & Riv., U.S.S.R.	48N	70E	39
Sarzeau, France.	47¼N	2¾w	31
Sasebo, Japan.	33¼N	129¼E	49
SASKATCHEWAN, Can.	54N	106w	66
Saskatchewan R., Can.	54N	101¼w	66
Saskatoon, Sask., Can.	52¼N	106¾w	70
Sasovo, U.S.S.R.	54N	41¼E	38
Saskylakh, U.S.S.R.	72N	114¼E	39
Sassabaneh, Ethiopia.	8N	43¼E	59
Sassandra, Ivory Coast.	5N	6¼w	50
Sassari, Sardinia.	40¼N	8¼E	36
Sassnitz, Germany.	54¼N	13¼E	33
Sasykoli, U.S.S.R.	47¼N	46¼E	38
Satara, India.	17¼N	74E	45
Satoraljaujhely, Hung.	48¼N	21¼E	33
Satpura Mts., India.	21¼N	76E	43
Sattur, India.	9¼N	77¼E	45
Satu Mare, Romania.	47¼N	23E	37
Satun, Thailand (ins.).	6¼N	100E	47
SAUDI ARABIA. S.W. Asia.	23N	48E	40
Saugor, India.	23¼N	78¼E	44
Saujbulagh, Iran.	36¼N	45¼E	41
Sault Ste. Marie, Ont.	46¼N	84¼w	68
Saumur, France.	47¼N	0	32
Saunders, C., S.I., N.Z. (inset D).			63
Sava, Riv., Yugoslavia.	44¼N	20¼E	37
Savaii I., Samoa, Pac.	13¼s	172¼w	64
Savanna La Mar, Jam.	18¼N	78¼w	77
Savannah, Ga., U.S.A.	32¼N	81w	75
Savannah River, U.S.A.	32N	81w	75
Savannakhet, Laos.	17N	105E	47
Savanne, Ontario, Can.	49N	90¼w	71
Savastepe, Turkey.	39¼N	27¼E	37
Save River, Mozam.	21¼s	35E	51
Saveh, Iran.	35N	50E	41
Savenay, France.	47¼N	2w	31
Saverne, France.	48¼N	7¼E	30
Savigliano, Italy.	44¼N	7¼E	36
Savigny, France.	47¼N	¼E	31
SAVOIE, France.	45¼N	6¼E	32
Savona, Italy.	44¼N	8¼E	36
Savonlinna, Finland.	61¼N	28¼E	29
Sawan Kaloke, Thai.	17¼N	100E	43
Sawu Is., Indonesia.	10¼s	122E	47
Sawu Sea, E. Indies.	9¼s	122E	47
Saxby R., Queens. Aust.	18s	141¼E	60
Saxmundham, Eng.	52¼N	1¼E	23
Sayan Mts., U.S.S.R.	52N	100E	39
Sazava, Riv., Czecho.	50N	14¼E	33
Scaddan, W. Aust.	33¼s	122E	61
Scaer, France.	48N	3¾w	31
Scafell Pike, Mt., Eng.	54¼N	3¼w	25
Scalloway, Scotland.	60¼N	1¼w	24
Scalpay, Scotland.	57¼N	6w	24
Scalpay, I. of, Scot.	57¼N	6¼w	24
Scapa Flow, Scotland.	59N	3w	24
Scaramia, C. of, Sicily.	36¼N	14¼E	36
Scarba, I. of, Scotland.	56¼N	5¾w	25
Scarborough, Eng.	54¼N	¼w	25
Scarborough, Tobago.	12N	60w	77
Scarpanto, I. of, Gr.	35¼N	27E	37
Sceaux, France.	48¼N	2¼E	31
Schaffhausen, Switz.	47¼N	8¼E	31
Schagen, Netherlands.	52¼N	4¼E	30
Scheerpoort, T'vaal.	25¼s	27¼E	55
Schefferville, Que., Can.	54N	67w	66
Schelde, R., Belgium.	51¼N	4¼E	30
Schenectady, N.Y., U.S.A.	42¾N	74w	75
Scherfede, Germany.	51¼N	8¼E	30
Scheveningen, Neth.	52¼N	4¼E	30
Schiedam, Nether.	51¼N	4¼E	30
Schiehallion, Scotland.	56¼N	4w	24
Schiengen, Germany.	47¼N	7¼E	30
Schiermonnikoog, Netherlands.	53¼N	6E	30
Schifferstadt, Ger.	49¼N	8¼E	30
Schillig, Germany.	53¼N	8E	30
Schiltach, Germany.	48¼N	8¼E	30
Schio, Italy.	45¼N	11¼E	31
Schirmeck, France.	48¼N	7E	30
Schleiden, Germany.	50¼N	6¼E	30
Schleswig, Germany.	54¼N	9¼E	33
Schluchtern, Germany.	50¼N	9¼E	33
Schmidt I., U.S.S.R.	81N	90E	39
Schmidtsdrif, C.Pr.	28¼s	24E	52
Schonebeck, Germany.	52N	11¼E	33
Schombie, C.Pr., S.Af.	31¼s	25¼E	53
Schopfheim, Germany.	47¼N	7¼E	30
Schotten, Germany.	50¼N	9E	33
Schouten Is., N. Guin.	1s	136E	47
Schouwen Is., Nether.	51¼N	4E	30
Schramberg, Germany.	48¼N	8¼E	32
Schreiber, Ont., Can.	48¼N	87¼w	71
Schruns, Austria.	47N	10E	31
Schull, Ireland.	51¼N	9¼w	26
Schuls, Switzerland.	46¼N	10¼E	31
Schwandorf, Germany.	49¼N	12E	33
Schwarzenburg, Switz.	46¼N	7¼E	31
Schwarzwald, Ger.	48¼N	8¼E	33
Schwaz, Austria.	47¼N	11¼E	33
Schwedt, Germany.	53N	14¼E	33
Schweich, Germany.	49¼N	7E	30
Schweinfurt, Germany.	50N	10¼E	33
Schweizer Reneke,S.Af.	27¼s	25¼E	54
Schwerin, Germany.	53¼N	11¼E	33
Schwerve, Ger. (ins.).	51¼N	7¼E	33
SCHWYZ, Switzerland.	47N	8¼E	31
Sciacca, Sicily.	37¼N	13E	36
Scilly Is., Atlantic.	50N	6¼w	22
Scone, N.S.W., Aust.	32s	150¼E	59
Scordia, Sicily.	37¼N	15E	36
Scorpionsdrif, C. Pr.	31s	21¼E	52
Scotia, Ontario, Can.	45¼N	79¼w	68
Scott, Sask., Canada.	52¼N	108¼w	70
Scott Inlet, N.W. Can.	72N	70w	66
Scott Is. & C., Br. Col.	50¼N	128¼w	72
Scottsbluff, Neb., U.S.	41¼N	103¾w	74
Scottburgh, Natal.	30¼s	30¼E	55
Scottsdale, Tasmania.	41¼s	147¼E	59
Scourie, Scotland.	58¼N	5¼w	24
Scranton, Pa., U.S.A.	41¼N	75¼w	75
Scerifos, I. of, Greece.	37N	24¼E	37
Scunthorpe, England.	53¼N	¼w	23
Scutari & L., see SHKODER			
Seabrook, L., W. Aust.	31s	119¼E	61
Seacliff, S.I., N.Z. (inset D).			63
Seaford, England.	50¼N	¼E	23
Seaforth, Ontario, Can.	43¼N	81¼w	68
Seaham Harb., Eng.	54¼N	1¼w	25
Sea Lake, Vict., Aust.	35¼s	142¼E	59
Seal R., Manitoba (ins.).	58¼N	94¼w	71
Seaton, England.	50¼N	3w	22
Seattle, Wash., U.S.A.	47¼N	122¼w	74
Sebha, Libya.	27N	14¼E	34
Sebou, Riv., Morocco.	34N	7¼w	34
Sebring, Fla., U.S.A.	27¼N	81¼w	75
Seclin, France.	50¼N	3E	30
Secunderabad, India.	17¼N	78¼E	45
Sedalia, Mo., U.S.A.	38¼N	93¼w	75
Sedan, France.	49¼N	5E	32
Sedan, S. Australia.	34¼s	139¼E	59
Sedbergh, England.	54¼N	2¼w	25
Seddonville, S.I., N.Z.	41¼s	172E	63
Sedgefield, England.	54¼N	1¼w	25
Sedhiou, Senegal, (Ins).	12¼N	15¼w	57
Seeheim, S.W. Africa.	26¼s	17¼E	50
Sees, France.	48¼N	1E	32
Seg, L., U.S.S.R.	63¼N	34E	38
Segamat, Malaysia(Ins.).	2¼N	102¾E	47
Segovia, Spain.	41N	4¼w	35
Segre, France.	47¼N	1w	32
Segre, Riv., Spain.	41¼N	1¼E	35
Segura, Riv., Spain.	38N	1w	35
Sehore, India.	23¼N	77E	44
Sehwan, Pakistan.	26¼N	67¼E	46
Seiches, France.	47¼N	¼w	31
Seiland I., Norway.	70¼N	23E	29
Sein, I. de, France.	48N	5w	32
Seinajoki, Finland.	63N	22E	38
Seine, B. de la, France.	49¼N	1w	31
Seine, Riv., France.	49¼N	1E	32
SEINE ET MARNE, Fr.	48¼N	3E	32
SEINE MARITIME, Fr.	49¼N	1E	32
Sejny, Poland.	54N	23¼E	33
Sekaju, Sumatra, Indon.	3s	104E	47
Sekondi, Ghana.	5N	1¼w	57
SELANGOR, Malay. (ins.)	3N	101¼E	47
Selaton, C., Borneo.	4s	114¼E	47
Selbo Fjord, Norway.	60N	5E	29
Selby, England.	53¼N	1w	23
Selemdzha R., U.S.S.R.	52N	128E	39
Selenga Riv., U.S.S.R.	52N	107E	39
Selennyakh R., U.S.S.R.	68N	144E	39
Selestat, France.	48¼N	7¼E	30
Selima Oasis, Sudan.	22N	29E	40
Selipuk, China.	32N	82¼E	43
Selkirk, Man., Can.	50¼N	97w	71
SELKIRK & Tn., Scot.	55¼N	2¾w	25
Selkirk, Yukon,Can.	62¼N	137¼w	66
Selkirk Mts., Br. Col.	51N	117¼w	66
Selles-s-Cher, France.	47¼N	1¼E	31
Selma, Ala., U.S.A.	32¼N	87w	75
Selsey Bill, England.	50¼N	¼w	23
Selukwe, Rhodesia.	19¼s	30E	51
SEL VAS, Brazil.	9s	65w	78
Selwyn, L., N.W. Can.	60N	105w	66
Selwyn Riv., S.I., N.Z. (inset C).			63
Selwyn, Queens., Aust.	21¼s	140¼E	60
Semans, Sask., Can.	51¼N	104¼w	70
Semarang, Java.	7s	110¼E	47
Sembe, Congo (B.).	1¼N	14E	56
Semenovskoe, U.S.S.R.	63N	42¼E	38
Semipalatinsk,U.S.S.R.	50¼N	80¼E	39
Semiyarka, U.S.S.R.	52N	78E	39
Semmering, Austria.	47¼N	15¼E	33
Semois, Riv., Belgium.	49¼N	5¼E	30
Senanga, Zambia.	16¼s	23E	51
Sendai, Japan.	32N	131E	49
Sendai, Japan.	38¼N	140¼E	49
Sendenhorst, Germany.	51¼N	7¼E	30
Senegal R., Senegal.	14N	15w	50
Senekal, O.F.S., S.Afr.	28¼s	27¼E	53
Senftenberg, Germany.	51N	14E	33
Sengwa Riv., Rhodesia.	17s	28E	51
Senigallia, Italy.	43¼N	13¼E	36
Senj, Yugoslavia.	45N	15E	34
Senja, I. of, Norway.	69N	17E	29
Senlis, France.	49¼N	2¼E	32
Sennar, Sudan.	13N	32¼E	56
Sennen, England.	50N	5¼w	22
Senny Br., Wales.	52N	3¾w	22
Senorbi, Sardinia.	39¼N	9¼E	36
Sens, France.	48¼N	3¼E	32
Sensuntepeque, Hond.	14N	88w	77
Senta, Yugoslavia.	46N	20E	37
Sentinel Mts., Antarc.	78s	87w	80
Seo De Urgel, Spain.	42¼N	1¼E	35
Seoni, India.	22N	79¼E	44
Seoul, Korea.	37¼N	127E	49
Sepik R., N. Guin. (ins.).	3¼s	144E	60
Sepolno, Poland.	53¼N	17¼E	33
Sepulveda, Spain.	41¼N	4w	35
Seraing, Belgium.	50¼N	5¼E	30
Serang I., Indonesia.	3s	130E	47
Serasan I., Indonesia.	3N	109E	47
SERBIA, Yugoslavia.	43N	21E	37
Serdobsk, U.S.S.R.	52¼N	44¼E	38
Seregno, Italy.	45¼N	9¼E	31
Seremban, Malaysia.	2¼N	102E	47
Serena, La, Chile.	30s	71w	78
Serenje, Zambia.	13s	31E	51
Seres, Greece.	41N	23¼E	37
SERGIPE, Brazil.	10¼s	37¼w	78
Seria, Brunei.	4¼N	114¼E	47
Seringapatam, India.	12¼N	76¼E	45
Serifos, I. of, Greece.	37N	24¼E	37
Serobanyane, Lesotho.	29¼s	29E	55
Serock, Poland.	52¼N	21E	33
Serov, U.S.S.R.	59¼N	60¼E	38
Serowe, Botswana.	22¼s	27E	51
Serpa, Portugal.	38N	7¼w	35
Serpent's Mth., Venez.	10N	62w	77
Serpukhov, U.S.S.R.	55N	37¼E	38
Serrat, C., Tunisia.	37¼N	9E	36
Serqueux, France.	49¼N	4w	32
Serviceton, Vict., Aust.	36¼s	141E	59
Seseke, R., Ger. (ins.).	51¼N	7¼E	33
Sesheke, Zambia.	17¼s	24¼E	51
Setana, Japan.	42¼N	139¼E	49
Sete, France.	43¼N	3¼E	32
Setif, Algeria.	36¼N	5¼E	50
Setit, Riv., Ethiopia.	14N	37¼E	56
Sette Cama, Gabon.	2¼s	9¼E	56
Settle, England.	54N	2¼w	25
Settlers, Transvaal.	25s	28¼E	54
Setubal, Portugal.	38¼N	9w	35
Seui, Sardinia.	40N	9¼E	36
Sevan, L., U.S.S.R.	40¼N	45¼E	38
Sevastopol, U.S.S.R.	44¼N	33¼E	38
Seven Is. & B., Quebec.	50¼N	66¼w	67
Sevenoaks, England.	51¼N	¼E	23
Severn, Riv., England.	51¼N	2¼w	23
Severn, R., N.S.W., Aust.	29s	151E	59
Sev. Dvina R., U.S.S.R.	64¼N	40¼E	38
Severnaya Zemlya, Arc.	79N	96E	60
Severodvinsk, U.S.S.R.	64¼N	40E	38
Severouralsk, U.S.S.R.	60N	59¼E	38
Seville, Spain.	37¼N	6w	35
Seward, Alaska, U.S.A.	60¼N	150w	74
Seward Pen., Alaska.	65N	161w	74
Sexsmith, Alberta, Can.	55¼N	118¾w	73
SEYCHELLES IS., Ind. Oc.	4s	55E	19
Seydhisfjordhur, Ice.	65N	14w	29
Seymchan, U.S.S.R.	63N	152¼E	39
Seymour, C. Pr., S.Af.	32¼s	26¼E	53
Seymour, Texas, U.S.A.	34N	99w	74
Seymour, Vict., Aust.	37s	145¼E	59
Seyssel, France.	46N	5¼E	31
Sezanne, France.	48¼N	3¼E	32
Sfax, Tunisia.	34¼N	10¼E	36
Sgurr na Ciche, Scot.	57N	5¼w	24
Shabani, Rhodesia.	20¼s	30E	51
Shackleton In., Antarc.	82¼s	163E	80
Shadi, Kashmir (ins.).	33¼N	77¼E	44
Shaftesbury, England.	51N	2¼w	23
Shahdadpur, Pakistan.	26¼N	68¼E	46
Shahjahanpur, India.	27¼N	80E	43
Shahr Kurd, Iran.	32¼N	51E	40
Shahriza, Iran.	32N	52w	40
Shahrud, Iran.	36N	54¼E	40
Shahsien, China.	26N	117¼E	48
Shaikh Shuaib, Iran.	27N	53E	46
Shaikhabad, Afghan.	33¼N	68¼E	43
Shajeungtrao, Thai.	14N	101E	43
Shakhti, U.S.S.R.	47N	40E	38
Shakhunya, U.S.S.R.	58N	46E	38
Shallal, U.A.R.	24N	33E	40
Shalym, U.S.S.R.	52N	88E	39
Shama, Ghana.	5N	1¼w	57
Shamrock, Texas, U.S.A.	35N	101w	74
Shamva, Rhodesia.	17¼s	31¼E	51
SHAN STATES, Burma.	22N	98E	43
Shangani Riv., Rhodesia.	18s	27E	51
Shanghai, China.	31¼N	121¼E	48
Shangjao, China.	28N	117¼E	48
Shangyiu, China.	26N	114¼E	48
Shanklin, England.	50¼N	1¼w	23

Place	Lat.	Long.	No.
Shannon, & R., Eire.	52¼N	9¼w	26
Shannon, N.I., N.Z.	40¼s	175½E	62
SHANSI, China.	38N	112E	48
Shantarski Is., U.S.S.R.	55N	138E	39
Shantow, China.	23½N	117E	48
SHANTUNG, China.	36N	118E	48
Shanwa, Tanzania.	3½s	33½E	56
Shaohing, China.	30N	120½E	48
Shaokwan, China.	24½N	113½E	48
Shaoyang, China.	27N	111E	48
Shap, England.	54½N	2¾w	25
Shapinsay, Scotland.	59N	2¾w	24
Shaqiq, Saudi Arabia.	29N	40E	41
Shaqra, Saudi Arabia.	25½N	46E	40
Shara River, China.	43N	121E	39
Sharasume, China.	47½N	88E	39
Share, Nigeria.	9N	5E	57
Shari River, Chad.	13N	15E	56
Sharia R., Israel (ins.).	31¼N	34½E	40
Sharja, Trucial St.	25¼N	55E	40
Shark B., W. Aust.	25¼s	114E	61
Sharkh, Mus. & Oman.	21¼N	58½E	40
Sharqat, Iraq.	36N	43E	41
Sharya, U.S.S.R.	58¼N	45½E	38
Shashi R., Botswana.	21½s	27¼E	51
Shasi, China.	30¼N	112¼E	48
Shasta, Mt., Cal. U.S.A.	41¼N	122¼w	74
Shaunavon, Sask., Can.	49½N	108¼w	70
Shawinigan Falls, Can.	46½N	72¾w	69
Shaw River, W. Aust.	20¼s	119E	61
Sheboygan, Wis. U.S.A.	43½N	87¾w	75
Shediac, New Bruns.	46¼N	64¼w	67
Sheelin, L., Ireland.	53¾N	7¼w	26
Sheep Haven, Ireland.	55¼N	8w	26
Sheepmoor, T'vaal.	26¼s	30¼E	55
Sheerness, England.	51¼N	1E	23
Sheffield, England.	53¼N	1½w	23
Sheffield, Tasmania.	41¼s	146¼E	59
Shefford, England.	52N	¼w	23
Sheho, Sask., Canada.	51¼N	103½w	70
Shehy Mts., Ireland.	51¾N	9¼w	26
Sheklung, China.	23N	114E	48
Shelagski, C., U.S.S.R.	70N	171E	39
Shelburne, No. Sc. Can.	43½N	65¼w	67
Shelburne, Ont., Can.	44¼N	80¼w	68
Shelby, Montana, U.S.A.	48N	111¼w	74
Shelekhova B., U.S.S.R.	60N	158E	39
Shellbrook, Sask., Can.	53½N	106¼w	70
Shendam, Nigeria.	9N	9¼E	57
Shendi, Sudan.	16¾N	33½E	50
Shengo, Botswana.	18s	22E	51
Shenkursk, U.S.S.R.	62N	43E	38
SHENSI, China.	35N	109E	49
Shentos Dzong, Tibet.	31N	88E	43
Shenyang, China.	42½N	122E	48
Shepparton, Victoria.	36½s	145½E	59
Sheppey, I. of, Eng.	51¼N	¾E	23
Shepton Mallet, Eng.	51¼N	2½w	22
Sherada, Ethiopia.	7¼N	36½E	56
Sherborne, England.	51N	2½w	22
Sherbro I. & R., S. Leone.	7¼N	12¾w	57
Sherbrooke, Que., Can.	45¼N	72w	69
Shereik, Sudan.	18N	33½E	40
Sheridan, Wyo., U.S.A.	44½N	107w	74
Sheringham, England.	53N	1¼E	23
Sherridon, Man., Can.	55N	100w	66
s'Hertogenbosch,Neth.	51¾N	5¼E	30
Shetlands, S., Antarc.	62s	60w	80
Shetland Is., Scotland.	60N	2w	24
Shiant Is., Scotland.	57¾N	6¼w	24
Shibam, S. Yem. (ins.).	15¾N	49½E	40
Shibarghan, Afghan.	36¼N	66E	43
Shibata, Japan.	38N	139E	49
Shibin El Kom, U.A.R.	30¼N	31E	50
Shifnal, England.	52¾N	2¼w	22
Shigar, Kash. (ins.).	35¼N	76E	44
Shigatse, Tibet.	29¼N	89E	43
Shihkiachwang, China.	38N	114½E	48
Shihtsien, China.	27¼N	108E	48
SHIKOKU, Japan.	33¼N	133E	49
Shikurpur, Pakistan.	28N	68E	43
Shillelagh, Eire.	52¾N	6¼w	26
Shilka, U.S.S.R.	52N	115E	39
Shillong, India.	26N	92E	43
Shiloh, Jordan (ins.).	32N	35¼E	40
Shimanovsk, U.S.S.R.	52N	127E	39
Shimo I., Japan.	33¼N	130E	49
Shimoga, India.	14N	75¼E	45
Shimonoseki, Japan.	34N	131E	49
Shin, L. & Riv., Scot.	58¼N	4¾w	24
Shinano, Riv., Japan.	38N	139E	49
Shingu, Japan.	33¾N	136E	49
Shinjo, Japan.	38¼N	140E	49
Shinkafe, Nigeria.	13N	6¼E	57
Shinko R., Cent. Afr. Rep.	5N	24E	56
Shinkolobwe, Congo (K.).	11s	26¼E	51
Shinyanga, Tanzania.	3¼s	33¼E	56
Shiogama, Japan.	38N	141E	49
Shippigan & I., Can.	47¼N	64¾w	67
Shipston-on-Stour, Eng.	52N	1¾w	23
Shirane, Mt., Japan.	37N	139¼E	49
Shiraz, Iran.	29¼N	52½E	40
Shirbin, U.A.R. (ins.).	31¼N	31½E	50
Shire Riv., Mozam.	17¼s	35E	51
Shiriya, C., Japan.	41¼N	141½E	49
Shiuden Gomba, China.	29N	97E	43
Shizuoka, Japan.	35N	138½E	49
Shkodër & L., Albania.	42N	19½E	37
Shoa, C., W. Aust.	33¼s	121E	61
Shoa Ghimirra, Eth.	7N	35½E	56
Shoal, C., W. Aust.	33¼s	121E	61
Shoal Lake, Man., Can.	50¼N	100¾w	70
Shoalhaven R., N.S.W.	34¼s	150½E	59
Shoalwater B., Queens.	22s	151E	60
Shobando, China.	31¼N	96E	43
Shoeburyness, Eng.	51¼N	¾E	23

Place	Lat.	Long.	No.
Shohsien, China.	39¼N	112E	48
Shoina, U.S.S.R.	68N	45E	38
Sholapur, India.	17¼N	75¾E	45
Shoreham-by-Sea, Eng.	50¾N	¼w	23
Shoshoni, Wyo., U.S.A.	43¼N	108w	74
Shott Djerid, L., Tunis.	33¾N	8¼E	35
Shott Ech Chergui, L., Algeria.	34¼N	½E	35
Shott El Hodna, L., Alg.	35½N	4¼E	35
Shott Melrhir, L., Alg.	34¼N	6¼E	35
Showa, China.	30N	95E	43
Shreveport, La., U.S.A.	32¼N	93¾w	75
Shrewsbury, England.	52¾N	2¾w	22
Shrewton, England.	51¼N	2w	22
SHROPSHIRE, CO., Eng.	52½N	2¾w	22
Shuikow, China.	26¼N	118¼E	48
Shujaabad, Pakistan.	29¾N	71½E	44
Shunning, China.	24¼N	100E	43
Shunyi, China.	40N	116¼E	48
Shuqra, S. Yem. (ins.).	14¼N	45E	40
Shuru, Iran.	29N	60E	40
Shuryshkary, U.S.S.R.	66N	65E	38
Shusha, U.S.S.R.	40N	47E	38
Shushal, Kash. (ins.).	33¼N	78¼E	44
Shushtar, Iran.	32N	49E	40
Shuswap, L., Br. Col.	51N	119w	72
Shuya, U.S.S.R.	57N	41¼E	38
Shuyang, China.	34N	119E	48
Shwangchen, China.	45¼N	126E	49
Shwebo, Burma.	22¼N	96E	43
Shyok & R., Kash.(ins.).	34N	78E	44
Sialkot, Pakistan.	32¼N	74¼E	44
Siam, G. of, Thailand.	11N	100E	43
Sian, China.	34¼N	109E	48
Siang Riv., China.	23¼N	111¼E	48
Siangyang, China.	32N	112E	48
Siangyin, China.	28¼N	112¼E	48
Siatsing, China.	37N	116E	48
Siauliai, U.S.S.R.	56N	23¼E	38
Sibenik, Yugoslavia.	43¼N	16E	37
Siberut I., Sumatra.	1¼s	99E	47
Sibi, Pakistan.	29¼N	67¼E	46
Sibiti, Congo (B.).	3¼s	13¼E	56
Sibiu, Romania.	45¼N	24E	37
Sibolga, Indonesia.	1¼N	98¼E	47
Sibsey, England.	53N	0	23
Sibu, E. Malaysia.	2¼N	112E	47
Sicamous, Br. Col.	50¼N	119w	72
Sicie, C., France.	43N	5½E	32
SICILY, Italy.	37¼N	14E	36
Sicuani, Peru.	14¼s	71¼w	78
Sid, Yugoslavia.	45¼N	19w	37
Sidcup, England.	51¼N	¼E	23
Siderno, Italy.	38¼N	16¼E	36
Sidhirokastron, Gr.	41¼N	23¼w	37
Sidi Barrani, U.A.R.	32N	27E	40
Sidi-bel-Abbes, Algeria.	35N	¾w	35
Sidmouth, England.	50¼N	3¼w	22
Sidney, Montana, U.S.A.	48N	104w	74
Sidorovsk, U.S.S.R.	66¼N	83E	39
Sidra, G. of, Libya.	32N	17¼E	34
Siedlce, Poland.	52¼N	22¼E	33
Siegburg, Germany.	50¾N	7¼E	30
Siegen, Germany.	50¾N	8E	30
Sieg, Riv., Germany.	50¾N	7E	30
Sielec, U.S.S.R.	52¼N	25E	33
Siena, Italy.	43¼N	11¼E	36
Sienne, Riv., France.	49N	1¼w	31
Sieradz, Poland.	51¼N	18¼E	33
Sierck, France.	49¼N	6¼E	30
Sierpc, Poland.	52¾N	19¼E	33
Sierra Blanca, U.S.A.	33N	106w	74
Sierra de Alcaraz, Sp.	39N	2w	35
Sierra de Gata, Spain.	40¼N	6¼w	35
Sierra de Gredos, Spain.	40N	6w	35
SierradeGuadalupe,Sp.	39¼N	5¼w	35
Sierra de Perija, Colom.	10N	72¼w	77
SIERRA LEONE, W. Africa.	8¼N	12w	50
Sierra Madre, Mexico.	27N	102w	76
Sierra Maestra, Cuba.	20N	76w	77
Sierra Pacaraima, Venez.	4N	62w	78
SierraTaguating,Braz.	12s	47w	78
Sierre, Switzerland.	46¼N	7¼E	31
Sifnos, I. of, Greece.	37N	24¼E	37
Sigean, France.	43N	3E	32
Sighet, Romania.	48N	23¼E	38
Sighisoara, Romania.	46¼N	24¼E	37
Siglufjordhur, Iceland.	66N	19w	29
Sigmaringen, Germany.	48N	9¼E	33
Sigoules, France.	44¾N	¼E	32
Siguenza, Spain.	41N	2¾w	35
Sikar, India.	27¾N	75¼E	44
Sikea, Greece.	36¼N	23E	37
Sikhota Alin Range, Mts., U.S.S.R.	45N	136E	49
Si-Kiang Riv., China.	22N	113¼E	48
SIKKIM, India.	27¼N	88¼E	44
Sila, Trucial States.	24N	52E	40
Silandro, Italy.	46¼N	10¼E	31
Silao, Mexico.	21¼N	102w	76
Silchar, India.	25N	93E	43
Silifke, Turkey.	36¼N	34E	41
Silistra, Bulgaria.	44N	27¼E	37
Siliqua, Sardinia.	39N	8¼E	36
Silivri, Turkey.	41N	28¼E	37
Siljan, L. of, Sweden.	61N	15E	29
Sille le Guillaume, Fr.	48¼N	0	31
Sillon de Talbert, Fr.	48¾N	3w	31
Silloth, England.	55N	3¼w	25
Silute, U.S.S.R.	55¼N	21¼E	33
Silver Centre, Ontario.	47¼N	79¼w	68
Silver City, U.S.A.	32¾N	108¼w	74
Silvermine Mts., Ire.	52¾N	8¼w	26
Silver Peak, S.I., N.Z. (inset D).			63
Silver Streams, C. Pr.	28¼s	23¼E	53

Place	Lat.	Long.	No.
Silverton, N.S.W., Aust.	32s	141½E	59
Silves, Portugal.	37¼N	8¼w	35
Simalu I., Sumatra.	2¼N	96E	47
Simbirsk, see ULYANOVSK.			
Simcoe, Ontario, Can.	42¾N	80¼w	68
Simcoe, L., Ont., Can.	44¼N	79¼w	68
Simferopol, U.S.S.R.	45N	34E	38
Simi, I. of, Greece.	36¼N	28E	37
Simla, India.	31N	77¼E	44
Simmern, Germany.	50N	7¼E	30
Simonstown, C. Pr.	34¼S	18¼E	52
Simplon Tunnel, Switz.-Italy.	46¼N	8¼E	31
Simpson Des., N. Terr.	25s	137E	60
Simpson, N.W.T., Can.	61¼N	122w	66
Simpson, Sask., Can.	51¼N	105¼w	70
Simrishamn, Sweden.	55¼N	14¼E	29
Sinai, Mt., U.A.R.	28¼N	34E	50
SINALOA, Mexico.	26N	108¼w	76
Sinalunga, Italy.	43¼N	11¼E	36
Sinanju, Korea.	39¼N	125E	49
Sinauen, Libya.	31N	10¼E	34
Since, Colombia.	9N	75¼w	77
Sinclair Head, N.I., N.Z. (inset B).			63
Sinclair, Mt., S.I., N.Z. (inset C).			63
Sindara, Gabon.	1s	11E	56
Sindjai, Celebes, Indon.	5s	120¼E	47
Sines, C., Portugal.	38N	9w	35
Singa, Sudan.	12¼N	33E	56
SINGAPORE, S.E. Asia.	1¼N	103¼E	47
Singida, Tanzania.	4¼s	34¼E	56
Singitic G. of Greece.	40N	24E	37
Singkawang, Kal., Indon.	1N	109E	47
Singkep, Sumatra, Indon.	1s	104E	47
Singleton, N.S.W., Aust.	32¼s	151¼E	59
Singleton Mt., W.Aust.	29¼s	117E	61
Singosan, Korea.	39N	127¼E	49
Sinhsien, China.	38N	112¼E	48
Sinhung, Korea.	40N	128E	49
Sinhwa, China.	27¼N	111E	48
Siniscola, Sardinia.	40¼N	9¼E	36
Sinj, Yugoslavia.	43¼N	16¼E	37
SINKIANG-UIGHUR, China.	42N	85E	42
Sinmin, China.	42N	122¼E	49
Sinnamary, Fr. Guiana.	6N	53w	78
Sinneh, Iran.	35¼N	47E	41
Sinning, China.	27N	110¼E	48
Sinoe, L., Romania.	44¼N	28¼E	37
Sinop, Turkey.	41N	35¼E	41
Sinpo, Korea.	40N	128E	49
Sintaluta, Sask., Can.	50¼N	103¼w	70
Sintang, Kal., Indon.	1N	111¼E	47
Sinuiji, Korea.	40N	124E	48
Sioma, Zambia.	17s	23E	51
Sion, Switzerland.	46¼N	7¼E	31
Sioux City, Io., U.S.A.	42¼N	96¼w	75
Sioux Falls, S.D., U.S.A.	43¼N	96¼w	75
Sioux Lookout,Ont.,Can.	50N	91¼w	71
Sipura I., Sumatra.	2¼s	99¼E	47
Siraiganj, Pakistan.	24¼N	90E	44
Sir Darya R., U.S.S.R.	45N	65E	42
Sir Edward Pellew's Is., N. Terr., Aust.	16s	136E	60
Sirino, Mt., Italy.	40N	16E	36
Sirohi, India.	24¼N	72¼E	44
Sironj, India.	24¼N	77¼E	44
Siros, I. of, Greece.	37¼N	25E	37
Sirsa, India.	29¼N	75E	44
Sir Samuel, W. Aust.	27¼s	121E	61
Sirte, Libya.	31N	16¼E	34
Sirur, India.	18¼N	74¼E	45
Sisak, Yugoslavia.	45¼N	16¼E	36
Sisteron, France.	44¼N	6E	32
Sisters I., Tas. (inset).	39¼N	148E	59
Sitapur, India.	27N	80¼E	44
Sitges, Spain.	41¼N	2E	35
Sitka, Alaska, U.S.A.	57N	137w	74
Sittang Riv., Burma.	17N	97E	43
Sittingbourne, Eng.	51¼N	¾E	23
Sivas, Turkey.	39¼N	37E	41
Siwa & Oasis, U.A.R.	29N	26E	40
Sixt, France.	46N	6¼E	31
Skagastolstind, Nor.	61¼N	8E	29
Skagastrond B., Iceland.	66N	21w	29
Skagerrak, Nor.-Den.	58N	10E	29
Skagway, Alaska, U.S.A.	59N	138w	74
Skaill, (Ork. Is.), Scot.	59N	2¾w	24
Skanevik, Norway.	59¾N	6E	29
Skardu, India.	35¼N	75¾E	43
Skarzysko-Kamienna, Poland.	51¼N	21E	33
Skaw, The, Denmark.	58N	10E	29
Skeena R., Br. Col., Can.	54¼N	130w	72
Skegness, England.	53¼N	¼E	23
Skelleftea, Sweden.	64¼N	21E	29
Skibbereen, Eire.	51¼N	9¼w	26
Skiddaw, Mt., Eng.	54¾N	3¼w	25
Skien, Norway.	59¼N	9¼E	29
Skierniewice, Poland.	52N	20¼E	33
Skikda, Algeria.	36¾N	6¼E	35
Skillaion, C., Greece.	37¾N	23¼E	37
Skipton, England.	54N	2w	25
Skopelos, I. of, Greece.	39N	23¼E	37
Skoplje, Yugoslavia.	42N	21¼E	37
Skovde, Sweden.	58¼N	14E	29
Skovorodino, U.S.S.R.	54N	124E	39
Skowhegan, Me., U.S.A.	45N	70w	75
Skudeneshavn I., Nor.	59¼N	5E	29
Skutskar, Sweden.	61N	17E	29
Skye, Is. of, Scotland.	57¼N	6¼w	24
Slabberts, O.F.S.,S. Afr.	28¼s	28¼E	53
Slane, Ireland.	53¾N	6¼w	26
Slaney, Riv., Ireland.	52¾N	6¼w	26
Slangfontein, C. Pr.	31¼s	22¼E	52
Slany, Czechoslovakia.	50¼N	14E	33

Place	Lat.	Long.	No.
Slatina, Yugoslavia.	45¼N	17¼E	37
Slatina, Romania.	44¼N	24¼E	37
Slave R., N.W.T., Can.	61¼N	113¼w	66
Slavgorod, U.S.S.R.	53N	78¼E	39
Slavkov, Czecho.	49¼N	16¼E	33
SLAVONIA, Yugoslavia.	45N	18E	37
Slavyansk, U.S.S.R.	49N	37¼E	38
Sleaford, England.	53N	¼w	23
Slea Head, Ireland.	52N	10¼w	26
Sledmere, England.	54N	¼w	25
Slesin, Poland.	52¼N	18¼E	33
Slesvig, Denmark.	55N	9E	29
Slieve Bloom Mts., Ire.	53N	7¾w	26
Slieve Donard Mt., Ire.	54¼N	6w	52
Slieve League, Ireland.	54¼N	8¾w	26
Slieve Mish Mts., Ire.	52¼N	9¾w	26
Sligachan, Scotland.	57¼N	6¼w	24
SLIGO B. & Co., Ireland.	54¼N	8¼w	26
Slite, Sweden.	57¼N	19E	29
Sliven, Bulgaria.	42¾N	26¼E	37
Slobodskoy, U.S.S.R.	58¾N	50¼E	38
Slobozia Veche, Rom.	44¼N	27¼E	37
Slocan &R & L., Br. Col.	49¼N	117¼w	73
Slonim, U.S.S.R.	53N	25¼E	38
Sloten, Netherlands.	52¾N	5¼N	30
Slough, England.	51¼N	¾w	23
SLOVAKIA, Czecho.	49N	20E	33
SLOVENIA, Yugoslavia.	46N	15E	37
Sluis, Netherlands.	51¼N	3¼E	30
Slupsk, Poland.	54¼N	17E	33
Slurg, Yugoslavia.	45N	15¼E	36
Slutsk, U.S.S.R.	59N	30¼E	38
Slutsk, U.S.S.R.	53N	27¼E	38
Slyne Head, Ireland.	53¼N	10¼w	26
Slyudyanka, U.S.S.R.	52N	103¼E	39
Smeeth, England.	51¼N	1E	23
Smith, Alberta, Can.	55¼N	114w	73
Smithers, Br. Col., Can.	54¾N	127¼w	72
Smiths Falls, Ont., Can.	45N	76w	69
Smoky Falls, Ont., Can.	50N	82¼w	71
Smoky Hill R., Kan.,U.S.	38N	97¼w	75
Smolen, Norway.	63¼N	8E	29
Smolensk, U.S.S.R.	54¼N	32E	38
Smolnik, Czecho.	48¼N	20¼E	33
Smolyan, Bulgaria.	41¾N	24¼E	37
Smyrna, see IZMIR.			
Snaefell Mt., I. of M.	54¼N	4¼w	25
Snaefellsnes Pen., Ice.	64¼N	23w	29
Snaith, England.	53¾N	1w	23
Snake R., Idaho, U.S.A.	43N	116w	74
Sneek, Netherlands.	53N	5¼E	30
Snehoetta, Norway.	62¼N	9E	29
Snina, Czechoslovakia.	49N	22¼E	33
Snowdon, Wales.	53N	4w	22
Snowy R., Vict., Aust.	37¼s	148¼E	59
Soave, Italy.	45¼N	11¼E	31
Soay, I. of, Scotland.	57¼N	6¼w	24
Sobat R., Sudan.	9¼N	31E	56
Sobernheim, Germany.	49¾N	7¼E	30
Sobeslav, Czecho.	49¼N	14¼E	33
Sobolev, U.S.S.R.	52N	51¼E	38
Sochaczew, Poland.	52¼N	20¼E	33
Sochi, U.S.S.R.	43¼N	40E	38
Society Is., Pacific.	17¼s	151w	64
Socorro, N. Mex., U.S.A.	34N	107w	74
Socotra I., Indian Oc.	12N	54E	19
Soderhamn, Sweden.	61¼N	17¼E	29
Sodertalje, Sweden.	59¼N	17¼E	29
Soekmekaar, S. Africa.	23¼s	30E	54
Soest, Germany.	51¼N	8E	30
Sofala, Mozambique.	20s	35¼E	51
Sofia, Bulgaria.	42¾N	23¼E	37
Sofia R., Malagasy.(ins.).	15s	46¼E	56
Sofisk, U.S.S.R.	52N	134E	39
Sogamoso, Colombia.	6N	73¼w	77
Sogne Fiord, Norway.	61N	4¼E	29
Sohag, U.A.R.	26N	32E	41
Soham, England.	52¼N	¼E	23
Sohana, Bougainville, Pac.	5s	155E	60
Sohar, Mus. & Oman.	24¼N	56¼E	40
Soignies, Belgium.	50¼N	4¼E	30
Soissons, France.	49¼N	3¼E	32
Sokal, U.S.S.R.	50¼N	24¼E	38
SOKE, Norway.	57¼N	9¼E	29
Soke, Turkey.	37¼N	27¼E	37
Sokna, Libya.	29N	16E	34
Sokode, Togo.	9N	1E	57
Sokol, U.S.S.R.	59N	40E	38
Sokolka, Poland.	53¼N	23¼E	33
Sokolow, Poland.	52¼N	22¼E	33
Sokoly, Poland.	53N	22¼E	33
Sokoto, Nigeria.	13N	5¼E	57
Solai, Kenya.	1N	36¼E	56
Soledad, Colombia.	11N	74¼w	77
Soledad, La, Mexico.	25N	105w	76
Soledad, Venezuela.	8¼N	63¼w	77
Solent, England.	50¾N	1¼w	23
Solenzara, Corsica.	41¾N	9¼E	36
Solihull, England.	52¼N	1¾w	23
Solikamsk, U.S.S.R.	59¼N	56¼E	38
Sol'Iletsk, U.S.S.R.	51¼N	55¼E	38
Solingen, Germany.	51¼N	7E	33
Soller, Balearic Is.	39¾N	3E	35
Sollum, U.A.R.	32N	25E	40
SOLOMON IS., Pacific.	8s	160E	64
Solomon R., Kan.,U.S.A.	38N	97¼w	75
Solothurn, Switz.	47¼N	7¼E	31
Solovetski Is., U.S.S.R.	65N	35¼E	38
Solsona, Spain.	42N	1¼E	32
Soltau, Germany.	53N	9¾E	33
Soluk, Libya.	31¼N	20E	34
Solunshan, China.	39N	117¼E	48
Solway Firth, U.K.	54¾N	3¼w	25
Solwezi, Zambia.	12¼s	26¼E	51
Soma, Turkey.	39¼N	27¼E	37

Place	Lat.	Long.	No.
Somabula, *Rhodesia.*	19s	29E	51
Somain, *France.*	50¼N	3¼E	30
SOMALI REPUBLIC, *Afr.*	5N	47E	56
Sombor, *Yugoslavia.*	45¾N	19E	37
SOMERSET, *England.*	51¼N	3W	22
Somerset, E., *C.Pr.,S.A.*	32¼s	25½E	53
Somerset I.,*N.W.T.,Can.*	73N	94w	66
Somerset, W., *C. Pr.*	34¼s	18¼E	52
Somes Riv., *Romania.*	47¼N	23E	37
Somkele, *Natal.*	28¼s	32¼E	55
Sommen, L. of, *Sweden.*	58N	15E	29
SOMME, R. & DEP., *Fr.*	50¼N	1¾E	32
Somme Py, *France.*	49¼N	4¼E	30
Sommesous, *France.*	48¼N	4E	30
Somoto, *Nicaragua.*	13N	86¼w	77
Somovit, *Bulgaria.*	43¼N	24½E	37
Sompuis, *France.*	48¼N	4¼E	30
Son, Riv., *India.*	26N	85E	46
Sona, *Panama.*	8N	81¼w	79
Sonchon, *Korea.*	40N	124E	47
Soncino, *Italy.*	45¼N	9¼E	30
Sonderhausen, *Ger.*	51¼N	10¼E	34
Sondre Stromfiord, *Gr.*	67N	51w	67
Sondrio, *Italy.*	46¼N	9¼E	30
Song Cau, *Vietnam.*	13N	109E	41
Songea, *Tanzania.*	10¼s	35¼E	53
Songjin, *Korea.*	41N	129E	46
Songkla, *Thailand.*	7¼N	100¼E	41
Songnim, *Korea.*	39N	126E	49
Sonhat, *India.*	23¼N	82¼E	44
Sonneberg, *Germany.*	50¼N	11¼E	33
Sonoita, *Mexico.*	32¼N	112¼w	76
SONORA, *Mexico.*	30N	111w	76
Sonora, *Texas, U.S.A.*	30¼N	100¼w	74
Sonpur Raj, *India.*	20¼N	84E	44
Sonsonate, *Salvador.*	13¾N	90w	76
Sopor, *Kashmir* (ins.).	34¼N	74¼E	44
Sopot, *Poland.*	54¼N	18¼E	33
Sopron, *Hungary.*	47¼N	16¼E	37
Sora, *Saudi Arabia.*	27¼N	35¼E	41
Soragna, *Italy.*	45N	10¼E	31
Sore, *France.*	44¼N	1w	32
Sorel, *Quebec, Canada.*	46N	73¼w	69
Sorell, *Tasmania, Aust.*	42¼s	147¼E	59
Sorell, C., *Tasmania.*	42¼s	145¼E	59
Soresina, *Italy.*	45¼N	9¼E	31
Soria, *Spain.*	42N	2¼w	35
Soro I., *Norway.*	71N	22¼E	29
Sorocaba, *Brazil.*	23¼s	47¼w	79
Sorochinsk, *U.S.S.R.*	52¼N	53E	38
Sorol I., *Pacific.*	8N	140E	64
Soroti, *Uganda.*	2N	33¼E	56
Sorrento, *Italy.*	40¼N	14¼E	36
Sorrento, *Vict., Aust.*	38¼s	144¼E	59
Sorsele, *Sweden.*	65N	18E	29
Sorsogon, *Luzon, P.I.*	12¼N	124E	47
Sort, *Spain.*	42¼N	1¼E	32
Sortavala, *U.S.S.R.*	62N	31E	38
Sos, *Spain.*	42¼N	1w	32
Sosan, *Korea.*	37N	126¼E	49
Sosnowiec, *Poland.*	50¼N	19¼E	33
Sosva Riv., *U.S.S.R.*	64N	65E	38
Sosva, *U.S.S.R.*	58¼N	62E	38
Sosvinskaya, *U.S.S.R.*	63N	62¼E	38
Sotok, *Poland.*	52¼N	15¼E	33
Sotteville, *France.*	49¼N	1¼E	32
Souan Ke, *Congo (B.).*	2N	14E	56
Soufflay, *Congo (B.).*	2N	15E	56
Souk Ahras, *Algeria.*	36¼N	8E	35
Sound of Harris, *Scot.*	57¼N	7w	24
Sound of Sleat, *Scot.*	57N	6w	24
Sound, The, *Denmark.*	56N	13E	29
Sounion, C., *Greece.*	37¼N	24E	37
Souppes, *France.*	48¼N	2¼E	30
Sour, *Lebanon.*	33¼N	35¼E	41
Sources, Mt. aux, *S. Afr.*	28¼s	28E	55
Sour el Ghozlane, *Alg.*	36N	3¼E	35
Souris, *Man., Can.*	49¼N	100¼w	70
Souris, *Pr. Ed. I., Can.*	46¼N	62¼w	69
Sousse, *Tunisia.*	35¼N	10¼E	35
SOUTH AFRICA, *Rep. of.*	30s	25E	50
Southam, *England.*	52¼N	1¼w	23
Southampton, *Eng.*	50¼N	1¼w	23
Southampton, *Can.*	44¼N	81¼w	68
Southampton I., *Can.*	64N	85w	66
SOUTH AUCKLAND—BAY OF PLENTY, *N.I., N.Z.*	38s	176E	62
SOUTH AUSTRALIA.	30s	135E	58
South Bend, *Ind., U.S.A.*	41¼N	86¼w	75
S. Brent, *England.*	50¼N	4w	22
Southbridge,*S.I.,N.Z.*	43¼s	172¼E	63
S. CAROLINA, *U.S.A.*	34N	81w	75
S. Cave, *England.*	53¾N	¾w	23
South China Sea, *Asia.*	15N	115E	47
SOUTH DAKOTA, *U.S.A.*	45N	100w	74
South East C., *Tas.*	43¼s	146¼E	59
Southend, *Scotland.*	55¼N	5¼w	24
Southend-on-Sea, *Eng.*	51¼N	¾E	23
Southern Alps, *N.Z.*	44s	170E	63
Southern Cross,*W.Aust.*	31¼s	119¼E	61
S. Indian L., *Man., Can.*	57N	100w	66
Southern Oc., *Antarc.*	50s	19E	19
Southey, *Sask., Can.*	51N	104¼w	70
South Foreland, *Eng.*	51¼N	1¼E	23
SOUTH ISLAND, *N.Z.*	44s	171E	63
SOUTHLAND, *S.I.,N.Z.*	45¼s	168E	63
Southminster, *Eng.*	51¼N	¾E	23
South Molton, *Eng.*	51N	3¼w	22
S. Natuna Is., *Indon.*	3N	109E	47
South Negril Pt., *Jam.*	18¼N	78¼w	77
South Patani, *Malay.* (ins.).	5¼N	100¼E	41
Southport, *England.*	53¼N	3w	25
Southport,*N.Terr.,Aust.*	13s	130¼E	60

Place	Lat.	Long.	No.
Southport, *Queens.*	28s	153¼E	60
South Riv., *Ont., Can.*	50N	79¼w	68
South Shetland Is., *Ant.*	63s	60w	80
South Shields, *Eng.*	55N	1¼w	25
South Sioux City, *U.S.*	42¼N	96w	75
South Sound, *Ireland.*	53N	9¼w	26
South Uist, *Scotland.*	57¼N	7¼w	24
Southwell, *C.Pr., S.Af.*	33¼s	26¼E	53
Southwell, *England.*	53N	1w	23
South Wellesley Is.,*Aust.*	17s	140E	60
S.W. AFRICA, *Africa.*	25s	17E	50
Southwood, *England.*	52¼N	1¼E	23
SOUTH YEMEN, *Asia* (ins.)	15N	47E	40
Soutpansberg, *S. Afr.*	23s	30E	54
Sovetsk *U.S.S.R.*	55N	22E	38
Soviet Hr., *U.S.S.R.*	49¼N	140E	39
Soya Strait, *Japan.*	45¼N	142E	49
Spa, *Belgium.*	50¼N	5¼E	30
SPAIN, *Europe.*			33
Spala, *Poland.*	51¼N	20¼E	33
Spalding, *England.*	52¼N	¾w	23
Spalding, *S. Aust.*	33¼s	138¼E	59
Spandau, *Germany.*	52¼N	13¼E	33
SPANISH SAHARA, *Afr.*	25N	13w	50
Spanish Town, *Jam.*	18N	77w	77
Sparkford, *England.*	51N	2¼w	22
Sparta, *Greece.*	37N	22¼E	37
Spartanburg, *U.S.A.*	35N	82w	75
Spartivento, C., *Italy.*	38N	16E	36
Spartivento, C., *Italy.*	38¼N	8¼E	36
Spassk Dalni, *U.S.S.R.*	44¼N	133E	39
Spatha, C., *Crete.*	35¼N	23¼E	37
Spean Bridge, *Scot.*	57N	5w	24
Speightstown, *W.I.*	13N	60w	77
Spencer,C. & G.,*S.Aust.*	35¼s	137E	59
Spence's Br., *Br. Col.*	50¼N	121¼w	72
Spennymoor, *Eng.*	54¼N	1¼w	25
Sperone, C. of, *Sard.*	39N	8¼E	36
Sperrin Mts., *Ireland.*	54¼N	7w	26
Spey B. & R., *Scot.*	57¼N	3w	24
Speyer, *Germany.*	49¼N	8¼E	33
Spezia, *Italy.*	44¼N	9¼E	36
Spicer Is., *N.W. Can.*	69N	80w	66
Spiekaer-Neufeld, *Ger.*	53¼N	8E	30
Spiekeroog, *Germany.*	53¼N	7¼E	30
Spiez, *Switzerland.*	46¼N	7¼E	31
Spigno, *Italy.*	44¼N	8¼E	31
Spilsby, *England.*	53¼N	¼E	23
Spirit Riv., *Alb., Can.*	55¼N	119w	73
Spisska Nova Ves, *Cz.*	49N	20¼E	33
Spitsbergen, *Arctic.*	77N	15E	80
Spittal, *Austria.*	46¼N	13¼E	33
Spittal of Glenshee, *Sc.*	56¼N	3¼w	24
Spitskop, C., *Pr., S. Afr.*	28¼s	24¼E	53
Split, *Yugoslavia.*	43¼N	16¼E	37
Splugen, *Switzerland.*	46¼N	9¼E	31
Spokane,*Wash.,U.S.A.*	47¼N	117¼w	74
Spoleto, *Italy.*	42¼N	12¼E	36
Spree, Riv., *Germany.*	52¼N	13E	33
Spremberg, *Germany.*	51¼N	14¼E	33
Springbok, *C.Pr., S.Af.*	29¼s	17¼E	52
Springburn,*S.I., N.Z.*	43¼s	171¼E	63
Springfield, *Ill., U.S.A.*	39¼N	89¼w	75
Springfield, *Mass., U.S.*	42N	72¼w	75
Springfield, *Missouri.*	37¼N	93¼w	75
Springfield, *Ohio.*	39¼N	83¼w	75
Springfield, *Colorado.*	37¼N	103¼w	74
Springfontein,*O.F.S.*	30¼s	25¼E	53
Spring Garden, *Guy.*	7N	58w	77
Springhill, *No.Sc., Can.*	45¼N	64¼w	67
Springlands, *Guyana.*	6N	56w	77
Springs, *Transvaal.*	26¼s	28¼E	55
Springs Junc.,*S.I.,N.Z.*	42¼s	172¼E	63
Springston, *S.I., N.Z.* (inset C).			63
Springsure, *Queens.*	24s	148¼E	60
Springvale, *Queens.*	23¼s	140¼E	60
Spring Valley, *C. Pr.*	32¼s	26¼E	53
Spungabera, *Moz.*	21s	33E	51
Spurn Head, *England.*	53¼N	¼E	23
Squillace, G. of, *Italy.*	38¼N	16¼E	36
Srebrenica, *Yugo.*	44¼N	19¼E	37
Sredne Kolymsk, *U.S.S.R.*	67N	151E	39
Srem, *Poland.*	52¼N	17¼E	33
Sretensk, *U.S.S.R.*	52¼N	117¼E	39
Srikakulam, *India.*	18¼N	84E	45
Srinagar, *Kashmir.*	34N	75E	43
Sroda, *Poland.*	52¼N	17¼E	33
Srzeziny, *Poland.*	51¼N	19¼E	33
Staarhelm, *Norway.*	62N	5E	29
Staaten Riv., *Queens.*	16s	141¼E	60
Stade, *Germany.*	53¼N	9¼E	33
Stadtlohn, *Germany.*	52N	7E	30
Staffin, *Scotland.*	57¼N	6¼w	24
STAFFORD & Tn.,*Eng.*	52¼N	2¼w	22
Staines, *England.*	51¼N	¾w	23
Staithes, *England.*	54¼N	¾w	25
Stalbridge, *England.*	51N	2¼w	22
Stalham, *England.*	52¼N	1¼E	23
Stalingrad, see VOLGOGRAD			
Stamford, *Con., U.S.A.*	41N	74w	75
Stamford, *England.*	52¼N	¾w	23
Stamford, *Queens.,Aust.*	21¼s	143¼E	60
Stamford Br., *Eng.*	54N	¾w	23
Stanchik, *U.S.S.R.*	71N	150E	39
Standerton, *T'vaal,S.Af.*	27s	29¼E	55
Stanfold, *Que., Can.*	46N	66¼w	69
Stanford, *C. Pr., S. Afr.*	34¼s	19¼E	52
Stanger, *Natal.*	29¼s	31¼E	55
Stangvik, *Norway.*	63N	8¼E	29
Stanhope, *England.*	54¼N	2w	25
Stanley, *England.*	54¼N	1¼w	25
Stanley, *Falkland Is.*	52s	60w	78
Stanley, *N. B. Can.*	46¼N	66¼w	67

Place	Lat.	Long.	No.
Stanley Mission, *Sask.*	55¼N	104¼w	70
Stanley, *Tasmania.*	40¼s	145¼E	59
Stanley Falls, *Congo (K.)*	1N	25E	50
Stanley Pool, *Congo (K.)*	4s	15¼E	56
Stanleyville, see KISANGANI.			
Stann Crk., *Br. Hond.*	17N	88¼w	77
Stannington, *Eng.*	55¼N	1¼w	25
StanovoyMts.,*U.S.S.R.*	56N	125E	39
Stanthorpe, *Queens.*	28¼s	152E	59
Stanton, *U.S.A.*	43¼N	85¼w	68
Stapleton, *N.Terr., Can.*	13s	131E	60
Star City, *Sask., Can.*	53N	104¼w	70
Staraya Russa, *U.S.S.R.*	58N	31¼E	38
Stara Zagora, *Bulg.*	42¼N	25¼E	37
Starbuck I., *Pacific.*	5s	155w	64
Stargard, *Poland.*	53¼N	15E	33
Staritsa, *U.S.S.R.*	56¼N	35E	38
Starodub, *U.S.S.R.*	52¼N	32¼E	38
Starogard, *Poland.*	54N	18¼E	33
Staro Oskol, *U.S.S.R.*	51¼N	38E	38
Start Pt., *England.*	50¼N	3¼w	22
Staszow, *Poland.*	50¼N	21¼E	33
Staten I., *N.Y., U.S.A.*	40¼N	74w	75
Statland, *Norway.*	62¼N	5E	29
Stavanger, *Norway.*	59N	5¼E	29
Staveley, *England.*	53¼N	1¼w	23
Stavelot, *Belgium.*	50¼N	5¼E	30
Stavely, *Alberta, Can.*	50¼N	113¼w	73
Stavoren, *Netherlands.*	53N	5¼E	30
Stavropol, *U.S.S.R.*	53N	49¼E	38
Stavropol, *U.S.S.R.*	45N	42E	38
Stavros, *Greece.*	40¼N	23¼E	37
Stawell, *Vict., Aust.*	37s	142¼E	59
Stawell R., *Queens., Aust.*	20s	142¼E	60
Steeg, *Austria.*	47¼N	10¼E	31
Steelpoort, *T'vaal.*	24¼s	30¼E	54
Steenwijk, *Nether.*	52¼N	6E	30
Stegi, *Swaziland.*	26¼s	32E	55
Steinach, *Austria.*	47¼N	11¼E	31
Steinhausen, *S.W.Afr.*	22s	18¼E	51
Steinkopf, *C. Pr.*	29¼s	17¼E	52
Stellarton,*No.Sc.,Can.*	45¼N	62¼w	67
Stellenbosch, *C. Pr.*	34s	18¼E	52
Stelvio Pass, *Sw.-It.*	46¼N	10¼E	31
Stem Reap, *Cambodia.*	13N	104E	47
Stenay, *France.*	49¼N	5¼E	30
Stendal, *Germany.*	52¼N	11¼E	33
Stephens, C., *S.I., N.Z.*	40¼s	174E	62
Stepnyak, *U.S.S.R.*	53N	70¼E	39
Sterkrade, *Germany.*	51¼N	6¼E	30
Sterkstroom,*C.Pr.,S.A.*	31¼s	26¼E	53
Sterlitamak, *U.S.S.R.*	53¼N	56E	38
Sternberk, *Czecho.*	49¼N	17¼E	33
Stettin, see SZCZECIN.			
Stettiner Haff, *Ger.*	53¼N	14E	33
Stettler, *Alberta, Can.*	52¼N	112¼w	73
Steubenville, *Ohio.*	40¼N	81w	75
Stevenage, *England.*	52N	1¼w	23
Stewart I., *S.I., N.Z.*	47s	168E	63
Stewarton, *Scotland.*	55¼N	4¼w	25
Stewartstown, *Ire.*	54¼N	6¼w	26
Stewiacke,*No.Sc., Can.*	45¼N	63¼w	67
Steyning, *England.*	51N	1¼w	23
Steynsburg, *C. Pr.*	31¼s	25¼E	53
Steynsrus, *O.F.S.*	28s	27¼E	55
Steyr, *Austria.*	48N	14¼E	33
Steytlerville, *C. Pr.*	33¼s	24¼E	53
Stia, *Italy.*	43¼N	11¼E	36
Stikine Mts., *Canada.*	62N	135w	66
Still Bay, *C. Pr., S. Af.*	34¼s	21¼E	52
Stillwater,*Okl.,U.S.A.*	36¼N	97w	75
Stilo, C. of, *Italy.*	38¼N	16¼E	36
Stilton, *England.*	52¼N	¼w	23
Stip, *Yugoslavia.*	41¼N	22¼E	37
Stirling, *Alb., Can.*	49¼N	112¼w	73
STIRLING & Co.,*Scot.*	56¼N	4w	24
Stirling Sta., *N.Terr.*	22s	133E	60
Stjerno I., *Norway.*	70¼N	22E	29
Stockbridge, *England.*	51¼N	1¼w	23
Stockerau, *Austria.*	48¼N	16¼E	33
Stockholm, *Sweden.*	59¼N	18E	29
Stockport, *England.*	53¼N	2¼w	25
Stockton, *Calif., U.S.A.*	38N	121¼w	74
Stockton-on-Tees, *Eng.*	54¼N	1¼w	25
Stoer, Pt. of, *Scotland.*	58¼N	5¼w	24
Stoffberg, *T'vaal, S.Af.*	25¼s	29¼E	54
Stoke, *England.*	53N	2¼w	22
Stoke Ferry, *England.*	52¼N	¼E	23
Stokesley, *England.*	54¼N	1¼w	25
Stokes Valley, *N.I., N.Z.* (inset B).			62
Stolberg, *Germany.*	50¼N	6¼E	30
Stolp, see SLUPSK.			
Stolzenfels, *S.W.Afr.*	28¼s	19¼E	51
Ston, *Yugoslavia.*	42¼N	17¼E	36
Stone, *England.*	52¼N	2¼w	22
Stonehaven, *Scotland.*	57N	2¼w	24
Stonehenge, *England.*	51¼N	2w	22
Stonehouse, *Scotland.*	55¼N	4w	25
Stonewall, *Man., Can.*	50N	97¼w	71
Stony Plain, *Alb., Can.*	53¼N	114w	73
Stony Stratford, *Eng.*	52N	1w	23
Stor, L. of, *Sweden.*	63N	15E	29
Stordalen, *Norway.*	62¼N	6¼E	29
Storen, *Norway.*	63N	10E	29
Storm Bay, *Tasmania.*	43s	147¼E	59
Stormberg, *C.Pr., S.Af.*	31¼s	26¼E	53
Storms River, *C. Pr.*	34s	24E	53
Stornoway, *Scotland.*	58¼N	6¼w	24
Storr, The, *Scotland.*	57¼N	6¼w	24
Stoughton, *Sask., Can.*	49¼N	103w	70
Stour, Riv., *England.*	50¼N	2w	22
Stour, Riv., *England.*	51¼N	1¼E	23
Stourbridge, *Eng.*	52¼N	2¼w	22

Place	Lat.	Long.	No.
Stourport, *England.*	52¼N	2¼w	22
Stow, *Scotland.*	55¼N	2¼w	25
Stowmarket, *Eng.*	52¼N	1E	23
Stow-on-the-Wold, *Eng.*	52N	1¾w	23
Strabane, *N. Ireland.*	54¼N	7¼w	26
Strachur, *Scotland.*	56¼N	5w	25
Stradbroke I., *Queens.*	27¼s	153¼E	60
Stradella, *Italy.*	45N	9¼E	31
Strahan, *Tasmania.*	42¼s	145E	59
Strakonice, *Czecho.*	49¼N	14E	33
Stralsund, *Germany.*	54¼N	13E	33
Strand, *C. Pr., S. Afr.*	34¼s	18¼E	52
Strangford, *L., N.Ire.*	54¼N	5¼w	26
Strangways Spr., *S. Aust.*	29s	136¼E	60
Stranraer, *Scotland.*	54¼N	5w	25
Strasbourg, *France.*	48¼N	7¼E	32
Strasbourg, *Sask., Can.*	51N	105w	70
Strasswalchen,*Austria.*	48N	13¼E	33
Stratford, *N.I., N.Z.*	39¼s	174¼E	62
Stratford, *Ont., Can.*	43¼N	81w	68
Stratford-on-Avon,*En.*	52¼N	1¾w	23
Strathalbyn, *S. Aust.*	35¼s	139E	59
Strathaven, *Scotland.*	55¼N	4w	25
Strathcanaird, *Scot.*	58N	5¼w	24
Strathcona Pk., *Can.*	49¼N	125¼w	72
Strathmore, *Alberta.*	51N	113¼w	73
Strathmore, *Scotland.*	58¼N	3¼w	24
Strath Nairn, R., *Scot.*	57¼N	4w	24
Strathpeffer, *Scot.*	57¼N	4¼w	24
Strath Spey, *Scotland.*	57¼N	3¼w	24
Strathy Pt., *Scotland.*	58¼N	4w	24
Stratton, *England.*	50¼N	4¼w	22
Straubing, *Germany.*	48¼N	12¼E	33
Strehaia, *Romania.*	44¼N	23¼E	37
Strelka, *U.S.S.R.*	58N	92E	39
Strelley, *W. Aust.*	20¼s	119E	61
Stresa, *Italy.*	45¼N	8¼E	31
Strichen, *Scotland.*	57¼N	2w	24
Strokestown, *Ireland.*	53¼N	8w	26
Stroma I., *Scotland.*	58¼N	3¼w	24
Stromboli I., *Italy.*	38¼N	15¼E	36
Strome Ferry, *Scot.*	57¼N	5¼w	24
Stromemore, *Scot.*	57¼N	5¼w	24
Stromness, *Scotland.*	59N	3¼w	24
Stromo, *Faeroe Is.*	62N	8w	29
Stroms, L. of, *Sweden.*	64N	15E	29
Stromstad, *Sweden.*	59N	11¼E	29
Strongoli, *Italy.*	39¼N	17¼E	37
Stronsay & F., *Scot.*	59¼N	2¼w	24
Strontian, *Scotland.*	56¼N	5¼w	24
Strood, *England.*	51¼N	¼E	23
Stroud, *England.*	51¼N	2¼w	22
Struga, *Yugoslavia.*	41¼N	20¼E	37
Struma, R., *Greece.*	40¼N	21¼E	37
Struy, *Scotland.*	57¼N	4¼w	24
Stryj & R., *U.S.S.R.*	49¼N	23¼E	33
Strzelce, *Poland.*	50¼N	18¼E	33
Stuart Highway, *Aust.*	20s	133E	60
Stuart, Mt., *W. Aust.*	22s	116E	61
Stuben, *Austria.*	47¼N	10¼E	31
Stung-Treng, *Camb.*	13¼N	106E	47
Stura, Riv., *Italy.*	45N	7¼E	31
Sturgeon Falls, *Can.*	46¼N	79¼w	68
Sturgis, *Sask., Can.*	52N	102¼w	70
Sturminster New., *Eng.*	51N	2¼w	22
Sturt Creek, *W. Aust.*	19s	129E	61
Sturt Desert, *S. Aust.*	28¼s	141E	59
Sturt, Mt., *N.S.W.*	29s	141E	59
Stutterheim, *C. Pr.*	32¼s	27¼E	53
Stuttgart, *Germany.*	48¼N	9¼E	33
Styx, *Queens., Aust.*	22¼s	149E	60
Suakin, *Sudan.*	19N	37¼E	40
Suancheng, *China.*	31N	118E	48
Suanhwa, *China.*	40¼N	115E	48
Subi I., *Indon.*	3N	109E	47
Subotica, *Yugoslavia.*	46N	19¼E	37
Suceava, *Romania.*	47¼N	26¼E	37
Suchan, *U.S.S.R.*	43N	133E	49
Suchitoto, *Salvador.*	13¼N	89w	76
Suchow, *China.*	31¼N	120¼E	48
Suck, Riv., *Ireland.*	53¼N	8¼w	26
Sucre, *Bolivia.*	19s	65¼w	79
SUDAN, *N. Africa.*	10N	30E	50
Sudbury, *England.*	52N	¾E	23
Sudbury, *Ont., Can.*	46¼N	81w	68
Suddie, *Guyana* (inset).	7¼N	58w	77
Sudeten Mts., *Czecho.*	50¼N	15¼E	33
Sueca, *Spain.*	39¼N	¼w	35
Suez Canal, *U.A.R.*	31N	32¼E	50
SUFFOLK, *England.*	52¼N	1E	23
Suget Karaul, *Kash.*	36¼N	78E	44
Suglan, *U.S.S.R.*	70N	141E	39
Suhl, *Germany.*	50¼N	10¼E	33
Suiaraw J., L., *Poland.*	53¼N	21¼E	33
Suifenho, *China.*	44¼N	131E	49
Suihwa, *China.*	47N	127E	49
Suining, *China.*	30¼N	105E	48
Suining, *China.*	34N	118E	48
Suippes, *France.*	49N	4¼E	30
Suir, Riv., *Eire.*	52¼N	7¼w	26
Suiteh, *China.*	37¼N	110E	48
Sukadana, *Kal., Indon.*	1¼s	110E	47
Sukarnapura, *Indonesia.*	2¼s	141E	47
Sukhana, *U.S.S.R.*	68N	118E	39
Sukhona R., *U.S.S.R.*	59N	40E	38
Sukhumi, *U.S.S.R.*	43N	41E	38
Suki, *Papua* (inset).	8s	142E	60
Sukkertoppen, *Green.*	65N	52w	66
Sukkur, *Pakistan.*	27¼N	68E	43
Sukotai, *Thailand.*	17N	100E	43
Sukumo, *Japan.*	33N	133E	49
SULA IS., *Indonesia.*	2s	125E	47
Sulaco, *Honduras.*	15N	86w	76
Sulaimaniya, *Iraq.*	35¼N	45¼E	41

Place	Lat.	Long.	No.
Sulaiyil, *Saudi Arabia.*	20½N	45½E	40
Sulby, *England.*	54¼N	4½W	25
Sulima, *S. Leone.*	7¼N	12W	57
Sulina, *Romania.*	45¼N	29½E	37
Sulingen, *Germany.*	52¾N	8¾E	30
Sullivan, L., *Alb., Can.*	52N	112W	73
Sully, *France.*	47¾N	2½E	30
Sulmona, *Italy.*	42N	14E	36
Sultanabad, *Iran.*	34N	49¾E	41
Sulu Sea & Arch., *P.I.*	7N	120E	47
Sulzberger B., *Antarc.*	76½S	152W	80
Sumarokovo, *U.S.S.R.*	62N	90E	39
SUMATRA I., *Indonesia.*	0	102E	47
Sumba I., *Indonesia.*	10S	120E	47
Sumbawa I., *Indonesia.*	8½S	118E	47
Sumbawanga, *Tanzania.*	8S	31½E	56
Sumburgh Hd., *Scot.*	59¾N	1W	24
Summer Is., *Scotland.*	58N	5½W	24
Summerland, *Can.*	49½N	119½W	72
Summerside, *Can.*	46½N	63¾W	67
Summit, L., *Canada.*	54¼N	122½W	72
Summit, *N.I., N.Z.*	(inset B).		62
Sumner, L., *S.I., N.Z.*	42¾S	172¼E	63
Sumner, *S.I., N.Z.*	(inset C).		63
Sumy, *U.S.S.R.*	51N	34¾E	38
Sun Valley, *Id., U.S.A.*	43½N	115W	74
Suna, *Tanzania.*	5½S	35E	56
Sunchon, *Korea.*	35N	127½E	49
Sunda Strait, *Java.*	6S	105¾E	47
Sundalen, *Norway.*	62¾N	8½E	29
Sundarbans, *Pak.-Ind.*	22N	89E	43
Sundays R., *C. Pr.*	33¾S	25¾E	53
Sunderland, *England.*	54¾N	1¼W	25
Sundridge, *Ont., Can.*	45¾N	79¼W	68
Sundsvall, *Sweden.*	62½N	17½E	29
Sungari Resr., *China.*	43N	128E	39
Sunkiang, *China.*	31½N	121E	48
Sunshine, *Vict., Aust.*	37¾S	145E	59
Suntar, *U.S.S.R.*	62¼N	117½E	39
Sunyani, *Ghana.*	7¼N	2¼W	57
Suoyarvi, *U.S.S.R.*	62N	32½E	38
Superior, *Wis., U.S.A.*	46¾N	92W	75
Superior Junc., *Can.*	50¼N	91¾W	71
Superior, L., *U.S.-Can.*	48N	87W	66
Sur, *Muscat & Oman.*	22½N	60E	40
Surabaja, *Java.*	7¼S	112¾E	47
Surakarta, *Java.*	7½S	110¾E	47
Surakhani, *U.S.S.R.*	40N	50E	38
Surama, *Guyana* (ins.).	4N	58½W	77
Surat, *India.*	21¼N	73E	44
Surat, *Queens., Aust.*	27S	149E	59
Surbiton, *C. Pr., S. Afr.*	32½S	27¾E	53
Suretka, *Costa Rica.*	10N	83W	77
Surfdale, *N.I., N.Z.*	(inset A).		62
Surgut, *U.S.S.R.*	61¼N	73½E	39
Surigao, *Mind., P.I.*	9¾N	125½E	47
Surin, *Thailand.*	15N	103E	47
Surinam, *S. America.*	4N	55½W	78
SURREY, *England.*	51¼N	¼W	23
Surt, *Turkey.*	38N	42E	41
Sus, *Switzerland.*	46¾N	10½E	31
Susa, *Italy.*	45¼N	7E	36
Susa, see SOUSSE.			
Susak, *Yugoslavia.*	45¼N	14½E	37
Susquehanna, *Pa., U.S.*	42N	75¾W	69
SUSSEX, *England.*	51N	0	23
Sussex Inlet, *N.S.W.*	35S	150½E	58
Susurluk, *Turkey.*	40N	28½E	37
Sutherland Ra., *W. Aust.*	26S	125½E	61
Sutherland, *Sask.*	52¼N	106½W	70
SUTHERLAND, *Scot.*	58¼N	4½W	24
Sutlej Riv., *Pakistan.*	29½N	71½E	46
Sutsien, *China.*	34N	118E	48
Sutterton, *England.*	53N	0	23
Sutton Coldfield, *Eng.*	52½N	1¾W	23
Sutton in Ashfield, *Eng.*	53¼N	1¼W	23
Sutton-on-Sea, *Eng.*	53¼N	¼E	23
Sutton Scotney, *Eng.*	51¼N	1¼W	23
Suttsu, *Japan.*	42¾N	140E	49
Suva, *Fiji, Pacific.*	18S	178E	64
Suvorov I., *Pacific.*	15S	162W	64
Suwaih, *Mus. & Oman.*	22N	60E	40
Suwalki, *Poland.*	54N	23E	33
Suwannee R., *Fla., U.S.*	29N	83W	75
Suwon, *Korea.*	37N	127E	49
Suzu, C., *Japan.*	37½N	137E	49
Suzzara, *Italy.*	45N	10¾E	31
Svartisen, *Norway.*	67N	14E	29
Svatovo, *U.S.S.R.*	49N	38E	38
Svendborg, *Denmark.*	55¼N	10½E	33
Svenljuga, *Sweden.*	57N	13E	29
Sventoji R., *U.S.S.R.*	55N	24½E	33
Sverdlovsk, *U.S.S.R.*	56¾N	60½E	38
Sverdrup Is., *N.W. Can.*	78N	100W	66
Sveti Vrach, *Bulgaria.*	41½N	23½E	37
Svetlaya, *U.S.S.R.*	47N	138¼E	39
Svir Riv., *U.S.S.R.*	61N	33E	38
Svishtov, *Bulgaria.*	43½N	25¼E	37
Svitavy, *Czecho.*	49¾N	16½E	33
Svoboda, *U.S.S.R.*	51¼N	40E	38
Svobodny, *U.S.S.R.*	51¼N	128E	39
Swaffham, *England.*	52¾N	¾E	23
Swains I., *Pacific.*	11S	171W	64
Swainsboro, *Ga., U.S.*	32½N	82W	75
Swakopmund, *S.W. Af.*	22¾S	14½E	51
Swale, Riv., *England.*	54¼N	1¾W	25
Swan Hill, *Vict., Aust.*	35¼S	143½E	59
Swan Is., *Caribbean S.*	17½N	84W	77
Swan Riv., *Man., Can.*	52¼N	101¼W	70
Swanage, *England.*	50¾N	2W	23
Swanlinbar, *Ireland.*	54¼N	7¾W	26
Swansea, *Tasmania.*	42¼S	148E	59
Swansea, *Wales.*	51¾N	4W	22
Swanson B., *Canada.*	53N	128½W	72
Swanson, *N.I., N.Z.* (inset A).			62
Swanton, *Vt., U.S.A.*	44¾N	73¼W	69
Swartberg Ra., *C. Pr.*	33S	22½E	52
Swartruggens, *T'vaal.*	25¾S	26¾E	54
Swastika, *Ont., Can.*	48N	80W	68
Swatow see SHANTON.			
SWAZILAND, *S. Africa.*	26½S	31½E	50
SWEDEN, *Europe.*	63N	15E	28
Sweetwater, *Tex., U.S.*	32½N	101½W	74
Swellendam, *C.Pr., S.A.*	34S	20½E	72
Swidnica, *Poland.*	50¾N	16½E	33
Swiebodzin, *Poland.*	52¼N	15½W	33
Swift Current, *Can.*	50¼N	108W	60
Swilly, L., *Eire.*	55¼N	7½W	26
Swindon, *England.*	51½N	1¾W	23
Swinford, *Ireland.*	54N	9W	26
Swinoujscie, *Germany.*	54N	14¼E	33
SWITZERLAND, *Europe.*			31
Sybil Pt., *Ireland.*	52¼N	10½W	26
Sydero, *Faer. Is.* (ins.).	61N	7W	29
Sydney, *C.Br.I., Can.*	46¼N	60¼W	67
Sydney, *N.S.W., Aust.*	33¾S	151¼E	59
Sydney I., *Pacific.*	5S	172W	64
Sydney Mines, *Canada.*	46¼N	60¼W	67
Sydproven, *Greenland.*	61N	45W	66
Syktyvkar, *U.S.S.R.*	61½N	50½E	39
Sylhet, *Pakistan.*	25N	91½E	43
Sylt I., *Germany.*	54¾N	8½E	29
Sylvan Lake, *Alb., Can.*	52¼N	114¼W	73
Syr Darya R., *U.S.S.R.*	46N	61½E	39
Syracuse, *N.Y., U.S.A.*	43N	76¼W	75
Syracuse *Sicily.*	37N	15¼E	36
SYRIA, *Asia.*	35N	39E	41
Syrian Desert, *Arabia.*	32N	40E	41
Syzran, *U.S.S.R.*	53¼N	48½E	38
Szamoluly, *Poland.*	52¼N	16½E	33
Szczecin, *Poland.*	53½N	14¼E	33
Szczecinek, *Poland.*	53¾N	16¾E	33
Szczytno, *Poland.*	53½N	21E	33
SZECHWAN, *China.*	31N	105E	48
Szeged, *Hungary.*	46¼N	20¼E	37
Szekesfehervar, *Hung.*	47¼N	18¼E	37
Szekszard, *Hungary.*	46¼N	18½E	36
Szemao, *China.*	22½N	101E	43
Szenan, *China.*	27½N	108E	48
Szepingkai, *China.*	43N	123E	39
Szigetvar, *Hungary.*	46N	17¾E	36
Szolnok, *Hungary.*	47¼N	20¼E	37
Szombathely, *Hung.*	47¼N	16½E	37
Szprotawa, *Poland.*	51½N	15½E	33
Szubin, *Poland.*	53N	17¾E	33
Szydlowiec, *Poland.*	51¼N	20¾E	33
TABANKULU, *S.Afr.*	31S	29½E	53
Tabar Is., *Pac.* (inset).	3S	152E	60
Tabarka, *Tunisia.*	37N	8¾E	35
Tabas, *Iran.*	33¾N	57¼E	40
Tabas, *Iran.*	32½N	60E	40
TABASCO, *Mexico.*	18N	93W	76
Tabelbala, *Algeria.*	29N	3½W	34
Taber, *Alberta, Can.*	49¾N	112¼W	73
Table Cape, *N.I., N.Z.*	39S	178E	62
Table Mt., *C. Pr., S. Afr.*	34S	18½E	52
Tabor, *Czechoslovakia.*	49½N	14¾E	33
Tabora, *Tanzania.*	5S	32¾E	56
Tabut, *S. Yemen* (ins.).	16N	51E	40
Tabriz, *Iran.*	38N	46¼E	40
Tachira, *Venezuela.*	8N	72¼W	77
Tachu, *China.*	31N	107½E	48
Tacloban, *Samar., P.I.*	11½N	125E	47
Tacna, *Peru.*	18S	70¼W	78
Tacoma, *Wash., U.S.A.*	47N	122½W	74
Tacuarembo, *Urug.*	31¾S	56W	79
Tadcaster, *England.*	53¾N	1¼W	23
Tadoussac, *Que., Can.*	48¼N	69¾W	69
Taedong Riv., *Korea.*	39N	125E	49
Taegu, *Korea.*	35¾N	128½E	49
Taejon, *Korea.*	36¼N	127½E	49
Tafalla, *Spain.*	42¾N	1½W	32
Tafelberg, *C. Pr., S. Af.*	31¾S	25¼E	53
Taganrog, *U.S.S.R.*	47¼N	39E	38
Tagbilaran, *Negros, P.I.*	10N	123E	47
Tagdempt, *Algeria.*	35¼N	1½E	35
Taghassa, *Morocco.*	31½N	6½W	34
Tagrifet, *Libya.*	29N	17½E	34
Tagula I., *Pac.* (inset).	11S	153E	60
Tagus Riv., *Portugal.*	38¼N	9W	35
Tahan, Mt., *Malaysia.* (ins.).	4¾N	102¼E	47
Tahcheng, *China.*	46¾N	82¼E	39
Taheiho, *China.*	51N	128E	39
Tahiti I., *Pacific.*	17¾S	149¼W	64
Tahsien, *China.*	32N	107½E	48
Tahuata I., *Pacific.*	10S	140W	64
Tai, L., *China.*	31½N	120E	48
Taian, *China.*	36N	116E	48
Taiaroa Hd., *S.I., N.Z.*	(inset D).		63
Taichung, *Formosa.*	24N	121E	48
Taieri, *S.I., N.Z.*	(inset D).		63
Taihape, *N.I., N.Z.*	39¾S	175¾E	62
Taihsien, *China.*	39N	112½E	48
Tailem Bend, *S. Aust.*	35¼S	139½E	59
Taimura R., *U.S.S.R.*	63N	99E	39
Taimyr Pen., *U.S.S.R.*	74½N	101E	39
Tain, *Scotland.*	57¾N	4W	24
Tainan, *China.*	23N	120¼E	48
Taipei, *Formosa.*	25N	121½E	48
Taiping, *Malaysia.*	4¾N	100¾E	47
Taira, *Japan.*	37N	140¾E	49
Taisha, *Japan.*	35½N	132E	49
Taishet, *U.S.S.R.*	55¾N	97½E	39
Taishun, *China.*	27½N	120E	48
Taitao Pen., *Chile.*	45S	76W	78
Taitapu, *S.I., N.Z.*	(inset C).		63
Taitung, *Formosa.*	23N	121E	48
TAIWAN *or* Formosa.	23½N	121E	48
Taiwara, *Afghanistan.*	33N	65E	43
Taiyuan, *China.*	38N	112½E	48
Taizz, *Yemen* (inset).	14N	44½E	40
TAJIK S.S.R., *U.S.S.R.*	39N	71E	39
Tajura, *Afars & Issas.*	11¾N	43E	56
Takada, *Japan.*	37N	138E	49
Takamatsu, *Japan.*	34¼N	134E	49
Takaoka, *Japan.*	37N	137E	49
Takapuna, *N.I., N.Z.*	36¾S	174¾E	62
Takasaki, *Japan.*	36N	139E	49
Takayama, *Japan.*	36N	137E	49
Takefu, *Japan.*	36N	136E	49
Takikawa, *Japan.*	43½N	142E	49
Takla, L., *Br. Col., Can.*	55½N	125½W	72
Takla-Makan Des., *Ch.*	37N	82½E	43
Taklakot, *Tibet.*	30¼N	81E	43
Takoradi, *Ghana.*	5N	1¾W	57
Taku, *China.*	38½N	117½E	48
Takuapa, *Thailand.*	9N	98E	43
Takum, *Nigeria.*	7¼N	10E	57
Takutea I., *Pacific.*	20S	158W	64
Takwanhs, *China.*	27¾N	104E	43
Talagang, *Pakistan.*	33N	72½E	46
Talaimanaar, *Ceylon.*	9¼N	79¾E	45
Talanga, *Honduras.*	14N	87W	76
Talasea, *Pacific* (inset).	5S	150E	60
Talaud Is., *Indonesia.*	4N	126¾E	47
Talca, *Chile.*	35½S	71¾W	79
Talcahuano, *Chile.*	37S	72W	78
Taldy Kurgan, *U.S.S.R.*	46N	79E	39
Talgarth, *Wales.*	52N	3¼W	22
Tali, *China.*	35N	110E	48
Tali, *China.*	25¾N	100E	43
Taliabu I., *Indonesia.*	2S	125E	47
Tallahassee, *Fla., U.S.*	30¼N	84¼W	75
Tallangatta, *Vic., Aust.*	36¼S	147¼E	59
Tallinn, *U.S.S.R.*	59½N	24¾E	38
Tallow, *Ireland.*	52N	8W	26
Tallulah, *La., U.S.A.*	32½N	91W	75
Talovka, *U.S.S.R.*	63N	165E	39
Talsi, *U.S.S.R.*	57¼N	22½E	38
Taltal, *Chile.*	25½S	70¾W	79
Taluk, *Sumatra, Indon.*	1S	102E	47
Talvik, *Norway.*	70N	23E	29
Talwood, *Queens., Aust.*	28½S	149½E	60
Tamaki Str., *N.I., N.Z.*	(inset A).		62
Tamale, *Ghana.*	9½N	¾W	57
Tamana I., *Pacific.*	3S	175S	64
Tamar, R., *England.*	50½N	4¼W	22
Tamas, *Kash.* (ins.).	35½N	75¾E	44
Tamasi, *Hungary.*	46½N	18¼E	36
Tamatave, *Malagasy.*	18¼S	49½E	56
TAMAULIPAS, *Mexico.*	25N	98W	76
Tambacounda, *Seneg.*	13¾N	13¾W	57
Tambelan Is., *Indonesia.*	1N	107½E	47
Tambellup, *W. Aust.*	34S	117¾E	61
Tambov, *U.S.S.R.*	52¾N	41½E	38
Tambura, *Sudan.*	5½N	27½E	56
Tame, *Colombia.*	6½N	72W	77
Tamega R., *Portugal.*	41N	8¾W	35
Tamiahua, L. de, *Mex.*	21½N	97¾W	76
Tampa, *Fla., U.S.A.*	28N	82¼W	75
Tampere, *Finland.*	61½N	23¾E	29
Tampico, *Mexico.*	22¼N	97¾W	76
Tamsui, *Formosa.*	25N	121E	48
Tamsweg, *Austria.*	47¼N	13¾E	33
Tamtsak Bulak, *Mong.*	47N	117E	39
Tamu, *Burma.*	24¼N	94¼E	46
Tamworth, *England.*	52¾N	1¾W	23
Tamworth, *N.S.W.*	31S	151E	59
Tana & Fd., *Norway.*	70½N	28E	29
Tana I., *N. Heb., Pac.*	19½S	169½E	64
Tana, L., *Ethiopia.*	12N	37½E	56
Tana R., *Kenya.*	3S	40E	56
Tanabe, *Japan.*	33¾N	135½E	49
Tanabu, *Japan.*	41¼N	141¼E	49
Tanahgrogot, *Indon.*	2S	116¼E	47
Tanana, *Alaska, U.S.A.*	65N	152W	66
Tananarive, *Malagasy.*	19S	47½E	56
Tanaro, Riv., *Italy.*	45N	8¾E	31
Tanchon, *Korea.*	40½N	129E	49
Tandil, *Argentina.*	37¼S	59W	79
Tandjung, *Kal., Indon.*	2¼S	115½E	47
Tandjungbalai, *Sum.*	3N	99¾E	47
Tandou, L., *N.S.W.*	32¾S	142E	59
Taneatua, *N.I., N.Z.*	38S	177E	62
Tanega, *Japan.*	30½N	131E	49
Tang Pass, *China.*	32½N	92½E	43
Tanga, *Tanzania.*	5S	39E	56
Tanga Is., *Pacific* (ins.).	3S	153E	60
Tangalla, *Ceylon.*	6N	80¾E	45
TANGANYIKA, see TANZANIA.			
Tanganyika, L., *Tanz.*	7S	30E	56
Tangar, *China.*	36½N	101½E	43
Tangermunde, *Ger.*	52½N	12E	33
Tangier, *N. Africa.*	35¾N	5¾W	35
Tangku, *China.*	39N	117E	48
Tangla Mts., *Tibet.*	34N	92E	43
Tangshan, *China.*	39¾N	118½E	48
Tangshan, *China.*	34½N	116E	48
Tangtu, *China.*	32N	118E	48
Tanimbar Is. *Indon.*	7½S	132E	47
Taninges, *France.*	46¼N	6¾E	31
Tanjore, *India.*	10¾N	79½E	45
Tank, *Pakistan.*	32¼N	70½E	46
Tanktse, *Kashmir.*	34N	78E	43
Tanque, *Mexico.*	28N	103¾W	76
Tanta, *U.A.R.*	30¾N	31E	50
Tanyang, *Korea.*	37N	128½E	49
TANZANIA, *Africa*	6S	34E	56
Tao River, *China.*	35½N	102½E	48
Taoan, *China.*	46N	122E	39
Taonan, *China.*	45N	122E	39
Taouz, *Morocco.*	31½N	4W	34
Tapachula, *Mexico.*	15N	92½W	76
Tapah, *Malaysia* (ins.).	4½N	101½E	47
Tapajoz, Riv., *Brazil.*	2S	53W	78
Tapanui, *S.I., N.Z.*	46S	169½E	63
Tapti, Riv., *India.*	21½N	72¾E	43
Tapuaenuku, Mt., *N.Z.*	42S	173½E	63
Taqa, *Muscat & Oman.*	17N	55E	40
Tara, *Queens., Aust.*	27S	150½E	59
Tara, *U.S.S.R.*	56¾N	74½E	39
Tara & Hill, *Eire.*	53¾N	6½W	22
Taradale, *N.I., N.Z.*	39½S	176¾E	62
Tarago, *N.S.W., Aust.*	35S	149½E	59
Tarakan I., *Indon.*	3½N	117¾E	47
TARANAKI, *N.I., N.Z.*	39S	174½E	62
Taransay, *Scotland.*	57¾N	7W	24
Taranto & G., *Italy.*	40½N	17½E	36
Tarapaca, *Chile.*	20S	69¼W	79
Tarascon, *France.*	43¾N	4½E	32
Tarawera, L., *N.Z.*	38¼S	176½E	62
Tarazona, *Spain.*	42N	1¾W	35
Tarbat Ness, *Scotland.*	57¾N	3¾W	24
Tarbert, *Ireland.*	52½N	9½W	26
Tarbert, *Scotland.*	55¾N	5½W	25
Tarbert (*Harris*), *Scot.*	58N	6¾W	24
Tarbes, *France.*	43¼N	¼E	32
Tarbet, *Scotland.*	56¼N	4¾W	25
Tarcoles, *Costa Rica.*	10N	85W	77
Tarcoola, *S. Aust.*	30¾S	134½E	58
Tarcutta, *N.S.W., Aust.*	35¼S	147½E	59
Tardre, *France.*	46N	4½E	32
Tardun, *W. Aust.*	28S	116E	61
Taree, *N.S.W., Aust.*	32S	152½E	59
Tarf, Riv., *Scotland.*	54¾N	4½W	25
Targoviste, *Romania.*	45N	25½E	37
Targuist, *Morocco.*	35N	4½W	35
Targu Jiu, *Romania.*	45N	23¼E	37
Targu Mures, *Rom.*	46½N	24½E	37
Targu Ocna, *Rom.*	46¼N	26½E	37
Tarifa, *Spain.*	36N	5¾W	35
TARIJA & Tn., *Bolivia.*	21½S	64½W	79
Tarim R., *China.*	41N	85E	42
Tarkastad, *C. Pr., S. Afr.*	32S	26½E	53
Tarko Sale, *U.S.S.R.*	65N	78E	39
Tarkwa, *Ghana.*	5¼N	2W	57
Tarland, *Scotland.*	57¼N	2¾W	24
TARN, R. & DEP., *Fr.*	43¾N	2E	32
TARN ET GARONNE, *Fr.*	44N	1½E	32
Tarna, *Sweden.*	65¼N	16E	29
Tarnak, *Afghanistan.*	32N	65E	43
Tarnogrod, *Poland.*	50¼N	22¾E	33
Tarnow, *Poland.*	50N	21E	33
Tarnowskie Gory, *Pol.*	50½N	18¾E	33
Taro, Riv., *Italy.*	45N	10½E	31
Taroom, *Queens., Aust.*	25½S	149¾E	60
Tarragona, *Spain.*	41¼N	1¼E	35
Tarrasa, *Spain.*	41½N	2E	35
Tarshiha, *Isr.* (ins.).	32¾N	35½E	40
Tarsus, *Turkey.*	37N	35E	41
Tarta, *U.S.S.R.*	40N	53E	38
Tartary, G. of, *U.S.S.R.*	50N	141E	39
Tartu, *U.S.S.R.*	58½N	27E	38
Tarutino, *U.S.S.R.*	46¼N	29E	37
Taschereau, *Que.* (ins.).	49N	79W	71
Tash Kurghan, *China.*	37N	75E	43
Tashauz, *U.S.S.R.*	42N	60E	40
Tashi Gomba, *China.*	33N	95E	43
Tashigong, *Tibet.*	32½N	79¾E	44
Tashkent, *U.S.S.R.*	41¼N	69¼E	39
Taskan, *U.S.S.R.*	63N	150E	39
Tasman B., *S.I., N.Z.*	41S	173½E	63
Tasman Hd., *Tas., Aust.*	42¾S	147½E	59
Tasman Mts., *S.I., N.Z.*	41S	173¾E	62
Tasman Pen., *Tas.*	43½S	148E	59
Tasman S., *N.I., N.Z.*	38S	173E	62
TASMANIA, *Australia.*	42S	147E	58
TATAR A.S.S.R., *U.S.S.R.*	55N	51E	38
Tatarsk, *U.S.S.R.*	55¼N	76E	39
Tatla Lake, *Canada.*	51¾N	124½W	72
Tatnam, C., *Man.*	57¼N	91W	66
Tatong, *Vict., Aust.*	36¾S	146E	59
Tatta, *Pakistan.*	25N	67½E	43
Tatu River, *China.*	30N	104E	48
Tatung, *China.*	40N	113½E	48
Tauberbischofsheim, *Germany.*	49½N	9½E	33
Taumarunui, *N.Z.*	38¾S	175½E	62
Taunggyi, *Burma.*	20¾N	97E	43
Taunton, *England.*	51N	3¼W	22
Taunton, *Mass., U.S.A.*	41¾N	71W	69
Taupo, *N.I., N.Z.*	38¾S	176½E	62
Taupo, L., *N.I., N.Z.*	38¾S	176E	62
Tauranga, *N.I., N.Z.*	37¾S	176½E	62
Tauroa Pt., *N.I., N.Z.*	35¼S	173E	62
Taurus Mts., *Turkey.*	37N	34E	41
Tavda & Riv., *U.S.S.R.*	57N	66E	39
Tavernole, *Italy.*	45¾N	10½E	31
Taveta, *Kenya.*	3½S	37½E	56
Tavira, *Portugal.*	37N	7¾W	35
Tavistock, *England.*	50½N	4¼W	22
Tavolara, *Sardinia.*	40¾N	9¾E	36
Tavoy, *Burma.*	14¼N	98¼E	47
Taw, Riv., *England.*	51¼N	4¼W	22
Tawa Flat, *N.I., N.Z.*	40¾S	174½E	62
Tawau, *E. Malaysia.*	4¼N	118E	47
Tawitawi Is., *Sulus, P.I.*	5¼N	120E	47
Tay, Firth of, *Scot.*	56½N	3W	25
Tay, Loch, *Scotland.*	56½N	4¼W	25
Tay, L., *W. Australia.*	33S	121E	61
Taygonos Pen., *U.S.S.R.*	61N	161E	39
Taylor Mt., *U.S.A.*	35½N	108W	74
Taynuilt, *Scotland.*	56½N	5¼W	25
Tayport, *Scotland.*	56½N	3W	25
Tayung, *China.*	29½N	110½E	48
Taza, *Morocco.*	34¼N	4W	35
Tazovskaya, G., *U.S.S.R.*	68N	76E	39
Tazovskoye, *U.S.S.R.*	67½N	78½E	39

Place	Lat.	Long.	No.
Tbilisi, *U.S.S.R.*	41½N	44½E	38
Tchang, *Cameroon.*	5½N	10E	57
Tchibanga, *Gabon.*	3s	11E	56
Tczew, *Poland.*	54N	18½E	33
Teague, L., *W. Aust.*	26s	121E	61
Te Anau, L., *S.I., N.Z.*	45½s	167½E	63
Te Aroha, *N.I., N.Z.*	37½s	175½E	62
Te Awamutu, *N.I., N.Z.*	38s	175½E	62
Te Kaha, *N.I., N.Z.*	37½s	177½E	62
Te Kuiti, *N.I., N.Z.*	38½s	175½E	62
Te Puke, *N.I., N.Z.*	37½s	176½E	62
Te Teko, *N.I., N.Z.*	38s	176½E	62
Tebessa, *Algeria.*	35½N	8½E	35
Tebuk, *Saudi Arabia.*	28N	36½E	40
Tecolutla, *Mexico.*	21N	97w	76
Tecpan de Galeana, *Mexico.*	17½N	100½w	76
Tecuci, *Romania.*	45½N	27½E	37
Teddington, *S.I., N.Z.*	(inset C).		63
Tedzhen &R., *U.S.S.R.*	37N	61E	40
Tees, Riv., *England.*	54½N	1¼w	25
Tegal, *Java.*	6½s	109½E	47
Tegerhi, *Libya.*	23½N	15E	50
Tegucigalpa, *Hond.*	14½N	87w	77
Teguise, *Can. Is.* (ins).	29N	13½w	35
Tegur, *Kash.* (inset).	34½N	77½E	44
Tehran, *Iran.*	35½N	51½E	40
Tehsien, *China.*	37½N	116E	48
Tehuacan, *Mexico.*	18½N	97½w	76
Teifi, Riv., *Wales.*	52N	4w	22
Teignmouth, *Eng.*	50½N	3½w	22
Tekapo, L., *S.I., N.Z.*	43½s	170½E	63
Tekirdag, *Turkey.*	41N	27½E	41
Tel Aviv, *Israel.*	32N	34½E	41
Tela, *Honduras.*	16N	87w	77
Telegraph Cr., *Canada.*	58N	131¼w	66
Tellicherry, *India.*	11½N	75½E	45
Telok Anson, *Malaysia.* (ins.).	4N	100½E	47
Telok Datoh, *Malaysia.* (ins.).	2½N	101½E	47
Telshai, *U.S.S.R.*	56½N	22E	33
Telukbetung, *Sumatra.*	5½s	105½E	47
Temax, *Mexico.*	21½N	89w	76
Temba, Riv., *Nigeria.*	8N	10E	56
Tembi, *N. Guin.* (ins.).	6½s	146E	60
Temerloh, *Malaysia.* (ins.).	3½N	102½E	47
Temir, *U.S.S.R.*	49N	57E	38
Temora, *N.S.W., Aust.*	34½s	147½E	59
Tempe, *O.F.S., S. Afr.*	29s	26½E	55
Tempio, *Sardinia.*	41N	9E	36
Temple, *Tex., U.S.A.*	31½N	97½w	75
Temple B., *Queens., Aust.*	12s	143E	60
Templemore, *Ireland.*	52½N	7½w	26
Templeton, *S.I., N.Z.*	(inset C).		63
Templeton, *Wales.*	51½N	4½w	22
Temptation, Mt. of, *Jordan* (inset).	31½N	35½E	40
Temuco, *Chile.*	38½s	72½w	78
Temuka, *S.I., N.Z.*	44½s	171½E	63
Tenasserim, *Burma.*	12N	99E	43
Tenbury, *England.*	52½N	2½w	22
Tenby, *Wales.*	51½N	4½w	22
Tendeka, *Natal.*	27½s	30½E	55
Tenedos, I. of, *Greece.*	40N	26E	37
Tenerife I., *Can. Is.*	28½N	16½w	35
Tenes, *Algeria.*	36½N	1½E	35
Tenggol Pt., *Mal.* (ins.).	4½N	103½E	47
Tenghai, *China.*	23½N	117½E	48
Tenghsien, *China.*	35N	117E	48
Tengiz, L., *U.S.S.R.*	50N	69E	39
Tengyueh, *China.*	25N	98½E	43
Tenke, *Congo.*	11s	26E	56
Tenkodogo, *Senegal.*	12N	½w	57
Tennant Crk., *N. Terr.*	19½s	134½E	60
TENNESSEE & R., *U.S.A.*	36N	88w	75
Tenryu, Riv., *Japan.*	34½N	138E	49
Tenterden, *England.*	51½N	½E	23
Tenterden, *W. Aust.*	34½s	117½E	61
Tenterfield, *N.S.W., Aus.*	29s	152E	59
Tepic, *Mexico.*	21½N	105w	76
Tepich, *Mexico.*	20N	88½w	76
Teplice-Sanov, *Czech.*	50½N	13½E	33
Tequila, *Mexico.*	21N	103½w	76
Ter, Riv., *Spain.*	42N	3E	35
Teramo, *Italy.*	42½N	13½E	36
Terampa I., *E. Indies.*	3N	107E	47
Terang, *Vict., Aust.*	38½s	143E	59
Ter Apel, *Holland.*	53N	7E	30
Terceira I., *Azores.*	38½N	27½w	35
Terek Riv., *U.S.S.R.*	43½N	47½E	38
Terezina, *Brazil.*	5s	43w	78
Teriberka, *U.S.S.R.*	69½N	35½E	38
Tergnier, *France.*	49½N	3½E	30
Terkos, *Turkey.*	41½N	29E	37
Termini, *Sicily.*	38N	13½E	36
Termoli, *Italy.*	42N	15E	36
Termonde, *Belgium.*	51N	4E	30
Ternate I., *Indonesia.*	1N	127½E	47
Terneuzen, *Holland.*	51½N	3½E	30
Terni, *Italy.*	42½N	12½E	36
Terowie, *S. Australia.*	33½s	139E	59
Terpeniya B., *U.S.S.R.*	49N	144E	39
Terra Nova B., *Antarc.*	75s	165E	80
Terrace, *Br. Col., Can.*	54½N	128½w	72
Terracina, *Italy.*	41½N	13½E	36
Terralba, *Sardinia.*	39½N	8½E	36
Terranova, *Sardinia.*	41N	9½E	36
Terre Haute, *Ind., U.S.*	39½N	87½w	75
Terryglass, *Ireland.*	53N	8½w	26
Terschelling, *Holl.*	53½N	5E	30
Teruel, *Spain.*	40½N	1w	35
Tesanj, *Yugoslavia.*	44½N	18E	36
Teshio, *Japan.*	45N	142E	49
Tesin, Riv., *Mongolia.*	50N	92E	39
Tessenberg, *Austria.*	46½N	12½E	31
Test, Riv., *England.*	51N	1½w	23
Testa, C., *Sardinia.*	41½N	9½E	36
Tetang, *China.*	24N	100E	43
Tetbury, *England.*	51½N	2½w	22
Tete, *Mozambique.*	16½s	33½E	51
Tete Jaune, *Br. Col.*	53N	119½w	72
Teterchen, *France.*	49½N	6½E	30
Tetova, *Yugoslavia.*	42N	21E	37
Tetuan, *Morocco.*	35½N	5½w	35
Tetyukhe, *U.S.S.R.*	44N	136E	49
Teulada, *Sardinia.*	39N	8½E	36
Teviot, Riv., *Scotland.*	55½N	2½w	25
Teviothead, *Scotland.*	55½N	2½w	25
Tewaewae B., *S.I., N.Z.*	46½s	167½E	63
Tewkesbury, *England.*	52N	2½w	22
Texarkana, *U.S.A.*	33½N	94w	75
Texas, *Queens., Aust.*	29s	151½E	59
TEXAS, *U.S.A.*	32N	100w	74
Texel, *Holland.*	53N	4½E	30
Texoma, L., *Okla., U.S.*	34N	96½w	75
Texutlan, *Mexico.*	19½N	97w	76
Tezpur, *India.*	20½N	92½E	46
Tg. Malim, *Mal.* (ins.).	3½N	101½E	47
Thaba Nchu, *O.F.S., S.A.*	29s	26½E	53
Thabazimbi, *T'vaal.*	24½s	27½E	54
THAILAND, *Asia.*	16N	102E	47
Thakhek, *Laos.*	17½N	105E	47
Thal, *Pakistan.*	33½N	70½E	46
Thal Desert, *Pakistan.*	31N	71½E	46
Thallon, *Queens., Aust.*	28½s	148½E	60
Thame, *England.*	51½N	1w	23
Thames, *N.I., N.Z.*	37½s	175½E	62
Thames, Riv., *Eng.*	51½N	½E	23
Thames R., *Ont., Can.*	43N	82w	68
Thane, *Queens., Aust.*	28s	151½E	59
Thangool, *Queens., Aus.*	24½s	150½E	60
Thangra, *Kash.* (ins.).	33N	78½E	44
Thanh Hoa, *Vietnam.*	20N	106E	47
Thann, *France.*	47½N	7½E	32
Thar Desert, *India.*	27½N	72E	44
Thargomindah, *Aust.*	28s	143½E	60
Tharrawaddy, *Burma.*	17½N	95½E	43
Thasos I., *Greece.*	40½N	24½E	37
Thatcham, *England.*	51½N	1½w	23
Thaton, *Burma.*	16½N	97½E	43
Thato Pass, *Kashmir.*	33½N	77½E	43
Thaungdut, *Burma.*	24½N	94½E	46
Thaxted, *England.*	52N	½E	23
Thayetmyo, *Burma.*	19½N	95½E	43
Thebes, *Egypt.*	26N	32½E	40
Thebes, *Greece.*	38½N	23½E	37
The Coorong, *S. Aust.*	36s	139½E	59
The Pas, *Man., Can.*	53½N	101½w	70
Thebus, *C Pr., S. Afr.*	31½s	25½E	53
Theebine, *Queens., Aust.*	26s	152½E	60
Theodore, *Sask., Can.*	51½N	102½w	70
Theophilo Ottoni, *Brazil.*	17s	40w	78
Theo. Roosevelt R., *Braz.*	3s	59w	78
Thermai, G. of, *Gr.*	40½N	23E	37
Thessalon, *Ont., Can.*	46½N	83½w	68
Thessaloniki, *Greece.*	40½N	23E	37
Thetford, *England.*	52½N	½E	23
Thetford Mines, *Can.*	46½N	71½w	69
The Twelve Pins, *Ire.*	53½N	10w	26
Theunissen,*O.F.S.,S.A.*	28½s	26½E	55
Thevenard, I., *W.Aust.*	21½s	115E	61
Thevenard, S. Aust.	32½s	133½E	58
Thicket, *Man., Can.*	55½N	97½w	71
Thielt, *Belgium.*	51N	3½E	30
Thiers, *France.*	46N	3½E	32
Thies, *Senegal.*	14½N	17w	50
Thionville, *France.*	49½N	6½E	30
Thira, I. of, *Greece.*	36½N	25½E	37
Thirlmere, *England.*	54½N	3½w	25
Thirsk, *England.*	54½N	1½w	25
Thisted, *Denmark.*	57N	9E	29
Thistil Fiord, *Iceland.*	66½N	16w	29
Thistle I., S. *Aust.*	35s	136½E	59
Tholen, *Holland.*	51½N	4E	30
Tholey, *Germany.*	49½N	7E	30
Thomas R., *C.Pr., S.A.*	32½s	27½E	53
Thomastown, *Ire.*	52½N	7½w	26
Thompson R., *Canada.*	50½N	121½w	72
Thompson's Falls, *Ken.*	0	36½E	56
Thonon, *France.*	46½N	6½E	32
Thornaby-on-Tees, *England.*	54½N	1½w	25
Thornbury, *Ont., Can.*	44½N	80½w	68
Thorne, *England.*	53½N	1w	23
Thornhill, *C.Pr., S.A.-r.*	34s	25½E	53
Thornhill, *Scotland.*	55N	3½w	25
Thouarce, *France.*	47½N	½w	31
Thouars, *France.*	47N	½w	32
Thouin, C., *W. Aust.*	20½s	118E	61
Thousand Is., L., *Can.*	44½N	76w	69
THRACE, *Greece.*	41N	26E	37
Thrapston, *England.*	52½N	½w	23
Three Rivers, *Canada.*	46½N	72½w	66
Three Sisters, *C. Pr.*	31½s	23½E	52
Three Springs, *W.Aust.*	29½s	115½E	61
Throk Pass, *China.*	31N	93E	43
Throssell, L., *W.Aust.*	27½s	124E	61
Thule, *Greenland.*	76N	69w	66
Thun & L., *Switz.*	46½N	7½E	31
THURGAU, *Switz.*	47½N	9E	31
Thurles, *Eire.*	52½N	7½w	26
Thurn Pass, *Austria.*	47½N	12½E	31
Thursday I., *Aust.*	10½s	142½E	58
Thurso, *Scotland.*	58½N	3½w	24
Thury-Harcourt, *Fr.*	49N	½w	31
Thusis, *Switzerland.*	46½N	9½E	31
Tiaret, *Algeria.*	35½N	1½E	35
Tibati, *Cameroon.*	6½N	12½E	56
Tiber River, *Italy.*	42N	12E	36
Tiberias, L., *Isr.* (ins.).	33N	35½E	40
TIBET, *Asia.*	32N	85E	42
Tibula, *W. Australia.*	26½s	125E	61
Tibooburra, *N.S.W.*	29½s	142E	59
Tiburon, *Haiti, W.I.*	18N	74½w	77
Tichit, *Mauritania.*	19½N	8½w	50
TICINO, *Switzerland.*	46½N	8½E	31
Ticino, Riv., *Italy.*	45½N	9E	36
Tickhill, *England.*	53½N	1w	23
Ticul, *Mexico.*	20½N	89½w	76
Tiddim, *Burma.*	23½N	93½E	46
Tiehling, *China.*	42N	123E	39
Tiehling, *Holland.*	51½N	5½E	30
Tienchen, *China.*	40½N	114E	48
Tien Shan Mts., *China.*	44N	84E	39
Tienshui, *China.*	34½N	106E	48
Tientsin, *China.*	39N	117½E	48
Tien Yen, *Vietnam.*	21N	107E	47
Tientung, *China.*	23½N	107E	48
Tierra Del Fuego I.	54s	68w	78
Tiflis, see TBILISI.			
Tiger B., *Angola.*	17s	11½E	56
Tigil, *U.S.S.R.*	58N	159E	39
Tigris R., *Iraq-Turk.*	32½N	46E	41
Tihama Des., *S.Arabia.*	25N	36E	40
Tijuana, *Mexico.*	32½N	117w	76
Tikamgarh, *India.*	25N	78½E	44
Tikhoretsk, *U.S.S.R.*	46N	40E	38
Tikhvin, *U.S.S.R.*	59½N	33½E	38
Tiksi & B., *U.S.S.R.*	72N	129E	39
Tilburg, *Holland.*	51½N	5E	30
Tilbury, *England.*	51½N	½E	23
Tilbury, *Ont., Can.*	42½N	82½w	68
Tili-Iki, *U.S.S.R.*	60N	167E	39
Till, Riv., *Scotland.*	55½N	2w	25
Tillsonburg, *Ont., Can.*	43N	80½w	68
Tilos, I. of, *Greece.*	36½N	27½E	37
Tilsit, see SOVETSK.			
Timagami, *Ont., Can.*	47N	79½w	68
Timaru, *S.I., N.Z.*	44½s	171½E	63
Timbo, *Guinea.*	11N	13w	50
Timboon, *Vict., Aust.*	38½s	143E	59
Timbuktu, *Mali.*	16½N	2½w	50
Timerein, *Sudan.*	17N	37E	40
Timisoara, *Romania.*	45½N	21½E	37
Timka Paul, *U.S.S.R.*	61½N	62E	38
Timmins, *Ont., Can.*	48½N	81½w	68
TIMOR I., *S.E. Asia.*	9s	125E	47
Timor Sea, *Australia.*	12s	125E	58
Timpton R., *U.S.S.R.*	58N	126E	39
Tinaca Pt., *Mind., P.I.*	6N	125E	47
Tinahely, *Eire.*	52½N	6½w	22
Tinajo, *Can. Is.* (ins.).	29N	13½w	35
Tineo, *Spain.*	43½N	6½w	35
Tingha, *N.S.W., Aust.*	30s	151½E	59
Tingnan, *China.*	24½N	115E	48
Tinguere, *Cameroon.*	7½N	12½E	57
Tinian I., *Pacific.*	14N	145E	64
Tinogasta, *Argentina.*	28s	67½w	79
Tinos I., *Aegean Sea.*	37½N	25½E	37
Tintagel, *England.*	50½N	4½w	22
Tintinara, *S. Australia.*	36s	140E	59
Tinto, *Nigeria.*	5½N	9½E	57
Tinto Hill, *Scotland.*	55½N	3½w	25
Tinwald, *S.I., N.Z.*	44s	171½E	63
Tioman I., *Mal.* (ins.).	3N	104½E	47
Tione, *Italy.*	46N	10½E	31
TIPPERARY, *Eire.*	52½N	8½w	26
Tirana, *Albania.*	41½N	19½E	37
Tirano, *Italy.*	46½N	10½E	31
Tiraspol, *U.S.S.R.*	46½N	29½E	38
Tirau, *N.I., N.Z.*	38s	175½E	62
Tire, *Turkey.*	38N	27½E	41
Tirebolu, *Turkey.*	41N	38½E	41
Tiree I., *Scotland.*	56½N	7w	25
Tirlemont, *Belgium.*	50½N	5E	30
Tirlyanski, *U.S.S.R.*	54½N	59E	38
Tirnavos, *Greece.*	39½N	22½E	37
Tiruchirapalli, *India.*	11N	78½E	45
Tirukkovil, *Ceylon.*	7½N	81½E	45
Tirunelveli, *India.*	8½N	77½E	45
Tisa R., *Hung.-Yugo.*	47½N	20½E	37
Tisdale, *Sask., Can.*	53N	104w	70
Tit, *Algeria.*	23N	5E	50
Titicaca, L., *Bolivia.*	15½s	69w	79
Titograd, *Yugoslavia.*	42½N	19½E	37
Tiverton, *England.*	50½N	3½w	22
Tivoli, *Italy.*	42N	12½E	36
Tizimin, *Mexico.*	21N	88½w	76
Tizi-Ouzou, *Algeria.*	36N	4E	50
Tjilatjap, *Java.*	7½s	109E	47
Tlaxcala, *Mexico.*	19½N	98½w	76
Tlemcen, *Algeria.*	34½N	1½w	50
Tobago I., *Wind. Is.*	11½N	60½w	77
Tobermory, *Ont., Can.*	45½N	81½w	68
Tobermory, *Aust.*	27½s	144½E	60
Tobermory, *Scotland.*	56½N	6½w	24
Tobolsk, *U.S.S.R.*	58½N	68½E	39
Tobruk, *Libya.*	32N	24E	34
Tocantins, R., *Brazil.*	10s	48w	78
Toce R., *Italy.*	45½N	8½E	31
Toco, *Trinidad* (ins.).	11½N	60½w	77
Tocopilla, *Chile.*	22s	70½w	79
Tocumwal, *Aust.*	35½s	145½E	59
Tocuya Riv., *Venez.*	11N	69w	77
Todd River, *Aust.*	25s	136E	60
Todenyang, *Kenya.*	4½N	36E	56
Todi Spoleto, *Italy.*	42½N	12½E	36
Todmorden, *Eng.*	53½N	2w	22
Todmorden, *S. Aust.*	27½s	135E	60
Todos Santos, *Mex.*	23½N	110½w	76
Todtnau, *Germany.*	47½N	8E	31
Toe Head, *Ireland.*	51½N	9½w	26
Tofield, *Alberta, Can.*	53½N	112½w	73
Tofua I., *Pacific.*	20s	178w	64
Togian Is., *Celebes.*	½s	122E	47
Togo, *Sask., Canada.*	51½N	101½w	70
TOGO, *West Africa.*	8N	2E	50
Togral Ombo, *China.*	35N	82E	43
Toinya, *Sudan.*	6N	29½E	56
Toise River, *C.Pr., S.A.*	32½s	27½E	53
Tokanui, *S.I., N.Z.*	46½s	169E	63
Tokar, *Sudan.*	18N	37½E	40
Tokat, *Turkey.*	40½N	36½E	41
Tokelau Is., *Pacific.*	8½s	170w	18
Tokiwa, *Japan.*	45N	142E	49
Tokoroa, *N.I., N.Z.*	38½s	175½E	62
Tokushima, *Japan.*	34N	134½E	49
Tokwe Riv., *Rhodesia.*	21½s	32E	51
Tokyo, *Japan.*	35½N	139½E	49
Tola Riv., *Mongolia.*	49N	105E	39
Tolaga B., *N.I., N.Z.*	38½s	178½E	62
Toledo, *Ohio, U.S.A.*	41½N	83½w	75
Toledo, *Spain.*	39½N	4w	34
Tolentino, *Italy.*	43N	13½E	36
Tolima, Mt., *Colombia.*	5N	74½w	78
Tolitoli, *Celebes.*	1N	120½E	47
Tolmezzo, *Italy.*	46½N	13E	36
Tolstoy, C., *U.S.S.R.*	59N	154E	39
Toluca, *Mexico.*	19½N	99½w	76
Tolun, *China.*	42½N	116E	39
Tomakomi, *Japan.*	42½N	141½E	49
Tomar, *Portugal.*	39½N	8½w	35
Tomari, *U.S.S.R.*	47½N	144E	39
Tomaszow, *Poland.*	50½N	23½E	33
Tomaszow, *Poland.*	51½N	20E	33
Tomatin, *Scotland.*	57½N	4w	24
Tomatlan, *Mexico.*	20N	105½w	76
Tomdoun, *Scotland.*	57N	5½w	24
Tornintoul, *Scotland.*	57½N	3½w	24
Tommot, *U.S.S.R.*	59N	126½E	39
Tompa, *U.S.S.R.*	56N	110E	39
Tompo Riv., *U.S.S.R.*	64N	134E	39
Tomsk, *U.S.S.R.*	56½N	85E	39
Tonala, *Mexico.*	16N	93½w	76
Tonbridge, *England.*	51½N	½E	23
Tonder, *Denmark.*	55N	9E	29
Tonkin, G. of, *China.*	20N	108E	48
Tonga Is., *Pacific.*	20s	174w	64
Tongaat, *Natal.*	29½s	31E	55
Tongareva I., *Pacific.*	9s	159w	64
Tongjuk Dzong, *China.*	30N	95E	43
Tongres, *Belgium.*	50½N	5½E	30
Tongue, *Scotland.*	58½N	4½w	24
Tonichi, *Mexico.*	28N	109½w	76
Tonj, *Sudan.*	7½N	28½E	56
Tonk, *India.*	26N	75½E	44
Tonopah, *Nev., U.S.A.*	37½N	117½w	74
Tonle Sap L., *Cambod.*	13N	104E	47
Tonnerre, *France.*	47½N	4E	32
Tonning, *Germany.*	54½N	9E	33
Tonosi, *Panama.*	7½N	80w	77
Tonsberg, *Norway.*	59½N	10½E	29
Toodvay, *W. Aust.*	31½s	116½E	61
Toolondo, *Vict., Aust.*	37s	142E	59
Toompine, *Queens.*	27½s	144E	60
Toowoomba, *Aust.*	27½s	152E	60
Topeka, *Kan., U.S.A.*	39N	96w	75
Topo, *Azores* (inset).	38½N	28w	35
Topola, *Yugoslavia.*	45½N	19½E	37
Topolobampo, *Mexico.*	25½N	109½w	76
Topsham, *England.*	50½N	3½w	22
Tor, *Egypt.*	28N	33½E	41
Torbali, *Turkey.*	38½N	27½E	37
Torgau, *Germany.*	51½N	13E	33
Torigny, *France.*	49N	1w	31
Torit, *Sudan.*	4N	32½E	56
Tornahaish, *Scotland.*	57½N	3½w	24
Tornala, *Czecho.*	48½N	20½E	33
Torne, L. of, *Sweden.*	68N	19E	29
Tornea Riv., *Sweden.*	66N	24E	29
Torness, *Scotland.*	56½N	5½w	24
Tornio, *Finland.*	66N	24E	29
Toro, *Spain.*	41½N	5½w	35
Toro, Mt., *Argentina.*	30s	70w	78
Torom, *U.S.S.R.*	54N	137E	39
Toroni, G. of, *Greece.*	40N	23½E	37
Toronto, *Ont., Can.*	43½N	79½w	68
Toronto L., *Mexico.*	27½N	106w	76
Toropets, *U.S.S.R.*	56½N	31½E	38
Tororo, *Kenya* (inset).			56
Torp, *Sweden.*	62½N	16E	29
Torpoint, *England.*	50½N	4½w	22
Torre Annunziata, *It.*	40½N	14½E	36
Torquay, *England.*	50½N	3½w	22
Torre Del Greco, *It.*	40½N	14½E	36
Torrelavega, *Spain.*	43½N	4w	35
Torres, L., *S. Aust.*	31s	137½E	59
Torrens Crk., *Queens.*	20½s	145E	60
Torreon, *Mexico.*	25½N	103½w	76
Torre Pellice, *Italy.*	44½N	7½E	31
Torres Is., *Pacific.*	13½s	166½E	64
Torres Novas, *Port.*	39½N	8½w	35
Torres Str., *N. Aust.*	10½s	142½E	60
Torres Vedras, *Port.*	39½N	9½w	35
Torrevieja, *Spain.*	38N	½w	35
Torridge, R., *England.*	51N	4½w	22
Torridon & L., *Scot.*	57½N	5½w	24
Torriglia, *Italy.*	44½N	9½E	36
Torrington, *England.*	51N	4½w	22
Torrington, *Wyo., U.S.*	42N	104½w	74
Torrowangee, *Aust.*	31½s	141½E	59
Torshavn, *Faeroes Is.*	62N	7w	29
Tortola I., *W. Indies.*	18½N	64½w	77
Tortoli, *Sardinia.*	40N	9½E	36

[132] Tortona—Ulundi

Place	Lat.	Long.	No.
Tortona, Italy.	45N	9E	31
Tortorici, Sicily.	38N	15E	36
Tortosa, C. de, Spain.	41N	1E	35
Tortue, I. de la, Haiti.	20¼N	72¾W	77
Tortuga I., Venezuela.	11N	65W	77
Torun, Poland.	53N	18½E	33
Tory I. & Sd., Eire.	55¼N	8¼W	26
Torzhok, U.S.S.R.	57N	35E	38
Toston, Can. Is. (ins.).	28¾N	14W	35
Tosu Nor, L., China.	35N	99E	43
Totana, Spain.	38N	1¼W	35
Toteng, Bech'land.	20½S	23E	51
Totma, U.S.S.R.	60N	42½E	38
Totnes, England.	50½N	3¾W	22
Totoya I., Pacific.	20S	180W	64
Tottenham, Aust.	32¼S	147½E	59
Tottori, Japan.	35½N	134¼E	49
Toucy, France.	47¾N	3¼E	30
Touggourt, Algeria.	33N	6E	35
Toul, France.	48¾N	6E	32
Toulon, France.	43¼N	6E	32
Toulouse, France.	43½N	1½E	32
Toungoo, Burma.	18¼N	96½E	43
TOURAINE, France.	47¼N	½E	31
Tourane, Vietnam.	16N	108E	47
Tourcoing, France.	50¾N	3¼E	30
Tournai, Belgium.	50¾N	3½E	30
Tourouvre, France.	48½N	½E	31
Towera, W. Aust.	22½S	115E	61
Tournon, France.	46¾N	1E	32
Tournus, France.	46½N	4¾E	32
Tours, France.	47½N	¾E	32
Tovar, Venezuela.	8N	72W	77
Touws R., C. Pr., S. Af.	33¼S	20E	52
Towcester, England.	52¼N	1W	23
Townshend I., Aust.	22S	151E	60
Townsville, Aust.	19¼S	146¾E	60
Towyn, Wales.	52½N	4W	22
Toyama, Japan.	36¾N	137¼E	49
Toyohashi, Japan.	34¾N	137½E	49
Tozeur, Tunisia.	34N	8E	35
Trabzon, Turkey.	41N	39¾E	41
Tracadie, Canada.	47½N	65W	67
Tradom, Tibet.	30N	84E	43
Trafalgar, C., Spain.	36¼N	6W	35
Trail, Br. Col., Can.	49N	117¾W	73
Tralee, Eire.	52¼N	9¾W	26
Tralee B., Ireland.	52¼N	10W	26
Tralleborg, Sweden.	55½N	13E	29
Tramore & B., Ire.	52¼N	7W	26
Trang, Thailand.	7½N	100E	43
Trangie, N.S.W., Aust.	32S	148E	59
Trani, Italy.	41¼N	16½E	36
Tranquebar, India.	11N	79¾E	45
Transcona, Man., Can.	49¾N	96¾W	71
TRANSKEI, C. Pr.	32S	29E	53
TRANSVAAL, S. Africa.	25S	29E	55
TRANSYLVANIA, Rom.	47N	24E	37
Trapani, Sicily.	38N	12½E	36
Trapiche, Guatemala.	17N	91W	76
Trasimeno, L., Italy.	43¼N	12¼E	36
Traunstein, Germany.	47¾N	12¾E	33
Travers, Mt., S.I.,N.Z.	42S	172½E	63
Traverse City, U.S.A.	44¾N	85¾W	75
Traversetolo, Italy.	44½N	10½E	31
Travnik, Yugoslavia.	44¼N	17¾E	37
Trayning, W. Aust.	31S	117¾E	61
Trebinje, Yugoslavia.	42¾N	18½E	36
Trebon, Czecho.	49N	14½E	33
Tredegar, England.	51¾N	3¼W	22
Trefoil, Alberta, Can.	51¼N	112¼W	73
Tregaron, Wales.	52¼N	4W	22
Tregastel, France.	48¾N	3½W	31
Tregoney, England.	50¼N	5W	22
Treguier, France.	48¾N	3¼W	31
Treinta-y-Tres, Urug.	33¼S	54W	79
Trekelano, Aust.	21½S	140E	60
Tremadoc B., Wales.	52¾N	4¼W	22
Tremaudan, Man., Can.	54N	101¼W	70
Tremiti Is., Italy.	42N	15½E	36
Trencin, Czecho.	48¾N	18E	33
TRENGGANU, Malaysia.	5N	103E	47
Trent, Riv., England.	53½N	¾W	23
TRENTINO-ALTO ADIGE, Italy.	46½N	11E	31
Trenton, Mo., U.S.A.	40N	93½W	75
Trento, Italy.	46N	11E	36
Trenton, N.J., U.S.A.	40¼N	74¾W	75
Trenton, No. Scotia.	45¾N	62¾W	67
Trenton, Ont., Can.	44¼N	77½W	69
Trepassey & B., Newf.	46¾N	53¼W	67
Trerap, Spain.	42¼N	1E	35
Tres Arroyos, Arg.	38½S	60½W	79
Treslove, W. Aust.	33S	122E	61
Treviglio, Italy.	45½N	9½E	36
Treviso, Italy.	45¾N	12¼E	36
Trevose Hd., Eng.	50½N	5W	22
Treysa, Germany.	51N	9¼E	33
Triabunna, Tasmania.	42½S	148E	59
Triang, Malaysia (ins.).	3¼N	102¼E	47
Trichardt, T'vaal, S.A.	26½S	29½E	55
Trida, N.S.W., Aust.	33S	145E	59
Trier, Germany.	49¾N	6¾E	33
Trieste, Italy.	45¾N	13¾E	36
Trikeri Strait, Greece.	39N	23E	37
Trikkala, Greece.	39½N	21¾E	37
Trim, Eire.	53½N	6¾W	26
Trincomalee, Ceylon.	8¾N	81¼E	45
Tring, England.	51¾N	¾W	23
Trinidad, Bolivia.	15S	65W	79
Trinidad, Colombia.	5¼N	72½W	77
Trinidad, Col., U.S.A.	37¼N	104½W	74
Trinidad, Cuba.	21¾N	80W	77
TRINIDAD I., W.Indies.	10½N	61¼W	77
Trinitapoli, Italy.	41¼N	16E	36
Trinite, Martinique.	15N	61W	77
Trinity, Newf., Can.	48¼N	53¼W	67
Trinkitat, Sudan.	18½N	37½E	40
Trino, Italy.	45¼N	8¼E	31
Trionto, C., Italy.	39½N	17E	37
Tripoli, Lebanon.	34½N	35¾E	41
Tripoli, Libya.	33¼N	13¼E	34
Tripolis, Greece.	37½N	22½E	37
TRIPURA, India.	24N	92E	43
Trivandrum, India.	8½N	77E	45
Trn, Bulgaria.	42¾N	22½E	37
Trnava, Czecho.	48¼N	17½E	33
Trnovo, Bulgaria.	43¼N	25½E	37
Trobriand Is., Pac.(ins.)	8S	151E	60
Trochu, Alb., Can.	51¾N	113¼W	73
Trodir, Yugoslavia.	43½N	16E	36
Troenan Is., Norway.	66¾N	12E	29
Troina, Sicily.	38N	14¾E	36
Trois Pistoles, Can.	48¼N	69¼W	69
Troitsk, U.S.S.R.	54N	62½E	38
Trollhattan, Sweden.	58¼N	12¼E	29
Trompsburg, O.F.S.	30S	25¾E	55
TROMSO & Tn., Nor.	69¾N	18½E	29
Tronador, Mt., Chile.	41S	71W	78
Trondheim, Norway.	63½N	10½E	29
Troon, Scotland.	55½N	4¾W	25
Tropea, Italy.	38½N	16E	36
Trosh, U.S.S.R.	66½N	56E	38
Trossachs, Scotland.	56¼N	4½W	25
Trout Creek, Ont., Can.	46N	79¾W	68
Trout Lake, Ont., Can.	51½N	93¼W	71
Trouville, France.	49½N	0	31
Trowbridge, Eng.	51¼N	2¼W	22
Troy, Ala., U.S.A.	31¾N	86W	75
Troy, N.Y., U.S.A.	42¾N	73¾W	69
Troyes, France.	48¼N	4E	32
TRUCIAL STATES, Asia.	23¾N	54E	42
Trujillo, Honduras.	16N	86W	77
Trujillo, Peru.	8S	79W	78
Trujillo, Spain.	39½N	6W	35
Trujillo, Venezuela.	9½N	70½W	78
Truk I., Pacific.	7½N	151¾E	64
Trumpington, Eng.	52¼N	0	23
Trun, France.	48¾N	0	31
Trundle, N.S.W., Aust.	33S	147¾E	59
Truro, England.	50¼N	5W	22
Truro, S. Australia.	34½S	139¼E	58
Trutnov, Czecho.	50½N	16E	33
Trzebiatowa, Poland.	54N	15½E	33
Trzebnica, Poland.	51¼N	17E	33
Tsabong, Botswana.	26½S	22½E	51
Tsagan Olom, Mong.	47N	97E	39
Tsagan Sanji, China.	43N	94E	39
Tsaidam Marsh, China.	36N	95E	43
Tsamaea, Botswana.	21S	27½E	54
Tsamai, Nigeria.	13½N	6E	57
Tsane, Botswana.	24S	22E	51
Tsangwu, China.	23½N	111¼E	48
Tsaratanana, Malagasy.	14S	47½E	56
Tsela Dzong, China.	30N	94E	43
Tselingrad, U.S.S.R.	51¼N	71½E	39
Tsenogory, U.S.S.R.	65N	46E	38
Tsessebe, Botswana.	21S	27½E	54
Tsetserlig, Mongolia.	47N	101E	39
Tshela, Congo (K.).	5S	12½E	56
Tshikapa, Congo (K.).	6½S	20¾E	56
Tsian, Korea.	41N	126½E	49
Tsina Riv., U.S.S.R.	56N	116E	39
Tsinan, China.	36¼N	117E	48
Tsincheng, China.	36N	112½E	48
Tsingchen, China.	37N	117E	48
Tsinkiang, China.	25N	118E	48
Tsingkiang, China.	28N	115E	48
Tsingkow, China.	35N	119¼E	48
Tsingtao, China.	36N	120¼E	48
Tsingyun, China.	24N	112½E	48
Tsining, China.	35¼N	117E	48
Tsining, China.	42½N	112½E	48
Tsingkiangpu, China.	33½N	119E	48
Tsinling Shan Mts., Ch.	34N	108E	48
Tsinyang, China.	35N	112½E	48
Tsolo, C. Pr., S. Afr.	31¼S	28¾E	53
Tsomo, C. Pr., S. Afr.	32S	27¾E	53
Tsu, Japan.	34¾N	136½E	49
Tsu Is. Japan.	34N	129E	49
Tsugaru Str., Japan.	42N	141E	49
Tsumeb, S.W. Africa.	19¼S	17¾E	51
Tsungfu, China.	23½N	114½E	48
Tsungshan, China.	22½N	107E	48
Tsunhwa, China.	40N	117½E	48
Tsunyi, China.	27¾N	107E	48
Tsuruga, Japan.	35¾N	136E	49
Tsuruoka, Japan.	38½N	140E	49
Tsuyama, Japan.	35N	134E	49
Tsuyung, China.	25N	101½E	43
Tuakau, N.I., N.Z.	37¼S	174¾E	62
Tuam, Eire.	53½N	8¾W	26
Tuamotu Arch., Pac.	19S	140W	18
Tuapse, U.S.S.R.	44N	38½E	38
Tuatapere, S.I., N.Z.	46¼S	167¾E	63
Tubas, Jordan (ins.).	32¼N	35¼E	40
Tubingen, Germany.	48½N	9E	33
Tubuai I., Pacific.	23S	150W	64
Tubutama, Mexico.	31¼N	111½W	76
Tucacas, Venezuela.	10¾N	68¼W	77
Tuchola, Poland.	53½N	17¾E	33
Tuckanarra, W.Aust.	27S	118E	61
Tucson, Ariz., U.S.A.	32¼N	111W	74
Tucuman, Argentina.	27S	65W	79
Tucumcari, U.S.A.	35½N	104W	74
Tucupita, Venezuela.	9N	62W	77
Tudela, Spain.	42N	2W	35
Tufi, Papua (inset).	9S	149E	60
TUGELA & R., Natal.	29S	31½E	55
Tughina, U.S.S.R.	46¾N	29½E	37
Tuguegarao, Luzon.	17½N	121¾E	47
Tuhshan, China.	26N	107½E	48
Tuinplaats, T'vaal, S.A.	25S	28¾E	54
Tuitan, Mexico.	24N	104W	76
Tukangbesi Is., Indon.	6S	124E	47
Tukums, U.S.S.R.	57N	23¼E	38
Tukuyu, Tanzania.	9S	33½E	56
Tula, U.S.S.R.	54¼N	37½E	38
Tula, Hidalgo, Mexico.	20N	99½W	76
Tulak, Afghanistan.	33¾N	64E	43
Tulancingo, Mexico.	20N	98W	76
Tulbagh, C. Pr., S. Afr.	33¼S	19¼E	52
Tulcea, Romania.	45¼N	28¾E	37
Tulear, Malagasy.	23½S	43¾E	56
Tuli, Rhodesia.	22S	29¼E	51
Tulkarm, Jordan (ins.)	32¼N	35E	40
Tullamore, Ireland.	53¼N	7½W	26
Tulle, France.	45¼N	1¾E	32
Tullow, Eire.	52¾N	6¾W	26
Tully, Queens., Aust.	17½S	146E	60
Tulsa, Okla., U.S.A.	36¼N	96W	75
Tulun, U.S.S.R.	54½N	100½E	39
Tumaco, Colombia.	1¾N	79W	78
Tumba, L., Congo (K.).	¾S	18E	56
Tumbala, Mexico.	17N	92½W	76
Tumbarumba, Aust.	35¾S	148E	59
Tumby Bay, S. Aust.	34¼S	136E	59
Tumen, Riv., Korea.	42½N	130½E	49
Tumeremo, Venez.	7N	61¼W	77
Tumereng, Guyana.	6½N	60W	77
Tumkur, India.	13¼N	77E	45
Tummel, R., Scotland.	56½N	4W	25
Tump, Pakistan.	26N	62½E	43
Tumpat, Malaysia (ins.).	6¼N	102¼E	47
Tumuc-Humac Mts., Brazil.	2N	55W	78
Tumut, N.S.W., Aust.	35¼S	148¼E	59
Tuna, Ghana.	9½N	2¼W	57
Tunapuna, Trinidad.	11N	61W	77
Tunbridge, Tasmania.	42¼S	147¼E	59
Tunbridge Wells, Eng.	51¼N	¼E	23
Tunduru, Tanzania.	11S	37¼E	56
Tung Ho Riv., China.	28N	104E	43
Tungabhadra R., India.	15N	76E	45
Tungchwah, China.	26½N	103E	43
Tunghai, China.	34½N	119¼E	48
Tunghwa, China.	41½N	126E	49
Tungjen, China.	27¾N	109E	48
Tungkiang, China.	48N	132E	39
Tungkun, China.	23N	113½E	48
Tungkwan, China.	34¾N	110¼E	48
Tungla, Nicaragua.	13½N	84¾W	77
Tungliao, China.	43N	122E	39
Tung-Ling, L., China.	29N	112½E	48
Tungtai, China.	33N	120E	48
Tunguska, Lower R., U.S.S.R.	64N	95E	39
Tunguska Stony R., U.S.S.R.	62N	95E	39
Tunis & G. of, Tunis.	36¾N	10½E	35
TUNISIA, N. Africa.	35N	9E	35
Tunja, Colombia.	5½N	73½W	78
Tunja, Riv., Turkey.	41¾N	26½E	37
Tunnel Crk, W. Aust.	24S	119E	61
Tunstall, England.	53N	2W	22
Tuoy-Khaya, U.S.S.R.	63N	111E	39
Tupelo, Miss., U.S.A.	34¼N	88¾W	75
Tupik, U.S.S.R.	55N	120E	39
Tupiza, Bolivia.	21¾S	66W	79
Tura, U.S.S.R.	64N	100E	39
Turaba, Saudi Arabia.	28N	43E	41
Turakirae Hd., N.I., N.Z. (inset B).			62
Turano, Riv., Italy.	42¾N	12¾E	36
Turbat, Pakistan.	26N	62½E	43
Turbat-i-Haidari, Iran.	35¼N	59½E	40
Turbo, Colombia.	8N	77W	77
Turda, Romania.	47N	24E	38
Tureia I., Pacific.	20S	139W	64
Turek, Poland.	52N	18½E	33
Tureta, Nigeria.	12½N	5½E	57
Turfan, China.	43N	89½E	39
Turfbult, T'vaal, S. Af.	24¾S	28¾E	54
Turgay, U.S.S.R.	50N	62E	39
Turin, Italy.	45N	7¾E	36
Turkestan, U.S.S.R.	43N	69E	39
Turkey Creek, W. Aust.	17S	129E	61
TURKEY, Asia-Eur.	40N	35E	41
TURKMENISTAN, U.S.S.R.	40N	55E	38
Turks Is., W. Indies.	21½N	71W	77
Turku, Finland.	60½N	22¼E	38
Turna, Czecho.	48¾N	21E	33
Turnagain, C., N.Z.	40½S	176½E	62
Turnberry, Man., Can.	53½N	101¾W	70
Turnberry, Scotland.	55¼N	4¾W	25
Turneffe Is., Br.Hond.	17½N	88W	77
Turner, Mt., W. Aust.	22½S	117½E	61
Turnhout, Belgium.	51½N	5E	30
Turnu Magurele, Rom.	43¾N	24¾E	37
Turnu Severin, Rom.	44¾N	22¾E	37
Turo River, U.S.S.R.	64N	100E	39
Turobin, Poland.	50¾N	22¾E	33
Turriff, Scotland.	57½N	2½W	24
Turtkul, U.S.S.R.	42N	62E	40
Turtleford, Sask., Can.	53½N	108¾W	70
Turtu, Mongolia.	52N	100E	39
Turukhansk, U.S.S.R.	65¾N	88½E	39
Turut, Iran.	35N	55E	40
Tuscaloosa, Ala., U.S.	33¼N	87½W	75
TUSCANY, Italy.	43N	11E	36
Tuskar Rock, Irish S.	52¼N	6¼W	26
Tutaev, U.S.S.R.	58N	39½E	38
Tuticorin, India.	8¾N	78¼E	45
Tuttlingen, Germany.	48N	8¾E	30
Tutuila I., Pacific.	15S	170W	64
Tutuko, Mt., S.I., N.Z.	44½S	168E	63
TUVA, U.S.S.R.	51N	94E	39
Tuwairifa, Sau. Arab.	22N	50E	40
Tuxedo, Man., Can.	49¾N	97¼W	71
Tuxford, England.	53¼N	¾W	23
Tuxpan, Nayarit, Mex.	22N	105¾W	76
Tuxpan, Vera C., Mex.	21N	97½W	76
Tuz Golu, L., Turk.	38¾N	33¼E	41
Tuzla, Yugoslavia.	44½N	18½E	36
Tweed, Ontario, Can.	44½N	77¼W	69
Tweed Heads, Aust.	28S	153½E	59
Tweed, Riv., Scotland.	55¾N	2½W	25
Tweeling, O.F.S., S.Af.	27½S	28½E	55
Tweespruit, O.F.S.	29¼S	27E	55
Twilight Cove, W.Aust.	32½S	126½E	61
Twinbrook, T'vaal.	25¾S	26¾E	54
Twin Falls, Id., U.S.A.	42½N	115W	74
Two Bridges, Eng.	50½N	4W	22
Tygda, U.S.S.R.	53N	126E	39
Tygerberg, C.Pr., S.Af.	33¾S	18½E	52
Tylden, C. Pr., S. Afr.	32S	27E	53
Tyler, Texas, U.S.A.	32½N	95¼W	75
Tym River, U.S.S.R.	59N	80E	39
Tyndinski, U.S.S.R.	55N	124E	39
Tyndrum, Scotland.	56½N	4¾W	25
Tyne, Riv., England.	55N	2W	25
Tynemouth, England.	55N	1½W	25
Tynisti, Czecho.	50¼N	16E	33
Tyrol, Austria.	47N	11E	33
TYRONE, N. Ireland.	54½N	7¼W	26
Tyrrel, L., Vict., Aust.	35¼S	142¾E	59
Tyrrhenian S., Italy.	40N	12E	36
Tyumen, U.S.S.R.	57¼N	65½E	39
Tyung River, U.S.S.R.	64N	122E	39
Tzaneen, T'vaal, S.Af.	23¾S	30½E	54
Tzekwei, China.	31N	110½E	48
Tzeli, China.	29¾N	111E	48
Tzeya River, China.	38N	117½E	48
Tzeyang, China.	35½N	117E	48
UAHUKA I., Pacific.	9S	140W	64
Uanda Jale, C. Afr. Rep.	9N	22½E	56
Uanetze, Mozambique.	24S	32E	51
Uaroo, W. Australia.	22½S	115E	61
Ubaila, S. Arabia.	22N	51E	40
Ubangi R., Cen. Af. Rep.	3N	18E	56
Ubari, Libya.	26N	12½E	34
Ubaye, Riv., France.	44½N	6¾E	31
Ube, Japan.	34N	131E	49
Ubeda, Spain.	38N	3½W	35
Uberaba, Brazil.	20S	48W	78
Uberlingen, Germany.	47¾N	9¼E	33
Ubiaja, Nigeria.	6½N	6½E	57
Ubombo, Natal.	27½S	32E	55
Ubon, Thailand.	15¼N	104½E	47
Ucayali River, Peru.	4S	74W	78
Uchte, Germany.	52½N	9E	30
Uch Turfan, China.	41N	79E	39
Uckfield, England.	51N	0	23
Uda River, U.S.S.R.	54N	135E	39
Udaipur, India.	24½N	73¾E	44
Uddevalla, Sweden.	58½N	12E	29
Uddjaur, L., Sweden.	66N	17E	38
Uden, Netherlands.	51¾N	5½E	30
Udine, Italy.	46N	13¼E	36
Udipi, India.	13¼N	74¾E	45
UDMURT, U.S.S.R.	57N	53E	38
Udskaya, G., U.S.S.R.	54N	135E	39
Ueda, Japan.	36½N	138¼E	31
Uele River, Congo (K.).	3¾N	27¾E	56
Uelen, U.S.S.R.	66N	170W	39
Ufa River, U.S.S.R.	53N	50E	38
Ufa, U.S.S.R.	54¾N	56E	38
Uffculme, England.	50¾N	3¼W	22
Ugab R., S.W.Afr.(ins.)	21S	13½E	51
Ugalla R., Tanzania.	5S	30E	56
UGANDA, East Africa.	2N	33E	56
Ugie, C. Pr., S. Afr.	31¼S	28¼E	53
Ugines, France.	45¾N	6½E	31
Uglegorsk, U.S.S.R.	49N	141E	39
Uglich, U.S.S.R.	57½N	38E	38
Uig, Scotland.	57½N	6½W	24
Uil River, U.S.S.R.	48N	53E	38
Uil, U.S.S.R.	49N	55E	38
Uitenhage, C.Pr., S.Af.	33¾S	25½E	53
Uithuizen, Nether.	53¼N	6½E	30
Uitzoek, O.F.S., S. Af.	27¾S	27¼E	54
Ujadbai, Kash. (ins.).	37½N	75½E	44
Ujae I., Pacific.	10N	165E	64
Ujelang I., Pacific.	10N	162E	65
Ujiji, Tanzania.	5S	29¾E	56
Ujjain, India.	23¼N	75¾E	44
Ujpest, Hungary.	47½N	19E	37
Uka, U.S.S.R.	58N	161E	39
Ukhta, U.S.S.R.	65N	31E	38
Ukhta, U.S.S.R.	63N	54E	38
Ukmerge, U.S.S.R.	55¼N	24¾E	38
UKRAINE, U.S.S.R.	49N	32E	38
Ulan, U.S.S.R.	46½N	45E	38
Ulan Bator, Mongolia.	48N	106¾E	39
Ulangom, Mongolia.	50N	92E	39
Ulan-Ude, U.S.S.R.	51¾N	107½E	39
Ulbanski B., U.S.S.R.	54N	139E	39
Ulbster, Scotland.	58¼N	3¼W	24
Ulchin, Korea.	37N	129½E	49
Uleaborg, see OULU.			
Ulithi I., Pacific.	10N	139E	64
Ulladulla, N.S.W.	35¼S	150½E	59
Ulladulla, Australia.	35¼S	150½E	59
Ullapool, Scotland.	58N	5¼W	24
Ullswater, England.	54½N	2¾W	23
Ullung I., Korea.	37½N	131E	49
Ulm, Germany.	48½N	10E	33
ULSTER, N. Ireland.	54½N	7W	26
Ultima, Vict., Aust.	35½S	143¼E	59
Ulundi, Natal.	28¼S	31½E	55

Place	Lat.	Long.	No.
Ulverston, *England.*	54¼N	3½W	25
Ulverstone, *Tasmania.*	41¼s	146½E	59
Ulya, *U.S.S.R.*	59N	141E	39
Ulyanovsk, *U.S S.R.*	54½N	48½E	38
Ulzburg, *Ger.* (inset).	53½N	10E	30
Ulzen, *Germany.*	53N	10½E	33
Umadaia, *Papua* (ins.).	7½s	143½E	60
Uman, *U.S.S.R.*	48¼N	30½E	38
Umbeluzi, *Moz.*	26s	32E	51
Umboi I., *Pac.* (inset).	6s	148E	60
UMBRIA, *Italy.*	43N	12½E	36
Umea, Riv., *Sweden.*	63½N	20E	29
Umea, *Sweden.*	63½N	20½E	29
Umfolozi, *Natal.*	28¼s	31½E	55
Umfuli Riv., *Rhodesia.*	17½s	29E	51
Umiat, *Alaska, U.S.A.*	68½N	151W	74
Umkomaas, *Natal.*	30¼s	30½E	55
Umm Lajj, *Sau. Arab.*	25N	37E	40
Umm Ruwaba, *Sud.*	12½N	31E	56
Umm Timman, *Chad.*	11N	20E	56
Umm Qasr, *Kuwait.*	30N	48E	41
Umniati Riv., *Rhodesia.*	19s	31E	51
Umtali, *Rhodesia.*	19s	32½E	51
Umtata, *C. Pr., S. Af.*	31¼s	28¼E	53
Umudhia, *Nigeria.*	5½N	7½E	57
Umvuma, *Rhodesia.*	19¼s	30¼E	51
Umzinto, *Natal.*	30¼s	30¼E	55
Umzumbe, *Natal.*	30¼s	30½E	55
Una, Riv., *Yugoslavia.*	45N	17E	36
Unalakleet, *Alaska.*	62½N	160W	74
Underberg, *Natal.*	29¼s	29½E	55
Underbool, *Vict., Aust.*	35¼s	141½E	59
Undoalya, *N.Terr.,Aust.*	24s	133½E	60
Undur Khan, *Mong.*	47N	110E	39
Unea I., *Pacific* (inset).	5s	149E	60
Unecha, *U.S.S.R.*	53N	33E	38
Ungarie, *N.S.W., Aust.*	33¼s	147½E	59
Ungava B., *Que., Can.*	60N	68W	66
Unggi, *Korea.*	42½N	131E	39
Uniket, *China.*	45N	116E	39
Uniondale, *C.Pr., S.Af.*	33¼s	23½E	52
Union, La., *Salvador.*	13N	87½W	76
Union, La. *Spain.*	37½N	1W	35
UNITED ARAB REPUBLIC, *Africa.*	27N	30E	40
Unity, *Sask., Canada.*	52½N	109¼W	70
Unna, *Germany.* (ins.).	51N	7½E	33
Unst I., (*Shet.*), *Scot.*	60¾N	1W	24
UNTER-WALDEN, *Switz.*	46½N	8½E	31
Unye, *Turkey.*	41½N	37½E	41
Unzha Riv., *U.S.S.R.*	57¼N	43½E	38
Upata, *Venezuela.*	8N	62¼W	77
Upavon, *England.*	51½N	1¾W	22
Upernavik, *Greenl'd.*	72½N	56W	66
Upington, *C.Pr., S.Af.*	28¼s	21½E	52
Upolu I., *Samoa, Pac.*	14s	171¾W	64
Upper L., *Ireland.*	52N	9¼W	26
Upper Hutt, *N.I., N.Z.*	41¼s	175E	62
Upper Liveinga,*W.Aus.*	18s	124E	61
Upper Sheikh, *Som. R.*	10N	45E	56
UPPER VOLTA, *Africa.*	13N	2W	57
Uppingham, *Eng.*	52½N	¾W	23
Uppsala, *Sweden.*	59¾N	17½E	29
Upstart B. & C., *Aust.*	20s	148E	60
Upton, *England.*	52N	2¼W	22
Uraba, G. of, *Colombia.*	9N	77W	77
Urakawa, *Japan.*	42¼N	142½E	48
Ural Mts., *U.S.S.R.*	59N	60E	38
Ural River, *U.S.S.R.*	47N	52E	59
Uralla, *N.S.W., Aust.*	30¼s	151½E	59
Uralsk, *U.S.S.R.*	51¼N	51½E	38
Urambo, *Tanzania.*	5s	32E	56
Urandangie, *Aust.*	21¼s	138E	60
Uranium City, *Canada.*	60N	109W	66
Urapunga, *Australia.*	14¼s	134½E	60
Uraricoera, R., *Brazil.*	2¼N	61W	77
Urawa, *Japan.*	36N	139¼E	48
Urbino, *Italy.*	43¾N	12¼E	36
Urda, *U.S.S.R.*	48¼N	47½E	38
Urdzhar, *U.S.S.R.*	47N	81½E	39
Ure, Riv., *England.*	54¼N	2W	25
Urfa, *Turkey.*	37¼N	38¼E	41
Uri, *Kashmir* (inset).	34N	74E	44
URI, *Switzerland.*	46¾N	8½E	31
Uribia, *Colombia.*	12N	72¼W	77
Urlingford, *Ireland.*	52¾N	7½W	26
Urmia, *U.S.S.R.*	37¼N	45½E	40
Ur of the Chaldees, *Ir.*	31N	46E	40
Urosevac, *Yugoslavia.*	42¼N	21E	37
Uruapan, *Mexico.*	19¼N	102W	76
URUGUAY, *S. America.*	33s	56W	79
Uruguayana, *Brazil.*	29¼s	57W	78
Urumchi, *China.*	43¾N	87½E	39
Urungu River, *China.*	47N	87E	39
Uruyen, *Venezuela.*	6N	62W	77
Uryupinsk, *U.S.S.R.*	51N	42E	38
Usa River, *U.S.S.R.*	65¼N	57E	38
Usak, *Turkey.*	38¼N	29½E	41
Usedom I., *Germany.*	54N	14E	33
Ushakova I., *U.S.S.R.*	80N	80E	39
Ushant I., *France.*	48N	5¼W	32
Ush Tobe, *U.S.S.R.*	47N	78E	39
Ushuaia, *Argentina.*	54¼s	68W	78
Usk, Riv., *Wales.*	52N	3¼W	22
Usk, *England.*	51¾N	3W	22
Uskudar, *Turkey.*	41N	29E	41
Usman, *U.S.S.R.*	52N	40E	38
U.S.S.R., *Europe-Asia.*			38,39
Ussuriysk, *U.S.S.R.*	44N	132E	49
Ust Amginskoye, *U.S.S.R.*	63N	134E	39
Ust Belaya, *U.S.S.R.*	66N	172E	39
UstBolsheretsk,*U.S.S.R.*	54N	155E	39
Ustica, *Mediterranean.*	38½N	13½E	36
Usti, *Czechoslovakia.*	50N	16½E	33
Usti (Aussig), *Czecho.*	50½N	14E	33
Ust Izhma, *U.S.S.R.*	65½N	53E	38
Ust Kamenogorsk, *U.S.S.R.*	50N	82½E	39
Ust Kulom, *U.S.S.R.*	62N	54E	38
Ust Kut, *U.S.S.R.*	57N	105E	39
Ust Maya, *U.S.S.R.*	60½N	134½E	39
Ust Nyukzhu, *U.S.S.R.*	56N	121E	39
Ust Ordynski, *U.S.S.R.*	53N	102E	39
Ust Pinyega, *U.S.S.R.*	64N	41E	38
Ust Port, *U.S.S.R.*	69N	84E	39
Ust Shchugor, *U.S.S.R.*	64N	57E	38
Ust Tsilma, *U.S.S.R.*	65½N	52½E	38
Ust Usa, *U.S.S.R.*	66N	56½E	38
Ust Urt Plat., *U.S.S.R.*	44N	56E	38
Ust Vorkuta, *U.S.S.R.*	67N	64E	38
Usumbura, *Congo (K.).*	3¼s	29½E	56
Usutu, Riv., *Moz.*	27s	32½E	51
Utah Beach, *France.*	49¼N	1¼W	31
Utan Muren R., *China.*	34N	95E	43
Utaradit, *Thailand.*	17¼N	100E	47
Utena, *Lith., U.S.S.R.*	55¼N	25½E	33
Utete, *Tanzania.*	8s	38½E	56
Utica, *N.Y., U.S.A.*	43N	75¼W	74
Utiel, *Spain.*	39½N	1¼W	35
Utirik I., *Pacific.*	12N	170E	64
Uto, *Japan.*	32½N	130½E	48
Utrecht, *Natal.*	27¼s	30½E	55
UTRECHT & Tn., *Neth.*	52½N	5½E	30
Utrera, *Spain.*	37N	6W	35
Utsunomiya, *Japan.*	36½N	139¾E	48
Uttar Pradesh, *India.*	28N	80E	44
Uttoxeter, *England.*	52¾N	1¾W	23
Utupua I., *Pacific.*	11s	168E	64
Uvac, *Yugoslavia.*	43¼N	19½E	37
Uvalde, *Texas, U.S.A.*	29¼N	100W	74
Uvea I., *Pacific.*	11s	178W	64
Uvea I., *Pacific.*	20s	166E	64
Uvria, *Congo (K.).*	3¼s	28½E	56
Uwajima, *Japan.*	33¼N	132½E	49
Uxbridge, *England.*	51½N	¾W	23
Uyo, *Nigeria.*	5N	8E	57
Uyuni, *Bolivia.*	20½s	67W	79
UZBEKISTAN, *U.S.S.R.*	42N	62E	40
Uzel, *France.*	48¼N	3W	31
Uzes, *France.*	44N	4½E	32
Uzhorod, *U.S.S.R.*	48¼N	22¼E	33
Uzice, *Yugoslavia.*	43¾N	19½E	37
Uzunkopru, *Turkey.*	41¼N	26½E	37
V			
VAAGO, *Faeroe Islands.*	62N	8w	29
Vaags Fiord, *Norway.*	68½N	16½E	29
Vaal R., *T'vaal-O.F.S.*	27¼s	26E	55
Vaalbank, *T'vaal, S. Af.*	27¼s	30¼E	55
Vaasa, *Finland.*	63¼N	21½E	29
Vac, *Hungary.*	47¾N	19E	37
Vadheim, *Norway.*	61¼N	5E	29
Vadhlavik, *Iceland.*	65N	14W	29
Vadso, *Norway.*	70¼N	30E	29
Vaduz, *Liechtenstein.*	47¼N	9½E	31
Vaga Riv., *U.S.S.R.*	62¼N	42¾E	38
Vah Riv., *Czecho.*	47¼N	18½E	33
Vahsel B., *Antarctica.*	76s	40W	80
Vaigach I., *U.S.S.R.*	70N	59E	38
Vaigai. Riv., *India.*	9¼N	79E	45
Vaiges, *France.*	48N	¾W	31
Vaitupu I., *Pacific.*	9s	180E	64
Vakh Riv., *U.S.S.R.*	61N	77E	39
Val Marie, *Sask., Can.*	49¼N	107¾W	70
VALAIS, *Switzerland.*	46¼N	7½E	31
Valbondione, *Italy.*	46N	10E	31
Valdai Hills, *U.S.S.R.*	57¼N	33E	38
Valdepenas, *Spain.*	38¾N	3¼W	35
Valderaduey, R., *Sp.*	41¼N	5½W	35
Valdez Pen., *Arg.*	42¼s	64W	78
Valdivia, *Chile.*	40s	73¼W	78
Valdosta, *Ga., U.S.A.*	31N	83W	75
Valencay, *France.*	47¼N	1½E	31
Valence, *France.*	44¾N	4½E	32
Valencia, *Venezuela.*	10N	67¾W	77
VALENCIA & Tn., *Sp.*	39¼N	1w	35
Valencia Harb., *Ire.*	52N	10¼W	26
Valencia de Alcantara, *Spain.*	39¼N	7¼W	35
Valenciennes, *France.*	50¼N	3½E	32
Valentano, *Italy.*	42¼N	11½E	36
Valentia I., *Ireland.*	52N	10¼W	26
Valentine, *Neb., U.S.A.*	43N	100¾W	74
Valentigny, *France.*	48¼N	4½E	30
Valentine, *U.S.A.*	43N	100¾W	74
Valenza, *Italy.*	45N	8½E	31
Valera, *Venezuela.*	9½N	70¼W	77
Valga, *U.S.S.R.*	57¾N	26E	38
Valjevo, *Yugoslavia.*	44¼N	20E	37
Valladolid, *Spain.*	41¾N	4¾W	34
Valladolid, *Mexico.*	20¼N	88¼W	76
Vallecillo, *Mexico.*	27N	99W	76
VALLE D'AOSTA, *Italy.*	45¾N	7½E	31
Valledupar, *Colombia.*	10¼N	73W	77
Vallejo, *Calif., U.S.A.*	38¼N	122½W	74
Vallenar, *Chile.*	28¼s	71W	78
Vallet, *France.*	47¼N	1¼W	31
Valletta, *Malta.*	37¼N	14½E	34
Valley City, *U.S.A.*	47N	98W	74
Valley Falls, *Ore., U.S.*	42¼N	120¼W	74
Valleyfield, *Que., Can.*	45¼N	74¼W	69
Vallorbe, *Switzerland.*	46¾N	6½E	31
Valls, *Spain.*	41¼N	1E	35
Valmont, *France.*	49¾N	0½E	31
Valognes, *France.*	49¼N	1½W	31
Valona & B., *Albania.*	40½N	19½E	37
Valparaiso, *Chile.*	33s	71¾W	78
Vals Platz, *Switz.*	46¼N	9½E	31
Vals River, *O.F.S.,S.A.*	28¼s	28E	53
Valuiki, *U.S.S.R.*	50N	38E	38
Valverde, *Canary Is.*	27¼N	18W	35
Van & L., *Turkey.*	38¼N	43½E	41
Van Diemen G., *Aust.*	12s	132E	60
Van Horn, *Tex., U.S.A.*	31N	105W	74
Van Reenen, *Natal.*	28¼s	29½E	55
Vanrhynsdorp, *S. Afr.*	31¼s	18½E	52
Vanstadensrus, *S. Afr.*	30s	27E	53
Vanwyksvlei, *C.Pr.*	30¼s	21½E	52
Vancouver, *Canada.*	49¼N	123W	72
Vancouver, *U.S.A.*	45¼N	122½W	74
Vancouver I., *Canada.*	50N	126W	72
Vancouver, C., *W. Aust.*	35s	118E	61
Vanderhoof,*Br.Col.,Can.*	54N	124W	72
Vanegas, *Mexico.*	24N	101¼W	76
Vaner, L., *Sweden.*	59N	14E	29
Vanersborg, *Sweden.*	58¼N	12½E	29
Vangaindrano,*Malag.*	23¼s	47E	56
Vanguard, *Sask., Can.*	50N	107¼W	70
Vanikoro Is., *S. Pac.*	11¼s	166¼E	64
Vannas, *Sweden.*	64N	20E	38
Vannes, *France.*	47¾N	2¾W	31
Vansittart B., *W. Aust.*	13¼s	126¼E	61
Vanua Levu I., *Fiji.*	16¼s	179¼E	64
VAR, *France.*	43¼N	6E	32
Varades, *France.*	47¼N	1W	31
Varallo, *Italy.*	45¼N	8¼E	31
Varanasi, *India.*	25¼N	83E	44
Varanger Fiord, *Nor.*	70N	30E	29
Varano, L. of, *Italy.*	42N	15¼E	36
Varazdin, *Yugoslavia.*	46¼N	16¼E	37
Varberg, *Sweden.*	57¼N	12¼E	29
Vardar R., *Yugo.-Gr.*	41¼N	22¼E	37
Vardo, *Norway.*	70¼N	31¼E	29
Varel, *Germany.*	53¼N	8¼E	30
Varese, *Italy.*	45¼N	8¼E	36
Varna, *Bulgaria.*	43¼N	28E	37
Varnamo, *Sweden.*	57¼N	14E	29
Varniai, *U.S.S.R.*	55¼N	22¼E	33
Varzi, *Italy.*	44¼N	9¼E	31
Vascau, *Romania.*	46¼N	22¼E	37
Vasht, *Iran.*	28N	62E	40
Vaslui, *Romania.*	46¼N	27¼E	37
Vasteras, *Sweden.*	59¼N	16¼E	29
Vastervik, *Sweden.*	58N	17E	29
Vasto, *Italy.*	42N	14¼E	37
Vasyugan R., *U.S.S.R.*	58N	82E	39
Vatersay, *Scotland.*	57N	7¼W	24
Vatnajokull, *Iceland.*	64¼N	17W	29
Vatomandry, *Malagasy.*	19s	49E	56
Vatter, L., *Sweden.*	58¼N	14¼E	29
Vatyna, *U.S.S.R.*	61N	170E	39
VAUCLUSE, *France.*	44N	5E	32
Vaucouleurs, *France.*	48¼N	5½E	30
VAUD, *Switzerland.*	46¾N	6½E	31
Vaughn, *N.M., U.S.A.*	35N	105W	74
Vauville, *France.*	49¼N	2W	31
Vavau I., *Pacific.*	20s	177W	64
Vaxholm, *Sweden.*	59¼N	19E	29
Vaxjo, *Sweden.*	57N	15E	29
Vecht, Riv., *Nether.*	52¾N	6E	30
Vechta, *Germany.*	52¾N	8½E	30
Vega, La, *Dom. Rep.*	19¼N	70¼W	77
Vega I., *Norway.*	65N	12E	29
Vegesack, *Germany.*	53¼N	8½E	30
Vegreville, *Alb., Can.*	53¼N	112W	73
Veile, *Denmark.*	56N	9E	29
Vejer, *Spain.*	36¼N	6W	35
Velbert, *Germany* (ins.).	51¼N	7E	33
Velddrif, *C. Pr., S. Afr.*	32¼s	18½E	52
Veles, *Yugoslavia.*	41¼N	21¼E	37
Velestinon, *Greece.*	39¼N	22¼E	37
Velez Malaga, *Spain.*	36¼N	4W	35
Velez Rubio, *Spain.*	37¼N	2W	35
Veliki Ustyug, *U.S.S.R.*	61N	46E	38
Velikie Luki, *U.S.S.R.*	56¼N	30¼E	38
Velizh, *U.S.S.R.*	56N	31E	38
Velletri, *Italy.*	41¼N	12¼E	36
Vellore, *India.*	13N	79¼E	45
Velsk, *U.S.S.R.*	61N	42¼E	38
Vemdalen, *Sweden.*	62¼N	15E	29
Venado, *Mexico.*	23N	101¼W	76
VENDEE, *France.*	46¼N	1¼W	32
Vendenheim, *France.*	48¼N	7¼E	30
Vendeuvre-s-Barse, *Fr.*	48¼N	4½E	30
Vendome, *France.*	47¾N	1¼E	31
Vendrell, *Spain.*	41¼N	1¼E	35
VENETO, *Italy.*	46N	12E	36
VENEZUELA, *S. America.*	7N	65W	77
Vengurla, *India.*	15¼N	73¼E	45
Venice & G. of, *Italy.*	45¼N	12¼E	36
Venkatagiri, *India.*	14N	79¼E	45
Venlo, *Netherlands.*	51¼N	6E	30
Ventersburg,*O.F.S.,S.A.*	28s	27E	55
Ventersdorp, *T'vaal.*	26¼s	26¼E	55
Venterstad, *C.Pr.,S.Af.*	30¼s	25¼E	53
Ventimiglia, *Italy.*	43¾N	7¼E	36
Ventnor, *I. of W., Eng.*	50¼N	1¼W	23
Ventotene, *I. of, Italy.*	40¼N	13¼E	36
Ventspils, *U.S.S.R.*	57¼N	21¼E	29
Venus B., *Vict., Aust.*	38¼s	145¼E	59
Vera, *Spain.*	37¼N	2w	35
VERA CRUZ & Tn., *Mex.*	20N	97¼W	76
Veraval, *India.*	21N	70¼E	43
Vercelli, *Italy.*	45N	8¼E	36
Verde, C., *Senegal.*	14¼N	17¼W	50
Verden, *Germany.*	53N	9¼E	30
Verdon, Riv., *France.*	43¾N	6¼E	32
Verdun, *France.*	49¼N	5¼E	30
Vereeniging, *T'vaal.*	26¼s	28E	55
Vergennes, *Vt., U.S.A.*	44¼N	73¼W	69
Verin, *Spain.*	42N	7¼W	35
Verkeerdevlei, *O.F.S.*	28¼s	26¼E	55
Verkhne Kolymsk, *U.S.S.R.*	65N	150E	39
Verkhoyansk, *U.S.S.R.*	68N	133½E	39
Vermaas, *T'vaal, S. Af.*	26¼s	26E	55
Vermilion, *Alb., Can.*	53¼N	110¼W	73
Vermilion P., *Br. Col.*	51N	116W	73
Vermilion B., *Ont., Can.*	50N	93¼W	71
VERMONT, *U.S.A.*	44N	73W	69
Vernal, *Utah, U.S.A.*	40¼N	109¼W	74
Verneuil, *France.*	48¼N	3E	31
Vernon, *Br. Col., Can.*	50¼N	119¼W	72
Vernon, *France.*	49N	1½E	31
Vernon Is., *Australia.*	12s	131E	60
Verolanuova, *Italy.*	45¼N	10E	31
Veroia, *Greece.*	40¼N	22¼E	37
Verona, *Italy.*	45¼N	11E	36
Verres, *Italy.*	45¾N	7¾E	31
Verrettes, *Haiti, W.I.*	19N	72¼W	77
Versailles, *France.*	48¼N	2½E	32
Vershina, *U.S.S.R.*	61N	63E	38
Vertus, *France.*	48¾N	4E	32
Verulam, *Natal.*	29¼s	31E	55
Verviers, *Belgium.*	50¼N	5½E	30
Vervins, *France.*	49¾N	4E	32
Verwood, *Sask., Can.*	49¼N	105¼W	70
Vesoul, *France.*	47¾N	6¼E	32
Vesta, *Costa Rica.*	10N	83W	77
Vesteraalen, *Norway.*	69N	15E	29
Vestfiorden, *Norway.*	68N	15E	29
Vestvadgo I., *Norway.*	68N	14E	29
Vesuvius, Mt., *Italy.*	40¼N	14½E	36
Veszprem, *Hungary.*	47N	18E	37
Vetluga, *U.S.S.R.*	58N	46E	38
Vet River, *O.F.S., S.Af.*	28¼s	26¼E	55
Vettore, Mt., *Italy.*	43N	13½E	36
Vevey, *Switzerland.*	46¼N	6¼E	31
Veynes, *France.*	44¼N	5½E	32
Vezelise, *France.*	48¼N	6E	30
Vezzano, *Italy.*	46N	11E	31
Viadana, *Italy.*	45N	10½E	31
Viana, *Spain.*	42¼N	2¼W	35
Vianden, *Germany.*	50N	6¼E	30
ViandodoCastelo,*Port.*	41¼N	9W	35
Viareggio, *Italy.*	43¾N	10¼E	36
Vibank, *Sask., Canada.*	50¼N	104W	70
Vibo Valentia, *Italy.*	38¼N	16¼E	36
Viborg, *Denmark.*	56¼N	9½E	29
Viborg, *U.S.S.R.*	60¾N	28¼E	38
Vicenza, *Italy.*	45¼N	11¼E	36
Viceroy, *Sask., Can.*	49¼N	105¼W	70
Vich, *Spain.*	42N	2¼E	32
Vichegda R., *U.S.S.R.*	61¼N	46E	38
Vichy, *France.*	46¼N	3¼E	32
Vicksburg, *Miss., U.S.*	32¼N	90¼W	75
Victor Harb., *S. Aust.*	35¼s	138¼E	59
VICTORIA, *Australia.*	37s	145E	59
Victoria, *Br. Col., Can.*	48¼N	123¼W	72
Victoria, *China.*	22N	114¼E	46
Victoria, *Mexico.*	23¼N	98W	76
Victoria, *Nigeria.*	4N	9¼E	57
Victoria, *Tex., U.S.A.*	28¼N	97W	74
Victoria Beach, *Can.*	50¼N	96¼W	71
Victoria Falls, *Rhod.*	18s	25¼E	51
Victoria Ft., *Rhodesia.*	20s	30¼E	51
Victoria I., *N.W. Can.*	70N	110W	66
Victoria, L., *Aust.*	34s	141¼E	59
Victoria, L., *Tanzania.*	1s	33E	56
Victoria Riv., *Aust.*	15¼s	129¼E	60
Victoria Str., *N.W. Can.*	69N	100W	66
Victoria West, *S. Afr.*	31¼s	23E	52
Victoriaville, *Que., Can.*	46¼N	72W	69
Videle, *Romania.*	44¼N	25¼E	37
Vidin, *Bulgaria.*	44N	23E	37
Viedma, *Argentina.*	41s	63W	78
Viella, *Spain.*	42¼N	1E	35
Vielsalm, *Belgium.*	50¼N	5¼E	30
Vienna, *Austria.*	48¼N	16¼E	33
Vienna, *U.S.A.*	45¼s	42E	32
VIENNE, R. & DEP., *Fr.*	46¼N	¾E	32
Vientiane, *Laos.*	18N	102¼E	47
Vieques I., *Puerto Rico.*	18N	65W	77
Vierfontein, *O.F.S.,S.A.*	27s	26¼E	55
Vierzon, *France.*	47¼N	2E	32
Vieste, *Italy.*	42N	16¼E	36
VIETNAM, *Indo-China.*	17N	107¼E	47
Vif, *France.*	45N	5½E	32
Vig, L., *U.S.S.R.*	63¼N	34¼E	38
Vigan, *Luzon, P.I.*	17¼N	120¼E	47
Viggiano, *Italy.*	40¼N	16E	36
Vignacourt, *France.*	50N	2E	32
Vigo, *Spain.*	42¼N	8¼W	35
Vihiers Nuaille, *Fr.*	47¼N	¾W	31
Viipuri, see VIBORG.			
Vijayavada, *India.*	16¼N	80¼E	45
Vijose, Riv., *Albania.*	40¼N	19¼E	37
Vik, *Iceland* (inset).	63¼N	19W	29
Vikten Is., *Norway.*	64¼N	11¼E	29
Vila Cabral, *Moz.*	13s	35¼E	51
Vila Fontes, *Moz.*	18s	35¼E	51
Vila L., *N. Heb., Pacific.*	17¼s	168E	64
Vila Luiza, *Moz.*	26s	32¼E	51
Vila Luso, *Angola.*	11¼s	19¼E	56
Vila Manica, *Moz.*	19s	33E	51
Vila Real, *Portugal.*	41¼N	8W	35
Vila Real de Santo Antonio, *Portugal.*	37N	7¼W	35
Vilaine. Riv., *France.*	47¼N	2¼W	32
Vileika, *U.S.S.R.*	54¼N	27E	38
Vilhelmina, *Sweden.*	64¼N	16¼E	38
Viliga, *U.S.S.R.*	61¼N	156E	39
Viljoenskroon, *O.F.S.*	27¼s	27E	55
Vilkitskogo, C., *U.S.S.R.*	76N	68E	39
Villa Cisneros, *Sp. Sah.*	24N	16w	50
Villa de Cura, *Venez.*	10N	67¼W	77

Place	Lat.	Long.	No.
Villa Hermosa, Mex.	17¾N	92¾w	76
Villa Maria, Arg.	32½s	63w	79
Villa Santina, Italy.	46½N	13E	36
Villach, Austria.	46½N	13¾E	33
Villacidro, Sardinia.	39½N	8¾E	36
Villafranca, Spain.	41½N	1¼E	35
Villaguay, Argentina.	32s	59w	79
Villajoyosa, Spain.	38½N	¼w	35
Villalba, Spain.	43½N	1¾w	35
Villaldama, Mexico.	26½N	100¼w	76
Villany, Hungary.	46N	18½E	36
Villapiana, Italy.	39½N	16¼E	36
Villard Bonnot, Fr.	45½N	6E	31
Villarreal, Spain.	40N	0	35
Villarrica, Paraguay.	25½s	56¼w	79
Villaviciosa, Spain.	43½N	5¼w	35
Villedieu, France.	48½N	1¼w	31
Villefranche, France.	44½N	2E	32
Villefranche, France.	46N	4¾E	32
Villena, Spain.	38½N	¾w	35
Villenauxe, France.	48½N	3¾E	30
Villers-Bocage, France.	49N	1w	31
Villers-Cotterets, Fr.	49¼N	3E	30
Villeurbanne, France.	45¾N	5E	32
Villiers, O.F.S., S. Afr.	27s	28¼E	55
Villiersdorp, C. Pr., S.A.	34s	19¼E	52
Villingen, Germany.	48N	8¼E	33
Vilnius, U.S.S.R.	54¾N	25¼E	38
Vilshofen, Germany.	48½N	13¼E	33
Vilvorde, Belgium.	51N	4½E	30
Vilyuy Riv., U.S.S.R.	64N	126E	39
Vilyuysk, U.S.S.R.	63¾N	121¼E	39
Vimeiro, Portugal.	39¼N	9¼w	35
Vimercate, Italy.	45½N	9¼E	31
Vimoutiers, France.	49N	¼E	31
Vimy, France.	50½N	3E	30
Vinaroz, Spain.	40½N	¾E	35
Vindel. Riv., Sweden.	63½N	20¼E	28
Vindhya Mts., India.	23N	77E	44
Vinh, Vietnam.	18½N	105½E	47
Vinkovci, Yugoslavia.	45¼N	18¼E	37
Vinnitsa, U.S.S.R.	49¼N	28¼E	38
Vipiteno, Italy.	47N	11¼E	31
Viramgam, India.	23¼N	72E	44
Virden, Manitoba, Can.	49¾N	100¾w	70
Vire, France.	48¾N	1w	31
Vire, Riv., France.	49¼N	1¼w	31
Virgin I., W. Indies.	18N	64w	77
Virginia, N.Terr., Aust.	12½s	131E	60
Virginia, O.F.S., S.Afr.	28s	27E	55
VIRGINIA, U.S.A.	38N	78w	75
Virovitica, Yugoslavia.	45¼N	17¼E	36
Virton, Belgium.	49½N	5¼E	30
Vis I., Adriatic Sea.	43N	16¼E	36
Visakhapatnam, India.	17½N	83½E	45
Visalia, Calif., U.S.A.	36¼N	119¼w	74
Visby, Gotland, Baltic.	57¼N	18¼E	28
Viscount, Sask., Can.	52N	105¾w	70
Vise, Belgium.	50¾N	5½E	30
Visegrad, Yugoslavia.	43¼N	19¼E	37
Viso Mts., Italy.	44½N	7E	31
Visoko, Yugoslavia.	44N	18¼E	36
Visp, Switzerland.	46¼N	8E	31
Vistula, Riv., Poland.	54¼N	19¼E	33
Vitiaz Strait, Pacific.	7s	148E	60
Vitebsk, U.S.S.R.	55¼N	30¼E	38
Viterbo, Italy.	42¼N	12E	36
Viti Levu I., Fiji, Pac.	17¾s	178E	64
Vitim & R., U.S.S.R.	59¼N	112¼E	39
Vitoria, Brazil.	20½s	40¼w	78
Vitoria, Spain.	42½N	2¾w	35
Vitre, France.	48¼N	1¼w	32
Vitry, France.	50½N	3E	30
Vittoria, Sicily.	37N	14¼E	36
Vittorio, Italy.	46N	12¼E	36
Viver, Spain.	40N	¼w	35
Vivero, Spain.	43¾N	7¾w	35
Vivi Riv., U.S.S.R.	64N	98E	39
Vize, Turkey.	41¼N	27¾E	37
Vizeu, Portugal.	40¾N	8w	35
Vizianagram, India.	18N	83½E	45
Vizille, France.	45N	5½E	31
Vizinga, U.S.S.R.	61½N	50E	38
Vlaardingen, Nether.	52N	4E	30
Vladimir, U.S.S.R.	56¼N	40½E	38
Vladimir P., U.S.S.R.	69¼N	33E	38
Vladimirovka, U.S.S.R.		47E	38
Vladimir Volynskiy, U.S.S.R.	50¾N	24¼E	38
Vladivostok, U.S.S.R.	43¼N	132E	39
Vlakte, T'vaal, S. Afr.	24s	29E	54
Vlakteplaas, C.Pr.,S.A.	33½s	22¼E	52
Vleifontein, C.Pr.,S.A.	33½s	21E	52
Vlieland, Netherlands.	53¼N	5E	30
Vltava, Riv., Czecho.	49¼N	14¼E	33
Voe, Scotland (inset).	60N	1¼w	24
Voerne Is., Nether.	51¾N	4¼E	30
Voghera, Italy.	45N	9E	31
Voi, Kenya.	3¼s	38¼E	56
Voiron, France.	45¼N	5¼E	31
VOJVODINA, Yugo.	46N	20E	37
Volga Riv., U.S.S.R.	46¼N	48E	38
Volgograd, U.S.S.R.	48½N	44¼E	38
Volkhov, U.S.S.R.	59¼N	32¼E	38
Volkhov Riv., U.S.S.R.	59¼N	31¼E	29
Volksdorf, Ger. (ins.).	53¾N	10E	30
Volksrust, T'vaal, S.Af.	27¼s	30E	55
Volme, R., Ger. (ins.).	51¼N	7½E	33
Volochanka, U.S.S.R.	72N	94E	39
Vologda, U.S.S.R.	59¼N	39¼E	38
Volonga, U.S.S.R.	67N	48E	38
Volos, Greece.	39¼N	23E	37
Volsk, U.S.S.R.	52N	47¼E	38
Volta, Riv., Ghana.	8N	¼w	50
Volterra, Italy.	43¼N	10¾E	36
Volturno, Riv., Italy.	41N	14E	36
Volvi, L. of, Greece.	40½N	23¼E	37
Volzhskiy, U.S.S.R.	49N	44¼E	38
Vonda, Sask., Canada.	52½N	106¼w	70
Vonda, U.S.S.R.	67N	54E	38
Vondeling, C.Pr.,S.Af.	33¼s	23E	52
Vopna Fiord, Iceland.	66N	14w	29
VORARLBERG, Austria.	47¼N	9½E	31
Vorde, Germany (ins.).	51¼N	7¼E	33
Vorkuta, U.S.S.R.	67¼N	64E	39
Voronezh, U.S.S.R.	51½N	39¼E	38
Voroshilov, U.S.S.R.	43N	132E	39
VOSGES, France.	48¼N	6½E	32
Vosges Mts., France.	48¼N	7¼E	32
Voss Harbou, Nor.	60¼N	6E	29
Vostok I., Pacific.	10¼s	155w	64
Votkinsk, U.S.S.R.	57N	54E	38
Vouvray, France.	47¼N	1E	31
Vouziers, France.	49¼N	4¼E	30
Voves, France.	48¼N	1¼E	30
Vozhega, U.S.S.R.	60¼N	40E	38
Voznesensk, U.S.S.R.	47¼N	32E	38
Vranje, Yugoslavia.	42¼N	22E	37
Vrattsa, Bulgaria.	43¼N	23¼E	37
Vrbno, Czecho.	50N	17¼E	33
Vrede, O.F.S., S. Afr.	27¼s	29¼E	55
Vredefort, O.F.S., S.Af.	27s	27¼E	55
Vredenburg, C.Pr.,S.A.	33s	18E	52
Vredendal, C.Pr.,S.Af.	31¼s	18¼E	52
Vreed-en-Hoop, Guyana.	7N	58w	77
Vrsac, Yugoslavia.	45N	21E	37
Vryburg, C. Pr., S. Afr.	27s	24¼E	51
Vryheid, Natal.	27¼s	30¼E	55
Vukovar, Yugoslavia.	45¼N	19E	37
Vulcan, Alberta, Can.	50¼N	113¼w	73
Vulcano, Mediter.	38¼N	15E	36
Vuollerim, Sweden.	66¼N	21F	29
Vyakta, Riv.,U.S.S.R.	57¼N	50E	38
Vyazma, U.S.S.R.	55¼N	34¼E	38
Vyrnwy Lake, Wales.	52¾N	3¼w	22
Vyshny Volochek, U.S.S.R.	57¼N	34¼E	38
Vyshka, U.S.S.R.	39N	54E	38
Vytegra, U.S.S.R.	61¼N	37E	38
W.A., Ghana.	10N	2¼w	57
Waal, Riv., Nether.	51¾N	4¼E	39
Wabamun, Alb., Can.	53¼N	114¼w	73
Wabash R., Ind., U.S.A.	40¼N	85¼w	75
Wabowden, Man., Can.	55N	98¼w	70
Waco, Texas, U.S.A.	31N	97¼w	75
Wad Hamid, Sudan.	17N	32¼E	40
Wad Medani, Sudan.	14¼N	33¼E	56
Waddan, Libya.	29¼N	16¼E	34
Wadden Is., Nether.	53¼N	5E	30
Wadden Zee, Nether.	53¼N	5¼E	30
Wadebridge, England.	50¼N	4¾w	23
Wadena, Sask., Can.	52N	103¾w	70
Wadern, Germany.	49¼N	7E	30
Wadhwan, India.	22¼N	71¼E	43
Wadi, India.	17N	77E	45
Wadi Al Birk, Sau. Arab.	23N	46E	40
Wadi Ar Rima, Sau., Ar.	26N	43E	40
Wadi Batha, Chad.	13N	19E	56
Wadi Duwasir, Sau Ar.	20N	45E	40
Wadi Fajr, Saudi Arab.	29N	38E	41
Wadi Habuna, Sau. Ar.	19N	45E	40
Wadi Halfa, Sudan.	21¼N	31¼E	40
Wadi Hauran, Iraq.	33N	41E	41
Wadi Sababa, Sau. Ar.	24N	49E	40
Wadi Sibai, Sau. Arab.	22N	43E	40
Wadi Sirhan, Sau., Ar.	32N	37E	41
Wadi Sirra, Sau. Arab.	22N	46E	40
Wager B., Canada.	65¼N	90w	66
Wagga Wagga, N.S.W.	35¼s	147¼E	59
Wagin, W. Australia.	33¼s	117¼E	61
Wagram, Austria.	48¼N	16¼E	33
Wagrowiec, Poland.	52¾N	17¼E	33
Waiau Riv., S.I., N.Z.	46¼s	167¾E	63
Waiau & R.S.I., N.Z.	42¼s	173E	63
Waidhofen, Austria.	48N	14¼E	33
Walgeo I., Indonesia.	¼s	131E	47
Waiheke, N.I., N.Z. (inset A).			62
Waiheke I., N.I., N.Z. (inset A).			62
Waihi, N.I., N.Z.	37¼s	175¾E	62
Waikaia, S.I., N.Z.	45¼s	168¾E	63
Waikare, L., N.I., N.Z.	37¼s	175¼E	62
Waikato R., S.I., N.Z.	37¼s	174¼E	62
Waikato R., N.I., N.Z.	38¼s	176E	62
Waikerie, S. Aust.	34¼s	140E	59
Waikouaiti, S.I., N.Z.	45¼s	170¾E	63
Waimate, S.I., N.Z.	44¼s	171E	63
Wainfleet, England.	53¼N	¼E	23
Wainganga Riv., India.	19N	79E	43
Waingapu, Indonesia.	9½s	120E	47
Wainuiomata, N.I.,N.Z.(inset B).			62
Wainwright, Alb., Can.	52¾N	110¼w	73
Waiotira, N.I. N.Z.	36s	174¼E	62
Waipa Riv., N.I., N.Z.	37¼s	174¾E	62
Waipara, S.I., N.Z.	43s	172¾E	63
Waipari, L. & R.,S.I., N.Z. (ins. D).			63
Waipawa, N.I., N.Z.	40s	176¼E	62
Waipiro, N.I., N.Z.	38s	178¼E	62
Waipukurau, N.I., N.Z.	40s	176¼E	62
Wairakei, N.I., N.Z.	38½s	176E	62
Wairarapa,L.,N.I.,N.Z.	41¼s	175¼E	62
Wairau R., S.I., N.Z.	41¼s	173¼E	63
Wairio, S.I., N.Z.	46s	168E	63
Wairoa & R., N.I., N.Z.	39s	177¼E	62
Waitaki R., S.I., N.Z.	44¼s	171E	63
Waitara, N.I., N.Z.	39s	174¼E	62
Waitati, S.I., N.Z.		(inset D).	63
Waitemata Harb., N.I., N.Z.(ins.A).			62
Waitoa, N.I., N.Z.	37¼s	175¼E	62
Waitomo Caves, N.Z.	38¼s	175E	62
Waiuku, N.I., N.Z.	37¼s	174¾E	62
Waiyeung, China.	23N	114¼E	48
Wajima, Japan.	37¼N	137E	49
Wajir, Kenya.	2¼N	40E	56
Wakamatsu, Japan.	37¼N	140E	49
Wakaputa Pt.,S.I.,N.Z.	46¼s	167¼E	63
Wakasa B., Japan.	36N	136E	49
Wakatipu, L., S.I., N.Z.	45s	168¼E	63
Wakaw, Sask., Canada.	52¼N	105¾w	70
Wakayama, Japan.	34¼N	135E	49
Wake Island, Pacific.	19N	166¼E	64
Wakefield, England.	53¾N	1¼w	22
Wakkanai, Japan.	45N	141¼E	49
WALACHIA, Romania.	44¼N	26E	37
Walbrzych, Poland.	50¾N	16¼E	33
Walcha, N.S.W., Aust.	31s	151¼E	59
Walcheren Is., Nether.	51¼N	3¼E	30
Walcourt, Belgium.	50¼N	4¼E	30
Walcz, Poland.	53¼N	16¼E	33
Waldbrol, Germany.	50¾N	7¼E	30
Waldheim, Sask., Can.	52¼N	106¾w	70
Waldsee, Germany.	48N	9¼E	33
Waldshut, Germany.	47¼N	8¼E	30
WALES, United King.	52¼N	3¾w	22
Walgett, N.S.W., Aust.	30s	148E	59
Walkerton, Ont., Can.	44¼N	81¼w	68
Walkerville, Ont., Can.	42¼N	83¼w	68
Walla Walla, Wash.,U.S.	46N	118¼w	74
Wallaceburg, Ont., Can.	42¼N	82¼w	68
Wallal, Queens., Aust.	26¼s	146¼E	60
Wallangarra, Aust.	29s	152E	59
Wallaroo, S. Australia.	34s	137¾E	59
Wallasey, England.	53¼N	3w	22
Wallen, L., Switz.	47¼N	9¼E	31
Wallenstadt, Switz.	47¼N	9¼E	31
Wallingford, England.	51¼N	1¼w	22
Walls, Scotland.	60¼N	1¾w	24
Wallsend, England.	55N	1¼w	25
Wallsend, N.S.W. Aust.	33s	151¾E	59
Walmer, C. Pr., S. Afr.	34s	25¼E	53
Walmer, England.	51¼N	1¼E	23
Walney I., England.	54¼N	3¼w	25
Walpole I., Pacific.	22s	170E	64
Walsall, England.	52¼N	2w	23
Walsenburg, Col., U.S.	37¼N	105w	74
Walsingham, England.	52¾N	¼E	23
Walsingham, C., Can.	66N	61w	66
Walterboro, S.C., U.S.A.	33N	81w	75
Walton-on-Naze, Eng.	51¾N	1¼E	23
Walvis Bay, S.W. Africa.	23s	14¼E	50
Walwale, Ghana.	10¼N	¼w	57
Wamako, Nigeria.	13N	5E	57
Wamba, Congo (K.).	2¼N	27¼E	56
Wana, Pakistan.	32¼N	70E	43
Wanaaring, N.S.W.	29¼s	144¼E	59
Wanaka, L., S.I., N.Z.	44¼s	169E	63
Wanaka, S.I., N.Z.	44¼s	169E	63
Wanapiri, W. Irian.	4¼s	136E	47
Wanchuan, China.	41N	115E	48
Wandsbek, Ger. (ins.).	53¾N	10E	30
Wandoan, Queen., Aust.	26¼s	150E	60
Wanganui, N.I., N.Z.	40s	175E	62
Wangaratta, Vic., Aust.	36¼s	146¼E	59
Wangching, China.	43¼N	130E	49
Wangerooge I., Ger.	53¾N	7¾E	30
Wanhsien, China.	30¼N	108¼E	48
Wankie, Rhodesia.	18½s	26¼E	51
Wanle Wein, Som. Rep.	2¼N	45E	56
Wanne-Eickel, Ger.	51¼N	7¼E	33
Wansbeck, R., Eng.	55¼N	1¼w	25
Wantage, England.	51¼N	1¼w	23
Wantagh, N.Y., U.S.A.	40¼N	74¼w	75
Wapella, Sask., Can.	50¼N	102w	70
Waqra, Saudi Arabia.	25N	51¼E	40
Waqu, C. Pr., S. Afr.	31¼s	27¼E	53
Warangal, India.	18N	79¼E	45
Waratah, Tasmania.	41¼s	145¼E	59
Waratah B., Vict., Aust.	38¼s	146¼E	59
Warburg, Germany.	51¼N	9¼E	33
Warburton, Vict., Aust.	37¼s	145¼E	59
Warburton R., S. Aust.	28s	137¼E	59
Warden, O.F.S., S. Afr.	27¼s	29E	55
Wardha, India.	20¼N	78¼E	44
Ware, England.	51¾N	0	23
Wareham, England.	50¾N	2¼w	22
Warendorf, Germany.	52N	8E	30
Warialda, N.S.W., Aust.	29¼s	150¼E	59
Wariri Mine, Guyana.	7N	58¼w	77
Wark, England.	55¼N	2¼w	25
Warka, Poland.	51¾N	21¼E	33
Warman, Sask., Can.	52¼N	106¼w	70
Warmbad, S.W. Africa.	28s	18¼E	51
Warmbad, T'vaal, S.Af.	24¼s	28¼E	54
Warminster, England.	51¼N	2¼w	22
Warnemunde, Ger.	54¼N	12E	33
Warner, Alberta, Can.	49¼N	112¼w	73
Warnsdorf, Czecho.	51N	14¼E	33
Waroona, W. Aust.	32¼s	115¼E	61
Warra Hallu, Ethiopia.	11N	39E	56
Warracknabeal, Aust.	36¼s	142¼E	59
Warragul, Vict., Aust.	38s	146E	59
Warrawagine, W. Aust.	21s	120¼E	61
Warrego R., Aust.	30¼s	145¼E	59
Warren, Ohio, U.S.A.	41¼N	80¾w	68
Warren Riv., W. Aust.	34¼s	116E	61
Warrenpoint, Eire.	54N	6¼w	26
Warri, Nigeria.	5N	5¼E	57
Warrina, S. Australia.	28s	135¼E	60
Warriner's R., S. Aust.	29¼s	137¼E	59
Warrington, England.	53¼N	2¼w	22
Warrington, S.I., N.Z.		(inset D).	63
Warrnambool, Aust.	38¼s	142¼E	59
Warroobpah, W. Aust.	18s	122E	61
Warsaw, Poland.	52¼N	21E	33
Warta, Poland.	52¼N	18¼E	33
Warwick, Queens., Aust.	28¼s	152E	60
Warwick, Queensland.	28s	152E	60
Warwick, R.I., U.S.A.	41¾N	71¼w	69
Wasbank, Natal.	28¼s	30¼E	55
Wasen, Switzerland.	47N	7¾E	31
Wash. The, England.	53N	¼E	23
WASHINGTON, U.S.A.	48N	120w	74
Washington, U.S.A.	39N	77w	75
Washington, I., Pacific.	5N	160w	64
Washington Mt., U.S.	44¼N	71¼w	69
Wasser, S.W. Africa.	26¼s	18E	51
Wassy, France.	48¼N	5E	30
Wast Water, England.	54¼N	3¼w	25
Watchet, England.	51¼N	3¼w	22
Waterbury, Conn., U.S.	41¼N	73w	74
Waterbury, Vt., U.S.A.	44¼N	72¼w	69
Wateree R., S.C., U.S.A.	33N	80w	75
Waterford, C. Pr., S.Af.	33s	25E	53
WATERFORD, Eire.	52¼N	7¼w	26
Waterklip, C. Pr., S.Af.	31¼s	18¼E	52
Waterkloof,O.F.S.,S.A.	30¼s	25¼E	55
Waterloo, Belgium.	50¾N	4¼E	30
Waterloo, Iowa, U.S.A.	42¼N	92¼w	75
Waterloo, Ont., Can.	43¼N	80¼w	68
Waterloo, Que., Can.	45¼N	72¼w	69
Waterloo, Trin. (ins.).	11N	61w	77
Waterpoort, T'vaal, S.A.	23s	29¼E	54
Watertown, N.Y., U.S.A.	44¼N	76w	69
Watertown, S.D., U.S.A.	45N	97w	74
Waterval B., T'vaal,S.A.	25¼s	30¼E	54
Waterville, Ireland.	51¼N	10¼w	26
Watford, England.	51¼N	¼w	23
Watheroo, W. Aust.	30¼s	116E	61
Watlington, England.	51¼N	1w	23
Watrous, Sask., Can.	51¼N	105¼w	70
Watsa, Congo (K.).	3N	29¼E	56
Watson, Sask Can.	52¼N	104¼w	70
Watten, France.	51N	2¼E	30
Wattenscheid, Germany	51¼N	7E	33
Watton, England.	52¼N	¼E	23
Wau, Sudan.	7¾N	28E	56
Wauchope, Aust.	31¼s	152¼E	59
Waukegan, Ill., U.S.A.	42N	88w	75
Wausau, Wis., U.S.A.	45N	89¼w	75
Wauwatosa,Wis.,U.S.A.	43N	88w	75
Wave Hill, Aust.	17¼s	131E	60
Waveney, R., England.	52¼N	1¼E	23
Waverley, C. Pr., S. Af.	32s	26¼E	53
Wavre, Belgium.	50¾N	4¼E	30
Wawota, Sask., Can.	49¼N	102w	70
Way, L., W. Australia.	27s	121E	61
Waycross, Ga., U.S.A.	31¼N	82¼w	75
Wear, Riv., England.	55N	1¼w	25
Webb, Sask., Canada.	50¼N	108¼w	70
Webbwood, Ont., Can.	46¼N	81¼w	68
Webi, Riv., Ethiopia.	5N	42E	56
Weda B., Moluccas.Indon.	0	128E	47
Weddell Sea, Antarc.	65s	45w	80
Wedel, Germany (ins.).	53¾N	9¼E	30
Wednesbury, England.	52¼N	2w	22
Wee Waa, N.S.W., Aust.	30¼s	149¼E	59
Weedon, England.	52N	1¼w	23
Weeley, England.	52N	1E	23
Weenen, Natal.	28¼s	30E	55
Weert, Netherlands.	51¼N	5¾E	30
Wegorzewo, Poland.	54¼N	21¼E	33
Wegrow, Poland.	52¼N	22E	33
Weichang, China.	42N	117¼E	48
Weiden, Germany.	49¼N	12¼E	33
Weifang, China.	36¼N	119E	48
Weihai, China.	37¼N	122E	48
Weilburg, Germany.	50¼N	8¼E	30
Weilheim, Germany.	47¾N	11¼E	33
Weimar, Germany.	51N	11¼E	33
Weinheim, Germany.	49¼N	8¼E	30
Weipa, Queens., Aust.	12¾s	141¼E	60
Weir R., Queens., Aust.	28¼s	149E	59
Weiser, Idaho, U.S.A.	44¼N	116¼w	74
Weismes, Belgium.	50¼N	6E	30
Weissenfels, Germany.	51¼N	12E	33
Weitmar, Ger. (inset).	51¼N	7¼E	33
Weiyuan, China.	23¼N	101E	48
Wejherowo, Poland.	54¼N	18E	33
Welcome, Queens.,Aust.	15¼s	145E	60
Welgelee, O.F.S., S. Af.	28s	26¼E	55
Welkom, O.F.S., S.Afr.	28s	26¼E	55
Welland, R., England.	52¼N	¼w	22
Welland, Ontario, Can.	42¾N	79¼w	68
WELLESLEY, Malaysia.	5¼N	100¼E	47
Wellesley Is., Queens.	16¼s	139¼E	60
Well Found, C.Pr.,S.A.	32¼s	24¼E	53
Wellingborough, Eng.	52¼N	¾w	23
Wellington, C.Pr.,S.Af.	33¼s	19E	52
Wellington, England.	52¾N	2¼w	22
Wellington, England.	51N	3¼w	22
Wellington, Aust.	32¼s	149E	59
WELLINGTON,N.I.,N.Z.	41¼s	174¾E	62
Wellington, Ont., Can.	44N	77¼w	69
Wellington I., Chile.	49¼s	75w	78
Wells, England.	53N	2¼E	23
Wells, England.	51¼N	2¼w	22
Wells, Nevada, U.S.A.	41¼N	115w	74
Wellsboro, Pa., U.S.A.	41¾N	77¼w	75
Wellsford, N.I., N.Z.	36¼s	174¼E	62
Wels, Austria.	48¼N	14E	22
Welshpool, Wales.	52¾N	3¼w	22
Welverdiend, T'vaal.	26¼s	27¼E	54
Welwyn, England.	51¾N	¼w	23
Wem, England.	52¾N	2¾w	22
Wembley, Alb., Can.	55¼N	119w	73
Wenatchee, Wash.,U.S.	47¼N	120w	74
Wenchi, Ghana.	7¾N	2w	57
Wenchow, China.	28N	120¼E	48

Wendover—Yao [135]

Place	Lat.	Long.	No.
Wendover, *England.*	51¾N	1w	23
Wendover, *Ut., U.S.A.*	40¾N	114w	74
Wenlau, *U.S.S.R.*	54¾N	21¼E	33
Wenshan, *China.*	23½N	104E	48
Wentworth, *Aust.*	34s	142E	59
Wepener, *O.F.S., S.Af.*	29¾s	27E	55
Werden, *Ger.* (inset).	51¼N	7E	33
Werlte, *Germany.*	52¾N	7½E	30
Wernberg, *Germany.*	49½N	12¼E	33
Werra, Riv., *Germany.*	51¼N	9¾E	33
Werris Creek, *N.S.W.*	31¼s	150¼E	59
Wesel, *Germany.*	51¾N	6½E	33
Weser, Riv., *Germany.*	52½N	9E	33
Wessel Is., *Australia.*	12s	136½E	60
Wesselsbron, *O.F.S.*	27¾s	26½E	55
West Allis, *Wis., U.S.A.*	43N	88w	75
WEST BENGAL, *India.*	26½N	89E	44
West Bromwich, *Eng.*	52½N	2w	23
W. FLANDERS, *Belgium.*	51N	3E	30
West Ham, *England.*	51½N	0	23
W. Hartlepool, *Eng.*	54¾N	1½w	25
WEST INDIES, *Caribbean.*	20N	75w	77
WEST IRIAN, *Indonesia.*	4s	137E	47
West Lorne, *Ont., Can.*	42¾N	81½w	68
WEST LOTHIAN, *Scot.*	56N	3¾w	25
WEST MALAYSIA, *Asia.*	4N	102E	47
W. Nicholson, *Rhodesia.*	21s	29¼E	51
W. Palm Beach, *U.S.A.*	26¾N	80¼w	75
W. Plains, *Mo., U.S.A.*	37N	92w	75
W. Point, *N.Y., U.S.A.*	41¼N	74w	75
West Riding, *England.*	53¾N	1½w	23
W. VIRGINIA, *U.S.A.*	39N	81½w	75
Westacre Jn., *Rhodesia.*	20¼s	28½E	54
Westbury, *England.*	51¼N	2¼w	22
Westbury, *Tasmania.*	41½s	146¾E	59
West Calder, *Scotland.*	55¾N	3½w	25
West Ems, *Nether.*	53½N	6½E	30
Westerham, *England.*	51½N	0	23
WESTERN AUSTRALIA.	23s	122E	58
Western Desert, *U.A.R.*	27N	27E	40
Western Ghats, *India.*	16N	74E	45
West Felton, *Wales.*	52¾N	3w	22
Westgate, *England*	51½N	1½E	23
Westgate, *Queens., Aust.*	26½s	146½E	60
WESTLAND, *S.I., N.Z.*	43s	170½E	63
W. Leichhardt, *Queens., Australia*	21s	139E	60
Westleigh, *O.F.S., S.Af.*	27½s	27½E	55
Westlock, *Alb., Can.*	54¼N	113¾w	73
WESTMEATH, *Eire.*	53½N	7½w	26
Westminster, *S. Africa.*	29s	27½E	55
WESTMORLAND, *Eng.*	54½N	2¾w	25
Weston, *Ontario, Can.*	43¾N	79½w	68
Weston-Super-Mare, *England.*	51½N	3w	22
Westport, *Ont., Can.*	44¾N	76½w	69
Westport, *S.I., N.Z.*	41¾s	171½E	63
Westport, *Eire.*	53¾N	9½w	26
Westray & Firth, *Scot.*	59¼N	3w	24
Westterschelling, *Neth.*	53½N	5E	30
Westville, *No. Sc., Can.*	45¾N	62¾w	67
Wetar I., *Indonesia.*	7¾s	126½E	47
Wetaskiwin, *Alb., Can.*	53N	113¼w	73
Wetherby, *England.*	54N	1¼w	23
Wetter, *Germany.*	50¾N	8¾E	30
Wetter, Riv., *Germany.*	50¼N	8¾E	30
Wetzlar, *Germany.*	50½N	8½E	30
Wewak, *N. Guin.* (ins.).	3½s	143½E	60
WEXFORD & Harb, *Eire.*	52¼N	6½w	26
Wey, Riv., *England.*	51¼N	¾w	23
Weyburn, *Sask., Can.*	49¾N	103¾w	70
Weymouth, *England.*	50¾N	2½w	22
Whymouth, C., *Aust.*	12½s	143½E	60
Whakataki, *N.I., N.Z.*	40½s	176½E	62
Whakatane, *N.I., N.Z.*	38s	177E	62
Whale River & R., *Can.*	58N	68w	66
Whalsey I., *Scot.* (ins)	60¼N	1w	24
Whangaehu Riv., *N.Z.*	40s	175E	62
Whangarei, *N.I., N.Z.*	35¾s	174¼E	62
Wharfe, Riv., *England.*	53¾N	1¼w	25
Wheeler Pk., *U.S.A.*	36½N	105w	74
Wheeling, *W. Va., U.S.A.*	40N	80¾w	75
Whinuapai, *N.I., N.Z.*, (inset A).			62
Whirnside, *England.*	54¼N	2¼w	25
Whitby, *England.*	54½N	½w	25
Whitby, *Ont., Can.*	43¾N	79w	69
Whitchurch, *England.*	51¼N	1¼w	23
Whitchurch, *Ireland.*	52¼N	7w	26
Whitchurch, *England.*	53N	2¾w	22
White Bay, *Newf., Can.*	50N	56½w	67
White Cliffs, *Aust.*	30¾s	143E	59
Whitecliffs, *S.I., N.Z.*	43½s	172E	63
Whitecourt, *Alb., Can.*	54¼N	115½w	73
Whitefish, *Mon., U.S.A.*	48N	114w	74
Whitehaven, *England.*	54½N	3¾w	25
White Hope, *W. Aust.*	31½s	122E	61
Whitehorse, *Yukon.*	60¾N	135w	66
White I., *N.I., N.Z.*	37½s	177¼E	62
White, L., *N. Terr., Aust.*	22s	129E	60
Whitemark, *Tas.* (ins.).	40s	148E	59
White Mts., *U.S.A.*	44¼N	71¼w	69
White Nile R., *Sudan.*	12N	32½E	56
White Plains, *N.Y., U.S.*	41N	74w	75
White R., *Ark., U.S.A.*	35½N	91w	75
White River, *Ont., Can.*	48½N	85½w	68
White R., *S. Dak., U.S.A.*	43N	99¾w	74
White R., *Texas, U.S.A.*	34N	100w	74
White River, *S. Afr.*	25¼s	31E	54
WHITE RUSSIA, *U.S.S.R.*	53½N	27½E	38
White Sea, *U.S.S.R.*	66N	40E	38
Whitewater, *Br. Col.*	57N	126w	66
Whitewood, *Sask., Can.*	50¼N	102¼w	70
Whitfield, *Vict., Aust.*	36¾s	146½E	59
Whithorn, *Scotland.*	54¾N	4½w	25
Whiting Bay, *Scotland.*	55½N	5w	25
Whitley B., *England.*	55N	1½w	25
Whitney, Mt., *U.S.A.*	36½N	118¾w	74
Whitstable, *England.*	51½N	1E	23
Whitsunday I., *Aust.*	20s	149E	60
Whittlesea, *C.Pr., S.Af.*	32½s	26¾E	53
Whittlesea, *Vict., Aust.*	37½s	145E	59
Whittlesey, *England.*	52½N	0	23
Wholdaia, L., *N.W.Can.*	61N	105w	66
Whyalla, *S. Australia.*	33s	137½E	59
Wiaga, *Ghana.*	10¾N	1½w	57
Wiarton, *Ont., Can.*	44¾N	81¼w	68
Wiawso, *Ghana.*	6¼N	2½w	57
Wichita, *Kan., U.S.A.*	37¾N	97¼w	75
Wichita Falls, *U.S.A.*	33¾N	98½w	74
Wick, *Scotland.*	58½N	3¼w	24
Wickenburg, *U.S.A.*	34N	113w	74
Wickepin, *W. Aust.*	32½s	117½E	61
Wickham Mkt., *Eng.*	52¼N	1½E	23
WICKLOW & Tn., *Eire*	53N	6w	26
Wicklow Mts., *Eire.*	53N	6½w	22
Wide B., *Queens., Aust.*	26s	153E	60
Widnes, *England.*	53½N	2¾w	22
Wieliczka, *Poland.*	50N	20E	33
Wielun, *Poland.*	51½N	18½E	33
Wiener Neustadt, *Austria.*	47¾N	16½E	33
Wieprz, Riv., *Poland.*	51½N	22E	33
Wierden, *Netherlands.*	52½N	6½E	30
Wierzbnik, *Poland.*	51N	21E	33
Wierzchowo, *Poland.*	53½N	16E	33
Wiesbaden, *Germany.*	50¼N	8¼E	33
Wigan, *England.*	53½N	2¾w	22
Wight, I. of, *England.*	50¾N	1¼w	23
Wigton, *England.*	54¾N	3¼w	25
WIGTOWN, & B., *Scot.*	54¾N	4½w	25
Wil, *Switzerland.*	47½N	9E	31
Wilberforce, C., *Aust.*	11½s	136½E	60
Wilcannia, *Australia*	31½s	143½E	59
Wilcox, *Sask., Canada.*	50¼N	104½w	70
Wild Horse, *Alb., Can.*	49N	110¼w	73
Wild Spitze Mt., *Aust.*	47N	11E	31
Wildbad, *Germany.*	48¾N	8½E	30
Wildeshausen, *Ger.*	52¾N	8½E	30
Wildhorn, Mt., *Switz.*	46½N	7½E	31
Wilhelmshaven I., *Ger.*	53½N	8E	33
Wilkes Ld., *Antarctica.*	66½s	120E	80
Wilkes-Barre, *Pa., U.S.*	41¼N	76w	69
Wilkie, *Sask., Canada.*	52½N	108¾w	70
Willcox, *Ariz., U.S.A.*	32N	110w	74
Willemstad, *Nether.*	51¾N	4½E	30
Willemstad, *Neth. W.I.*	12N	69w	77
Willenhall, *England,*	52½N	2w	22
Willeroo, *N. Terr., Aust.*	15¼s	132E	60
William Creek, *S. Aust.*	29s	136½E	59
Williambury, *W. Aust.*	24s	115E	61
Williams, *W. Aust.*	33s	117E	61
Williamsport, *U.S.A.*	41½N	77w	75
Williamstown, *Aust.*	38s	144E	59
Willingdon, *Alb., Can.*	53¾N	112w	73
Williston, *C.Pr., S.Af.*	31¼s	21E	52
Williston, *N.D., U.S.A.*	48¼N	103¾w	74
Williton, *England.*	51¼N	3¼w	22
Willmar, *Minn., U.S.A.*	45N	95w	75
Willowmore, *S.Afr.*	32¾s	23½E	52
Willowvale, *C.Pr., S.A.*	32¼s	28½E	53
Wills Creek, *Aust.*	23½s	139¾E	60
Wills, L., *N. Terr., Aust.*	22s	129E	60
Willunga, *S. Aust.*	35¼s	138½E	59
Wilmer, *Br. Col., Can.*	50¾N	116w	73
Wilmington, *U.S.A.*	39¾N	75½w	75
Wilmington, *S. Aust.*	32¾s	138E	59
Wilmington, *U.S.A.*	34¼N	78w	75
Wilmslow, *England.*	53¼N	2¼w	22
Wilno, see VILNIUS.			
Wilpena Riv., *S. Aust.*	31½s	139¾E	59
Wilson Riv., *Aust.*	28s	141¾E	59
Wilson's Prom., *Vict.*	39½s	146½E	59
Wilton, *England.*	51¼N	1¾w	23
WILTSHIRE, *England.*	51¼N	2w	22
Wiltz, *Luxembourg.*	50N	6E	30
Wiluna, *W. Australia.*	26¾s	120¼E	61
Wimbledon, *England.*	51½N	¼w	23
Wimborne, *Alb., Can.*	51¾N	113½w	73
Wimborne, *England.*	50¾N	2w	23
Wimereux, *France.*	50¾N	1¾E	30
Wimmera, *Vict., Aust.*	36½s	142E	59
Winburg, *O.F.S., S.Af.*	28½s	27E	55
Wincanton, *England.*	51N	2½w	22
Winchelsea, *England.*	51N	¾E	23
Winchester, *England.*	51N	1¼w	23
Winchester, *Ont., Can.*	45¼N	75½w	69
Windermere, *Br. Col.*	50½N	116w	73
Windermere, *England.*	54¼N	3w	25
Windhoek, *S.W.Africa.*	22½s	17E	51
Windorah, *Queens., Aust.*	25½s	142½E	60
Windsor, *England.*	51½N	½w	23
Windsor, *N.S.W.* (ins.).	34s	150½E	58
Windsor, *N.S., Can.*	45N	64¼w	67
Windsor, *Ont., Can.*	42¼N	83w	68
Windsorton, *C.Pr., S.A.*	28¼s	24¾E	53
Windward Is., *W. Ind.*	12½N	62½w	77
Windward Passage, *W.I.*	20N	75w	77
Wingham, *England.*	51¼N	1½E	23
Wingham, *N.S.W.*	31¾s	152½E	59
Wingham, *Ont., Can.*	44N	81½w	68
Winisk, L., *Ont., Can.*	53N	88w	66
Winneba, *Ghana.*	5½N	¾w	56
Winnemucca, *Nev., U.S.*	41N	117¾w	74
Winnfield, *La., U.S.A.*	32N	92¾w	75
Winning Pool, *W. Aust.*	23s	114E	61
Winnipeg, *Man., Can.*	49¾N	97w	71
Winnipeg, L., *Man.*	52½N	98w	71
Winnipegosis, L., *Man.*	52½N	100w	71
Winnweiler, *Germany.*	49½N	7¾E	30
Winona, *Minn., U.S.A.*	44N	91¾w	75
Winschoten, *Nether.*	53¼N	7E	30
Winslow, *Ariz., U.S.A.*	35N	110¾w	74
Winslow, *England.*	52N	¾w	23
Winstead, *C. Pr., S. Afr.*	29s	22½E	52
Winston-Salem, *U.S.A.*	36¼N	80¼w	75
Winter Haven, *Fla., U.S.*	28N	82w	75
Winterberg, *Germany.*	51¼N	8½E	30
Winterborne Abbas, *England.*	50½N	2½w	22
Winter's Rush, *C. Pr.*	28½s	24½E	53
Winterswijk, *Nether.*	52N	6¾E	30
Winterthur, *Switz.*	47½N	8¾E	31
Winterton, *Natal.*	28¾s	29½E	55
Winton, *Queens., Aust.*	22½s	143E	60
Winton, *S.I., N.Z.*	46½s	168½E	63
Wirksworth, *England.*	53N	1½w	23
Wirraminna, *S. Aust.*	31¼s	136E	59
Wisbech, *England.*	52¾N	¼E	23
WISCONSIN, *U.S.A.*	45N	90w	75
Wishaw, *Scotland.*	55¾N	4w	25
Wishbone, *W. Aust.*	33s	117½E	61
Wismar, *Guyana* (ins.).	6½N	58w	77
Wismar, *Germany.*	53¾N	11½E	33
Wissant, *France.*	51N	2E	30
Wissembourg, *France.*	49N	8E	32
Witbank, *T'vaal, S. Afr.*	26s	29¼E	55
Witham, *England.*	51¾N	¾E	23
Witham, R., *England.*	53¼N	¼w	23
Witheridge, *England.*	51N	3¾w	22
Withernsea, *England.*	53¾N	0	23
Witmos, *C. Pr., S. Afr.*	32½s	25¾E	53
Witney, *England.*	51¾N	1½w	23
Witten, *Germany.*	51½N	7½E	30
Wittenberg, *Germany.*	51¾N	12½E	33
Wittenberge, *Germany.*	53N	11¾E	33
Wittengen, *Germany.*	52¾N	10½E	33
Wittlich, *Germany.*	50N	6¾E	33
Wittstock, *Germany.*	53N	12½E	33
Witvley, *S.W. Africa.*	22½s	18E	51
WITWATERSRAND, *S.Afr.*	26s	27½E	51
Wiveliscombe, *Eng.*	51N	3¼w	22
Wkra, Riv., *Poland.*	52½N	21E	33
Wloclawek, *Poland.*	52¾N	19E	33
Wlodawa, *Poland.*	51½N	23½E	33
Woburn, *England.*	52N	½w	23
Wodonga, *Vict., Aust.*	36s	147E	59
Woking, *England.*	51¼N	½w	23
Wokingham, *England.*	51½N	¾w	23
Woleai I., *Pacific.*	8N	143E	64
Wolfsberg, *Austria.*	46¾N	14¾E	33
Wolfville, *N.S., Can.*	45¼N	64¼w	67
Wolgast, *Germany.*	54N	13¾E	33
Wolhuterskop, *T'vaal.*	25¾s	27¾E	54
Wolin I., *Poland.*	54N	14½E	33
Wolkowysk, *U.S.S.R.*	53¼N	24½E	33
Wolla Wolla, *W. Aust.*	28s	117E	61
Wollaston, C., *N.W.Can.*	71N	122w	66
Wollaston, L., *Sask.*	58¼N	103¼w	66
Wollaston Pen., *Can.*	69N	116w	66
Wollongong, *Aust.*	34½s	151E	59
Wolmaransstad, *S.Afr.*	27¼s	26E	55
Wolseley, *C.Pr., S.Af.*	33½s	19¼E	52
Wolseley, *Sask., Can.*	50½N	103¼w	70
Wolsingham, *Eng.*	54¾N	1¾w	25
Wolstenholme, C., *Can.*	62N	78w	66
Wolverhampton, *Eng.*	52¾N	2¼w	22
Wolverton, *England.*	52N	¾w	23
Wolwehoek, *O.F.S., S.Af.*	27s	27¾E	55
Wonderboom, *S.Afr.*	25¾s	28½E	54
Wonderfontein, *S.Afr.*	25¾s	29¾E	55
Wongal-Burra, *W. Aust.*	25s	115½E	61
Wonju, *Korea.*	37½N	128E	49
Wonnerup, *W. Aust.*	33¾s	115½E	61
Wonsan, *Korea.*	39½N	127½E	49
Wonthaggi, *Vict., Aust.*	38½s	145½E	59
Woodbridge, *England.*	52¼N	1½E	23
Woodburn, *N.S.W., Aust.*	29s	153½E	59
Woodford, *Ireland.*	53N	8½w	26
Woodgreen, *Aust.*	22½s	134E	60
Woodlark I., *Pacific.*	9s	152¾E	60
Woodridge, *Man., Can.*	49½N	96½w	71
Woods, L., *Aust.*	17½s	132½E	60
Woods, L. of the, *Ont.*	49½N	94½w	71
Woodside, *Vict., Aust.*	38½s	147E	59
Woodstock, *England.*	51¾N	1¼w	23
Woodstock, *Can.*	46¼N	67½w	67
Woodstock, *Ont., Can.*	43¼N	80¾w	68
Woodstock, *Vt., U.S.A.*	43¾N	72½w	69
Woodstock, *W. Aust.*	22s	119E	61
Woodville, *N.I., N.Z.*	40½s	175¾E	62
Woodward, *Okl., U.S.A.*	36½N	100w	74
Wooler, *England.*	55½N	2w	25
Woolgangie, *W. Aust.*	31s	121E	61
Woomera, *S. Aust.*	31s	137½E	59
Woondoola, *Queens.*	18½s	141E	60
Woonsocket, *R.I., U.S.A.*	42N	71½w	69
Wooramel, *W.Australia*	25¾s	114¼E	61
Wootton Bassett, *Eng.*	51½N	2w	23
Worcester, *C.Pr., S.Af.*	33¾s	19½E	52
WORCESTER, *England.*	52¼N	2¼w	22
Worcester, *Mass., U.S.A.*	42¼N	71¾w	75
Worgl, *Austria.*	47½N	12E	33
Workington, *England.*	54¾N	3½w	25
Worksop, *England.*	53½N	1w	25
Workum, *Netherlands.*	53N	5½E	30
Worland, *Wyo., U.S.A.*	44N	108w	74
Wormhoudt, *France.*	51N	2½E	30
Worms, *Germany.*	49½N	8¼E	33
Worth, *France.*	49N	7¾E	32
Worth, *Germany.*	49N	8¼E	30
Worthing, *England.*	50¾N	½w	23
Worthington, *U.S.A.*	43½N	95¾w	75
Wotton-under-Edge, *England.*	51¾N	2½w	22
Wowoni I., *Celebes.*	4½s	123E	47
Woy Woy, *N.S.W., Aust.*	33½s	151½E	59
Wragby, *England.*	53¼N	¼w	23
Wrangel I., *U.S.S.R.*	71N	180E	39
Wrangell, *Alaska, U.S.A.*	56N	132w	66
Wrath, C., *Scotland.*	58½N	5w	24
Wray, *Colorado, U.S.A.*	40N	103w	74
Wremen, *Ger.* (inset).	53½N	8½E	30
Wrentham, *England.*	52½N	1½E	23
Wrexham, *England.*	53N	3w	22
Wroclaw, *Poland.*	51N	17E	33
Wrotham, *England.*	51¼N	¼E	23
Wroxham, *England.*	52½N	1½E	23
Wrzesnia, *Poland.*	52½N	17½E	33
Wschawa, *Poland.*	51¾N	16½E	33
Wubin, *W. Australia.*	30s	116½E	61
Wuchang, *China.*	30¾N	114¼E	48
Wuhan, *China.*	30½N	114¼E	48
Wuhing, *China.*	31¼N	120E	48
Wuhu, *China.*	31¼N	118½E	48
Wukang, *China.*	27N	110½E	48
Wukari, *Nigeria.*	7¾N	9½E	57
Wulfrath, *Ger.* (ins.).	51¼N	7E	33
Wumme, Riv., *Ger.*	53½N	8½E	30
Wuonta, *Nicaragua.*	13½N	83½w	77
Wupper, Riv., *Germany.*	51N	7E	30
Wuppertal, *Germany.*	51¼N	7¼E	33
Wurarga, *W. Aust.*	28s	117E	61
Wurno, *Nigeria.*	13¼N	5½E	57
Wurzburg, *Germany.*	49¾N	10E	33
Wusheng, *China.*	30¼N	106E	48
Wusih, *China.*	31½N	120E	48
Wuwei, *China.*	37¾N	103E	48
Wuyuan, *China.*	42N	108E	48
Wuyun, *China.*	49¼N	130E	39
Wyalkatchem, *W.Aust.*	31¼s	117½E	61
Wyalong, *N.S.W., Aust.*	34s	147¼E	59
Wyandotte, *Mich., U.S.*	42¼N	83¼w	68
Wyandra, *Queens., Aust.*	27s	146E	59
Wyangala Dam, *Aust.*	34s	149E	59
Wycheproof, *Vict., Aust.*	36s	143¼E	59
Wye, *England.*	51¼N	1E	23
Wye, Riv., *Wales.*	51½N	2¾w	22
Wylye, *England.*	51¼N	2w	22
Wymark, *Sask., Can.*	50¼N	107¾w	70
Wymondham, *Eng.*	52½N	1¼E	23
Wynberg, *C. Pr., S. Afr.*	34s	18½E	52
Wynbring, *S. Aust.*	30½s	133½E	58
Wyndham, *S.I., N.Z.*	46¼s	168¾E	63
Wyndham, *W. Aust.*	15¼s	128E	60
Wynnum, *Queens., Aust.*	27s	153¼E	59
Wynyard, *Sask., Can.*	51¾N	104¼w	70
Wynyard, *Tasmania.*	41s	145¾E	59
WYOMING, *U.S.A.*	43N	108w	74
Wyong, *N.S.W., Aust.*	33½s	151½E	59
Wyszkow, *Poland.*	52½N	21½E	33
XANTHE, *Greece.*	41¼N	24¾E	37
Xilokastron, *Greece.*	38N	22½E	37
Xingu, Riv., *Brazil.*	2s	52w	78
Xuka Drift, *C.Pr., S.Af.*	31¼s	28E	53
YAAMBA, *Queens., Aust.*	23s	151E	60
Yaan, *China.*	30N	102½E	48
Yaapeet, *Vict., Aust.*	35¾s	142E	59
Yabassi, *Cameroon.*	4½N	10E	56
Yablonovy Mts., *U.S.S.R.*	53N	115E	39
Yabo, *Nigeria.*	12¾N	5E	57
Yachow, *China.*	30N	103E	43
Yackandandah, *Vict.*	36¼s	146¾E	59
Yacke Yackine, *W. Aust.*	30s	119E	61
Yagman, *U.S.S.R.*	40N	54E	38
Yahk, *Br. Col., Can.*	49¼N	116¼w	73
Yaita, *Japan.*	37N	140E	49
Yakhtul, *Yemen* (ins.).	14N	44E	40
Yakima, *Wash., U.S.A.*	46½N	120½w	74
Yaku I., *Japan.*	30N	131E	49
Yakumo, *Japan.*	42¼N	140¼E	49
YAKUT, *U.S.S.R.*	65N	130E	39
Yakutat, *Alaska, U.S.A.*	60N	140w	66
Yakutsk, *U.S.S.R.*	62N	130E	39
Yala, *Thailand* (ins.).	6½N	101¼E	47
Yale, *Br. Col., Canada.*	49¾N	121¼w	72
Yalgoo, *W. Australia.*	28¼s	116¾E	56
Yalinga, *Cen.Afr.Rep.*	7N	23½E	61
Yaloginda, *W. Aust.*	27s	118E	38
Yalta, *U.S.S.R.*	44½N	34¼E	49
Yalu R., *China-Korea.*	40¾N	125¾E	43
Yalung River, *China.*	27N	102E	49
Yamagata, *Japan.*	38¼N	140½E	49
Yamaguchi, *Japan.*	34¼N	131½E	39
Yamal Pen., *U.S.S.R.*	71N	70E	56
Yamankhalinsk, *U.S.S.R.*	47½N	52E	38
Yamba, *N.S.W., Aust.*	29½s	153¼E	59
Yambio, *Sudan.*	4¾N	28E	46
Yambol, *Bulgaria.*	42½N	26½E	37
Yambura, *U.S.S.R.*	67N	69E	38
Yamethin, *Burma.*	20¼N	96¼E	43
Yamma Yamma, L., *Queensland, Aust.*	26¼s	141¾E	60
Yamsk, *U.S.S.R.*	60N	154E	39
Yanac, *Victoria, Aust.*	36¼s	141½E	59
Yanaul, *U.S.S.R.*	56½N	55E	38
Yangdok, *Korea.*	39N	127E	49
Yangi Langar, *Kash.*	36½N	79½E	44
Yangkao, *China.*	40¾N	113½E	48
Yankton, *S.D., U.S.A.*	43N	97½w	75
Yangtze-Kiang, *China*	28N	105½E	48
Yannarie & R., *W.Aust.*	22½s	115E	61
Yannina, *Greece.*	39¾N	20¾E	37
Yanski, *U.S.S.R.*	70N	135E	39
Yao, *Chad.*	13N	17½E	56

Place	Lat.	Long.	No.
Yaoundé, Cameroon.	4N	11½E	56
Yap I., Pacific.	9½N	138½E	64
Yar, U.S.S.R.	58N	52E	38
Yaraka, Queens., Aust.	25S	144E	60
Yare, Riv., England.	52½N	1½E	23
Yarensk, U.S.S.R.	62½N	49E	38
Yarkand, Sinkiang, Chi.	38½N	77½E	42
Yarkand R., Kash.(ins.)	36½N	76E	44
Yarkand R., China.	40½N	80E	42
Yarm, England.	54½N	1¼W	25
Yarmouth, England.	52½N	1½E	23
Yarmouth, England.	50½N	1¼W	23
Yarmouth, No. Scotia.	43¾N	66W	67
Yarmuk R., Jord.(ins.)	32½N	35½E	40
Yaroslavl, U.S.S.R.	57½N	40E	38
Yarram, Vict., Aust.	38½N	146½E	59
Yarrawonga, Vict., Aust.	36S	146E	59
Yartsevo, U.S.S.R.	55N	33E	38
Yashi, Nigeria.	12½N	8E	57
Yasin, Kashmir (ins.).	36½N	73½E	44
Yass, N.S.W., Aust.	34½S	148½E	59
Yatsushiro, Japan.	32½N	130½E	49
Yatta, Jordan (inset).	31½N	35E	40
Ye, Burma.	15½N	97¾E	43
Yea, Victoria, Aust.	37½S	145½E	59
Yealmpton, Eng.	50½N	4W	22
Yecla, Spain.	38½N	1W	35
Yefira, Greece.	40½N	22½E	37
Yegorevsk, U.S.S.R.	55N	39E	38
Yehposhow, China.	42N	120E	48
Yehsien, China.	37½N	120E	48
Yei, Sudan.	4½N	30½E	56
Yelabuga, U.S.S.R.	55½N	52E	38
Yelets, U.S.S.R.	52½N	38½E	38
Yelizavety, C., U.S.S.R.	54N	143E	39
Yell I., Shet Is., Scot.	60½N	1W	24
Yellow Grass, Can.	49½N	104½W	70
Yellow Sea, China.	35N	123E	48
Yellowdine, W. Aust.	31¼S	119½E	61
Yellowhead Pass, Alb.	52¾N	118½W	73
Yellowknife Can.	62½N	114½W	66
Yellowstone L., U.S.A.	44½N	110W	74
Yelverton, England.	50½N	4¼W	22
Yelwa, Nigeria.	11N	4½E	57
YEMEN, Arabia.	15½N	44E	40
Yenbai, Vietnam.	21½N	105E	48
Yenbo, Saudi Arabia.	24N	38½E	40
Yencheng, China.	33N	120E	48
Yende, Ghana.	9½N	0	57
Yengki, China.	43N	129E	48
Yenisei Riv., U.S.S.R.	70N	68E	42
Yeniseisk, U.S.S.R.	58½N	29E	42
Yenotaevsk, U.S.S.R.	47N	74E	38
Yentai, China.	37½N	121½E	48
Yeo, L., W. Australia.	28S	124E	61
Yeotmal, India.	0½N	78½E	45
Yeovil, England.	51N	2½W	22
Yepi, Guyana (inset).	1N	58W	77
Yeppoon, Queens.Aust.	23S	151E	60
Yeraki, Greece.	37N	22½E	37
Yerbent, U.S.S.R.	39N	58E	40
Yerbogachen, U.S.S.R.	61½N	109E	39
Yeres, Riv., France.	48½N	2½E	30
Yeropol, U.S.S.R.	66N	169E	39
Yershov, U.S.S.R.	51½N	48E	32
Yes Tor (Hill), Eng.	50½N	4W	22
Yetman, N.S.W., Aust.	29S	150½E	59
Yevlakh, U.S.S.R.	41N	47½E	38
Yevpatoriya, U.S.S.R.	45N	33½E	38
Yezd, Iran.	32N	54½E	40
Yealousa, Cyprus.	35½N	34E	41
Yebna, Israel (inset).	31½N	34½E	40
Yelliminning, W. Aust.	33S	117½E	61
Yinchuan, China.	38½N	106½E	48
Yinghsien, China.	39½N	113E	48
Yingkow, China.	40½N	122½E	48
Yingtak, China.	24½N	113E	48
Yingtan, China.	28N	117E	48
Yinkanie.S. Australia.	34½S	140½E	59
Yinnie Tharra, W.Aust.	24½S	116½E	61
Yirol, Sudan.	7N	30½E	56
Yitu, China.	36¾N	118½E	48
Yiyang, China.	29½N	112½E	48
Yogou, Ghana.	10½N	½E	57
Yoho Park, Br. Col., Canada.	51½N	116½W	73
Yokkaichi, Japan.	35N	136½E	49
Yoko, Cameroon.	5½N	12½E	56
Yokohama, Japan.	35½N	139½E	49
Yokosuka, Japan.	35½N	139½E	49
Yokote, Japan.	39N	140½E	49
Yola, Nigeria.	9½N	12½E	57
Yonago, Japan.	35½N	133½E	49
Yonezawa, Japan.	38N	140E	49
Yongdok, Korea.	36½N	129½E	49
Yongdungpo, Korea.	37½N	127E	49
Yonghung, Korea.	39½N	127½E	49
Yonkers, N.Y., U.S.A.	41N	74W	75
YONNE, France.	48N	3½E	32
York & Tn., England.	54N	1¼W	25
York, W. Australia.	32S	116½E	61
York, C., Greenland.	76N	66½W	66
York, C., Queens., Aust.	10½S	142½E	60
York Factory, Canada	57N	92½W	71
Yorke Pen., S. Aust.	35S	137½E	59
Yorkton, Sask., Can.	57N	102½W	70
Yoshkar-Ola, U.S.S.R.	56½N	47½E	38
Youanmi, W. Aust.	28½S	118½E	61
Youghal & B., Eire.	52N	7½W	26
Youkadouma, Camer.	3½N	15E	56
Young, N.S.W., Aust.	34½S	148½E	59
Young, Sask., Can.	51½N	105½W	70
Youngstown, Alb., Canada.	51½N	111¼W	73
Youngstown, U.S.A.	41½N	80½W	75
Yo-yang, China.	29½N	113½E	48
Yozgat, Turkey.	39½N	34½E	41
Ypres, Belgium.	50½N	2½E	30
Ystad, Sweden.	55½N	13½E	29
Ystan, U.S.S.R.	65½N	143½E	39
Ythan, Riv., Scotland.	57½N	2¼W	24
Ytre Sulen I., Norway.	61N	4½E	29
Yuan River, China.	28½N	111E	48
Yuanling, China.	28½N	110½E	48
Yuba City, Calif., U.S.A.	39N	122W	74
Yubari, Japan.	43N	142E	49
YUCATAN, Mexico.	21N	89W	76
Yudam-Ni, Korea.	40½N	127E	49
Yudoma Riv., U.S.S.R.	59½N	135E	39
YUGOSLAVIA, Europe.	44N	20E	37
Yuin, W. Australia.	28S	116E	61
Yukon R., Alaska, U.S.A.	64N	164W	65
YUKON, Canada.	64N	136W	65
Yule River, W. Aust.	20½S	118E	61
Yuleba, Queens., Aust.	26½S	149½E	60
Yulin, China.	38N	109½E	48
Yülin, China.	22½N	110½E	48
Yuma, Arizona, U.S.A.	32½N	114½W	74
Yuna, W. Australia.	28½S	115E	61
Yuncheng, China.	36N	115½E	48
Yungchang, China.	25N	99E	43
Yungera, Vict., Aust.	34½S	143½E	59
Yungnien, China.	37N	115E	48
Yugning, China.	22½N	107½E	48
Yungpeh, China.	27N	101E	43
Yungshun, China.	29N	110E	48
Yungsin, China.	27N	114E	48
Yunhsien, China.	33N	110½E	48
Yunlungchow, China.	26N	99E	43
YUNNAN, China.	25N	100E	43
Yunta, S. Australia.	32½S	139½E	59
Yunyang, China.	32N	109E	48
Yuroma, U.S.S.R.	65N	45½E	38
Yurungkash R., China.	38N	80E	43
Yuscaran, Honduras.	13½N	87W	76
Yushino, U.S.S.R.	68N	55E	38
Yusun Bulak, Mongolia.	47N	96E	39
Yuyang, China.	28½N	109E	48
Yuyao, China.	30N	121E	48
Yuyu, China.	40N	112E	48
Yuzhny, C., U.S.S.R.	58N	157E	39
Yverdon, Switzerland.	46½N	6½E	31
Yvetot, France.	49½N	½E	31
Zaandam, Nether.	52½N	4½E	30
Zabaikalski, U.S.S.R.	50N	111E	39
Zabid, Yemen (inset).	14½N	43½E	40
Zabkowice, Poland.	50½N	16½E	33
Zabludow, Poland.	53N	23½E	33
Zabrze, Poland.	50½N	18½E	33
ZACATECAS, Mexico.	23N	103W	76
Zacatecoluca, Salvador.	13N	88½W	76
Zadar, Yugoslavia.	44N	15½E	36
Zafra, Spain.	38½N	6¾W	35
Zagan, Poland.	51½N	15½E	33
Zagazig, U.A.R.	30½N	32E	40
Zaghouan, Tunisia.	36½N	10E	36
Zagorsk, U.S.S.R.	56½N	38E	38
Zagreb, Yugoslavia.	45½N	16E	37
Zagros Mts., Iran.	34N	47½E	40
Zahidan, Iran.	29½N	61E	40
Zaidiya, Yemen (ins.).	15N	44E	40
Zaima, Saudi Arabia.	22N	40E	40
Zair, Algeria.	29N	6W	34
Zaire, Angola.	6½S	12½E	56
Zaisan, L., U.S.S.R.	48N	83E	39
Zajecar, Yugoslavia.	43½N	22½E	37
Zakho, Iraq.	37N	42½E	41
Zakinthos, Greece.	37½N	20½E	37
Zaklikow, Poland.	50½N	22E	33
Zakopane, Poland.	49½N	20E	33
Zakros, Crete.	35N	26½E	37
Zakynthos, Greece.	37½N	20½E	37
Zalaegerszeg, Lung.	47N	17E	37
Zalau, Romania.	47½N	23E	37
Zalew Wislany, Pol.	54½N	19E	33
Zalingei, Sudan.	12½N	24E	56
Zambesi Riv., Africa.	19½S	35E	50
Zambezia, Mozam.	17S	37E	51
ZAMBIA, Africa.	15S	25E	50
Zamboanga, Mind., P.I.	7N	122E	47
Zamora, Mexico.	20N	102½W	76
Zamora, Spain.	41½N	5½W	35
Zamosc, Poland.	50½N	23½E	33
Zanaga, Congo (B.).	3S	13½E	56
Zanesville, Oh., U.S.A.	40N	82W	75
Zangla, Kash. (inset).	33½N	77E	44
Zanthus, W. Aust.	31S	123½E	61
Zanzibar, Tanzania.	5½S	39½E	56
Zapala, Argentina.	39S	70W	79
Zaporozhye, U.S.S.R.	47½N	35E	38
Zaragoza, Mexico.	32N	106½W	76
Zarand, Romania.	46½N	22½E	37
Zarand, Iran.	31N	56E	40
Zaria, Nigeria.	11N	7½E	57
Zary, Poland.	51½N	15E	33
Zastron, O.F.S.&S.Afr.	30½S	27E	55
Zatec, Czechoslovakia.	50N	13½E	33
Zauiet Msus, Libya.	31N	21E	34
Zavitinsk, U.S.S.R.	50½N	130E	39
Zawi, Rhodesia.	17S	30E	51
Zawiercie, Poland.	50½N	19½E	33
Zayarsk, U.S.S.R.	57N	102E	39
Zdunska Wola, Pol.	51½N	19E	33
Zealand, Denmark.	55½N	12E	29
Zebediela, T'vaal.,S.Afr.	24½S	29½E	54
Zeebrugge, Belgium.	51½N	3½E	30
ZEELAND, Nether.	51½N	4E	30
Zeerust, Transvaal.	25½S	26E	54
Zeidab, Sudan.	17½N	33½E	40
Zeil, Germany.	50N	10½E	33
Zeila, Somali Republic.	11½N	43½E	56
Zeist, Netherlands.	51N	5½E	30
Zeitz, Germany.	51N	12E	33
Zelechow, Poland.	51½N	22E	33
Zell, Austria.	47½N	12E	31
Zell, Germany.	50N	7½E	30
Zella, Libya.	28½N	17½E	34
Zemio, Cen.Afr.Rep.	5N	25½E	56
Zemun, Yugoslavia.	44½N	20½E	37
Zenica, Yugoslavia.	44½N	18E	37
Zenjan, Iran.	37N	47½E	41
Zepce, Yugoslavia.	44½N	18E	36
Zermatt, Switzerland.	46N	7½E	31
Zesfontein, S.W.Africa.	19S	13½E	51
Zeven, Germany.	53½N	9½E	30
Zevenaar, Nether.	52N	6E	30
Zeya & R., U.S.S.R.	53½N	127½E	39
Zgierz, Poland.	51½N	19½E	33
Zharyk, U.S.S.R.	49N	72E	39
Zhdanov, U.S.S.R.	47N	37½E	38
Zhigalovo, U.S.S.R.	55N	105E	39
Zhigansk, U.S.S.R.	66½N	123½E	39
Zhirkova, U.S.S.R.	67N	157E	39
Zhitomir, U.S.S.R.	50½N	28½E	38
Zhlobin, U.S.S.R.	53N	30E	38
Zidanimost, Yugo.	46N	15½E	36
Zielona Gora, Poland.	52N	15½E	33
Zierikzee, Nether.	51½N	3½E	30
Zifta, U.A.R. (inset).	31N	31½E	50
Zilfi, Saudi Arabia.	26½N	45E	40
Zilina, Czechoslovakia.	49¼N	18½E	33
Zima, U.S.S.R.	54N	102E	39
Zimapan, Mexico.	20½N	99½W	76
Zimbabwe, Rhodesia.	20½S	31E	51
Zinder, Niger.	13½N	9E	57
Zingst, Germany.	54½N	12½E	33
Zittau, Germany.	50½N	14½E	33
Zlatoust, U.S.S.R.	55½N	59½E	38
Zlotow, Poland.	53½N	17E	33
Znojmo, Czecho.	48½N	16E	33
Zobak, Afghanistan.	37N	70½E	43
Zogno, Italy.	45½N	9½E	31
Zolotonosha, U.S.S.R.	50N	32E	38
Zomba, Malawi.	15½S	35½E	51
Zonguldak, Turkey.	41½N	31½E	41
Zouerate, Mauritania.	22½N	12½W	50
Zuarungu, Ghana.	10½N	1W	57
Zug & L., Switzerland.	47½N	8½E	31
Zugdidi, U.S.S.R.	42½N	42E	38
Zuider Zee, see IJSSELMEER.			
Zuidhorn, Nether.	53½N	6½E	30
Zulpich, Germany.	50½N	6½E	30
Zululand, Natal.	28N	32E	55
Zumbo, Mozambique.	16N	31½E	51
Zuney, C. Pr., S. Afr.	33½S	26½E	53
Zungeru, Nigeria.	9½N	6½E	57
Zurich, & L. Switz.,	47½N	8½E	31
Zuromin, Poland.	53S	20E	33
Zuru, Nigeria.	11N	5E	57
Zutphen, Nether.	52½N	6E	30
Zuurfont ,C.Pr.,S.A.	32½S	25E	53
Zvolen, Czecho.	48½N	19E	33
Zwai, L., Ethiopia.	7½N	38½E	56
Zwartsluis, Nether.	52½N	6E	30
Zweibrucken, Ger.	49½N	7½E	33
Zweisimmen, Switz.	46½N	7½E	31
Zwettel, Austria.	48½N	15½E	33
Zwickau, Germany.	50½N	12½E	33
Zwischenahn, Ger.	23½N	8E	30
Zwolle, Netherlands.	52½N	6E	30
Zyrardow, Poland.	52N	20½E	33
Zyaryanovsk, U.S.S.R.	50N	84E	39

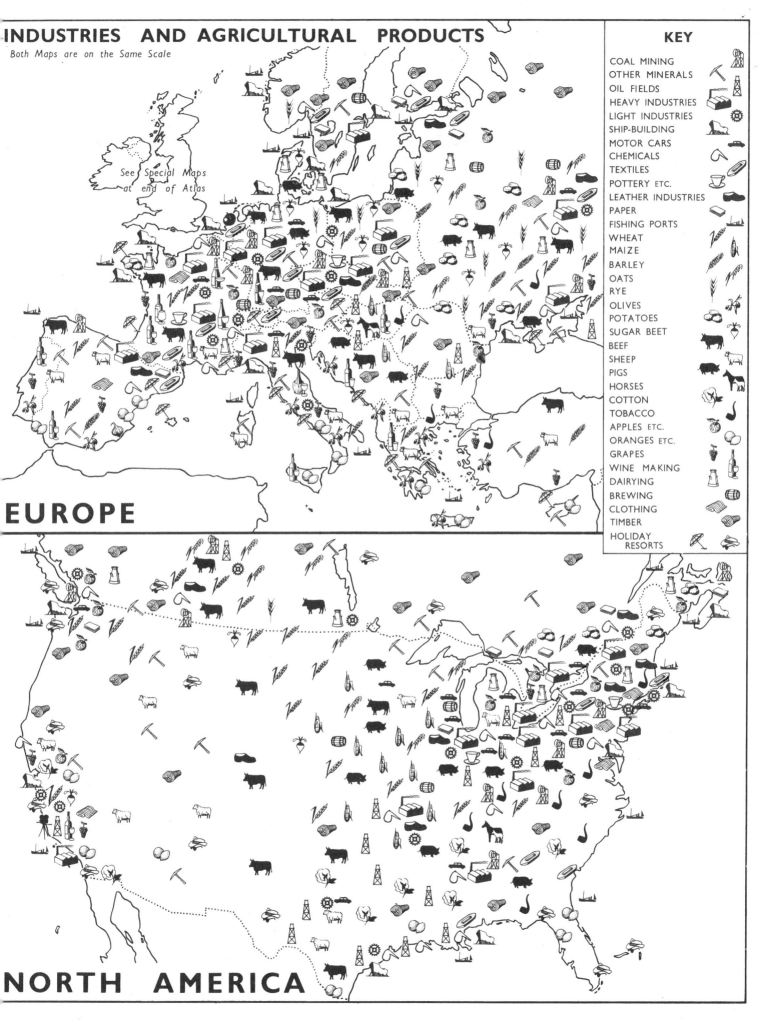

INDUSTRIES AND AGRICULTURAL PRODUCTS

Both Maps are on the Same Scale

See Special Maps
at end of Atlas

EUROPE

NORTH AMERICA

KEY

COAL MINING
OTHER MINERALS
OIL FIELDS
HEAVY INDUSTRIES
LIGHT INDUSTRIES
SHIP-BUILDING
MOTOR CARS
CHEMICALS
TEXTILES
POTTERY ETC.
LEATHER INDUSTRIES
PAPER
FISHING PORTS
WHEAT
MAIZE
BARLEY
OATS
RYE
OLIVES
POTATOES
SUGAR BEET
BEEF
SHEEP
PIGS
HORSES
COTTON
TOBACCO
APPLES ETC.
ORANGES ETC.
GRAPES
WINE MAKING
DAIRYING
BREWING
CLOTHING
TIMBER
HOLIDAY
 RESORTS

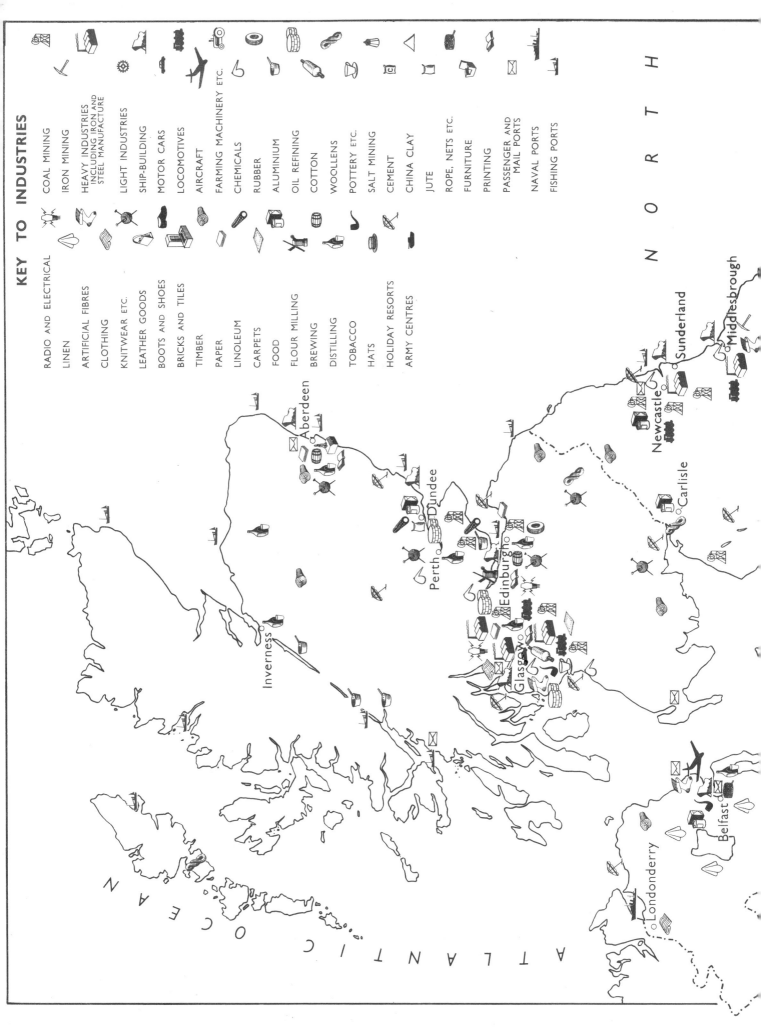

KEY TO INDUSTRIES

COAL MINING	
IRON MINING	
HEAVY INDUSTRIES INCLUDING IRON AND STEEL MANUFACTURE	
LIGHT INDUSTRIES	
SHIP-BUILDING	
MOTOR CARS	
LOCOMOTIVES	
AIRCRAFT	
FARMING MACHINERY ETC.	
CHEMICALS	
RUBBER	
ALUMINIUM	
OIL REFINING	
COTTON	
WOOLLENS	
POTTERY ETC.	
SALT MINING	
CEMENT	
CHINA CLAY	
JUTE	
ROPE, NETS ETC.	
FURNITURE	
PRINTING	
PASSENGER AND MAIL PORTS	
NAVAL PORTS	
FISHING PORTS	

RADIO AND ELECTRICAL	
LINEN	
ARTIFICIAL FIBRES	
CLOTHING	
KNITWEAR ETC.	
LEATHER GOODS	
BOOTS AND SHOES	
BRICKS AND TILES	
TIMBER	
PAPER	
LINOLEUM	
CARPETS	
FOOD	
FLOUR MILLING	
BREWING	
DISTILLING	
TOBACCO	
HATS	
HOLIDAY RESORTS	
ARMY CENTRES	

Aberdeen

Inverness

Dundee

Perth

Edinburgh

Glasgow

Carlisle

Newcastle

Sunderland

Middlesbrough

Belfast

Londonderry

NORTH

ATLANTIC OCEAN